THE HERITAGE OF
WORLD CIVILIZATIONS

TEACHING AND LEARNING CLASSROOM EDITION

BRIEF THIRD EDITION

VOLUME TWO: SINCE 1500

Albert M. Craig
HARVARD UNIVERSITY

William A. Graham
HARVARD UNIVERSITY

Donald Kagan
YALE UNIVERSITY

Steven Ozment
HARVARD UNIVERSITY

Frank M. Turner
YALE UNIVERSITY

Upper Saddle River, New Jersey 07458

Library of Congress Cataloging-in-Publication Data

The heritage of world civilizations / Albert M. Craig … [et al].- Brief 3rd ed., volume two
    p. cm.
    Includes bibliographical references and index.
    ISBN 0-13-219695-6
      1. Civilizations–History–Textbooks.   I. Craig, Albert M.
    CB69.H45 2005

VP, Editorial Director: Charlyce Jones Owen
Executive Editor: Charles Cavaliere
Associate Editor: Emsal Hasan
Editorial Assistant: Maria Guarascio
Senior Media Editor: Deborah O'Connell
Editor-in-Chief, Development: Rochelle Diogenes
**AVP, Director of Production
  and Manufacturing:** Barbara Kittle
Senior Managing Editor: Joanne Riker
Production Liaison: Randy Pettit
Prepress and Manufacturing Manager: Nick Sklitsis
Prepress and Manufacturing Buyer: Ben Smith
Director of Marketing: Brandy Dawson
Marketing Manager: Emily Cleary
Creative Design Director: Leslie Osher
Interior and Cover Designer: Laura Gardner

Cartographer: CartoGraphics
Electronic Artists: Maria Piper, Mirella Signoretto,
  Bruce Killmer, Carey Davies
Director, Image Resource Center: Melinda Reo
Interior Image Specialist: Beth Brenzel
Cover Image Specialist: Karen Sanatar
Image Permission Coordinator: Michelina Viscusi
Photo Researcher: Elaine Soares
Color Scanning Services: Joe Conti, Greg Harrison, Cory
  Skidds, Rob Uibelhoer, Ron Walko
Editorial Production and Composition: GEX Publishing
  Services
Printer/Binder: The Courier Companies
Cover Printer: The Lehigh Press, Inc.

 Born in Argentina in 1928, Ernesto "Che" Guevara was one of the leaders of the revolutionary force that seized power in Cuba in 1959. Gifted with great charisma and intellectual acumen, Che advocated guerilla warfare as a means to overthrow corrupt regimes across the world and he was killed in Bolivia in 1967 while trying to organize a guerilla movement there. In 1960, during a state funeral in Havana, Che briefly appeared and was instantly photographed while he scanned the crowd. Widely reproduced throughout the world, Che's heroic gaze is one of the great icons of contemporary times.

Credits and acknowledgments borrowed from other sources and reproduced, with permission, in this textbook appear on appropriate page within text or on page C-1

Pearson Education Ltd., London
Pearson Education Australia Pty., Limited, Sydney
Pearson Education Singapore, Pte., Ltd.
Pearson Education North Asia Ltd., Hong Kong

Pearson Education Canada, Ltd., Toronto
Pearson Educación de Mexico, S.A. de C.V.
Pearson Education — Japan, Tokyo
Pearson Education Malaysia, Pte., Ltd.

PEARSON
Prentice
Hall

10 9 8 7 6 5 4 3 2 1

ISBN 0-13-219695-6

Preface xxii

PART 2
EMPIRES AND CULTURES OF THE ANCIENT WORLD   54

3

Greek and Hellenistic Civilization   56

4

Iran, India, and Inner Asia to 200 C.E.   84

Visualizing The Past

5 *Africa, Early History to 1000* C.E.   104

6 *Republican and Imperial Rome*   122

China's First Empire
221 B.C.E.– 589 C.E.   152

Visualizing The Past

PART 3
CONSOLIDATION AND INTERACTION OF WORLD CIVILIZATIONS 172

Religions of the World
Buddhism 224

Visualizing The Past

Ancient Civilizations of the Americas 310

Visualizing The Past

*Europe to the Early 1500s: Revival, Decline,
and Renaissance* 336

PART 4
THE WORLD IN TRANSITION 370

16

Europe 1500–1650: Expansion, Reformation and Religious Wars 372

Religions of the World

Christianity 412

17

Africa, ca. 1000–1800 414

18

*Conquest and Exploitation: The Development
of the Transatlantic Economy* 434

19

East Asia in the Late Traditional Era 456

20
*State Building and Society
in Early Modern Europe* 484

21

Visualizing The Past

PART 5
ENLIGHTENMENT AND REVOLUTION IN THE WEST 534

22

23

Revolutions in the Transatlantic World 556

24

Political Consolidation in Nineteenth-Century Europe and North America, 1815–1880 582

Visualizing The Past

**Imagining Women in the Eighteenth
and Nineteenth Centuries   614**

PART 6

INTO THE MODERN WORLD   616

*Northern Transatlantic Economy
and Society, 1815–1914*   618

28

Modern East Asia 696

Visualizing The Past

PART 7
GLOBAL CONFLICT AND CHANGE 726

29

Imperialism and World War I 728

30

Depression, European Dictators, and the American New Deal 750

31

World War II 772

32

The West Since World War II 794

33

East Asia, The Recent Decades 818

34

Postcolonialism and Beyond: Latin America, Africa, Asia, and the Middle East 836

Visualizing The Past

Imperialism and Race in Modern Art 862

History's Voices

Maps

SPECIAL FEATURES

SPECIAL FEATURES

SPECIAL FEATURES

Visualizing the Past

Religions of the World

PREFACE

The response of the United States to the events of September 11, 2001, including the war in Iraq and Afghanistan, have brought upon the world a new awareness of human history in a global context. Prior to the attacks on New York and Washington and the subsequent U.S. intervention in the Middle East, readers in North America generally understood world history and globalism as academic concepts. They now understand them as realities shaping their daily lives and experience. The immediate pressures of the present and of the foreseeable future draw us to seek a more certain and extensive understanding of the past.

The idea of globalization is now a pressing reality on the lives of nations, affecting the domestic security of their citizens, the deployment of armed forces, their standard of living, and the environment. Whether, as Samuel Huntington, the distinguished Harvard political scientist, contends, we are witnessing a clash of civilizations, we have certainly entered a new era in which no active citizen or educated person can escape the necessity of understanding the past in global terms. Both the historical experience and the moral, political, and religious values of the different world civilizations now demand our attention and our understanding. It is our hope that in these new, challenging times *The Heritage of World Civilizations* will provide one path to such knowledge.

THE ROOTS OF GLOBALIZATION

Globalization—that is, the increasing interaction and interdependency of the various regions of the world—has resulted from two major historical developments: the closing of the European era of world history and the rise of technology.

From approximately 1500 C.E. to the middle of the twentieth century, Europeans gradually came to dominate the world through colonization (most particularly in North and South America), state-building, economic productivity, and military power. That era of European dominance ended during the third quarter of the twentieth century after Europe had brought unprecedented destruction on itself during World War II and as the nations of Asia, the Near East, and Africa achieved new positions on the world scene. Their new political independence, their control over strategic natural resources, and the expansion of their economies (especially those of the nations of the Pacific rim of Asia), and in some cases their access to nuclear weapons have changed the shape of world affairs.

Further changing the world political and social situation has been a growing discrepancy in the economic development of different regions that is often portrayed as a problem between the northern and southern hemispheres. Beyond the emergence of this economic disparity has been the remarkable advance of radical political Islamism during the past forty years. In the midst of all these developments, as a result of the political collapse of the former Soviet Union, the United States has emerged as the single major world power.

The second historical development that continues to fuel the pace of globalization is the advance of technology, associated most importantly with transportation, military weapons, and electronic communication. The advances in transportation over the past two centuries including ships, railways, and airplanes have made more parts of the world and its resources accessible to more people in ever shorter spans of time. Over the past century and a half, military weapons of increasingly destructive power enabled Europeans and then later the United States to dominate other regions of the globe. Now, the spread of these weapons means that any nation with sophisticated military technology can threaten other nations, no matter how far away. Furthermore, technologies that originated in the West from the early twentieth century to the present have been turned against the West. More recently, the electronic revolution associated with computer technology and most particularly the internet has sparked unprecedented speed and complexity in global communications. It is astonishing to recall that personal computers have been generally available for less than twenty-five years and the rapid personal communication associated with them has existed for less than fifteen years.

Why not, then, focus only on new factors in the modern world, such as the impact of technology and the end of the European era? To do so would ignore the very deep roots that these developments have in the past. More important, the events of recent years demonstrate, as the authors of this book have long contended, that the major religious traditions continue to shape and drive the modern world as well as the world of the past. The religious traditions link today's civilizations to their most ancient roots. We believe this emphasis on the great religious traditions recognizes not only a factor that has shaped the past, but one that is profoundly and dynamically alive in our world today.

STRENGTHS OF THE TEXT

Balanced and Flexible Presentation   In this edition, as in past editions, we have sought to present world history fairly, accurately, and in a way that does justice to its great variety. History has many facets, no one of which can account for the others. Any attempt to tell the story of civilization from a single perspective, no matter how timely, is bound to neglect or suppress some important part of that story.

Historians have recently brought a vast array of new tools and concepts to bear on the study of history. Our coverage introduces students to various aspects of social and intellectual history as well as to the more traditional political, diplomatic, and military coverage. We firmly believe that only through an appreciation of all pathways to understanding of the past can the real heritage of world civilizations be claimed.

The Heritage of World Civilizations, TLC Edition, is designed to accommodate a variety of approaches to a course in world history, allowing teachers to stress what is most important to them. Some teachers will ask students to read all the chapters. Others will select among them to reinforce assigned readings and lectures.

Clarity and Accessibility   Good narrative history requires clear, vigorous prose. Our goal has been to make our presentation fully accessible to students without compromising on vocabulary or conceptual level. We hope this effort will benefit both teachers and students.

Current Scholarship   As in previous editions, changes in this edition reflect our determination to incorporate the most recent developments in historical scholarship and the expanding concerns of professional historians. To better highlight the dynamic processes of world history, significant new coverage of the Silk Road, Byzantium, the Crusades, Southeast Asia, women in Islam, nineteenth-century European science, the homefront during World War II, and recent events in the Middle East has been added.

Pedagogical Features   This edition retains many of the pedagogical features of previous editions, while providing increased assessment opportunities.

- **NEW • Chapter Highlights** begin each chapter and provide a preview of the key developments and themes that are to follow.

- **Part Timelines** show the major events in five regions—Europe, the Near East and India, East Asia, Africa, and the Americas—side by side. Appropriate photographs enrich each timeline.

- **Chapter-Opening Questions**, organized by the main subtopics of each chapter, encourage careful consideration of important themes and developments. Each question is repeated at the appropriate place in the margin of the text.

- **Chronologies** within each chapter help students organize a time sequence for key events.

- **History's Voices**, including selections from sacred books, poems, philosophy, political manifestos, letters, and travel accounts, introduce students to the raw material of history, providing an intimate contact with the people of the past and their concerns. Questions accompanying the source documents direct students toward important, thought-provoking issues and help them relate the documents to the material in the text. They can be used to stimulate class discussion or as topics for essays and study groups.

- **Map Explorations** and **Critical-Thinking Questions** prompt students to engage with maps, often in an interactive fashion. Each Map Exploration is found on the Companion Website for the text.

- **NEW • Religions of the World** essays examine the historical impact of each of the world's great religious traditions: Judaism, Christianity, Islam, Buddhism, and Hinduism.

- **Visualizing the Past** essays, found at the end of selected chapters, analyze important aspects of world history through photographs, fine art, sculpture, and woodcuts. Focus questions and a running narrative guide students though a careful examination of the historical issues raised by each topic in question. Four new Visualizing the Past essays have been added to this edition: "Humans and Nature in the Ancient World," "The Silk Road," "Mapping the World before 1500," and "Imagining Women in the 18th and 19th Centuries."

- **Chapter Review** Questions help students focus on and interpret the broad themes of a chapter. These questions can be used for class discussion and essay topics.

- **Overview Tables** in each chapter summarize complex issues.

- **Quick Reviews**, found at key places in the margins of each chapter, encourage students to review important concepts.

- **Key Terms**, boldfaced in the text, are listed (with page reference) at the end of each chapter, and defined in the book's glossary.

- **Documents CD-ROM**, containing over 200 documents in world history, is bound with all new copies of the text. Relevant documents are listed at appropriate places in the margin of the text and at the end of each chapter.

- NEW • **Study in Time**, a laminated six-panel timeline of world history, provides a succinct overview of key developments in social, political, and cultural history in global history from earliest times to the present.

- NEW • **Online Essays**, located on the companion website for *The Heritage of World Civilizations*, provide additional learning opportunities. One set of essays examines technology and civilization from a cross-cultural perspective, while a second set introduces each chapter's content from a wider global viewpoint.

Content and Organization   The many changes in content and organization in this edition of *The Heritage of World Civilizations* reflect our ongoing effort to present a truly global survey of world civilizations that at the same time gives a rich picture of the history of individual regions:

- **Strengthened Global Approach.** This new TLC edition more explicitly highlights the connections and parallels in global history among regions of the world.

Greater emphasis is now placed on cultural exchange, trade, encounter, and the diffusion of ideas.

- **Expanded and Improved Map Program.** The entire map program has been completely clarified and expanded. Several new maps graphically illustrate key global developments, such as trade in the classical world, the spread of Buddhism, the Islamicization of Southeast Asia, the Columbian exchange, world slavery, European global conflicts in the eighteenth century, global migration, and the Holocaust. Every single map in the text has been redesigned for greater visual appeal and accuracy. A listing of all the maps in the text can be found on pp. xxiv–xxvi.

- **Improved, Streamlined Organization.** To better accommodate typical teaching sequences, the number of chapters has been reduced to 34, with coverage of European society and state-building in the seventeenth and eighteenth centuries now treated in a single chapter. In addition, coverage of Han China (chapter 7) now immediately succeeds coverage of the Rome (chapter 6) making it easier to draw connections and parallels between these two empires. The final chapter has been exensively reorganized to better examine important recent events in the Middle East.

- **New Design and Photo Program.** The entire text has been set in a lively and engaging new design. Each of the 34 chapters includes photos never before included in previous editions of the text, the total number of illustrations in the text has been increased.

A Note on Dates and Transliteration   We have used B.C.E. (before the common era) and C.E. (common era) instead of B.C. (before Christ) and A.D. (anno domini, the year of our Lord) to designate dates.

Until recently, most scholarship on China used the Wade-Giles system of romanization for Chinese names and terms. China, today, however, uses another system known as pinyin. Virtually all Western newspapers have adopted it. In order that students may move easily from the present text to the existing body of advanced scholarship on Chinese history, we now use the pinyin system throughout the text.

Also, we have followed the currently accepted English transliterations of Arabic words. For example, today Koran is being replaced by the more accurate Qur'an; similarly Muhammad is preferable to Mohammed and Muslim to Moslem. We have not tried to distinguish the letters 'ayn and hamza; both are rendered by a simple apostrophe (') as in shi'ite.

With regard to Sanskritic transliteration, we have not distinguished linguals and dentals, and both palatal and lingual s are rendered sh, as in Shiva and Upanishad.

ANCILLARY INSTRUCTIONAL MATERIALS

The Heritage of World Civilizations, TLC Edition, comes with an extensive package of ancillary materials.

For the Instructor

- **Instructor's Resource Binder** This innovative, all-in-one resource organizes the instructor's manual, the Test-Item File, and the transparency pack by each chapter of *The Heritage of World Civilizations* to facilitate class preparation. The Instructor's Resource Binder also includes an **Instructor's Resource CD-ROM**, which contains all of the maps, graphs, and many of the illustrations from the text in easily downloadable electronic files.

- The *Instructor Resource CD-ROM*, compatible with both Windows and Macintosh environments, provides instructors with such essential teaching tools as hundreds of digitized images and maps for classroom presentations, PowerPoint lectures, and other Instructional material. The assets on the IRCD-ROM can be easily exported into online courses, such as WebCT and Blackboard.

- *Test Manager* is a computerized test management program for Windows and Macintosh environments. The program allows instructors to select items from the test-item file to create tests. It also allows online testing.

- The *Transparency Package* provides instructors with full color transparency acetates of all the maps, charts, and graphs in the text for use in the classroom.

For the Student

- *History Notes* (Volumes I and II) provides practice tests, essay questions, and map exercise to help reinforce key concepts.

- *Documents in World History* (Volumes I and II) is a collection of 200 primary source documents in global history. Questions accompanying the documents can be used for discussion or as writing assignments.

- Produced in collaboration with Dorling Kindersley, the world's most respected cartography publisher, *The Prentice Hall Atlas of World History* includes approximately 100 maps fundamental to the study of world history—from early hominids to the twenty-first century.

- *Reading Critically About History* is a brief guide to reading effectively that provides students with helpful strategies for reading a history textbook.

- *Understanding and Answering Essay Questions* suggest helpful analytical tools for understanding different types of essay questions, and provides precise guidelines for preparing well-crafted essay answers.

- Prentice Hall is pleased to provide adopters of *The Heritage of World Civilizations* with an opportunity to receive significant discounts when copies of the text are bundled with Penguin Classics titles in world history. Contact your local Prentice Hall representative for details.

MEDIA RESOURCES

OneKey Prentice Hall's Online Resource, **OneKey** lets instructors and students in to the best teaching and learning resources–all in one place. This all-inclusive online resource is designed to help you minimize class preparation and maximize teaching time. Conveniently organized by chapter, OneKey for *The Heritage of World Civilizations*, TLC Edition, reinforces what students have learned in class and from the text. Among the student resources available for each chapter are: a complete, media-rich e-book version of *The Heritage of World Civilizations* TLC Edition; quizzes organized by the main subtopics of each chapter; over 200 primary-source documents; and interactive map quizzes.

For instructors, OneKey includes images and maps from *The Heritage of World Civilizations* TLC Edition, instructional material, hundreds of primary-source documents, and PowerPoint presentations.

Research Navigator.com *Prentice Hall One Search with Research Navigator: History 2005* This brief guide focuses on developing critical-thinking skills necessary for evaluating and using online sources. It provides a brief introduction to navigating the Internet with specific references to History web sites. It also provides an access code and instruction on using Research Navigator, a powerful research tool that provides entry to three exclusive databases of reliable source material: ContentSelect Academic Journal Database, the *New York Times* Search by Subject Archive, and Link Library.

The *Companion Website with Grade Tracker*™ (*www.prenhall.com/craig*) works in tandem with the text and features objectives, study questions, web links to related Internet resources, document exercises, interactive maps, online essays on technology and global history, and map labelling exercises.

World History Document CD-ROM Bound into every new copy of this textbook is a free World History Documents CD-ROM. This is a powerful resource for research and additional reading that contains more than 200 primary source documents central to World History. Each document provides essay questions that are linked directly to a website where short-essay answers can be submitted oline or printed out. A complete list of documents on the CD-ROM is found at the end of the text.

Pearson Prentice Hall is pleased to serve as a sponsor of the **The World History Association Teaching Prize** and **The World History Association and Phi Alpha Theta Student Paper Prize** (undergraduate and graduate divisions). Both of these prizes are awarded annually. For more information, contact *thewha@hawaii.edu*

ACKNOWLEDGMENTS

We are grateful to the many scholars and teachers whose thoughtful and often detailed comments helped shape this as well as previous editions of *The Heritage of World Civilizations.* The advice and guidance provided by Magnus T. Bernhardsson of Williams College in the revision of the coverage of Islam is especially appreciated. We also thank Tianyuan Tan of Harvard University, who helped with conversion of Chinese words to the pinyin system and Gayle K. Brunelle, California State University (Fullerton), who provided invaluable input on strengthening the book's global approach.

Special thanks to A. Dan Frankforter of Pennsylvania State University who helped edit this new TLC edition.

Wayne Ackerson, *Salisbury State University*

Jack Martin Balcer, *Ohio State University*

Charmarie J. Blaisdell, *Northeastern University*

Deborah Buffton, *University of Wisconsin at La Crosse*

Loretta Burns, *Mankato State University*

Gayle K. Brunelle, *California State University, Fullerton*

Chun-shu Chang, *University of Michigan, Ann Arbor*

Mark Chavalas, *University of Wisconsin at La Crosse*

Anthony Cheeseboro, *Southern Illinois University at Edwardsville*

William J. Courteney, *University of Wisconsin*

Samuel Willard Crompton, *Holyoke Community College*

James B. Crowley, *Yale University*

Bruce Cummings, *The University of Chicago*

Stephen F. Dale, *Ohio State University, Columbus*

Clarence B. Davis, *Marian College*

Raymond Van Dam, *University of Michigan, Ann Arbor*

Bill Donovan, *Loyola University of Maryland*

Jaime Dunlap, *Olivet College*

Wayne Farris, *University of Tennessee*

Anita Fisher, *Clark College*

Suzanne Gay, *Oberlin College*

Katrina A. Glass, *United States Military Academy*

Robert Gerlich, *Loyola University*

Samuel Robert Goldberger, *Capital Community-Technical College*

Andrew Gow, *University of Alberta*

Katheryn L. Green, *University of Wisconsin, Madison*

David Griffiths, *University of North Carolina, Chapel Hill*

Louis Haas, *Duquesne University*

Joseph T. Hapak, *Moraine Valley Community College*

Kenneth E. Hendrickson, *Sam Houston State University*

Hue-Tam Ho Tai, *Harvard University*

David Kieft, *University of Minnesota*

Frederick Krome, *Northern Kentucky University*

Lisa M. Lane, *Mira Costa College*

Richard Law, *Washington State University*

David Lelyveld, *Columbia University*

Jan Lewis, *Rutgers University, Newark*

James C. Livingston, *College of William and Mary*

Moira Maguire, *University of Arkansas, Little Rock*

Richard L. Moore Jr., *St. Augustine's College*

Beth Nachison, *Southern Connecticut State University*

Robin S. Oggins, *Binghamton University*

Louis A. Perez Jr., *University of South Florida*

Jonathan Perry, *University of Central Florida*

Cora Ann Presley, *Tulane University*

Norman Raiford, *Greenville Technical College*

Norman Ravitch, *University of California, Riverside*

Thomas M. Ricks, *University of Pennsylvania*

Philip F. Riley, *James Madison University*

Thomas Robisheaux, *Duke University*

William S. Rodner, *Tidewater Community College*

David Ruffley, *United States Air Force Academy*

Dankwart A. Rustow, *The City University of New York*

James J. Sack, *University of Illinois at Chicago*

William Schell, *Murray State University*

Marvin Slind, *Washington State University*

Daniel Scavone, *University of Southern Indiana*

Roger Schlesinger, *Washington State University*

Charles C. Stewart, *University of Illinois*

Nancy L. Stockdale, *University of Central Florida*

Carson Tavenner, *United States Air Force Academy*

Truong-buu Lam, *University of Hawaii*

Harry L. Watson, *Loyola College of Maryland*

William B. Whisenhunt, *College of DuPage*

Paul Varley, *Columbia University*

Finally, we would like to thank the dedicated people who helped produce this revision: our acquisitions editor, Charles Cavaliere; Laura Gardner who created the handsome new design for this edition; Randy Pettit, our production Liaison; and Ben Smith our manufacturing buyer.

A.M.C.
W.A.G.
D.K.
S.O.
F.M.T.

ANNOUNCING A NEW SERIES IN WORLD HISTORY

❋ CONNECTIONS: KEY THEMES IN WORLD HISTORY
Series Editor: Alfred J. Andrea

The increasing pace and specialization of historical inquiry has caused an ever-widening gap between professional research and general surveys of world history. The titles in the Connections series are designed to bridge that gap by placing the latest research on selected topics of global significance, such as disease, trade, slavery, imperialism, decolonization, holy war, and revolution, into an easily accessible context for students. Brief and tightly focused, each Connections title examines cross-cultural themes by employing a combination of narrative, documents, and analysis to show students connections in world history.

PUBLISHED

- TRADING TASTES: *Commodity and Cultural Exchange to 1750*
  Erik Gilbert, *Arkansas State University*
  Jonathan Reynolds, *Northern Kentucky University*

- THE FIRST HORSEMAN: *Disease in Human History*
  John Aberth, *Castleton State College*

FORTHCOMING TITLES

- THE GLOBE ENCOMPASSED: *The Age of European Discovery*
  Glen Ames, *University of Toledo*

- JIHAD AND CRUSADE: *Islamic and Christian Holy Wars Through the Ages*
  Alfred J. Andrea, *University of Vermont*

- GENDER AND POWER: *Women and Nationalism, 1880–1960*
  Nupur Chaudhuri, *Texas Southern University*

- CHANGING THE COURSE OF HISTORY: *Revolutions Past and Present*
  Jack Goldstone, *George Mason University*

- CAPTIVES AS COMMODITIES: *The Trans-Atlantic Slave Trade*
  Lisa Lindsay, *University of North Carolina, Chapel Hill*

- AN IMPERIAL WORLD: *Empires and Colonies, 1750–1945*
  Douglas Northrop, *University of Michigan*

- CONFRONTING THE WEST: *Modernization in the Developing World, 1877–1936*
  Cyrus Veeser, *Bentley College*

Contact your local Prentice Hall representative for additional information regarding the Connections series.

ALBERT M. CRAIG is the Harvard-Yenching Research Professor of History at Harvard University, where he has taught since 1959. A graduate of Northwestern University, he took his Ph.D. at Harvard University. He has studied at Strasbourg University and at Kyoto, Keio, and Tokyo universities in Japan. He is the author of *Choshu in the Meiji Restoration* (1961), *The Heritage of Chinese Civilization* (2001), and, with others, of *East Asia, Tradition and Transformation* (1989). He is the editor of *Japan, A Comparative View* (1973) and co-editor of *Personality in Japanese History* (1970). At present he is engaged in research on the thought of Fukuzawa Yukichi. For eleven years (1976–1987) he was the director of the Harvard-Yenching Institute. He has also been a visiting professor at Kyoto and Tokyo Universities. He has received Guggenheim, Fulbright, and Japan Foundation Fellowships. In 1988 he was awarded the Order of the Rising Sun by the Japanese government.

WILLIAM A. GRAHAM is Albertson Professor of Middle Eastern Studies and Professor of the History of Religion at Harvard University, and Master of Currier House at Harvard University. From 1990–1996 he directed Harvard's Center for Middle Eastern Studies. He has taught for twenty-six years at Harvard, where he received the A.M. and Ph.D. degrees. He also studied in Göttingen, Tübingen, and Lebanon. He is the author of *Divine World and Prophetic World in Early Islam* (1977), awarded the American Council of Learned Societies History of Religions book prize in 1978, and of *Beyond the Written Word: Oral Aspects of Scripture in the History of Religion* (1987). He has published a variety of articles in both Islamic studies and the general history of religion and is one of the editors of the *Encyclopedia of the Qur'an*. He serves currently on the editorial board of several journals and has held John Simon Guggenheim and Alexander von Humboldt research fellowships. *Three Faiths, One God*, co-authored with Jacob Neusner and Bruce Chilton, published in January 2003.

DONALD KAGAN is Sterling Professor of History and Classics at Yale University, where he has taught since 1969. He received the A.B. degree in history from Brooklyn College, the M.A. in classics from Brown University, and the Ph.D. in history from Ohio State University. During 1958–1959 he studied at the American School of Classical Studies as a Fulbright Scholar. He has received three awards for undergraduate teaching at Cornell and Yale. He is the author of a history of Greek political thought, *The Great Dialogue* (1965); a four-volume history of the Peloponnesian war, *The Origins of the Peloponnesian War* (1969); *The Archidamian War* (1974); *The Peace of Nicias and the Sicilian Expedition* (1981); *The Fall of the Athenian Empire* (1987); and a biography of Pericles, *Pericles of Athens and the Birth of Democracy* (1991); *On the Origins of War* (1995), and *The Peloponnesian War* (2003). He is coauthor, with Frederick W. Kagan of *While America Sleeps* (2000). With Brian Tierney and L. Pearce Williams, he is the editor of *Great Issues in Western Civilization*, a collection of readings. He was awarded the National Humanities Medal for 2002.

STEVEN OZMENT is McLean Professor of Ancient and Modern History at Harvard University. He has taught Western Civilization at Yale, Stanford, and Harvard. He is the author of eleven books. *The Age of Reform, 1250–1550* (1980) won the Schaff Prize and was nominated for the 1981 National Book Award. Five of his books have been selections of the History Book Club: *Magdalena and Balthasar: An Intimate Portrait of Life in Sixteenth Century Europe* (1986), *Three Behaim Boys: Growing Up in Early Modern Germany* (1990), *Protestants: The Birth of A Revolution* (1992), *The Burgermeister's Daughter: Scandal in a Sixteenth Century German Town* (1996), and *Flesh and Spirit: Private Life in Early Modern Germany* (1999). His most recent publications are *Ancestors: The Loving Family of Old Europe* (2001), *A Mighty Fortress: A New History of the German People* (2004), and "Why We Study Western Civ," *The Public Interest* 158 (2005).

FRANK M. TURNER is John Hay Whitney Professor of History at Yale University, where he served as University Provost from 1988 to 1992. He received his B.A. degree at the College of William and Mary and his Ph.D. from Yale. He has received the Yale College Award for Distinguished Undergraduate Teaching. He has directed a National Endowment for the Humanities Summer Institute. His scholarly research has received the support of fellowships from the National Endowment for the Humanities and the Guggenheim Foundation and the Woodrow Wilson Center. He is the author of *Between Science and Religion: The Reaction to Scientific Naturalism in Late Victorian England* (1974), *The Greek Heritage in Victorian Britain* (1981), which received the British Council Prize of the Conference on British Studies and the Yale Press Governors Award, *Contesting Cultural Authority: Essays in Victorian Intellectual Life* (1993), and *John Henry Newman: The Challenge to Evangelical Religion* (2002). He has also contributed numerous articles to journals and has served on the editorial advisory boards of *The Journal of Modern History, Isis,* and *Victorian Studies.* He edited *The Idea of a University,* by John Henry Newman (1996). Since 1996 he has served as a Trustee of Connecticut College. In 2003, Professor Turner was appointed Director of the Beinecke Rare Book and Manuscript Library at Yale University.

When writing history, historians use maps, tables, graphs, and visuals to help their readers understand the past. What follows is an explanation of how to use the historian's tools that are contained in this book.

TEXT

Whether it is a biography of Gandhi, an article on the Ottoman Empire, or a survey of world history such as this one, the text is the historian's basic tool for discussing the past. Historians write about the past using narration and analysis. Narration is the story line of history. It describes what happened in the past, who did it, and where and when it occurred. Narration is also used to describe how people in the past lived, how they passed their daily lives and even, when the historical evidence makes it possible for us to know, what they thought, felt, feared, or desired. Using analysis, historians explain why they think events in the past happened the way they did and offer an explanation for the story of history. In this book, narration and analysis are interwoven in each chapter.

STUDY AIDS

A number of features in this book are designed to aid in the study of history. Each chapter begins with **Chapter Highlights**, mini-summaries that preview key themes and developments, and **Questions**, organized by the main subtopics of each chapter, which encourage careful consideration of important themes and developments. Each question is repeated at the appropriate place in the margin of the text.

CHAPTER HIGHLIGHTS

North Africa Developments in African history from 1000 to 1800 varied from region to region. In North Africa, the key new factor was the imperial expansion of the Ottoman Empire as far west as Morocco. But regionalism soon rendered Ottoman authority in North Africa purely nominal.

Empires of the Sudan Several substantial states arose south of the Sahara: Ghana, Mali, Songhai, and Kanem. The ruling elites of these states converted to or were heavily influenced by Islam, although most of their populations clung to their older traditions. Much of the wealth of these states was tied to their control of the trans-Saharan trade routes. Farther south, in Central Africa, another substantial kingdom arose in Benin, famous for its brass sculptures.

East Africa On the east coast, Islam influenced the development of the distinctive Swahili culture and language, and Islamic traders linked the region to India and East Asia.

The Coming of the Europeans The key development of the fifteenth century was the arrival of European traders, missionaries, and warships. The Portuguese and later Europeans came in search of commerce, converts to Christianity, and spheres of influence. Their arrival disrupted indigenous African culture and political relations and presaged Africa's involvement in a new, expanding global trading system dominated by Europeans.

WHICH ECONOMIC factors led to the spread of slavery in the New World?

SLAVERY IN THE AMERICAS

Black slavery was the final mode of forced or subservient labor in the New World. It extended throughout the Americas.

ESTABLISHMENT OF SLAVERY

As the numbers of Native Americans in South America declined, the Spanish and Portuguese turned to African slaves. By the late 1500s, in the West Indies and the cities of South America, black slaves surpassed the white population.

On much of the South American continent dominated by Spain, slavery declined during the late 17th century, but it continued to thrive in Brazil and in the Caribbean. In British North America, it began with the importation of slaves to Jamestown in 1619, and quickly became a fundamental institution.

The spread of slavery in Brazil and the West Indies was promoted by the market for sugar. Only slave labor could provide enough workers for the sugar

MAPS

Maps are important historical tools. They show how geography has affected history and concisely summarize complex relationships and events. Knowing how to read and interpret a map is important to understanding history. Map 11–1 from Chapter 11 shows Muslim conquests from 622–750 C.E. It has three features to help you read it: a **caption**, a **legend**, and a **scale**. The caption explains the rapid rise of Islam from its beginnings in Arabia to its domination of much of the Mediterranean and Persia.

The legend is situated on the bottom left corner of the map. The legend provides information for what each colored area of the map represents. The purple region is the Byzantine Empire. The dark orange represents Muhammad's conquests from 622–632. The areas in light orange were conquered in 632–661. The territories in brown were conquered between 661–750.

The scale, located on the top of the map, informs us that three-quarters of an inch equals 1000 miles (or about 1600 kilometers). With this information, estimates of distance between points on the map are easily made.

The map also shows the topography of the region—its mountains, rivers, and seas. This helps us understand the interplay between geography and history. For example, note how the spead of Islam stops at the Caucasus Mountains. Do you think the topography of this region played a role in limiting the Muslim advance?

Finally, a **critical-thinking question** asks for careful consideration of the spatial connections between geography and history.

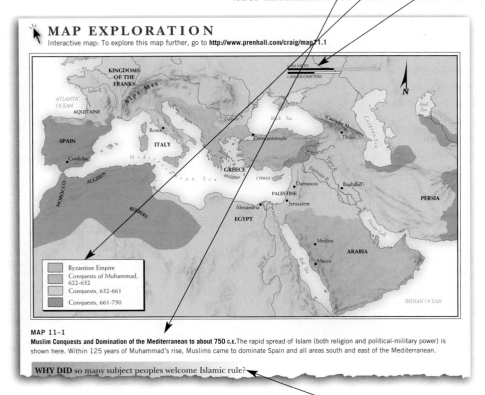

MAP EXPLORATION
Interactive map: To explore this map further, go to **http://www.prenhall.com/craig/map11.1**

Legend:
Byzantine Empire
Conquests of Muhammad, 622-632
Conquests, 632-661
Conquests, 661-750

MAP 11-1
Muslim Conquests and Domination of the Mediterranean to about 750 c.e. The rapid spread of Islam (both religion and political-military power) is shown here. Within 125 years of Muhammad's rise, Muslims came to dominate Spain and all areas south and east of the Mediterranean.

WHY DID so many subject peoples welcome Islamic rule?

MAP EXPLORATIONS

Many of the maps in each chapter are provided in a useful interactive version on the text's Companion Website. These maps are easily identified by a bar along the top (see example above) that reads "**Map Exploration.**" An interactive version of Map 11.1 can be found at **www.prenhall.com/craig/map11.1**. The interactive version of this particular map provides an opportunity to move a timeline from left to right to see the progress of Muslim conquests.

ANALYZING VISUALS

Visual images embedded thoughout the text can provide as much insight into world history as the written word. Within photographs and pieces of fine art lies emotional and historical meaning. Captions also provide valuable information, such as in the example below. When studying the image, consider questions such as: "Who are these people?"; "What are their relationships to each other?"; "What are they doing?"; and "What can we learn from the way the people are dressed?" Such analysis allows for a fuller understanding of the way people lived in the past.

VISUALIZING THE PAST

These essays, found at the end of selected chapters, analyze important aspects of world history through photographs, fine art, sculpture, maps, and woodcuts. Focus questions and a running narrative guide the reader though a careful examination of the historical implications of each topic in question.

Plantation. In the American South, the islands of the Caribbean, and in Brazil, slaves labored on sugar plantations under the authority of overseers.

The Granger Collection.

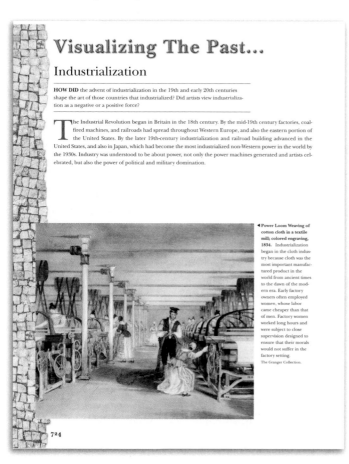

Visualizing The Past...

Industrialization

HOW DID the advent of industrialization in the 19th and early 20th centuries shape the art of those countries that industrialized? Did artists view industrialization as a negative or a positive force?

The Industrial Revolution began in Britain in the 18th century. By the mid-19th century factories, coal-fired machines, and railroads had spread throughout Western Europe, and also the eastern portion of the United States. By the later 19th-century industrialization and railroad building advanced in the United States, and also in Japan, which had become the most industrialized non-Western power in the world by the 1930s. Industry was understood to be about power, not only the power machines generated and artists celebrated, but also the power of political and military domination.

◄ **Power Loom Weaving of cotton cloth in a textile mill; colored engraving, 1834.** Industrialization began in the cloth industry because cloth was the most important manufactured product in the world from ancient times to the dawn of the modern era. Early factory owners often employed women, whose labor came cheaper than that of men. Factory women worked long hours and were subject to close supervision designed to ensure that their morals would not suffer in the factory setting.
The Granger Collection.

724

RELIGIONS OF THE WORLD

Each of these special, two-page essays examines one of the world's great religions and the impact it has had on history.

OVERVIEWS

The **Overview** tables in this text are a special feature designed to highlight and summarize important topics within a chapter. The Overview table shown here, for example, summarizes the Columbian exchange.

OVERVIEW — THE COLUMBIAN EXCHANGE

The same ships that carried Europeans and Africans to the Americas also transported animals, plants, and diseases that had never before appeared in the New World. There was a similar transport back to Europe and Africa. Historians call this cross-continental flow "the Columbian exchange." The overall result was an ecological transformation that continues to shape the world.

To the Americas

Animals:	cattle, chickens, goats, horses, pigs, and sheep
Plants:	almonds, apples, apricots, bananas, barley, cabbage, cherries, dandelions, grapes, lemons, mangos, melons, oats, okra, olives, onions, oranges, peaches, pears, plums, radishes, rice, sugar cane, wheat, and other green vegetables
Diseases:	bubonic plague, chicken pox, diphtheria, influenza, malaria, measles, smallpox, typhoid, and typhus

From the Americas

Animals:	turkeys
Plants:	avocados, beans, blueberries, chilis, cocoa, guavas, maize, manioc (tapioca), peanuts, pecans, pineapples, potatoes, pumpkins, squash, sweet peppers, sweet potatoes, tobacco, and tomatoes
Diseases:	syphilis

QUICK REVIEWS

Quick reviews, placed at key locations in the margins of each chapter, provide pinpoint summaries of important concepts.

QUICK REVIEW

Women Under the Qing and Ming
- Confucian family ideals changed little during the Ming and Qing eras
- Footbinding spread among the upper classes and some commoners
- As population grew, more women worked at home

Church and Empire

910	Monastery of Cluny founded
918	Henry I becomes King of Germany
951	Otto I invades Italy
955	Otto I defeats the Hungarians at Lechfeld
962	Otto I crowned emperor by Pope John XII
1077	Gregory VII pardons Henry IV at Canossa
1122	Concordat of Worms settles the investiture controversy
1152–1190	Reign of Frederick Barbarossa
1198–1215	Reign of Innocent III
1214	Collapse of the claims of Otto IV
1220	Frederick II crowned emperor
1232	Frederick II devolves authority to the German princes
1257	The German monarchy becomes elective

CHRONOLOGIES

Each chapter includes **Chronologies** that list, in chronological order, key events discussed in the chapter. The chronology shown here from Chapter 12, lists the dates of key events in the history of the Holy Roman Empire. Chronologies provide a review of important events and their relationship to one another.

WORLD HISTORY DOCUMENT CD-ROM

Bound into every new copy of this textbook is a free world. History Document CD-ROM. This is a powerful resource for research and additional reading that contains more than 200 primary source documents central to world History. Each document provides essay questions that are linked directly to a website where short-essay answers can be submitted online or printed out. Particularly relevant or interesting documents are called out at appropriate places in the margin of each chapter (see example). A complete list of documents on the CD-ROM is found at the end of the text.

11.1
Mansa Musa: The "King Who Sits on a Mountain of Gold"

PRIMARY SOURCE DOCUMENTS

Historians find most of their information in written records, original documents that have survived from the past. These include government publications, letters, diaries, newspapers—whatever people wrote or printed, including many private documents never intended for publication. Each chapter in the book contains a feature called **History's Voices**—a selection from a primary source document. The example shown here is a description by a Chinese traveler of India. Each **History's Voices** begins with a brief introduction followed by questions on what the document reveals.

HISTORY'S VOICES

A CHINESE TRAVELER'S REPORT ON THE GUPTA REALM

Fa-Hsien, a Chinese Buddhist monk, was the first of several Chinese known for traveling to India to study and bring back Buddhist scriptures from the intellectual centers of Buddhist thought there. He wrote an account of his travels, first through Central Asia, then all over India, and finally through Ceylon and Indonesia again to China (399–414 C.E.).

WHAT THINGS about India seem most to surprise Fa-Hsien? Is his image of Indian rule a positive one? What do his remarks say about the prestige of the Buddhist tradition and its monks in the Indian state? What does he tell us about Indian society?

On the sides of the river, both right and left, are twenty san ghârâmas [monasteries], with perhaps 3,000 priests. The law of the Buddha is progressing and flourishing. Beyond the deserts are the countries of Western India. The kings of these countries are all firm believers in the law of Buddha. They remove their caps of state when they make offerings to the priests. The members of the royal household and the chief ministers personally direct the food-giving; when the distribution of food is over, they spread a carpet on the ground opposite the chief seat (the president's seat) and sit down before it. They dare not sit on couches in the presence of the priests. The rules relating to the almsgiving of kings have been handed down from the time of Buddha till now. Southward from this is the so-called middle-country (Mâdhyade´sa). The climate of this country is warm and equable, without frost or snow. The people are very well off, without poll tax or official restrictions. Only those who till the royal lands return a portion of profit of the land. If they desire to go, they go; if they like to stop, they stop. The kings govern without corporal punishment; criminals are fined, according to circumstances, lightly or heavily. Even in cases of repeated rebellion they only cut off the right hand. The king's personal attendants, who guard him on the right and left, have fixed salaries. Throughout the country the people kill no living thing nor drink wine, nor do they eat garlic or onions, with the exception of Chandâlas [outcasts] only. The Chandâlas are named "evil men" and dwell apart from others; if they enter a town or market, they sound a piece of wood in order to separate themselves; then men, knowing who they are, avoid coming in contact with them. In this country they do not keep swine nor fowls, and do not deal in cattle; they have no shambles or wine-shops in their market places. In selling they use cowrie shells. The Chandâlas only hunt and sell flesh. Down from the time of Buddha's Nirvâna, the kings of these countries, the chief men and householders, have raised vihâras [monasteries] for the priests, and provided for their support by bestowing on them fields, houses, and gardens, with men and oxen. Engraved title-deeds were prepared and handed down from one reign to another; no one has ventured to withdraw them, so that till now there has been no interruption. All the resident priests having chambers (in these vihâras) have their beds, mats, food, drink, and clothes provided without stint; in all places this is the case. The priests ever engage themselves in doing meritorious works for the purpose of religious advancement (karma—building up their religious character), or in reciting the scriptures, or in meditation.

Source: "Buddhist Country Records," in Si-Yu-Ki, *Buddhist Records of the Western World*, trans. by Samuel Beal (London, 1884; reprint, Delhi: Oriental Books Reprint Corporation, 1969), pp. xxxvii–xxxviii. Reprinted by permission of Motilal Banarsidass Publishers Pvt. Ltd., Delhi, India.

Indigenous Reactions The vitality of so many of the cultures and traditions that bore the brunt of the Western onslaught has been striking. Arab, Iranian, Indian, African, and other encounters with Western material and intellectual domination produced different responses and initiatives. These have borne full fruit in political, economic, and intellectual independence only since 1945; however, most began much earlier, some even well before 1800.

One result of the imperial-colonial experience almost everywhere has been the sharpening of cultural self-consciousness and self-confidence among those peoples most negatively affected by Western dominance. The imperial-colonial experiences of the Third World nations may well prove to have been not only ones of misery and reversal, but also of transition to positive development and resurgence, despite the looming economic, educational, and demographic problems that plague many of them.

REVIEW QUESTIONS

1. What kind of policies did the British follow in India? What were the kinds of political activism against British rule were there in India after 1800?

2. How was the Islamic world internally divided after 1800? How did those divisions influence the coming of European powers?

3. How did nationalism affect European control in south Asia, Africa, and the Middle East?

4. What was the role of African nationalism in resisting foreign control?

KEY TERMS

bazaari (p. 681)
cantonments (p. 677)
Great Trek (p. 684)

mfecane (p. 684)
mujtahid (p. 680)
pan-Islamism (p. 682)

raj (p. 675)
scramble for Africa (p. 689)
Wahhabis (p. 679)

For additional study resources for this chapter, go to:
www.prenhall.com/craig/chapter27

IMAGE KEY
for pages 672–673

a. A fez.
b. Kemal Ataturk.
c. ivory for sale, congo.
d. An Imperial procession, or *durbar*.
e. Mahatma Ghandi.
f. Bungandan Kabaka Mutesa I and members of his court.
g. A page from a 19th-century Moroccan Koran.
h. Imam Shamil of Dagestan.
i. Sepoy cavalry attacking British infantry at the Battle of Cawpore in 1857.

SUMMARIES, REVIEW QUESTIONS, AND ADDITIONAL STUDY RESOURCES

At the end of each chapter **summaries** and **review questions** reconsider the main topics. An Image Key provides information about the illustrations that appear at the beginning of the chapter. The URL for the Companion Website ™ is also found at the end of each chapter; this is an excellent resource for additional study aids. In addition, a laminated "Study in Time" chart is found at the front of the text and provides a succinct timeline of world history.

GLOSSARY/KEY TERMS

Significant historical terms are called out in heavy type throughout the text, defined in the margin, and listed at the end of each chapter with appropriate page numbers. These are listed alphabetically and defined in a glossary at the end of the book.

EXPLORE THE POWER OF ONEKEY

OneKey is Prentice Halls' premium exclusive online resource for instructors and students. **OneKey** gives you access to the best online teaching and learning tools—all available 24/7. Harnessing the power of WebCT *WebCT*, Blackboard **Bb**, and Course Compass *CourseCompass*, OneKey puts all of your resources in one place for maximum convenience, simplicity and success.

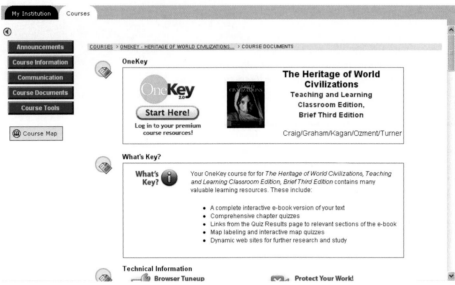

PRESENTATION RESOURCES FOR INSTRUCTORS

VISUALS

- Images
- Maps, Tables, Figures
- Map Outlines

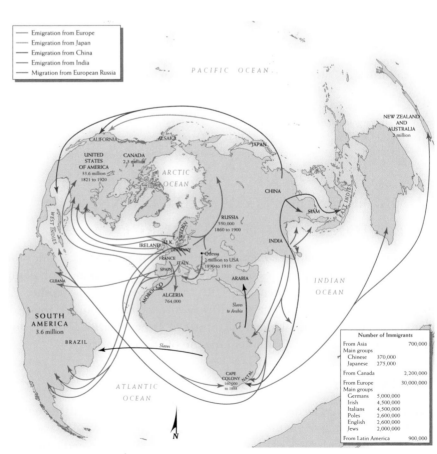

POWERPOINT™ PRESENTATIONS

- Lecture Aids—Visuals
- Lecture Aids—Text
- Lecture Aids—Lecture Outline

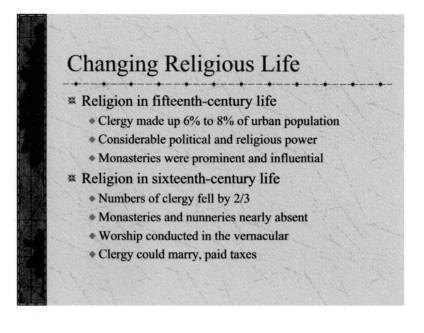

ANIMATIONS AND ACTIVITIES

- Interactive Maps

TEXT

- Instructor's Manual

ASSESSMENT RESOURCES FOR STUDENTS

HOMEWORK

- Review Questions
- e-book

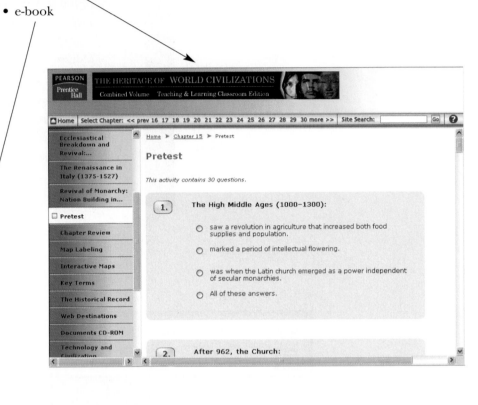

ADDITIONAL STUDENT RESOURCES

LINKS

- Companion Website
- e-themes in World History

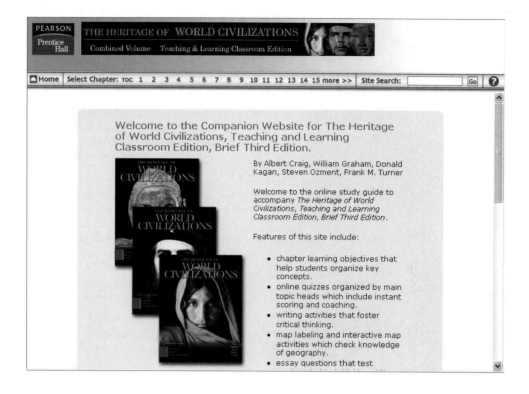

ADDITIONAL RESOURCES

 • Research Navigator

Take a tour at www.prenhall.com/onekey

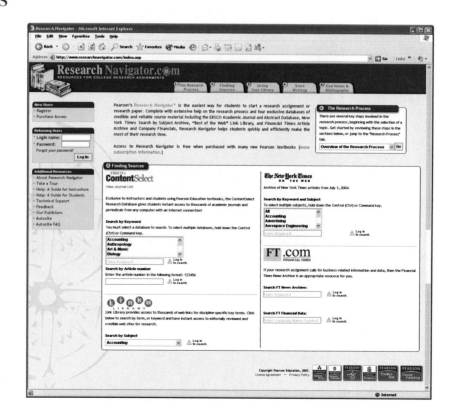

15 Europe to the Early 1500s
Revival, Decline, and Renaissance

CHAPTER HIGHLIGHTS

Medieval Society Medieval society was divided, in theory, into three main groups: clergy, nobility, and laborers. The rise of merchants, self-governing towns, and universities helped break down this division. By supporting rulers against the nobility, towns gave kings the resources to build national governments. Much of medieval history involves the struggle by rulers to assert their authority over powerful local lords and the church.

Church and State The medieval papacy sought to extend its power over both church and state. In the tenth century, the Cluny reform movement increased popular respect for the church and strengthened the papacy. In the Investiture Struggle, the papacy secured the independence of the clergy, in the process weakening imperial power in Germany. The First Crusade further strengthened papal prestige. But, by the end of the thirteenth century, kings had become more powerful than popes. In the fourteenth century, the Great Schism further weakened papal prestige.

Nation Building By the fifteenth century, England, France, and Spain had developed into strong national monarchies with centralized bureaucracies and professional armies. The Great Schism, the Hundred Years' War, and the Black Death had weakened the church and the nobility, while townspeople supported kings. A similar process began in Russia where rulers of Moscow extended their authority after throwing off Mongol rule.

The Renaissance The Renaissance, which began in the Italian city-states in the late fourteenth century, marked the transition from the medieval to the modern world. Humanism promoted a rebirth of ancient norms and values and the classical ideal of an educated, well-rounded person. The growth of secular values led to a great burst of artistic activity. The political weakness of the Italian states invited foreign intervention by France, Spain, and the Habsburgs. The sack of Rome by imperial forces in 1527 marked the end of the Renaissance.

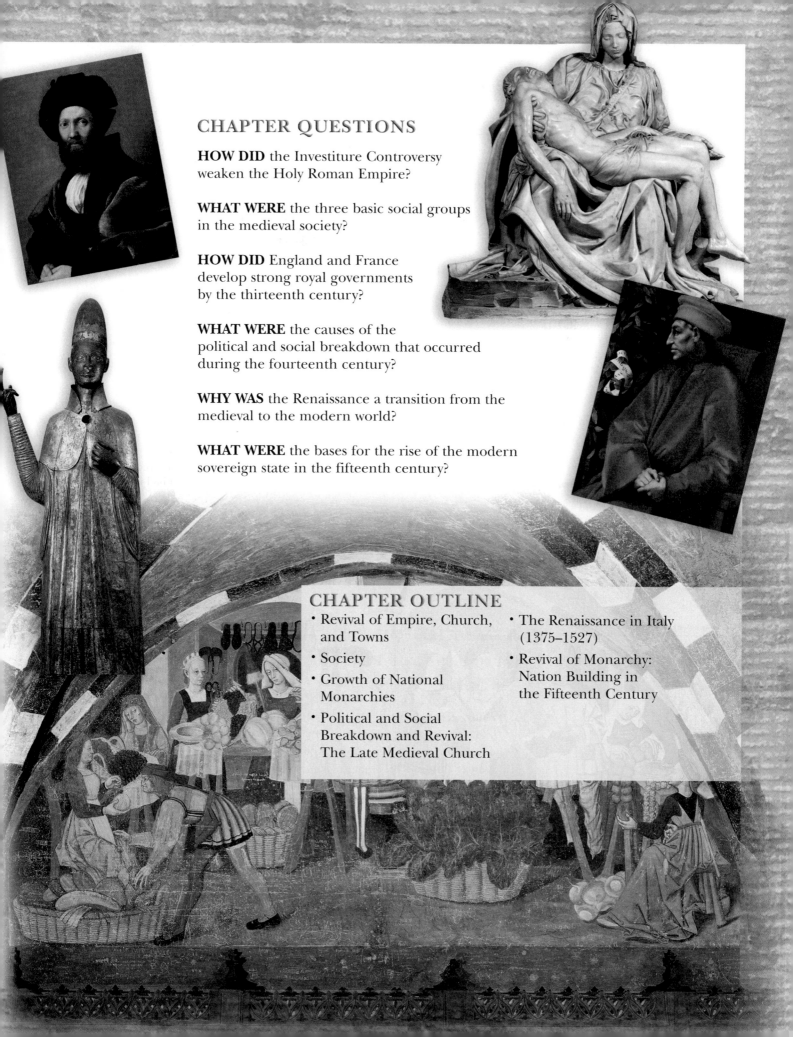

CHAPTER QUESTIONS

HOW DID the Investiture Controversy weaken the Holy Roman Empire?

WHAT WERE the three basic social groups in the medieval society?

HOW DID England and France develop strong royal governments by the thirteenth century?

WHAT WERE the causes of the political and social breakdown that occurred during the fourteenth century?

WHY WAS the Renaissance a transition from the medieval to the modern world?

WHAT WERE the bases for the rise of the modern sovereign state in the fifteenth century?

CHAPTER OUTLINE

- Revival of Empire, Church, and Towns
- Society
- Growth of National Monarchies
- Political and Social Breakdown and Revival: The Late Medieval Church
- The Renaissance in Italy (1375–1527)
- Revival of Monarchy: Nation Building in the Fifteenth Century

The High Middle Ages (from the eleventh through the thirteenth centuries) were a period of both political expansion and consolidation and intellectual flowering and synthesis. The Latin, or Western, church established itself as a spiritual authority independent of secular monarchies, which themselves became more powerful and self-aggrandizing. The parliaments and popular assemblies that accompanied the rise of these monarchies pioneered modern representative institutions.

The High Middle Ages saw a revolution in agriculture that increased food supplies and populations. Trade and commerce revived, towns expanded, protomodern forms of banking and credit developed, and a "new rich" merchant class rose to power in Europe's cities. Universities were established, and contact with the Arab world led to the beginning of the recovery of the works of the ancient Greek philosophers. This helped to stimulate the great expansion of Western education and culture that was achieved during the late Middle Ages and the Renaissance.

The late Middle Ages and the Renaissance (the fourteenth, fifteenth, and early sixteenth centuries) were a time of unprecedented calamity and of bold new beginnings in Europe. France and England grappled with each other in a bitter conflict, the Hundred Years' War (1337–1453). Between 1348 and 1350, Bubonic plague, which contemporaries called the Black Death, reduced the population in many regions by approximately one-third. A schism divided the papacy and the church (1378–1417), and in 1453 the Turks captured Constantinople and expanded into Europe. From this perspective, Western civilization seemed to be collapsing.

But the late Middle Ages also witnessed an intellectual and artistitic renaissance that continued into the seventeenth century. Scholars criticized medieval assumptions about the nature of God, humankind, and society. Italian and northern humanists made a full recovery of classical learning and languages and conceived of ideas that would spread and transform life in Europe. The "divine art" of printing was invented. The vernaculars, the languages of ordinary people, began to take their place alongside Latin as vehicles for art and serious discourse, and patriotism and incipient nationalism became important factors in the politics of Europe's independent nation-states.

HOW DID the Investiture Controversy weaken the Holy Roman Empire?

REVIVAL OF EMPIRE, CHURCH, AND TOWNS

OTTO I AND THE REVIVAL OF THE EMPIRE

The fortunes of both the old empire and the papacy began to revive in 918, when the Saxon Henry I ("the Fowler"; d. 936) became the first non-Frankish king of Germany. Henry rebuilt royal power and left his son and successor Otto I (r. 936–973) in a strong territorial position. Otto maneuvered his own kin to dominate Bavaria, Swabia, and Franconia. Then, in 951, he invaded Italy and proclaimed himself its king. In 955, he defeated the Hungarians at Lechfeld, which secured German borders against barbarian attacks. All this earned Otto the title "the Great."

Otto enlisted the help of the church in rebuilding his realm. As agents to administer his lands, he preferred to appoint bishops and abbots. These men possessed a sense of universal empire but they could not marry and found families to compete with his own. In 961, Otto responded to a call for help from Pope John XII (955–964), and on February 2, 962, Otto received from the pope in return the imperial coronation he had long desired. The church was brought ever more under royal control, but it was increasingly determined to assert its independence.

THE REVIVING CATHOLIC CHURCH

Otto's successors became so preoccupied with Italy that they allowed their German base to disintegrate. As the revived empire began to crumble in the 11th century, the church, long unhappy with imperial domination, declared its independence by embracing a reform movement pioneered by a monastic order.

Cluny Reform Movement   In 910, a monastery was founded at Cluny in east-central France, and the Cluniac monks launched a campaign to free the church from lay control. Their cause was aided by the popular respect the church commanded. The church was medieval society's most democratic institution. Theoretically, any man could become pope, for the pope was usually elected by the people and the clergy of Rome. The grace and salvation the church dispensed were available to everyone, and the church promised a better life to come to the great mass of ordinary people, who found their earthly circumstances brutish and hopeless.

The Cluny reformers maintained that clergy should not be subservient to kings, and that all clergy should come directly under the authority of the pope. They denounced "secular" parish clergy, who by living with concubines in a relationship akin to marriage, fell short of Cluny's ascetic ideals. Distinctive features of Western religion—separation of church and state and the celibacy of the Catholic clergy—had their definitive origins in the Cluny reform movement. From Cluny, reformers were dispatched throughout France and Italy, and in the late 11th century the papacy embraced their reforms.

Otto I and the Church. Otto I presents the Magdeburg Cathedral to Christ, as the pope (holding the keys to the kingdom of heaven) watches, a testimony to Otto's guardianship of the Church.

"Christ Enthroned with Saints and Emperor Otto I" (r. 962–973). One from a series of 19 known as the Magdeburg Ivories. Ivory H 5" × W 41/2" (12.7 × 11.4 cm).

Investiture Struggle: Gregory VII and Henry IV   In 1075, Pope Gregory VII (r. 1073–1085), a fierce advocate of church reform, condemned under penalty of excommunication the well-established custom of king's appointing bishops to administer their estates and "investing" them with the ring and staff that symbolized their ecclesiastical office. The emperor Henry IV of Germany considered Gregory's action a direct challenge to his authority. Germany's territorial princes, on the other hand, were inclined to support the pope, for they believed that anything that weakened the emperor strengthened them.

The lines of battle were quickly drawn. Henry assembled his loyal German bishops at Worms in January 1076 and had them declare their independence from Gregory. Gregory promptly excommunicated Henry and absolved all Henry's subjects from loyalty to him. The German princes were delighted. Henry, facing a general revolt, had to come to terms with Gregory. In a famous scene, he prostrated himself outside Gregory's castle retreat at Canossa in northern Italy. Reportedly he stood barefoot in the snow off and on for three days before the pope absolved him. Papal power seemed to triumph, but the struggle was not yet over.

The investiture controversy was not settled until 1122. In the Concordat of Worms, Emperor Henry V (r. 1106–1125) agreed not to invest bishops with the ring and staff that signified their spiritual authority, and Pope Calixtus II (r. 1119–1124) recognized the emperor's right to be present at episcopal consecrations and to grant bishops their secular fiefs before or after their investment

QUICK REVIEW

Church and State

- Investiture crisis centered on authority to appoint and control clergy
- Pope Gregory excommunicated Henry IV when he proclaimed his independence from papacy
- Crisis settled in 1122 with Concordat of Worms

Struggle Between Emperor and Pope. A 12th-century German manuscript portrays the struggle between Emperor Henry IV and Pope Gregory VII. In the top panel, Henry installs the puppet pope Clement III and drives Gregory from Rome. Below, Gregory dies in exile. The artist was a monk, whose sympathies were with Gregory, not Henry.

Thuringer Universities and Landesbibliothek, Jena: Bos. q. 6, Blatt 79r.

Crusades Religious wars directed by the church against infidels and heretics.

with the spiritual symbols by the church. The emperor effectively retained the right to nominate or veto a candidate. The settlement had the effect of separating spheres of ecclesiastical and secular authority and setting the stage for future and greater conflicts between church and state.

THE CRUSADES

If evidence of a surge of popular piety and support for the pope in the High Middle Ages is needed, the **Crusades** provide it. What the Cluniac reform was to the clergy, the First Crusade to the Holy Land was to the laity: an outlet for heightened religious zeal.

Late in the 11th century, the Byzantine Empire was under severe pressure from the Seljuk Turks, and Emperor Alexius I Comnenus (r. 1081–1118) appealed for Western aid. At the Council of Clermont in 1095, Pope Urban II (r. 1088–1099) responded by launching the First Crusade. Scholars debate the motives of the Crusaders. Genuine religious piety played a major part. The papacy promised crusaders forgiveness for all their sins should they die in battle, and a crusade to the Holy Land was the ultimate religious pilgrimage. But the pope and others may also have hoped to stabilize the West by sending large numbers of restless, feuding young nobles off to foreign lands. (About 100,000 took part in the First Crusade.) Younger sons of nobleman, for whom there were no estates at home, may have hoped that the crusade would make their fortunes. Urban also saw the crusade as an opportunity to reconcile Eastern and Western Christianity.

7.6
Launching the Crusades (1095): "It Is the Will of God!"

The First Victory   Drawn by the dream of liberating the holy city of Jerusalem, which the Seljuk Turks had held since the seventh century, three great armies gathered in France, Germany, and Italy. As the crusaders marched by different overland routes toward Constantinople, they seized the opportunity to rid Europe of Jews as well as Muslims. Jewish communities, especially in the Rhineland, suffered bloody pogroms (see Map 15-1).

The eastern emperor was suspicious of the uncouth, spirited soldiers who gathered at his capital, and his subjects, whose villages the Europeans plundered, were openly hostile. Nevertheless, the Crusaders succeeded in doing what Byzantine armies had failed to do. They routed the Seljuks and on July 15, 1099,

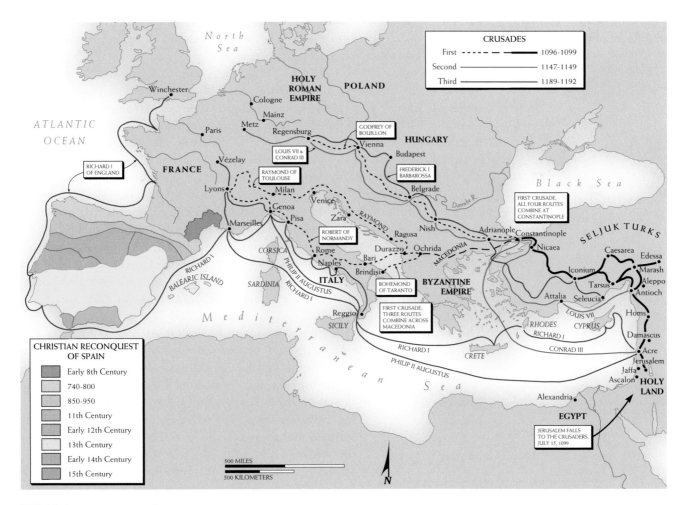

MAP 15–1
The Early Crusades. Routes and several leaders of the Crusades during the first century of the movement are shown. The names on this map do not exhaust the list of great nobles who went on the First Crusade. The even showier array of monarchs of the Second and Third Crusades still left the Crusades, on balance, ineffective in achieving their goals.

WHAT obstacles did the Crusaders encounter?

Seige of Jerusalem. Godfrey of Bouillon leads the attack on Jerusalem in 1099. The capture of the city was hailed as a miracle, followed by the massacre of its inhabitants.

Bibliotheque Nationale, Paris, France.

took the city of Jerusalem. They owed their success to their superior military discipline and weaponry and to the fact that the Muslims failed to unite to oppose them.

The Crusaders set up a "kingdom of Jerusalem" composed of a number of tiny feudal states. These were tenuously held islands in a sea of Muslims intent on their destruction. As the crusaders built castles for the defense of their new territories, their focus shifted from conquest to economic development. Some, like the military-religious order of the Knights Templar, acquired vast fortunes.

The Second and Third Crusades Europeans held their own for about 40 years, and then the crusader states began to fall. The first to go was Edessa. Its loss in 1144 sparked a drive for a Second Crusade (1147–1149), which was effectively preached by Bernard of Clairvaux (1091–1153), a Cistercian monk and one of Europe's most eminent religious leaders. The venture was a dismal failure.

In October 1187, Saladin (r. 1138–1193), king of Egypt and Syria, retook Jerusalem. Its loss inspired the Third Crusade (1189–1192), a joint effort by three of Europe's greatest kings: Richard the Lion-Hearted of England, Frederick Barbarossa of the Holy Roman Empire, and Philip Augustus of France. Barbarossa died in an accident en route to the front, and Philip Augustus soon returned to France to prey on Richard's lands. Left alone, Richard could do little. When he finally acknowledged that fact and headed home, he was captured by Emperor Henry VI. England paid a huge ransom to win his release. Popular resentment at the failed, costly venture contributed to the events that produced the Magna Carta in 1215, an effort to curb the power of England's kings.

The Crusades did not change the international political situation. The Holy Land reverted as firmly as ever to Muslim control. But the Crusades did transform international commerce by creating new trade routes and reopening old ones. Italy's great port cities—particularly Venice, Pisa, and Genoa—profited greatly.

The Fourth Crusade Venetian commercial ambitions helped to make the Fourth Crusade a travesty. In 1202, 30,000 crusaders gathered at Venice, intending to sail to Egypt. When they could not raise the money to pay for their transport, they negotiated a deal with the Venetians. In exchange for passage, they agreed to take the rival Christian port of Zara for Venice. Europe was stunned, but worse was to come. The Crusaders were next diverted to Constantinople, which fell to their assault in 1204. A Latin ascended the Byzantine throne, and Venice became the dominant commercial power in the eastern Mediterranean.

Pope Innocent III was chagrined by the misdirection of a crusade he had authorized, but once Constantinople was in Latin hands, he changed his mind. The opportunity to bring Greek Christians under the control of the Latin church was too tempting. The Greeks, however, could not

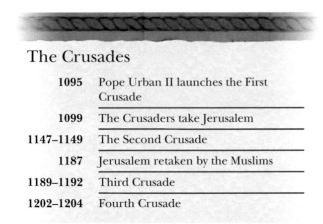

The Crusades

1095	Pope Urban II launches the First Crusade
1099	The Crusaders take Jerusalem
1147–1149	The Second Crusade
1187	Jerusalem retaken by the Muslims
1189–1192	Third Crusade
1202–1204	Fourth Crusade

be reconciled to Latin rule, and in 1261 the man they recognized as their legitimate emperor, Michael Paleologus, recaptured the city. He had help from Venice's rival, Genoa. The Fourth Crusade did nothing to heal the political and religious divisions that separated East and West.

Towns and Townspeople

In the 11th and 12th centuries, most towns were small. Only about 5 percent of western Europe's population lived in an urban context, but they were some of the most creative members of medieval society.

The Chartering of Towns   Towns were originally dominated by the feudal lords who issued charters spelling out terms for their organization. The lords' purpose was to court skilled laborers who could manufacture the finished goods the feudal nobility desired. A charter guaranteed a town's safety and gave its residents a degree of independence unknown to a rural peasant.

As towns grew and their privileges beckoned, many serfs migrated to the new urban centers. There they found the freedom and opportunity to earn the wealth that elevated an industrious craftsperson's social standing. As movement of serfs to towns accelerated, the lords in the countryside were forced to offer serfs more favorable terms of tenure to keep them on the land. The growth of towns thus improved the lot of serfs in several ways.

The Rise of Merchants   Rural society not only provided craftspeople and day laborers for towns, but the first merchants may have been enterprising serfs. Certainly, some of the long-distance traders were people who had nothing to lose and everything to gain from the enormous risks of foreign trade. They traveled together in armed caravans and convoys, buying goods and products as cheaply as possible at the source, and selling them for all they could get.

At first the merchants were disliked because they were outside the traditional social groups of nobility, clergy, and peasantry. Over time, however, the powerful came to respect the merchants and the weak to imitate them. Merchants brought prosperity and a higher standard of living.

As traders established themselves in towns and grew in wealth and numbers, they formed their own protective associations. These soon challenged seigneurial authority over their communities. Merchants especially wanted to end the arbitrary tolls and tariffs that regional magnates imposed on the goods merchants moved through the countryside.

Townspeople needed simple, uniform laws and a government sympathetic to their new forms of business activity. Commerce was incompatible with the defensive, fortress mentality of the lords of the countryside. The result was often a struggle with the old nobility within and outside the towns. This conflict led townspeople in the High and late Middle Ages to form independent communes and to ally themselves with kings against the rural nobility, a development that rearranged the centers of power in medieval Europe and ended classic feudal government.

QUICK REVIEW

Town Charters
- Towns originally dominated by feudal lords
- Town charters granted townspeople safety and independence
- Growth of towns improved conditions for serfs generally

Foundry in Florence. Skilled workers were an integral component of the commerce of medieval towns. This scene shows the manufacture of cannons in a foundry in Florence.

Scala/Art Resource, N.Y.

MAP EXPLORATION

 Interactive map: To explore this map further, go to **http://www.prenhall.com/craig/map15.2**

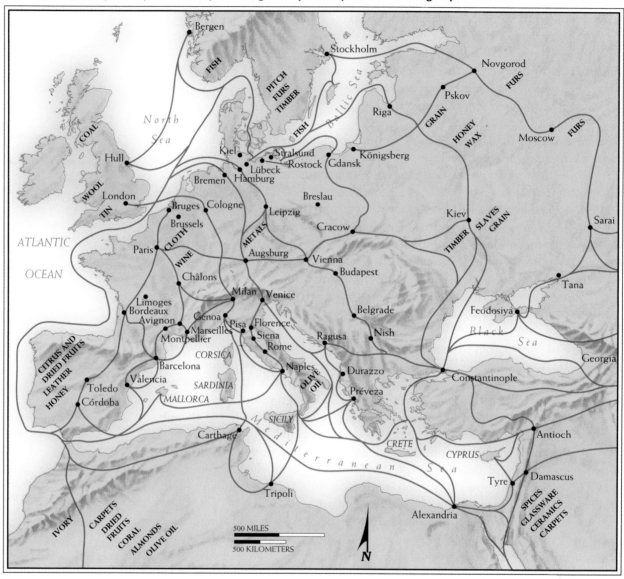

MAP 15–2

Medieval Trade Routes and Regional Products. Trade in Europe varied in intensity and geographical extent in different periods during the Middle Ages. The map shows some of the channels that came to be used in interregional commerce. Labels tell part of what was carried in that commerce.

HOW STRONG were the connections among Europe, the Middle East, and Africa at this time?

Because the merchants were the engine of the urban economy, small shopkeepers and artisans identified far more with them than with the aloof lords and bishops who were medieval society's traditional masters. The lesser nobility (small knights) also recognized the new mercantile economy as the wave of the future. During the 11th and 12th centuries, the burgher upper classes increased their economic strength and successfully challenged the old noble urban lords for control of towns.

New Models of Government   With urban autonomy came new models of self-government. Around 1100 the old urban nobility and the new burgher upper class merged to form an urban patriciate. It was a marriage between those wealthy by birth (inherited property) and those who made their fortunes in long-distance trade. From this new ruling class was born the aristocratic town council, which henceforth governed towns.

Enriching and complicating the situation, small artisans and craftspeople also slowly developed their own protective associations or **guilds** and began to gain a voice in government. The opportunities towns created for the "little people" established a new principle: "Town air brings freedom." Within town walls people thought of themselves as citizens with basic rights, not subjects liable to a master's whim.

Towns and Kings   By providing kings with the resources they needed to curb factious noblemen, towns became a major force in the transition from feudal societies to national governments. Towns were a ready source of educated bureaucrats and lawyers who knew Roman law, an effective tool for building royal government. The money that towns could provide for kings also enabled kings to hire their own armies and free themselves from dependence on the nobility. In turn, towns won political recognition and had their privileges guaranteed by national governments. In France, towns were integrated early into the royal administration. In Germany, they came under ever-tighter control by princes. In Italy, uniquely, they grew into genuine city-states that reached the peak of their power and influence during the Italian Renaissance.

Jews in Christian Society   Towns also attracted Jews who plied trades in small businesses. Many became wealthy as moneylenders to kings, popes, and business-people. Jewish intellectual and religious culture both dazzled and threatened Christians. These various factors encouraged suspicion and distrust among Christians, and led to a surge in anti-Jewish sentiment in the late 12th and early 13th centuries.

Schools and Universities   In the 12th century, translations and commentaries by Byzantine and Spanish Islamic scholars introduced western Europeans to the philosophical works of Aristotle, the writings of Euclid and Ptolemy, the texts of Greek physicians and Arab mathematicians, and the corpus of Roman law. The intellectual ferment created by this explosion of information began the development of the modern universities. The first important Western university was established in 1158 in Bologna. It specialized in the study of Roman law and became the model for the universities of Spain, Italy, and southern France. Paris provided a different model for northern European universities, and it was leading school for theologians

At the start of the High Middle Ages, learning involved mastering what was already known. People assumed that all truth had been discovered and only needed to be properly organized, elucidated, and defended. Students wrote commentaries on authoritative texts, especially those of Aristotle and the church fathers. Teachers did not encourage students to strive independently for undiscovered truth. They taught them to organize and harmonize the accepted truths of tradition and drilled these into them.

Under this method of study, called **Scholasticism**, students summarized the opinions of the received authorities in their field, debated their arguments pro

guild Association of merchants or craftsmen that offered protection to its members and set rules for their work and products.

Scholasticism Method of study based on logic and dialectic that dominated the medieval schools. It assumed that truth already existed; students had only to organize, elucidate, and defend knowledge learned from authoritative texts, especially those of Aristotle and the Church Fathers.

Dominicans (left) and Franciscans (right). Unlike the other religious orders, the Dominicans and Franciscans did not live in cloisters but wandered about preaching and combating heresy. They depended for support on their own labor and the kindness of the laity.

Cliche Bibliothèque Nationale de France, Paris.

and con, and then drew logical conclusions. The arrival of Aristotle's works in the West honed the tools of logic and dialectic they used to discipline their thinking. Dialectic is the art of testing a truth by examining arguments against it. The assumption that truth could be discovered by debating authoritative texts was accepted even in fields such as medicine—to the detriment of practical experience and empirical research.

Abelard   Peter Abelard (1079–1142) was the boldest and most controversial of the advocates for the new Aristotelian learning. As the leading philosopher and theologian of his day, he was the first European scholar to attract a large student following. His audacious logical critique of religious doctrine, however, earned him powerful enemies. His thinking was unique in its appreciation of subjectivity. He claimed, for instance, that the motives of an act's agent determined whether that act was good or evil, not the act itself. He also said that an individual's feeling of repentance was a more important factor in receiving God's forgiveness than the church's sacrament of penance.

Abelard, as he laments in his autobiography, played into the hands of his enemies by seducing Heloise, a young woman he was hired to tutor. She was the niece of a powerful canon of Paris's cathedral of Notre Dame. After she became pregnant, Abelard wed her—but kept the marriage secret, for university teachers, like clergy, were required to be celibate. Her chagrined uncle hired men to break into Abelard's rooms and castrate him.

Abelard sought refuge in the monastic life and induced Heloise to enter a convent. They exchanged letters in which he denigrated his love for her as wretched desire. Repentance failed, however, to ingratiate him with the church authorities. In 1121, his works were burned, and in 1140, 19 propositions that he had taught were condemned as heresies. Heloise outlived him by 20 years and won renown for her efforts to improve conditions for cloistered women.

SOCIETY

THE ORDER OF LIFE

WHAT WERE the three basic social groups in the medieval society?

Medieval commentators described society as consisting of only three categories of people: those who fought as mounted knights (the landed nobility), those who prayed (the clergy), and those who labored in fields and shops (the peasantry and village artisans). After the revival of towns in the 11th century, a fourth social group emerged: the long-distance traders and merchants.

Nobles By the late Middle Ages, separate classes of higher and lower nobility had evolved. The higher were the great landowners and territorial magnates, long the dominant powers in their regions; the lower were petty landlords, the descendants of minor knights, newly rich merchants, or wealthy farmers.

Arms were the nobleman's profession and waging war his sole occupation. In the eighth century, the adoption of stirrups made mounted warriors Europe's most valued military assets. The chief virtues of these knights were physical strength, courage, and beligerancy. For them, warfare was an opportunity to win wealth, honor, and glory. Peace, on the other hand, meant economic stagnation and boredom.

No medieval social group was absolutely uniform. Noblemen formed a broad spectrum—from minor vassals without subordinate vassals to mighty barons, the principal vassals of a king or prince, who had many vassals of their own. Dignity and status within the nobility were directly proportional to how much authority one exercised over others; a chief with many vassals far excelled the small country nobleman who was lord over none but himself.

By the late Middle Ages, several developments were forcing the landed nobility into a steep economic and political decline from which it never recovered. Climatic changes and agricultural failures created large famines, while the great plague (discussed later in this chapter) brought about unprecedented population losses. Changing military tactics and the appearance of heavy artillery during the Hundred Years' War empowered infantry and made the noble cavalry nearly obsolete. The support wealthy towns gave to kings enabled strong royal governments to reduce the power nobles once had over their private domains. After the 14th century, land and wealth counted for far more than noble lineage as qualifications for entrance into the highest social class.

Clergy Unlike a noble or a peasant, one was not born into the clerical estate. It was acquired by religious training and ordination and was, in theory at least, open to anyone. There were two fundamental categories of clergy. The **regular clergy** were the monks who lived according to a special ascetic rule (*regula*) in cloisters apart from the world. In the 13th century, the papacy authorized a different kind of monastic order. The friars—the Franciscans and the Dominicans—stayed in the world to preach, combat heresy, and provide social services. The **secular clergy** lived and worked among the laity in the world (*saeculum*). They staffed a vast hierarchy. At the top were the wealthy cardinals, archbishops, and bishops who were drawn almost exclusively from the nobility. Below them were the urban priests, cathedral canons, and court clerks. Finally, there was the great mass of poor parish priests, who were neither financially nor intellectually much above the common people they served.

During most of the Middle Ages, the clergy were honored as the first estate, and theology was the queen of the sciences. There was great popular respect and reverence for the clergy's function as mediators between God and humanity. The priest brought the Son of God down to earth when he celebrated the sacrament of the Eucharist, and his absolution released penitents from punishment for sin. Mere laypeople were not to presume to sit in judgment on such a priest.

Peasants The largest and lowest social group in medieval society was the one on whose labor the welfare of all the others depended: the agrarian peasantry. Many peasants lived and worked on the manors of the nobility, the vital cells of rural social life. The lord of a manor was owed a fixed amount of produce (grain,

regular clergy Monks and nuns who belong to religious orders.

secular clergy Parish clergy who did not belong to a religious order.

OVERVIEW   MEDIEVAL UNIVERSITIES

In the 12th century, Latin translations of of ancient texts in law, astronomy, philosophy, and mathematics, and of learned commentaries on them by Islamic and Byzantine scholars, reached the West. The resulting intellectual ferment gave rise to the medieval universities. The first university was established at Bologna in Italy in 1158. By 1500, there were almost 50 universities across Europe from Scotland to Poland. Universities helped bring wealth and prestige to towns; graduated professionals, such as lawyers, physicians, and theologians; and provided rulers with trained bureaucrats for their increasingly complex administrations. The following is a list of the medieval universities and the dates of their founding:

University	Country	Date of Founding	University	Country	Date of Founding
Bologna	Italy	1158	Erfurt	Germany	1379
Paris	France	ca. 1150–1160	Heidelberg	Germany	1385
Oxford	England	1167	Ferrara	Italy	1391
Vicenza	Italy	1204	Wurzburg	Germany	1402
Cambridge	England	1209	Leipzig	Germany	1409
Salamanca	Spain	1218	St. Andrews	Scotland	1411
Padua	Italy	1222	Turin	Italy	1412
Naples	Italy	1224	Louvain	Belgium	1426
Toulouse	France	1229	Poitiers	France	1431
Rome	Italy	1244	Caen	France	1437
Siena	Italy	1247	Bourdeaux	France	1441
Piacenza	Italy	1248	Barcelona	Spain	1450
Montpellier	France	1289	Trier	Germany	1450
Lisbon	Portugal	1290	Glasgow	Scotland	1451
Avignon	France	1303	Freiburg	Germany	1455
Orleans	France	1305	Ingolstadt	Germany	1459
Perugia	Italy	1308	Basel	Switzerland	1460
Coimbra	Portugal	1308	Nantes	France	1463
Grenoble	France	1339	Bourges	France	1465
Pisa	Italy	1343	Ofen	Germany	1475
Valladolid	Spain	1346	Tubingen	Germany	1477
Prague	Bohemia	1348	Uppsala	Sweden	1477
Pavia	Italy	1361	Copenhagen	Denmark	1479
Vienna	Austria	1364	Aberdeen	Scotland	1494
Cracow	Poland	1364			

eggs, and the like) and services from its peasant families, and he held judicial and police authority over them. He owned and operated the machines that processed their crops into food and drink, and he had the right to subject his tenants to exactions called *banalities*. He could, for example, force them to breed their cows with his bull, to grind their bread grains in his mill, to bake their bread in his oven, and to make their wine in his wine press—all for a fee. He might also compel them to buy their beer from his brewery and even give him the choice parts of all animals slaughtered on his lands. He collected as an inheritance tax a serf's best animal. Without the lord's permission, a serf could neither travel nor marry outside the manor to which he was attached.

However, the serfs' status was not chattel slavery. It was to a lord's advantage to keep his serfs healthy and happy, for his welfare, like theirs, depended on the quality of their work. Serfs had their own dwellings and strips of land that produced their incomes. They organized their own labor and could market for their own profit any surpluses that remained after they met their obligations. Serfs could pass their property (their dwellings, fields, and personal possessions) on to their children.

Two basic changes transformed conditions of life for the peasantry during the course of the Middle Ages. The first was increasing importance of single-family holdings. As families acquired and retained property from generation to generation, family farms replaced manorial units. The second was the conversion of the serf's dues into money payments, a change made possible by the revival of trade, the rise of town markets, and the return of a monetary economy. By the 13th century, many peasants held their land as rent-paying tenants and no longer had servile status.

In the mid-14th century, when the great plague and the Hundred Years' War created a labor shortage, nobles in England and France tried to turn back the clock by increasing taxes on the peasantry and restricting their migration to the cities. Their efforts triggered rebellions. The revolts of the agrarian peasantry, like those of the urban proletariat, were brutally crushed, but they were only one of the stresses that were threatening to destabilize European society at the end of the Middle Ages.

MEDIEVAL WOMEN

The image of women and the reality of their lives were quite different in the Middle Ages. The image was sketched by celibate male clergy who viewed virginity as morally superior to marriage. Drawing on ancient pagan as well as biblical sources, they claimed that women were physically, mentally, and morally inferior to men. They defined only two respectable roles for them: subjugated housewife, or confined nun. Many medieval women were neither.

Image and Status   The clerical view of women was contradicted both within the church itself and in secular society. During the 12th and 13th centuries, the burgeoning popularity of the cult of the Virgin Mary, of chivalric romances, and of courtly love literature celebrated women as natural moral superiors of men. The church also condemned extreme misogyny.

Virgin and Child, surrounded by angels, by Giovanni Cimabue (1240–1302).

SuperStock, Inc.

Medieval Marketplace. A 15th-century rendering of an 11th- or 12th-century marketplace. Medieval women were active in all trades, but especially in the food and clothing industries.

Scala/Art Resource, N.Y.

10.3
The Goodman of Paris

vernacular Everyday language spoken by the people as opposed to Latin.

HOW DID England and France develop strong royal governments by the 13th century?

Peter Lombard (1100–1169), an influential theologian, taught that God created Eve from Adam's rib because God intended woman neither to rule nor be ruled, but to be at man's side as his partner in a mutual relationship.

Germanic customary law also treated women better than Roman law. German women married men of their own age, and a German bride was entitled to a gift of property from her husband that she retained in case of his death. German law gave women the right to inherit, administer, dispose of, and confer property, and it allowed women to take men to court and sue for bodily injury and rape.

Life Choices   The nunnery was an option only for women from the propertied classes, for admission to a cloister was contingent on payment of a substantial dowry. The number of nuns was never very large in the Middle Ages, but the cloister was an appealing refuge for some. Within a nunnery a woman could rise to a position of leadership and exercise a kind of authority often denied her sisters in the outside world. Even cloistered women, however, had to submit to supervision by male clergy.

In the ninth century, the Carolingian monarchs obeyed the church and began to enforce monogamy. This was both a gain and a loss for women. Wives were accorded greater dignity and legal security, but their burdens as household managers and bearers of children multiplied. The mortality rates of Frankish women increased and their longevity decreased in the ninth century.

Working women   The vast majority of medieval women were neither housewives nor nuns, but working women. Evidence suggests that they were respected and loved by their husbands, perhaps because they worked shoulder to shoulder with them. Between the ages of 10 and 15, girls were apprenticed to learn productive trades, much like boys. If they married, they might operate businesses of their own or go to work in their husband's shops. Women appeared in virtually every "blue-collar" trade, but were especially prominent in the food and clothing industries. They belonged to guilds, and they could become craftmasters, but working women were paid less than men who did the same jobs. In the late Middle Ages, townswomen had opportunities to get some schooling and acquire **vernacular** literacy, but they were excluded from the learned professions.

GROWTH OF NATIONAL MONARCHIES

ENGLAND AND FRANCE: HASTINGS (1066) TO BOUVINES (1214)

William the Conqueror   Medieval England's political destiny was determined by the response to the death of the childless Anglo-Saxon ruler Edward the Confessor (r. 1042–1066). Through a connection with Edward's mother, a Norman princess, Duke William of Normandy (d. 1087) laid claim to the vacant English throne. The Anglo-Saxon assembly preferred a native nobleman, Harold Godwinsson (ca. 1022–1066). William reacted by invading England and defeating Harold's army at Hastings on October 14, 1066. William I "the Conqueror" was crowned king of England in Westminster Abbey within weeks of the invasion.

Battle of Hastings. William the Conqueror on horseback urging his troops into combat with the English at the Battle of Hastings (October 14, 1066). From the Bayeux Tapestry, about 1073–1083.

Giraudon/Art Resource, N.Y.

As England's conqueror, William was free to establish a strong monarchy. He kept the Anglo-Saxon tax system and practice of issuing court writs (legal warnings). He continued the Anglo-Saxon quasi-democratic tradition of frequent *parleying*; that is, conferring with the lesser powers who had vested interests in royal decisions. This led eventually to the balance between monarchical and parliamentary elements that remains a characteristic of England's government.

Popular Rebellion and Magna Carta The Duke of Normandy, who after 1066 was master of England, was also a vassal of the French king in Paris. France's Capetian kings understandably watched with alarm as the power of their Norman vassal grew alarmingly during the reign of William's grandson, Henry II (r. 1154–1189). From his mother Henry inherited Normandy. His father left him Maine, Touraine, and Anjou. Marriage to Eleanor of Aquitaine (1122–1204) brought him her huge duchy in southern France and completed the so-called Angevin or English-French empire. Henry used his resources to promote royal power, but this was met by strong resistance from both the nobility and the clergy.

Under Henry's successors, the brothers Richard the Lion-Hearted (r. 1189–1199) and John (r. 1199–1216), burdensome taxes levied to support Crusades and a failing war with France turned resistance into rebellion. With the full support in 1215 of the clergy and the townspeople, England's barons forced King John grudgingly to agree to terms spelled out in the **Magna Carta** ("Great Charter") in 1215. This famous cornerstone of modern English law limited royal power and secured the right of the privileged classes to representation when the government considered important matters like taxation. The Great Charter charted a path between dissolution of the monarchy by the nobility and the abridgment of the rights of the nobility by the monarchy.

Philip II Augustus Powerful feudal princes dominated France from the beginning of the Capetian dynasty (987) until the reign of Philip II Augustus (1180–1223). During this period the Capetian kings wisely concentrated their limited resources on securing the territory surrounding Paris, the Île-de-France. By the time of Philip II, Paris had become the center of French government and culture, and the Capetian dynasty had acquired a secure hereditary right to the throne. Thereafter, the kings of France steadily enhanced their power over the French nobles.

Philip Augustus waged both internal and international campaigns, and he succeeded at both. His armies reclaimed all of England's continental fiefdoms,

Magna Carta The "Great Charter" limiting royal power, which the English nobility forced King John to sign in 1215.

Gothic Cathedral. The portal of Reims Cathedral, where the kings of France were crowned. The cathedral was built in the Gothic style—emblematic of the High and late Middle Ages—that originated in France in the mid–12th century. The earlier Romanesque (Roman-like) style from which it evolved is characterized by fortresslike buildings with thick stone walls, rounded arches and vaults, and few windows. The Gothic style, in contrast, is characterized by soaring structures, their interiors flooded with colored light from vast expanses of stained glass.

Scala/Art Resource, N.Y.

except for Aquitaine. At Bouvines on July 27, 1214, the French won a decisive victory over the English and their German allies. Philip solidly united France behind its king and laid the foundation for French ascendancy in the late Middle Ages.

FRANCE IN THE 13TH CENTURY: REIGN OF LOUIS IX

Louis IX (r. 1226–1270), the grandson of Philip Augustus, embodied the medieval ideal of kingly authority. Louis's greatest achievements were on the domestic front. Under him, the efficient French bureaucracy established order and fair play in local government. He dispatched commissioners to monitor the conduct of the royal officials who were responsible for local administration and enforcing justice. These royal ambassadors were perceived as genuine champions of the people. Louis abolished private wars among nobles and serfdom within the royal domain, gave his subjects the right of appeal from local to higher courts, and made the tax system more equitable. The French people came to associate their king with justice, and their awareness of themselves as possessors of a unifying national identity grew strong during his reign.

French society and culture, during Louis's lifetime, set a standard for all of Europe, a pattern that continued into the modern period. Northern France became the showcase of monastic reform, chivalry, and Gothic art and architecture. Louis's reign also coincided with the golden age of Scholasticism, in which Europe's greatest thinkers converged on Paris, among them the famous Thomas Aquinas.

THE HOHENSTAUFEN EMPIRE (1152–1272)

Frederick I Barbarossa While different, but stable, monarchies developed in France and England, the Holy Roman Empire fragmented (see Map 15-3). Frederick I Barbarossa (1152–1190), founder of the Hohenstaufen dynasty, reestablished imperial authority but also initiated a new phase in the contest between popes and emperors. Frederick attempted to consolidate an empire uniting Germany and Italy by stressing feudal bonds, but his reign ended with stalemate in Germany and rising tensions in Italy. In 1186 his son—the future Henry VI (r. 1190–1197)—married Constance, heiress to the kingdom of Sicily. This union of the empire with Sicily threatened the papacy by encircling the Papal States, and turned the popes into determined opponents of the German emperor.

When Henry VI died in September 1197, chaos followed. Civil war erupted in Germany. Henry VI's four-year-old son, Frederick, the heir to the imperial crown, had for his own safety been made—fatefully, it would prove—a ward of Pope Innocent III (r. 1198–1215). Innocent had both the will, the means, and the opportunity to challenge the power of the Hohenstaufens.

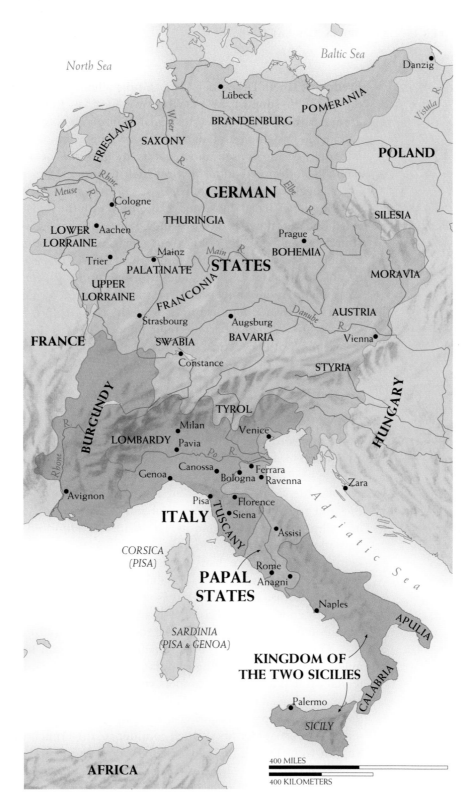

MAP 15–3

Germany and Italy in the Middle Ages. Medieval Germany and Italy were divided lands. The Holy Roman Empire (Germany) embraced hundreds of independent territories that the emperor ruled only in name. The papacy controlled the Rome area and tried to enforce its will in the Romagna. Under the Hohenstaufens (mid–12th to mid–13th centuries), internal German divisions and papal conflict reached new heights; German rulers sought to extend their power to southern Italy and Sicily.

WHY WERE the emperors unable to unite Germany and Italy in the Middle Ages?

Frederick II In December 1212, shifting alliances in the German war induced the pope to support his ward's coronation as Emperor Frederick II. But Frederick soon disappointed his papal sponsor. He was a Sicilian by upbringing, and he was to spend only 9 of the 38 years of his reign in Germany. To secure the imperial title for himself and his sons, he gave the German princes what they wanted—undisputed authority over their territories. Germany was fragmenting into a gaggle of petty kingdoms.

Frederick had a disastrous relationship with the papacy. Popes excommunicated him four times and roused the German princes against him, launching the church into European politics on a massive scale. Efforts by the papacy to become a formidable political and military power made the church highly vulnerable to criticism from religious reformers and royal apologists.

When Frederick died in 1250, the German monarchy died with him. The princes established an electoral college in 1257 to pick the emperor, and the "king of the Romans" became their puppet. The Hohenstaufen dynasty effectively ended with Frederick.

POLITICAL AND SOCIAL BREAKDOWN

HUNDRED YEARS' WAR

WHAT WERE the causes of the political and social breakdown that occurred during the 14th century?

The Causes of the War The Hundred Years' War, which began in May 1337 and lasted until October 1453, started when the English king Edward III (r. 1327–1377), the grandson of Philip the Fair of France (r. 1285–1314), claimed the French throne. But the war was more than a dynastic quarrel. England and France were territorial and economic rivals with a long history of mutual prejudice and animosity This made the Hundred Years' War a struggle for national identity.

Although France had three times the population of England, was far wealthier, and fought on its own soil, most of the major battles were stunning English victories. The primary reason for France's failure was internal disunity caused by endemic social conflict. France lagged behind England in making the transition from a fragmented feudal society to a centralized modern state.

France's defeats also owed much to incompetent leadership and English military superiority. The English infantry was more disciplined than the French feudal cavalry, and English archers could fire six arrows a minute with enough force to pierce an inch of wood or the armor of a knight at 200 yards. Eventually, thanks in part to the inspiring leadership of Joan of Arc (1412–1431), and a sense of national identity and self-confidence, the French were able to expel the English from France. By 1453, all that remained to the English was a coastal enclave at Calais.

Joan was poorly repaid by the king she helped to the throne. When the Burgundians captured her in May 1430, Charles could have secured her release but did not. The Burgundians and the English wanted her publicly discredited, believing this would demoralize French resistance. She was turned over to the Inquisition in English-held Rouen, where, after 10 weeks of interrogation, she was executed on May 30, 1431.

The Hundred Years' War had lasting political and social consequences. It devastated France, but it also awakened French nationalism and hastened the country's transition from a feudal monarchy to a centralized state. In both France and England the burden of the war fell most heavily on the peasantry, who were forced to support it with taxes and services.

THE BLACK DEATH

Preconditions and Causes   In the late Middle Ages, improvements in agriculture increased the food supply, spurring a growth in population. It is estimated that Europe's population doubled between the years 1000 and 1300, and then began to outstrip food production. Finally, there were more people than food to feed them or jobs to employ them. The average European

10.7
"A Most Terrible Plague:"
Giovanni Boccaccio

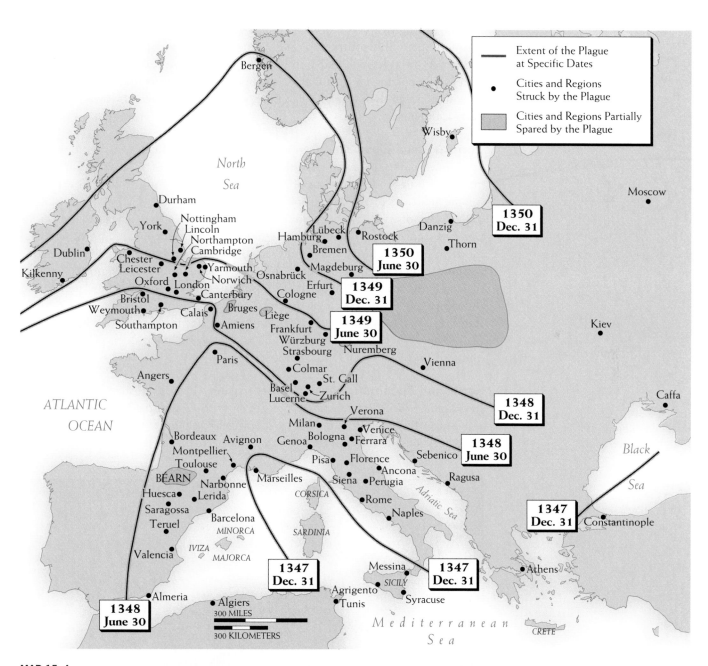

MAP 15–4

Spread of the Black Death.   Apparently introduced by sea-borne rats from areas around the Black Sea where plague-infested rodents have long been known, the Black Death had great human, social, and economic consequences. According to one of the lower estimates, it killed 25 million in Europe. The map charts the spread of the plague in the mid–14th century. Generally following trade routes, it reached Scandinavia by 1350, and some believe it then went on to Iceland and even Greenland. Areas off the main trade routes were largely spared.

WHAT WERE the social and economic consequences of the plague?

faced the probability of famine at least once during his or her average 35-year life-span.

Between 1315 and 1317, crop failures produced the greatest famine of the Middle Ages. Decades of overpopulation, economic depression, famine, and bad health made Europeans vulnerable to a virulent plague that struck with full force in 1348.

This **Black Death**, so called because it discolored the body, travelled the trade routes from Asia into Europe. Appearing in Sicily in late 1347, it entered Europe through Venice, Genoa, and Pisa in 1348, and from there it swept rapidly through Spain and southern France and into northern Europe. Areas outside the major trade routes, like Bohemia, appear to have remained virtually unaffected. The plague made numerous reappearances after its first onslaught, and it is estimated that the population of Europe had been reduced by two-fifths by the early 15th century.

Popular Remedies   The plague was transmitted by fleas and rats, but it also sometimes entered the lungs and was spread by sneezes. Contemporary physicians had little understanding of how diseases worked and no idea how to help people fend off or recover from infection. Popular wisdom held that bad air caused the disease. Some thought that earthquakes had released poisonous fumes. Psychological reactions sometimes went to extremes. Some hoped that moderation and temperance would save them; some wildly indulged their bodily appetites; some fled in panic, and some developed a morbid religiosity. Parades of flagellants whipped themselves, hoping to induce God to show mercy and intervene. Jews were baselessly accused of spreading the disease, and pogroms flared again. The church tried to maintain order, but across Western Europe people developed an obsession with death and dying and a deep pessimism that endured for decades.

Social and Economic Consequences   Whole villages vanished in the wake of the plague. With them went much of the labor force that made the estates of the nobility profitable. Demand for farm laborers and skilled artisans drove wages up. Many serfs negotiated substitution of money payment for their traditional servile

Black Death   Bubonic plague that killed millions of Europeans in the 14th century.

Black Death.   Men and women carrying plague victims in coffins to the burial ground in Tournai, Belgium, 1349.

The Granger Collection, N. Y.

obligations, or they abandoned the farm altogether and sought jobs in cities. Agricultural prices fell because of lowered demand from a shrunken market, but the price of luxury and manufactured goods—the scarce work of skilled artisans—rose. The standard of living of the nobility was seriously threatened by these developments. Landed aristocrats had to pay more for finished products and for farm labor, but received less for their agricultural produce. Their rents also declined.

Peasants Revolt   To recoup their losses, some landowners converted arable land to sheep pasture. Wool production was less labor-intensive than grain farming. The properties classes also used their political influence to pass repressive legislation that forced peasants to stay on their farms and froze wages at low levels. The result was the eruption of peasant rebellions in France and England.

Cities Rebound   Although the plague hit urban populations especially hard, the cities and their skilled industries ultimately prospered from its effects. Cities had always protected their interests by regulating competition and immigration from rural areas. After the plague the reach of such laws was extended beyond the cities to include the lands of nobles and landlords, many of whom were now integrated into urban life.

The omnipresence of death whetted the appetite for goods that only skilled urban industries could produce. Expensive cloths, jewelry, furs, and silks were in great demand. Faced with life at its worst, people insisted on having the best. Initially this new demand could not be met, for the first wave of plague transformed an already limited supply of skilled artisans into a shortage almost overnight. As a result, the prices of manufactured and luxury items soared to new heights. This, however, encouraged workers to migrate to the city to become artisans. Urban dwellers enjoyed every advantage. Their products sold at premium prices, but the depressed market for agricultural goods reduced the cost of the things they bought from the countryside.

There was gain and loss for the church as well. As a great landhold, its income and therefore its political influence declined. But it received new revenues from the vastly increased demand for religious services for the dead and the dying and from the multiplication of gifts and bequests.

New Conflicts and Opportunities   The plague contributed to social conflicts within cities. The merchant and patrician classes had long dominated urban government, but they lost ground to the growing economic and political power of artisan and trade guilds. Guilds used their political influence to pass restrictive legislation that protected their markets. Master artisans wanted to keep their numbers low to limit competition, but the journeymen they employed wanted access to the guild so that they could set up shops of their own. To the old conflict between the urban patriciate and the guilds was now added a struggle within the guilds themselves.

In the years following the plague, two groups that had helped to contain the growth of royal power, the landed nobles and the church, were thrust onto the defensive, and kings seized the opportunity to exploit growing national sentiment and work toward the centralization of governments and economies. The nobles lost clout as the new infantry forces that appeared during the Hundred Years' War diminished the importance of the feudal cavalry. The church suffered a reduction in the numbers of clergy—up to one-third in places. To make things worse, the leadership of the church blundered badly.

WHAT ISSUES led to the papal crisis of the late Medieval ages?

ECCLESIASTICAL BREAKDOWN AND REVIVAL: THE LATE MEDIEVAL CHURCH

BONIFACE VIII AND PHILIP THE FAIR

By the 14th century, popes faced rulers far more powerful than the they were. When Pope Boniface VIII (r. 1294–1303) issued the bull, *Clericis Laicos*, which forbade lay taxation of the clergy without prior papal approval, King Philip the Fair of France (r. 1285–1314) unleashed a ruthless antipapal campaign. On November 18, 1302, Boniface made a last-ditch stand against attempts by states to assert their authority over the churches within their borders. He issued the bull *Unam Sanctam*, which declared that temporal authority was "subject" to the spiritual power of the church. The French, however, responded with force. Philip sent troops into Italy who captured the pope, beat him badly, and might have executed him had not an aroused populace rescued him. No pope ever again seriously tried to threaten a king or emperor. Relations between church and state henceforth were characterized by increasing state control of religion.

THE GREAT SCHISM (1378–1417) AND THE CONCILIAR MOVEMENT TO 1449

After Boniface VIII's death, his successor, Clement V (r. 1305–1314), moved the papal court to Avignon on the southeastern border with France, where it remained until Pope Gregory XI (r. 1370–1378) returned the papacy to Rome in January 1377. His successor, Pope Urban VI (r. 1378–1389), proclaimed his intention to reform the **Curia**. This announcement alarmed the cardinals, most of whom were French. Not wanting to surrender the benefits of a papacy under French influence, the French king, Charles V (r. 1364–1380), supported a schism in the church, and on September 20, 1378, 13 cardinals, all but one of whom was French, elected a cousin of the French king as Pope Clement VII (r. 1378–1397). Clement's papacy was seated in Avignon. This **Great Schism** created two papal courts, and support for them divided along political lines: England and its allies (the **Holy Roman Empire**, Hungary, Bohemia, and Poland) acknowledged Urban VI, whereas France and its allies (Naples, Scotland, Castile, and Aragon) backed Clement VII. Today, only the Roman line of popes is recognized as legitimate by the church.

In 1409, a council at Pisa deposed both the Roman and the Avignon popes and elected its own new pope. But neither Rome nor Avignon accepted its action, so after 1409 there were three contending popes. This intolerable situation ended when Emperor Sigismund (r. 1410–1437) prevailed on the Pisan pope to summon a council of the church in Constance in 1414. The Roman pope Gregory XII (r. 1406–1415) also eventually recognized its legitimacy. After the three contending popes had either resigned or been deposed, the council elected a new pope, Martin V (r. 1417–1431), in November 1417. After nearly 30 years of schism, the church was again reunited

Under Pope Eugenius IV (r. 1431–1447), the papacy regained much of its prestige and authority, and in 1460 the papal bull *Execrabilis* condemned all appeals to councils as "completely null and void." But the conciliar movement had planted deep within the conscience of all western peoples the conviction that the leader of an institution must be responsive to its members and not act against their best interests.

Curia Papal government.

Great Schism Appearance of two and at times three rival popes between 1378 and 1415.

Holy Roman Empire Revival of the old Roman Empire, based mainly in Germany and northern Italy, that endured from 870 to 1806.

THE RENAISSANCE IN ITALY (1375–1527)

Most scholars agree that the **Renaissance** was a transition from the medieval to the modern world. Medieval Europe, especially before the 12th century, had been a fragmented feudal society with an agricultural economy, its thought and culture dominated by the church. Renaissance Europe, especially after the 14th century, was characterized by growing national consciousness and political centralization, an urban economy based on organized commerce and capitalism, and ever greater lay and secular control of thought and culture.

The distinctive features and achievements of the Renaissance are most strikingly revealed in Italy from roughly 1375 to 1527, the year Rome was sacked by imperial soldiers. What was achieved in Italy during these centuries also deeply influenced northern Europe.

THE ITALIAN CITY-STATE: SOCIAL CONFLICT AND DESPOTISM

The Renaissance began in the cities of late medieval Italy. Italy was the natural gateway between East and West. Its vibrant urban societies, such as Venice, Genoa, and Pisa, traded uninterruptedly with the Middle East throughout the Middle Ages. During the 13th and 14th centuries, the trade-rich Italian cities became powerful city-states, dominating the political and economic life of their surrounding countrysides. By the 15th century, the great Italian cities had become the bankers for much of Europe. There were five major and competing states in Italy: the duchy of Milan, the republics of Florence and Venice, the Papal States, and the kingdom of Naples.

Social strife and competition for political power were so intense within the cities that to maintain order and survive, most had, by the 15th century, found it necessary to submit to the control of a despot. Venice, ruled by a successful merchant oligarchy, was the notable exception. Elsewhere, the new social classes and divisions within society produced by rapid urban growth fueled chronic, near-anarchic conflict.

In Florence, divisions created turmoil at every level of society. True stability was not established until the ascent to power in 1434 of Cosimo de' Medici (1389–1464), the wealthiest man in Florence and a most astute statesman. Cosimo controlled the city internally from behind the scenes, skillfully manipulating its constitution and influencing elections. His grandson Lorenzo the Magnificent (1449–1492, r. 1478–1492) exercised near totalitarian authority.

Despotism was less subtle elsewhere in Italy. To prevent internal social conflict and foreign intrigue from paralyzing their cities, the dominant groups in many cities cooperated to install a hired strongman,

WHY WAS the Renaissance a transition from the medieval to the modern world?

Renaissance Revival of ancient learning and the supplanting of traditional religious beliefs by new secular and scientific values that began in Italy in the 14th and 15th centuries.

Cosimo de' Medici (1389–1464). Florentine banker and statesman, in his lifetime the city's wealthiest man and most successful politician. This portrait is by Jacopo da Pontormo (1494–1556).

Jacopo Pontormo (1494–1556), "Cosimo de' Medici the Elder, Pater Patriae," (1389–1464). Oil on wood, 87 × 65 cm. Inv. 3574. Uffize, Florence. Photograph © Erich Lessing/Art Resource, N.Y.

Church and Empire

910	Monastery of Cluny founded
918	Henry I becomes King of Germany
951	Otto I invades Italy
955	Otto I defeats the Hungarians at Lechfeld
962	Otto I crowned emperor by Pope John XII
1077	Gregory VII pardons Henry IV at Canossa
1122	Concordat of Worms settles the investiture controversy
1152–1190	Reign of Frederick Barbarossa
1198–1215	Reign of Innocent III
1214	Collapse of the claims of Otto IV
1220	Frederick II crowned emperor
1232	Frederick II devolves authority to the German princes
1257	The German monarchy becomes elective

humanism Study of the Latin and Greek classics and of the Church Fathers both for their own sake and to promote a rebirth of ancient norms and values.

studia humanitatis During the Renaissance, a liberal arts program of study that embraced grammar, rhetoric, poetry, history, philosophy, and politics.

a *podesta,* to maintain law and order. Because these despots could not depend on the cooperation of a divided populace, they relied on mercenary armies to maintain order.

Political turbulence and warfare motivated the development of diplomacy. Most city-states established resident embassies during the 15th century, and their ambassadors were their watchful eyes and ears at rival courts. They stayed abreast of foreign military developments and, if shrewd enough, gained power and advantage without actually going to war.

HUMANISM

Humanism was the scholarly study of the Latin and Greek classics and the ancient Church Fathers both for their own sake and to promote a rebirth of ancient norms and values. Humanists advocated the *studia humanitatis*, a liberal arts program consisting of rhetoric, poetry, history, politics, and moral philosophy.

The first humanists were orators and poets. They wrote in both the classical and the vernacular languages and drew their inspiration from newly discovered works of the ancients. They taught rhetoric within the universities, and they were sought as secretaries, speech writers, and diplomats in princely and papal courts.

Classical and Christian antiquity had been studied before the Italian Renaissance. However, the Italian Renaissance of the late Middle Ages was more secular and lay dominated, had broader interests, recovered more manuscripts, and possessed far superior technical skills than the earlier medieval rebirths of interest in antiquity.

Unlike their Scholastic rivals, humanists were not content only to summarize and compare the views of recognized authorities on a question, but instead went directly to original sources and drew their own conclusions. Avidly searching out manuscript collections, Italian humanists made the full corpus of Greek and Latin antiquity available to scholars during the 14th and 15th centuries. Mastery of Latin and Greek was their primary instrument. There is a kernel of truth—but only a kernel—in the arrogant boast of the humanists that the period between themselves and classical civilization was a "dark middle age."

Petrarch, Dante, and Boccaccio Francesco Petrarch (1304–1374), the father of humanism, left the legal profession to pursue his love of letters and poetry. Petrarch celebrated ancient Rome in his writings and tirelessly collected ancient manuscripts; among his finds were letters by Cicero. His critical textual studies, elitism, and contempt for the allegedly useless learning of the Scholastics were shared by many later humanists.

Petrarch had a far more secular orientation than Dante Alighieri (1265–1321), whose *Vita Nuova* and *Divine Comedy* form, with Petrarch's sonnets, the cornerstones of Italian vernacular literature. Petrarch's student and friend Giovanni Boccaccio (1313–1375), author of the *Decameron,* 100 bawdy tales told by three men and seven women in a country retreat from the plague that ravaged Florence in 1348, also pioneered humanist studies. An avid

HISTORY'S VOICES

PICO DELLA MIRANDOLA STATES THE RENAISSANCE IMAGE OF MAN

One of the most eloquent Renaissance descriptions of the abilities of humankind comes from the Italian humanist Pico della Mirandola (1463–1494). In his famed *Oration on the Dignity of Man* (ca. 1486), Pico described humans as free to become whatever they choose.

IN WHAT does the dignity of humankind consist? Does Pico reject the biblical description of Adam and Eve's fall? Does he exaggerate a person's ability to choose freely to be whatever he or she wishes? What inspired such seeming hubris during the Renaissance?

The best of artisans [God] ordained that that creature (man) to whom He [God] had been able to give nothing proper to himself should have joint possession of whatever had been peculiar to each of the different kinds of being. He therefore took man as a creature of indeterminate nature and, assigning him a place in the middle of the world, addressed him thus: "Neither a fixed abode nor a form that is thine alone or any function peculiar to thyself have we given thee, Adam, to the end that according to thy longing and according to thy judgment thou mayest have and possess what abode, what form, and what functions thou thyself shalt desire. The nature of all other beings is limited and constrained within the bounds of laws prescribed by Us. Thou, constrained by no limits, in accordance with thine own free will, in whose hand We have placed thee, shalt ordain for thyself the limits of thy nature. We have set thee at the world's center that thou mayest from thence more easily observe whatever is in the world. We have made thee neither of heaven nor of earth, neither mortal nor immortal, so that with freedom of choice and with honor, as though the maker and molder of thyself, thou mayest fashion thyself in whatever shape thou shalt prefer. Thou shalt have the power to degenerate into the lower forms of life, which are brutish. Thou shalt have the power, out of thy soul's judgment, to be reborn into the higher forms, which are divine." O supreme generosity of God the Father, O highest and most marvelous felicity of man! To him it is granted to have whatever he chooses, to be whatever he wills.

Source: Giovanni Pico della Mirandola, *Oration on the Dignity of Man*, in *The Renaissance Philosophy of Man*, ed. by E. Cassirer et al. Phoenix Books, 1961, pp. 224–225. Reprinted by permission of The University of Chicago Press.

---

collector of manuscripts, Boccaccio assembled an encyclopedia of Greek and Roman mythology.

Educational Reforms and Goals   The classical ideal of a useful education that produces well-rounded people inspired far-reaching reforms in traditional education. The most influential Italian Renaissance tract on education, Pietro Paolo Vergerio's (1349–1420) *On the Morals That Befit a Free Man*, was derived directly from classical models. Vittorino da Feltre (d. 1446) guided his students through a highly disciplined curriculum that combined the reading of ancient authors with vigorous physical exercise (see "Pico della Mirandola States the Renaissance Image of Man").

Educated and cultured noblewomen also had a prominent place at Renaissance courts, among them Christine de Pisan (1363?–1434). She was an expert in classical, French, and Italian languages and literature and became a well-known woman of letters in the courts of Europe. Her most famous work, *The City of Ladies*, describes the accomplishments of the great women of history.

RENAISSANCE ART

In Renaissance Italy, as later in Reformation Europe, the values and interests of the laity were less subordinated to those of the clergy. In education, culture, and religion, medieval Christian values were adjusting to a more this-worldly spirit. Men and women began again to appreciate and even to glorify the secular world, secular learning, and purely human pursuits as ends in themselves.

This perspective on life is especially prominent in the painting and sculpture of the High Renaissance (late 15th and early 16th centuries), when Renaissance art reached its full maturity. In imitation of Greek and Roman art, painters and sculptors attempted to create harmonious, symmetrical, and properly proportioned figures, portraying the human form with a glorified realism. Whereas Byzantine and Gothic art had been religious and idealized in the extreme, Renaissance art, especially in the 15th century, realistically reproduced nature and human beings as a part of nature.

Renaissance artists took advantage of new technical skills and materials developed during the 15th century: the use of slow-drying oil paints, of contrast of light and shade to enhance realism (**chiaroscuro**), and of linear perspective to give the viewer the illusion of three-dimensional space. Compared with their flat Byzantine and Gothic counterparts, Renaissance paintings seem filled with energy and life. The great masters of the High Renaissance include Leonardo da Vinci (1452–1519), Raphael (1483–1520), and Michelangelo Buonarroti (1475–1564).

chiaroscuro Use of shading to enhance naturalness in painting and drawing.

Aviation Drawings by Leonardo da Vinci (1452–1519). He imagined a possible flying machine with a retractable ladder for boarding.

David Forbert/SuperStock, Inc.

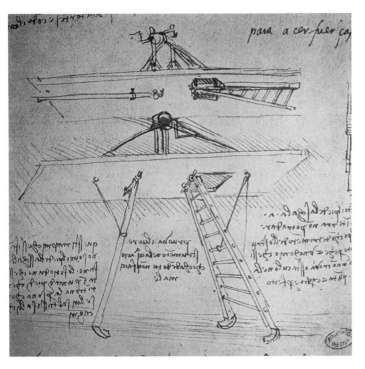

Leonardo da Vinci Leonardo personified the Renaissance ideal of the universal person, one who is not only a jack-of-all-trades but also a master of many. A military engineer and advocate of scientific experimentation, he dissected corpses to learn anatomy and was a self-taught botanist. He sketched designs for such modern machines as airplanes and submarines. The variety of his interests tended, however, to shorten his attention span, so that he constantly moved from one activity to another. As a painter, his great skill lay in conveying inner moods through complex facial features. This is the intriguing characteristic of his most famous painting, the *Mona Lisa*.

Raphael Raphael, who died young (37), is reknowned for his tender depictions of the Virgin Mary and the infant Jesus. Art historians also consider his fresco *The School of Athens*, which depicts Plato and Aristotle surrounded by philosophy and science, one of the best examples of Renaissance artistic theory and technique.

Michelangelo This melancholy genius also excelled in a variety of arts and crafts. His 18-foot statue *David* is a perfect example of the Renaissance artist's devotion to harmony, symmetry, and proportion, and to the extreme glorification of the human form. Four different popes commissioned works by Michelangelo, the best known of which are the frescoes for the Sistine Chapel, which he painted for Pope Julius II (r. 1503–1513).

His later works mark the passing of High Renaissance painting and the advent of a new, experimental style called *mannerism,* which flourished in the late 16th and early 17th centuries. Mannerism derived its name from the "mannered" or "affected" way in which artists expressed their individual perceptions and feelings. Tintoretto (d. 1594) and especially El Greco (d. 1614) are its supreme representatives.

ITALY'S POLITICAL DECLINE: THE FRENCH INVASIONS (1494–1527)

Italy's autonomous city-states had always worked together to oppose foreign invaders. But in 1494, when Naples, backed by Florence and the Borgia pope Alexander VI (1492–1503), prepared to attack Milan, the Milanese despot Ludovico il Moro (r. 1476–1499) invited the French to invade to assert a dynastic claim France had to Naples. France, however, also laid claim to Milan, and the French appetite for territory became insatiable once French armies had crossed the Alps and reestablished themselves in Italy.

The French king Charles VIII (r. 1483–1498) quickly responded to Ludovico's call. Within five months, he had crossed the Alps (August 1495) and raced as conqueror through Florence and the Papal States into Naples. Charles's lightning march through Italy alarmed Ferdinand (r. 1479–1516), king of Aragon and Sicily. He organized a counteralliance (the League of Venice) that forced Charles to retreat.

The French returned to Italy under Charles's successor, Louis XII (r. 1498–1515), this time assisted by the Borgia pope Alexander VI (1492–1503). Alexander, probably the most corrupt pope in history, wanted to carve out a duchy for his son Cesare, in Romagna, officially part of the Papal States. Hoping that a French alliance would allow him to regain control of the region, Alexander abandoned the League of Venice. This made the league too weak to defend Milan, which Louis successfully invaded in August 1499. In 1500, he and Ferdinand of Aragon divided Naples, while the pope and Cesare Borgia conquered the Romagna without opposition.

In 1503, Cardinal Giuliano della Rovere became Pope Julius II (1503–1513). He suppressed the Borgias and placed their newly conquered lands in Romagna under papal jurisdiction. After securing the Papal States with French aid, Julius changed sides and sought to rid Italy of his former allies. Julius, Ferdinand of Aragon, and Venice formed the Holy League in October 1511, which was soon joined by Emperor Maximilian I (r. 1493–1519) and the Swiss. By 1512 the French were in full retreat.

The French invaded Italy again under Louis's successor, Francis I (r. 1515–1547). French armies massacred the Holy League's Swiss army at Marignano in September 1515, and forced the Medici pope Leo X (r. 1513–1521) to agree to the Concordat of Bologna (August 1516). The agreement gave the French king control over the French clergy and the right to collect

mannerism A style of art in the mid to late 16th century that permitted artists to express their own "manner" or feelings in contrast to the symmetry and simplicity of the art of the High Renaissance.

Major Political Events of the Italian Renaissance (1375–1527)

1378–1382	Ciompi revolt in Florence
1434	Medici rule in Florence established by Cosimo de' Medici
1454–1455	Treaty of Lodi allies Milan, Naples, and Florence (in effect until 1494)
1494	Charles VIII of France invades Italy
1495	League of Venice unites Venice, Milan, the Papal States, the Holy Roman Empire, and Spain against France
1499	Louis XII invades Milan (the second French invasion of Italy)
1500	The Borgias conquer Romagna
1512–1513	The Holy League (Pope Julius II, Ferdinand of Aragon, Emperor Maximilian I, and Venice) defeat the French
1513	Machiavelli writes *The Prince*
1515	Francis I leads the third French invasion of Italy
1516	Concordat of Bologna between France and the papacy
1527	Sack of Rome by imperial soldiers

Niccolò Machiavelli. Santi di Tito's portrait of Machiavelli, perhaps the most famous Italian political theorist, who advised Renaissance princes to practice artful deception and inspire fear in their subjects if they wished to succeed.

Scala/Art Resource, N.Y.

WHAT WERE the bases for the rise of the modern sovereign state in the 15th century?

taxes from them in exchange for France's recognition of the pope's superiority to church councils. The terms helped keep France Catholic after the outbreak of the Protestant Reformation. But France's thrust into Italy began the first of four major wars with Spain, the Habsburg-Valois wars. These wars stretched over the first half of the 16th century, and France won none of them.

NICCOLÒ MACHIAVELLI

Invasions and wars made a shambles of Italy, and Niccolò Machiavelli (1469–1527) watched as French, Spanish, and German armies wreaked havoc on his country. The more he saw, the more convinced he became that the creation of a unified, independent Italy was an end that justified any means needed to achieve it. Machiavelli admired the heroic acts of ancient Roman rulers, what Renaissance people called their *Virtu.* Romanticizing the old Roman citizenry, he lamented the absence of comparable heroism among his compatriots. His perspective led him to pen distorted interpretations of both ancient and contemporary history.

Machiavelli's comparison of the noble achievements of idealized ancient Romans with the failures of his "Roman" contemporaries led him to conclusions that have made *Machiavellian* synonymous with cynicism. Only an unscrupulous strongman, he argued, using duplicity and terror, could impose order on so divided and selfish a people as his countrymen. Machiavelli was probably in earnest when he advised rulers to consider the advantages of fraud and brutality. He apparently hoped to see a strong ruler emerge from the Medici family. The Medicis, however, were not destined to be Italy's deliverers. The second Medici pope, Clement VII (r. 1523–1534), watched helplessly as Rome was sacked by the army of Emperor Charles V (r. 1519–1556) in 1527, the year of Machiavelli's death.

REVIVAL OF MONARCHY: NATION BUILDING IN THE 15TH CENTURY

After 1450, unified national monarchies progressively replaced fragmented and divisive feudal governance. The dynastic and chivalric ideals of feudalism did not, however, disappear. Minor territorial princes survived, and representative assemblies even gained influence in some regions. But by the late 15th and early 16th centuries, the old problem of the one and the many was being decided clearly in favor of monarchy.

The feudal monarchies of the High Middle Ages split the basic powers of government between a king and his semiautonomous vassals. The nobility and the towns worked with varying degrees of unity and success through evolving representative bodies, such as the English Parliament, the French Estates General, and the Spanish Cortes, to thwart the centralization of royal power. However, the Hundred Years' War and the schism in the church undercut the power of the landed nobility and the clergy respectively in the late Middle Ages, and the increasingly important towns sided with the kings. Loyal, businesswise townspeople, not the nobles and the clergy, staffed offices in royal governments, becoming the king's lawyers, bookkeepers, military tacticians, and diplomats. This alliance between king and town slowly broke the bonds of feudal society and promoted the rise of the modern sovereign state.

In a sovereign state, the powers of taxation, war making, and law enforcement are no longer the right of local semiautonomous vassals but are concentrated at the center in the monarch and exercised by his chosen agents. Taxes, wars, and laws become national rather than merely regional matters. Only as monarchs won free of the nobility and representative assemblies could they overcome the decentralization that was the chief obstacle to nation building.

Monarchies also began to create standing national armies in the 15th century. As the aristocratic cavalry receded in importance and the infantry and the artillery emerged as the primary forces, many kings employed mercenary soldiers recruited from Switzerland and Germany. The growing cost of warfare increased a king's need to develop new sources of income, but expansion of royal revenues was hampered by the upper classes' stubborn belief that they were immune from taxation. The nobility guarded their properties and traditional rights and despised taxation as an insult and a humiliation. Royal revenues accordingly grew at the expense of those least able to resist and least able to pay. Monarchs had several options. As feudal lords they collected rents from their personal domains. They might also levy national taxes on basic food and clothing, such as the *gabelle* or salt tax in France and the *alcabala* or 10 percent sales tax on commercial transactions in Spain. Kings could also levy direct taxes on the peasantry (such as the French *taille*) and on commercial transactions in towns that were under royal protection. They did this with the cooperation of assemblies that represented the privileged classes but not the peasants who paid the taxes. In the 15th century innovative fund-raising devices, such as sale of public offices and issuance of high-interest government bonds, appeared. But kings still did not levy taxes on the powerful aristocrats. Instead, they turned to rich nobles, as they did to the great bankers of Italy and Germany, for loans, bargaining with the privileged classes, who were often as much the kings' creditors and competitors as their subjects.

MEDIEVAL RUSSIA

In the late 10th century, Prince Vladimir of Kiev (r. 972–1015), then Russia's chief city, converted to Greek Orthodoxy. It became the religion of Russia and added a new cultural bond to the long-standing commercial ties the Russians had with the Byzantine Empire.

Vladimir's successor, Yaroslav the Wise (r. 1016–1054), turned Kiev into a magnificent political and cultural center, but after his death, rivalry among princes challenged Kiev's dominance, and it became just one of several national centers.

Mongol Rule (1243–1480)   Mongol (or Tatar) armies (see Chapters 8 and 13) invaded Russia in 1223, and Kiev fell to them in 1240. Russia's cities became tribute-paying principalities of the portion of the Mongol Empire called the **Golden Horde**. It had its capital at Sarai, on the lower Volga. Mongol rule drew Russia away from the West but left Russia's traditional political institutions and religion largely intact. Mongolian power and trade contacts also enhanced the peace and prosperity of Russia.

taille   Direct tax on the French peasantry.

Golden Horde   Name given to the Mongol rulers of Russia from 1240 to 1480.

Exterior of a Russian Orthodox Church in Novgorod, Russia.

UNESCO, Ann Ronan/ The Image Works.

11.8
Kuyuk Khan, Letter to
Pope Innocent IV

Russian Liberation   The princes of Moscow cooperated with the Mongols, grew wealthy, and gradually expanded their principality through land purchases, colonization, and conquest. In 1380, Grand Duke Dimitri of Moscow (1350–1389) defeated Tatar forces at Kulikov Meadow in a victory that marked the beginning of the decline of Mongolian hegemony. Another century passed before Ivan III, called Ivan the Great (d. 1505), brought all of northern Russia under Moscow's control and ended Mongol rule (1480). By the last quarter of the 15th century, Moscow had replaced Kiev as the political and religious center of Russia. After the fall of Constantinople to the Turks in 1453, Russians laid claim to the legacy of the Byzantine Empire and proclaimed Moscow the "third Rome."

FRANCE

There were two cornerstones of French nation building in the 15th century. The first was England's retreat from the continent following its loss of the Hundred Years' War. The second was the defeat of Charles the Bold (r. 1467–1477) and his duchy of Burgundy. The dukes of Burgundy were probably Europe's strongest rulers in the mid-15th century, and they hoped to build a dominant middle kingdom between France and the Holy Roman Empire. They might have succeeded had not the Continental powers joined forces to oppose them. The dream of Burgundian empire died in 1477, when Charles the Bold was killed in battle at Nancy.

The dissolution of Burgundy removed a serious threat to France and cleared the way for its King Louis XI (r. 1461–1483) to build a powerful monarchy. By annexing and adding Burgundian lands to his own Angevin inheritance, Louis doubled the size of his kingdom. He harnessed the nobility and expanded trade and industry.

Strength does not necessarily ensure a healthy future for a nation. It was because Louis left his successors such a secure and efficient government that they were able to pursue Italian conquests in the 1490s and to fight a long series of losing wars with the Habsburgs in the first half of the 16th century. By the mid-16th century, France was again a defeated nation and almost as divided internally as it had been during the Hundred Years' War.

SPAIN

Spain, too, became a strong country in the late 15th century. Both Castile and Aragon had been poorly ruled, divided kingdoms in the mid-15th century, but the marriage in 1469 of Isabella of Castile (r. 1474–1504) and Ferdinand of Aragon (r. 1479–1516) changed that trend. Their union was strongly protested by their neighbors, Portugal and France, who foresaw the formidable European power it would create. Castile was by far the richer and more populous of the two kingdoms, having an estimated five million inhabitants to Aragon's less than one million. Castile also had a lucrative sheep-farming industry. An example of the growing trend toward centralized economic planning, it was run by a government-backed organization called the *Mesta*. Although the two kingdoms were dynastically united by the marriage of Ferdinand and Isabella in 1469, each retained its own laws, armies, coinage, tax systems, and cultural traditions.

Ferdinand and Isabella could do together what neither could accomplish alone: subdue their realms, secure their borders, and conduct foreign military ventures. Townspeople allied themselves with the crown and progressively replaced nobles within the royal administration. The crown further circumscribed the power of the nobility by extending its authority over the wealthy chivalric orders.

Spain had long been remarkable as a place where three religions—Islam, Judaism, and Christianity—coexisted with a certain degree of toleration. This changed dramatically as Ferdinand and Isabella exerted state control over religion. They totally dominated the Spanish church and made religion serve the cause of national unity. They appointed the higher clergy and the officers of the Inquisition. The Inquisition was a key national agency established in 1479 to monitor the activity of Spain's converted Jews (*conversos*) and Muslims (*Moriscos*). It was run by Isabella's confessor, Tomás de Torquemada (d. 1498). In 1492, Ferdinand and Isabella exiled all Jews from Spain and confiscated their properties. In 1502, nonconverting Moors in Granada were driven into exile. The state imposed regimented, uniform spiritual practices on its subjects. Spain remained a loyal Catholic country through the era of the Reformation and provided a base of operation for the Counter-Reformation resurgence of the Catholic Church.

Ferdinand and Isabella had wide horizons. The anti-French marriage alliances they arranged for their children determined much of European history in the 16th century. In 1496, their eldest daughter, Joanna, later known as "the Mad" (1479–1555), married Archduke Philip (1478–1506), the son of Emperor Maximilian I (r. 1493–1519). Their son, Charles I, the first king of a united Spain, acquired by inheritance and his election as Emperor Charles V in 1519 a European realm almost equal in size to Charlemagne's. A second daughter, Catherine of Aragon (1485–1536), married King Henry VIII of England. The failure of this marriage led to the English Reformation.

Ferdinand and Isabella's vision for Spain's future was also revealed by their sponsorship of overseas exploration. They sent the Genoese adventurer Christopher Columbus (1451–1506) west in search of a shorter route to the spice markets of the Far East. The islands he discovered in the Caribbean began the creation of the Spanish Empire in Mexico and Peru. Gold and silver from their mines helped to make Spain Europe's dominant power in the 16th century.

ENGLAND

The last half of the 15th century was a difficult period for England. Following its loss of the Hundred Years' War, civil war broke out in England between two rival branches of the royal family, the House of York and the House of Lancaster. This conflict, named the Wars of the Roses (York's symbol, according to legend, was a white rose, and Lancaster's a red rose), kept England in turmoil from 1455 to 1485.

The Lancastrian, King Henry VI (r. 1422–1461), was challenged by the Duke of York and his supporters in the prosperous southern towns. In 1461 the Duke of York's son seized power and became King Edward IV (r. 1461–1483). Assisted by loyal and able ministers, he bent Parliament to his will. His brother and successor, Richard III (r. 1483–1485), was confronted by growing support for the exiled Lancastrian leader Henry Tudor. Henry defeated Richard on Bosworth Field in August 1485 to become King Henry VII (r. 1485–1509), founder of a Tudor dynasty that endured until 1603.

To bring the rival royal families together and give his offspring an incontestable hereditary claim to the throne, Henry married Edward IV's daughter, Elizabeth of York. With the aid of a much-feared instrument of royal power, the Court of Star Chamber, he imposed discipline on the English nobility. He shrewdly construed legal precedents to the advantage of the crown and used English law to further his own ends. He confiscated so much noble land and so many fortunes that he was able to govern without depending on Parliament for grants. Henry constructed a powerful monarchy that became one of early modern Europe's most exemplary governments during the reign of his granddaughter, Elizabeth I (r. 1558–1603).

SUMMARY

Medieval Society Medieval society was divided in theory into three main groups: clergy (those who prayed), nobility (those who fought as mounted warriors), and laborers (peasants and artisans). The rise of merchants, self-governing towns, and universities helped break down this division. By supporting rulers against the nobility, towns gave kings the resources—money and university-trained bureaucrats and lawyers—to build national governments. Much of medieval history involves the struggle by rulers to assert their authority over powerful local lords and the church.

Church and State The medieval papacy sought to extend its power over both church and state. In the 10th century, the Cluny reform movement increased popular respect for the church and strengthened the papacy. In the Investiture Struggle, the papacy secured the independence of the clergy by enlisting the support of the German princes against the Holy Roman Emperors, thus weakening imperial power in Germany. The First Crusade further strengthened papal prestige. But, by the end of the 13th century, kings had become more powerful than popes, and the French king, Philip the Fair, was able to defy the papacy. In the 14th century, the Great Schism further weakened papal prestige. Although the papacy was able to fend off a movement to make church councils superior to popes, it never recovered its authority over national rulers.

Nation Building By the 15th century, England, France, and Spain had developed into strong national monarchies with centralized bureaucracies and professional armies. Although medieval institutions, such as the English Parliament, in theory limited royal power, in practice monarchs in these countries held unchallenged authority. The Great Schism, the Hundred Years' War, and the Black Death had weakened the church and the nobility, while townspeople supported kings. A similar process was beginning in Russia where the rulers of Moscow were extending their authority after throwing off Mongol rule. In the empire, however, regional lords had defeated the emperors' attempts to build a strong central state.

The Renaissance The Renaissance, which began in the Italian city-states in the late 14th century, marks the transition from the medieval to the modern world. Humanism, the scholarly study of the Greek and Latin classics and the ancient Church fathers, promoted a rebirth of ancient norms and values and the classical ideal of an educated, well-rounded person. The growth of secular values led to a great burst of artistic activity by artists such as da Vinci, Raphael, and Michelangelo. The political weakness of the Italian states invited foreign intervention by France, Spain, and the Habsburgs. The sack of Rome by imperial forces in 1527 marks the end of the Renaissance.

IMAGE KEY
for pages 336–337

a. Two-handed sword, circa 1600
b. Raphael's portrait (ca.1515) of Baldassare Castiglione (1478–1529)
c. Students attending a lecture, detail of the Tomb of Giovanni da Legnano
d. From the Bayeux Tapestry (ca. 1073–1083), William the Conqueror on horseback
e. An eleventh- or twelfth-century marketplace in a fifteenth-century rendering
f. Pope Innocent III
g. Michelangelo's *Pietà* (ca. 1498–1500)
h. Statue of Pope Boniface VIII
i. Cosimo de' Medici
j. Joan of Arc

REVIEW QUESTIONS

1. What were the objectives of the Cluny reform movement? Why did it succeed?

2. Was the investiture controversy a political or a religious conflict?

3. Why did Germany remain divided while France and England were able to begin forming strong, unified states during the High Middle Ages?

4. How did the Hundred Years' War, the Black Death, and the Great Schism in the church affect the course of history?

5. What gave rise to towns? How did they change medieval society?

6. What was "reborn" in the Renaissance?

KEY TERMS

Black Death (p. 356)

chiaroscuro (p. 362)

Crusades (p. 340)

Curia (p. 358)

Golden Horde (p. 365)

Great Schism (p. 358)

guild (p. 345)

Holy Roman Empire (p. 358)

humanism (p. 360)

Magna Carta (p. 351)

mannerism (p. 363)

regular clergy (p. 347)

Renaissance (p. 359)

Scholasticism (p. 345)

secular clergy (p. 347)

studia humanitatis (p. 360)

taille (p. 365)

vernacular (p. 350)

 For additional study resources for this chapter, go to:
www.prenhall.com/craig/chapter15

EUROPE

1517–1555	Protestant Reformation
1533–1584	Ivan the Terrible of Russia reigns
1540	Jesuit Order founded by Ignatius Loyola
1543–1727	Scientific Revolution
1556–1598	Philip II of Spain reigns
1558–1603	Elizabeth I of England reigns
1562–1598	French Wars of Religion
1581	The Netherlands declares its independence from the Spanish Habsburgs
1588	Defeat of the Spanish Armada
1589–1610	Henry IV, Navarre, founds Bourbon dynasty of France

▲ Queen Elizabeth I

NEAR EAST/ INDIA

1500–1722	Safavid Shi'ite rule in Iran
1512–1520	Ottoman ruler Selim I
1520–1566	Ottoman ruler Suleiman the Magnificent
1525–1527	Babur founds Mughai dynasty in India
1540	Hungary under Ottoman rule
1556–1605	Akbar the Great of India reigns
1571	Battle of Lepanto; Ottomans defeated
ca. 1571–1640	Safavid philosopher-writer Mullah Sadra
1588–1629	Shah Abbas I of Iran reigns

Leaf from "Divan" ▶
by the poet, Hafiz

EAST ASIA

1500–1800	Commercial revolution in Ming-Ch'ing China; trade with Europe; flourishing of the novel
1543	Portuguese arrive in Japan
1568–1600	Era of unification follows end of Warring States Era in Japan
1587	Spanish arrive in Japan
1588	Hideyoshi's sword hunt in Japan
1592–1598	Ming troops battle Hideyoshi's army in Korea

AFRICA

Feluccas ▶
on the Nile

1506	East coast of Africa under Portuguese domination
1507	Mozambique founded by Portuguese
1517	Spanish crown authorizes slave trade to its South American colonies; rapid increase in importation of slaves to the New World
1554–1659	Sa'did Sultanate in Morocco
1575	Union of Bornu and Kanem by Idris Alawma (r. 1575–1610); Kanem-Bornu state the most fully Islamic in West Africa
1591	Moroccan army defeats Songhai army; Songhai Empire collapses

THE AMERICAS

1519	Conquest of the Aztecs by Cortes; Aztec ruler, Montezuma (r. 1502–1519) killed; Tenochtitlán destroyed
1529	Mexico City becomes capital of the viceroyalty of New Spain
1533	Pizarro begins his conquest of the Incas
1536	Spanish under Mendoza arrive in Argentina
1544	Lima becomes capital of the viceroyalty of Peru
1584	Sir Walter Raleigh sends expedition to Roanoke Island (North Carolina)

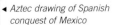

◀ Aztec drawing of Spanish conquest of Mexico

▲ Algonquin village of Secotton

1618–1648	Thirty Years' War
1640–1688	Frederick William, the Great Elector, reigns in Brandenburg-Prussia
1642–1646	Puritan Revolution in England
1643–1715	Louis XIV of France reigns
1682–1725	Peter the Great of Russia reigns
1688	Glorious Revolution in England
1690	"Second Treatise of Civil Government," by John Locke

◄ *Louis XIV of France*

1701	Act of Settlement provides for Protestant succession to English throne
1702–1713	War of Spanish Succession
1740–1748	War of Austrian Succession
1756–1763	Seven Years' War
ca. 1750	Industrial Revolution begins in England
1772	First partition of Poland
1789	First French Revolution
1793 and 1795	Last two partitions of Poland

▲ *"Evening" by Francis Wheatley*

1628–1657	Shah Jahan reigns; builds Taj Mahal as mausoleum for his beloved wife
1646	Founding of Maratha Empire
1648	Delhi becomes the capital of Mughal Empire
1658–1707	Shah Aurangzeb, the "World Conqueror," reigns in India; end of religious toleration toward Hindus; beginning Mughal decline
1669–1683	Last military expansion by Ottomans: 1669, seize Crete; 1670s, the Ukraine; 1683, Vienna

▲ *The Taj Mahal*

1700	Sikhs and Marathas bring down Mughal Imperial Power
1708	British East India Company and New East India Company merge
1722	Last Safavid ruler forced to abdicate
1724	Rise in the Deccan of the Islamic state of Hyderabad
1725	Nadir Shah of Afganhistan becomes ruler of Persia
1739	Persian invasion of northern India, by Nadir Shah
1748–1761	Ahmad Shah Durrani of Afghanistan invades India
1757	British victory at Plassey, in Bengal

1600	Tokugawa Ieyasu wins battle of Sekigahara, completes unification of Japan
1600–1868	Tokugawa shogunate in Edo
1630s	Seclusion adopted as national policy in Japan
1644–1694	Bashō, Japanese poet
1644–1911	Ch'ing (Manchu) dynasty in China
1661-1722	K'ang Hsi reign in China
1673–1681	Revolt of southern generals in China
1699	British East India Company arrives in China

1701	Forty-seven ro-nin incident in Japan
1716–1733	Reforms of Tokugawa Yoshimune in Japan
1737–1795	Reign of Qianlong in China
1742	Christianity banned in China
1784	American traders arrive in China
1787–1793	Matsudaira Sadanobu's reforms in Japan
1798	White Lotus Rebellion in China

Manchu emperor ▶ *Ch'ien Lung*

◄ *"White Heron" castle in Jimeji*

1600s	English, Dutch, and French enter the slave trade; slaves imported to sugar plantations in the Caribbean
1619	First African slaves in North America land in Virginia
1652	First Cape Colony settlement of Dutch East India Company
1660–1856	Omani domination of East Africa; Omani state centered in Zanzibar; 1698, takes Mozambique from Portuguese

◄ *Slave labor on sugar plantation in Brazil*

1702	Asiento Guinea Trade Company founded for slave trade between Africa and the Americas
1700s	Transatlantic slave trade at its height
1741–1856	United Sultanate of Oman and Zanzibar
1754–1817	Usman Dan Fodio, founder of sultanate in northern and central Nigeria; the Fulani become the ruling class in the region
1762	End of Funj Sultanate in eastern Sudanic region

◄ *The Friday Mosque at Shela*

1607	The London Company establishes Jamestown Colony (Virginia)
1608	Champlain founds Quebec
1619	Slave labor introduced at Jamestown (Virginia)

1733	Georgia founded as last English colony in North America
1739–1763	Era of trade wars in Americas between Great Britain and the French and Spanish
1763	Peace of Paris establishes British government in Canada
1776–1781	American Revolution
1783–1830	Simón Bolívar, Latin American soldier, statesman
1789	U.S. Constitution
1791	Negro slave revolt in French Santo Domingo
1791	Canada Constitution Act divides the country into Upper and Lower Canada

16 Europe 1500–1650: Expansion, Reformation and Religious Wars

CHAPTER HIGHLIGHTS

Voyages of Discovery In the late fifteenth century, Europe began to expand around the globe. The Portuguese pioneered a sea route around Africa to India and the Far East, and the Spanish discovered the Americas. The consequences were immense for Europeans, native Americans, Africans, and Asians. In time, a truly global society would emerge.

The Reformation The Reformation began in Germany with Martin Luther's attack on indulgences in 1517. Despite the opposition to the Reformation of Emperor Charles V, Luther had the support of many German princes. The Reformation shattered the religious unity of Europe. In Switzerland, Zwingli and Calvin launched their own versions of Protestantism. In England, Henry VIII repudiated papal authority when the pope refused to grant him a divorce. The Reformation also led to far-reaching changes in religious practices and social attitudes, including steps toward the advancement of women.

The Roman Catholic Church also acted to reform itself. The Council of Trent tightened church discipline and reaffirmed traditional doctrine. The Jesuits converted many Protestants back to Catholicism.

The Wars of Religion The religious divisions of Europe led to more than a century of warfare from the 1520s to 1648. When the Thirty Years' War ended in 1648, Europe was permanently divided into Catholic and Protestant areas.

Superstition and Enlightenment The Reformation led to both dark and constructive views of human nature. Perhaps the darkest view was the witch crazes that erupted across Europe. Thousands of innocent people, mostly women, were persecuted and executed as witches between 1400 and 1700.

In literature and philosophy, however, these years witnessed an outpouring of creative thinking. Among the greatest writers of the age were Cervantes, Shakespeare, Pascal, Spinoza, Hobbes, and Locke.

CHAPTER QUESTIONS

WHAT WERE the motives for the European voyages of discovery in the late fifteenth and sixteenth centuries?

WHY DID Martin Luther break with the Roman Catholic Church?

HOW DID the Reformation change religious and social life?

WHAT WAS the final result of the wars of religion in France, the Netherlands, and Germany?

WHY DID witch hunts and panics erupt across Western Europe between 1400 and 1700?

CHAPTER OUTLINE

- The Discovery of a New World
- The Reformation
- The Reformation's Achievements
- The Wars of Religion
- Superstition and Enlightenment: The Battle Within

In the second decade of the 16th century, a powerful religious movement began in Saxony in Germany and rapidly spread throughout northern Europe, deeply affecting society and politics as well as spiritual life. Attacking what they believed to be burdensome superstitions that robbed people of their money and their peace of mind, Protestant reformers led a revolt against the medieval church. In a short time, hundreds of thousands of people from all social classes set aside the beliefs of centuries and adopted a more simplified religious practice.

The Protestant Reformation challenged aspects of the Renaissance, especially its loyalty to traditional religions and humanism's tendency to follow classical sources in glorifying human nature. Protestants were more convinced of the human potential for evil than by any human inclination to do good. This led them to urge parents, teachers, and magistrates to be firm disciplinarians. On the other hand, Protestants also embraced many Renaissance ideas, especially educational reform and the study of ancient languages. These provided the tools they used to interpret Scripture and challenge the papacy.

Protestantism was not the only reform movement to grow out of the religious grievances of the late Middle Ages. Within the Catholic Church itself a reform was emerging that would give birth to new religious orders, rebut Protestantism, and win back a great many of its converts.

As different groups identified their political and social goals with either Protestantism or Catholicism, a hundred years of bloody war between Protestants and Catholics darkened the second half of the 16th century and the first half of the 17th. In the second half of the 16th century, the political conflict that had previously been confined to central Europe and a struggle for Lutheran rights and freedoms shifted to Western Europe—to France, the Netherlands, England, and Scotland—where it became a struggle for Calvinist recognition. In France, Calvinists fought Catholic rulers for the right to form their own communities, to practice their chosen religion openly, and to exclude from their lands those they deemed heretical. During the Thirty Years' War (1618–1648), international armies of varying religious persuasions clashed in central and northern Europe. By 1649 English Puritans had overthrown the Stuart monarchy and the Anglican Church.

For Europe the late 15th and the 16th centuries were also a period of unprecedented territorial expansion. Permanent colonies were established within the Americas, and the exploitation of the New World's human and mineral resources began. Imported American gold and silver spurred scientific invention and a new weapons industry. The new bullion helped fund an international traffic in African slaves as rival tribes sold their captives to the Portuguese. These slaves were brought in ever-increasing numbers to work the mines and the plantations of the New World as replacements for faltering American natives.

THE DISCOVERY OF A NEW WORLD

WHAT WERE the motives for the European voyages of discovery in the late 15th and 16th centuries?

The discovery of the Americas dramatically expanded the geographical and intellectual horizons of Europeans. Knowledge of the New World's inhabitants and exploitation of its vast wealth set new cultural and economic forces in motion throughout Western Europe. Beginning with the successful voyages of Christopher Columbus (1451–1506) in the late 15th century, commercial supremacy started to shift from the Mediterranean and the Baltic to the Atlantic seaboard, and western Europe's global expansion began in earnest (see Map 16–1).

The Portuguese Chart the Course Seventy-seven years before Columbus sailed for Spain, Portugal's Prince Henry the Navigator (1394–1460) began exploration of Africa's Atlantic coast. The Portuguese first sought gold and slaves. During the second half of the 15th century, the Portuguese delivered

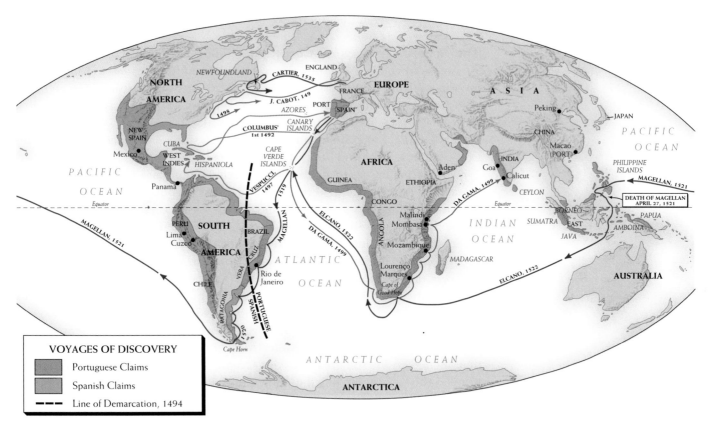

MAP 16–1
European Voyages of Discovery and the Colonial Claims of Spain and Portugal in the 15th and 16th Centuries. The map dramatizes Europe's global expansion in the 15th and 16th centuries.

WHY DID the Europeans want to find a sea route to Asia?

150,000 slaves to Europe. By the end of that century, however, they were hoping to find a sea route around Africa to Asia's spice markets. Spices, especially pepper and cloves, were in great demand both as preservatives and taste enhancements to food. Overland routes to India and China had long existed, but they were difficult and expensive and monopolized by the Venetians and Turks. The first exploratory voyages were slow and tentative, but the experience they provided taught sailors the skills needed to cross the oceans to the Americas and and Orient.

In 1455, a pope gave the Portuguese rights to all the lands, goods, and slaves they might discover from the coast of Guinea to the Indies. The church hoped that conquests would be followed by mass conversions and the development of allies against the Muslims. Bartholomew Dias (d. 1500) opened the Portuguese Empire in the East when he rounded the Cape of Good Hope at the tip of Africa in 1487. A decade later, in 1498, Vasco da Gama (d. 1524) stood on the shores of India. When he returned to Portugal, his cargo was worth 60 times the cost of the voyage. Later, the Portuguese established colonies in Goa and Calcutta and successfully challenged the Arabs and the Venetians for control of the European spice trade.

While the Portuguese concentrated on the Indian Ocean, the Spanish set sail across the Atlantic, hoping to establish a shorter route to the rich spice markets of

14.5
Christopher Columbus

the East Indies. Rather than beat the Portuguese at their own game, however, Columbus discovered the Americas—although he did not at first realize that.

The Spanish Voyages of Christopher Columbus   On October 12, 1492, after a 33-day voyage from the Canary Islands, Columbus landed in San Salvador (Watlings Island) in the eastern Bahamas. He thought San Salvador was an outer island of Japan, for his knowledge of geography was based on Marco Polo's account of his years in China during the 13th century and a global map by Martin Behaim, a Nuremberg map-maker, which showed only ocean between the west coast of Europe and the east coast of Asia.

The friendly naked natives, who greeted Columbus and his crew on the beaches of the New World, were Taino Indians. They spoke a variant of a language known as Arawak. Mistaking the island for the East Indies, Columbus called the people Indians, and the name stuck even after it became known that he had discovered a new continent. The natives' generosity amazed Columbus. They freely gave his men all the corn and yams—and sexual favors—they desired. "They never say no," Columbus marveled and predicted that they could easily be enslaved.

On the heels of Columbus, Amerigo Vespucci (1451–1512), after whom America is named, and Ferdinand Magellan (1480–1521) carefully explored the coastline of South America. Their travels proved that the lands discovered by Columbus were not the outermost territory of the Far East, but a new continent that opened on the still greater Pacific Ocean. Magellan, in search of a westward route to the East Indies, sailed to the Philippines, where he died.

Impact on Europe and America   Columbus's voyage of 1492 marked, unknowingly to those who undertook and financed it, the beginning of more than three centuries of Spanish conquest, exploitation, and administration of a vast American empire. What had begun as voyages of discovery soon became expeditions of conquest. The wars Christian Aragon and Castile waged against the Islamic Moors had just ended in 1492, and they imbued the early Spanish explorers with a zeal for conquering and converting non-Christian peoples.

The voyages to the New World had important consequences for both Europe and America. For Spain, the venture created Europe's largest and longest-surviving trading bloc and yielded the wealth that financed Spain's commanding role in the era's religious and political conflicts. It also fueled European-wide economic expansion, and spurred other European countries to undertake their own colonial ventures.

European expansion had major consequences for ecosystems. Numerous species of fruits, vegetables, and animals were introduced to Europe from America and vice versa. European diseases also devasted America's natives. The imprint that Spain left on the new territories—Roman Catholicism, economic dependence, and a hierarchical society—is visible today.

THE REFORMATION

*T*he **Reformation** was a religious reform movement that began in Germany in the sixteenth Century and led to the establishment of Protestant Christianity.

Religion and Society   The Reformation broke out first in the free imperial cities of Germany and Switzerland. There were about 65 of these, and each was a

---

QUICK REVIEW

Impact on Europe and America
- Spurred other European nations to colonial expansion
- Financed Spain's role in the age's political and religious conflicts
- For native peoples of the Americas, contact brought disease, war, and destruction

WHY DID Martin Luther break

with the Roman Catholic Church?

Reformation   Sixteenth-century religious movement that sought to reform the Roman Catholic Church and led to the establishment of Protestantism.

little kingdom unto itself. Most developed Protestant movements, but with mixed success and duration. Some quickly turned Protestant and remained so. Some were Protestant for only a short time. Others developed mixed confessions and let Catholics and Protestants coexist.

The cities not only struggled with higher princely or royal authority, they also suffered deep internal social and political divisions. Certain groups favored the Reformation more than others. In many places, guilds like that of the printers, whose members were prospering both socially and economically and who had a history of conflict with local authority, were in the forefront of the Reformation. Evidence suggests that people who felt pushed around and bullied by either local or distant authority—a guild by an autocratic local government; a city or region by a prince or king—initially perceived an ally in the Protestant movement.

Social and political experience thus coalesced with the larger religious issues in both town and countryside. When Martin Luther and his comrades wrote, preached, and sang about a priesthood of all believers, scorned the authority of ecclesiastical landlords, and ridiculed papal laws as arbitrary human inventions, they touched political as well as religious nerves in German and Swiss cities. This was also true in villages, for the peasants also heard in the Protestant sermon and pamphlet a promise of political liberation and even a degree of social betterment.

Popular Movements and Criticism of the Church The Protestant Reformation could not have occurred without the monumental crises of the late medieval church and the Renaissance papacy. For many people, the church had ceased to provide a viable vehicle for the expression of their piety. Laity and clerics alike began to seek more heartfelt, idealistic, and often—in the eyes of the pope—increasingly heretical religious outlets. The late Middle Ages were marked by independent lay and clerical efforts to reform local religious practice and by widespread experimentation with new religious forms that shared a common goal: the recovery of religious simplicity in imitation of Christ.

A variety of factors contributed to the growth of lay criticism of the church. The laity in the cities were becoming increasingly knowledgeable about the world and those who controlled their lives. They traveled widely—as soldiers, pilgrims, explorers, and traders. New postal systems and the printing press increased the information at their disposal. The new age of books and libraries raised literacy and heightened curiosity. Laypersons were increasingly able to take the initiative in shaping the cultural life of their communities.

Secular Control over Religious Life On the eve of the Reformation, Rome's international network of church offices began to be pulled apart by a growing awareness of regional identity (incipient nationalism) and the increasing competence of local secular administrations. The late medieval church had permitted important ecclesiastical posts ("benefices") to be sold to the highest bidders and had not enforced residency requirements in parishes. Rare was the late medieval German town that did not have complaints about the maladministration, concubinage, or fiscal conduct of its clergy, especially the higher clergy (bishops, abbots, and prelates).

City governments also sought to restrict the growth of ecclesiastical properties and clerical privileges and to improve local religious life by bringing the clergy under the local tax code and by endowing new clerical positions for well-trained and conscientious preachers.

Gutenberg Bible. The printing press made possible the diffusion of Renaissance learning. But no book stimulated thought more at this time than did the Bible. With Gutenberg's publication of a printed Bible in 1454, scholars gained access to a dependable, standardized text, so that Scripture could be discussed and debated as never before.

Huntigton Library.

QUICK REVIEW

Criticism of the Church
- Many people did not see church as a foundation for religious piety
- Laity and clerics interested in alternatives and reform
- Layperson increasingly willing to take the initiative

THE NORTHERN RENAISSANCE

The scholarly works of northern humanists created a climate favorable to religious and educational reforms. Northern humanism was initially stimulated by the importation of Italian learning through such varied intermediaries as students who had studied in Italy, merchants, and a religious organization called the Brothers of the Common Life. The northern humanists tended to come from more diverse social backgrounds and to be more devoted to religious reforms than were their Italian counterparts. They were also more willing to write for lay audiences.

The growth of schools and lay education combined with the invention of cheap paper to create a mass audience for printed books. It was well served when, around 1450, Johann Gutenberg (d. 1468) invented printing with movable type in the German city of Mainz. Thereafter, books were rapidly and handsomely produced on topics both profound and practical. By 1500, printing presses operated in at least 60 German cities and in more than 200 throughout Europe. The provided politicians, humanists, and reformers with a new medium through which to promote their causes.

The most famous of the northern humanists was Desiderius Erasmus (1466–1536), the "prince of the humanists." Idealistic and pacifistic, Erasmus gained fame as both an educational and a religious reformer. He aspired to unite the classical ideals of humanity and civic virtue with the Christian ideals of love and piety. He believed that disciplined study of the classics and the Bible, if begun early enough, was the best way to reform both individuals and society. He summarized his own beliefs with the phrase *philosophia Christi*, a simple, ethical piety in imitation of Christ. He set this ideal against what he believed to be the dogmatic, ceremonial, and factious religious practice of the late Middle Ages. To promote his own religious beliefs, Erasmus edited the works of the Church Fathers and made a Greek edition of the New Testament (1516), which became the basis for a new, more accurate Latin translation (1519). Martin Luther later used both these works as the basis for his famous German translation.

The best known of early English humanists was Sir Thomas More (1478–1535), a close friend of Erasmus. While visiting More, Erasmus wrote his most famous work, *The Praise of Folly* (1511), an amusing and profound exposé of human self-deception. It was quickly translated from the original Latin into many vernacular languages. More's *Utopia* (1516), a criticism of contemporary society, depicts an imaginary society based on reason and tolerance that requires everyone to work and has rid itself of all social and political injustice. Although More remained a staunch Catholic, humanism in England, as in Germany, paved the way for the Reformation. A circle of English humanists, under the direction of Henry VIII's minister Thomas Cromwell, translated and disseminated late medieval criticisms of the papacy and many of Erasmus's satirical writings as well.

Whereas humanism helped the Protestants in Germany, England, and France, in Spain it entered the service of the Catholic Church. Here the key figure was Francisco Jiménez de Cisneros (1437–1517), a confessor to Queen Isabella, and after 1508 Grand Inquisitor—a position from which he was able to enforce the strictest religious orthodoxy. Jiménez was a conduit for humanist scholarship and learning. He founded the University of Alcalá near Madrid in 1509, printed a Greek edition of the New Testament, and translated many religious tracts that aided clerical reform and control of lay religious life. His greatest achievement, taking 15 years to complete, was the Complutensian Polyglot Bible. It is a six-volume work that prints, side by side, Hebrew, Greek, and Latin versions of the Bible. Such scholarly projects and internal church reforms joined with the repressive measures of Ferdinand and Isabella to keep Spain strictly Catholic.

MARTIN LUTHER AND THE GERMAN REFORMATION TO 1525

Late medieval Germany lacked the political unity to enforce "national" religious reforms during the late Middle Ages. What happened on a unified national level in England and France occurred only locally and piecemeal in Germany. As popular resentment of clerical immunities and ecclesiastical abuses spread among German cities and towns—especially regarding the selling of indulgences—an unorganized "national" opposition to Rome formed. German humanists had long voiced such criticism, and by 1517 it provided a solid foundation for Martin Luther's reform.

Luther (1483–1546), the son of a successful Thuringian miner, was educated by teachers who had been influenced by the Northern Renaissance. He received his master of arts degree from the University of Erfurt in 1505 and registered with the law faculty. He never began that course of study, for to the shock and disappointment of his parents, he joined the Order of the Hermits of Saint Augustine in Erfurt on July 17, 1505. This decision had apparently been forming in his mind for some time and was precipitated by a terrifying storm that caused him to promise the saint to whom he prayed that he would enter a monastery if he escaped death.

Luther was ordained in 1507 and was sent to Rome in 1510 on business for his order. There he witnessed the abuses for which the papacy was being criticized. In 1511, he was transferred to the Augustinian monastery in Wittenberg, where he earned his doctorate in theology (1512)—thereafter to become a leader within the monastery, the new university, and the spiritual life of the city.

Justification by Faith Alone Reformation theology grew out of a problem common to many clergy and laity at this time: the failure of traditional medieval religion to provide full personal or intellectual satisfaction. Luther was especially plagued by the disproportion between his own sense of sinfulness and the perfect righteousness that medieval theology taught that God required for salvation. Traditional church teaching and the sacraments were no consolation. Luther wrote that he came to despise the phrase "righteousness of God," for it seemed to demand of him a perfection he knew neither he nor any other human being could ever achieve. His insight into the meaning of "justification by faith alone" was a gradual process that extended over several years, between 1513 and 1518. The righteousness God demands, he concluded, does not come from religious works but is present in full measure in those who believe and trust in the redemptive life and death of Christ, who alone exhibits the righteousness satisfying to God. To believe in Christ is to stand before God clothed in Christ's righteousness.

13.4
Martin Luther

John Tetzel. A contemporary caricature depicts John Tetzel, the famous indulgence preacher. The last lines of the jingle read: "As soon as gold in the basin rings, right then the soul to heaven springs." It was Tetzel's preaching that spurred Luther to publish his 95 theses.

Courtesy Stiftung Luthergedenkstaten in Sachsen-Anhalt/Lutherhalle, Wittenberg.

The Attack on Indulgences An **indulgence** was a remission of the temporal penalty imposed by the priest on penitents as a "work of satisfaction" for their sins. According to medieval theology, after the priest had absolved penitents of guilt for their sins, God still imposed on them a temporal penalty, a manageable "work of satisfaction" that the penitent could perform here and now (for example, through prayers, fasting, almsgiving, retreats, and pilgrimages). Penitents who defaulted on such prescribed works of satisfaction could expect to suffer for their sins in purgatory.

Originally, indulgences had been given only for the true self-sacrifice of going on a crusade to the Holy Land. But they came over time to be more commonly issued as a comfort to laity who were genuinely anxious that forgotten or unrepented sins would condemn them to suffering in purgatory. In 1343, Pope Clement VI (r. 1342–1352) proclaimed the existence of a "treasury of merit," on which popes could draw to issue "letters of indulgence" that canceled the works of satisfaction owed by penitents. By Luther's time, they were regularly dispensed for small cash payments (modest sums that were regarded as almsgiving) and were said to remit not only future punishment of the living, but also those of the dead in purgatory for whom they were purchased.

In 1517, a Jubilee indulgence, proclaimed under Pope Julius II (r. 1503–1513) to raise funds for the rebuilding of Saint Peter's in Rome, was revived and preached on the borders of Saxony in the territories of Archbishop Albrecht of Mainz, who had large debts. The selling of the indulgence was a joint venture by Albrecht, the Augsburg banking house of Fugger, and Pope Leo X (r. 1513–1521), half the proceeds going to the pope and half to Albrecht and his creditors. The famous indulgence preacher John Tetzel (d. 1519) exhorted the crowds:

> Don't you hear the voices of your dead parents and other relatives crying out, "Have mercy on us, for we suffer great punishment and pain. From this you could release us with a few alms.... We have created you, fed you, cared for you, and left you our temporal goods. Why do you treat us so cruelly and leave us to suffer in the flames, when it takes only a little to save us?"[1]

When on October 31, 1517, Luther posted his **ninety-five theses** against indulgences on the door of Castle Church in Wittenberg, he especially protested the impression Tetzel gave his customers that indulgences actually remitted sins and released the dead from purgatory. Luther thought that this was excessive and created the impression that salvation could be bought.

Election of Charles V Luther's theses made him famous overnight. Humanists endorsed them, but the church began official proceedings to discipline him. As sanctions were being prepared against Luther, Emperor Maximilian I died (January 12, 1519), diverting attention from heresy in Saxony to the contest for a new emperor. The pope backed the French king, Francis I. However, Charles I of Spain, then 19, succeeded his grandfather and became Emperor Charles V (r. 1519–1556). Charles was assisted by a long tradition of Habsburg imperial rule and massive Fugger loans, which secured the votes of the seven electors. The electors also won political concessions from Charles that prevented him from taking unilateral action against Germans, something for which Luther eventually had cause to be grateful.

[1] *Die Reformation in Augenzeugen Berichten*, ed. by Helmar Junghans (Dusseldorf: Karl Rauch Verlag, 1967), p. 44.

indulgences Remission of the temporal penalty of punishment in purgatory that remained after sins had been forgiven.

ninety-five theses Document posted on the door of Castle Church in Wittenberg, Germany on October 31, 1517 by Martin Luther protesting, among other things, the selling of indulgences.

A Catholic portrayal of Martin Luther tempting Jesus (1547). Reformation propaganda often portrayed the pope as the Antichrist or the devil. Here Catholic propaganda turns the tables on the Protestant reformers by portraying a figure of Martin Luther as the devil (note the monstrous feet and tail under his academic robes).

Versuchung Christi, 1547, Gemälde, Bonn, Rheinisches Landesmuseum, Inv. Nr. 58.3.

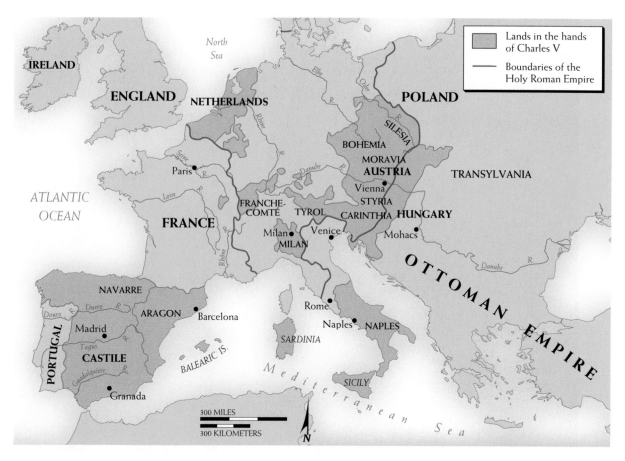

MAP 16–2

The Empire of Charles V. Dynastic marriages and good luck concentrated into Charles's hands rule over the lands shown here, plus Spain's overseas possessions. Crowns and titles rained down on him; election in 1519 as emperor gave him new burdens and responsibilities.

WHAT WERE the geographical advantages and disadvantages of the empire of Charles V?

Luther's Excommunication and the Diet of Worms In the same month in which Charles was elected emperor, Luther debated the Ingolstadt professor John Eck (1486–1543) in Leipzig (June 27, 1519). Luther challenged the infallibility of the pope and the inerrancy of church councils, and argued for the first time for Scripture as the sole and sovereign authority over faith. He burned all his bridges to the old church when he defended John Huss, a condemned heretic.

In 1520, Luther made his position clear by issuing three famous pamphlets. The *Address to the Christian Nobility of the German Nation* urged the German princes to force reforms on the Roman Church and especially to curtail its political and economic power in Germany. The *Babylonian Captivity of the Church* attacked the traditional seven sacraments and claimed that only two were legitimate. It also exalted the authority of Scripture and the decisions of church councils and secular princes over the judgments of popes. The last pamphlet, *Freedom of a Christian*, eloquently summarized his new teaching: that salvation came by faith alone— that it was the consequence of a "happy union" between the soul and Christ.

In April 1521, Luther presented his views before the imperial **Diet of Worms**, over which Charles V presided. Ordered to recant, Luther refused. On

Diet of Worms Meeting of the representatives (diet) of the Holy Roman Empire, presided over by the Emperor Charles V at the German city of Worms in 1521, at which Martin Luther was ordered to recant his ninety-five theses. Luther refused and was declared an outlaw although he was protected by the Elector of Saxony and other German princes.

May 26, 1521, he was placed under the imperial ban and became an "outlaw" within the empire. Friends hid him in Wartburg Castle. There he spent almost a year in seclusion (April 1521 to March 1522), translating Erasmus's new Greek text of the New Testament into German. He also attempted by correspondence to oversee the first stages of the Reformation in Wittenberg.

Imperial Distractions: France and the Turks   The Reformation was greatly assisted at its start by the fact that the emperor was forced to focus his attention on a war with France and the advance of the Ottoman Turks into eastern Europe. Against both adversaries, Charles V, who was also Spain's king and had dynastic responsibilities outside the empire, needed German troops. Consequently, he pursued friendly relations with the German princes. Between 1521 and 1559, Spain (the Habsburg dynasty) and France (the Valois dynasty) fought four major wars. In 1526, the Turks overran Hungary at the Battle of Mohacs, while in western Europe the French-led League of Cognac pushed Charles toward a second Habsburg-Valois war. Thus preoccupied, the emperor agreed at the German Diet of Speyer in 1526 that each German territory could be free to enforce the Edict of Worms (1521) against Luther "so as to be able to answer in good conscience to God and the emperor." That concession, in effect, gave the German princes territorial sovereignty in religious matters while giving the Reformation time to put down deep roots. In 1555, the Peace of Augsburg enshrined this princely privilege as imperial law.

How the Reformation Spread   The Reformation soon passed from the hands of theologians and pamphleteers into those of magistrates and princes. In many cities, Protestant preachers built sizable congregations that pressured urban governments to adopt religious reforms. Many magistrates had long pushed for reform and welcomed the preachers as allies. Reform slogans thus became laws binding on all townspeople.

Religious reform became a territorial political movement as well. It was led by the elector of Saxony and the prince of Hesse. Like the urban magistrates, the princes recognized political and economic opportunities for themselves in the demise of the Roman Catholic Church, and they urged the reform on their neighbors. By the 1530s, there was a powerful Protestant alliance prepared for war with the Catholic emperor.

The Peasants' Revolt   In its first decade, the Protestant movement suffered more from internal division than from imperial interference. By 1525, Luther had become as much an object of protest within Germany as was the pope. Original allies and sympathizers declared their independence from him.

The German peasants had at first believed Luther to be an ally. Since the late 15th century, they had organized to resist efforts by princes to jettison traditional customs and impose new regulations and taxes on them. Peasant leaders saw in Luther's teaching of religious freedom and his criticism of monastic landowners a point of view close to their own. They openly solicited his support of their political and economic rights, including their revolutionary request for release from serfdom.

Luther and his followers sympathized with the peasants, but the Lutherans were no social revolutionaries. Luther believed that Christian freedom was an inner release from guilt and anxiety, not the right to an egalitarian society. When the peasants revolted in 1524–1525, Luther condemned them in the strongest

Execution of a Peasant Leader. The punishment of a peasant leader in a village near Heilbronn. After the defeat of rebellious peasants in and around the city of Heilbronn, Jacob Rorbach, a well-to-do peasant leader from a nearby village, was tied to a stake and slowly roasted to death.

© Badische Landesbibliothek.

possible terms as "unchristian" and urged the princes to crush their revolt without mercy. Tens of thousands of peasants (estimates run between 70,000 and 100,000) had died by the time the revolt was put down.

For Luther, the freedom of the Christian was an inner release from guilt and anxiety, not a right to restructure society by violent revolution. Had Luther supported the Peasants' Revolt, he would have also ended any chance of his reform surviving beyond the 1520s.

Luther and the Jews   Luther's stand toward the Jews has also been controversial. In 1523 he published a pamphlet, "Jesus Christ was Born a Jew," in which he urged Christians to be kind to Germany's Jews in the hope that they might convert to reformed Christianity. But Luther came to regret his pamphlet and decided that the Jews were just another in a long history of foreign predators who threatened German Christians. He expressed these views in a series of pamphlets in the late 1530s and early 1540 in which he urged German princes to forcibly expel Jews who refused to convert. Fortunately, the Jews found a protector in Emperor Charles V, and Luther's colleagues were not inclined to abandon the hope that the Jews would eventually convert. However, in Hesse and Saxony rulers tightened restrictions on Jews, and Luther did not, as he might have, use his influence on their behalf.

ZWINGLI AND THE SWISS REFORMATION

Although Luther's was the first, reform movments occurred in Switzerland and France almost simultaneously with the German Reformation. Switzerland was a loose confederacy of 13 autonomous cantons or states and allied areas. Some became Protestant, some remained Catholic, and a few managed to effect a compromise. The two preconditions of the Swiss Reformation were the growth of national sentiment and a desire for church reform.

The Reformation in Zurich   Ulrich Zwingli (1484–1531), the leader of the Swiss Reformation, was widely known for opposition to the sale of indulgences and religious superstition. As a priest in Zurich, he made the city his base for reform. Zwingli's reform guideline was simple and effective: whatever lacked literal support in Scripture was to be neither believed nor practiced. After a public disputation in January 1523, based on his Scripture test, Zurich became, to all intents and purposes, a Protestant city and the center of the Swiss Reformation. Its rigorous enforcement of its religious ideals made it one of the first examples of a "puritanical" Protestant city.

The Marburg Colloquy   Landgrave Philip of Hesse (1504–1567) sought to unite Swiss and German Protestants in a mutual defense pact, a potentially significant political alliance. His efforts were spoiled, however, by theological disagreements between Luther and Zwingli over the nature of Christ's presence in the Eucharist. Zwingli maintained a symbolic interpretation of Christ's words, "This is my body"; Christ, he argued, was only spiritually, not bodily, present in the bread and wine of the Eucharist. Luther, to the contrary, insisted that Christ's human nature could share the properties of his divine nature. Hence, where Christ was spiritually present, he could also be bodily present, for his was a special nature (***transubstantiation***).

Philip of Hesse brought the two Protestant leaders together in his castle in Marburg in early October 1529, but they were unable to work out their differences

transubstantiation Doctrine that the entire substances of the bread and wine are changed in the Eucharist into the body and blood of Christ.

on this issue. Luther left thinking Zwingli a dangerous fanatic. The disagreement splintered the Protestant movement theologically and politically.

ANABAPTISTS AND RADICAL PROTESTANTS

The moderate pace and seemingly small ethical results of the Lutheran and Zwinglian reformations discontented many people, among them some of the original coworkers of Luther and Zwingli. Many desired a more rapid and thorough implementation of primitive Christianity and accused the major reformers of going only halfway. The most important of these radical groups were the Anabaptists, the 16th-century ancestors of the modern Mennonites and Amish. The Anabaptists take their name from their rejection of infant baptism and their insistence that only baptism as a consenting adult conformed to Scripture and was respectful of human freedom. (*Anabaptism* derives from the Greek word meaning "to rebaptize.")

Anabaptists withdrew from society to form more perfect communities modeled on what they believed to be the example of the first Christians. Due to the close connection between religious and civic life in this period, however, political authorities believed that their separatism was a threat to basic social bonds.

At first, Anabaptism drew adherents from all social classes. But as Lutherans and Zwinglians joined with Catholics in opposing it, a more rural, agrarian class came to make up the great majority of Anabaptists. In 1529, rebaptism became a capital offense throughout the Holy Roman Empire. It has been estimated that between 1525 and 1618 at least 1,000 and perhaps as many as 5,000 men and women were executed for rebaptizing themselves as adults.

JOHN CALVIN AND THE GENEVAN REFORMATION

Calvinism was the religious ideology that inspired or accompanied massive political resistance in France, the Netherlands, and Scotland. Believing in both divine predestination and the individual's responsibility to create a godly society, Calvinists were zealous reformers. In a famous and controversial study, *The Protestant Ethic and the Spirit of Capitalism* (1904), the German sociologist Max Weber argued that this peculiar combination of religious confidence and self-disciplined activism produced an ethic congenial to emergent capitalism.

Political Revolt and Religious Reform in Geneva

Whereas in Saxony religious reform paved the way for a political revolution against the emperor, in Geneva a political revolution against the local prince-bishop laid the foundation for religious change. In late 1533, the Protestant city of Bern sent Protestant reformers to Geneva and by the summer of 1535, after much internal turmoil, the Protestants triumphed. On May 21, 1536, the city voted officially to adopt the Reformation: "to live according to the Gospel and the Word of God ... without ... any more masses, statues, idols, or other papal abuses."

A portrait of the young John Calvin.
Bibliotheque Publique et Universitaire, Geneva.

John Calvin (1509–1564), a reform-minded humanist and lawyer, arrived in Geneva after these events, in July 1536. The local Protestant reformer persuaded him to stay and assist the Reformation. Before a year had passed, Calvin had drawn up articles for the governance of the new church, as well as a catechism to guide and discipline the people. As a result of the strong measures proposed to govern Geneva's moral life, the reformers were accused of trying to create a "new papacy," and in February 1538 they were exiled from the city.

Calvin went to Strasbourg, a model Protestant city, where he became pastor to a group of French exiles. During his two years in Strasbourg, he wrote biblical commentaries and a second edition of his masterful *Institutes of the Christian Religion*, which many consider the definitive theological statement of the Protestant faith. He also married and participated in the ecumenical discussions urged on Protestants and Catholics by Charles V. Most important, he learned from the Strasbourg reformer Martin Bucer (1491–1551) how to implement the Protestant Reformation successfully.

Calvin's Geneva   In 1540, Geneva elected officials favorable to Calvin, and he was invited to return. Within months of his arrival, new ecclesiastical ordinances were implemented that allowed the magistrates and the clergy to cooperate in matters of internal discipline.

Calvin and his followers were motivated above all by a desire to make society godly. The "elect," Calvin taught, should live a manifestly God-pleasing life, if they were truly God's elect. The majesty of God demanded nothing less. The *consistory*, a judicial body composed of clergy and laity, was established to enforce the strictest moral discipline. It meted out punishments for a broad range of moral and religious transgressions and became unpopular among many Genevans.

After 1555 the city's magistrates were all devout Calvinists, and Geneva became a refuge for thousands of exiled Protestants driven out of France, England, and Scotland. Refugees (more than 5,000), most of them utterly loyal to Calvin, constituted over one-third of the population of Geneva. From this time until his death in 1564, Calvin's position in the city was greatly strengthened and the magistrates were very cooperative.

POLITICAL CONSOLIDATION OF THE LUTHERAN REFORMATION

By 1530 the Reformation was irreversible, but it would take several decades and major attempts to eradicate it before this was accepted. The political success of Lutheranism in the empire, by the 1550s, gave Protestant movements elsewhere a new lease on life.

Expansion of the Reformation   In the 1530s, German Lutherans formed regional consistories, which oversaw and administered the new Protestant churches. These consistories replaced the old Catholic episcopates. Under the leadership of Philip Melanchthon (1497–1560), Luther's most admired colleague, educational reforms were enacted that provided for compulsory primary education, schools for girls, a humanist revision of the traditional curriculum, and catechetical instruction of the laity in the new religion.

The Reformation also dug in elsewhere. Introduced into Denmark by Christian II (r. 1513–1523), Lutheranism became the state religion under Christian III (r. 1536–1559). In Sweden, Gustavus Vasa (r. 1523–1560), supported by a nobility greedy for church lands, confiscated church property and subjected the clergy to royal authority at the Diet of Vesteras (1527). In politically splintered Poland, Lutherans, Calvinists, and others found room to practice their beliefs. The absence of a central political authority made Poland a model of religious pluralism and toleration in the second half of the 16th century.

Reaction Against Protestants: The "Interim"   Charles V made abortive efforts in 1540–1541 to enforce a compromise agreement between Protestants and Catholics. When these and other conciliar efforts failed, he sought a military solution. In 1547 imperial armies crushed a Protestant alliance called the Schmalkaldic League.

The emperor established puppet rulers in Saxony and Hesse and issued as imperial law the Augsburg Interim. It ordered Protestants everywhere to readopt Catholic beliefs and practices. The Reformation was, however, too entrenched by 1547 to be ended even by brute force. Confronted by fierce Protestant resistance and weary from three decades of war, the emperor was forced to relent.

The Peace of Augsburg in September 1555 made the division of Christendom permanent. This agreement recognized in law what had already been well established in practice: *cuius regio, eius religio*, meaning that the ruler of a land would determine the religion of the land. Lutherans were permitted to retain all church lands forcibly seized before 1552. Those discontented with the religion of their region were permitted to migrate to another.

Calvinism was not recognized as a legal form of Christian belief and practice by the Peace of Augsburg. Calvinists remained determined not only to secure the right to worship publicly as they pleased, but also to shape society according to their own religious convictions. They organized to lead national revolutions throughout northern Europe.

Progress of Protestant Reformation on the Continent

1517	Luther posts 95 theses against indulgences
1519	Charles I of Spain elected Holy Roman emperor (as Charles V)
1519	Luther challenges infallibility of pope and inerrancy of church councils at Leipzig Debate
1521	Papal bull excommunicates Luther for heresy
1521	Diet of Worms condemns Luther
1521–1522	Luther translates the New Testament into German
1524–1525	Peasants' Revolt in Germany
1529	Marburg Colloquy between Luther and Zwingli
1530	Diet of Augsburg fails to settle religious differences
1531	Formation of Protestant Schmalkaldic League
1536	Calvin arrives in Geneva
1540	Jesuits, founded by Ignatius of Loyola, recognized as order by pope
1546	Luther dies
1547	Armies of Charles V crush Schmalkaldic League
1555	Peace of Augsburg recognizes rights of Lutherans to worship as they please
1545–1563	Council of Trent institutes reforms and responds to the Reformation

THE ENGLISH REFORMATION TO 1553

Late medieval England had a well-earned reputation for defending the rights of the crown against the pope. It was, however, the unhappy marriage of King Henry VIII (r. 1509–1547) that precipitated England's break with the papacy.

The King's Affair   Henry had married Catherine of Aragon (d. 1536), a daughter of Ferdinand and Isabella of Spain, and the aunt of Emperor Charles V. By 1527, the union had produced only one surviving child, a daughter, Mary Tudor. Henry was justifiably concerned about the political consequences of leaving only a female heir. People in this period believed it unnatural for women to rule over men. At best, a woman ruler meant a contested reign; at worst, turmoil, revolution, and possible foreign invasion. After Henry's queen Catherine had numerous miscarriages and stillbirths, the king concluded

Main Events of the English Reformation

that their union had been cursed by God. Catherine had briefly been the wife of his late brother, Arthur.

By 1527, Henry was thoroughly enamored of Anne Boleyn (ca. 1504–1536), one of Catherine's young ladies in waiting. He decided to put Catherine aside and marry Anne, but this required papal annulment of the marriage—and therein lay a problem. In 1527, the reigning pope, Clement VII (r. 1523–1534), was a prisoner of Charles V, Catherine's nephew. Even if this had not been the case, it would have been virtually impossible for the pope to grant Henry an annulment. Not only had his marriage lasted for 18 years, but it had been made possible in the first place by a special papal dispensation. This had been required because of Catherine's previous marriage to Henry's deceased brother, Arthur.

After Cardinal Wolsey (1475–1530), Lord Chancellor of England since 1515, failed to secure the annulment the king wanted, Henry chose as advisers Thomas Cranmer (1489–1556) and Thomas Cromwell (1485–1540), both of whom harbored Lutheran sympathies. They urged the king to take a different course: Why not simply declare himself supreme in English spiritual affairs as he was in English temporal affairs? The king could then rule on the status of his own marriage.

Reformation Parliament   In 1529 Parliament convened for the seven-year session that earned it the title "Reformation Parliament." It passed a flood of legislation that subjected the clergy to royal authority. In January 1531, the clergy publicly recognized Henry as head of the church in England "as far as the law of Christ allows." In 1532, Parliament passed the Submission of the Clergy, effectively placing canon law under royal control and the clergy under royal jurisdiction.

In January 1533 Henry wed the pregnant Anne Boleyn, with Thomas Cranmer, his newly appointed archbishop of Canterbury, officiating. In 1534, Parliament ended all payments by the English clergy and laity to Rome and gave Henry sole jurisdiction over high ecclesiastical appointments. The Act of Succession in the same year made Anne Boleyn's children legitimate heirs to the throne, and the Act of Supremacy declared Henry "the only supreme head in earth of the church of England."

The Protestant Reformation Under Edward VI   Despite his political break with Rome, Henry remained decidedly conservative in his religious beliefs and continued to endorse Catholic doctrine and practices, despite agitation for Protestant reforms by some of his subjects. Henry forbade the English clergy to marry and threatened to execute clergy caught twice in concubinage. The Six Articles of 1539 reaffirmed belief in transubstantiation, denied the Eucharistic cup to the laity, declared that vows of celibacy could not be voided, provided for private Masses, and ordered the continuation of oral confession to a priest.

Edward VI (r. 1547–1553), Henry's son by his third wife, Jane Seymour, became king at age 10. Under his regents, England enacted much of the

Protestant Reformation. Henry's Six Articles and laws against heresy were repealed, and clerical marriage and Communion with the cup were sanctioned. An Act of Uniformity imposed Thomas Cranmer's Book of Common Prayer on all English churches, which were stripped of their images and altars. His 42-article confession of faith set forth a moderate Protestant doctrine.

These changes were short-lived because in 1553 young Edward died, and his half-sister, Catherine of Aragon's daughter, Mary Tudor (d. 1558), succeeded to the throne. She restored Catholic doctrine and practice with a single-mindedness that rivaled that of her father. It was not until the reign of Anne Boleyn's daughter, Elizabeth I (r. 1558–1603), that a lasting religious settlement was worked out in England.

CATHOLIC REFORM AND COUNTER-REFORMATION

The Protestant Reformation did not take the medieval church completely by surprise. There had been much criticism and many calls for reform before the **Counter-Reformation** began in response to Protestant successes.

Sources of Catholic Reform Before the Reformation began, ambitious proposals had been made for church reform. But 16th-century popes were mindful of how the Councils of Constance and Basel had tried to strip the pope of his traditional powers, and they squelched efforts to bring about basic changes in the laws and institutions of the church. Despite papal foot-dragging, the church was not without reformers. Many new religious orders sprang up in the 16th century to champion renewal within the church.

Ignatius of Loyola and the Society of Jesus Of the various reform groups, none was more instrumental in the success of the Counter-Reformation than the Society of Jesus, the new order of Jesuits. Organized by Ignatius of Loyola in the 1530s, it was officially recognized by the papacy in 1540. Within a century, the society had more than 15,000 members scattered throughout the world and had established thriving missions in India, Japan, and the Americas.

Ignatius of Loyola (1491–1556) was a heroic figure. A dashing courtier and caballero in his youth, he began his spiritual pilgrimage in 1521 while recouperating from a serious battle wound. During a lengthy and painful convalescence, he read Christian classics. So impressed was he with the heroic self-sacrifice of the church's saints and their methods of overcoming mental anguish and pain that he underwent a profound religious conversion. Henceforth, he too would serve the church as a soldier of Christ.

Counter-Reformation
Sixteenth-century reform movement in the Roman Catholic Church in reaction to the Protestant Reformation.

The Ecstasy of Saint Teresa of Avila, by Gianlorenzo Bernini (1598–1680). Catholic mystics like Saint Teresa and Saint John of the Cross helped revive the traditional piety of medieval monasticism.

© Scala/Art Resource, N.Y.

HISTORY'S VOICES

IGNATIUS OF LOYOLA'S "RULES FOR THINKING WITH THE CHURCH"

As leaders of the Counter-Reformation, the Jesuits attempted to live by and instill in others the strictest obedience to church authority. The following are some of the 18 rules included by Ignatius in his Spiritual Exercises to give Catholics positive direction. These rules also indicate the Catholic reformers' refusal to compromise with Protestants.

WOULD PROTESTANTS find any of Ignatius's "rules" acceptable? Might any of them be controversial among Catholic laity as well as among Protestant laity?

In order to have the proper attitude of mind in the Church Militant we should observe the following rules:

1. Putting aside all private judgment, we should keep our minds prepared and ready to obey promptly and in all things the true spouse of Christ our Lord, our Holy Mother, the hierarchical Church.

2. To praise sacramental confession and the reception of the Most Holy Sacrament once a year, and much better once a month, and better still every week. . . .

3. To praise the frequent hearing of Mass. . . .

4. To praise highly the religious life, virginity, and continence; and also matrimony, but not as highly. . . .

5. To praise the vows of religion, obedience, poverty, chastity, and other works of perfection and supererogation. . . .

6. To praise the relics of the saints . . . [and] the stations, pilgrimages, indulgences, jubilees, Crusade indulgences, and the lighting of candles in the churches.

7. To praise the precepts concerning fasts and abstinences . . . and acts of penance. . . .

8. To praise the adornments and buildings of churches as well as sacred images. . . .

9. To praise all the precepts of the church. . . .

10. To approve and praise the directions and recommendations of our superiors as well as their personal behaviour. . . .

11. To praise both the positive and scholastic theology. . . .

12. We must be on our guard against making comparisons between the living and those who have already gone to their reward, for it is no small error to say, for example: "This man knows more than St. Augustine"; "He is another Saint Francis, or even greater." . . .

13. If we wish to be sure that we are right in all things, we should always be ready to accept this principle: I will believe that the white that I see is black, if the hierarchical Church so defines it. For I believe that between . . . Christ our Lord and . . . His Church, there is but one spirit, which governs and directs us for the salvation of our souls.

Source: *The Spiritual Exercises of St. Ignatius,* trans. by Anthony Mottola. Copyright © 1964 by Doubleday, a division of Bantam, Doubleday, Dell Publishing Group, Inc., pp. 139–141. Used by permission of Doubleday, a division of Random House, Inc.

Ignatius devised a program of religious and moral self-discipline called the *Spiritual Exercises,* which outlined a path to absolute spiritual self-mastery. Ignatius believed that a person could shape his or her own behavior, even create a new religious self, through disciplined study and regular practice (see Ignatius of Loyola's "Rules for Thinking with the Church").

Whereas in Jesuit eyes Protestants had distinguished themselves by disobedience to church authority and by religious innovation, Ignatius's exercises were intended to teach good Catholics to submit without question to higher church authority and spiritual direction. Perfect discipline and self-control were essential for achieving such obedience, as were a passion for traditional spirituality and mystical experience. This potent combination helped counter the Reformation and win many Protestants back to the Catholic fold, especially in Austria and Germany.

The Council of Trent (1545–1563) The broad success of the Reformation and the insistence of the emperor Charles V forced Pope Paul III (r. 1534–1549) to call a general council of the church to reassert church doctrine. The pope also appointed a reform commission, whose report, presented in February 1537, bluntly criticized the fiscality and simony[2] of the papal Curia (court) as the primary source of the church's loss of esteem. The report was so critical that Pope Paul III attempted unsuccessfully to suppress its publication, and Protestants reprinted and circulated it to justify their criticism.

The long-delayed council met in 1545 in the imperial city of Trent in northern Italy. There were three sessions spread over 18 years with long interruptions due to war, plague, and politics. Unlike the general councils of the 15th century, Trent was strictly under the pope's control, with high Italian prelates prominent in the proceedings.

The council's most important reforms concerned internal church discipline. The selling of church offices and other religious goods was forbidden. Trent strengthened the authority of local bishops so they could effectively discipline popular religious practice. Bishops who resided in Rome were forced to move to their appointed seats of authority. They had to preach regularly and conduct annual visitations. Parish priests were required to be neatly dressed, better educated, strictly celibate, and active among their parishioners. To train better priests, Trent also called for the establishment of a seminary in every diocese.

The Council did not make a single doctrinal concession to the Protestants, however. In the face of Protestant criticism, the Council of Trent reaffirmed the traditional scholastic education of the clergy; the role of good works in salvation; the authority of tradition; the seven sacraments; transubstantiation; the withholding of the Eucharistic cup from the laity; clerical celibacy; the reality of purgatory; the veneration of saints, relics, and sacred images; and the granting of letters of indulgence.

Rulers initially resisted Trent's reform decrees, fearing a revival of papal political power within their lands. But in time the new legislation took hold, and parish life revived under the guidance of a devout and better-trained clergy.

THE REFORMATION'S ACHIEVEMENTS

*A*lthough politically conservative, the Reformation changed traditional religious practices and institutions in many lands. By the end of the 16th century, what had disappeared or was radically altered was often dramatic.

HOW DID the Reformation change religious and social life?

Religion in 15th-Century Life Prior to the Reformation, the streets of the great cities of central Europe that later turned Protestant (for example, Zurich, Strasbourg, Nuremberg, or Geneva) were filled with people who had clerical vocations. They made up 6 to 8 percent of the total urban population, and they exercised considerable political as well as spiritual power. They legislated and taxed; they tried cases in special church courts; and they enforced their laws with threats of excommunication.

The church calendar regulated daily life. About one-third of the year was devoted to some kind of religious observance or celebration. There were frequent

---

[2]The sin of selling sacred or spiritual things, such as church offices.

periods of fasting. On almost a hundred days out of the year, a pious Christian could not, without special dispensation, eat eggs, butter, fat, or meat.

Monasteries and especially nunneries were prominent, influential institutions. Sons of society's most powerful citizens resided there. Local aristocrats were closely identified with particular churches and chapels, whose walls recorded their lineage and proclaimed their generosity. Friars from near and far worked the streets begging alms. The Mass and liturgy were read entirely in Latin. Images of saints were regularly displayed, and on certain holy days their relics were paraded about and venerated. Pilgrims gathered by the hundreds and thousands at religious shrines, many sick and dying in search of a cure or a miracle, but also "tourists" seeking diversion and entertainment. Several times during the year, special preachers appeared with letters of indulgence to sell. Many clergy lived openly with concubines and had children, although they were sworn to celibacy and forbidden marriage. The church tolerated such relationships if penitential fines were paid.

People everywhere could be heard complaining about the clergy's exemption from taxation and, in many instances, also from the civil criminal code. People also grumbled about having to support local church officials who actually lived and worked elsewhere. Townspeople expressed concern that the church had too much influence over education and culture.

Religion in 16th-Century Life After the Reformation, few changes in politics and society were evident in these cities. The same aristocratic families governed, and the rich generally got richer and the poor poorer. But overall numbers of clergy fell by two-thirds and religious holidays shrank by one-third. Monasteries and nunneries were almost all gone. Many were turned into hospices for the sick and poor or into educational institutions, their endowments to these new purposes. A few cloisters remained for very devout old monks and nuns, who could not be pensioned off or who lacked families and friends to care for them. But these remaining cloisters died out with their inhabitants.

The number of churchgoers had been reduced by at least a third, and worship was conducted almost completely in the vernacular. In some, particularly those in Zwinglian cities, the walls were stripped bare and white-washed to make sure their congregations meditated only on God's Word. The laity observed no obligatory fasts. Indulgence preachers no longer appeared. Local shrines were closed down, and anyone found openly venerating saints, relics, and images was subject to fine and punishment.

Copies of Luther's translation of the New Testament, or more often excerpts from it, could be found in private homes, and meditation on them was encouraged by the new clergy. The clergy could marry, and most did. They paid taxes and were punished for their crimes in civil courts. Domestic moral life was regulated by committees composed of roughly equal numbers of laity and clergy, over whose decisions secular magistrates had the last word.

Not all Protestant clergy were enthusiastic about the new authority the laity enjoyed in religious affairs, and the laity themselves were ambivalent about some aspects of the Reformation. More than half of the original converts returned to the Catholic fold before the end of the 16th century. Half of Europe could be counted in the Protestant camp in the mid-16th century, but only a fifth were still there by the mid-17th century.[3]

[3]Geoffrey Parker, *Europe in Crisis, 1598–1648* (Ithaca, NY: Cornell University Press, 1979), p. 50.

FAMILY LIFE IN EARLY MODERN EUROPE

Changes in the timing and duration of marriage, family size, and child care suggest that social and economic pressures were altering family life in the 16th and 17th centuries. The Reformation was only one factor—and not the chief—of these changes.

Later Marriages   Between 1500 and 1800 men and women married later than in previous centuries: men in their mid-to late 20s and women in their early to mid-20s. The medieval church had recognized marriages made by a private exchange of vows between competent adults, but after the Reformation both Catholics and Protestants required parental consent and public vows for a licit union.

Late marriages reflected the difficulties couples had in accumulating the capital needed to set up independent households. There was a large population of single women: one in five never married, and 15 percent were widowed. Late marriages meant shorter unions, older first-time mothers, and higher mortality in childbirth. That led to more frequent remarriages for men. Delayed marriage also increased incidences of premarital sex and the numbers of children born out of wedlock.

Arranged Marriages   By the 15th century, it was usual for a future bride and groom to have known each other and to have had a prior relationship. Parents did not force strangers to wed, and the law protected children from coercion. Forced marriages where by definition invalid. But marriages were "arranged" in the sense that parents met and discussed terms before the prospective bride and groom began preparations.

Family Size   Nuclear families were the rule in Western Europe: a father, a mother, and their children. They might live in larger households with in-laws, servants, and boarders. Children were conceived on the average of every two years. About one-third died by age five, and one-half by their teens.

Birth Control   Artificial birth control methods had been known since antiquity. They were, however, not very effective, and the church opposed anything that might be done to prevent conception. St. Thomas Aquinas had argued that acts were moral only when they served nature's ends, and the production of children was the natural purpose of sex.

Wet Nursing   The church and physicians both encouraged women to suckle their own newborns rather than hand them off to wet nurses (lactating women who sold their services). Wet nursing increased the risk of infant mortality, for the women who provided this service were not always as healthy, clean, or caring as the well-off women who employed them. Upper-class women, however, tended for reasons of vanity and convenience to employ wet nurses. Because nursing has a contraceptive effect, some women nursed to space out their pregnancies, and those who wanted many children used wet nurses.

A Young Couple in Love (ca. 1480) by an anonymous artist.

Bildarchiv Preussischer Kulturbesitz.

Loving Families Some features of family life in this period may seem cold to modern people. Between the ages of 8 and 13, children were usually sent away from home to school or to begin apprenticeships and take up employment. The widowed often remarried within a few months of their bereavement. Marriages between spouses of vastly different ages were common.

In context, these practices made sense. Parents showed love and affection for their children by ensuring that they acquired the skills needed to be self-supporting. The labor involved in maintaining a household pushed people to remarry rapidly, but extreme disparity in age did invite criticism and ridicule.

THE WARS OF RELIGION

WHAT WAS the final result of the Wars of Religion in France, the Netherlands, and Germany?

After the Council of Trent adjourned in 1563, Protestants were met by a Jesuit-led Catholic counteroffensive. At the time of John Calvin's death in 1564, Geneva had become both a refuge for Europe's persecuted Protestants and an international school training Protestant resisters—leaders fully equal to the new Catholic challenge.

Genevan Calvinism and the reformed Catholicism of the Council of Trent were equally dogmatic, aggressive, and unwilling to compromise. Calvinists may have looked like "new papists" to their critics in the cities they dominated, but when they were a minority fighting for civil and religious rights, they could become firebrands and revolutionaries.

Calvinists favored a presbyterian form of church government. Congregations elected boards of *presbyters* (elders) to govern them and represent them at synods and meetings that shaped the policy of the church at large. Calvinism, therefore, encouraged local and regional religious authority. By contrast, the Counter-Reformation affirmed Catholicism's dedication to a centralized episcopal system, a church governed by a clerical hierarchy and owing absolute obedience to the pope. The higher clergy—the pope and bishops—not synods of local churches, ruled supreme. Calvinism attracted proponents of political decentralization who opposed totalitarian rulers, whereas Catholicism was congenial to proponents of absolute monarchy who believed that order required "one king, one church, one law."

The wars of religion that erupted between these camps were both internal national conflicts and international wars. Catholic and Protestant struggled for control of France, the Netherlands, and England. The Catholic governments of France and Spain fought the Protestant regimes in England and the Netherlands. The Thirty Years' War, which began in 1618, illustrated the international nature of religious conflict. Before it ended, it drew in every major European nation.

FRENCH WARS OF RELIGION (1562–1598)

When Henry II (r. 1547–1559) died accidentally during a tournament in 1559, his sickly 15-year-old son, Francis II (d. 1560), came to the throne under the regency of the queen mother, Catherine de Médicis (1519–1589). With the monarchy so weakened, three powerful families competed to control France: the Bourbons based in the south and west, the Montmorency-Châtillons from the center, and the Guises from eastern France. The Guises were by far the strongest, and the name *Guise* was synonymous with militant, ultra-Catholicism. The Bourbon and Montmorency-Châtillon families, by contrast, had strong **Huguenot** sympathies,

Huguenots French Calvinists.

primarily for political reasons. (French Protestants were called Huguenots after Besançon Hughes, the leader of a Genevan political revolt in the late 1520s.) The Bourbon Louis I, prince of Condé (d. 1569), and the Montmorency-Châtillon admiral Gaspard de Coligny (1519–1572) were the leaders of the French Protestant cause.

Ambitious aristocrats and discontented townspeople often joined Calvinist churches to oppose the Guise-dominated French monarchy. By 1561, there were more than 2,000 Huguenot congregations in France. Huguenots made up only about a 1/15 of the population, but they held important geographic areas and were well represented among the leaders of French society. More than 2/5 of the French aristocracy became Huguenots. Many apparently hoped to establish in France a principle of territorial sovereignty akin to the arrangement that the German princes won from the emperor in the Peace of Augsburg (1555). In this sense, Calvinism served the forces of political decentralization.

Catherine de Médicis and the Guises After Francis II's death in 1560, Catherine de Médicis continued as regent for her second son, Charles IX (r. 1560–1574). Fearing the Guises, Catherine, whose first concern was to

The St. Bartholemew's Day Massacre. In this notorious event, here depicted by the contemporary Protestant painter François Dubois, 3,000 Protestants were slaughtered in Paris and an estimated 20,000 others died throughout France. The massacre transformed the religious struggle in France from a contest for political power into an all-out war between Protestants and Catholics.

Le Massacre de la St–Barthelemy, entre 1572 et 1584. Oil on wood, 94 × 154 cm. Musée Cantonal des Beaux Arts, Lausanne. Photo: J.–C. Ducret Musée Cantonal des Beaux–Arts, Lausanne.

preserve the monarchy, sought allies among the Protestants. Early in 1562, she granted Protestants freedom to worship publicly outside towns—although only privately within them—and to hold synods, or church assemblies. In March 1562, the Duke of Guise surprised and massacred a Protestant congregation worshiping illegally at Vassy. This began the French Wars of Religion. Perpetually caught between fanatical Huguenot and Guise extremes, Queen Catherine tried to play one side against the other. She wanted a Catholic France but not under Guise domination.

On August 22, 1572, four days after the Huguenot Henry of Navarre had married Charles IX's sister—a royal alliance based on the queen mother's belief that Protestant power was growing—the Huguenot leader Coligny, who had influence over the king, was wounded by an assassin's bullet. Catherine may have been privy to this Guise plot to eliminate Coligny. After its failure, she feared both the king's response to her complicity and the Huguenots reaction to the attack on their leader. Catherine convinced Charles that a Huguenot coup was afoot and that only the swift execution of Protestant leaders could save the crown from a Protestant attack on Paris. On the eve of Saint Bartholomew's Day, August 24, 1572, Coligny and 3,000 fellow Huguenots were butchered in Paris. Within three days an estimated 20,000 Huguenots were killed in coordinated attacks throughout France.

This event changed the nature of the struggle between Protestants and Catholics throughout Europe. In France, it was no longer an internal political contest between Guise and Bourbon factions, nor was it simply a Huguenot campaign to win basic religious freedoms. Henceforth, Protestants viewed it as an international struggle to the death for survival against an adversary whose cruelty justified any means of resistance.

The Rise to Power of Henry of Navarre Henry III (r. 1574–1589), who was Catherine's third son and the last Valois king, was caught between a radical Catholic League, formed in 1576 by Henry of Guise, and vengeful Huguenots. Like his mother, he tried to steer a middle course, which won him support from a growing body of neutral Catholics and Huguenots, who put the political survival of France above its religious unity. Such *politiques*, as they were called, were prepared to compromise religious creeds to save the nation.

In the mid-1580s the Catholic League, with Spanish help, totally dominated Paris. Henry III tried to rout the league with a surprise attack in 1588, but he failed and had to flee Paris. Resorting to guerrilla tactics, the king had both the Duke and the Cardinal of Guise assassinated. The Catholic League reacted with a fury that matched the earlier Huguenot response to the Massacre of Saint Bartholomew's Day. In April 1589, the king was forced into an alliance with his Protestant cousin and heir, Henry of Navarre.

However, as the two Henrys prepared to attack Paris, a fanatical Dominican friar murdered Henry III, clearing the way for the Bourbon Huguenot Henry of Navarre to become Henry IV of France (r. 1589–1610).

Henry IV was a *politique*, who valued peace more than religious unity. He believed that a policy of tolerant Catholicism would best achieve his objectives. On July 25, 1593, he abjured the Protestant faith and embraced the majority religion of his subjects. He is reported to have said: "Paris is worth a Mass."

The Edict of Nantes Five years later, on April 13, 1598, Henry IV issued the Edict of Nantes, a formal religious settlement. In 1591, he had assured the

Huguenots of at least qualified religious freedoms, and the edict fulfilled his promise by sanctioning minority religious rights within what was to remain an officially Catholic country. This religious truce—and it was never more than that—granted the Huguenots, who by this time numbered well over a million, freedom of public worship, the right of assembly, admission to public offices and universities, and permission to maintain fortified towns. Most of these freedoms, however, were confined to specific Huguenot localities. Concession of the right to fortify towns reveals the continuing distrust between French Protestants and Catholics. The edict only transformed a long hot war between enemies into a long cold war. Critics believed the edict created a state within a state.

A Catholic fanatic assassinated Henry IV in May 1610. Although Henry is best remembered for the Edict of Nantes, his political and economic policies were equally important. They laid the foundations for the transformation of France into the absolutist state it became in the 17th century. His grandson Louis XIV (r. 1643–1715), renewing the slogan "one king, one church, one law," revoked the Edict of Nantes in 1685 (see Chapter 20). Religion again violently disrupted French society. Rare is the politician who learns from the lessons of history.

The Milch Cow. A 16th-century satirical painting depicting the Netherlands as a land all the great powers of Europe wish to exploit. Elizabeth of England is feeding her (England had long-standing commercial ties with Flanders); Philip II of Spain is attempting to ride her (Spain was trying to reassert its control over the entire region); William of Orange is trying to milk her (he was the leader of the anti-Spanish rebellion); and the king of France holds her by the tail (France hoped to profit from the rebellion at Spain's expense).

Rijksmuseum, Amsterdam.

IMPERIAL SPAIN AND THE REIGN OF PHILIP II (1556–1598)

Until the English defeated his mighty Armada in 1588, no ruler was greater in the second half of the sixteenth century than Philip II of Spain. During the first half of his reign, Philip II focused attention on the Mediterranean and Turkish expansion. On October 7, 1571, a Holy League of Spain, Venice, and the pope defeated the Turks at Lepanto in the largest naval battle of the 16th century. About 30,000 Turks were killed and more than one-third of the Turkish fleet was sunk or captured.

Revolt in the Netherlands   The spectacular Spanish military success in southern Europe was not repeated in northern Europe, where Philip tried to impose his will within the Netherlands and on England and France. The resistance of the Netherlands was key to undoing Spanish dreams of world empire.

The Netherlands were the richest area in Europe. The merchant towns of the region were, however, Europe's most independent. Many, like the great port of Antwerp, were Calvinist strongholds. Opposition to the Spanish overlords found a leader in a native nobleman, William of Nassau, the Prince of Orange (r. 1533–1584). Like other successful rulers in this period, William of Orange was a politique who valued the Netherlands' political autonomy above religious creeds. He was at various times Catholic, Lutheran, and Calvinist.

In 1564, political and religious opponents to Spain's rule united for the first time under Philip II's unwise insistence that the decrees of the Council of Trent be enforced throughout the Netherlands. They formed a national covenant called the Compromise, a solemn pledge to resist the decrees of Trent and the Inquisition.

Philip ordered the Duke of Alba (1508–1582) to lead an army of 10,000 men into the Netherlands from Milan in 1567, a show of combined Spanish and papal might. Alba put down the revolt and established a tribunal—known to the Spanish as the Council of Troubles and to the Netherlanders as the Council of Blood—to govern the land. Several thousand suspected heretics were publicly executed before Alba's reign of terror ended.

William of Orange, who was an exile in Germany during these turbulent years, emerged as the leader of a broad movement for the Netherlands' independence. In 1576, after a decade of persecution and warfare, the 10 predominantly Catholic southern provinces (roughly modern Belgium) joined the 7 largely Protestant northern provinces (roughly the modern Netherlands) in opposition to Spain. Their union, the Pacification of Ghent, granted each region of the country sovereignty in matters of religion—a Netherlands version of the Peace of Augsburg.

In January 1579, the southern provinces formed the Union of Arras and made peace with Spain. The northern provinces formed the Union of Utrecht and continued the struggle. Spanish preoccupation with France and England in the 1580s gave the northern provinces their chance to evict Spain's armies (1593), and in 1596, France and England formally recognized their independence. However, the northern provinces did not formally conclude peace with Spain until 1609, and Spain did not fully recognize their independence until the Peace of Westphalia in 1648.

ENGLAND AND SPAIN (1558–1603)

Elizabeth I   Elizabeth I (r. 1558–1603), daughter of Henry VIII and Anne Boleyn, was perhaps the most astute politician of the 16th century in both domestic and foreign policy. She repealed the anti-Protestant legislation of her predecessor Mary Tudor and guided a religious settlement through Parliament that prevented England from being torn asunder by religious differences in the 16th century, as the Continent was.

Catholic extremists hoped to replace Elizabeth with the Catholic Mary Stuart, Queen of Scots. But Elizabeth fended off Catholic assassination plots and rarely let emotion override her political instincts.

Elizabeth also dealt cautiously with England's Puritans, Protestants who wanted to "purify" the national church of every vestige of "popery" and make its theology purely Protestant. The Puritans had two special grievances: (1) the retention of Catholic ceremony and vestments by the Church of England, and (2) the continuation of the episcopal system of church governance. Sixteenth-century Puritans were not separatists, however. They worked through Parliament to create an alternative national church of semiautonomous congregations governed by representative presbyteries, following the model of Calvin and Geneva. These were the Presbyterians. The more extreme Puritans, who wanted every congregation to be autonomous and a law unto itself, were called Congregationalists. Elizabeth considered their views subversive.

Deterioration of Relations with Spain A series of events led inexorably to war between England and Spain, despite the sincere desires of both Philip II and Elizabeth to avoid it. Following Spain's victory at Lepanto in 1571, England signed a mutual defense pact with France. Also in the 1570s, Elizabeth's famous seamen, John Hawkins (1532–1595) and Sir Francis Drake (?1545–1596), began to prey on Spanish shipping in the Americas. Drake's circumnavigation of the globe (1577–1580) was one in a series of dramatic demonstrations of England's growing sea power. In 1585, Elizabeth signed a treaty that committed English soldiers to aid the Netherlands. These events pushed England and Spain toward a showdown, and the breakpoint was Elizabeth's reluctant decision to execute Mary, Queen of Scots (1542–1587) for complicity in a plot to assassinate her.

Philip assembled a great armada for an invasion of England, and on May 30, 1588, his fleet of 130 ships bearing 25,000 sailors and soldiers under the command of the Duke of Medina-Sidonia set sail for England. The English, however, ably countered his attack. The barges sent to transport Spanish soldiers from the galleons onto English shores were prevented from leaving Calais and Dunkirk. The swifter English and Netherlands ships, assisted by an "English wind (a storm)", dispersed the Spanish fleet, over a third of which never returned to Spain. The Armada's defeat gave heart to Protestant resistance everywhere, and Spain never fully recovered. By the time of Philip's death on September 13, 1598, his forces had been rebuffed by the French and the Dutch. His 17th-century successors were all inferior leaders, and Spain never again had an era of imperial grandeur comparable to Philip's reign. The French seized the opportunity to dominate the Continent, while the Dutch and the English whittled away at Spain's overseas empire.

Elizabeth died on March 23, 1603, leaving behind her a strong nation poised to expand into a global empire (see Map 16–3).

THE THIRTY YEARS' WAR (1618–1648)

The Thirty Years' War in the Holy Roman Empire was the last and most destructive of the Wars of Religion. Religious and political differences had long set Catholics against Protestants and Calvinists against Lutherans. What made the Thirty Years' War so devastating was the entrenched hatred of the various sides and their seeming determination to sacrifice everything for territorial sovereignty and religion. As conflicts multiplied, virtually every major European land became involved either directly or indirectly. When the hostilities ended in 1648, the peace terms redrew much of the map of northern Europe to conform to the pattern we know today.

Fragmented Germany During the second half of the 16th century, Germany was an almost ungovernable land of 360 autonomous political entities. The Peace of Augsburg (1555) had given each a significant degree of sovereignty within its own borders. Each levied its own tolls and tariffs and coined its own money, practices that made land travel and trade between the various regions difficult, if not impossible. Many of these little "states" had political ambitions. Unlike France, Spain, and England at the start of the 17th century, Germany was radically decentralized and fragmented (see Map 16–3).

Religious Division Religious conflict accentuated international and internal political divisions. The Holy Roman Empire was about equally divided between Catholics and Protestants, the latter having perhaps a slight numerical

MAP EXPLORATION

 Interactive map: To explore this map further, go to **http://www.prenhall.com/craig/map16.3**

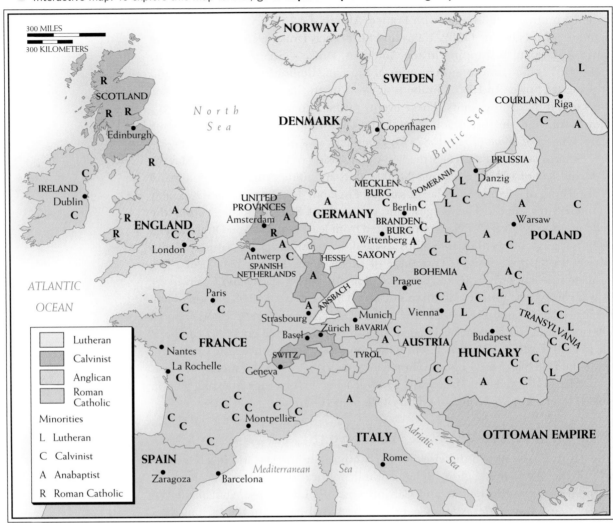

MAP 16–3

Religious Division ca. 1600. By 1600 few could expect Christians to return to a uniform religious allegiance. In Spain and southern Italy, Catholicism remained relatively unchallenged, but note the existence elsewhere of large religious minorities, both Catholic and Protestant.

WHY DID the Wars of Religion fail to reestablish religious uniformity in the Holy Roman Empire?

edge by 1600. The terms of the Peace of Augsburg (1555) had attempted to freeze the amount of territory held by Lutherans and the Catholics. In the intervening years, however, the Lutherans had gained political control in many Catholic areas, and Catholics had taken over a few previously Lutheran areas. There was also religious strife between liberal and conservative Lutherans and between Lutherans and the growing numbers of Calvinists.

As elsewhere in Europe, Calvinism operated as political and religious leaven within the Holy Roman Empire. Calvinism was not recognized as a legal religion by the Peace of Augsburg, but in 1559 it established a strong foothold within the empire when Elector Frederick III (r. 1559–1576) of the Palatinate, a devout convert to Calvinism, made it his domain's official religion. By 1609,

MAP 16–4

The Holy Roman Empire ca. 1618. On the eve of the Thirty Years' War, the empire was politically and religiously fragmented, as this somewhat simplified map reveals. Lutherans dominated the north and Catholics the south, while Calvinists controlled the United Provinces and the Palatinate and also had an important presence in Switzerland and Brandenburg.

DID THE Holy Roman Empire emerge from the Wars of Religion stronger or weaker?

Palatine Calvinists had organized a Protestant defensive alliance supported by Spain's enemies: England, France, and the Netherlands.

If the Calvinists were active within the Holy Roman Empire, so were their Catholic counterparts, the Jesuits. Staunchly Catholic Bavaria, with Spanish backing, was militarily and ideologically for Counter-Reformation Catholicism what the Palatinate was for Protestantism. From Bavaria, the Jesuits launched successful missions throughout the empire. In 1609, Maximilian, Duke of Bavaria (1573–1651), organized a Catholic League to counter a new Protestant

The Reformation permanently shattered the religious unity of Western Europe that had existed since the fifth century C.E. It also gave rise to more than a century of warfare, in which Catholics fought Protestants, and Protestants fought each other all in the name of faith. By 1648, when the Treaty of Westphalia ended the Thirty Years' War, Europe remained divided into mostly Catholic regions, mostly Protestant regions, and those areas with large religious minorities. Most of these divisions have persisted to the present day.

Country	Religion
Austria	Catholic
Belgium	Catholic
Bohemia (modern Czech Republic)	Catholic
Croatia	Catholic
England	Protestant (Anglicans, Calvinists, and Anabaptists); a declining Catholic minority
Estonia	Lutheran
France	Catholic, but with substantial numbers of Calvinists
Germany	North was predominately Protestant (Lutheran, Calvinist, Anabaptist); south and the Rhineland were mostly Catholic; but each area had religious minorities
Hungary	Mostly Catholic, but with a large Calvinist minority
Ireland	Mostly Catholic, but with a Protestant minority (Anglicans and Calvinists) mainly in the north
Italy	Catholic
Latvia	Lutheran
Lithuania	Catholic
Netherlands	Calvinist majority, but with a large Catholic minority
Poland	Catholic
Portugal	Catholic
Scandinavia	Lutheran
Scotland	Calvinist
Slovakia	Catholic
Slovenia	Catholic
Spain	Catholic
Switzerland	Almost evenly divided between Catholics and Protestants (both Calvinists and Lutherans)

alliance that had been formed by the Calvinist Elector Palatine, Frederick IV (r. 1583–1610). When the league fielded a great army under the command of Jean't Senclaes, Count of Tilly (1559–1632), the stage was set for the Thirty Years' War, the worst European catastrophe since the Black Death of the 14th century.

The Treaty of Westphalia   In 1648, all hostilities within the Holy Roman Empire were ended by the Treaty of Westphalia. The treaty reasserted the major feature of the religious settlement of the Peace of Augsburg (1555). Rulers were again permitted to determine the religion of their lands. Calvinists were given the legal recognition they had long-sought, but they were denied such status to various sectarians. The independence of the Swiss Confederacy and of the United Provinces of Holland was officially recognized.

By confirming the territorial sovereignty of Germany's many political entities, the Treaty of Westphalia prolonged Germany's division and political weakness into the modern era. However, two German states attained international significance during the 17th century: Austria and Brandenburg-Prussia. The petty regionalism within the empire reflected on a small scale the drift of larger European politics. During the 17th century Europe's distinctive nation-states, each with its own political, cultural, and religious identity, reached maturity and firmly established the competitive nationalism of the modern world.

SUPERSTITION AND ENLIGHTENMENT: THE BATTLE WITHIN

*R*eligious reform and warfare permanently changed religious institutions in major European countries. They also motivated rethinking traditional assumptions about human nature and society. On the one hand, this had dark consequence, for the peak years of religious warfare were also those of the great European witch hunts. On the other hand, however, the era spawned a constructive skepticism that inaugurated a period of significant scientific progress.

WITCH HUNTS AND PANIC

Nowhere is the dark side of the period better seen than in the witch hunts and panics that erupted in almost every western land. Between 1400 and 1700, courts sentenced an estimated 70,000 to 100,000 people to death for harmful magic (*malificium*) and diabolical witchcraft. In addition to threatening their neighbors, witches were said to attend mass meetings known as *sabbats*, to which they were believed to fly. They were accused of indulging in sexual orgies with the devil, who appeared in animal form, most often as a he-goat. They were said to practice cannibalism (having a taste for Christian children) and a variety of ritual acts and practices that denied or perverted Christian beliefs.

Many factors may have contributed to the great witch panics of the second half of the 16th and the early 17th centuries. Religious division and warfare were major influences. The Reformation's rejection of the defenses against the devil and demons that the chuch had traditionally provided forced people to find alternative ways to handle their anxieties. The growing strength of governments intent on weeding out nonconformists also played a part.

WHY DID witch hunts and panics erupt across Western Europe between 1400 and 1700?

Village Origins In village societies, "cunning folk," those who were both revered and feared by their neighbors, played a positive role in helping people cope with calamity. Neighbors turned to them for help in the face of natural disasters or physical disabilities, for they provided consolation and hope that, through magic, something might be done to avert or overcome difficulties.

Possession of magical powers, for good or ill, gave one status in village society. Not surprisingly, therefore, claims to such powers most often were made by the people most in need of security and influence—the old and the impoverished, especially single or widowed women. For villagers, witch beliefs may also have been a way of resisting pressure from urban Christian societies that wanted to impose their laws and institutions on the rural populace. From the perspective of church authorities, entrenched local fertility cults (semipagan practices intended to ensure good harvests) may have looked like diabolical witchcraft.

Influence of the Clergy Had ordinary people not believed that "gifted persons" could help or harm them by magical means and had they not been willing to make accusations against them, witch hunts would not have occurred. But the highly educated also contributed to the witch craze. The Christian clergy believed in and practiced magic—the holy sacraments and exorcism of demons. In the late 13th century the church declared its magic to be the only legitimate magic. Given that magical powers were not human, theologians reasoned that they had to come either from God or the devil. Anyone who practiced magic outside the church obviously derived their power from the devil. From such reasoning grew accusations of "pacts" between non-Christian magicians and Satan.

Attacking witches was one way in which the church brought regions into conformity with its doctrines and established its spiritual hegemony. The clergy viewed the cunning folk as competitors and obstacles. A campaign to root them out was a way to establish moral and policial authority over a village or territory.

Why Women? Roughly 80 percent of the victims of witch hunts were women, most of whom were single and between 45 and 60 years of age, suggesting to some that misogyny fueled the witch hunts. At a time when women threatened to break out from under male control, witch hunts, it has been argued, were simply a conspiracy of males against females.

Older single women may, however, have been vulnerable for more basic social reasons. They were a largely dependent social group in need of public assistance and natural targets for the "social engineering" of the witch hunts. For economic reasons, such women sometimes sought to protect and empower themselves by claiming supernatural powers. They thus found themselves on the front lines in disproportionate numbers when the church declared war against all who practiced magic without its blessing. Also, the practice by many of these women of midwifery

Combating Witchcraft. Three women are burned to death as witches in Baden, Germany. Their alleged crimes are depicted on the right, where they are seen feasting with demons.

"Three witches burned alive from a German Broadside," circa 1555. Courtesy of Stock Montage, Inc.

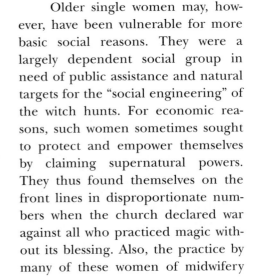

associated them with the deaths of beloved wives and infants and made them targets of local resentment and accusations. Both the church and their neighbors were prepared to think and say the worst about these women. It was a deadly combination.

End of the Witch Hunts   Many factors helped end the witch hunts. The emergence of a new, more scientific worldview made it difficult to believe in the powers of witches. When, in the 17th century, mind and matter came to be viewed as independent realities, the belief faded that a witch's curse, mere words, could affect things. Advances in medicine and the beginning of insurance companies improved people's ability to cope with calamities and physical affliction and dissuaded them from thoughts of the supernatural. Witch hunts also tended to get out of hand. Accused witches sometimes alleged that important townspeople had attended their sabbats, sometimes even their judges. At this point the trials ceased to serve the purposes of those who were conducting them. They not only became dysfunctional but threatened anarchy as well.

WRITERS AND PHILOSOPHERS

By the end of the 16th century, many could no longer accept either old Catholic or new Protestant absolutes. Intellectually as well as politically, the 17th century was a period of transition for which the humanists and scientists of the Renaissance and post-Renaissance (see Chapter 22) had prepared the way. Writers and philosophers of the era were aware that they lived in a time of change. Some embraced emerging science attitudes wholeheartedly (Hobbes and Locke), some tried to straddle the two ages (Cervantes and Shakespeare), and still others ignored or opposed developments that seemed to threaten traditional values (Pascal).

Miguel de Cervantes Saavedra   Spanish literature of the 16th and 17th centuries was influenced by Spain's peculiar religious and political situation. Spain was dominated by a Catholic Church that enjoyed vigorous state support. The intertwining of Catholic piety and Spanish political power created a preoccupation with medieval chivalric virtues—in particular, honor and loyalty.

Generally acknowledged to be the greatest Spanish writer of all time, Cervantes (1547–1616) explored the strengths and weaknesses of religious idealism. The son of a nomadic physician, he received only a smattering of formal education. Cervantes educated himself by insatiable reading in vernacular literature and immersion in the school of life. As a young man, he worked in Rome for a Spanish cardinal. In 1570, he became a soldier and was decorated for gallantry at Lepanto (1571). He began to write his most famous work, *Don Quixote*, in 1603, while languishing in prison after conviction for theft.

The first part of *Don Quixote* appeared in 1605, and a second part in 1615. If, as many argue, the intent of this work was to satirize the chivalric romances so popular in Spain, Cervantes failed to conceal his deep affection for the character he created as an object of ridicule, Don Quixote. Don Quixote, a none-too-stable middle-aged man, is driven mad by reading too many romances. He comes to believe that he is an aspirant to knighthood and must prove his worthiness. To this end, he acquires a rusty suit of armor, mounts an aged horse, and chooses for his inspiration a quite unworthy peasant girl whom he imagines to be a noble lady to whom he can, with honor, dedicate his life.

Don Quixote's foil in the story—his squire, Sancho Panza, a clever, worldly wise peasant—watches with bemused skepticism and genuine sympathy, as his lord does battle with a windmill (which he mistakes for a dragon) and repeatedly makes a fool of himself. The story ends tragically with Don Quixote's humiliating defeat by a well-meaning friend, who, disguised as a knight, bests Don Quixote in combat and forces him to renounce his quest for knighthood. The humiliated Don Quixote does not, however, come to his senses as a result. He returns sadly to his village to die a shamed and broken-hearted old man.

Throughout *Don Quixote*, Cervantes juxtaposed the down-to-earth realism of Sancho Panza with the old-fashioned religious idealism of Don Quixote. Cervantes admired the one as much as the other. He wanted his readers to realize that to be truly happy, men and women need dreams just as much as a sense of reality.

William Shakespeare   There is much less factual knowledge about William Shakespeare (1564–1616), the greatest playwright in the English language, than one would expect of such an important figure. Shakespeare may have worked as a schoolteacher for a time and in this capacity acquired his broad knowledge of Renaissance learning and literature. His work shows none of the Puritan distress over worldliness. He took the new commercialism and the bawdy pleasures of the Elizabethan Age in stride and with amusement. In politics and religion, he was a man of his time and not inclined to offend his queen.

That Shakespeare was interested in politics is apparent from his historical plays and the references to contemporary political events that fill all his works. He seems to have viewed government simply as a function of the character of a ruler, whether a Richard III or an Elizabeth Tudor, not as the realization of a social ideal. By modern standards he was a political conservative, accepting the social rankings and the power structure of his day and demonstrating unquestioned patriotism.

Shakespeare knew the theater as an insider. A member and principal dramatist of a famous company of actors, the King's Men, he was a playwright, actor, and part owner of a theater. He synthesized the best of the past and current achievements in the dramatic arts. He was particularly skilled at exploring human motivation and passion and had a unique talent for psychological penetration.

Shakespeare wrote histories, comedies, and tragedies. The tragedies are his greatest achievements. Four were written within a three-year period: *Hamlet* (1603), *Othello* (1604), *King Lear* (1605), and *Macbeth* (1606). The most original of the tragedies, *Romeo and Juliet* (1597), transformed an old popular story into a moving drama of "star-cross'd lovers."

In his lifetime and ever since, Shakespeare has been immensely popular with both audiences and readers. As Ben Jonson (1572–1637), a contemporary classical dramatist who created his own school of poets, put it in a tribute affixed to the *First Folio* edition of Shakespeare's plays (1623): "He was not of an age, but for all time."

Blaise Pascal   Blaise Pascal (1623–1662) was a French mathematician and a physical scientist widely acclaimed by his contemporaries. Torn between the continuing dogmatism and the new skepticism of the 17th century, Pascal aspired to write a work that would refute both the Jesuits, whose *casuistry* (confessional tactics designed to minimize or excuse sinful acts) he considered a distortion of Christian teaching, and the skeptics, who either denied religion altogether (atheists) or accepted it only as it conformed to reason (deists). Pascal failed to complete such a definitive work, and his views on these matters exist only in piecemeal form. He opposed the Jesuits in his *Provincial Letters* (1656–1657), and he left behind a provocative collection of reflections on humankind and religion that was published posthumously under the title *Pensées*.

Pascal was early influenced by the Jansenists, 17th-century Catholic opponents of the Jesuits. Although good Catholics, the Jansenists shared with the Calvinists St. Augustine's belief in the total sinfulness of human beings, their eternal predestination by God, and their complete dependence on faith and grace for knowledge of God and salvation.

Pascal believed that reason and science, although attesting to human dignity, remained of no avail in religion. Only the reasons of the heart and a "leap of faith" could found belief. Pascal saw two essential truths in the Christian religion: that a loving God, worthy of human devotion, exists; and that human beings, because they are corrupted in nature, are utterly unworthy of God. Pascal believed that the atheists and deists of the age had spurned the lesson of reason. For him, rational analysis of the human condition attested to humankind's utter mortality and corruption and exposed the inability of reason to resolve the problems of human nature and destiny. Those who truly heed reason should be driven by it to faith and dependence on divine grace.

Pascal made a famous wager with skeptics. It is a better bet, he argued, to believe that God exists and to stake everything on His promised mercy than not to do so; if God does exist, everything will be gained by the believer, whereas the loss incurred by having believed in God should He prove not to exist is, by comparison, slight.

Pascal was convinced that belief in God measurably improved earthly life psychologically and disciplined it morally, regardless of whether God proved in the end to exist. He thought that great danger lay in the surrender of traditional religious values. He urged his contemporaries to seek self-understanding through "learned ignorance" and to discover humankind's greatness by recognizing its misery. This, he hoped, would counter what he believed to be the false optimism of the new rationalism and science.

Baruch Spinoza   The most controversial thinker of the 17th century was Baruch Spinoza (1632–1677), the son of a Jewish merchant of Amsterdam. Spinoza's philosophy caused his excommunication by his own synagogue in 1656. In 1670, he published his *Treatise on Religious and Political Philosophy*, a work that criticized the dogmatism of Dutch Calvinists and championed freedom of thought. During his lifetime, both Jews and Protestants attacked him as an atheist.

Spinoza's most influential writing, *Ethics*, appeared after his death in 1677. Religious leaders universally condemned it for its apparent espousal of pantheism. God and nature were so closely identified by Spinoza that little room seemed left either for divine revelation in Scripture or for the personal immortality of the soul, denials equally repugnant to Jews and to Christians.

The most controversial part of *Ethics* deals with the nature of substance and of God. According to Spinoza there is only one substance, which is self-caused, free, and infinite, and God is that substance. From this definition, it follows that everything that exists is in God and cannot even be conceived of apart from him.

Pascal's calculator. Pascal invented this adding machine, the ancestor of mechanical calculators, around 1644. It has eight wheels with ten cogs each, corresponding to the numbers 0 through 9. The wheels move forward for addition, backward for subtraction.

Bildarchiv Preussischer Kulturbesitz

Leviathan. The famous title page from Hobbes's book depicts the ruler as absolute lord of his lands, but note that he incorporates the mass of individuals whose self interests are best served by their willing consent to accept him and cooperate with his rule.

Such a doctrine is not precisely pantheistic, because God is still seen to be more than the created world that he, as primal substance, embraces. Nonetheless, in Spinoza's view, statements about the natural world are also statements about divine nature. Mind and matter are seen to be extensions of the infinite substance of God; what transpires in the world of humankind and nature is a necessary outpouring of the Divine.

Such teaching clearly ran the danger of portraying the world as eternal and human actions as unfree and inevitable, the expression of a divine fatalism. Such points of view had been considered heresies by Jews and Christians because these views deny the creation of the world by God and destroy any voluntary basis for personal reward and punishment.

Thomas Hobbes Thomas Hobbes (1588–1679) was the most original political philosopher of the 17th century. Although he never broke with the Church of England, he came to share basic Calvinist beliefs, especially the low view of human nature and the ideal of a commonwealth based on a covenant, both of which find eloquent expression in his political philosophy.

Hobbes, an urbane and much-traveled man, was one of the most enthusiastic supporters of the new scientific movement. During the 1630s he visited Paris, where he came to know Descartes. After the outbreak of the Puritan Revolution (see Chapter 20) in 1640, he lived as an exile in Paris until 1651. Hobbes also spent time with Galileo (see Chapter 22) in Italy. He took a special interest in the works of William Harvey, a physiologist famed for the discovery of how blood circulated through the body; Harvey's scientific writings influenced Hobbes's own tracts on bodily motions.

Hobbes was driven to the vocation of political philosophy by the English Civil War (see Chapter 20). In 1651, his *Leviathan* appeared in which he examined the political consequences of human passions. This work's originality lay in (1) its making natural law, rather than common law (i.e., custom or precedent), the basis of all positive law; and (2) its defense of a representative theory of absolute authority against the theory of the divine right of kings. Hobbes maintained that statute law found its justification only as an expression of the law of nature and that rulers derived their authority from the consent of the people.

Hobbes viewed humankind and society in a thoroughly materialistic and mechanical way. Human beings are defined as a collection of material particles in motion. All their psychological processes begin with and are derived from bare sensation, and all their motivations are egotistical, intended to increase pleasure and minimize pain. Despite this seemingly low estimate of human beings, Hobbes believed much could be accomplished by the reasoned use of science. All was contingent, however, on the correct use of that greatest of all human powers, a commonwealth that unites people by their consent as one all-powerful person.

The key to Hobbes's political philosophy is a brilliant myth of the original state of humankind. According to this myth, human beings in the natural state are generally inclined to a "perpetual and restless desire of power after power that ceases only in death."[4] As all people desire—and in the state of nature have a natural right to—everything, their equality breeds enmity, competition, and

[4]*Leviathan*, Parts I and II, ed. By H. W. Schneider (Indianapolis, IN: Bobbs-Merrill, 1958), p. 86.

diffidence, and the desire for glory begets perpetual quarreling—"a war of every man against every man."[5]

Whereas earlier and later philosophers saw the original human state as a paradise from which humankind had fallen, Hobbes saw it as a corruption from which social life had delivered people. Contrary to the views of Aristotle and of Christian thinkers like St. Thomas Aquinas, Hobbes saw human beings not as sociable, political animals, but as self-centered beasts, laws unto themselves, utterly without a master unless one is imposed by force.

According to Hobbes, people escape the impossible state of nature only by entering a social contract that creates a commonwealth tightly ruled by law and order. The social contract obliges every person, for the sake of peace and self-defense, to agree to set aside personal rights to all things. We should impose restrictions on the liberty of others only to the degree that we would allow others to restrict our own.

Because words and promises are insufficient to guarantee this state, the social contract also establishes the coercive force necessary to compel compliance with the covenant. Hobbes believed that the dangers of anarchy were far greater than those of tyranny, and he conceived of the ruler's power as absolute and unlimited. There is no room in Hobbes's political philosophy for political protest in the name of individual conscience, nor for resistance to legitimate authority by private individuals—features of *Leviathan* criticized by his contemporaries, Catholics and Puritans alike.

John Locke John Locke (1632–1704) has proved to be the most influential political thinker of the 17th century.[6] His political philosophy came to be embodied in the so-called Glorious Revolution of 1688–1689 (Chapter 20). Although he was not as original as Hobbes, his political writings were a major source of the later Enlightenment Era's criticism of absolutism, and they inspired both the American and French Revolutions.

Locke's two most famous works are the *Essay Concerning Human Understanding* (1690) (discussed in Chapter 22) and *Two Treatises of Government* (1690). He wrote the latter to refute the argument that rulers had absolute power. Rulers, Locke argued, are bound to the law of nature, which is the voice of reason that teaches that "all mankind [are] equal and independent, [and] no one ought to harm another in his life, health, liberty, or possessions,"[7] inasmuch as all human beings are the images and property of God. According to Locke, people enter social contracts, empowering legislatures and monarchs to "umpire" their disputes, precisely to preserve their natural rights and not to surrender them to an absolute authority.

"Whenever that end [namely, the preservation of life, liberty, and property for which power is given to rulers by a commonwealth] is manifestly neglected or opposed, the trust must necessarily be forfeited and the power devolved into the hands of those that gave it, who may place it anew where they think best for their safety and security."[8] From Locke's point of view, absolute monarchy was "inconsistent" with civil society and could be "no form of civil government at all."[9]

18.1
The Mortal God:
Leviathan (1651)

QUICK REVIEW

Important European writers and philosophers, 1600–1700
- Cervantes (1547–1616), Spain
- Shakespeare (1564–1616), England
- Pascal (1623–1662), France
- Spinoza (1632–1677), Netherlands
- Hobbes (1588–1679), England
- Locke (1632–1704), England

[5] Ibid., p. 106.
[6] Locke's scientific writings are discussed in Chapter 24.
[7] *The Second Treatise of Government*, ed. By P. T. Peardon (Indianapolis, IN: Bobbs-Merrill, 1952), chap. 2, sects. 4–6, pp. 4–6.
[8] Ibid., chap. 13, sect. 149, p. 84.
[9] Ibid.

IMAGE KEY

for pages 370–371

a. Fifteenth century Italian silver cross
b. Martin Luther tempting Jesus
c. *The Milch Cow* a sixteenth-century satirical painting
d. Gutenberg's Bible
e. Miguel de Cervantes Saavedra (1547–1616)
f. *The Ecstacy of Saint Teresa of Avila*, by Bernini
g. Le Massacre de la St-Barthelemy, entre 1572 et 1584
h. John Calvin
i. Elizabeth I

SUMMARY

Voyages of Discovery In the late 15th century, Europe began to expand around the globe. Driven by both mercenary and religious motives, the Portuguese pioneered a sea route around Africa to India and the Far East, and the Spanish discovered the Americas. The consequences were immense for Europeans, Native Americans, Africans, and Asians. In time, a truly global society would emerge.

The Reformation The Reformation began in Germany with Martin Luther's attack on indulgences in 1517. Despite the opposition to the Reformation of Emperor Charles V, Luther had the support of many German princes. The Reformation shattered the religious unity of Europe. In Switzerland, Zwingli and Calvin launched their own versions of Protestantism. In England, Henry VIII repudiated papal authority when the pope refused to grant him a divorce. The different Protestant sects were often as hostile to each other as they were to Catholicism. The Reformation also led to far-reaching changes in religious practices and social attitudes, including steps toward the advancement of women.

The Roman Catholic Church also acted to reform itself. The Council of Trent tightened church discipline and reaffirmed traditional doctrine. The Jesuits converted many Protestants back to Catholicism.

The Wars of Religion The religious divisions of Europe led to more than a century of warfare from the 1520s to 1648. The chief battlegrounds were in France, the Netherlands, and Germany. When the Thirty Years' War ended in 1648, Europe was permanently divided into Catholic and Protestant areas.

Superstition and Enlightenment The Reformation led to both dark and constructive views of human nature. Perhaps the darkest view was the witch crazes that erupted across Europe. Thousands of innocent people, mostly women, were persecuted and executed as witches between 1400 and 1700 by both Catholic and Protestant authorities.

In literature and philosophy, however, these years witnessed an outpouring of creative thinking. Among the greatest writers of the age were Cervantes, Shakespeare, Pascal, Spinoza, Hobbes, and Locke.

REVIEW QUESTIONS

1. What were the main problems of the church that contributed to the Protestant Reformation? Why was the church unable to suppress dissent as it had earlier?

2. Why did the Reformation begin in Germany?

3. What was the Catholic Reformation?

4. Why did Henry VIII break with the Catholic Church? Was the "new" religion he established really Protestant?

5. Were the Wars of Religion really over religion?

KEY TERMS

Counter-Reformation   (p. 389)   **indulgences**   (p. 380)   **Reformation**   (p. 376)
Diet of Worms   (p. 382)   **ninety-five theses**   (p. 380)   **transubstantiation**   (p. 384)
Huguenot   (p. 394)

 For additional study resources for this chapter, go to:
www.prenhall.com/craig/chapter16

CHRISTIANITY

Christianity is based on the teaching of Jesus of Nazareth, a Jew who lived in Palestine during the Roman occupation. His simple message of faith in God and self-sacrificial love of one's neighbor attracted many people. Roman authorities, perceiving his large following as a threat, crucified him. After Jesus' crucifixion, his followers proclaimed that he had been resurrected from the dead and that he would return in glory, to defeat sin, death, and the devil, and take all true believers with him to heaven—a radical vision of judgment and immortality that has driven Christianity's appeal since its inception. In the teachings of the early church, Jesus became the Christ, the son of God, the long-awaited Messiah of Jewish prophecy. His followers called themselves Christians.

Christianity proclaimed the very incarnation of God in a man, the visible presence of eternity in time. According to early Christian teaching, the power of God's incarnation in Jesus lived on in the preaching and sacraments of the church under the guidance of the Holy Spirit. According to the Christian message, in Jesus, eternity has made itself accessible to every person here and now and forevermore.

The new religion attracted both the poor and powerless and the socially rising and well-to-do. For some, the gospel of Jesus promised a better material life. For others, it imparted a sense of spiritual self-worth regardless of one's place or prospects in society.

In the late second century, the Romans began persecuting Christians as "heretics" (because of their rejection of the traditional Roman gods) and as social revolutionaries (for their loyalty to a lord higher than the emperor of Rome). At the same time, dissenting Christians, particularly sects claiming direct spiritual knowledge of God apart from Scripture, internally divided the young church. To meet these challenges the church established effective weapons against state terrorism and Christian heresy: an ordained clergy, a hierarchical church organization, orthodox creeds, and a biblical canon (the New Testament). Christianity not only gained legal status within the Roman Empire, but also, by the fourth century, most favored religious status thanks to Emperor Constantine's embrace of it.

After the fall of the Western Roman Empire in the fifth century C.E., Christianity became one of history's great success stories. Aided by the enterprise of its popes and the example of its monks, the church cultivated an appealing lay piety centered around the Lord's Prayer, the Apostles' Creed, veneration of the Virgin, and the sacrament of the Eucharist. Clergy became both royal teachers and bureaucrats within the kingdom of the Franks. Despite a growing schism between the Eastern (Byzantine) and Western churches, and a final split in 1054, by 1000 the church held real economic and political power. In the 11th century reform-minded prelates put an end to presumptuous secular interference in its most intimate spiritual affairs by ending the lay investiture of clergy in their spiritual offices. For several centuries thereafter the church remained a formidable international force, able to challenge kings and emperors and inspire crusades to the Holy Land.

Pentecost. This exquisite enamel plaque, from the Mosan school that flourished in France in the 11th and 12th centuries, shows the descent of the Holy Spirit upon the apostles, 50 days after the resurrection of Jesus on the ancient Jewish festival called the "feast of weeks," or Pentecost.

Courtesy Metropolitan Museum of Art.

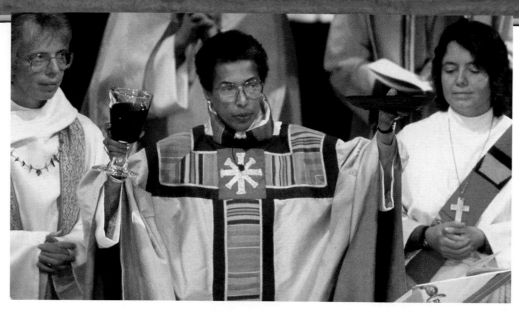

▲ **Female Bishop.** Women are entering the ministry and priesthood of many Christian denominations. The first woman bishop of the Episcopal Church of North America is here shown consecrating the Eucharist. The Church of England has also voted to admit women to the priesthood.

Ira Wyman/Corbis/Sygma.

By the 15th century the new states of Europe had stripped the church of much of its political power. It was thereafter progressively confined to spiritual and moral authority. Christianity's greatest struggles ever since have been not with kings and emperors over political power, but with materialistic philosophies and worldly ideologies, matters of spiritual and moral hegemony within an increasingly pluralistic and secular world. Since the 16th century a succession of humanists, skeptics, Deists, Rationalists, Marxists, Freudians, Darwinians, and atheists have attempted to explain away some of traditional Christianity's most basic teachings. In addition, the church has endured major internal upheavals. After the Protestant Reformation (1517–1555) made the Bible widely available to the laity, the possibilities for internal criticism of Christianity multiplied exponentially. Beginning with the split between Lutherans and Zwinglians in the 1520s, Protestant Christianity has fragmented into hundreds of sects each claiming to have the true interpretation of Scripture. The Roman Catholic Church, by contrast, has maintained its unity and ministry throughout perilous times, although present-day discontent with papal authority threatens the modern Catholic Church almost as seriously as the Protestant Reformation once did.

Christianity has remained remarkably resilient. It possesses a simple, almost magically appealing gospel of faith and love in and through Jesus. In the present-day world where religious needs and passions still run deep, evangelical Christianity has experienced a remarkable revival. The Roman Catholic Church, still troubled by challenges to papal authority, has become more pluralistic than in earlier periods. The pope has become a world figure, traveling to all continents to represent the church and advance its position on issues of public and private morality. A major ecumenical movement emerging in the 1960s has promoted unprecedented cooperation among evangelical Christian denominations. Everywhere Christians of all sects are politically active, spreading their divine, moral, and social messages. Meanwhile, old hot-button issues, such as the ordination of women, are being overtaken by new ones, particularly the marriage of gay men and women and the removal of clergy who do not maintain the moral discipline of their holy orders.

- Over the century what have been some of the chief factors attracting people to Christianity?

- What forces have led to disunity among Christians in the past? What factors cause tensions among modern Christians?

17 Africa
ca. 1000–1800

CHAPTER HIGHLIGHTS

North Africa Developments in African history from 1000 to 1800 varied from region to region. In North Africa, the key new factor was the imperial expansion of the Ottoman Empire as far west as Morocco. But regionalism soon rendered Ottoman authority in North Africa purely nominal.

Empires of the Sudan Several substantial states arose south of the Sahara: Ghana, Mali, Songhai, and Kanem. The ruling elites of these states converted to or were heavily influenced by Islam, although most of their populations clung to their older traditions. Much of the wealth of these states was tied to their control of the trans-Saharan trade routes. Farther south, in Central Africa, another substantial kingdom arose in Benin, famous for its brass sculptures.

East Africa On the east coast, Islam influenced the development of the distinctive Swahili culture and language, and Islamic traders linked the region to India and East Asia.

The Coming of the Europeans The key development of the fifteenth century was the arrival of European traders, missionaries, and warships. The Portuguese and later Europeans came in search of commerce, converts to Christianity, and spheres of influence. Their arrival disrupted indigenous African culture and political relations and presaged Africa's involvement in a new, expanding global trading system dominated by Europeans.

CHAPTER QUESTIONS

HOW DID Islam spread south of the Sahara?

WHAT WERE the four most important states in the Sahel between 1000 and 1600?

WHY DID Christianity gradually disappear in Nubia?

HOW DID the arrival of Europeans affect the peoples of West and Central Africa?

HOW DID Swahili language and culture develop?

HOW DID slavery affect race relations in the Cape Colony?

CHAPTER OUTLINE

- North Africa and Egypt
- The Spread of Islam South of the Sahara
- Sahelian Empires of the Western and Central Sudan
- The Eastern Sudan
- The Forestlands—Coastal West and Central Africa
- East Africa
- Southern Africa

In this chapter we explore, region by region, some salient developments in Africa from 1000 to 1800. While the Atlantic slave trade is treated in Chapter 18, its importance must be kept in mind as we review the period's other developments. We begin with Africa above the equator, where the influence of Islam increased and where substantial empires and kingdoms developed and flourished. Then we discuss west, east, central, and southern Africa and the effects of first Arab-Islamic and then European influence in both regions.

NORTH AFRICA AND EGYPT

WHY WAS no single power able to control North Africa for long?

*I*n politics, this period witnessed the influential dynasties of the Fatimids (909–969 in Tunisia; 969–1171 in Egypt), the Almoravids (1056–1147 in Senegal and the western Sudan; 1062–1118 in Marrakesh and western North Africa; 1086–1147 in Spain), the Almohads (1130–1269 in western North Africa; 1145–1212 in Spain), the Ayyubids (1169–1250 in Egypt), the Mamluks (1250–1517 in Egypt and the eastern Mediterranean); and the Ottomans (from the 14th century) across most of Mediterranean Africa. In general, a feisty regionalism characterized states, city-states, and tribal groups north of the Sahara and along the lower Nile, especially vis-à-vis external power centers, such as Baghdad and Spain. No single power controlled them for long. Regionalism persisted even after 1500, when most of North Africa came under the influence— and often direct control—of the Ottoman Empire.

By 1800, the nominally Ottoman domains from Egypt to Algeria were effectively independent principalities. In Egypt, the Ottomans had established direct rule after their defeat of the Mamluks in 1517, but by the 17th and 18th centuries, power had already passed to Egyptian governors descended from the former ruling Mamluks. The Mediterranean coastlands between Egypt and Morocco were officially Ottoman provinces, or regencies, whether under local governors or Ottoman deputies. By the 18th century, however, Algiers, Tripoli (in modern Libya), and Tunisia were virtually independent of the Ottomans. Morocco was the only North African sultanate to remain fully independent after 1700. Its most important dynasty was that of the Sa'dis (1554–1659).

THE SPREAD OF ISLAM SOUTH OF THE SAHARA

HOW DID Islam spread south of the Sahara?

*B*y 1800, Islamic influence in sub-Saharan Africa affected most of the Sudanic belt and the coast of East Africa as far south as modern Zimbabwe. Typically, Islam did not penetrate beyond the ruling or commercial classes of a region and tended to coexist or blend with indigenous ideas. Nevertheless, Islam and its carriers brought commercial and political changes as well as the Qur'an, new religious practices, and literate culture.

In East Africa, Islamic city-states along the coast from Mogadishu to Kilwa became a major factor. By contrast, in the western and central parts of the continent, Islam penetrated south of the Sahara into the Sudan by overland routes, primarily from North Africa and the Nile valley. Its agents were sometimes traders, but primarily emigrants from the east seeking new land.

From the 1030s, zealous militants known as Almoravids began an overt conversion campaign that extended to the western Sahel and Sahara. This movement eventually swept into Ghana, and finally Kumbi in 1076. Farther west, the Fulbe rulers of Takrur along the Senegal became Muslim in the 1030s and propagated their new faith among their subjects.

SAHELIAN EMPIRES OF THE WESTERN AND CENTRAL SUDAN

WHAT WERE the four most important states in the Sahel between 1000 and 1600?

*U*rbanization and state formation in sub-Saharan Africa did not occur only in response to trans-Saharan trade with the Islamic world, which dates largely from the end of the first millennium. Substantial states had risen in the first millennium C.E. in the Sahel regions just south of the Sahara proper (see Chapter 5). From about 1000 to 1600, four of these developed into notable and relatively long-lived empires: Ghana, Mali, and Songhai in the western Sudan, and Kanem-Bornu in the central Sudan.

GHANA

Ghana was located north of modern Ghana between and north of the inland Niger delta and the upper Senegal. It emerged as a regional power near the end of the first millennium and flourished for about two centuries. Its capital, Kumbi (or Kumbi Saleh), on the desert's edge, was well sited for the Saharan and Sahelian trade networks. Ghana's major population group were the Soninke. (*Ghana* is the Soninke term for "ruler.")

Ghanaian rulers were matrilineally descended. The king was supreme judge and held court regularly to hear grievances. Royal ceremonies were embellished with the full trappings of regal wealth and power appropriate to a king held to be divinely blessed if not semi-divine himself.

Tribute from the empire's many chieftaincies and taxes on royal lands and crops supplemented the duties levied on all incoming and outgoing trade. This trade involved a variety of goods—notably imported salt, cloth, and metal goods such as copper—probably in exchange for gold and perhaps kola nuts from the south. The regime apparently also controlled the gold (and, presumably, the slave) trade that originated in the savannah to the south and west.

Although the king and court of Ghana did not convert to Islam, they made elaborate arrangements to accommodate Muslim traders and government servants in their own settlement a few miles from the royal preserve in Kumbi Saleh. Muslim traders were prominent in the court, literate Muslims administered the government, and Muslim legists advised the ruler. In Ghana's hierarchical society, slaves were at the bottom; farmers and draftsmen above them; merchants above them; and the king, his court, and the nobility on top.

A huge, well-trained army secured royal control and enabled the kings to extend their sway in the late 10th century to the Atlantic shore and to the south as well (see Map 17–1). Ghanaian troops captured Awdaghast, the important southern terminus of the trans-Saharan trade route to Morocco, from the Berbers in 992. The empire was, however, vulnerable to attack from the desert fringe, as Almoravid Berber forces proved in 1054 when they took Awdaghast in a single raid.

Ghana's rulers may have converted to Islam soon after 1100. Ghana's empire was probably

The Great Mosque in Timbuktu. This mud and wood building is typical of western Sudanese mosques. The distinctive tower of the mosque was a symbol of the presence of Islam, which came to places like Timbuktu in central and West Africa by way of overland trade routes.

Werner Forman/Art Resource, N.Y.

MAP EXPLORATION

Interactive map: To explore this map further, go to **http://www.prenhall.com/craig/map17.1**

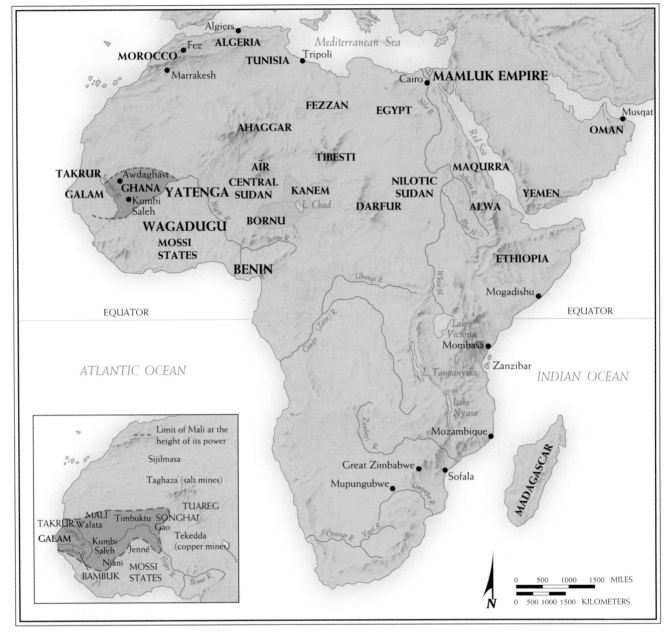

MAP 17–1

Africa ca. 900–1500. Shown are major cities and states referred to in the text. The main map shows the region of West Africa occupied by the empire of Ghana from ca. 990 to ca. 1180. The inset shows the region occupied by Mali between 1230 and 1450.

WHY WAS Ghana's location important for its prosperity?

destroyed in the late 12th century by the militantly anti-Muslim Soso people from the mountains southeast of Kumbi Saleh.

MALI

After the Almoravids brought their reform movement to the western Sahel at the end of the 11th century, their proselytizing zeal led to conversion of many of the region's ruling classes. It was, however, over a half-century after the breakup of

Ghana's empire before anyone in the western Sahel, Muslim or non-Muslim, could reestablish an empire of comparable extent. With Ghana's collapse and the Almoravids' failure to build a new empire below the Sahara (largely because of their focus on North Africa), the western Sudan broke up into smaller kingdoms. The former Ghanaian provinces of Mande and Takrur were already independent before 1076, and in the early 12th century Takrur's control of the Senegal valley and the gold-producing region of Galam made it briefly the strongest state in the western Sudan. Like Ghana, however, it was soon eclipsed by developments to the east, along the upper Niger—first the brief Soso ascendancy and then the rise of Mali.

In the mid-13th century, the Keita ruling clan of a Ghanaian successor kingdom, Mali, forged a new and lasting empire. The Keita kings dominated enough of the Sahel to control the flow of West African gold from the Senegal regions and the forestlands south of the Niger to the trans-Saharan trade routes, and the influx of copper and especially salt in exchange. Because they were farther south, in the fertile land along the Niger, than their Ghanaian predecessors had been, they were better placed to control all trade on the upper Niger and to add to it the Gambia and Senegal trade to the west. They were also able to use war captives for plantation labor in the Niger inland delta to produce surplus food for trade.

Agriculture and cattle farming were the primary occupations of Mali's population and, together with the gold trade, the mainstays of the economy. Rice was grown in the river valleys and millet in the drier parts of the Sahel. Together with beans, yams, and other agricultural products, this made for a plentiful food supply. Fishing flourished along the Niger and elsewhere. Animal husbandry was strongest among pastoralists of the Sahel, such as the Fulani (or Fulbe), but cattle, sheep, and goats were also plentiful in the Niger valley by the 14th century. Many of the Fulani seem to have been attracted by excellent pasturages to the riverine regions. The chief craft specialties were metalworking (iron and gold) and weaving of cotton grown within the empire.

The Malinke, a southern Mande-speaking people of the upper Niger region, formed the core population of the new state. They lived in walled urban settlements typical of the western savannah region. Each walled town was surrounded by its own agricultural land, and held perhaps 1,000 to 15,000 people.

The Keita dynasty had converted early to Islam (ca. 1100). During Mali's heyday in the 13th and 14th centuries, its kings often made the pilgrimage to Mecca. From their travels in the central Islamic lands, they brought back ideas about political and military organization. Through Muslim traders' networks, Islam also connected Mali to other areas of Africa.

Mali's imperial power was built largely by one leader, the Keita King Sundiata (or Sunjaata; r. 1230–1255). Sundiata and his successors, aided by significant population growth in the western savannah, exploited their agricultural resources and Malinke commercial skills to build an empire even more powerful than its Ghanaian predecessor. Sundiata extended his control well beyond the former domains of Ghana, west to the Atlantic coast and east beyond Timbuktu. By controlling the commercial entrepôts of Gao, Walata, and Jenne, he was able to dominate the Saharan as well as the Niger trade. He built his capital, Niani, into a major city. Niani was located on a tributary of the Niger in the savannah at the edge of the forest in a gold- and iron-rich region, well away from the lands of the Sahel nomads and well south of Ghana's capital, Kumbi. Niani had access to the forest trade products of gold, kola nuts, and palm oil; it was easily defended by virtue of its surrounding small hills; and it was easily reached by river.

QUICK REVIEW

Mali

- Keita clan forged Mali in mid-13th century
- Keita kings controlled the flow of West African gold
- Agriculture and cattle farming were primary occupations of Mali's people

11.3
Ibn Battuta in Mali

QUICK REVIEW

King Sundiata (r. 1230–1255)

- Built Mali's imperial power
- Mali's empire was more powerful than its Ghanaian predecessor
- Empire encompassed three major regions: Senegal, the central Mande states, and the peoples of the Niger in the Gao region

The Great Mosque at Jenne. Jenne was one of the important commercial centers controlled by the empire of Mali in the 13th and 14th centuries.

Ann Stalcup.

 11.1

Mansa Musa: The "King Who Sits on a Mountain of Gold"

Mansa Musa, King of Mali. The 14th-century Catalan Atlas shows King Mansa Musa of Mali, seated on a throne. A rider on a camel approaches him.

The Granger Collection.

The empire that Sundiata and his successors built ultimately encompassed three major regions and language groups of Sudanic West Africa: (1) the Senegal region (including Takrur), occupied by speakers of the West Atlantic Niger-Kongo language group (including Fulbe, Tukulor, Wolof, Serer); (2) the central Mande states between Senegal and Niger, occupied by the Niger-Kongo-speaking Soninke and Mandinke peoples; and (3) the peoples of the Niger in the Gao region who spoke Songhai, the only Nilo-Saharan language west of the Lake Chad basin.

Mali was less a centralized bureaucratic state than the center of a vast sphere of influence that included provinces and tribute-paying kingdoms. Many chieftaincies retained much of their independence but recognized the sovereignty of the supreme, sacred *mansa*, or "emperor," of the Malian realms.

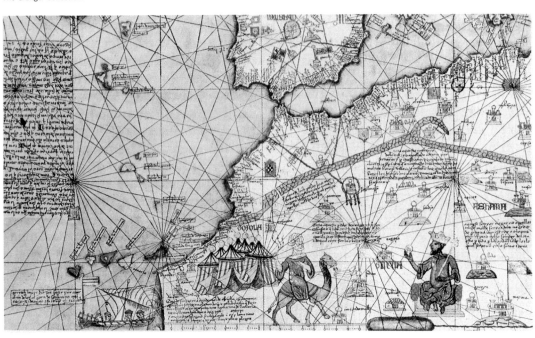

The greatest Keita king proved to be Mansa Musa (r. 1312–1337), whose pilgrimage through Mamluk Cairo to Mecca in 1324 became famous. At home, he consolidated Mali's power, securing peace for most of his reign throughout his vast dominions. Musa's devoutness as a Muslim fostered the further spread of Islam in the empire and beyond. Under his rule, Timbuktu became known far and wide for its *madrasas* (religious schools), libraries, poets, scientists, and architects—making the city the leading intellectual center of sub-Saharan Islam as well as a major trading city of the Sahel.

Mali's dominance waned in the 15th century as the result of competition for its throne. As time went on, subject dependencies became independent, and the empire withered. After 1450, a new Songhai power in Gao to the east ended Mali's imperial authority.

SONGHAI

Gao became an imperial power in the reign of Sonni Ali (1464–1492). Sonni Ali made the Songhai Empire so powerful that it dominated the political history of the western Sudan for more than a century and was arguably the most powerful state in Africa (see Map 17–2).

Askia Muhammad al-Turi (r. 1493–1528) continued Sonni Ali's expansionist policies. Between them, Sonni Ali and Askia Muhammad built an empire that stretched from near the Atlantic into the Sahara and the central Sudan. The ancient caravan trade across the Sahara to the North African coasts provided their major source of wealth. Muhammad al-Turi was an enthusiastic Muslim. He built up the Songhai state after the model of the Islamic empire of Mali. In his reign, Muslim scholars made Timbuktu a major intellectual and legal training center for the whole Sudan. Nevertheless, his reforms failed to Islamize the empire or to ensure a strong central state under his less able successors.

The last powerful Askia leader was Askia Dawud (r. 1549–1583), under whom Songhai economic prosperity and intellectual life peaked. Still, difficulties mounted. Civil war broke out over succession to the throne in 1586, and the empire was divided. The once-great state became only one among many regional competitors in the western Sudan.

KANEM AND KANEM-BORNU

A fourth sizable Sahelian empire, Kanem, in the central Sudan, arose after 1100. Roughly contemporaneous with the Malian Empire to the west, Kanem began as a southern Saharan confederation of the black nomadic tribes known as Zaghawah. Their key leader, Mai Dunama Dibbalemi (r. ca. 1221–1259), was probably the first Kanuri leader to embrace Islam, which appears to have entrenched itself among the Kanuri ruling class during his reign. Dibbalemi used Islam to sanction his rule and provide a rationale for expansion through *jihad*, or holy "struggle" against polytheists. Dibbalemi and his successors expanded Kanuri power to control important trade routes to Libya and Egypt.

Sahelian Empires of the Western Sudan

ca. 990–ca. 1180?	Empire of Ghana
1076	Ghana loses Awdaghast to Almoravids
1180–1230	Soso clan briefly controls the old Ghanaian territories
ca. 1230–1450	Empire of Mali, founded by Sundiata
1230–1255	Reign of Sundiata
1312–1337	Reign of Mansa Musa
1374	Independent Songhai state emerges in Gao after throwing off Malian rule
ca. 1450–1600	Songhai Empire at Gao
1464–1591	Askia dynasty
1464–1492	Reign of Sonni Ali
1493–1528	Reign of Askia Muhammad al-Turi
1549–1583	Reign of Askia Dawud
1590s	Collapse of the Songhai Empire

MAP EXPLORATION

Interactive map: To explore this map further, go to **http://www.prenhall.com/craig/map17.2**

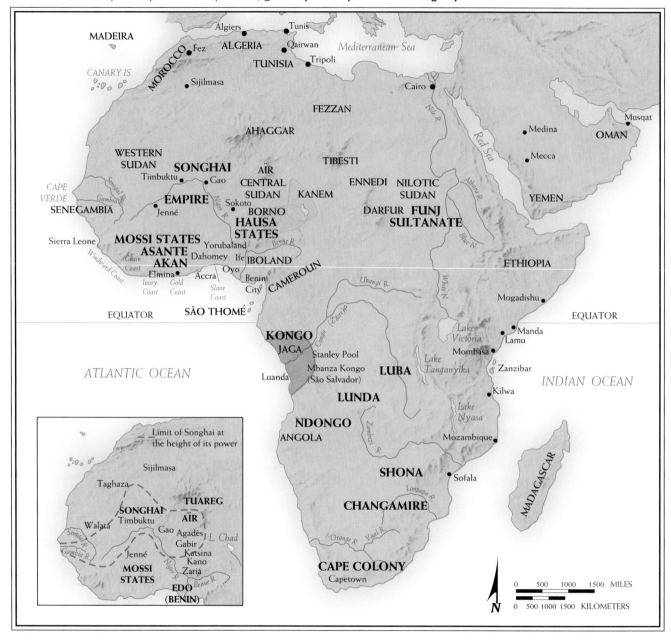

MAP 17–2

Africa ca. 1500–1800. Important towns, regions, peoples, and states are presented in the main map. The inset shows the empire of Songhai at its greatest extent in the early 16th century.

WHAT WAS Songhai's major source of wealth?

Civil strife, largely over the royal succession, weakened the Kanuri state from the later 14th century, and after 1400, the locus of power shifted from Kanem proper westward, to the land of Bornu, southwest of Lake Chad. Near the end of the 16th century, firearms and Turkish military instructors enabled the Kanuri leader Idris Alawma (r. ca. 1575–1610) to unify Kanem and Bornu. He set up an avowedly Islamic state and extended his rule even into Hausaland, between Bornu and the Niger River. The center of trading activity as well as political power and security now shifted from the Niger bend east to the territory under Kanuri control.

Deriving its prosperity from the trans-Saharan trade, Idris Alawma's regional empire survived for nearly a century, but by 1700, its power had been reduced by the Hausa states to the west.

THE EASTERN SUDAN

The Christian states of Maqurra and Alwa in the Nilotic Sudan, or Nubia, lasted for more than 600 years from their early seventh-century beginnings. Often thought of as isolated, Christian Nubia in fact maintained political, religious, and commercial contact with Egypt, the Red Sea world, and the east-central and even central Sudan. From late Fatimid times onward, both Maqurra and Alwa were subject to growing Muslim minorities. The result was a long-term intermingling of Arabic and Nubian cultures and the creation of a new Nilotic Sudanese people and culture.

Islam spread slowly with Arab immigration into the upper Nile region. A significant factor in the gradual disappearance of Christianity in Nubia was the apparently elite character of Christianity there and its association with foreign Egyptian Coptic Christianity. Maqurra became officially Muslim at the beginning of the 14th century. The Islamization of Alwa came somewhat later, under the Funj sultanate that replaced the Alwa state.

The Funj state flourished from just after 1500 until 1762. The Funj developed an Islamic society whose Arabized character was unique in sub-Saharan Africa. A much-reduced Funj state held out until an Ottoman-Egyptian invasion in 1821.

THE FORESTLANDS—COASTAL WEST AND CENTRAL AFRICA

WEST AFRICAN FOREST KINGDOMS: THE EXAMPLE OF BENIN

Many states had developed in West Africa centuries before the first Portuguese reports of their existence in 1485. Benin, the best known of these kingdoms, reflects, especially in its art, the sophistication of West African culture before 1500.

Benin State and Society   A distinct kingdom of Benin likely existed as early as the 12th century, and the power of the king, or *oba*, at this time was sharply limited by the *uzama*, an order of hereditary indigenous chiefs. Only in the 15th century, with King Ewuare, did Benin become a royal autocracy and a large state of major regional importance.

Ewuare apparently established a government in which he had sweeping authority, although he exercised it in light of the deliberations of a royal council formed from the palace uzama and the townspeople. He gave each chief specific administrative responsibilities and rank in the government hierarchy. Ewuare and his successors engaged in major wars of expansion and claimed for the office of oba an increasing ritual authority.

Central Sudanic Empires

ca. 1100–1500	Kanuri Empire of Kanem
ca. 1220s–1400	Height of Empire of Kanem
1221–1259	Reign of Mai Dunama Dibbalemi
1575–1846	Kanuri Empire of Kanem-Bornu
1575–1610	Reign of Idris Alawma, major architect of the state

WHY DID Christianity gradually disappear in Nubia?

HOW DID the arrival of Europeans affect the peoples of West and Central Africa?

oba   Title of the king of Benin.

uzama   Order of hereditary chiefs in Benin.

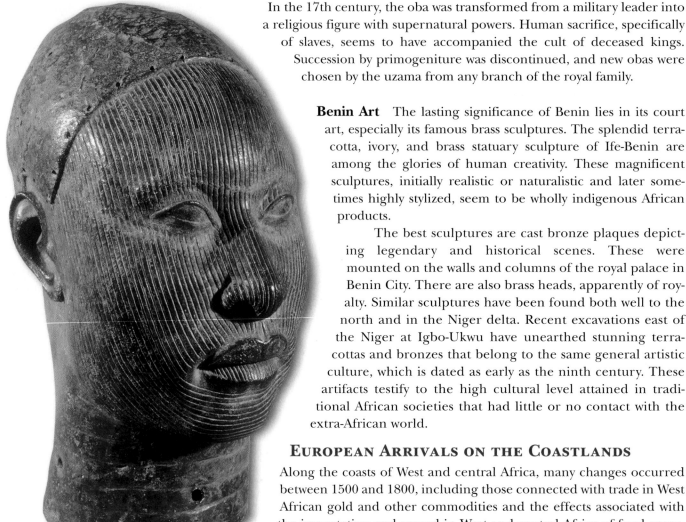

Brass head. This naturalistic brass head (29 cm high), which dates to the 13th century, conveys a serenity remarkably similar to classical Greek sculpture.

© Frank Willet.

Benin

ca. 1100–1897	Benin state
ca. 1300	First Ife king of Benin state
1440–1475	Reign of Ewuare

In the 17th century, the oba was transformed from a military leader into a religious figure with supernatural powers. Human sacrifice, specifically of slaves, seems to have accompanied the cult of deceased kings. Succession by primogeniture was discontinued, and new obas were chosen by the uzama from any branch of the royal family.

Benin Art The lasting significance of Benin lies in its court art, especially its famous brass sculptures. The splendid terracotta, ivory, and brass statuary sculpture of Ife-Benin are among the glories of human creativity. These magnificent sculptures, initially realistic or naturalistic and later sometimes highly stylized, seem to be wholly indigenous African products.

The best sculptures are cast bronze plaques depicting legendary and historical scenes. These were mounted on the walls and columns of the royal palace in Benin City. There are also brass heads, apparently of royalty. Similar sculptures have been found both well to the north and in the Niger delta. Recent excavations east of the Niger at Igbo-Ukwu have unearthed stunning terracottas and bronzes that belong to the same general artistic culture, which is dated as early as the ninth century. These artifacts testify to the high cultural level attained in traditional African societies that had little or no contact with the extra-African world.

EUROPEAN ARRIVALS ON THE COASTLANDS

Along the coasts of West and central Africa, many changes occurred between 1500 and 1800, including those connected with trade in West African gold and other commodities and the effects associated with the importation and spread in West and central Africa of food crops, such as maize, peanuts, squash, sweet potatoes, cocoa, and cassava (manioc) from the Americas. The gradual involvement of Africa in the emerging global economic system paved the way for eventual colonial domination of the continent, especially its coastal regions, by the Europeans. The European names for segments of the coastline—the Grain (or Pepper) Coast, the Ivory Coast, the Gold Coast, and the Slave Coast—identify the main exports that could be extracted by ship and vividly indicate the nature of the emerging relationship.

Senegambia In West Africa, Senegambia—which takes its name from the Senegal and Gambia Rivers—was one of the earliest regions affected by European trade. Its maritime trade with European powers, like the older overland trade, was primarily in gold and products such as salt, cotton goods, hides, and copper. Senegambian states also provided perhaps a third of all African slaves exported during the 16th century. Thereafter, the focus of the slave trade shifted south and east along the coast. Over time, Portuguese-African mulattos and the British came to control the Gambia River trade, while the French won the Senegal River markets.

The Gold Coast The Gold Coast derives its name from its importance after 1500 as the outlet for West Africa's gold fields. Here, beginning with the Portuguese at Elmina in 1481, European states and companies built coastal forts to protect their trade. The trade encouraged the growth of larger states—like the Akan forest states near the coast and the Gonja state just north of the forest—perhaps because they could better control commerce.

The intensive contact of the Gold Coast with Europeans also led to the spread of American crops, notably maize and cassava, into the region, which contributed to substantial population growth. Slaves became big business here in the late 17th century, especially in the Accra region. The economy was so disrupted by the slave trade that gold mining declined. Eventually more gold came into the Gold Coast from the sale of slaves than went out from its mines.

CENTRAL AFRICA

The vast center of the subcontinent is bounded by swamps in the north, coastal rain forests to the west, highlands to the east, and deserts in the south. Before 1500, these natural barriers impeded international contact and trade with the interior.

The coming of the Portuguese broke down this isolation, albeit slowly. The Portuguese came looking for gold and silver but found none. Instead, they exported such goods as ivory and palm cloth. Ultimately, their main export was slaves, first to the Portuguese sugar plantations on Sao Thomé island in the Gulf of Guinea, then to Brazil.

The Kongo Kingdom Kongo was the major state with which the Portuguese dealt after coming to central Africa in 1483. Dating from probably the 14th century, the Kongo kingdom was located on a fertile, well-watered plateau south of the lower Zaïre River valley, between the coast and the Kwango River in the east. Here, astride the border between forest and grassland, the Kongo kings had built a central government based on a pyramid structure of tax or tribute collection balanced by rewards for those faithful in paying their taxes. Kongo society was dominated by the king, whose authority was tied to acceptance of him as a kind of spiritual spokesman of the gods or ancestors. By 1600, Kongo was half the size of England and alongside farming boasted a high state of specialization in weaving and pottery, salt production, fishing, and metalworking.

The Portuguese brought Mediterranean goods, preeminently luxury textiles from North Africa, to trade for African goods. Such luxuries augmented the prestige and wealth of the ruler and his elites. However, slaves became the primary export that could be used to obtain foreign luxury goods. Imports, such as fine clothing, tobacco, and alcohol, did nothing to replace the labor pool lost to slavery.

At first the Portuguese put time and effort into education and Christian proselytizing, but the need for more slaves led to their concentrating on exploiting the human

Benin Bronze Plaque. From the palace of the Obas of Benin it dates to the Edo period of Benin culture, 1575–1625. It depicts two Portuguese males, perhaps a father and son, holding hands. It is likely that they represent the traders or government officials who came to the African coasts in increasing numbers from the end of the 15th century on.

Werner Forman, Art Resource, N.Y.

Central Africa

1300s	Kongo kingdom founded
1483	Portuguese come to central African coast
ca. 1506–1543	Reign of Affonso I as king of Kongo
1571	Angola becomes Portuguese proprietary colony

HISTORY'S VOICES

AFFONSO I OF KONGO WRITES TO THE KING OF PORTUGAL

I n 1526, Affonso, the Christian African king of Kongo, wrote to the Portuguese monarch ostensibly to complain about the effects of slaving on the Kongo people and economy. But the real issue was that the Portuguese were circumventing his own royal monopoly on the inland slave trade. One of the insidious effects of the massive demand of the Atlantic trade for slaves was the ever-increasing engagement in it of African monarchs, chieftains, and merchants.

HOW HAD the introduction of Portuguese merchants and European goods upset the social and political situation in Kongo? How had these goods tempted Affonso's subjects into the slave trade? How did Affonso wish to change the relationship of his people to Portugal? Was the king more worried about human rights or his economic losses?

Sir, Your Highness [of Portugal] should know how our Kingdom is being lost in so many ways that it is convenient to provide for the necessary remedy, since this is caused by the excessive freedom given by your factors and officials to the men and merchants who are allowed to come to this Kingdom to set up shops with goods and many things which have been prohibited by us, and which they spread throughout our Kingdoms and Domains in such an abundance that many of our vassals, whom we had in obedience, do not comply because they have the things in greater abundance than we ourselves; and it was with these things that we had them content and subjected under our vassalage and jurisdiction, so it is doing a great harm not only to the service of God, but the security and peace of our Kingdoms and State as well.

And we cannot reckon how great the damage is, since the mentioned merchants are taking every day our natives, sons of the land and the sons of our noblemen and vassals and our relatives, because the thieves and men of bad conscience grab them wishing to have the things and wares of this Kingdom which they are ambitious of; they grab them and get them to be sold; and so great, Sir, is the corruption and licentiousness that our country is being completely depopulated, and Your Highness should not agree with this nor accept it as in your service. And to avoid it we need from those [your] Kingdoms no more than some priests and a few people to teach in schools, and no other goods except wine and flour for the holy sacrament. That is why we beg of Your Highness to help and assist us in this matter, commanding your factors that they should not send here either merchants or wares, because it is *our will that in these Kingdoms there should not be any trade of slaves nor outlet for them.**

Concerning what is referred above, again we beg of Your Highness to agree with it, since otherwise we cannot ... remedy such an obvious damage. Pray Our Lord in His mercy to have Your Highness under His guard and let you do for ever the things of His service. I kiss your hands many times. ...

From *The African Past*, trans. by J. O. Hunwick, reprinted in Basil Davidson (Grosset and Dunlap, The Universal Library), pp. 191–193. Reprinted by permission of Curtis Brown Ltd. Copyright © 1964 by Basil Davidson.

*Emphasis in the original.

resources of central Africa. Regional rulers sought to procure slaves from neighboring kingdoms, as did Portuguese traders who went inland themselves. As the demand grew, local rulers increasingly attacked neighbors to garner slaves for Portuguese traders (see Chapter 18).

The Kongo ruler Affonso I (r. ca. 1506–1543), a Christian convert, began by welcoming Jesuit missionaries and supporting conversion. But in time he broke with the Jesuits and encouraged traditional practices, even though he himself remained a Christian. Affonso had constant difficulty curbing slaving practices and provincial governors who often dealt directly with the Portuguese, undermining royal authority (see "Affonso I of Kongo Writes to the King of Portugal"). Affonso's successor restricted Portuguese activity to Mpinda harbor and the Kongo capital of Mbanza Kongo (São Salvador). A few years later, Portuguese attempts to name the Kongo royal successor caused a bloody uprising against them that led in turn to a Portuguese boycott on trade with the kingdom.

Thereafter, disastrous internal wars shattered the Kongo state. Kongo, however, enjoyed renewed vigor in the 17th century. Its kings ruled as divine-right monarchs at the apex of a complex sociopolitical pyramid that rose from district headmen through provincial governors to

East and Southeast Africa

900–1500	"Great Zimbabwe" civilization
ca. 1200–1400	Development of Bantu Kiswahili language
ca. 1300–1600	Height of Swahili culture
1698	Omani forces take Mombasa, oust Portuguese from East Africa north of the port of Mozambique
1741–1856	United sultanate of Oman and Zanzibar

Fort Jesus, Mombasa, Kenya. Built by the Portuguese in the sixteenth century, it is the most conspicuous reminder of their former presence in East Africa.

Robert Harding World Imagery.

the court nobility and king. Royal power came to depend on a guard of musket-armed hired soldiers. The financial base of the kingdom rested on tribute from officials holding positions at the king's pleasure and on taxes and tolls on commerce. Christianity, the state religion, was accommodated to traditional beliefs. Kongo sculpture, iron and copper technology, and dance and music flourished.

Angola To the south, in Portuguese Angola, the experience was even worse than in Kongo. By 1600, Angola was exporting thousands of slaves yearly through the port of Luanda. In less than a century, the hinterland had been plundered. The Portuguese arrival had brought economic and social catastrophe.

EAST AFRICA

SWAHILI CULTURE AND COMMERCE

HOW DID Swahili language and culture develop?

The participation of East African port towns in the lucrative southern seas trade was ancient. Arabs, Indonesians, and even Indians had trafficked there for centuries. From the eighth century onward, Islam traveled with Arab and Persian sailors and merchants to these southerly trading centers. In the 13th century, Muslim traders from Arabia and Iran began to come in increased numbers and to dominate the coastal cities. Henceforward, Islamic faith and culture were often predominant along the seacoast, from Mogadishu to Kilwa.

By this time, a common language had also developed from the interaction of Bantu and Arabic speakers along the coast. This tongue is called *Swahili*, or *Kiswahili*, from the Arabic *sawahil*, "coastlands." Swahili language and culture probably developed first in the northern towns of Manda, Lamu, and Mombasa, then farther south along the coast to Kilwa. Likewise, the spread of Islam was largely limited to the coastal civilization and did not reach inland. This contrasts with lands farther north, in the Horn of Africa, where Islamic kingdoms developed in the Somali hinterland as well as on the coast.

Swahili civilization reached its apogee in the 14th and 15th centuries. The harbor trading towns were the administrative centers of the local Swahili states, and most of them were sited on coastal islands or easily defended peninsulas. To these ports came merchants from abroad and from the African hinterlands, some to settle and stay. These towns had impressive mosques, fortress-palaces, harbor fortifications, fancy residences, and commercial buildings.

Today, historians recognize that the ruling dynasties of the Swahili states were probably African in origin, with an admixture of Arab or Persian immigrant blood. Swahili coastal centers boasted an advanced, cosmopolitan level of culture. By comparison, most of the populace in the small villages lived in mud houses and sometimes stone houses and earned their livings by farming or fishing, the two basic coastal occupations besides trade. Society consisted of three principal groups: local nobility, commoners, and resident foreigners engaged in commerce. Slaves constituted a fourth class, although their local extent (as opposed to their sale) is disputed.

The flourishing trade of the coastal centers was fed mainly by export of inland ivory. Other exports included gold, slaves, turtle shells, ambergris, leopard skins, pearls, fish, sandalwood, ebony, and local cotton cloth. The chief imports were cloth, porcelain, glassware, china, glass beads, and glazed pottery. Certain exports tended to dominate particular ports: cloth, sandalwood, ebony, and ivory at Mogadishu; ivory at Manda; and gold at Kilwa. Cowrie shells were a

Swahili Language and culture that developed from the interaction of native Africans and Arabs along the East African coast.

OVERVIEW MAJOR AFRICAN STATES, 1000–1800

North Africa	Sahel	Eastern Sudan	West and Central Africa	East Africa	Southern Africa
Morocco	Ghana	Maqurra	Benin	Zanzibar	"Great Zimbabwe"
Algiers	Mali	Alwa	Kongo		
Tunis	Songhai	Funj			
Tripoli	Kanem				
Egypt					

common currency in inland trade, but coins were used in the major trading centers. The gold trade itself apparently became important only in the 15th century.

THE PORTUGUESE AND THE OMANIS OF ZANZIBAR

The decline of the original Swahili civilization in the 16th century can be attributed primarily to the arrival of the Portuguese and their destruction of the old oceanic trade (in particular, the Islamic commercial monopoly) and the main Islamic city-states along the eastern coast.

In Africa, as everywhere, the Portuguese saw the "**Moors**" as implacable enemies. Many Portuguese viewed the struggle to wrest the commerce and seaports of Africa and Asia from Islamic control as a Christian crusade. The initial Portuguese victories along the African coast led to the submission of many small Islamic coastal ports and states. Still, there was no concerted effort to spread Christianity. Thus, the long-term cultural and religious consequences of the Portuguese presence were slight. After 1660, the eastern Arabian state of Oman ejected the Portuguese everywhere north of Mozambique.

The Omanis soon shifted their home base to Zanzibar, which became a major power in East Africa. Their control of the coastal ivory and slave trade fueled a substantial recovery of prosperity by the later 18th century. The domination of the east coast by Omani African sultans, descendants of the earlier invaders, continued until 1856. Thereafter, Zanzibar and its coastal holdings became independent, and then passed to the British. Still, the Islamic impact on the whole coast survives today.

SOUTHERN AFRICA

SOUTHEASTERN AFRICA: "GREAT ZIMBABWE"

At about the same time that the east-coast trading centers were beginning to flourish, a purely African civilization was enjoying its heyday inland in modern southern Zimbabwe. It was founded in the 10th or 11th century by Bantu-speaking Shona people, who still inhabit the same general area today. It seems to have become a large and prosperous state between the late 13th and the late 15th centuries. We know it only through the archaeological remains of an estimated 150 settlements in the Zambezi-Limpopo region.

QUICK REVIEW

East African Port Towns
- Part of trade with Middle East, Asia, and India
- Tied together by common language, *Swahili*
- Swahili civilization reached its peak in the 14th and 15th centuries

Moors Spanish and Portuguese term for Muslims.

HOW DID slavery affect race relations in the Cape Colony?

14.1

Kilwa, Mombasa, and the Portuguese: Realities of Empire

"Great Zimbabwe." The most impressive of 300 such stone ruins in modern Zimbabwe and neighboring countries. These sites give clear evidence of the advanced Iron Age mining and cattle-raising culture that flourished in this region between about 1000 and 1500 C.E. The people, thought to have been of Bantu origins, apparently had a highly developed trade in gold and copper with outsiders, including Arabs on the east coast. As yet, all too little is known about this impressive society.

Robert Aberman and Barbara Heller/
Art Resource, N.Y.

The most impressive of these ruins is known today as "Great Zimbabwe"—a huge, 60-odd-acre site encompassing two major building complexes. One—the so-called acropolis—is a series of stone enclosures on a high hill. It overlooks another, much larger enclosure that contains many ruins and a circular tower, all surrounded by a massive wall some 32 feet high and up to 17 feet thick. The acropolis complex may have contained a shrine, whereas the larger enclosure was apparently the royal palace and fort. The stonework reflects a wealthy and sophisticated society. Artifacts from the site include gold and copper ornaments, soapstone carvings, and imported beads, as well as china, glass, and porcelain of Chinese, Syrian, and Persian origins.

The state itself seems to have had partial control of the increasing gold trade between inland areas and the east coast. We can speculate that this large settlement was the capital city of a prosperous empire and the residence of a ruling elite. Its wider domain was made up mostly of smaller settlements whose inhabitants lived by subsistence agriculture and cattle raising and whose culture was considerably different from that of the capital. Without written or new archaeological sources, we shall likely never know exactly what allowed this impressive civilization to develop and to dominate its region for nearly 200 years.

THE PORTUGUESE IN SOUTHEASTERN AFRICA

The Portuguese destroyed Swahili control of both the inland gold trade and the overseas trade. Their chief objective was to obtain gold from the interior.

Although the Portugese derived little lasting profit from their enterprise, all along the Zambezi a lasting and destabilizing consequence of their intrusion was the creation of quasi-tribal chiefdoms led by mixed-blood Portuguese landholders, who were descended from the first Portuguese estate holders along the Zambezi. By the late 18th century, they were too strong for either the Portuguese or the regional African rulers to control. They remind us of how diverse the peoples of modern Africa are.

SOUTH AFRICA: THE CAPE COLONY

In South Africa, the Dutch planted the first European colonials almost inadvertently, yet the consequences of their action were to be ultimately as grave and far-reaching as any European incursion onto African soil. The first Cape settlement was built in 1652 by the Dutch East India Company as a resupply point and way station for Dutch vessels on their route between the Netherlands and the East Indies. The support station gradually became a settler community, the forebears of the Afrikaners of modern South Africa.

The local Khoikhoi (see Chapter 5) had neither a strong political organization nor an economic base beyond their herds. They bartered livestock freely to Dutch ships. As company employees established farms to supply the Cape station, they began to displace the Khoikhoi. Conflicts led to the consolidation of European landholdings and a breakdown of Khoikhoi society. Military success led to even greater Dutch control of the Khoikhoi by the 1670s.

The Khoikhoi became the chief source of colonial wage labor, but the colony also imported slaves. Slavery set the tone for relations between the emergent, and ostensibly "white," Afrikaner population and the "coloreds" of other races. Free or not, the latter were eventually identified with slave peoples.

After the first settlers spread out around the company station, nomadic white livestock farmers, or **Trekboers**, moved more widely afield, leaving the richer, but limited, farming lands of the coast for the drier interior tableland. There they contested still wider groups of Khoikhoi cattle herders for the best grazing lands. Again the Khoikhoi lost. By 1700, their way of life was destroyed.

The Cape society in this period was thus a diverse one. The Dutch Company officials (including Dutch Reformed ministers), the emerging Afrikaners (both settled colonists and Trekboers), the Khoikhoi, and the slaves of diverse nationalities played differing roles. Intermarriage and cohabitation of masters and slaves added to the complexity. The emergence of **Afrikaans**, a new vernacular language of the colonials, shows that the

Carving from Great Zimbabwe. This carving (steatite, 40.5 cm high) is thought to represent a mythical eagle that carries messages from man to the gods. It dates to ca. 1200–1400 C.E.

Werner Forman Archive/Art Resource, N.Y.

Trekboers White livestock farmers in Cape Colony.

Afrikaans New language, derived from Dutch, that evolved in the 17th- and 18th-century Cape Colony.

Southern Africa

1652	First Cape colony settlement of Dutch East India Company
1795	British replace Dutch as masters of Cape Colony

Cape Town, with European ships in its harbor. The colony relied on shipping for commercial links with the outside world.

National Archives of South Africa.

apartheid "Apartness," the term referring to racist policies enforced by the white-dominated regime that existed in South Africa from 1948 to 1992.

Dutch immigrants themselves were also subject to acculturation processes. By the time of English domination after 1795, the sociopolitical foundations—and the bases of the *apartheid* doctrine—of modern South Africa were firmly laid.

SUMMARY

North Africa Developments in African history from 1000 to 1800 varied from region to region. In North Africa, the key new factor was the imperial expansion of the Ottoman Empire as far west as Morocco. But regionalism soon rendered Ottoman authority in North Africa purely nominal.

Empires of the Sudan Several substantial states arose south of the Sahara: Ghana, Mali, Songhai, and Kanem. The ruling elites of these states converted to or were heavily influenced by Islam, although most of their populations clung to their older traditions. Much of the wealth of these states was tied to their control of the trans-Saharan trade routes. Farther south, in the coastal forestlands of Central Africa, another substantial kingdom arose in Benin, famous for its brass sculptures.

East Africa On the east coast, Islam influenced the development of the distinctive Swahili culture and language, and Islamic traders linked the region to India and East Asia.

The Coming of the Europeans The key development of the 15th century was the arrival of European traders, missionaries, and warships. The Portuguese and later Europeans came in search of commerce, converts to Christianity, and spheres of influence. Their arrival disrupted indigenous African culture and political relations and presaged Africa's involvement in and exploitation by a new, expanding global trading system dominated by Europeans.

IMAGE KEY
for pages 414–415
a. Moroccan Coin dating from Songhai Empire
b. Benin plaque
c. Golden rhino found at Mapungubwe
d. Thirteenth-century brass head from Benin
e. Mosque in Janne
f. Mansa Musa early medieval painting
g. The Djinquereber mosque in Timbuktu
h. Benin plaque
i. Fort Jesus, Mombasa, Kenya, Africa
j. "Great Zimbabwe," one of 300 stone ruins
k. Great Zimbabwe carving (stearite, 40.5cm high) representing a mythical eagle carrying messages to the gods.

REVIEW QUESTIONS

1. Why did Islam succeed in sub-Saharan and East Africa? How did warfare and trade affect its success?

2. What was the importance of the empires of Ghana, Mali, and Songhai to world history? Why was the control of the trans-Saharan trade so important to these kingdoms? What was the importance of Islamic culture to them? Why did each of these empires break up?

3. How did the Portuguese affect East and central Africa? How did European coastal activities affect the African interior?

4. How did the Portuguese and Dutch differ from or resemble the Arabs, Persians, and other Muslims who came as outsiders to sub-Saharan Africa?

5. Who were the Trekboers and what was their conflict with the Khoikhoi? How was the basis for apartheid formed in this period?

KEY TERMS

Afrikaans (p. 431)
apartheid (p. 432)
Moors (p. 429)

oba (p. 423)
Swahili (p. 428)

Trekboers (p. 431)
uzama (p. 423)

 For additional study resources for this chapter, go to:
www.prenhall.com/craig/chapter17

18 Conquest and Exploitation
The Development of the Transatlantic Economy

CHAPTER HIGHLIGHTS

European Conquest of the New World The contact between the native peoples of the American continents and the European explorers of the fifteenth and sixteenth centuries transformed world history. In the Americas, the native peoples had established a wide variety of civilizations, but until the European explorations, the civilizations of the Americas and Eurasia and Africa had no significant contact with each other.

Within half a century of the landing of Columbus, millions of America's native peoples had encountered Europeans intent on conquest, exploitation, and religious conversion. Because of their technology and the new diseases they brought with them, as well as internal divisions among the native Americans, the Europeans achieved a rapid conquest.

The Transatlantic Economy In both North and South America, economies of exploitation were established. From the mid-Atlantic English colonies through the Caribbean and into Brazil, slave-labor plantations forcibly imported slaves from Africa. The economies and peoples of Europe, Africa, and the Americas were thus drawn into a vast worldwide web of production based on slave labor.

Slavery The impact of slavery in the Americas was not limited to the life of the black slaves. Whites in the New World numbered about 12 million in 1820, compared to some six million blacks. However, only about two million whites had migrated there, compared to some 11 million or more Africans forcibly imported as slaves. Such numbers reveal the effects of brutal slave conditions and the high mortality and low birthrates of slave populations.

None of these statistics, however, enables us to asses the role that slavery has played in the Americas or, in particular, the United States. The United States actually received only a bit more than a quarter as many slaves as did Brazil, yet the consequences of the forced migration of just over a half-million Africans remain massive. The Atlantic slave trade's impact continues to be felt at both ends of the original "trade."

TO BE SOLD,

On THURSDAY the third Day of AUGUST next,

A CARGO OF NINETY-FOUR PRIME, HEALTHY

NEGROES,

CONSISTING OF

Thirty-nine MEN, Fifteen BOYS, Twenty-four WOMEN, and Sixteen GIRLS.

JUST ARRIVED,

In the Brigantine DEMBIA, *Francis Bare*, Master, from SIERRA LEON, by

DAVID & JOHN DEAS.

CHAPTER QUESTIONS

WHAT WAS mercantilism?

WHAT ROLES did the Roman Catholic Church play in Spanish America?

HOW WERE sugar production and slavery intertwined in colonial Brazil?

HOW WERE the economies of the French and British North American colonies integrated into the transatlantic economy?

WHY WAS the trans-atlantic slave trade so economically important?

CHAPTER OUTLINE

The European encounter with the American continents in the late 15th century made the region an area where European languages, legal and political institutions, trade, and religion prevailed. These developments in the Americas gave Europe more influence over other world cultures than it would otherwise have achieved.

Within decades of the European voyages of discovery, Native Americans, Europeans, and Africans began to interact in a manner unprecedented in human history. By the end of the 16th century, Europe, the Americas, and Africa had become linked in a vast transatlantic economy that extracted wealth from the American continents largely on the basis of the nonfree labor of impressed Native Americans and imported African slaves in a plantation economy that extended from Maryland to Brazil. The slave trade connected the economy of sections of Africa to the transatlantic economy and devastated the African people and cultures involved in it, but it also enriched the Americas with African culture.

PERIODS OF EUROPEAN OVERSEAS EXPANSION

Since the late 15th century, Europe's contacts with the rest of the world have passed through four stages. The first was the discovery, exploration, conquest, and settlement of the Americas and commercial expansion elsewhere. The second was an era of trade rivalry among Spain, France, and Great Britain. During this period (to 1820) the British colonies of North America and the Spanish colonies of Mexico and Central and South America broke free from European control. The third period spanned the 19th century and was characterized by the development of European empires in Africa and Asia. Imperial ideology at this time involved theories of trade, national honor, race, religion, and military strength. The last period of European experience with empire occupied the mid-20th century and was a time of decolonization—a retreat from empire.

It was technological advantages, not innate cultural superiority, that enabled Europeans for four and a half centuries to exercise global dominance beyond the proportions of Europe's size and population. However, the legacy of European imperialism—a memory of suffering, abuse, and exploitation—survives to complicate contemporary international relations.

MERCANTILIST THEORY OF ECONOMIC EXPLOITATION

The European empires of the 16th through the 18th centuries were based on commerce and were established primarily to promote trade. As a result, extensive trade rivalries sprang up around the world, and competitors developed navies to protect their interests. The empires also relied largely on slave labor. Indeed, the Atlantic slave trade was a major way in which European merchants profited. That trade in turn forcibly thrust the people of Africa into the life and culture of the New World.

If any formal economic theory lay behind these empires, it was *mercantilism*, a system in which governments heavily regulate trade and commerce to increase national wealth. From beginning to end, the economic well-being of the home country was the primary concern of mercantilist writers. They believed that a nation had to gain more gold and silver bullion than its rivals and that one nation's economy could grow only at the expense of others. Governments did this by establishing colonies overseas to provide markets and natural resources for the home country, which furnished military security and

---

WHAT IMPACT has European expansion had on the peoples of Asia, Africa, Australia, and the Americas?

WHAT WAS mercantilism?

mercantilism Term used to describe close government control of the economy that sought to maximize exports and accumulate as much precious metals as possible to enable the state to defend its economic and political interests.

Batavia. The Dutch established a major trading base at Batavia in the East Indies in the 17th century. Its geographical position allowed the Dutch to dominate the spice trade. Batavia is now Djakarta, capital of modern-day Indonesia.

Bildarchiv Preussicher Kulturbesitz.

political administration for these colonies. The home country and its colonies were to trade exclusively with each other. For decades, both sides assumed that the colonies were the inferior partner in a monopolistic relationship.

Mercantilist ideas were always neater on paper than in practice. By the early 18th century, it was clear that mercantilist assumptions did not correspond with reality. Colonial and home markets did not mesh. Spain, for instance, could not produce enough goods for South America, and manufacturing in the British North American colonies challenged production in England. Colonists of different countries also wanted to trade with one another. Governments could not control all their subjects, and they could be dragged into war by clashes among their colonies. Problems associated with the mercantile empires led to conflicts around the world.

ESTABLISHMENT OF THE SPANISH EMPIRE IN AMERICA

CONQUEST OF THE AZTECS AND THE INCAS

Within 20 years of the arrival of Columbus (1451–1506), Spanish explorers in search of gold had claimed the major islands of the Caribbean and suppressed the native peoples. These actions presaged what was to occur on the continent.

In 1519, Hernan Cortés (1485–1547) landed in Mexico with about 500 men and a few horses. He opened communication with Moctezuma II (1466–1520), the Aztec emperor. Moctezuma hesitated to confront Cortés, attempting at first to appease him with gifts of gold. Cortés forged alliances with subject peoples of the Aztecs. His forces then marched on the Aztec capital of Tenochtitlán (modern Mexico City), where Moctezuma welcomed him. Cortés soon made Moctezuma a prisoner in his own capital. After Moctezuma died from unknown circumstances, the Spaniards were driven from Tenochtitlán. But they returned, and the Aztecs were defeated in late 1521. Cortés proclaimed the Aztec Empire to be New Spain.

In 1532, Francisco Pizarro (c. 1478–1541) landed on the western coast of South America to take over the Inca Empire. His force included about 200 men

WHAT ROLES did the Roman Catholic Church play in Spanish America?

QUICK REVIEW

Francisco Pizarro (c. 1478–1541)

- Invasion force landed in South America in 1532
- Forces included 200 men, horses, guns, and swords
- 1533: Executed the Inca ruler and captured Cuzco

Spanish Conquest of Mexico. A 16th-century Aztec drawing depicts a battle during the Spanish conquest of Mexico. Note how the Spanish are assisted by a far greater number of Indian allies.

Corbis–Bettmann. Archivo Iconografico. S. A./Corbis.

armed with guns, swords, and horses, the military power of which the Incas did not understand. Pizarro lured the Inca ruler, Atahualpa (c. 1500–1533), into a conference, then seized him and had him garroted in 1533. The Spaniards then captured Cuzco, the Inca capital, ending the Inca Empire.

The conquests of Mexico and Peru are among the most dramatic and brutal events in modern world history. Small military forces armed with advanced weapons quickly subdued two advanced, powerful groups. European diseases, especially smallpox, aided the conquerors. Having never been explosed to European diseases, the native populations had no natural immunity to them.

Beyond the drama and bloodshed, these conquests marked a turning point. Whole civilizations with long histories and enormous social, architectural, and technological achievements were destroyed. Native American cultures endured, but European culture had the upper hand.

THE ROMAN CATHOLIC CHURCH IN SPANISH AMERICA

The Spanish conquest of the West Indies, Mexico, and South America opened these regions to the Roman Catholic faith. As it had in the Castilian reconquest of the Iberian peninsula from the Moors, religion played a central role in the conquest of the New World. In both cases, the obligation Christians felt to spread their faith was used to justify military conquest and the extension of political control

OVERVIEW   THE COLUMBIAN EXCHANGE

The same ships that carried Europeans and Africans to the Americas also transported animals, plants, and diseases that had never before appeared in the New World. There was a similar transport back to Europe and Africa. Historians call this cross-continental flow "the Columbian exchange." The overall result was an ecological transformation that continues to shape the world.

To the Americas

Animals:	cattle, chickens, goats, horses, pigs, and sheep
Plants:	almonds, apples, apricots, bananas, barley, cabbage, cherries, dandelions, grapes, lemons, mangos, melons, oats, okra, olives, onions, oranges, peaches, pears, plums, radishes, rice, sugar cane, wheat, and other green vegetables
Diseases:	bubonic plague, chicken pox, diphtheria, influenza, malaria, measles, smallpox, typhoid, and typhus

From the Americas

Animals:	turkeys
Plants:	avocados, beans, blueberries, chilis, cocoa, guavas, maize, manioc (tapioca), peanuts, pecans, pineapples, potatoes, pumpkins, squash, sweet peppers, sweet potatoes, tobacco, and tomatoes
Diseases:	syphilis

and dominance. The link between the goals of the church and the state meant that the Roman Catholic Church in the New World worked to protect the interests of the Spanish authorities.

The relationship between political authority and the propagation of religious doctrine was even closer in the New World than on the Iberian peninsula. The papacy recognized that it could not self-support such an extensive missionary effort and turned over much of the control of the church in the New World to the Spanish monarchy. A close relationship between the monarchy and the church was created. The zeal of both institutions increased in the 16th century as the papacy and the Habsburg monarchy attempted to prevent Protestantism from establishing a foothold in America. As a consequence, the Roman Catholicism that spread throughout Spanish America was the zealous faith of the Counter-Reformation.

The Roman Catholic Church, first with the aid of the Franciscans and Dominicans, and later the Jesuits, sought to convert the Native Americans and eradicate Indian religious practices. Religious conversion involved, among other things, an attempt to destroy still other aspects of Native American culture. Converts, however, did not enjoy equality with Europeans; even late in the 18th century there were few Native American Christian priests.

There were some tensions between the early Spanish conquerors and the friars. Without conquest, the church could not convert the Native Americans, but the priests often deplored the harsh treatment native peoples received from their conquerors. The most outspoken clerical critic of the Spanish conquerors was Bartolomé de Las Casas (1474–1566), a Dominican. He contended that conquest was not necessary for conversion, and after 1550 his agitation inspired the royal government to pass legislation aimed at improving conditions for the native peoples. Las Casas's writings inspired the "**Black Legend**," according to which all Spanish treatment of the Native Americans was inhumane. Although substantially true, the Black Legend exaggerated the case against Spain. Certainly the rulers of the native empires—as the Aztec demands for sacrificial victims attest—had often themselves been cruel to their subject peoples.

By the end of the 16th century, the church in Spanish America had become largely an institution upholding the colonial status quo. Although priests did defend the communal rights of Indian tribes, the colonial church prospered through its exploitation of the resources of the New World. Those who spoke for the church did not challenge Spanish domination, and the church only modestly moderated the forces exploiting human labor and material wealth. By the late 18th century, the Roman Catholic Church had become one of the most conservative forces in Latin American society.

15.1
The Black Legend of Spain: Bartolomé de Las Casas

Black Legend Argument that Spanish treatment of Native Americans was uniquely inhumane.

ECONOMIES OF EXPLOITATION IN THE SPANISH EMPIRE

HOW WERE sugar production and slavery intertwined in colonial Brazil?

Colonial Spanish America had an economy of exploitation in two senses. First, its organization of labor involved dependent servitude or slavery. Second, resources were exploited for the economic advantage of Spain.

VARIETIES OF ECONOMIC ACTIVITY

The early *conquistadores* ("conquerors") had been interested primarily in gold, but by the middle of the 16th century, silver mining provided the chief source of metallic wealth. Great silver mining centers were in Bolivia and northern Mexico.

conquistadores Meaning "conquerors." Spanish conquerors of the New World.

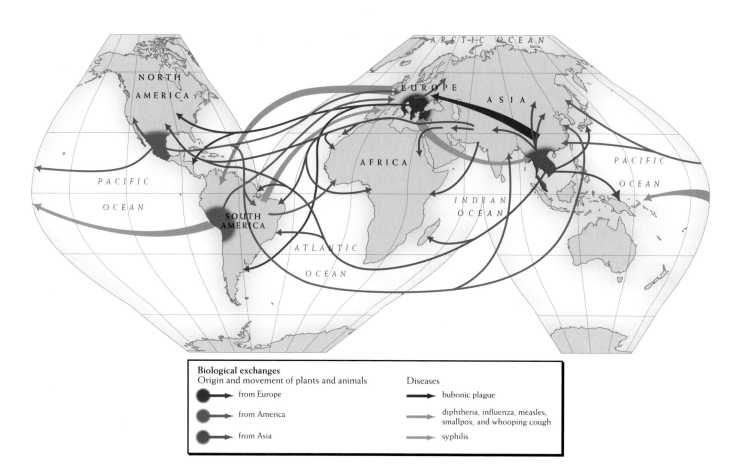

MAP 18–1

Biological Exchanges, 1000–1600 c.e. Though the transfer of plants, animals, and diseases had been going on for centuries, European expansion set in motion a global movement transformed the world.

HOW DID the Columbian exchange alter environments around the world?

The Spanish crown received one fifth of all mining revenues. Silver mining for the benefit of Spaniards and the Spanish crown epitomized the extractive economy on which Latin American colonial life was based.

This extractive economy required labor, but there were too few Spanish colonists to provide it, and most of the colonists who came to the Americas did not want to work for wages. So, the Spaniards turned first to the native population for workers and then to African slaves. Indian labor dominated on the continent and African labor in the Caribbean (see Map 18–1).

Encomienda The Spanish devised a series of institutions to exploit Native American labor. The first was the *encomienda*, a formal grant by the crown of the right to the labor of a specific number of Native Americans for a particular time. The Spanish crown disliked the encomienda system. The monarchy was distressed by reports from clergy that the Native Americans were being mistreated and feared that encomienda holders were becoming a powerful nobility in the New World. Encomienda as an institution declined by the middle of the 16th century.

Repartimiento The passing of the encomienda led to the *repartimiento*, largely copied from the draft labor practices of the Incas. Repartimiento required adult male Native Americans to devote a set number of days of labor annually to

encomienda Grant by the Spanish crown to a colonist of the labor of a specific number of Indians for a set period of time.

repartimiento Labor tax in Spanish America that required adult male Native Americans to devote a set number of days a year to Spanish economic enterprises.

Spanish economic enterprises. The time limitation on repartimiento led some Spanish managers to try to maximize productivity by working teams of men to exhaustion—sometimes to death—before replacing them with the next rotation.

The Hacienda   The *hacienda*, which dominated rural and agricultural life in Spanish colonies on the continent, developed when the crown made grants of land. These grants created large landed estates for ***peninsulares***, whites born in Spain, or creoles, whites born in America. This use of the resources of the New World for royal patronage did not directly burden Native Americans because the grazing that occurred on the haciendas required less labor than did the mines. But laborers on the hacienda were usually in formal servitude to the owner and had to buy goods for everyday living on credit from him. They were rarely able to repay the resulting debts and thus could not leave. This system was known as ***debt peonage***. The hacienda economy produced foodstuffs for mining areas and urban centers, and haciendas became one of the most important features of Latin American life.

THE DECLINE OF THE NATIVE AMERICAN POPULATION

Conquest, exploitation, forced labor, and European diseases decimated the Indian population (see Map 18–1). Beginning in the 16th century, Native Americans began to die off in huge numbers. In New Spain (Mexico) alone, the population probably declined from approximately 25 million to fewer than 2 million within the first century after the conquest. Thereafter, the Indian population began to expand slowly, but the precipitous drop eliminated the easy supply of exploitable labor.

COMMERCIAL REGULATION AND THE FLOTA SYSTEM

Because Queen Isabella of Castile (r. 1474–1504) had commissioned Columbus, the legal link between the New World and Spain was the crown of Castile. The governing of America was assigned to the Council of the Indies, which nominated the viceroys of New Spain and Peru, the chief executives in the New World.

hacienda   Large landed estates in Spanish America.

peninsulares   Persons born in Spain who settled in the Spanish colonies.

debt peonage   Requirement that laborers remain and continue to work on a hacienda until they had paid their debts to the owner for goods bought from him on credit.

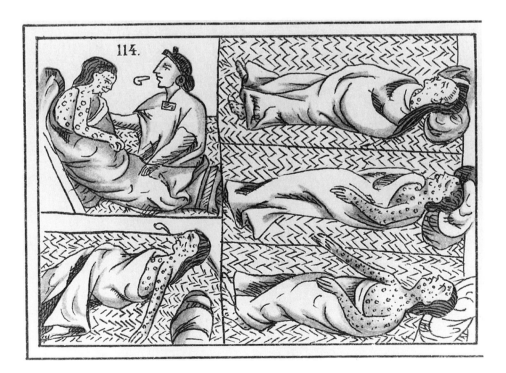

Smallpox. Introduced by Europeans to the Americas, smallpox had a devastating effect on Native American populations. The disease swept through the Aztec capital of Tenochtitlán soon after the Spaniards arrived, contributing to the fall of the city. This illustration of the effect of the plague in the Aztec capital is from a post-conquest history known as the Florentine Codex compiled for Spanish church authorities by Aztec survivors.

Sixteenth-century drawing of smallpox victims. Aztec original codex Florentino. Courtesy President and Fellows of Harvard College. Courtesy Peabody Museum of Archeology and Ethnology, Harvard University, photograph by Hillel Burger.

Each of the viceroyalties included subordinate judicial councils known as *audiencias.* A variety of local officers presided over municipal councils. Virtually all political power flowed from the top of this political structure downward; there was little local initiative or self-government (see Map 18–2).

Colonial political structures existed largely to support the commercial goals of Spain. But the system of monopolistic trade regulation was often breached. The Casa de Contratación (House of Trade) in Seville regulated all trade with the New World and was the most influential institution of the Spanish Empire. The entire organization was geared to benefit the Spanish monarchy and privileged merchant groups.

A complicated system of trade and bullion fleets administered from Seville maintained the trade monopoly. Each year a fleet of commercial vessels controlled by Seville merchants and escorted by warships carried merchandise from Spain to specified ports in America. These included Portobello, Veracruz, and Cartagena. There were no authorized ports on the Pacific Coast. Areas such as Buenos Aires received goods only after the shipments had been unloaded at one of the authorized ports. After selling their wares, the ships were loaded with silver and gold bullion. They then usually wintered in fortified Caribbean ports before sailing back to Spain. Regulations prohibited Spanish colonists from trading directly with each other and from building their own shipping and commercial industries. Foreign merchants were also forbidden to breach the Spanish monopoly.

COLONIAL BRAZIL AND SLAVERY

In 1494, by the Treaty of Tordesillas, the pope divided the overseas empires of Spain and Portugal by drawing a line west of the Cape Verde Islands. In 1500, a Portuguese explorer landed in present-day Brazil, east of the papal line. This gave Portugal a foothold in South America. Portugal, however, had fewer resources to devote to its New World empire than did Spain. Its rulers, therefore,

Sugar Plantation. Brazil and the West Indies were a major source of the demand for slave labor. Slaves are shown here grinding sugar cane and refining sugar, which was then exported to the consumer markets in Europe.

© Hulton-Deutsch Collection/Corbis.

DISPUTED BY
ENGLAND,
RUSSIA,
AND SPAIN

VICEROYALTY
OF
NEW SPAIN

ATLANTIC

EFFECTIVE FRONTIER OF *O C E A N*
SPANISH SETTLEMENT

Rio Grande

Gulf of Mexico

Mexico
City
Veracruz

Santo Domingo

Caribbean Sea

Cartagena   Caracas

Portobelo

**VICEROYALTY OF
NEW GRANADA**
Separated From
Bogotá   Viceroyalty of
Peru,
1717, 1739   **GUIANA**

Quito

Amazon R.

**VICEROYALTY
OF
PERU**

**VICEROYALTY
OF
BRAZIL**

Pernambuco

Lima

Bahia

PACIFIC

Portosi

OCEAN

São Paulo

**VICEROYALTY
OF
LA PLATA**
Separated From the
Viceroyalty of Peru,
1776

Rio de Janeiro

Santiago

Buenos
Aires

**AUDIENCIA
OF CHILE**

Claimed but not
settled by Spain

N

MAP 18–2
Viceroyalties in Latin America in 1780.   Spain organized its vast holdings in the New World into viceroyalties, each of which had its own governor and other administrative officials.

HOW EFFECTIVE was Spain's control over its New World colonies?

left exploitation of the region to private entrepreneurs. Because the native peoples in the lands that Portugal claimed were nomadic, the Portuguese, unlike the Spanish, imported Africans as slaves rather than using the native Indian population as their work force.

By the mid-16th century, sugar production had gained preeminence in the Brazilian economy, and the dominance of sugar meant the dominance of slavery. Slavery became even more important when, in the early 18th century, gold was discovered in southern Brazil. Nowhere, except perhaps in the West Indies, was slavery so important as it was in Brazil, where it persisted until 1888.

The taxation and administration associated with gold mining brought new wealth to Portugal's monarchs that strengthened them by allowing them to rule without recourse to Cortés or the parliament for taxation. Through transatlantic trade, the diffusion of Brazilian gold also promoted the economies of all the major trading nations.

FRENCH AND BRITISH COLONIES IN NORTH AMERICA

French explorers moved down the St. Lawrence River valley in Canada during the 17th century. French fur traders and missionaries followed, with the French government sponsoring the missionary effort. By the end of the 17th century, Canada was sparsely populated by the French. Their largest settlement was Quebec, founded in 1608. It was primarily through the fur trade that French Canada functioned as part of the early transatlantic economy.

HOW WERE the economies of the French and British North American colonies integrated into the transatlantic economy?

The Fur Trade. Europeans and Indians, from an engraving of 1777.

©The Granger Collection, New York.

Beginning with the first successful settlement in Jamestown, Virginia, in 1607, English colonies spread along the eastern seaboard of the future United States. With the exception of Maryland, these colonies were Protestant. The Church of England dominated the southern colonies. In New England, varieties of Protestantism associated with or derived from Calvinism were in the ascendancy. In their religious affiliations, the English-speaking colonies manifested two important traits derived from the English experience. First, much of their religious life was organized around self-governing congregations. Second, their religious outlook derived from those forms of Protestantism that were suspicious of central political authority. In this regard, their cultural and political outlook differed sharply from the cultural and political outlook associated with the Roman Catholics of the Spanish Empire. In a sense, the ideologies of the extreme Reformation and Counter-Reformation confronted each other in the Americas.

The English colonists had complex interactions with the Native American populations. They had only modest interest in missionizing the natives and, as in South America, European diseases took a high toll on the native population. Unlike Mexico and Peru, however, North America had no large Native American cities. The Native American populations were dispersed, and intertribal animosity was intense. The English often used one tribe against another, and the Native Americans also tried to use the English or the French in their own conflicts. From the late 17th century through the American Revolution, however, the Native Americans were drawn into the Anglo-French Wars that were fought in North America as well as Europe (see Chapter 20).

The economies of the English-speaking colonies were primarily agricultural. From New England through the Middle Atlantic states, there were mostly small farms tilled by free white labor; from Virginia southward a plantation economy dependent on slavery predominated. The principal ports—Boston, Newport, New York, Philadelphia, Baltimore, and Charleston—were the chief centers through which goods moved back and forth between the colonies and England and the West Indies. The commercial economies of these cities were all related to the transatlantic slave trade.

Until the 1760s, most Americans, like their English counterparts, were monarchists who were suspicious of monarchical power. Their politics involved patronage and individual favors. Their society was hierarchical. It had an elite that functioned like an aristocracy and many ordinary people who were dependent on that aristocracy. Throughout the colonies during the 18th century, the Anglican church grew in influence and membership. The prosperity of the colonies might eventually have led them to separate from England, but in 1750 few people anticipated that break.

Roanoke. The first successful English colonies in North America in the 17th century were preceded by two failed efforts on Roanoke Island in what is now North Carolina in the late 16th century. John White accompanied both attempts, the second as governor. White was a perceptive and sensitive observer whose watercolor paintings provide invaluable information about Native American life in the coastal Carolina region at the time of contact. This painting shows the Algonquian village of Secoton. The houses were bark-covered. In the lower left is a mortuary temple. Dancers in the lower right are performing a fertility ceremony. The man sitting in the platform in the upper right is keeping birds away from the corn crop.

The Bridgeman Art Library International Ltd.

Both England and France had important sugar islands in the Caribbean, with plantations worked by African slaves. The trade and commerce of the northern British colonies were focused on meeting the needs of these islands.

SLAVERY IN THE AMERICAS

 lack slavery was the final mode of forced or subservient labor in the New World. It extended throughout the Americas.

ESTABLISHMENT OF SLAVERY

As the numbers of Native Americans in South America declined, the Spanish and Portuguese turned to African slaves. By the late 1500s, in the West Indies and the cities of South America, black slaves surpassed the white population.

On much of the South American continent dominated by Spain, slavery declined during the late 17th century, but it continued to thrive in Brazil and in the Caribbean. In British North America, it began with the importation of slaves to Jamestown in 1619, and quickly became a fundamental institution.

The spread of slavery in Brazil and the West Indies was promoted by the market for sugar. Only slave labor could provide enough workers for the sugar plantations. As the production of sugar expanded, so did the demand for slaves.

By 1700, the Caribbean Islands were the world center for sugar production. As the European appetite for sugar grew, so did the slave population. By 1725, black slaves may have constituted almost 90 percent of the population of the West Indies. There and in Brazil and the southern British colonies, prosperity and slavery went hand in hand. The wealthiest colonies were those that raised consumer staples, such as sugar, rice, tobacco, or cotton, by slave labor.

THE PLANTATION ECONOMY AND TRANSATLANTIC TRADE

The **plantation economy** encompassed plantations that stretched from Maryland through the West Indies and into Brazil and formed a vast corridor of slave societies. This kind of society—defined by a total dependence on slave labor and racial difference—had not existed before the European discovery and exploitation of the Americas. The social and economic influence of plantation slavery also touched West Africa, Europe, and New England. It persisted from the 16th century through the second half of the 19th century. Every society in which it existed still contends with its effects.

The slave trade was part of the larger system of transatlantic trade that linked Europe, Africa, and the European colonies in the Americas. In this system, the Americas supplied labor-intensive raw materials (tobacco, sugar, coffee, precious metals, cotton, and indigo). Europe supplied manufactured goods (textiles, liquor, guns, metal wares, and beads) and cash. Africa supplied gold,

WHICH ECONOMIC factors led to the spread of slavery in the New World?

plantation economy Economic system stretching between Chesapeake Bay and Brazil that produced crops, especially sugar, cotton, and tobacco, using slave labor on large estates.

Slave Auction Notice. Africans who survived the voyage across the Atlantic were immediately sold into slavery in the Americas. This slave-auction notice describes a group of slaves whose ship had stopped at Charleston, South Carolina, and then landed elsewhere in the region to auction its human cargo. Notice the concern to assure potential buyers that the slaves were healthy.

Corbis-Bettmann.

TO BE SOLD on board the Ship *Bance-Island*, on tuesday the 6th of *May* next, at *Ashley-Ferry*; a choice cargo of about 250 fine healthy NEGROES, just arrived from the Windward & Rice Coast. —The utmost care has already been taken, and shall be continued, to keep them free from the least danger of being infected with the SMALL-POX, no boat having been on board, and all other communication with people from *Charles-Town* prevented. *Austin, Laurens, & Appleby.*

N. B. Full one Half of the above Negroes have had the SMALL-POX in their own Country.

ivory, wood, palm oil, gum, and other products, as well as the slaves who provided the labor to create the American products. By the 18th century, slaves were the predominant African export.

SLAVERY ON THE PLANTATIONS

The American plantations to which the African slaves arrived produced for an overseas market that was part of a larger integrated transatlantic economy. In turn, plantation owners imported virtually all the finished or manufactured goods they consumed.

The conditions of plantation slaves differed from colony to colony. Vast slave holdings were the exception. Black slaves living in Portuguese areas had the fewest legal protections. In the Spanish colonies, the church provided some protection, but devoted more effort to protecting Native Americans. Slave codes in the British and the French colonies provided only the most limited protection. Regulations were designed to prevent slave revolts and favored the master rather than the slave. Masters were permitted to punish slaves by harsh corporal punishment. Slaves were forbidden to gather in large groups lest they plan a rebellion. Slave marriages were usually not recognized by law. Children of slaves were owned by the owner of the parents, and slave families could be separated by sale or inheritance. The death rate among slaves was high. Their lives were sacrificed to the ongoing expansion of the plantations that made their owners wealthy and that produced goods for consumers in Europe.

The African slaves who were transported to the Americas were converted to Christianity: in the Spanish domains to Roman Catholicism, and in the English colonies to Protestantism. In both cases, they were largely separated from African religious traditions. Although slaves mixed Christianity with some African religion, the conversion of Africans to Christianity represented another example of the crushing of non-European cultural values in the New World.

Europeans were also prejudiced against black Africans. Many Europeans thought Africans were savages or looked down on them because they were slaves. These attitudes had been shared by both Christians and Muslims in the Mediterranean world, where slavery had long existed. Furthermore, many European cultures attached negative connotations to blackness. Although racial thinking in regard to slavery became more important in the 19th century, the fact that slaves were differentiated from the rest of the population by race as well as by their status as chattel property was fundamental to the system.

AFRICA AND THE TRANSATLANTIC SLAVE TRADE

*T*he establishment of plantations demanding slave labor drew Africa into the heart of the transatlantic economy. As Native Americans were decimated by conquest and disease or proved unsatisfactory as plantation laborers, colonial entrepreneurs began to look elsewhere for workers. The Portuguese first, and then the Spanish, Dutch, French, and English, turned to Africa for slaves. The Atlantic slave trade was not overtly the result of racist principles but of the economic needs of the colonial powers and their willingness (based on tacit racist assumptions) to exploit weaker peoples to satisfy those needs.

The Portuguese were the principal transporters throughout most of the history of the slave trade. During the 18th century, which saw the greatest shipments,

Job Ben Solomon. Captured by Mandingo enemies and sold to a Maryland tobacco planter, Job Ben Solomon accomplished the nearly impossible feat of returning to Africa as a free man. By demonstrating his talents as a Muslim scholar, including his ability to write the entire Qur'an from memory, he astonished his owners and eventually convinced them to let him go home.

"The Fortunate Slave," An Illustration of African Slavery in the early 18th century by Douglas Grant (1968). From "Some Memoirs of the Life of Job," by Thomas Bluett (1734). Photo by Robert D. Rubic/ Precision Chromes, Inc. The New York Public Library, Research Libraries.

WHY WAS the transatlantic slave trade so economically important?

15.3
Olaudah Equiano,
*The Interesting Narrative
of the Life of Olaudah
Equiano, or Gustavus
Vassa, the African*

the French and English carried almost half the total traffic. Americans were avid slavers who managed to make considerable profits even after Britain and the United States outlawed slaving in 1807 (see Map 18–3.)

Slaving was an important part of the massive new overseas trade that financed much of the European and American economic development that so changed the West during the 19th century. This trade, bought at the price of immense human suffering, helped propel Europe and some of its colonial off-shoots in the Americas to world dominance.

MAP EXPLORATION

Interactive map: To explore this map further, go to **http://www.prenhall.com/craig/map18.3**

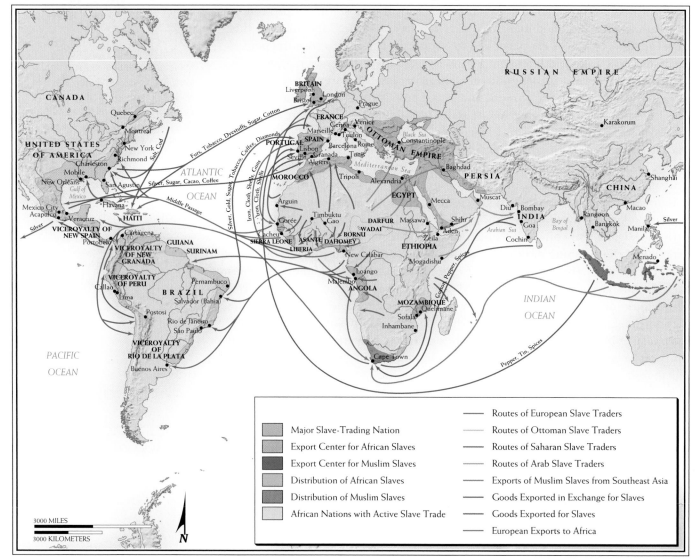

MAP 18–3

The Slave Trade, 1400–1860. Slavery is an ancient institution and complex slave-trading routes were in existence in Africa, the Middle East, and Asia for centuries, but it was the need to supply labor for the plantations of the Americas that led to the greatest movement of peoples across the face of the earth.

WHY WAS the slave trade so economically important?

THE BACKGROUND OF SLAVERY

Slavery seems to have been a tragic fact of human societies as far back as we can trace it. Although linked to warfare, it cannot be explained by military or economic necessity.

Virtually every premodern state around the globe depended on slavery. The Mediterranean and African worlds were no exception. Slave institutions in sub-Saharan Africa were ancient. The Islamic states of southwestern Asia and North Africa increased this traffic, although they took fewer slaves from Africa than from Eastern Europe and central Asia. (Hence it is not surprising that the word *slave* is derived ultimately from *Slav*.) Both Mediterranean-Christian and Islamic peoples were using slaves—mostly Greeks, Bulgarians, Turkish prisoners of war, and Black Sea Tartars, but also Africans—before the voyages of discovery opened sub-Saharan sources of slaves for the new European colonies.

Not all forms of slavery were as dehumanizing as the chattel slavery in the Americas. Islamic law, for example, ameliorated slavery. All slavery, however, involved the forceful exploitation and degradation of human beings, the denial of basic freedoms, and the sundering of family ties.

Africa suffered immense social devastation when it was the chief supplier of slaves to the world. Societies that were built on the exploitation of African slavery also suffered enduring consequences, not the least of which is racism.

A Slave Coffle. This 18th-century print shows bound African captives being forced to a slaving port. It was largely African middlemen who captured slaves in the interior and marched them to the coast.

North Wind Picture Archives.

15.2
"Our Kingdom is Being Lost," Nzinga Mbemba (Affonso I)

SLAVERY AND SLAVING IN AFRICA

The trade that supplied African slaves to the Islamic lands and Asia has been termed the "oriental" slave trade. The Sudan and the Horn of Africa were the two prime sources of slaves for this trade. The trade managed by Europeans is called the "occidental" slave trade. Voyages beginning in the 15th century by first the Portuguese and then other Europeans made the western coasts of Africa as far south as Angola the prime slaving areas.

Before the full development of the transatlantic slave trade (about 1650), slavery and slave trading had been no more significant in Africa than anywhere else.[1] Indigenous African slavery resembled that of other premodern societies. Estimates suggest that about 10,000 slaves per year, most of them female, were taken from sub-Saharan Africa through the oriental trade.

By about 1650, the newer occidental slave trade of the Europeans had become as large as the oriental trade and for the ensuing two centuries far surpassed it. It affected all of Africa, disrupting especially western and central African

Estimated Slave Imports into the Americas and Old World by Region, 1451–1870

British North America	523,000
Spanish America	1,687,000
British Caribbean	2,443,000
French Caribbean	1,655,000
Dutch Caribbean	500,000
Danish Caribbean	50,000
Brazil (Portuguese)	4,190,000
Old World	297,000
Total	**11,345,000**

Figures as calculated by James A. Rawley, *The Transatlantic Slave Trade: A History* (New York: W. W. Norton, 1981), p. 428, based on his and other more recent revisions of the careful but older estimates of Philip D. Curtin, *The Atlantic Slave Trade: A Census* (Madison: University of Wisconsin Press, 1969), especially pp. 266, 268.

[1]The summary follows closely that of P. Manning, *Slavery and African Life: Occidental, Oriental, and African Slave Trades* (Cambridge: Cambridge University Press, 1990), pp. 127–140.

Conquest of the Americas and the Transatlantic Slave Trade

1494	The Treaty of Tordesillas divides the overseas empires of Spain and Portugal
1500	The Portuguese arrive in Brazil
1519–1521	Hernan Cortés conquers the Aztec Empire
1531–1533	Francisco Pizarro conquers the Inca Empire
1607	Jamestown, Virginia, first permanent English settlement in North America, founded
1608	The French found Quebec
1619	First African slaves brought to British North America
1650	Transatlantic slave trade becomes bigger than the older oriental slave trade
1700s	More than 6 million slaves imported from Africa to the Americas
1807	Slavery abolished in British domains
1808	The importation of slaves abolished in the United States
1874–1928	Indigenous African slavery abolished
1888	Slavery abolished in Brazil

society. As a result of the demand for young male slaves on the plantations of the Americas, West Africa experienced a sharp drain on its productive male population. Between 1640 and 1690, the number of slaves sold to European carriers doubled, indicating the increasing participation of Africans in the trade. The demand for slaves increased internal warfare in western and central Africa. Moreover, as the external trade destroyed the male-female population balance, an internal market for female slaves arose.

These developments accelerated during the 18th century when African states and slave traders were most heavily involved in the trade. The population declined sharply in the coastal and inland areas hardest hit by the ravages of the trade.

As European and American nations began to outlaw slaving and slavery in the 19th century, the oriental and internal trades increased. Slave exports from East Africa and the Sudan and Horn increased after about 1780, and indigenous African slavery also expanded. This traffic was dominated by the same figures—merchants, warlords, and rulers—who had profited from external trade.

Indigenous African slavery began a real decline only at the end of the 19th century because of the dominance of European colonial regimes and internal changes. The formal end of African indigenous slavery occurred only in 1928 in Sierra Leone.

THE AFRICAN SIDE OF THE TRANSATLANTIC TRADE

Africans were actively involved in the transatlantic slave trade. European slave traders generally obtained their human cargoes from private or government-sponsored African middlemen along the coast. This situation was the result of both the ability of Africans to control inland trade and the vulnerability of Europeans to tropical disease. Thus, it was largely African middlemen who undertook the capture or procurement of slaves and the difficult task of marching them to the coast. These middlemen were generally either wealthy merchants or the agents of African chieftaincies or kingdoms.

The media of exchange for slaves varied. At first the items were usually gold dust, firearms, or alcohol. Increasingly, they involved monetary payments. This trade drained productive resources (human beings) in return for nonproductive wealth.

The chief West and central African slaving regions provided different numbers of slaves at different times, and the total number of exported slaves varied between periods. When one area could not meet demand, the European traders shifted to other locales. Traders went where population density and African merchant or state suppliers promised the best numbers and prices.

THE EXTENT OF THE SLAVE TRADE

The slave trade fluctuated greatly from period to period. It peaked between 1701 and 1810, accounting for more than 60 percent of the total. The final half-century of slaving (ending in 1870) accounted for more than 20 percent of the total. The Portuguese transported more than a million slaves to Brazil between

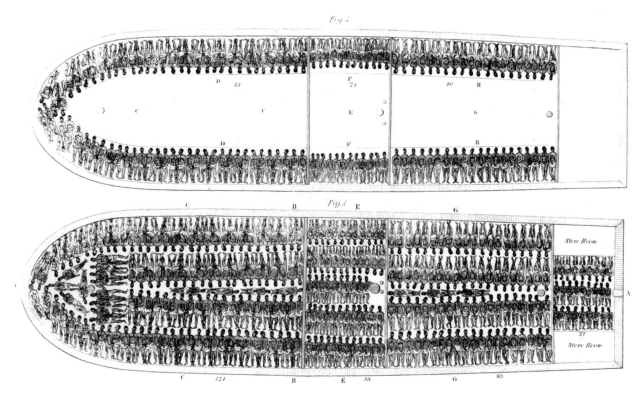

1811 and 1870. It is sobering to contemplate how long it took the "modern" occidental world to abolish the trade in African slaves.

The overall number of African slaves exported during the occidental trade—effectively, between 1451 and 1870—is still debated and must be seen in the larger context of all types of slaving in Africa in the same period. A major unknown is the number of slaves who died under the brutal conditions to which they were subjected when captured and transported overland and by sea. The most reliable estimates pertain only to those slaves who actually landed abroad. As the table on page 443 shows, just those who actually reached an American or Old World destination in the occidental trade totaled more than 11 million.

At a minimum, Africa lost some 13 million people to the Atlantic trade alone. Another 5 million or more were lost to the oriental trade. Finally, according to the estimate of one expert, an additional 15 million people were enslaved within African societies themselves.[2]

CONSEQUENCES OF THE SLAVE TRADE FOR AFRICA

Statistics hint at the massive impact slave trading had on African life, but the actual effects remain in dispute. We do not know for certain if the Atlantic trade brought net population loss or gain to specific areas of West Africa. The rapid spread of maize and cassava cultivation in forest regions after these plants were imported from the Americas may have fueled African population increases that offset regional human loss through slaving. We know, however, that slaving took away many of the strongest young men and, in the oriental-trade zones, most of the young women. Similarly, we do not know if more slaves were captured as byproducts of local wars or from pure slave raiding, but we do know they were captured and removed from their societies (see "Olaudah Equiano Recalls His Experience at the Slave Market in Barbados").

Slave Ship. Loading plan for the main decks of the 320-ton slave ship *Brookes*. The *Brookes* was only 25 feet wide and 100 feet long, but as many as 609 slaves were crammed onboard for the nightmarish passage to the Americas. The average space allowed each person was only about 78 inches by 16 inches.

Photographs and Prints Division, Schomburg Center for Research in Black Culture, The New York Public Library, Astor, Lenox, and Tilder Foundations.

[2]Ibid., pp. 37, 170–171.

HISTORY'S VOICES

OLAUDAH EQUIANO RECALLS HIS EXPERIENCE AT THE SLAVE MARKET IN BARBADOS

Olaudah Equiano composed one of the most popular and influential slave narratives of the late 18th and early 19th centuries. He also led a remarkable life. Born in West Africa in what is today Nigeria, he spent his early life among the Ibo. He was captured and sold into slavery, making the dreaded Atlantic crossing. In the passage that follows, Equiano recounts his arrival in Barbados and the experience of cultural disorientation, his sale into slavery, and seeing Africans separated from their families. His life did not end in slavery, the most destructive aspects of which he also described in vivid detail. He achieved his freedom and then had an adventuresome career sailing on various commercial and military ships plying the Caribbean, the Atlantic, and the Mediterranean. Equiano also made a trip to the Arctic Ocean. His account consequently describes not only the life of a person taken from Africa and sold into American slavery, but also the life of a person who, once free, explored the entire transatlantic world. His autobiographical narrative, which first appeared in 1789 and displayed Equiano's wide reading, served two purposes for the antislavery campaign that commenced in the second half of the 18th century. First, it provided a firsthand report of the slave experience in crossing from Africa to America. Second, his powerful rhetoric and clear arguments demonstrated that, if free, Africans could achieve real personal independence. Many defenders of slavery had denied that Africans possessed the character and intelligence to be free.

WHAT WERE the fears of the Africans on the slave ship as they approached the port? How were older slaves in Barbados used to calm their fears? How did the sale of slaves proceed? What happened to African families in the process of the sale?

At last, we came in sight . . . of Barbados, . . . and we soon anchored . . . off Bridgetown. Many merchants and planters now came on board. . . . They put us in separate parcels, and examined us attentively. They also made us jump, and pointed to the land, signifying we were to go there. We thought by this we should be eaten by these ugly men, as they appeared to us; and when, soon after we were all put down under the deck again, there was much dread and trembling among us, and nothing but bitter cries to be heard all the night from these apprehension, insomuch that at last the white people got some old slaves from the land to pacify us. They told us we were not to be eaten, but to work, and were soon to go on land, where we should see many of our country people. This report eased us much. . . . We were conducted immediately to the merchant's yard, where we were all pent up together like so many sheep in a fold, without regard to sex or age. As every object was new to me, everything filled me with surprise . . . and indeed I thought these people were full of nothing but magical arts. . . . We were not many days in the merchant's custody before we were sold after their usual manner which was this: On a signal given (as the beat of a drum), the buyers rush at once into the yard where the slaves are confined, and make choice of that parcel they like best. The noise and clamour with which this is attended, and the eagerness visible in the countenances of the buyers, serve not a little to increase the apprehension of the terrified Africans, who may well be supposed to consider them as the ministers of that destruction to which they think themselves devoted. In this manner, without scruple, relations and friends separate, most of them never to see each other again. I remember in the vessel in which I was brought over, in the men's apartment, there were several brothers who, in the sale, were sold in different lots; and it was very moving on this occasion to see and hear their cries at parting. . . . Surely this is a new refinement in cruelty, which, while it has no advantage to atone for it, thus aggravates distress, and adds fresh horrors even to the wretchedness of slavery.

Source: *The Interesting Narrative of the Life of Olaudah Equiano or Gustavus Vassa, The African, Written by Himself* (first published 1789), as quoted in Henry Louis Gates Jr., and William L. Andrews, eds., *Pioneers of the Black Atlantic: Five Slave Narratives from the Enlightenment, 1772–1815* (Washington, DC: Counterpoint, 1998), pp. 221–223.

Nor do we know if slaving inhibited trade or stimulated it. Commerce in African products from ivory to wood and hides often accompanied that in slaves. Still, we do know that the exchange of productive human beings for money or goods that were not used to build a productive economy was ultimately a loss for African society.

Finally, because we do not yet have accurate estimates of the total population of Africa at different times over the four centuries of the Atlantic slave trade, we cannot determine with certainty its demographic impact. We can, however, make educated guesses. If, for example, tropical Africa had 50 million inhabitants in 1600, it would then have had 30 percent of the combined population of the Americas, the Middle East, Europe, and Africa. If in 1900, after the depredations of the slave trade, it had 70 million inhabitants, its population would have dropped to about 10 percent of the combined population of the same world regions. Current estimates indicate that overall African population growth suffered significantly as a result of the slave trade. Figures like these also give some idea of slavery's probable impact on Africa's ability to keep up with the modern industrializing world.[3]

Even in West and central Africa, which bore the brunt of the Atlantic trade, its impact and the response to it were varied. In a few cases, kingdoms such as Dahomey (the present Republic of Benin) seem to have derived immense economic profit by making slaving a state monopoly. Other kingdoms derived no gain from it. In many instances, including the rise of Asante power or the fall of the Yoruba Oyo Empire, increased slaving was a result as well as a cause of regional change. Increased warfare meant increased prisoners to be sold; however, whether slaving was a motive for war is still unclear.

Similarly, if it can be established, as seems evident, that a major increase in indigenous slavery was a result of the external trade to occident and orient, we have to assume major social consequences for African society. The specific consequences would, however, differ according to regional situations. For example, in West Africa more men were taken as slaves than women, whereas in the Sahelian Sudanic regions, more women than men were taken. In the west, the loss of so many men increased the pressures for polygamy and possibly the use of female slaves, whereas in the Sahelian Sudanic regions, the loss of women may have stimulated polyandry and reduced the birthrate.

Even though slavery existed previously in Africa, the scale of the Atlantic trade was unprecedented and hence had an unprecedented impact. In general, the slave trade changed patterns of life and balances of power in the main affected areas, whether by stimulating trade or warfare, by disrupting market and political structures, by increasing slavery inside Africa, or by disturbing the male-female ratio (and hence the work-force balance and birthrate patterns) and consequently the basic social institution of monogamous marriage.

[3]Ibid., pp. 126–148, 168–176.

Plantation. In the American South, the islands of the Caribbean, and in Brazil, slaves labored on sugar plantations under the authority of overseers.

The Granger Collection.

QUICK REVIEW

Difficulties in Determining Consequences of the Slave Trade

- Do not know how slave trade affected specific West African regions
- Cannot determine number of slaves captured during wars and captured during pure slave raiding
- Do not know how slave trading affected commerce in African products

The overseas slave trade at the least siphoned off indigenous energy and channeled it in counterproductive or destructive directions. This inhibited economic development. The Atlantic slave trade was one of the most tragic aspects of European involvement in Africa.

SUMMARY

European Conquest of the New World   Contact between the native peoples of the American continents and the European explorers of the 15th and 16th centuries transformed world history. In the Americas, the native peoples had established a wide variety of civilizations. Some of their most remarkable architectural monuments and cities were constructed during the centuries when European civilizations were reeling from the collapse of Roman power. Until the European explorations, the civilizations of the Americas and Eurasia and Africa had no significant contact with one another.

Within half a century of Columbus's landing, millions of America's native peoples encountered Europe's intent on conquest, exploitation, and religious conversion. Because of their advanced weapons, navies, and the diseases they brought with them, as well as internal divisions among the Native Americans themselves, Europeans achieved a rapid conquest.

The Transatlantic Economy   In both North and South America, economies of exploitation were established. In Latin America, various institutions were developed to extract native labor. From the mid-Atlantic English colonies through the Caribbean and into Brazil, slave-labor plantation systems were established. Slaves were forcibly imported from Africa and sold in America to plantation owners. The economies and peoples of Europe, Africa, and the Americas were thus drawn into a worldwide web of production based on slave labor.

Slavery   The impact of slavery in the Americas was not limited to the life of the black slaves. Whites in the New World numbered about 12 million in 1820, compared to some 6 million blacks. However, only about 2 million whites had migrated there, compared to some 11 million or more Africans forcibly imported as slaves. Such numbers reveal the effects of brutal slave conditions and the high mortality and low birthrates of slave populations.

None of these statistics, however, enables us to asses the role that slavery has played in the Americas or, in particular, the United States. The United States actually received only a bit more than a quarter as many slaves as did Brazil alone or the British and French Caribbean regions together, yet the consequences of the forced migration of just over a half-million Africans remain massive. Consider just the American Civil War and the endurance of racism and inequality or, more positively, the African contribution to American industrial development, language, music, literature, and artistic culture. The Atlantic slave trade's impact continues to be felt at both ends of the original trade route.

IMAGE KEY

for pages 434–435

a. Job Ben Solomon, a freed slave who returned to Africa

b. A poster for a slave auction in Charleston

c. John Singleton Copley, "Watson and the Shark," ca. 1778

d. A chunk of silver metal and rock

e. Spanish map showing the seven cities of Cibola and Baja California, 16th century

f. Dried tobacco leaves

g. Slave ship, ca. 1790

h. Samuel Scott, "Old Custom House Quay"

i. Bartolomé de Las Casas

j. Slaves grinding sugar cane and refining sugar

k. Fur traders and Indians

l. Slaves harvest sugar cane on a plantation

REVIEW QUESTIONS

1. How were small groups of Spaniards able to conquer the Aztec and Inca Empires?

2. What was the the mercantilist economic theory? How accuately did it describe the relationship between the colonies and their homelands?

3. Why did forced labor and slavery develop in tropical colonies? How was slavery in the Americas different from slavery in earlier societies?

4. What was the effect of the transatlantic slave trade on African societies? What role did Africans themselves play in the slave trade?

KEY TERMS

Black Legend (p. 439)   *encomienda* (p. 440)   **peninsulares** (p. 441)
conquistadores (p. 439)   *hacienda* (p. 441)   **plantation economy** (p. 446)
debt peonage (p. 441)   **mercantilism** (p. 436)   *repartimiento* (p. 440)

 For additional study resources for this chapter, go to:
www.prenhall.com/craig/chapter18

19 East Asia in the Late Traditional Era

CHAPTER HIGHLIGHTS

China China's last two imperial dynasties were the Ming (1368–1644) and the Qing or Manchus (1644–1911). Although China could not match the dynamism of the West during these years, its society became more integrated and its government more sophisticated. The population reached 410 million, cities grew, and commerce expanded. Chinese government depended on the Confucian bureaucracy and the gentry class. Under the Manchus, China expanded to the east and annexed Taiwan. There also was growing trade with the West, especially Britain, but it was conducted under highly restricted terms by Chinese officials.

Japan After more than a century of civil war among the warrior aristocracy (the Warring States Era, 1467–1600), the Tokugawa shoguns (1600–1868) restored order. Their government controlled the aristocracy and encouraged economic growth. Christianity, which had made many converts in Japan, was driven underground, and Japan was closed to the outside world except for a small Dutch presence at Nagasaki. Japanese drama, literature, and art flourished, as did commercial life.

Korea and Vietnam China considered both Korea and Vietnam to be tributary states, and both countries adopted Chinese Confucian culture and forms of government while preserving their political independence.

CHAPTER QUESTIONS

WHY DID the Chinese accept
Manchu rule?

WHAT WAS the "Warring States Era"
in Japan?

HOW DID the Tokugawa
control Japan?

HOW DID Chinese
culture influence Korea
and Vietnam?

CHAPTER OUTLINE

LATE IMPERIAL CHINA
- Ming (1368–1644)
  and Qing (1644–1911) Dynasties

JAPAN
- Warring States Era (1467–1600)
- Tokugawa Era (1600–1868)

KOREA AND VIETNAM
- Korea
- Vietnam
- Southeast Asia

This chapter underlines the dynamism of China and Japan during the centuries between the "medieval" and the "modern" eras. "Late traditional society" does not mean "late static society." In both countries, social structures became more integrated and the apparatus of government became more sophisticated. These advances shaped Chinese and Japanese responses to the West during the 19th century. Even Korea and Vietnam did not lack dynamism. But during these centuries the West was transformed. As we view East Asia from the perspective of Europe, it appears to have been in slow motion, but the truth was that the West was rapidly accelerating.

LATE IMPERIAL CHINA

MING (1368–1644) AND QING (1644–1911) DYNASTIES

WHY DID the Chinese accept Manchu rule?

The Ming and the Qing were China's last dynasties. The former was Chinese, the latter a foreign dynasty (Manchus) established by conquest. The two were nevertheless remarkably similar in their institutions and pattern of rule.

LAND AND PEOPLE

China's population reached about 410 million people in the mid-19th century. This population density stimulated commerce and gave new prominence to the scholar-gentry. Population growth was paralleled by an increase in the food supply.

There are many unanswered questions regarding the population growth during these six centuries. Was there a decline in the death rate and, if so, why? Or did the development of new lands and technology enable more mouths to be fed? Certainly, the Ming–Qing Era was the longest continuous period of good government in Chinese history. But by the early 19th century, the Chinese standard of living may have begun to decline. An ever-increasing population was no blessing.

CHINA'S THIRD COMMERCIAL REVOLUTION

Early Ming emperors were isolationists with an agrarian orientation. They established government monopolies that stifled enterprise and depressed the southeastern coastal region by restricting maritime trade and shipping. In the mid-16th century, commerce started to grow again, buoyed by the surge of population and agriculture and a relaxation of government controls. If the growth during the Han and Song dynasties may be called China's first and second commercial revolutions, then the expansion between 1500 and 1800 was its third. By the early 19th century, China was the most highly commercialized nonindustrial society in the world.

One stimulus to commerce was imported silver. The Chinese balance of trade was favorable. Beginning in the mid-16th century, silver from Japan entered China, and from the 1570s, Spanish galleons brought in Mexican and Peruvian silver. In the 18th century, private **Shaanxi banks** opened branches throughout China to facilitate the transfer of funds and extend credit for trade. Eventually they opened offices in Singapore, Japan, and Russia. As in Europe, the influx of silver and the overall increase in liquidity led to inflation and commercial growth in China.

Urban growth between 1500 and 1800 was mainly at the level of market towns. These towns provided the link between the local markets and the larger

Shaanxi banks Private commercial banks in China under the Manchus.

provincial capitals and cities. Commercial integration of local, intermediate, and large cities spread over China. Interregional trade also gained, but China did not develop a national economy. Seven or eight regional economies, each the size of a large European nation, were the focus for most economic activity. But a new level of trade developed among them, especially where water transport made such trade economical.

Women and the Commercial Revolution   The Confucian family ideal changed little during the Ming and Qing dynasties. A woman was expected first to obey her parents, then her husband, and finally her son—when he succeeded his father as family head. Physically, women were more restricted as footbinding spread through the upper classes and to some commoners. One exception to the rule was the Manchus. One Manchu (Qing) emperor issued an edict banning footbinding, but it was ignored by the Chinese.

As population grew and the size of the average landholding shrunk, more women worked at home, making products for commercial markets. And as their contribution to the household income grew, their voice in household decisions often became larger than Confucian doctrines would suggest.

Political System   Despite these massive demographic and economic changes, political superstructure of China changed very little. Government during the Ming and Qing was much like that of the Song or Yuan, only stronger. Sources of strength of the Ming–Qing system were the spread of education, the use of Confucianism as an ideology, stronger emperors, better government finances, more competent officials, and a larger gentry class with an expanded role in local society.

Role of Confucianism   Confucian teachings were more widespread in late imperial China than ever before. There were more schools. Academies preparing candidates for the civil service examinations multiplied, and literacy outpaced population growth. The Confucian view of society was patriarchal. The family, headed by the father, was the basic unit. The emperor, the son of Heaven and the ruler-father of the empire, stood at its apex. In between were the district magistrates, the "father-mother officials." The idea of the state as the family *writ large* carried with it duties and obligations at every level.

In comparison to Europe, where religious philosophies were less involved with the state and where a revolution in science was reshaping religious and political doctrines, China had greater unity and a more integrated worldview.

Emperor   Ming–Qing emperors were more powerful than ever and made all important decisions. They wielded despotic powers at their courts. They had secret police and prisons where those who committed even minor offenses might be tortured. Even high officials might suffer humiliating and fatal punishment. The dedication and loyalty even of officials who were cruelly mistreated attest to the depth of their Confucian ethical training.

During the Qing, the life-and-death authority of emperors did not diminish, but officials were generally better treated. As foreign rulers, the Manchu emperors took care not to alienate Chinese officials.

The Forbidden Palace in Beijing was an icon of the emperor's majesty. The entire palace complex focused on the ruler. Its massive walls and vast courtyards progress to the audience hall where the emperor sat on an elevated dais above

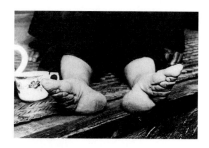

Foot Binding. As a young girl her arches were broken and her feet forced into iron training shoes. Later, her deformed feet were encased in silk slippers, forcing her to walk with a slow and swaying gait.

AP WideWorld Photos.

QUICK REVIEW

Women Under the Qing and Ming

- Confucian family ideals changed little during the Ming and Qing eras
- Footbinding spread among the upper classes and some commoners
- As population grew, more women worked at home

the officials, who knelt before him. Behind the audience hall were the emperor's private chambers and his harem. By the 17th century, there were 9,000 palace ladies and perhaps as many as 70,000 eunuchs. The glory of the emperor extended to his family, whose members were awarded vast estates in North China.

Bureaucracy   A second component of the Ming–Qing system was the government itself. At the top were the military, the censorate, and the administrative branch; beneath the administration were the six ministries and the web of provincial, prefectural, and district offices. Government was better financed than during earlier dynasties. As late as the 1580s, huge surpluses were accumulated at both the central and the provincial levels. Only during the last 50 years of the Ming did soaring military expenses bankrupt the government. When, in the second half of the 17th century, the Manchus reestablished a strong central government, they restored the flow of taxes to levels close to those of the Ming.

The good government of the Ming–Qing system in China was largely a product of the ethical commitment and ability of its officials. No officials in the world today approach in power or prestige those of the Ming and the Qing. When the Portuguese arrived early in the 16th century, they called these officials "mandarins." The rewards of an official career were so great that the competition to enter it was intense. As the population grew and schools increased, entrance became ever more competitive. (see "The Seven Transformations of an Examination Candidate").

After being screened at the district office, a candidate took the county examination. If he passed, he became a member of the gentry and was exempted from state labor service. This examination required years of study. About half a million passed each year. The second hurdle was the provincial examination held every third year. Only one in a hundred was successful. The final hurdle was the metropolitan examination, also held triennially. Fewer than 90 passed each year.

The great Manchu emperor Qianlong (r. 1736–1795).

© Metropolitan Museum of Art, Rogers Fund, 1942 (42.141.8).

gentry   In China, a largely urban, landowning class that represented local interests and functioned as quasi-bureaucrats under the magistrates.

Gentry   A final component in the Ming–Qing system was the **gentry** class. It was an intermediate layer between the elite bureaucracy above and the village below. The lowest level of bureaucratic government was the district magistrate. Although the population increased sixfold during the Ming and the Qing, the number of district magistrates increased only from 1,171 to 1,470. To prevent conflicts of interest, an outsider was appointed as district magistrate. His office compound had a large staff of secretaries and advisers, but to govern effectively, he had to obtain the cooperation of the local *literati* or gentry.

By *gentry* we do not mean a rural elite, like English squires. The Chinese gentry was largely urban, living in market towns or district seats. Socially and educationally, its members were of the same class as the magistrate—a world

HISTORY'S VOICES

THE SEVEN TRANSFORMATIONS OF AN EXAMINATION CANDIDATE

*T*he Chinese civil service examination was a grueling ordeal. Like a chess tournament, it required physical and mental strength. Chinese critics said, "To pass the provincial examination a man needed the spiritual strength of a dragon-horse, the physique of a donkey, the insensitivity of a wood louse, and the endurance of a camel." The following selection is by a 17th-century writer who never succeeded in passing.

Is the style of this passage overdone or effective? What is distinctively Chinese about it?

When he first enters the examination compound and walks along, panting under his heavy load of luggage, he is just like a beggar. Next, while undergoing the personal body search and being scolded by the clerks and shouted at by the soldiers, he is just like a prisoner. When he finally enters his cell and, along with the other candidates, stretches his neck to peer out, he is just like the larva of a bee. When the examination is finished at last and he leaves, his mind in a haze and his legs tottering, he is just like a sick bird that has been released from a cage. While he is wondering when the results will be announced and waiting to learn whether he passed or failed, so nervous that he is startled even by the rustling of the trees and the grass and is unable to sit or stand still, his restlessness is like that of a monkey on a leash. When at last the results are announced and he has definitely failed, he loses his vitality like one dead, rolls over on his side, and lies there without moving, like a poisoned fly. Then, when he pulls himself together and stands up, he is provoked by every sight and sound, gradually flings away everything within his reach, and complains of the illiteracy of the examiners. When he calms down at last, he finds everything in the room broken. At this time he is like a pigeon smashing its own precious eggs. These are the seven transformations of a candidate.

Source: From I. Miyazaki, *China's Examination Hell*, trans. by C. Schirokauer. Copyright © 1976 Weatherhill, pp. 57–58.

apart from clerks or village headmen. They usually owned land, which enabled them to avoid manual labor and to send their children to private academies. As absentee landlords whose lands were worked by sharecroppers, they were often exploitative. But they also acted as local leaders. They represented community interests vis-à-vis the bureaucracy. They also performed quasi-official functions on behalf of their communities: maintaining schools and Confucian temples and repairing roads, bridges, canals, and dikes. The gentry class was the matrix from which officials arose; it was the local upholder of Confucian values.

Pattern of Manchu Rule   The collapse of the Ming dynasty in 1644 and the establishment of Manchu (Qing) rule was less of a break than might be imagined. First, the transition was short. Second, the Manchus, unlike the Mongols, were already partially Sinicized. Even before entering China, they had ruled over the Chinese settled in Manchuria.

In the late 16th century, an able leader unified the Manchurian tribes, proclaimed a new dynasty, and established a Confucian government. When the Ming collapsed, the Manchus presented themselves as the conservative upholders of the Confucian order. The Chinese gentry preferred the Manchus to Chinese rebel leaders, whom they regarded as bandits. After the Manchu

Late Imperial China

Ming Dynasty 1368–1644

1368–1398	Reign of first Ming emperor; Chinese armies invade Manchuria, Mongolia, and eastern Central Asia
1402–1424	Reign of third Ming emperor; Chinese armies invade Vietnam and Mongolia
1405–1433	Voyage of Zheng He to India and Africa
1415	Grand Canal reopened
1472–1529	Wang Yang-ming, philosopher
1592–1598	Chinese army battles Japanese army in Korea

Qing (Manchu) Dynasty 1644–1911

1668	Manchuria closed to Chinese immigrants (by Willow Palisade)
1661–1722	Reign of Kangxi
1681	Suppression of revolts by Chinese generals
1683	Taiwan captured
1689	China and Russia sign Treaty of Nerchinsk
1736–1795	Reign of Qianlong
1793	Macartney mission

conquest, most officials served its new Qing dynasty. The Qing as a Chinese dynasty dates from 1644.

As a tiny fraction of the Chinese population, the Manchus adopted institutions to maintain themselves as an ethnically separate elite group. One was their military organization. Manchu garrison forces were segregated and not put under the jurisdiction of Chinese officials. They were given stipends and lands to cultivate. They were forbidden to marry Chinese, their children had to study Manchu, and they were not permitted to bind the feet of their daughters. In 1668, northern and central Manchuria were closed to Chinese immigrants.

The second institutional feature was the appointment of one Chinese and one Manchu to each key post in the central government. At the provincial level, Chinese governors were overseen by Manchu governor-generals. Most officials and all district magistrates beneath the governors were Chinese.

A particular strength of the Manchu dynasty was the long reigns of two extremely able emperors, Kangxi (1661–1722) and Qianlong (1736–1795). Kangxi was a man of great vigor. He rose at dawn to read official documents before meeting with officials. He presided over palace examinations. Well versed in the Confucian classics, he won the support of scholars.

Kangxi also displayed an interest in European science, a subject he studied with Jesuit court astronomers. He opened four ports to foreign trade and carried out public works, improving the dikes on the Huai and Yellow Rivers and dredging the Grand Canal. During his reign, he made six tours of China's southern provinces. Kangxi, in short, was a model emperor.

Qianlong began his reign in 1736. Under his rule the Qing dynasty attained its highest level of prosperity and power. Like Kangxi, he was vigorous, wise, conscientious, careful, and hard-working. He visited South China on inspection tours and patronized scholars on a grand scale.

Only in his last years did Qianlong lose his grip and permit a court favorite to practice corruption on an almost unprecedented scale. In 1796, the White Lotus Rebellion broke out. Qianlong's successor put down the rebellion, but the ample financial reserves that had existed throughout the 18th century were never reestablished. China nevertheless entered the 19th century with its government intact and with a peaceful and stable society. There were few signs of what was to come.

MING–QING FOREIGN RELATIONS

Ming　The first Ming emperor (r. 1368–1398) oversaw the expansion of China's borders. By the time he died, China controlled the northern steppe and had recovered jurisdiction over the southern tier of Chinese provinces (see Map 19–1). During the reign of the third Ming emperor (1402–1424), northern Vietnam became a Chinese province and remained so for two decades.

The Ming emperors "managed" China's frontiers using a tribute system. Ambassadors of vassal kings acted out their subordination to the universal ruler

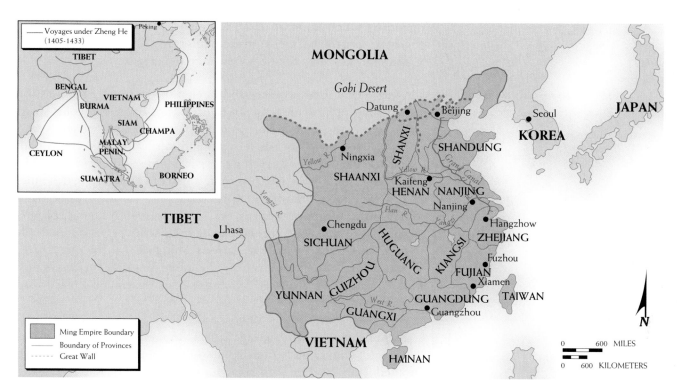

MAP 19–1

Ming Empire and the Voyages of Zheng He.   The inset map shows the voyages of Zeng He to Southeast Asia and India. Some ships of his fleet even reached East Africa. (Zheng himself did not.)

WHAT WAS the purpose of Zheng He's voyages?

16.2
Dynastic Change in China
Tears a Family Apart

of the celestial kingdom by approaching the emperor, performing the kowtow (kneeling three times and each time bowing his head to the floor three times), and presenting gifts. In return, the vassal kings were sent seals confirming their status, given permission to use the Chinese calendar and year-period names, and appointed to the Ming nobility.

The most far-ranging ventures of the third Ming emperor were the maritime expeditions that sailed to Southeast Asia, India, the Arabian Gulf, and East Africa between 1405 and 1433. They were commanded by the eunuch Zheng He, a Muslim from Yunnan (see Map 19–1). The first of these armadas had 62 major ships and carried 28,000 sailors, soldiers, and merchants. Trade was not the primary purpose. The expeditions were intended to make China's glory known to distant kingdoms and to enroll them in the tribute system.

The expeditions ended as abruptly as they had begun. They were costly at a time when the dynasty was fighting in Mongolia and building Beijing. What was remarkable about these expeditions was not that they came a half-century earlier than the Portuguese voyages of discovery, but that China had the maritime technology needed for exploration and chose not to use it. China lacked the combination of restlessness, greed, faith, and curiosity that motivated the Portuguese.

The chief threat to the Ming dynasty was the Mongols. In the 1430s, they captured the emperor, and in 1550 they overran Beijing. They were defeated by a Chinese army in the 1560s and signed a peace treaty in 1571.

A second threat came from Japan, whose pirates raided the Chinese coast in the 15th and 16th centuries. After Hideyoshi unifyied Japan, he twice invaded

16.5
Letter to King George:
China and Great Britain

Giraffe with Attendant. Some emperors had private zoos and gladly received exotic animals as gifts from tribute states. A painting by Shen Du (1357–1438).

Philadelphia. Museum of Art: Given by John T. Dorrance.

Western Factories in Canton (Guangzhou) c. 1800–1815. A factory was a trading post, not a manu-factory. This street scene shows many Chinese mingling with a few Westerners wearing tall hats. The factories were built on riverbanks outside the city walls. Western merchants were not allowed to bring their wives to China, they were tightly controlled by Chinese merchant guilds, and communicated with the Chinese in pidgin (business) English.

The Henry Francis du Pont Winterthur Museum, Inc.

and occupied Korea in 1592 between 1597 and 1598. China sent troops, and the Japanese withdrew after the death of Hideyoshi. But the strain on Ming finances weakened the dynasty.

Qing The final and successful foreign threat to the Ming was the Manchus. After coming to power in 1644, the Manchu court spent decades consolidating its rule within China. Chinese generals who had helped the Manchus revolted and were supported by a pirate state on Taiwan. The emperor Kangxi suppressed the revolts, and in 1683 he took Taiwan, which became a part of China for the first time.

As always, the principal foreign threats to China came from the north and northwest. By the 1660s, Russian traders, trappers, and adventurers had reached northern Manchuria, where they built forts and traded with the eastern Mongols. During the 1680s, Kangxi drove the Russians from the lower Amur River. This victory led to the 1689 Treaty of Nerchinsk, which excluded Russia from northern Manchuria.

In the west, the situation was more complex, with a three-corner relationship among Russia, the western Mongols, and Tibet. Kangxi, and then Qianlong, campaigned against the Mongols, invaded Tibet, and in 1727 signed a new treaty with Russia. During the campaigns, the Chinese temporarily came to control millions of square miles of new territories. It is a telling comment on the Chinese concept of empire that ever since that time, even after China's borders contracted during the 19th century, the Chinese have insisted that the Manchu conquests of non-Chinese peoples define their legitimate borders. The roots of the present-day contention over borders between China and the countries of the former Soviet Union go back to these events during the 18th century, as does the Chinese claim to Tibet.

Contacts with the West Europeans had made their way to China during the Tang and the Yuan dynasties. But only with Europe's oceanic expansion in the 16th century did they arrive in large numbers. Some came as missionaries, of whom the most successful were the Jesuits. They studied Chinese and the Confucian classics and conversed with scholars. They used their knowledge of astronomy, geography, engraving, and firearms to win entry to the court at Beijing and appointments in the bureau of astronomy.

When the Manchus came to power in 1644, the Jesuits kept their position. They appealed to the curiosity of the court with instruments such as telescopes, clocks, and clavichords. They tried to propagate Christianity. They attacked Daoism and Buddhism, but argued that Confucianism as a rational philosophy complemented Christianity, just as Aristotle's teaching complemented Christian theology in Europe. They interpreted the Confucian rites of ancestor worship as secular and nonantagonistic to Christianity. A few high court officials were converted.

Meanwhile, their Franciscan and Dominican rivals had reported to Rome that the Jesuits condoned the Confucian rites. Papal bulls in 1715 and

1742 forbade Chinese Christians to participate in the family rites of ancestor worship. Thereupon the emperor banned Christianity in China.

Other Europeans came to China to trade. The Portuguese came first in the early 16th century and were permitted to trade on a tiny peninsula at Macao. They were followed by the Dutch from the East Indies (Indonesia), by the British East India Company in 1699, and by Americans in 1784.

By the early 18th century, Westerners could trade only at Canton outside its walls along the river. They could not bring their wives to China. They were subject to Chinese law and were controlled by official merchant guilds. Nevertheless, the trade was profitable to both sides.

The British East India Company developed a triangular commerce among China, India, and Britain. For China, this trade produced an influx of specie, and the Chinese officials in charge grew immensely wealthy. Chafing under the restrictions, the British government in 1793 sent the Macartney mission to China to negotiate the opening of other ports, fixed tariffs, representation at Beijing, and so on. The emperor Qianlong permitted Lord Macartney (1736–1806) to present his gifts, which the Chinese described as tribute, but he turned down Macartney's requests. Western trade remained encapsulated at Canton.

MING–QING CULTURE

Chinese culture had begun to turn inward during the Song dynasty in reaction to Buddhism. This tendency continued into the Ming and Qing, when Chinese culture became virtually impervious to outside influences. This reflected a tradition and a social order that had stood the test of time, but it also indicated a closed system of ideas with weaknesses that would become apparent in the 19th century.

Ming and Qing Chinese highly esteemed the traditional categories of high culture: painting, calligraphy, poetry, and philosophy. Porcelains of great beauty were also produced. The pottery industry of Europe began during the 16th century to imitate these wares, and Chinese and Japanese influences have dominated Western ceramics ever since.

Chinese today see the novel as the characteristic cultural achievement of the Ming and Qing. The novel in China grew out of plot-books used by earlier storytellers. Like the stories, Chinese novels consisted of episodes strung together. As most novels were written in colloquial Chinese, which was not quite respectable in the society of scholars, their authors wrote under pseudonyms.

JAPAN

The two segments of late traditional Japan could not be more different. The Warring States Era (1467–1600), the last phase of Japan's medieval history, was marked by internal wars and anarchy. Within a century, all vestiges of the old manorial or estate system were scrapped and almost all of the Ashikaga lords were overthrown. The Tokugawa era (1600–1868) that followed saw Japan under a stronger government than ever before. During the Tokugawa era, Japanese

Ming Dynasty Ink Painting by Wu Wei (1479–1508). The seated human figure is a part of the tranquility of nature. Nature, densely concentrated at the left and lower portions of the painting, stretches off into space in the middle and upper-right portion.

Wu Wei, "Scholar Seated Under a Tree," China. Ink + traces of colour on silk. 14.7 × 8.25. Chinese and Japanese Special Fund. © 1996. All rights reserved. Courtesy of Museum of Fine Arts, Boston.

QUICK REVIEW

Chinese Contacts with the West

- Europeans arrived in China in large numbers after the 16th century
- The most successful missionaries were the Jesuits
- By the 18th century, Europeans could only trade at Canton

culture was transformed, preparing it for the challenge it would face during the mid-19th century.

WARRING STATES ERA (1467–1600)

*I*n 1467, a dispute arose over who would be the next Ashikaga shōgun. The dispute led to wars throughout Japan for 11 years. Most of Kyoto was destroyed in the fighting, and the authority of the Ashikaga bakufu came to an end. This first war ended in 1477, but the fighting resumed and continued for more than a century.

WAR OF ALL AGAINST ALL

Even before 1467, the Ashikaga equilibrium had been precarious. The regional **daimyo** lords had relied on their relationship to the *bakufu* to hold their stronger vassals in check, while relying on these vassals to preserve their independence against strong neighbors. The collapse of bakufu authority after 1467 left the regional lords standing alone, removing the last barrier to internecine wars. The regional lords became prey to the stronger among their vassals as well as to powerful neighboring states.

By the end of the 16th century, hundreds of little "Warring States daimyo" had emerged, each with his own warrior band. The constant wars among these men were not unlike those of the early feudal era in Europe. The most efficient in revamping their domains for military ends survived. The less ruthless, who clung to old ways, were defeated and absorbed.

As fighting continued, local states gave way to regional states until the late 16th century, all of Japan was brought under the hegemony of a single lord, Toyotomi Hideyoshi (1536–1598). But it was only with the victory of Tokugawa Ieyasu (1542–1616) at the Battle of Sekigahara in 1600 that true unification was finally achieved. Ieyasu radically transformed Japanese society.

daimyo Japanese territorial lord.

Warring States Japan and the Era of Unification (1467–1600)

1467–1568	Battles throughout Japan
1543	Portuguese arrive in Japan
1568	Oda Nobunaga takes Kyoto and partially unifies Japan
1575	Battle of Nagashino
1582	Nobunaga assassinated
1588	Hideyoshi starts sword hunt
1590	Hideyoshi completes unification
1592, 1597–1598	Hideyoshi sends armies to Korea
1597	Hideyoshi bans Christianity
1598	Hideyoshi dies, his generals battle for succession
1600	Battle of Sekigahara; Tokugawa reunifies Japan

FOOT SOLDIER REVOLUTION

During the Warring States period, the foot soldier replaced the aristocratic mounted warrior as the backbone of the military. Soldiers were still called *samurai* and were still vassals of a lord, but their numbers, social status, and techniques of warfare changed dramatically. All public lands and estates, including the emperor's, were seized and converted into fiefs, which were privately governed by the fief holder. A fief was not divided among heirs, but passed intact to the ablest son. Larger revenues made larger armies possible–in the tens of thousands. New weapons also appeared, a two-handed thrusting spear in the mid-14th century and muskets in the mid-16th century.

The society that emerged from the Warring States period might, in some sense, be described as feudal. By the late 16th century, all warriors in Japan were part of a pyramid of vassals and lords headed by a single overlord and warriors of rank held fiefs and vassals of their own. But in other respects, Japan was more like postfeudal Europe. First, most of the military class were soldiers, not aristocrats. Even though they were called samurai and were vassals, they were not given fiefs but were paid with stipends of rice. Second, unlike feudal England, where the military class was about one-quarter of 1 percent of the population, in mid-16th-century Japan the military may have reached 7 or 8 percent. It was comparable in size to European mercenary armies of the 14th or 16th centuries. Third, the recruitment of village warriors gave rise to problems. Taxes became harder to collect. Local samurai were often involved in uprisings that sometimes spread through whole provinces. Again, the parallels with postfeudal Europe seem closer. Fourth, even in a feudal society, not everything is feudal. Commercial growth continued in the Warring States Era.

16.7
The Laws for Military House (Buke Shohatto), 1615

FOREIGN RELATIONS AND TRADE

Japanese pirate-traders plied the seas of East Asia during the 15th and 16th centuries. To halt their depredations, the Ming emperor invited the third Ashikaga shōgun to trade with China. An agreement was reached in 1404. However, piracy stopped only after Japan was reunified at the close of the 16th century.

The content of the trade reflected the progress of Japanese crafts. Early Japanese exports to China were raw materials, but by the 16th century, manufactured goods were rising in importance. In exchange, Japan received copper cash, porcelains, paintings, books, and medicines. Then, in 1635, the imposition of a policy of national seclusion ended Japan's foreign trade. No Japanese were permitted to leave Japan, and the construction of large ships was prohibited.

Overlapping Japan's maritime expansion in the seas of East Asia was the arrival of European ships. Portuguese pirate-traders arrived in Japan in 1543. Spanish galleons came in 1587, and they were followed by the Dutch and the English after the turn of the century.

The Portuguese became important as shippers. They carried Southeast Asian goods and Japanese silver to China and Chinese silk to Japan, and they used their profits to buy spices for the European market.

Traders brought with them Jesuit missionaries, who concentrated their efforts on the samurai. Christian converts numbered about 300,000 in 1600—a higher percentage of Japanese were Christian than today. It is difficult to explain why Christianity met with greater success in Japan than in other Asian lands. When introduced, it was seen as a new Buddhist sect. There seemed little difference to the Japanese between the cosmic Buddha of Shingon and the Christian God, between the paradise of Amida and the Christian heaven, or between prayers to Kannon—the female *bodhisattva* of mercy—and to the Virgin Mary. The Japanese also noted the theological similarity between the pietism of the Pure Land sect and that of Christianity. The personal example of the Jesuits was also important.

The fortunes of Christianity began to decline in 1597, when six Spanish Franciscans and 20 Japanese converts were crucified in Nagasaki. Hideyoshi was aware of Spanish colonialism in the Philippines, and a Spanish pilot had apparently boasted that merchants

"The Arrival of the Portuguese in Japan." Portuguese merchants arrived in Japan in 1543 from India and the East Indies. Their crews were multiethnic, and they brought Jesuit priests as well.
Giraudon/Art Resource, N.Y.

and priests were preparing Japan for conquest. Sporadic persecutions continued until 1614, when Tokugawa Ieyasu formally banned the foreign religion. Some Christians recanted. More than 3,000 others were martyred. The last resistance was an uprising in 1637 and 1638 in which 37,000 Christians died. After that, Christianity survived in Japan only as a hidden religion. A few of these "hidden Christians" reemerged in the late 18th century.

HOW DID the Tokugawa control Japan?

TOKUGAWA ERA (1600–1868)

POLITICAL ENGINEERING AND ECONOMIC GROWTH DURING THE 17TH CENTURY

After the unifications of 1590 and 1600, Japan's leaders sought to create a peaceful, stable, orderly society. By the middle or late 17th century, Japan's society and political system had been radically reengineered. Vigorous economic and demographic growth had also occurred. This combination of political and economic change made the 17th century a period of great dynamism.

Hideyoshi's Rule   In the summer of 1588, Hideyoshi ordered a "sword hunt" to disarm the peasants. Once the hunt was completed, the 5 percent of the population who were still equipped as samurai used their monopoly on weapons to control the other 95 percent.

Hideyoshi next froze the social classes. Samurai were prohibited from quitting the service of their lord. Peasants were barred from abandoning their fields to become townspeople. Samurai, farmers, and townspeople tended to marry within their respective classes, and each class developed a unique cultural character.

Having disarmed the peasantry, Hideyoshi ordered surveys to define each parcel of land by location, size, soil quality, product, and cultivator's name. Hideyoshi's survey laid the foundations for a systematic land tax. Domains and fiefs were henceforth ranked in terms of their assessed yield.

Establishment of Tokugawa Rule   Hideyoshi assumed that his vassals would honor their oaths of loyalty to his heir, and he was especially trustful of his great ally Tokugawa Ieyasu. This trust, however, was misplaced. After his death in 1598, Hideyoshi's former vassals broke into two opposing camps. In 1600, they fought a great battle from which Tokugawa Ieyasu emerged victorious. Ieyasu established his headquarters in Edo (modern Tokyo), in the center of his military holdings in eastern Japan (see Map 19–2). He took the title of shōgun in 1603 and called his government the bakufu. Ieyasu then used his military power to reorganize Japan.

Ieyasu's first move was to confiscate the lands of his defeated enemies and use them to reward his vassals and allies. During the first quarter of the 17th century, the bakufu confiscated the domains of 150 daimyo and transferred 229 daimyo from one domain to another. The transfers severed long-standing ties between daimyo and their disarmed former village retainers. When a daimyo was transferred to a new fief, he took his samurai retainers with him. The rearrangement created a defensive system with the staunchest Tokugawa supporters nearest to the center of power.

The Tokugawa also established other controls. Legal codes regulated the imperial court, the temples and shrines, and the daimyo. Military houses were enjoined to use men of ability and to practice frugality. Only with bakufu consent could daimyo marry or repair their castles.

MAP EXPLORATION

Interactive map: To explore this map further, go to **http://www.prenhall.com/craig/map19.2**

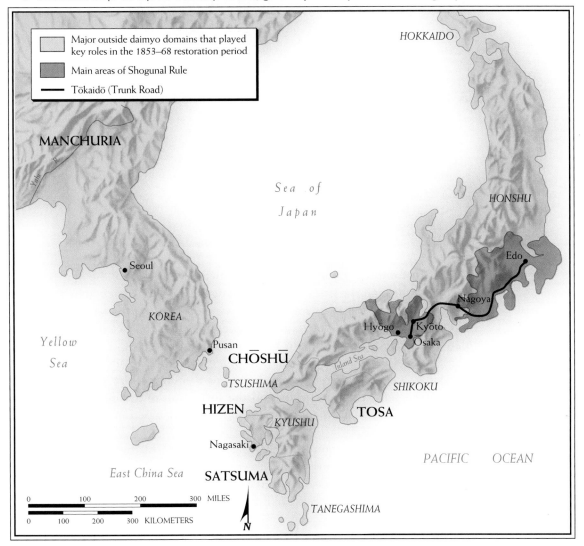

MAP 19–2
Tokugawa Japan and the Korean Peninsula.   The area between Edo and Osaka in central Honshu was both the political base of the Tokugawa bakufu and its rice basket. The domains that would overthrow the Tokugawa bakufu in the late 19th century were mostly in outlying areas of southwestern Japan.

WHAT CONTROLS did the Tokugawa impose to restrain the daimyo?

The Tokugawa also established a hostage system that required the wives and children of daimyo to reside permanently in Edo and the daimyo themselves to spend every second year in Edo. This transformed feudal lords into courtiers.

Another key control was the national policy of seclusion. Seclusion was no barrier to cultural imports from China and Korea. But except for small Chinese and Dutch trading contingents at Nagasaki, no foreigners were permitted to enter Japan, and on pain of death no Japanese were allowed to go abroad. Nor could oceangoing ships be built. This policy was strictly enforced until 1854. Seclusion enclosed the system of Tokugawa rule. Cut off from outside political contacts, for the Japanese, their homeland became the world.

The Commercial District of Osaka, the "kitchen" of Tokugawa Japan. Warehouses bear the crests of their merchant houses. Ships (upper right) loaded with rice, cotton goods, *sake*, and other goods are about to depart for Edo (Tokyo). Their captains vied with one another to arrive first and get the best price.

Courtesy Albert Craig.

QUICK REVIEW

The Japanese Economy
- Agricultural production doubled between 1600 and 1700
- Peace sustained economic growth
- Economic growth and national integration led to a rich and diverse urban society

Kabuki Realistic form of Japanese theater similar to English Elizabethan drama.

Nō play Highly stylized form of Japanese drama in which the chorus provides the narrative line as in classical Greek plays.

The 17th-Century Economy The political dynamism of the period from Hideyoshi through the first century of Tokugawa rule was matched by economic growth. Resources no longer needed for war were allocated to land reclamation and agriculture. This doubled food production, which led to a doubling of population from about 12 million in 1600 to 24 million in 1700.

Peace also sustained growth in commerce. Medieval guilds were abolished and Japan's central markets were freed from monopolistic restrictions. The result was a burgeoning of trade and the formation of a national market network. As this network expanded, economic functions became more differentiated and efficient.

Economic growth and the national integration of the economy led to a richness and diversity in urban life. Townsmen governed their districts. Samurai city managers watched over the city as a whole. Official services were provided by schools, police, and firefighters. But there were also servants, cooks, messengers, restaurant owners, priests, doctors, teachers, sword sharpeners, book lenders, instructors in the martial arts, prostitutes, and bathhouse attendants. In the world of popular arts, there were woodblock printers and artists, book publishers, puppeteers, acrobatic troupes, storytellers, and **Kabuki** and **Nō** actors. Merchant establishments included money changers, pawnbrokers, peddlers, small shops, single-price retail establishments like the House of Mitsui, and great wholesale merchants.

18TH AND EARLY 19TH CENTURIES

By the late 17th century, the political engineering of the Tokugawa state was complete. After that, few important changes were made in governing institutions. In the economy, too, dynamic growth gave way to slower growth within a high-level equilibrium. Yet changes of a different kind were under way.

The Forty-Seven Rōnin The 18th century began with a famous drama. In 1701, a daimyo at Edo Castle drew his sword and wounded an official who had insulted him. It was a capital crime to unsheath a sword within the castle, and the daimyo was ordered to commit *harakiri* (that is, to disembowel himself), which he promptly did. This made his retainers *rōnin*, masterless samurai. Almost two years later, they avenged their master by beheading the official whose insult had cost them their daimyo. All 47 of them then obeyed an order to kill themselves. They were widely acclaimed for the purity of their sense of duty and their loyalty to their lord, but Tokugawa society held law to be the only basis of social order. The law forbade personal vendettas, and the law could not be trumped by ethical considerations.

Cycles of Reform   Most political history of late Tokugawa Japan is written in terms of alternating cycles of laxity and reform. Even during the mid-17th century, the expenses of the bakufu and daimyo states were often greater than their income. In part, the reason was structural. Taxes were based on agriculture in an economy that was becoming commercial. It was simple mathematics. After the samurai were paid their stipends, not enough was left for the expenses of domain government and the costs of the Edo establishments. In part, it was the toll of extraordinary costs, such as a bakufu levy, the wedding of a daimyo's daughter, or the rebuilding of a castle after a fire. And finally, it was a taste for luxury among daimyo and retainers of rank.

Over the years a familiar pattern emerged. To make ends meet, domains would borrow from merchants. Then, as finances became even more difficult, a reformist clique of officials would return the domain to a more frugal and austere way of life. But since no one likes to practice frugality forever, a new round of spending would begin. The bakufu carried out three great reforms:

1716–1733	Tokugawa Yoshimune	17 years
1787–1793	Matsudaira Sadanobu	6 years
1841–1843	Mizuno Tadakuni	2 years

The first two reforms were long and successful; the third was not. Its failure set the stage for the ineffective response of the bakufu to the West in the mid-19th century.

Bureaucratization   The balance between centralization and decentralization lasted until the end of the Tokugawa era. Not a single domain ever tried to overthrow the bakufu hegemony, nor did the bakufu ever try to extend its control

Bridal Procession. The bridal procession of Yohime, the 21st daughter of the 11th Tokugawa shōgun, approaches the Edo mansion of the Kaga daimyo. The red gate (upper right), built in 1827 for this occasion, is today an entrance to the main campus of Tokyo University. The 11th shōgun had 28 sons and 27 daughters by his more than 40 concubines. Of his children, 13 sons and 12 daughters survived to maturity. This woodblock print by Kunisada is a "national treasure."
Courtesy Albert Craig.

over the domains. But bureaucracy grew steadily both within the bakufu and the domains. By 1850, all but the largest samurai fiefs were administered by district officials who collected the domain taxes and forwarded their income to the samurai. Along with the growth in bureaucracy came a proliferation of administrative codes and paperwork: records of births, adoptions, name changes, samurai ranks, fief registers, stipend registers, land and tax registers, court proceedings, and so on.

Of course, there were limits to bureaucratization. Only samurai could aspire to official posts, and decision-making posts were limited to upper-ranking samurai. But in periods of financial crises a demand arose for men of ability, and middle- or lower-middle-ranking samurai became staff assistants to bureaucrats of rank.

The Later Tokugawa Economy   By 1700, the economy approached the limit of expansion within the available technology. The population reached 26 million early in the 18th century and remained at that level into the mid-19th century, a period during which the population of China more than doubled.

After 1700, taxes were stabilized and land surveys were few. Evidence suggests little increase in grain production and only slow growth in agricultural byproducts. Some families made conscious efforts to limit their size to raise their standard of living. Contraception and abortion were commonplace, and infanticide was practiced in hard times. But periodic disease, shortages of food, and late marriages among the poor were more important factors in limiting population growth.

Some farmers remained independent cultivators, but by the mid-19th century, about a quarter of all cultivated lands were worked by tenants. Most landlords had small holdings. Though they were often village leaders, they were not at all like the Chinese gentry. The misery of the lower stratum of rural society contributed to an increase in peasant uprisings during the late 18th and early 19th centuries. Authorities had no difficulty quelling them, and no uprising in Japan approached those that erupted in late Manchu China.

Commerce grew slowly during the late Tokugawa. In the early 18th century, it was again subjected to regulation by guilds. Merchants paid set fees in return for monopoly privileges in central marketplaces. Guilds were also reestablished in the domains, and some domains created domain-run monopolies on products such as wax, paper, indigo, or sugar. The problem facing domain leaders was how to share in the profits without injuring the competitive standing of domain exports. Most late Tokugawa commercial growth was in rural industries— *sake*, soy sauce, dyes, silks, or cotton. Some were organized and financed by city merchants. Others competed with city merchants, shipping directly to the end markets to circumvent monopoly controls. The expansion of labor in rural industries may explain why the population of late Tokugawa cities declined.

The largest question about the Tokugawa economy concerns its relation to Japan's rapid industrialization in the late 19th century. Some scholars have suggested that Japan had a "running start." Others have stressed Japan's backwardness in comparison with European developers. The question is unresolved.

Tokugawa Era (1600–1868)

1600	Tokugawa Ieyasu reunifies Japan
1615	"Laws of Military Houses" issued
1639	Seclusion policy adopted
1642	Edo hostage system in place
1644–1694	Bashō, poet
1653–1724	Chikamatsu Monzaemon, dramatist
1701	The 47 rōnin avenge their lord
1853, 1854	Commodore Matthew Perry visits Japan

TOKUGAWA CULTURE

Two hundred fifty years of peace and prosperity provided a base for an ever-more complex culture and a broader popular participation in cultural life. In the villages, Buddhism became more deeply rooted, and new folk religions proliferated By the early 19th century, most well-to-do farmers could read and write. The aristocratic culture of the ranking samurai houses also remained vigorous. Nō plays continued to be staged. The medieval tradition of black ink painting was continued by the Kanō school and other artists.

The Ashikaga tradition of restraint, simplicity, and naturalness in architecture was extended. The imperial villa in Katsura outside of Kyoto, which has roots in medieval architecture, still inspires Japanese architects. The gilded and colored screen paintings that had surged in popularity during Hideyoshi's rule developed further, culminating in the powerful works of Ogata Kōrin (1658–1716).

Zen Buddhism, having declined during the Warring States period, was revitalized by the monk Hakuin (1686–1769). One of the great cultural figures of the Tokugawa era, Hakuin was also a writer, painter, calligrapher, and sculptor.

Some scholars have described Tokugawa urban culture as having two divisions. One was the work of serious, high-minded samurai, who produced a vast body of Chinese-style paintings, poetry, and philosophical treatises. The other was the product of the townspeople: low brow, irreverent, secular, satirical, and often scatological. The samurai esteemed Song-style paintings of mountains and waterfalls, often adorned with quotations from the Confucian classics or Tang poetry. The townspeople collected prints of local beauties, actors, courtesans, and scenes from everyday life. Samurai moralists saw money as the root of evil; merchants saw it as their goal in life.

Literature and Drama   Is cultural creativity more likely during periods of economic growth and political change or during periods of stability? The greatest works of literature and philosophy of Tokugawa Japan were produced between 1650 and 1725, just as the initial political transformation was being completed. The economy was still growing and the society was not yet set in its ways.

One of the major literary figures and certainly the most entertaining was Ihara Saikaku (1642–1693), who is generally credited with having re-created the Japanese novel. Saikaku was the heir to an Osaka merchant house. He was raised to be its master, but after his wife died he let the head clerk manage the business and devoted himself to poetry, the theater, and the pleasure quarters. At the age of 40, he wrote and illustrated *The Life of an Amorous Man*, the story of a modern and bawdy Prince Genji who cuts a swath through bathhouse girls, shrine maidens, courtesans, and boy actors. The success of the work led to a sequel, *The Life of an Amorous Woman*, the tale of a woman undone by passion.

A second major figure of Osaka culture at the turn of the century was the dramatist Chikamatsu Monzaemon (1653–1724). Born a samurai, Chikamatsu wrote for both the Kabuki and the puppet theater. Kabuki had begun early in the 17th century as suggestive skits and erotic dances performed by actresses. In 1629, the bakufu forbade women to perform on the stage. By the 1660s, Kabuki had evolved into a more serious drama with male actors playing both male and female roles.

The three main types of Kabuki plays were dance pieces, which were influenced by the tradition of the Nō; domestic dramas; and historical pieces. Chikamatsu wrote all three. In contrast to Saikaku's protagonists, the men and

Kabuki Theater, 1790. The male actors provide the drama—even female roles are played by men. A reprint of a three-panel woodblock print by Utagawa Toyokuni (1769–1825) from the late 1790s.

Toyokuni Utagawa. Interior of a Theater. Nineteenth Century © Musee Grimet, Paris, France. Giraudon/Art Resource, N.Y.

women in Chikamatsu's dramas struggle to fulfill the duties and obligations of their stations in life. Only when their passions become uncontrollable do the plays end in tragedy. The emotional intensity of the ending is heightened by the restraint shown by the actors before they reach their breaking point.

It is interesting to compare Kabuki and Nō drama. Nō is like early Greek drama in that the chorus provides the narrative line. In Nō, the stylization of action is extreme. In Kabuki, as in Elizabethan drama, the actors declaim their lines with the dramatic realism demanded by the commoner theatergoers of 17th-century Japan.

In the early 18th century, Kabuki was exceeded in popularity by the puppet theater (Bunraku). Many of Chikamatsu's plays were written for this genre. In the late 18th century, the puppet theater, in turn, declined, and Kabuki again blossomed as Japan's premier form of drama.

Confucian Thought The most important change in Tokugawa intellectual life was that the ruling elite abandoned the religious worldview of Buddhism in favor of the more secular values of Confucianism, opening many avenues for further changes.

The great figures of Tokugawa Confucianism lived in the late 17th and early 18th centuries. They adapted Chinese Confucianism to fit Japanese society. One problem, for example, was that in Chinese Confucianism there was no place for a shōgun, whereas in the Japanese tradition of sun-line emperors, there was no room for the Mandate of Heaven. Most Tokugawa thinkers handled this discrepancy by saying that heaven gave the emperor its mandate and that the emperor then entrusted political authority to the shōgun. One philosopher suggested that the divine emperor acted for heaven and gave the mandate to the shōgun. Neither solution was very realistic, for, in fact, the emperor was as much a puppet as the dolls used in the Osaka theater.

Another problem was the difference between China's centralized bureaucratic government and Japan's "feudal" system of lord-vassal relationships. Samurai loyalty was clearly not that of a scholar-official to the Chinese emperor. Some Japanese Confucianists solved this problem by saying that it was China that had deviated from the feudal society of the Zhou sages, whereas in Japan, Tokugawa Ieyasu had recreated that society.

A third problem concerned the "central flowery kingdom" and the barbarians around it. No philosopher could bring himself to say that Japan was the real middle kingdom and China the barbarian, but some argued that centrality was relative, and still others suggested that China under barbarian Manchu rule had lost its claim to universality. These are just a few of a large range of issues that were debated relative to Japanese political organization, Shinto, and Japanese family practices. By the early 18th century, the difficulties had been addressed, and a revised Confucianism acceptable for use in Japan had come into being.

Japanese thought retained its intellectual vitality into the mid-19th century. Thinkers were stimulated in part by disputes among different schools of Confucianism and, perhaps, by Japan's lack of an examination system. The best energies of its samurai youth were not channeled into writing the conventional and sterile "eight-legged essay" that was required for the Chinese examination system. Official preferment—within the constraints of Japan's hereditary system—was more likely to be obtained by writing a proposal for domain reforms.

The intellectual vitality was also a result of a rapid expansion of schools, which began in the early 18th century. By the early 19th century, every domain had its own official school. Commoner schools, in which reading, writing, and the rudiments of Confucianism were taught, grew apace. In the first half of the 19th century, private academies also appeared throughout the country. By the mid-19th century, about 40 to 50 percent of the male population and 15 to 20 percent of the female population was literate—a far higher rate than in most of the world, and on a par with some late developers in Europe.

Other Developments in Thought   For Tokugawa scholars, how to deal with China was a vexing, emotional problem. They praised China as the teacher country and respected its creative tradition. They studied its history, philosophy, and literature. But they also sought to preserve a separate Japanese identity. Most scholars dealt with this problem by adapting Confucianism to fit Japan. But two schools, National Studies and Dutch Studies, criticized the Chinese influence on Japanese life and culture.

National Studies began as a philological examination of ancient Japanese texts. Sources of its inspiration were Shinto and the Neo-Confucian School of Ancient Learning. Just as the School of Ancient Learning had sought to discover the original, true meanings of the Chinese classics before they were contaminated by Song metaphysics, so the scholars in the National Studies tradition tried to find in the Japanese classics the original true character of Japan before it had been contaminated by Chinese ideas. They concluded that the early Japanese spirit was free, spontaneous, clean, lofty, and honest, in contrast to the Chinese spirit, which they characterized as rigid, cramped, and artificial. National Studies also reaffirmed Japan's imperial institution.

National Studies became influential during the late Tokugawa Era and influenced the Meiji Restoration. Its doctrines continued thereafter as one strain of Japanese ultranationalism.

A second development was **Dutch Studies**. After Christianity had been proscribed and the policy of seclusion adopted, all Western books were banned in Japan. Some knowledge of Dutch was maintained by the official interpreters who dealt with the Dutch at Nagasaki. The ban on Western books (except for those propagating Christianity) was ended in 1720 by the shōgun Tokugawa Yoshimune (r. 1716–1745).

During the 18th century, a school of "Dutch medicine" was established in Japan. Japanese pioneers recognized early that Western anatomy texts were superior to Chinese. The first Japanese dissection of a corpse occurred in 1754. By the mid-19th century, there were schools of Dutch Studies in the main cities of Japan, and instruction was available in some domains as well. Medicine was the primary occupation of those who studied Dutch. But some knowledge of Western astronomy, geography, botany, physics, chemistry, and arts also entered Japan.

Starting in the late 18th century, the Japanese began to be aware of the West, and especially of Russia, as a threat to Japan. In 1791, a concerned scholar wrote *A Discussion of the Military Problems of a Maritime Nation*, advocating strong navy and coastal defenses. During the early 19th century, such concerns mounted. A sudden expansion in Dutch Studies occurred after Commodore Matthew Perry's visits to Japan in 1853 and 1854. During the 1860s, Dutch Studies became Western Studies, as English, French, German, and Russian were added to the languages studied at the bakufu Institute for the Investigation of Barbarian Books. In sum, Dutch Studies laid a foundation on which the Japanese built quickly when the need arose for knowledge of the West.

National Studies Japanese intellectual tradition that emphasized native Japanese culture and institutions and rejected the influence of Chinese Confucianism.

HOW DID Chinese culture influence Korea and Vietnam?

KOREA AND VIETNAM

A feature of world history, as noted earlier, is the spread of heartland civilizations into their surrounding areas. In East Asia, the heartland civilization was China. The surrounding areas it transformed were Japan, Korea, and Vietnam. Like the Japanese, Koreans and Vietnamese devised writing systems using Chinese ideographs. They partially modeled their governments on those of China. They accepted Chinese Buddhism and Confucianism and with them Chinese conceptions of the universe, state, and human relationships. The Confucian definitions of the relations between ruler and minister, father and son, and husband and wife were emphasized in Korea and Vietnam as they were in China. But at the same time, Koreans and Vietnamese, who spoke non-Chinese tongues, saw themselves as separate peoples and gradually came to take pride in their independence. In Europe, Germany might be a parallel case: it became civilized by borrowing the heartland Greco-Christian culture of the Mediterranean area, but it kept its original tongue and elements from its earlier culture.

KOREA

A range of mountains along its northern rim divides the Korean peninsula from Manchuria, making it a distinct geographical unit. Mountains continue south through the eastern third of Korea, while in the west and south are coastal plains and broad river valleys. Two additional geographical factors affected Korean history: (1) the northwestern corner of Korea was only 300 miles from the northeastern corner of historical China—close enough for Korea to be vulnerable to invasions by its powerful neighbor but far enough away so that most of the time China found it easier to treat Korea as a tributary; and (2) the southern rim of Korea was just 100 miles from Japan.

EARLY HISTORY

During the first millennium B.C.E., agriculture, bronze, and iron were introduced to Korea, transforming its primitive society. But Koreans were still ruled by tribal chiefdoms in 108 B.C.E., when the Han Emperor Wudi sent an army into North Korea to menace the flank of the Hunnish (Xiongnu) Empire that had spread across the steppe to the north of China. Wudi built a Chinese city, which survived into the fourth century C.E., and established commanderies and prefectures to administer the land.

Between the fourth and seventh centuries, three archaic states emerged from earlier tribal confederations. Silla, one of the three, together with armies from Tang China, conquered the other two in the seventh century. Silla was recognized by China in 675 as an autonomous tribute state. The period of Silla rule may be likened to Nara Japan: Korea borrowed Chinese writing, established some government offices on the Chinese model, sent annual embassies to the Tang court, and took in Chinese Buddhism and Chinese arts and philosophies. Yet within the Silla government, birth mattered more than scholarship and rule by aristocrats continued, while in village Korea, the worship of nature deities was only lightly affected by the Buddhism that spread among the ruling elites.

Glazed Pot. Celadon glazes spread from China to Korea during the Koryo period (918–1392). Pots such as this late 12th- or early 13th-century ewer are prized by collectors around the world for their graceful contours and detail.

Melon-shaped Ewer, Stoneware. Koryo dynasty, ca. 12th century H. 9"Diam. 19 1/2". Korea. The Avery Brundage Collection/Asian Art Museum of San Francisco.

Silla underwent a normal end-of-dynasty decline, and in 918, a warlord general founded a new dynasty, the Koryo. The English word "Korea" is derived from this dynastic name. This was a creative period. Korean scholars advanced in their mastery of Chinese principles of government. New genres of poetry and literature appeared. Korean potters made celadon vases rivaling those of China. Printing using moveable metallic type was invented during the 13th century. But most important was the growth of Buddhism. Temples, monasteries, and nunneries were built throughout the land, and Buddhist arts flourished.

Despite cultural advances, the Koryo state was weak. Its economy was undeveloped: trade was by barter, and Chinese missions commented on the extravagance of officials in the capital and the squalor of commoners and slaves in Korea's villages. The dynasty was aristocratic, and as centuries passed, private estates and armies arose, and civil officials were replaced by military men. Frequent incursions from across Korea's northern border weakened the state. The cost of wars with the Mongols was particularly high. The Koryo court survived as long as it did by becoming in succession the tributary of the Song, Liao, Chin, and Mongol dynasties.

Korea	
108 B.C.E.– 4th century C.E.	Chinese rule in northern Korea
4th century C.E.–675	Three archaic states
675–918	Silla Era
918–1392	Koryo dynasty
1392–1910	Choson Era
1592, 1596	Japanese invasions of Korea
1627, 1637	Manchu invasions of Korea
1671	Famine

THE CHOSON ERA: LATE TRADITIONAL KOREA

In 1392, a Koryo general, Yi Songgye, founded a new dynasty. It lasted until 1910; its amazing longevity was directly related to the stability of Ming–Qing China.

After seizing power, Yi carried out an extensive land reform and strengthened his government by absorbing into his officialdom members of the great Koryo families. During the Yi, or Choson period, these elite families, known as *yangban*, monopolized education, official posts, and land. Beneath them were the commoners, the "good people," tax-paying free subjects of the king. Beneath the commoners and constituting perhaps one third of the population were government and private slaves. Korean scholars argue that they were not like slaves in other lands, since there were no slave auctions, and, following Confucian teachings, husbands were not separated from their wives. But Korean slaves were nonetheless property. They were often attached to land, they could be given as gifts, and their children were slaves to be used as their owners willed.

Early Choson culture showed many signs of vigor. Lyrical poetry and then prose reached new heights. The most important intellectual trend was the gradual movement of the yangban away from Buddhism and their acceptance of Neo-Confucianism.

But at mid-dynasty, invasions dealt a severe blow to the well-being of Choson society. Hideyoshi, having brought all of Japan under his control, decided to conquer China through Korea. His samurai armies devastated Korea in 1592 and 1596. The invasions ended with his death in 1598. On both occasions the Ming court sent troops to aid its tributary, but the Chinese armies devastated the land almost as badly as the Japanese. A third disaster occurred in 1627 and 1637 when Manchu troops invaded pro-Ming Korea. The result of these multiple incursions was a drop in taxable land to about a quarter of its late-16th-century level. Behind this statistic lay famine, death, and misery.

Had the late-16th-century Choson government been stronger, it might have recovered. But cliques of officials had begun to fight among themselves

yangban Elite Korean families of the Choson period.

over official positions. Many in the losing factions were executed or imprisoned. As the struggles became more fierce, the effectiveness of government declined. High officials in Seoul used their power to garner private agricultural estates and established local academies to prepare their own kinsmen for the official examinations.

From the mid-17th century on, Korea offers a mixed picture. Literacy rose and a new popular fiction of fables, romances, and novels appeared. Women writers became important for the first time. Among some yangban there was a philosophic reaction against what was perceived as the emptiness of Neo-Confucianism. Calling for "practical learning" to effect a renewal of Korean society, scholars criticized the Confucian classics and outlined plans for administrative reforms and the encouragement of commerce. Unfortunately, their recommendations were not adopted, and the society continued its decline. More Koreans died in the famine of 1671 than during Hideyoshi's invasions. Overtaxation, drought, floods, pestilence, and famine became commonplace. Robberies occurred in daytime Seoul, and bandits plagued the countryside. Disgruntled officials led peasants in revolts in 1811 and 1862. Because of the concentration of officials, wealth, and military power at Seoul and because of Manchu support for the ruling house, neither revolt toppled the dynasty, but the revolts left Korea unable to meet challenges it was soon to face.

VIETNAM

EARLY VIETNAM

Until the 15th century C.E., the Vietnamese inhabited only the northern portion of the modern country of Vietnam, the basin of the Red River (centering on Hanoi). Central Vietnam and the southeastern coast were ruled by the state of Champa. Most of the Mekong River delta in the south (centering on Saigon, or Ho Chi Minh City) was ruled by Cambodian empires (see Map 19–3).

The political history of the Vietnamese began in 208 B.C.E., when a renegade Han dynasty general formed the state of Nan Yueh. It ruled over southeastern China and the Red River basin from its capital, which was near present-day Canton. In Vietnamese, the Chinese ideograph "Yueh" is read "Viet." The name "Vietnam," literally "Viet to the south," is derived from the name of this early state. In 111 B.C.E., Han Wudi brought it under Chinese rule.

For more than a millennium after 111 B.C.E., Vietnam was ruled by China. The administrative center was a fort with a Chinese governor and Chinese troops. The governor ruled through the heads of powerful Vietnamese families. Then, in 39 C.E., the Truong sisters led a revolt against Chinese rule—the husband of one sister had been executed by the Chinese. Thereafter, more officials were sent from China and direct bureaucratic rule was instituted. Later, Vietnamese historians made the two sisters into national heroes.

During these early centuries, change was slow. Buddhism was introduced into Vietnam from China.

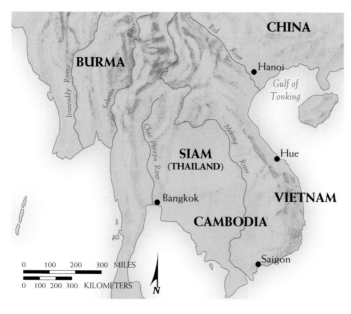

MAP 19–3
Vietnam and Neighboring Southeast Asia.

WHICH RELIGIONS intermingled in Southeast Asia?

Chinese officials and immigrants married Vietnamese women, which led to the formation of a Sino-Vietnamese political elite. The influence of Chinese higher culture was largely confined to this elite.

The pace of change increased during the Tang dynasty (618–907). Vietnam was still treated as a border region, but Chinese administration became stronger. Vietnam was divided into provinces, which the Chinese referred to as **Annam**, the "pacified south." This name was never forgotten. When the French came to Vietnam in the 19th century, they called its people the *Annamese*.

Japan and Korea reached out and took in Chinese learning during the Tang, and so in some ways did Vietnam. In all three societies, Buddhism entered, flourished in the capitals, and then percolated into local areas, where it absorbed earlier religious traditions. In all three, other aspects of China's higher culture affected mainly the elites, while an older way of life continued among villagers. But the differences were also significant. Japanese and Korean rulers wanted to imitate China's civilization and use it for their own ends. In Vietnam, the rulers were Chinese, and no such transformation occurred.

THE SECOND MILLENNIUM: POLITICS AND SOCIETY

Ten major revolts challenged Vietnam's Chinese rulers—not an unusual number for a Chinese border region with a non-Chinese population. The last revolt, in 939 when China was weak, established Vietnamese independence, and Vietnam never again became a part of China.

Several approaches have been taken to writing the history of Vietnam's second millennium. One divides it into dynastic periods:

Ly	1009–1225
Tran	1225–1400
Le	1428–1787
Nguyen	1802–1880s

As in China, dynasties began with strong military figures, who established courts, extended their control over the countryside, and collected taxes. Most founders of dynasties were members of the Sino-Vietnamese elite. Dynasties ended with the decentralization of power, the breakdown of taxation, and the rise of regional armies. But the idea of a "dynastic cycle" of slow administrative decline fits Vietnam less well than it does China. For one thing, even early in a dynasty, administrations were weaker than in China. Local magnates contested central control for longer periods. Also, each new Chinese dynasty invaded Vietnam to regain control over an area that had once been ruled by China. These invasions often reshaped dynasties. The Tran dynasty, for example, was extended for 20 more years by Ming forces. For still another, the dynastic name was sometimes kept even after its ruling house had lost power. During the 17th and 18th centuries, for example, Vietnam was divided into two states, one ruling from Hanoi and the other from Hue. In short, though the "dynasty" may be a convenient unit for dividing the second millennium into large blocks of time, it is less useful for analysis.

Another approach is to see Vietnam in relation to the Chinese state and Chinese civilization. Although Chinese invasions of Vietnam were unsuccessful, Vietnamese rulers found it easier to "manage" China than to defy it. Every Vietnamese dynasty became a "tributary" of China. Missions were sent to China bearing tribute. The head of the mission professed the Vietnamese ruler's submission to the Chinese emperor and performed the kowtow. In correspondence with

Annam Chinese term for Vietnam.

OVERVIEW THE RELIGIONS OF SOUTHEAST ASIA

The countries of Southeast Asia, the area between India and China, have been influenced by Indian, Chinese, Muslim, and, since the 16th century, Western culture and religion. Hinduism, Buddhism, Islam, and Christianity were all brought to the area by invaders, merchants, and missionaries. Their presence is reflected in the religious makeup of the countries of Southeast Asia in the 21st century. While most of these countries are predominately Buddhist, Muslim, or Christian, most of them also include many adherents of other religions.

Predominately Buddhist	Burma
	Thailand, but with a significant Muslim minority
	Cambodia
	Laos
	Vietnam, but with a large Christian, primarily Roman Catholic, minority
	Singapore, includes Muslim, Christian, and Hindu minorities
Predominately Muslim	Indonesia, but the island of Bali is Hindu, and there is a large Christian minority
	Malaysia, but with Hindu, Buddhist, and Christian minorities
	Brunei
Predominately Christian	Philippines, but with a large Muslim minority

the Chinese "emperor," the Vietnamese rulers styled themselves as "kings," a title indicating their subordinate status. But their submission was little more than formulaic. Within Vietnam, Vietnamese rulers styled themselves as "emperors." They claimed their mandate to rule came directly from heaven, equal to the mandate of China's ruler. They denied the universality of the Chinese imperium by referring to China not as the Middle Kingdom but as the Northern Court—their own government being the Southern Court. Yet over the centuries, the imprint of Chinese culture became more pronounced. One highpoint was the reign of Le Thanh Tong (1442–1497), one of the strongest rulers in Vietnamese history. Le used Chinese culture and institutions as an advanced technology to strengthen his government. He established schools, introduced Neo-Confucianism, institutionalized an examination system, and promulgated a legal code that remained in effect through the remainder of the Le dynasty.

A third approach to Vietnamese history is to see it as a steady "march to the south" continuing from the 15th through the 18th centuries. Until the 15th century, the Vietnamese inhabited only the northern portion of modern Vietnam, the Red River basin. Central and southeastern Vietnam was Champa, the kingdom of the Chams, a Malayan people who engaged in trade and piracy. The Chams converted to Islam and for centuries waged intermittent wars with the Vietnamese. In 1357, when Tran rule was weak, a Cham army pillaged Hanoi, but Le Thanh Tong destroyed Champa.

Le Thanh Tong's successors could not hold together the lands he conquered, but settlers from the crowded Red River delta began to drift into the south, and autonomous Vietnamese states arose in the area. By 1700, a southern Vietnamese state with a capital at Hue had conquered Saigon, and by 1757 it had occupied present-day southern Vietnam. This chain of events made south

Vietnam different from the north. It was less Confucian and, as a frontier society, less educated. It included large minority populations of Muslim Chams and Cambodians, who practiced a Southeast Asian form of Buddhism. Massive emigrations of Chinese into southeast Asia also began during these centuries. Today about 1 million Chinese live in south Vietnam alone and play key roles in its economy. Such ethnic and religious diversity made the south far more difficult to govern than the more homogeneous north.

During the last half of the 18th century, Vietnam was wracked by wars. In 1802, one warlord established Vietnam's last dynasty, the Nguyen. Its capital was at Hue. In coming to power, the new emperor had been aided by French advisers, several of whom were rewarded with high posts. The Nguyen dynasty, nonetheless, became more Chinese than any previous dynasty. It adopted the law codes of Manchu China and established institutions such as the Six Boards, Hanlin Academy, Censorate, and a hierarchy of civil and military officials recruited by examinations. These initiatives were intended to placate Confucian scholars in the north, to strengthen the court, and to weaken the military figures who had helped the dynasty's rise. From the time of its second emperor, the Nguyen dynasty also became anti-French and anti-Christian.

During the first half of the 19th century, Vietnam was probably governed better than any other Southeast Asian state, but it had weaknesses. There were tensions between the north, which was overpopulated, well schooled, and furnished most of the official class, and the south, which was ethnically diverse, educationally backward, and poorly represented in government. Trade and artisanal industries were less developed than in China and Japan, only small amounts of specie circulated, and periodic markets were more common than permanent market towns. The government rested on a society characterized largely by self-sufficient villages. In sum, Vietnam entered the second half of the 19th century even less prepared than China or Japan for the challenges posed by the West.

SOUTHEAST ASIA

The historical civilizations of Southeast Asia were shaped by four movements. One was the drift of peoples and languages from north to south. Ranges of mountains rising in Tibet and southern China divide Southeast Asia into river valleys. The Mon and Burmese peoples had moved from the southeast slopes of the Tibetan plateau into the Upper Irrawaddy by 500 B.C.E. and continued south, founding the kingdom of Pagan in 847 C.E. Thai tribes moved south from China down the valley of the Chao Phraya River later, founding the kingdoms of Sukhothai (1238–1419) and Ayutthaya (1350–1767). Even today, Thai-speaking tribes are found in south China. The Vietnamese, too, arose in the north and moved into present-day central and south Vietnam only in recent historical times.

A second movement was the Indianization of Southeast Asia. Between the 1st and 15th centuries, Indian traders and missionaries established outposts throughout southeast Asia. As Hinduism and Buddhism spread through the region, Indian-type states with god-kings were established, and Indian scripts, legal codes, literature, drama, art, and music were adopted. Today, Burma, Thailand, and Cambodia retain an Indian-type of Buddhism.

A third movement was of Arab and Indian traders who sailed across the Indian Ocean to dominate trade with the Spice Islands (the Moluccas of present-day Indonesia) between the 13th and 15th centuries. They married into local ruling families and spread Islam. Local rulers who converted became sultans. Today Malaysia and Indonesia are predominantly Muslim.

The fourth movement was the Chinese **diaspora**, an emigration of Chinese to most parts of the world but especially to Southeastern Asia. It was in full tide by 1842. Initially, most Chinese were indentured laborers on plantations, but many moved to cities to become shopkeepers. China's mercantile ethos was stronger than that of the southern peoples. In most of Southeast Asia, urban economies were largely developed and controlled by Chinese. The greatest concentrations of Chinese, apart from Singapore, were in Malaysia, Indonesia, and Thailand.

diaspora Dispersion of an originally homogeneous people or culture. Among the many diasporas in world history, some of the most famous are the Jewish, the Chinese, the African, the Irish, and the Armenian.

IMAGE KEY

for pages 456–457

a. Long grain rice
b. Kitagawa Utamaro (1753–1806), "Mother Bathing Her Son"
c. Chinese carved lacquer box
d. Karaori kimono
e. Tai Chin, "Fisherman on an Autumn River" (1390–1460)
f. Woodblock print of the commercial district of Osaka
g. Stoneware ewer from the the Koryo dynasty in Korea
h. A pile of table salt
i. Manchu emporer Ch'ien Lung
j. "The Arrival of the Portuguese in Japan."

SUMMARY

China China's last two imperial dynasties were the Ming (1368–1644) and the Qing, or Manchus (1644–1911). Although China could not match the dynamism of the West during these years, its society became more integrated and its government more sophisticated. The population reached 410 million, cities grew, and commerce expanded. Chinese government depended on the Confucian bureaucracy and the gentry class. Under the Manchus, China expanded to the east and annexed Taiwan. There also was growing trade with the West, especially Britain, but it was conducted under highly restricted terms by Chinese officials.

Japan After more than a century of civil war among the warrior aristocracy (the Warring States Era, 1467–1600), the Tokugawa shōguns (1600–1868) restored order. Their government controlled the aristocracy and encouraged economic growth. Christianity, which had made many converts in Japan, was driven underground, and Japan was closed to the outside world except for a small Dutch presence at Nagasaki. Japanese drama, literature, and art flourished, as did commercial life.

Korea and Vietnam China considered both Korea and Vietnam to be tributary states, and both countries adopted Chinese Confucian culture and forms of government while preserving their political independence.

Southest Asia Southeast Asian civilizations have been heavily influenced by the movement of peoples, religions (especially Hinduism and Buddism), and the Chinese diaspora, which increased in the 19th century.

REVIEW QUESTIONS

1. Why did the economy grow in late traditional China?

2. Did Manchu rule resemble Mongol rule, or was it different? In what regards were Kangxi and Qianlong indistinguishable from Chinese emperors?

3. How did Ming–Qing foreign relations set the stage for China's 19th-century encounter with the West?

4. How did military technology in Japan change during the 15th and 16th centuries?

5. How was Chinese culture a "technology" used by Japan, Korea, and Vietnam for state building? Why were the results in each country so different?

KEY TERMS

Annam (p. 479)

daimyo (p. 466)

diaspora (p. 482)

gentry (p. 460)

Kabuki (p. 470)

Nō play (p. 470)

National Studies (p. 475)

Shaanxi banks (p. 458)

yangban (p. 477)

For additional study resources for this chapter, go to:
www.prenhall.com/craig/chapter19

20 State Building and Society in Early Modern Europe

CHAPTER HIGHLIGHTS

Models of European Political Development In the seventeenth and eighteenth centuries, five great powers emerged in Europe: France, Britain, Austria, Prussia, and Russia. Through their military strength, economic development, and in some cases colonial empires, they would affect virtually every other world civilization.

The Old Regime Eighteenth-century European society was traditional, hierarchical, corporate, and privileged–features that had characterized Europe and the world for centuries. All societies also confronted the scarce food supplies. For the eighteenth century, however, an improved food supply helped support a larger population. New agricultural techniques and the expanding population created pressures on social structures. Commerce also grew during the eighteenth century. Agriculture became more commercialized. Cities expanded.

Changes in European Society European society stood on the brink of a new era in which the social, economic, and political relationships of centuries would be destroyed. The commercial spirit and the values of the marketplace clashed with the traditions of peasants and guilds. By the early nineteenth century it led to a conception of human beings as individuals rather than as members of communities.

The expansion of the European population further stimulated change and challenge to tradition and hierarchy. New wealth meant that birth would cease to determine social relationships.

The eighteenth century furthermore witnessed the beginning of industrial production in response to the demands for consumer goods by the expanding population. Industrialization also affected Europe's relations with much of the non-European world. For the first time in history, major changes in one region of Europe left virtually no corner of the globe untouched.

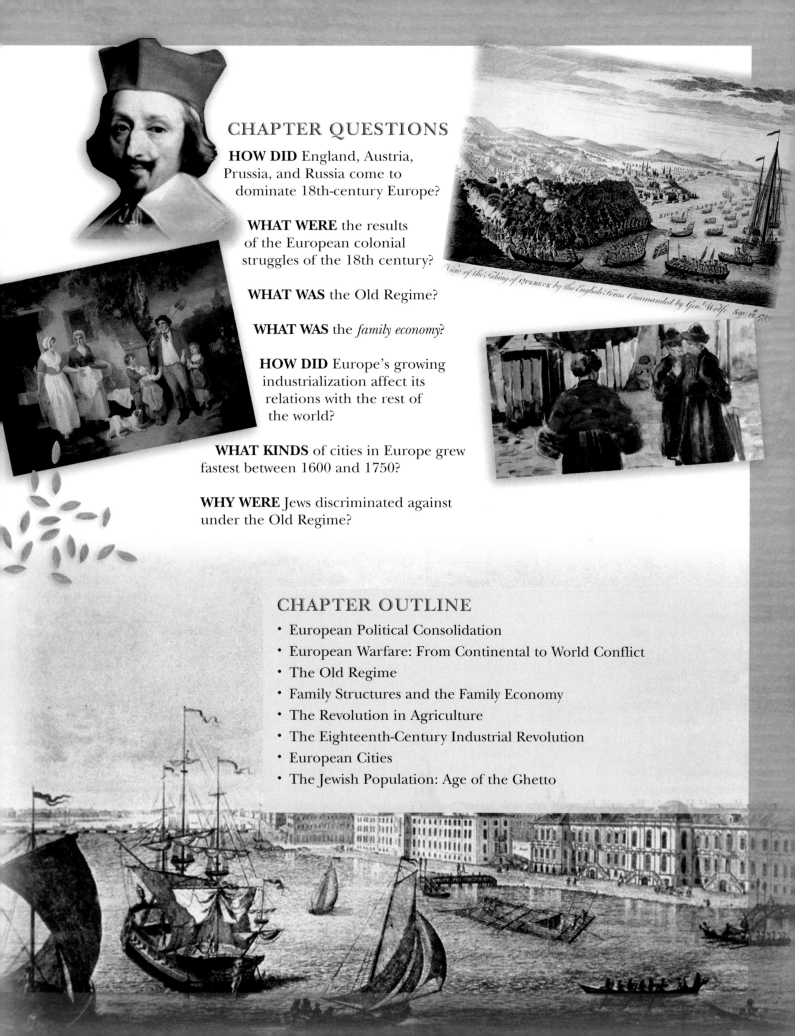

CHAPTER QUESTIONS

HOW DID England, Austria, Prussia, and Russia come to dominate 18th-century Europe?

WHAT WERE the results of the European colonial struggles of the 18th century?

WHAT WAS the Old Regime?

WHAT WAS the *family economy*?

HOW DID Europe's growing industrialization affect its relations with the rest of the world?

WHAT KINDS of cities in Europe grew fastest between 1600 and 1750?

WHY WERE Jews discriminated against under the Old Regime?

View of the taking of Quebeck by the English Forces Commanded by Genl. Wolfe Sepr. 13. 1759.

CHAPTER OUTLINE

- European Political Consolidation
- European Warfare: From Continental to World Conflict
- The Old Regime
- Family Structures and the Family Economy
- The Revolution in Agriculture
- The Eighteenth-Century Industrial Revolution
- European Cities
- The Jewish Population: Age of the Ghetto

From the early 17th century to the mid-20th century, Europe exercised unprecedented domination over other parts of the world. Two factors accounted for this situation. First, by the mid-18th century, five major states had become dominant in Europe: Great Britain, France, Austria, Prussia, and Russia. In the late 17th century these five states began to fight among themselves, first in Europe and then in their colonial empires. These conflicts had major consequences for the non-European world.

The second factor leading to Europe's dominance was a series of economic advances that laid the foundation for the social and economic transformation of the world. For the first time, Europeans developed a more or less stable food supply, and the population of Europe entered a major period of growth. New inventions, known collectively as the Industrial Revolution, gave Europe a productive capacity previously unknown in human history, and these advantages gave Europeans the power to dominate much of the world.

EUROPEAN POLITICAL CONSOLIDATION

TWO MODELS OF EUROPEAN POLITICAL DEVELOPMENT

In the second half of the 16th century, changes in European military organization, weapons, and tactics sharply increased the cost of warfare and forced monarchs to seek new revenues. Rulers like the king of France, who established secure financial bases without the support of nobles or assemblies, exercised absolute rule. The English monarch, however, by the end of the 17th century, could govern only with Parliament. These two governmental systems—**absolutism** in France and **parliamentary monarchy** in England—shaped Europe's political evolution.

TOWARD PARLIAMENTARY GOVERNMENT IN ENGLAND

When Elizabeth I died in 1603, the English crown passed to James VI of Scotland, the son of Mary Queen of Scots, who became James I of England, the first of the Stuart dynasty. The Stuart kings aspired to absolute power, and their pursuit of an income to support it threatened the economic well-being of the nobility and the landed and commercial elites represented in Parliament. These groups invoked traditional English liberties and effectively resisted the Stuarts. **Puritans** (Calvinists), who wanted a more radical reformation of the Anglican Church, also opposed the kings. Both James I (r. 1603–1625) and his son Charles I (r. 1625–1649), who had Catholic sympathies, confronted a combined political and religious opposition to their absolutist policies.

In 1642, the conflict between Charles I and Parliament erupted into civil war, which the parliamentary and Puritan forces won in 1645. In 1649, a "rump" Parliament (one from which the opposition had been removed) beheaded Charles I and abolished the monarchy, the House of Lords, and the established church. England became a Puritan republic led by Oliver Cromwell (1599–1658), the victorious general in the civil war. After Cromwell died in 1658, disillusionment with Puritan strictness and republican mismanagement prompted restoration of the Stuart monarchy under Charles II (r. 1660–1685). His Parliament was dominated by conservative members of the Church of England, and the policies it pursued severely restricted both Protestant Non-Conformists and Roman Catholics. Parliament's Test Act established an oath as a qualification for office that no Roman Catholic could take in good conscience.

James II (r. 1685–1688), the brother who succeeded Charles in 1685, was a Roman Catholic. He decreed toleration for both Roman Catholics and Protestant Non-Conformists and imprisoned seven Anglican bishops who refused to publicize his suspension of laws against Catholics. James's policy of toleration had as it goal the extension of royal authority over all English institutions.

Members of England's Parliament hoped that James would be succeeded by his eldest daughter, Mary (r. 1689–1694), a Protestant and the wife of William of Orange (1650–1702), stadtholder of the Netherlands. But on June 20, 1688, James II's Catholic second wife gave birth to a Catholic male heir to the throne. This prompted Parliament to invite William of Orange to invade England to preserve its "traditional liberties," that is, the Anglican Church and parliamentary government.

THE "GLORIOUS REVOLUTION"

William of Orange met no opposition when he landed an army in England in November 1688. James fled to France, and Parliament proclaimed William III and Mary II the new monarchs. This bloodless coup was celebrated as the **Glorious Revolution**, for the government it established limited the powers of the monarchy and guaranteed the civil liberties of the English privileged classes. Henceforth, England's monarchs would rule by the consent of Parliament, which convened every three years. Roman Catholics were declared ineligible to inherit the English throne. The Toleration Act of 1689 permitted all forms of Protestant worship but outlawed Roman Catholicism.

The Act of Settlement in 1701 ended a century of strife by bequeathing the English crown to Germany's Protestant House of Hanover if Anne (r. 1702–1714), the second daughter of James II and the heir to the childless William and Mary, died without issue. At Queen Anne's death in 1714, the Elector of Hanover became George I of England (r. 1714–1727), the third foreigner to occupy its throne in just more than a century.

During the first quarter of the 18th century, Britain enjoyed political stability and economic prosperity. Robert Walpole (1676–1745), George I's chief minister from 1721 to 1742, was adept at handling the House of Commons and exercising influence through control of government patronage. He maintained peace abroad and the status quo at home. The dominant economic interests were represented in Parliament, and their taxes funded a powerful army and navy that made Great Britain into a world power—with a commercial empire extending from New England to India.

The power of the British monarchs and their ministers were limited, and Parliament could not wholly ignore popular pressure. Many members of Parliament held independent views. Newspapers and public debate flourished. Free speech could be exercised, as could freedom of association. No standing army intimidated the populace. The English state showed how military power could coexist with political liberty, and Britain became the model for European progressives who opposed the absolutist regimes on the continent. The political ideas that emerged in the British Isles during the 17th century also took deep root in Britain's North American colonies.

Oliver Cromwell. His model army defeated the royalists in the English Civil War. After the execution of Charles I in 1649, Cromwell dominated the short-lived English republic, conquered Ireland and Scotland, and ruled as Lord Protector from 1653 until his death in 1658.

Stock Montage, Inc./Historical Pictures Collection.

Glorious Revolution Largely peaceful replacement of James II by William and Mary as English monarchs in 1688. It marked the beginning of constitutional monarchy in Britain.

18.2
The Ideal Absolute
State (1697): Jean Domat

RISE OF ABSOLUTE MONARCHY IN FRANCE: THE WORLD OF LOUIS XIV

The French monarchy took a different path. During the minority of Louis XIV (r. 1643–1715), who ascended the throne at age 5, Cardinal Mazarin (1602–1661), his regent, tried to strengthen royal control. The result was a series of widespread rebellions between 1649 and 1652 called the Fronde (after the slingshot used by street urchins).

YEARS OF PERSONAL RULE

After Mazarin's death in 1661, Louis XIV assumed personal control of the government. Louis concentrated unprecedented authority in the monarchy but, with the Fronde in mind, took care not to intrude excessively on local social and political institutions. Because he governed directly, rebels could not defend themselves from a charge of treason by claiming that they opposed only bad ministers and not the king.

Louis ruled through powerful councils, whose members he chose from families long in royal service or people just beginning to advance socially. Unlike the ancient noble families, they had no power bases in the provinces and depended solely on the king for their positions.

divine right of kings Theory that monarchs are appointed by and answerable only to God.

Louis XIV of France (r. 1643–1715). He was the dominant European monarch in the second half of the 17th century. The powerful centralized monarchy he created established the prototype for the mode of government later termed absolutism.

Bridgemann-Giraudon/Art Resource, N.Y.

Louis XIV was innovative in the use of the physical setting of his court to enhance his political power. The palace at Versailles, which was built between 1676 and 1708, was a temple to royalty. Its splendor proclaimed the majesty of the Sun King, as Louis was known. It housed thousands of the more important nobles, royal officials, and servants, and preoccupation with Versailles' elaborate court ceremonies kept nobles from the real business of government.

Louis owed his concept of royal authority to his devout tutor, the political theorist Bishop Jacques-Bénigne Bossuet (1627–1704). Bossuet defended what he called the "**divine right of kings**" by citing examples of Old Testament rulers divinely appointed by and answerable only to God. Medieval popes had insisted that only God could judge a pope, and Bossuet made the same claim for a king. As God's regents on Earth, kings could not be bound by nobles and parliaments, for as Louis XIV allegedly explained: "*L'état, c'est moi*" ("I am the state").

Louis insisted on religious conformity, and in October 1685 he revoked the Edict of Nantes (1598), which had protected France's Huguenots. Protestant churches and schools were closed, Protestant ministers exiled, nonconverting laity condemned as galley slaves, and Protestant children taken to be baptized by Catholic priests. More than a quarter million people fled and joined France's opponents in England, Germany, Holland, and the New World.

Louis used most of the wealth and authority he had amassed to lead France into a long series of wars (discussed later) that weakened the nation. Despite this, he established a model for strong

Versailles. As painted in 1668 by Pierre Patel the Elder (1605–1676), the central building is the hunting lodge built for Louis XIII earlier in the century. The wings that appear here were some of Louis XIV's first expansions.

Giraudon/Art Resource, N.Y.

centralized monarchy that other monarchs in central and eastern Europe copied. They saw Louis as more successful than the Stuarts of Great Britain, who could only rule through Parliament.

RUSSIA ENTERS THE EUROPEAN POLITICAL ARENA

The emergence of Russia as an active European power was a wholly new development in European politics. Previously, Russia had hardly been considered part of Europe, and prior to 1673 it maintained no permanent ambassadors in Western Europe. Hemmed in by Sweden on the Baltic and by the Ottoman Empire on the Black Sea, Russia had no warm-water ports. Its chief outlet for trade to the west was Archangel on the White Sea, which was ice-free for only part of the year.

BIRTH OF THE ROMANOV DYNASTY

The last half of the reign of Ivan IV (r. 1533–1584), or Ivan the Terrible, was a time of enormous political turmoil in Russia. An era called the Time of Troubles followed, and in 1613, an assembly of nobles tried to stabilize the situation by electing as tsar a 17-year-old boy, Michael Romanov (r. 1613–1645). He began the dynasty that ruled Russia until 1917, but his country remained weak and impoverished. The *boyars*, the old nobility, controlled its bureaucracy, and the *streltsy*, or guards of the Moscow garrison, constantly threatened mutiny.

PETER THE GREAT

In 1682, a 10-year-old boy named Peter (r. 1682–1725), the future Peter the Great, ascended the throne with the help of the streltsy, who expected to exploit

QUICK REVIEW

Versailles

- Palace of Versailles: Central element in the image of the French monarchy
- Nobles who wanted Louis's favor congregated at Versailles
- Life at Versailles governed by elaborate etiquette

boyars Russian nobility.

streltsy Professional troops who made up the Moscow garrison. They were suppressed by Peter the Great.

OVERVIEW GREAT POWERS AND DECLINING POWERS IN EUROPE

In the 17th and 18th centuries, five European states—Britain, France, Austria, Prussia, and Russia—became great European powers and remained so until and, in every case except Austria, even after the end of World War I in 1918. At the same time, four other states that had been major European powers declined permanently into secondary status. The table below lists the main strengths of the rising powers and the main sources of weakness of the declining states.

Five Great Powers

State	Government	Strengths
Britain	Constitutional Monarchy	Commercial and financial resources; navy; colonial Empire; overseas trade; intellectual liberty; growing industry; religious toleration
France	Absolute Monarchy	Army; large population; cultural preeminence; colonial empire; intellectual vibrancy
Austria	Absolute Monarchy	Imperial prestige; dynastic loyalty: army
Prussia	Absolute Monarchy	Army; efficient bureaucracy
Russia	Absolute Monarchy	Army; large population; extensive natural resources; imperial control over church and state

Four Declining Powers

State	Government	Weaknesses
Spain	Absolute Monarchy	Stagnant economy; inefficient government; weak military; enforced religious and intellectual conformity
Ottoman Empire	Absolute Monarchy	Backward economy; unstable government; resistance to change; outmoded military
Sweden	Constitutional Monarchy	Small population; weak economy
Netherlands	Republic	Divided government; small population; declining economy

him. Like Louis XIV, the turmoil of his youth convinced Peter that the power of the tsar had to be made supreme over the boyars and the streltsy and that the tsar needed a strong military.

The military resources of Europe's maritime powers fascinated Peter I, and in 1697, he toured Western Europe incognito (allowing him to avoid the ceremony that would have attended an official royal visit). He spent his happiest moments inspecting shipyards, docks, and shops that produced military hardware, and he returned to Moscow determined to copy the technology he had seen abroad. He also understood that his plans for making Russia into a great nation would require him to oppose the long-standing power and traditions of the Russian nobles.

Taming the Streltsy and Boyars In 1698, while Peter was abroad, the streltsy rebelled. On his return, Peter brutally suppressed their revolt. Approximately 1,000 of them were put to death and their corpses publicly displayed to discourage future disloyalty. Peter then built a new military that would serve him and not itself. He employed ruthless methods of conscription and over the course of his reign drafted about 300,000 men. He adopted policies for the officer corps and general military discipline patterned on those of West European armies.

Peter sustained a campaign against the boyars and their antiquated customs. He personally shaved their long beards and sheared off the hand-covering sleeves of their shirts and coats. These traditional emblems of their rank had made them the butt of jokes at the European courts. Peter skillfully played one group against another, as he set about rebuilding Russia's government and military after the pattern of the more powerful European states.

Developing a Navy   In the mid-1690s, Peter built a navy to compete in the Black Sea with the Ottoman Empire, and in 1695, he began a war with the Ottomans. He also constructed a Baltic fleet to fight the Great Northern War with Sweden (1700–1721). In 1721, the Peace of Nystad confirmed Russia's conquest of Estonia, Livonia, and part of Finland. Peter had acquired the ice-free ports that were to give Russia influence in European affairs.

Founding St. Petersburg   In 1703, Peter founded a new capital, the city of St. Petersburg, at a site on the Gulf of Finland. He compelled the boyars to construct townhouses there and joined the European monarchs who copied Louis XIV by constructing smaller versions of Versailles. However, the founding of St. Petersburg was more than the establishment of a central imperial court. It oriented Russia to the West and signaled Peter's determination to hold his position on the Baltic coast.

The Case of Peter's Son Aleksei and Reforms of Peter the Great's Final Years   Other reforms arose from Peter's family difficulties. Peter's son Aleksei had never demonstrated much intelligence or ambition, yet Peter distrusted him. Late in 1717, Peter suspected that Aleksei had become the focal point for a seditious plot, and he undertook an investigation. He personally interrogated Aleksei, who was eventually condemned to death and died under mysterious circumstances on June 26, 1718.

The interrogations surrounding Aleksei had revealed more opposition to Peter at court than he had suspected. He decided that force alone would not eliminate all his opponents, so he implemented radical administrative reforms designed to bring the nobility and the Russian Orthodox Church more closely under the authority of persons loyal to the tsar.

Administrative Colleges   In December 1717, Peter reorganized domestic administration, using the example of Swedish institutions called *colleges*—bureaus operating according to written instructions rather than departments headed by a single minister. He established eight colleges to handle such things as the collection of taxes, foreign relations, war, and economic affairs. Each college was given a foreign adviser, and by making careful appointments Peter balanced influence within these colleges between nobles and people personally loyal to himself.

England

1603	James VI of Scotland becomes James I of England
1625	Charles I becomes king of England
1629	Charles I dissolves Parliament and embarks on 11 years of personal rule
1640	April–May, Short Parliament; November, Long Parliament convenes
1642	Outbreak of the Civil War
1649	Charles I executed
1649–1660	Various attempts at a Puritan Commonwealth
1660	Charles II restored to the English throne
1670	Secret Treaty of Dover between France and England
1672	Parliament passes the Test Act
1685	James II becomes king of England
1688	Glorious Revolution
1689	William III and Mary II come to the throne of England
1701	Act of Settlement provides for Hanoverian Succession
1702–1714	Reign of Queen Anne, the last of the Stuarts
1714	George I of Hanover becomes king of England
1721–1742	Ascendancy of Sir Robert Walpole

Rise of Russian Power

1533–1584	Reign of Ivan the Terrible
1584–1613	Time of Troubles
1613	Michael Romanov becomes tsar
1682	Peter the Great becomes tsar as a boy
1689	Peter assumes personal rule
1697	European tour of Peter the Great
1698	Peter suppresses the streltsy
1700	The Great Northern War begins between Russia and Sweden; Russia defeated at Narva by Charles XII
1703	St. Petersburg founded
1709	Russia defeats Sweden at Poltava
1718	Death of Aleksei, son of Peter the Great
1721	Peace of Nystad ends the Great Northern War
1721	Peter establishes control over the Russian church
1722	The Table of Ranks
1725	Peter dies, leaving an uncertain succession

Table of Ranks Official hierarchy established by Peter the Great in imperial Russia that equated a person's social position and privileges with his rank in the state bureaucracy or army.

Achieving Secular Control of the Church Peter also curtailed the independence of the Russian Orthodox Church, some of whose clergy sympathized with the tsar's son. In 1721, Peter abolished the post of *patriarch* and submitted the church to a government department called the *Holy Synod*. It consisted of several bishops headed by a layman, the *procurator general*. It made sure that the church supported the tsar's secular agenda.

Table of Ranks In 1722, Peter drew the nobles into state service by means of a **Table of Ranks**. It used rank in the bureaucracy or military to determine a person's social position and privileges, not descent from the old landed families, who generally resisted his reforms. Peter made the social standing of individual boyars a function of their willingness to serve his new centralized government.

Peter took many decisive actions, but he never settled on a successor. When Peter died in 1725, he left no obvious heir to the throne. For about 30 years, soldiers and nobles decided who ruled Russia. Peter had laid the foundations of a modern Russia, but not a stable state.

THE HABSBURG EMPIRE AND THE PRAGMATIC SANCTION

In 1648, the Habsburg family established a permanent hold on the title of Holy Roman Emperor, but their power depended on eliciting cooperation from scores of political entities of various kinds. While establishing their authority over the German states, the Habsburgs also consolidated their power within their hereditary possessions outside the Holy Roman Empire: the kingdom of Bohemia (in modern Czechoslovakia), the duchies of Moravia

St. Petersburg. Peter the Great built St. Petersburg on the Gulf of Finland to provide Russia with better contact with Western Europe. He moved Russia's capital there from Moscow in 1703. This is an 18th-century view of the city.

The Granger Collection.

and Silesia, Hungary, Croatia, and Transylvania. In each of their territories, the Habsburgs needed help from local nobles, and they often had to bargain with nobles in one part of Europe to maintain their position in another.

Despite these internal weaknesses, Leopold I (r. 1658–1705) blocked the advances of the Turks into central Europe and thwarted aggression by Louis XIV. The Ottomans recognized his sovereignty over Hungary in 1699 and extended his territorial holdings over much of the Balkan Peninsula and western Romania.

In the early 18th century the Habsburg emperor Charles VI (r. 1711–1740) had no male heir, and Charles feared that after he died the Austrian Habsburg lands might fall prey to the surrounding powers. Determined to prevent that disaster, he devoted most of his reign to seeking the approval of his family, the estates of his realms, and the major foreign powers for a document called the ***Pragmatic Sanction***. This provided the legal basis for a single line of inheritance within the Habsburg dynasty through Charles VI's daughter Maria Theresa (1740–1780). When Charles VI died, he believed that he had secured legal recognition of the unity of the Habsburg Empire and the succession of his daughter. However, his failure to provide his daughter with a strong army or a full treasury left her lands vulnerable to foreign aggression. Less than two months after his death in December 1740, Frederick II of Prussia invaded the Habsburg province of Silesia, and Maria Theresa had to fight for her inheritance.

THE RISE OF PRUSSIA

Prussia expanded into a German power vacuum created by the Peace of Westphalia. It was built by the Hohenzollern family, rulers of Brandenburg since 1417. By inheritance, the Hohenzollerns acquired a series of territories, most of which were not contiguous with Brandenburg, but which, by the late 17th century, consituted a block of territory within the Holy Roman Empire second only to that of the Habsburgs. Beginning in the mid-17th century, Hohhenzollern rulers forged their geographically separated holdings into a powerful state and built an army that empowered them to rule without the approval of the local nobility.

There was, however, a political and social tradeoff between the Hohenzollerns and their nobles, the **Junkers**. In exchange for obedience to the Hohenzollerns, the Junkers received the right to total authority over the serfs on their estates. Furthermore, the heaviest taxes were imposed on the peasants and the urban classes. Junkers increasingly dominated the army officer corps, and all officials and army officers took an oath of loyalty to the Hohenzollern rulers. The army provided the state with a semblance of unity and made Prussia a desirable ally. In 1701, the Habsburg emperor repaid the Hohenzollerns for their help by granting them the title "King in Prussia."

Frederick William I (r. 1713–1740) of Prussia governed through a bureaucracy structured along military lines and mobilized his small realm to support the third or fourth largest army in Europe. Separate laws applied to soldiers and to civilians. Given that the officer corps was the highest social class, military service attracted the sons of Junkers. The army, the Junker nobility, and the monarchy fused into a single political entity. The military dominated Prussian government, society, and daily life as in no other state in Europe. Other nations had armies; the Prussian army had a nation.

Although Frederick William I built the best army in Europe, he avoided conflict. His army was a symbol of Prussian power and unity, not an instrument for foreign aggression. At his death in 1740, he passed the army to his son Frederick II (Frederick the Great, r. 1740–1786), but not the wisdom to refrain

Pragmatic Sanction Legal basis negotiated by Emperor Charles VI (r. 1711–1740) for the Habsburg succession through his daughter Maria Theresa (r. 1740–1780).

Junkers Noble landlords of Prussia.

from using it. Almost immediately, Frederick II voided the Pragmatic Sanction and invaded Silesia. This began an Austrian-Prussian competition for control of Germany that dominated central European affairs for more than a century.

EUROPEAN WARFARE: FROM CONTINENTAL TO WORLD CONFLICT

WHAT WERE the results of the European colonial struggles of the 18th century?

Whereas religious zeal had fueled the European wars of the Reformation Era, dynastic and commercial rivalry drove wars from the reign of the Louis XIV through the conclusion of the Seven Years' War in 1763. Through their conflicts with each other, the European powers developed the military weapons and naval prowess that they used against non-European peoples.

THE WARS OF LOUIS XIV

Thanks to France's consolidation under the power of its absolute king, Louis XIV could afford to raise and maintain a large and powerful army and entertain dreams of dominating Europe. In 1667, he led France into the first of four major wars designed to expand his territory, and he was soon regarded as a menace to the whole of Western Europe, Catholic and Protestant alike. In 1681, Louis's forces occupied the free city of Strasbourg, prompting defensive coalitions to form against him. One of these, the League of Augsburg, grew to include England, Spain, Sweden, the United Provinces, and the major German states, including the Habsburg emperor. Between 1689 and 1697, the League of Augsburg and France battled each other on European fronts in the Nine Years' War, while England and France also warred in North America. In 1697, the Peace of Ryswick secured Holland's borders and thwarted Louis's expansion into Germany.

18.3
The Sighs of Enslaved France (1690): Pierre Jurieu

On November 1, 1700, Charles II of Spain (r. 1665–1700) died and bequeathed his estate to Louis's grandson, Philip of Anjou, or Philip V of Spain (r. 1700–1746). This tipped the balance of power in Europe in France's favor, and England, Holland, and the Holy Roman Empire formed the Grand Alliance as a countermeasure. The War of the Spanish Succession (1701–1714) soon enveloped Western Europe. France finally made peace with England at Utrecht in July 1713 and with Holland and the emperor at Rastadt in March 1714. Philip V retained Spain, but England got Gibraltar, a base for action in the Mediterranean. The long war left France economically and politically exhausted (see Map 20–1).

France

1649–1652	The Fronde, a revolt of nobility and townspeople against the crown
1661	Louis XIV assumes personal rule
1667	Louis XIV invades Flanders
1672	France invades the United Provinces
1678–1679	Peace of Nijmwegen
1682	Louis establishes his court at Versailles
1685	Edict of Nantes revoked
1689–1697	Nine Years' War between France and the League of Augsburg
1697	Peace of Ryswick
1701–1714	War of the Spanish Succession
1713	Treaty of Utrecht between England and France
1714	Treaty of Rastadt between the emperor and France

THE 18TH-CENTURY COLONIAL ARENA

The Treaty of Utrecht in 1713 established boundaries for the colonial empires of the first half of the 18th century. Except for Portugal's Brazil, Spain claimed all of mainland South America, Mexico, Cuba, half of Hispaniola, Florida, and California. Britain held the North Atlantic seaboard, Nova Scotia, Newfoundland, Jamaica, and Barbados as well as a few trading stations on the Indian subcontinent. The Dutch controlled Surinam (Dutch Guiana) and various trading stations in Ceylon, Bengal, and Java (modern-day Indonesia). The French claimed the St. Lawrence River valley; the Ohio and Mississippi river valleys; Saint Domingue

MAP 20–1

Europe In 1714. The War of the Spanish Succession ended a year before the death of Louis XIV. The Bourbons had secured the Spanish throne, but Spain had forfeited its possessions in Flanders and Italy.

WHICH COUNTRIES benefitted the most from the war?

(Haiti), Guadeloupe, and Martinique in the West Indies; and trading stations in India and West Africa. French and English settlers in North America clashed throughout the 18th century.

The Treaty of Utrecht gave the British a 30-year *asiento*, or contract, to furnish slaves to the Spanish Empire and the right to send one ship each year to the trading fair at Portobello. The British cheated, and when the Spanish government under the Bourbon kings decided to enforce its monopoly over trade with its empire, the stage was set for conflict.

WAR OF JENKINS'S EAR

In 1731, when a Spanish coastal patrol boarded a British vessel to search for contraband, there was a fight, and an English captain, Robert Jenkins, had his ear cut off. He preserved it in a jar of brandy and in 1738 displayed it to the British Parliament as evidence of atrocities Spain was said to inflict on British merchants in the West Indies. Late in 1739, Great Britain went to war with Spain and, in junction with Prussia's aggression on the continent, began a series of worldwide European wars.

THE WAR OF THE AUSTRIAN SUCCESSION (1740–1748)

In December 1740, Frederick II of Prussia seized the Austrian province of Silesia. Maria Theresa of Austria preserved the Habsburg Empire by sacrificing some of the power of its crown. She ensured the loyalty of the Magyars of Hungary, the most important of her domains, by granting them considerable local autonomy. The link between her war with Prussia, the War of the Austrian Succession, and the British–Spanish commercial conflict was made by France. French aristocrats pushed their government to support Prussia against Austria, France's long-standing enemy. French aid to Prussia helped consolidate a new and powerful German state, a threat that brought Great Britain into the continental war against France and Prussia. In 1744, the conflict expanded beyond the continent when France decided to support Spain against Britain in the New World. The war ended in stalemate in 1748. By the Treaty of Aix-la-Chapelle, however, Prussia retained Silesia. There was a truce but not a permanent peace.

THE SEVEN YEARS' WAR (1756–1763)

In 1756, a dramatic shift of alliances occurred. Prussia and Great Britain signed the Convention of Westminster. The Prussians and the British hoped that their alliance would dissuade Russia and France from invading Germany. When Austria countered the loss of its British ally by turning to France, the European alliances of the previous century were reversed.

In August 1756, Frederick II's invaded Saxony to head off what he thought was a conspiracy against Prussia by Saxony, Austria, and France. This began the Seven Years' War. In the spring of 1757, France and Austria formed a new alliance targeted at Prussia, and Sweden, Russia, and the smaller German states joined them. Two factors in addition to Frederick's strong leadership saved Prussia: British financial aid, and the death in 1762 of Empress Elizabeth of Russia (r. 1741–1762). Her successor, Tsar Peter III, (d. 1762), fervently admired Frederick and immediately made peace with Prussia. The Treaty of Hubertusburg of 1763 ended the Seven Years' War with no changes in borders.

More impressive than Prussia's survival were Great Britain's victories in every theater of conflict. These were the work of William Pitt the Elder (1708–1778), who was named secretary of state in charge of the war in 1757. North America, however, was Pitt's real concern. He won control of all of North America east of the Mississippi for Great Britain in what American historians call the French and Indian War. Pitt's aspirations were global. He took Quebec from the French in 1759 and Montreal a year later. The French West Indies fell to the British fleet. British forces on the Indian subcontinent, under Robert Clive (1725–1774), defeated the French in 1757 and cleared the way for the conquest of all India by the British East India Company. By the Treaty of Paris of 1763, Britain received all of Canada, the Ohio River valley, and the eastern half of

European Conflicts of the Mid-18th Century

1739	Outbreak of War of Jenkins's Ear between England and Spain
1740	War of the Austrian Succession commences
1748	Treaty of Aix-la-Chapelle
1756	Convention of Westminster between England and Prussia
1756	Seven Years' War opens
1759	British forces capture Quebec
1763	Treaty of Hubertusburg
1763	Treaty of Paris

Parliament, the French *parlements*, their local estates, and provincial diets. Nobles also pressed the peasantry for higher rents or long-forgotten feudal dues as a way to shore up their position and reassert traditional privileges.

THE LAND AND ITS TILLERS

Land was the economic basis of life in the 18th century. Well over three-fourths of all Europeans lived on the land and never traveled more than a few miles from their birthplaces. Most were poor, and their lives were hard.

PEASANTS AND SERFS

Most people who worked the land were subject to domination by landowners. This was true to different degrees for free peasants, such as English tenants and most French cultivators, and for the serfs of Germany, Austria, and Russia, who were bound to individual plots of land and particular lords. Landlord power increased from west to east. Most French peasants owned some land, but nearly all peasants were subject to feudal dues and to forced labor on a lord's estate for a certain number of days each year.

In Prussia and Austria, despite attempts by the monarchies to improve the lot of serfs, landlords exercised almost complete control over them. Moreover, throughout continental Europe the burden of state taxation fell on the tillers of the soil. Through various legal privileges and the ability to demand concessions from their monarchs, the landlords escaped the payment of numerous taxes. The serf's condition was worst in Russia. Russian serfs were regarded merely as economic commodities. Their services were attached to an individual lord rather than to a particular plot of land. Their landlords could demand up to six days a week of labor from them, and like Prussian and Austrian landlords, they could punish their serfs. Although serfs had little recourse against their lords, custom, tradition, and law provided a few protections. For example, the marriages of serfs, unlike those of most slaves, were legally recognized. The landlord could not disband the family of a serf (see "Russian Serfs Lament Their Condition").

QUICK REVIEW

Servants under the Old Regime
- Worked in exchange for room, board, and wages
- Usually young and not socially inferior to employer
- Work as servants allowed young people to save toward independence

parlement French regional court dominated by hereditary nobility. The most important was the Parlement of Paris, which claimed the right to register royal decrees before they could become law.

Road Work. Eighteenth-century France had some of the best roads in the world, but they were often built with forced labor. French peasants were required to work part of each year on such projects. This system, called the *corvée*, was not abolished until the French Revolution in 1789.

Joseph Vernet, "Construction of a Road." Louvre, Paris, France/Bridgemann-Giraudon/ Art Resource, N.Y.

HISTORY'S VOICES

RUSSIAN SERFS LAMENT THEIR CONDITION

As with other illiterate groups in European history, it is difficult to recapture the voices of Russian serfs. The following verses from "The Slaves' Lament," a popular ballad from the era of the Pugachev Rebellion (1773–1775), indicate that serfs were aware of how the legislation of that era, which favored the landowning classes, affected their lives. Note how the verses suggest that the tsar may be more favorable to serfs than their landowners are. Throughout this ballad, serfs present themselves as slaves.

WHAT SPECIFIC complaints about landlords are expressed in these verses? What charges indicate that serfs may believe their situation has worsened? What hope do they seem to place in the tsar? What idealized picture of the world do the serfs believe they would themselves create?

O woe to us slaves living for the masters!
We do not know how to serve their ferocity!
Service is like a sharp scythe;
And kindness is like the morning dew.
* * * * *
Brothers, how annoying it is to us
And how shameful and insulting
That another who is not worthy to be equal with us
Has so many of us in his power.
* * * * *
And if we steal from the lord one half kopeck,
The law commands us to be killed like a louse.
And if the master steals ten thousand,
Nobody will judge who should be hanged.
The injustice of the Russian sheriffs has increased:
Whoever brings a present is right beyond argument.
They have stopped putting their trust in the Creator
for authority,
And have become accustomed to own us like cattle.
All nations rebuke us and wonder at our stupidity,
That such stupid people are born in Russia.
And indeed, stupidity was rooted in us long ago,

as each honour here has been given to vagrants.
The master can kill the servant like a gelding;
The denunciation by a slave cannot be believed.
Unjust judges have composed a decree
That we should be tyrannically whipped with a knout
for that.
* * * * *
Better that we should agree to serve the tsar.
Better to live in dark woods
Than to be before the eyes of these tyrants;
They look on us cruelly with their eyes
And eat us as iron eats rye. No one wants to serve
the tsar
But only to grind us down to the end.
And they try to collect unjust bribes,
And they are not frightened that people die cruelly.
* * * * *
Ah brothers, if we got our freedom,
We would not take the lands or the fields for
ourselves.
We would go into service as soldiers, brothers,
And would be friendly among ourselves,
Would destroy all injustice
And remove the root of evil lords.
* * * * *
They [the landlords] sell all the good rye to the
merchants,
And give us like pigs the bad.
The greedy lords eat meat at fast time,
And even when meat is allowed, the slaves
must cook meatless cabbage soup.
O brothers, it is our misfortune
always to have rye kasha.
The lords drink and make merry,
And do not allow the slaves even to burst out
laughing.

Source: Paul Dukes, trans. and ed., *Russia under Catherine the Great: Select Documents on Government and Society* (Oriental Research Partners, 1978), pp. 115–117. Reprinted by permission of Oriental Research Partners.

Peter the Great (r. 1682–1725) gave whole villages of serfs to favored nobles, and Catherine the Great (r. 1762–1796) confirmed the authority of the nobles over their serfs in exchange for the nobility's political cooperation. The result was considerable unrest: more than 50 peasant revolts between 1762 and 1769. They culminated between 1773 and 1774 in Pugachev's rebellion, the largest peasant uprising of the 18th century. When it was finally and brutally suppressed, any discussion of liberalizing the condition of Russia's serfs was postponed for a generation. Smaller peasant revolts or disturbances occurred in Bohemia in 1775, in Transylvania in 1784, in Moravia in 1786, and in Austria in 1789. The peasants and serfs normally directed their wrath against property rather than persons, and they sought to reassert traditional or customary rights against practices they perceived as innovations. In this respect, the peasant revolts were profoundly conservative.

FAMILY STRUCTURES AND THE FAMILY ECONOMY

*I*n preindustrial Europe, the household was the basic unit of production and consumption. In rural areas, small towns, and cities, the household mode of organization predominated: farms, artisans' workshops, and small merchants' shops. This created what is called the *family economy*.

THE FAMILY ECONOMY

Throughout Europe people saw themselves as family members working together in an interdependent rather than an independent or individualistic manner. Their goal was to sustain a family household by jointly producing or earning enough food to support its members. In the countryside, they usually farmed. In cities and towns, artisan crafts or paid employment produced their income. Almost everyone lived within a household because few could support themselves independently. Indeed, except for members of religious orders, people who were not part of a household were viewed as potentially criminal, disruptive, or a drain on the charity of others.

Every member of a family in the family economy had to work. Few peasant households in Western Europe had enough land to support themselves by farming alone. One or more of their family members had to work elsewhere and send wages home. It was not uncommon for a father to become a migrant worker and shift the burden of work on his own farm to his wife and younger children. Within the family economy, all of the goods and income produced benefitted the household, not individual family members. The need to survive poor harvests or economic slumps required everyone to work.

In the urban version of the family economy, the father was usually a chief craftsman who employed one or more servants. But he also expected his children to work in his shop. His eldest child was usually trained in the trade, and his wife

Emelyan Pugachev (1726–1775).
He led the largest peasant revolt in Russian history. In this contemporary propaganda picture, he is shown in chains. An inscription in Russian and German was printed below the picture decrying the evils of revolution and insurrection.

Bildarchiv Preussischer Kulturbesitz.

WHAT WAS the *family economy*?

family economy Basic structure of production and consumption in preindustrial Europe.

Women's Work. During the 18th century, with their employment opportunities tightly restricted, many unmarried women and widows served as governesses to children of the aristocracy and other wealthier groups in Europe.

Chardin, Jean-Baptiste-Simeon: "The Governess" (#6432), National Gallery of Canada, Ottawa.

QUICK REVIEW

Women in Preindustrial Society

- By age 7 girls contributed to household work
- Most girls left home between ages of 12 and 14
- A young woman's chief goal was to accumulate a dowry

---

might sell the wares he produced or pursue another trade. The wife of a merchant also often ran her husband's business, especially when he traveled to purchase new goods. When business was poor, family members looked for other employment to help the family unit survive.

WOMEN AND THE FAMILY ECONOMY

The family economy constrained the lives of women in preindustrial society. In Western Europe, a woman's life experience was largely a function of her ability to establish and maintain a household. Marriage was an economic necessity for her, for a woman outside a household was highly vulnerable. Unless she was an aristocrat or a member of a religious order, she could probably not support herself. Consequently, much of a woman's life was devoted first to serving her parents' household and then to establishing one of her own.

By the age of 7, a girl was expected to begin to do household work. On a farm, she might look after chickens or water animals or carry food to adult men and women working the land. In an urban artisan's household, she would do some form of light work, such as cleaning, carrying, sewing, or weaving. She remained in her parents' home until they found more remunerative work for her elsewhere. An artisan's daughter might not leave home until marriage because she was learning valuable skills from her parents. Girls who grew up on farms, however, soon became of little value to their families. These girls left home, usually by the age of 12 or 14. They were likely to migrate to a nearby town or city to become household servants, but would rarely travel more than 30 miles from their parents' home.

A young woman's chief goal was to accumulate a dowry, some capital she could contribute to setting up a household with her husband. Marriage within the family economy was a joint economic undertaking. It might take a young woman 10 years or more to accumulate a dowry. This meant that marriage was usually postponed until a woman's mid- to late 20s.

A married woman's work was in many ways a function of her husband's occupation, but at all stages in life women played active, often decisive roles in the family economy. Ensuring an adequate food supply for the household was always the dominant concern, and domestic duties, childbearing, and child rearing were subordinate to economic survival. Couples practiced birth control. Young children were placed with wet nurses so that their mothers could continue to work. Wet nursing was a way for some to contribute to their households. Industriousness was a woman's lot in life.

THE REVOLUTION IN AGRICULTURE

The main goal of peasant society was to ensure the stability of the local food supply. That supply was never certain and became more uncertain the farther east one traveled. A failed harvest meant not only hardship, but also death from either outright starvation or protracted debility. Poor harvests played havoc with prices, and even small increases in the cost of food could

---

WHY WAS land the economic basis of 18th-century life?

Farm Family. Painted by the English artist Francis Wheatley (1747–1801) near the close of the 18th century, this scene is part of a series illustrating a day in the life of an idealized country-side farm family. Note the artist's assumptions about the division of labor by gender. Men work in the fields, women work in the home or look after the needs of men and children. As other illustrations in this chapter show, many 18th-century women in fact worked outside the home, but considerable social pressure was developing at this time to restrict them to domestic roles. This painting and the others in the series are thus more prescriptive than descriptive, intended in part to persuade their viewers that women belonged in their separate family sphere. Many, perhaps most, families living in the country could not maintain the closeness that these paintings extol. To survive, many had to send members to work on other farms or even to other regions.

Francis Wheatley (RA) (1747–1801), "Evening," signed and dated 1799, oil on canvas, 17 1/2 × 21 1/2 in. (44.5 × 54.5 cm), Yale Center for British Art, Paul Mellon Collection, Bridgmann Art Library (B1977.14.118).

squeeze peasant or artisan families. If prices increased sharply, many of those families sought help from their local government or the church. Peasants felt helplessness before the whims of nature and the marketplace, and they resisted change on the assumption that traditional cultivation practices best ensured the food supply.

During the century, bread prices, spurred by demand from a growing population, slowly but steadily rose. Prices rose faster than urban wages and brought no advantage to the small peasant producer. The beneficiaries were landlords and the wealthier peasants who had surplus grain to sell. The increasing price of grain encouraged these people to innovate in farm production and begin an *agricultural revolution*.

New Crops and New Methods   The agricultural revolution began during the 16th and 17th centuries in the Low Countries, where Dutch landlords and farmers devised better ways to build dykes and to drain land so that they could farm more extensive areas. They experimented with new crops, such as clover and turnips, that would increase the supply of animal fodder and replenish the soil.

The Dutch innovations spread to England during the early 18th century and provided the increased food production needed to support the development of an industrial society. They ensured adequate food for cities and freed surplus agricultural labor for industrial work, but the landlords' new approach to farming undermined traditional peasant life. The objective of farming ceased to be the provision of a local food supply and became the pursuit of the largest possible profit.

Enclosure Replaces Open-Field Method   Many of the agricultural innovations were incompatible with Britain's traditional modes of working the land. Small cultivators in village communities usually tilled unconnected strips, and

agricultural revolution
Innovations in farm production that began in the eighteenth century and led to a scientific and mechanized agriculture.

French peasants. Throughout the age of splendor of Louis XIV, millions of French peasants endured lives of poverty and hardship.

Source to come

enclosures Consolidation or fencing in of common lands by British landlords to increase production and achieve greater commercial profits. It also involved the reclamation of waste land and the consolidation of strips into block fields.

their traditional two- or three-field systems of rotation left much land fallow and unproductive each year. Decisions about planting were made communally. The system discouraged innovation and aimed to produce a steady, but not a growing, supply of food.

In 1700, approximately half the arable land in Britain was farmed by the open-field method. By the second half of the century, the rising price of wheat encouraged landlords to consolidate or enclose their lands to increase production. **Enclosure** involved fencing common lands, reclaiming previously untilled waste, and transforming cultivated strips into block fields. These procedures disrupted the economic and social life of the countryside and incited riots. The larger landlords resorted to parliamentary acts for help in enclosing lands. Between 1761 and 1792, almost 500,000 acres were enclosed through parliamentary acts, as compared with 75,000 acres between 1727 and 1760. In 1801, a general enclosure act streamlined the process.

Enclosures expanded farming, promoted innovation, and increased food production on larger agricultural units. They also disrupted traditional communities and forced many people off the land, but they did not depopulate the countryside. As more land was reclaimed for farming and a demand for services subsidiary to farming grew, population began to increase.

POPULATION EXPANSION

Agricultural improvement was both a cause and a result of an immense growth in the population of Europe. Exact figures are lacking, but the best estimates suggest that in 1700 Europe's population was between 100 million and 120 million people. By 1800, the figure had risen to almost 190 million, and by 1850, to 260 million. Causes of this growth are unclear. The death rate declined, thanks to fewer wars and epidemics in the 18th century. But changes in the food supply itself may have been the chief reason for sustained population growth. One contributing factor was the introduction of widespread cultivation of a New World tuber, the potato. Enough potatoes could be raised on a single acre to feed one peasant's family for an entire year.

THE 18TH-CENTURY INDUSTRIAL REVOLUTION

AN EVENT IN WORLD HISTORY

In the second half of the18th century the European economy underwent an **Industrial Revolution**. This development, more than any other change, has distinguished the West from the rest of the world. Previously, economies had been relatively static. But since the late 18th century, Europe's ecomomy has expanded at a relatively steady rate. Depressions and recessions have been temporary, and even during economic downturns the Western economy has continued to grow.

At considerable social cost and dislocation, industrialism produced more goods and services than ever before in human history and overcame the ancient economy of scarcity. New means of production demanded new kinds of skills, new discipline in work, and a large labor force. The goods produced met consumer demand and created new demand. In the long run, the poverty in which most Europeans had always lived was overcome, and industrialization gave human beings more control over the forces of nature than they had ever known. But industrialism also upset the political and social structures of the Old Regime and prompted political and social reform. The economic elite of the emerging industrial society challenged the political dominance of the aristocracy. Traditional communities declined, people were displaced, and cities grew. This occurred wherever industrialization spread during the next two centuries.

Industrialization produced a flood of consumer products for Europeans to market to the world. It encouraged international trade in which Western nations supplied finished goods in exchange for raw materials. As a consequence, other areas of the globe became economically dependent on European and American demand. This uneven commerce allowed Europeans to accumulate the wealth that allowed them to dominate world markets for almost two centuries, and it helped the West develop the military forces that ensured political dominance as well.

Much of the history of the non-Western world from the middle of the 18th century to the present can be understood in terms of how the nonindustrialized nations

HOW DID Europe's growing industrialization affect its relations with the rest of the world?

Industrial Revolution
Mechanization of the European economy that began in Britain in the second half of the 18th century.

Major Inventions in the Textile-Manufacturing Revolution

1733	John Kay's flying shuttle
1765	James Hargreaves's spinning jenny (patent 1770)
1769	James Watt's steam engine patent
1769	Richard Arkwright's water frame patent
1787	Edmund Cartwright's power loom

initially reacted to the penetration of their world by Westerners made wealthy and powerful by industrialized economies. Africa and Latin America became generally dependent economies. Japan, in the middle of the 19th century, decided it had to imitate Europe. China succumbed to indirect rule by Europeans. Southeast Asia and the Middle East were drawn into the network of resource supply to the West. The process of industrialization that commenced in small factories in 18th-century Europe has changed the world more than any other single development in the last two centuries.

INDUSTRIAL LEADERSHIP OF GREAT BRITAIN

Great Britain was the home of the Industrial Revolution. Several factors contributed to the early start of industrialization in Britain. Britain was the single largest free-trade area in Europe, with good roads and waterways without tolls or other internal trade barriers. There were rich deposits of coal and iron ore. The political structure was stable, and property rights were secure. A sound system of banking and public credit created a good investment climate. Taxation was heavy, but fairly collected. In addition to domestic consumer demand, the British economy also benefitted from the demand for goods from the North

OVERVIEW — WHY THE INDUSTRIAL REVOLUTION BEGAN IN BRITAIN

Great Britain was the home of the Industrial Revolution, and until the middle of the 19th century, it maintained the industrial leadership of Europe. Several factors contributed to the early industrialization of Britain.

Natural Resources Infrastructure	1. Britain had extensive deposits of coal and iron ore. 2. Britain had an extensive network of roads and canals that facilitated the shipment of raw materials and goods.
Society	1. The predominance of London: London was the largest city in Europe and the social, commercial, financial, and political center of Britain. It was thus both an enormous market for consumer goods and created a demand for these goods in the rest of Britain, which sought to emulate London fashions. 2. The prevalence of newspapers: Newspapers thrived in Britain, and advertisements in them increased consumer demand for goods. 3. Wealth in Britain brought status: British society was relatively mobile. Wealthy merchants and entrepreneurs could rise socially, enter the aristocracy, and enjoy political influence.
Government, Financial Institutions, and Empire	1. The rule of law: Britain had a stable government that guaranteed property rights. 2. Britain was a free trade area. No internal tolls inhibited the shipment of goods and raw materials within Britain. 3. Britain had a sound system of banking and public credit that created a stable climate for investing in commerce and industry. 4. Taxes were collected efficiently and fairly. No class was exempt from paying taxes. 5. The colonial empire: British colonies were both a market for British goods and sources of raw materials for British manufacturers.

American colonies. Finally, British society was relatively open and allowed people who had money, or who could earn it, to rise socially.

New Methods of Textile Production   Eighteenth-century European society concentrated primarily on agriculture, but small-scale household manufacturing permeated the countryside. The same peasants who tilled the land in spring and summer often spun thread or wove textiles in winter. Under the **domestic** or *putting-out system*, agents of urban textile merchants distributed wool or other fibers to the homes of peasants, who spun it into thread. The agent then transported the thread to other peasants, who wove it into cloth, and the merchant sold the final product. Sometimes spinners or weavers owned their own equipment, but more often than not the merchant capitalist provided the machinery.

By mid-century production bottlenecks had developed within the domestic system. The demand for cotton textiles exceeded production as population increased in Great Britain and its colonies The most famous inventions of the Industrial Revolution were stimulated by consumer demand for cotton textiles. John Kay's invention of the flying shuttle in the 1730s gave weavers the technical capacity to produce enough fabric to satisfy demand, but spinners could not make enough thread for the weavers. Manufacturers offered prizes for the invention of a machine to correct this imbalance, and about 1765 James Hargreaves (d. 1778) invented the **spinning jenny**.

The spinning jenny was a piece of machinery for cottage use. The invention that moved cotton textile manufacture from the home to the factory was Richard Arkwright's (1732–1792) **water frame**, patented in 1769. When Arkwright lost his patent rights, other manufacturers used his invention, and numerous factories sprang up in the countryside near streams that provided water power. By 1815, cotton composed 40 percent of the value of British domestic exports, and by 1830 just over 50 percent.

The Steam Engine   The invention that more than any other enabled industrialization to spread from one industry to another was the steam engine. For the first time in history, human beings were able to tap an unlimited source of inanimate power. Unlike engines powered by water or wind, the steam engine, fueled by coal, provided a portable, steady source of power that could be applied to many industrial and transportation uses.

The first practical engine using steam power was invented by Thomas Newcomen (1663–1729) in the early 18th century. It was large, inefficient, and practically immovable, but English mine operators used it to pump water out of coal and tin mines. During the 1760s, James Watt (1736–1819) began to experiment with a model of a Newcomen machine at the University of Glasgow. In 1769, he patented an improved design, but it required precise metalwork. Watt's partner Matthew Boulton (1728–1809), a toy manufacturer, worked with John Wilkinson (1728–1808), a cannon manufacturer, to find ways to drill the precise

Blacksmith Shop. During the 18th century, most goods were produced in small workshops, such as this English blacksmith shop shown in a painting by Joseph Wright of Derby (1734–1797), or in the homes of artisans. Not until very late in the century, with the early stages of industrialization, did a few factories appear.

Joseph Wright of Derby, "The Blacksmith's Shop," signed and dated 1771, oil on canvas, 50 1/2 × 41 in. (128.3 × 104.0 cm). Yale Center for British Art, Paul Mellon Collection.

domestic or putting-out system of textile production Method of producing textiles in which agents furnished raw materials to households whose members spun them into thread and then wove cloth, which the agents sold as finished products.

spinning jenny Machine invented in England by James Hargreaves around 1765 to mass-produce thread.

water frame Water-powered device invented by Richard Arkwright to produce a more durable cotton fabric. It led to the shift in the production of cotton textiles from households to factories.

Dress Shop. Consumption of all forms of consumer goods increased greatly in the 18th century. This engraving illustrates a shop, probably in Paris. Here women, working apparently for a woman manager, are making dresses and hats to meet the demands of the fashion trade.

Bildarchiv Preussischer Kulturbesitz.

metal cylinders required by Watt's engines. In 1776, the Watt steam engine found its first commercial application pumping water from mines. Boulton persuaded a reluctant Watt to adapt the engines for use in running cotton mills, and by the early 19th century the steam engine had become the prime mover in every industry. Applied to ships and then to wagons on iron rails, it also revolutionized transportation.

Iron Production   The manufacture of high-quality iron was essential for industrial development. In the course of the 18th century, British ironmakers began to use coke (derived from coal) instead of charcoal to smelt ores, and the steam engine provided power for high temperature blast furnaces. Britain had large coal deposits, and the steam engine improved iron production while increasing demand for iron. In 1784, Henry Cort (1740–1800) introduced a new method for melting and stirring molten ore that yielded a purer iron. He also developed a rolling mill that shaped molten metal into bars, rails, or other forms. Previously, metal had to be pounded into shape. All of these innovations achieved a better, more versatile, and cheaper product, and by the early 19th century, annual British iron production amounted to more than a million tons.

EUROPEAN CITIES

PATTERNS OF PREINDUSTRIAL URBANIZATION

WHAT KINDS of cities in Europe grew fastest between 1600 and 1750?

Remarkable changes occurred in the pattern of city growth between 1500 and 1800. In 1500, there were approximately 156 cities within Europe (excluding Hungary and Russia) with a population greater than 10,000. Only Paris, Milan,

Venice, and Naples had more than 100,000 inhabitants. By 1800, approximately 363 cities had 10,000 or more inhabitants, and 17 of those had populations larger than 100,000. The percentage of the European population living in urban areas had risen from just over 5 percent to just over 9 percent. The urban concentration had also shifted from southern Mediterranean Europe to the north.

URBAN CLASSES

The Upper Classes   At the top of the urban social structure stood a generally small group of nobles, major merchants, bankers, financiers, clergy, and government officials. They usually constituted a self-appointed and self-electing oligarchy who governed the city through its corporation or city council. In a few cities on the continent, artisan guilds featured in urban governments, but most city councils were dominated by the local nobility and the commercial elite.

The Middle Class   Prosperous, but not wealthy, merchants, tradesmen, bankers, and professional people were a city's most dynamic citizens. They constituted its middle class, or *bourgeoisie*. The middle class had less wealth than most nobles, but more than urban artisans. Middle-class people lived in the cities and towns, and their sources of income had little or nothing to do with the land. They normally supported reform, change, and economic growth. They resented aristocratic privilege and social exclusiveness and wanted rational regulations for trade and commerce.

As the century passed, the bourgeoisie increasingly begrudged the aristocracy, and as the middle class grew in size and wealth and aristocratic control of political and ecclesiastical power tightened, tension increased. On the other hand, the middle class tended to fear the lower urban classes, a potentially violent element in society and a threat to property.

Artisans   The segment of the urban population that suffered most from the greed of the middle class and nobility consisted of shopkeepers, artisans, and wage earners—the largest single group in any city. They had their own culture, values, and institutions and, like the rural peasants, were conservative. Their economic position was highly vulnerable, and their lives centered on their work. They usually lived near or at their place of employment and worked in shops with fewer than a half dozen other people. They formed guilds to protect their interests, but by the 18th century these had declining influence and reinforced conservative values. Guilds were dedicated to preserving the jobs of their members, and they tried to prevent too many competitors from entering their markets.

THE JEWISH POPULATION: AGE OF THE GHETTO

*T*here were small Jewish communities in Amsterdam and other Western European cities, but most European Jews lived in eastern Europe. In 1762, Catherine the Great of Russia specifically excluded Jews from a manifesto that welcomed foreigners to settle in Russia, although she eased this a few years later. The first partition of Poland in 1772 (see Chapter 23) gave Russia a large Jewish population and created larger Jewish communities in Prussia and Austria.

QUICK REVIEW

Urban Classes

- Upper classes: Nobles, large merchants, bankers, financiers, clergy, government officials
- Middle class: Prosperous merchants, tradesmen, bankers, professionals
- Artisans: shopkeepers, wage earners, artisans

WHY WERE Jews discriminated against under the Old Regime?

Ghetto in Cracow. During the Old Regime, European Jews were separated from non-Jews, typically in districts known as ghettos. Relegated to the least desirable section of a city or to rural villages, most lived in poverty. This watercolor painting depicts a street in Kazimlesz, the Jewish quarter of Cracow, Poland.

Judaica Collection Max Berger, Vienna Austria/©Erich Lessing/Art Resource, N.Y.

Jews did not have the same rights as Christians, unless such rights were specifically granted to them by a sympathetic monarch. They were resident aliens whose status could change at the whim of a government. Under the Old Regime, they lived apart from non-Jews—in cities usually in districts called **ghettos**; and in the countryside in separate villages. They were treated as a distinct people religiously and legally and often bore the burden of discriminatory legislation.

During the 17th century, a few Jews helped finance wars for major rulers. The most famous of these "court Jews" was Samuel Oppenheimer (1630–1703), who helped the Habsburgs fund the struggle against the Turks that defended Vienna. The court Jews were exceptional, for most European Jews lived in poverty and worked at the lowest occupations. Their religious beliefs, rituals, and community set them apart, and numerous issues kept them in positions of social inferiority. But under the Old Regime, the discrimination they suffered was based on religious separateness, not racial prejudices. Jews who converted to Christianity were admitted to the political and social institutions of European society.

ghettos Separate communities in which Jews were required by law to live.

SUMMARY

Models of European Political Development In the 17th and 18th centuries, five great powers emerged in Europe: France, Britain, Austria, Prussia, and Russia. Through their military strength, economic development, and in some cases colonial empires, they would affect virtually every other world civilization.

Britain In the 17th century, conflict between the Stuart kings and Parliament arising out of political, religious, and economic issues led to civil war, the execution of Charles I, a short-lived English republic under Oliver Cromwell, and in 1688 and 1689 the Glorious Revolution that finally limited royal authority and established the supremacy of Parliament. Although 18th-century England was not a democracy, its people had more rights and liberties than the subjects of the absolutist monarchs who ruled the other European great powers. In a series of worldwide colonial struggles with France, Britain used its commercial resources and navy to profit from France's entanglements in Europe and emerge supreme in North America and India.

France   Under Louis XIV (r. 1643–1715), France became the model of an absolute monarchy. Louis used his splendid court at Versailles to overawe the French aristocracy and promote a glittering image of French culture that impressed all of Europe. However, he was not able completely to overcome opposition from the French elites who sought to reassert their influence under his successors. His revocation of the Edict of Nantes weakened France by driving thousands of French Protestants into exile. Louis pursued an aggressive foreign policy that expanded France's borders but cost France dearly in wealth and resources and provoked strong opposition from the other European powers. In the War of the Spanish Succession, he succeeded in placing his grandson on the throne of Spain, but the war left France exhausted.

Russia   Russia became a great power under Peter the Great (r. 1682–1725). Peter curbed the power of the Russian church and aristocracy and opened Russia to Western technology and military and commercial influences. He built his new capital at St. Petersburg. He also built an efficient army and navy and established a centralized bureaucracy to collect revenue.

Central Europe   The Habsburgs remained Holy Roman Emperors, but their power rested on their hereditary domains—Austria, Hungary, Bohemia, and northern Italy. Although the Habsburgs reconquered Hungary from the Ottomans, the rise of Prussia under the Hohenzollerns challenged Habsburg dominance in Central Europe. The Hohenzollern rulers built Prussia from a collection of scattered German states into a great power by developing an efficient bureaucracy and a powerful army. Under Frederick II (r. 1740–1786), Prussia emerged from a series of wars with Austria, France, and Russia as one of the strongest European states and the rival to Habsburg power in central Europe.

The Old Regime   Eighteenth-century European society was traditional, hierarchical, corporate, and privileged—features that had characterized Europe and the world for centuries. All societies also confronted scarce food supplies. For the 18th century, however, an improved food supply helped support a larger population. New agricultural techniques and the expanding population created pressures on social structures. Commerce also grew during the 18th century. Agriculture became more commercialized, with more money payments. Cities expanded.

Changes in European Society   European society stood on the brink of a new era in which the social, economic, and political relationships of centuries

IMAGE KEY
for pages 484–485

a. F. Boucher, *The Breakfast*, 1739. Francois Boucher (1703–1770). Louvre, Paris, France. Copyright Scala/Art Resource.

b. Grains of wild einkorn.

c. Maria Theresa of Austria. Kunsthistorisches Museum, Vienna.

d. The Crown of Louis XV, 1722.

e. A long-handled churn.

f. Cardinal Richelieu.

g. The taking of Quebec by British forces in September 1759. The Granger Collection, New York.

h. Francis Wheatley's *Evening*.

i. The Jewish quarter Kazimlesz in Krakow, Poland.

j. St. Petersburg, Russia.

would be destroyed. The commercial spirit and the values of the marketplace clashed with the traditions of peasants and guilds. That commercial spirit brought social change; by the early 19th century it led to a conception of human beings as individuals rather than as members of communities.

The expansion of the European population further stimulated change and challenge to tradition, hierarchy, and corporateness. The traditional economic and social organization (the family economy) had presupposed a stable or declining population. A larger population created the need for new ways to solve old problems. The social hierarchy had to accommodate more people. Corporate groups, such as the guilds, had to confront an expanded labor force. New wealth meant that birth would cease to determine social relationships.

The 18th century also witnessed the beginning of industrial production in response to the demands for consumer goods by the expanding population. New inventions greatly increasing productive capacity first appeared in the English textile industry. Thereafter industrial modes of production spread to the manufacture of iron. The steam engine provided a portable source of energy, allowing factories to be moved from the countryside into cities.

Industrialization also affected Europe's relations with much of the non-European world. For the first time in history, major changes in one region of Europe left virtually no corner of the globe untouched. By the close of the 18th century, a movement toward world interconnectedness and interdependence had begun.

REVIEW QUESTIONS

1. By the end of the 17th century, what differences had emerged between the governments of England and France? Why did each nation develop as it did?

2. How and why did Russia emerge as a great power?

3. What was the *family economy*? What roles did women play in preindustrial society?

4. What caused the agricultural revolution? What caused the Industrial Revolution?

5. How did population growth affect the development of Europe in the 18th century?

6. What was the status of European Jews in the Old Regime? What were the sources of prejudice against them?

KEY TERMS

absolutism (p. 486)

agricultural revolution (p. 503)

aristocratic resurgence (p. 498)

boyars (p. 489)

divine right of kings (p. 488)

domestic or putting-out system
      (p. 507)

enclosures (p. 504)

family economy (p. 501)

ghettos (p. 510)

Glorious Revolution (p. 487)

Industrial Revolution (p. 505)

Junkers (p. 493)

Old Regime (p. 498)

parliamentary monarchy (p. 486)

Pragmatic Sanction (p. 493)

Puritans (p. 486)

spinning jenny (p. 507)

streltsy (p. 489)

Table of Ranks (p. 492)

water frame (p. 507)

 For additional study resources for this chapter, go to:
      www.prenhall.com/craig/chapter20

21 The Last Great Islamic Empires
1500–1800

CHAPTER HIGHLIGHTS

The Last Islamic Empires The period from 1500 to 1800, marks the cultural and political blossoming of the last Islamic empires and their sharp decline. The Islamic vitality in the first half of this period was exemplified in the Ottoman, Safavid, and Mughal Empires. All three built vast bureaucracies and arguably the greatest cities in the world of their time. They patronized the arts. Yet they were conservative societies. Economically, they remained tied to agricultural production and taxation based on land. They did not undergo the social or religio-political revolutions that rocked the West after 1500 or the sort of generative changes in material and intellectual life that the Western world experienced during the same period. There was no compelling challenge to traditional Islamic ideals, even though numerous Islamic movements of the eighteenth century did call for reform.

Decline By the latter half of this period, all these empires were in economic, political, and military decline, even if intellectual and artistic vigor held on.

Thus, it is not surprising that European expansionism impinged in these three centuries upon Africa, India, Indonesia, and the Islamic heartland, rather than the reverse. None of the Islamic states, fared well in their encounters with Europeans during this age. Their growing domination of the world's seas allowed Europeans to contain or to bypass the major Islamic lands in their quest for commercial empires.

Industrial development joined economic wealth and political stability by the late 1700s to give the West global military supremacy for the first time. Before 1800, the Europeans were able to bring only minor Islamic states under colonial administrations. However, the footholds they gained in Africa, India, and Southeast Asia laid the groundwork for rapid colonial expansion after 1800. The age of the last great Muslim empires was the beginning of the first great modern European empires.

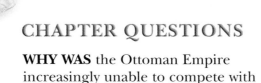

CHAPTER QUESTIONS

WHY WAS the Ottoman Empire increasingly unable to compete with the European powers?

WHAT ROLE did Shi'ite ideology play in the Safavid Empire?

WHAT ROLE did religious intolerance play in the decline of the Mughal Empire?

WHAT WERE the most important Islamic states in central and southern Asia?

HOW DID the arrival of Europeans affect the control of the commerce in Southeast Asia?

CHAPTER OUTLINE

ISLAMIC EMPIRES

*   The Ottoman Empire
*   The Safavid Shi'ite Empire
*   Mughals

ISLAMIC ASIA

*   Central Asia: Islamization and Isolation
*   Power Shifts in the Southern Seas

Between 1450 and 1650, Islamic culture and statecraft blossomed. The creation of the Ottoman, Safavid, and Mughal Empires marked the global apogee of Islamic culture and power.

In 1600, Islamic civilization seemed as strong and vital as that of Western Europe, China, or Japan. Yet by the late 17th century, Islamic power was in retreat before the rising tide of Western European military and economic imperialism, even though Islamic cultural life and Muslim religion flourished. Hindus were the chief religious group the Muslims displaced (see Map 21–1).

WHY WAS the Ottoman Empire increasingly unable to compete with the European powers?

Grand Mufti Chief religious authority of the Ottoman Empire. Also called "the Shaykh of Islam."

Shari'a Islamic religious law.

Süleyman the Lawgiver (r. 1520–1566). Süleyman the Lawgiver giving advice to the Crown Prince, Mehmed Khan. From a contemporaneous Ottoman miniature.

Folio 79a of the *Talikizade Shenamesi,* Library of the Topkapi Palace Museum, A3592/Photograph courtesy of Talat Halman.

ISLAMIC EMPIRES

THE OTTOMAN EMPIRE

ORIGINS AND DEVELOPMENT OF THE OTTOMAN STATE BEFORE 1600

The Ottomans were a Turkish dynasty that reached Anatolia (Asia Minor) in the time of the Seljuks of Rum (1098–1308). In the 14th century, the Ottomans expanded into central Anatolia and west across the Dardanelles (in 1356) onto European soil. The Ottomans built a formidable army, and by 1421, Ottoman control extended as far as the Danube. Constantinople fell in 1453 to Sultan Mehmed II, "the Conqueror" (r. 1451–1481). It became the Ottoman capital and was renamed Istanbul. After hundreds of years, Byzantium, the center of eastern Christendom, was no more. Its conquest stimulated the Ottoman appetite for European territory. As the extraordinary conquests of the Ottomans continued, Christian Europe again felt threatened by Islam.

By 1512, Ottoman rule was secure in southeastern Europe. Under Selim I (r. 1512–1520) and Süleyman, "the Lawgiver" ("Süleyman the Magnificent"; r. 1520–1566), this sovereignty was greatly expanded. Selim subjugated Egypt (1517), Syria-Palestine, and most of North Africa. The Yemen and western Arabia, including Mecca and Medina, also came under his control. Süleyman added the Caucasus, Mesopotamia, and most of Hungary to the Ottoman Empire (see Map 21–1).

These conquests enabled the Ottoman ruler legitimately to claim to be the caliph for all Muslims—a claim signified by the titles "Protector of the Sacred Places [Mecca and Medina]" and "emperor" (padishah). Ottoman military might was, at this point, unmatched by any world state, except possibly China.

THE "CLASSICAL" OTTOMAN ORDER

Mehmed II was the true founder of the Ottoman political system. He replaced tribal chieftains with men loyal to him and began a tradition of formal legislation. He organized the *ulama* into a hierarchy under a "Sheikh of Islam," the **Grand Mufti.** Süleyman the Lawgiver reconciled customary law and **Shari'a,** religious law, and regularized both the law and the bureaucracy. The Ottoman state was structured as one

MAP EXPLORATION

Interactive map: To explore this map further, go to **http://www.prenhall.com/craig/map21.1**

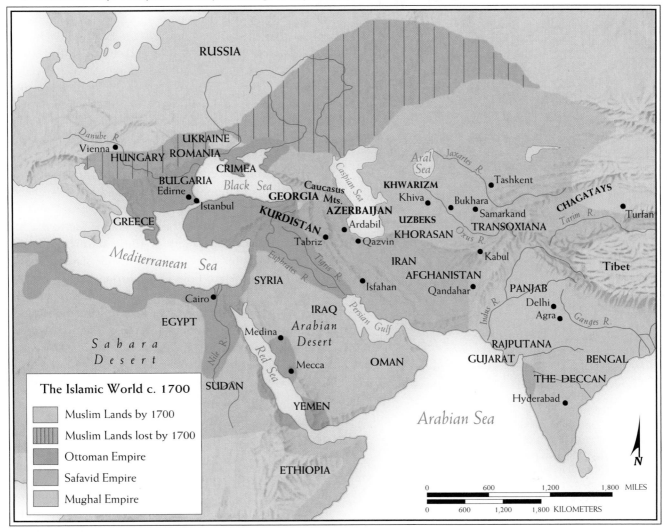

The Islamic World c. 1700

- ☐ Muslim Lands by 1700
- ▦ Muslim Lands lost by 1700
- ▩ Ottoman Empire
- ▨ Safavid Empire
- ▤ Mughal Empire

MAP 21–1
The Islamic World ca. 1700. The three rival "gunpowder" empires—the Safavid, Mughal, and Ottoman Empires—dominated the Islamic heartlands.

BY 1700, was the Islamic world in decline?

vast military institution. All its members held military rank. The ruling class were Muslim men who pledged total allegiance to the sultan. However, some women, although concealed from public eye, played important roles. They had ceremonial functions and influence over the appointment of officers and formulation of economic policy.

Several measures helped ensure the sultan's power. Young Ottoman princes received leadership training in the provinces, allowing them to experience life outside the capital. The succession was theoretically left to God in a power struggle that ended with the strongest aspirant to the sultanate seizing the throne. Stability of succession was guaranteed by the legal requirement that the man who won the throne would execute all his brothers, a policy that continued into the late 16th century.

12.2
Süleyman "The Lawgiver" and the Advantages of Islam: Oigier de Busbecq

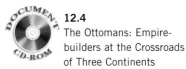

12.4
The Ottomans: Empire-builders at the Crossroads of Three Continents

Devshirme. An Ottoman portrayal of the *devshirme*. This miniature painting from about 1558 depicts the recruiting of young Christian children (located at the bottom of the picture) for the Sultan's elite Janissary corps.

Arifi, "Suleymanname," Topkapi Palace Museum, II 1517, fol. 31b, photograph courtesy of Talat Halman.

devshirme System under the Ottoman Empire that required each province to furnish a levy of Christian boys who were raised as Muslims and became soldiers in the Ottoman army.

Janissaries Elite Ottoman troops who were recruited through the *devshirme*.

The Ottomans organized the religious scholars, or *ulama*, as a department of government. A system of courts and judges rested on a comprehensive system of educational institutions ranging from local mosque schools to four elite madrasas in Istanbul. Scholars held graded rank with the hierarchy reflecting their level of schooling. The ulama enjoyed great prestige and usually functioned as part of the state apparatus. The religious establishment upheld the *Shari'a* and the sultan recognized its authority, but the functional law of the land was the ruler's legislation, or *Qanun*. The *Shari'a* theoretically governed the *Qanun*, but sometimes their conformity was only a pious fiction.

Ottoman rulers kept the military loyal by checking the power of the old landed aristocracy and by using slave soldiers whose only allegiance was to the sultan. To sustain the quality of these slave troops, the Ottomans established the provincial slave levy, or **devshirme**. Christian boys were chosen from the peasantry to be raised as Muslims and trained to serve in both army and bureaucracy. The most famous slave corps was the **Janissaries**, the elite infantry of the empire. They reduced the aristocratic cavalry's preeminence and, unlike the cavalry, were equipped with firearms.

AFTER SÜLEYMAN: CHALLENGES AND CHANGE

The reign of Süleyman marked the peak of Ottoman prestige and power (see Map 21–2). Beginning with his weak son, Selim II (1566–1574), the empire was plagued by corruption, decentralization, and maritime setbacks. Agricultural failures, commercial imbalances, and inflation were hard to check. Despite the fact that the empire seesawed between decline and vitality, its cultural achievements during the 17th and 18th centuries were impressive.

Political and Military Developments   The post-Süleyman era began with the loss of territory in the east to the Persian Safavids (1603). By this time the Ottoman military apparatus was weakening, partly from fighting two-front wars with the Safavids and the Habsburgs and partly because of European advances in technology. The Janissaries, once the backbone of Ottoman power, became disruptive and tried to influence decision making and even dynastic succession. Finally, the increasing employment of mercenaries resulted, whenever peace was declared, in the release of masses of unemployed armed men into the countryside. They sacked provincial towns and practiced banditry.

Economic Developments   Financing the Ottoman state grew more difficult. By 1600, the increase in the Janissary corps from 12,000 to 36,000 men had drained state coffers. Fluctuations in silver caused inflation. To avoid shortages that would raise prices for domestic consumers, the Ottomans encouraged imports and discouraged exports, a policy that hurt the Ottoman economy in the long run. Unemployment increased as the population doubled in the 16th century. As central authority weakened, provincial notables (*ayan*) grew stronger until, by the 18th century, they were virtually independent.

Culture and Society   The 17th and 18th centuries were an era of vitality in artistic and intellectual life. The sultan used patronage of the arts and sciences to back the Ottoman claim to universal authority. The ulama, however, became an aristocratic and increasingly corrupt elite. Major religious posts were controlled by a handful of families and became hereditary sinecures that were often sold or leased.

Notable among the scholars of the period is Katib Chelebi (d. 1657), the most illustrious of the many polymaths who wrote histories, social commentary, geographies, and encyclopedic works. Thanks to men like the imperial master architect Sinan (d. 1578), the Ottomans developed distinctive artistic and architectural forms in the late 16th century. The first half of the 18th century saw the introduction of the printing press to the Ottoman Empire and the flourishing of the golden age of Ottoman poetry and art.

Socially, the period saw the consolidation of Ottoman society as a multi-ethnic and multireligious state. All subjects, both Muslim and non-Muslim, were organized into small communities called ***millets***. These communities were responsible for their members from cradle to grave, providing education, justice, charitable aid, and liason with the sultan's government. They were usually headed by a religious leader and had considerable freedom to handle their own internal affairs. This made the empire a haven for minority groups, especially Jews. Many Jews settled in Ottoman lands following their expulsion from Spain in 1492. The large Christian population of the empire was well treated until the 17th century, when they began to suffer increasing discrimination. They then began to look to Europe and Russia for liberation.

During the 18th century, relations between Muslims and non-Muslims generally grew increasingly strained. This was, in part, a reaction to the rise in the economic and social status of non-Muslims—particularly in the rich mercantile middle class. Non-Muslims monopolized foreign trade and, in the 18th century, European countries gave many of them citizenship, which qualified them for trade privileges the sultan granted to foreign governments.

One of the characteristic social institutions of later Ottoman society, the coffeehouse, flourished from the mid-16th century on. It rapidly became a major common space for socializing, as people gathered to drink coffee, play games, read, and discuss public affairs. It stimulated the development of a common Ottoman urban culture among lower and middle classes.

millets   Small self-governing communities within the Ottoman Empire.

The Ottoman Empire

ca. 1280	Foundation of early Ottoman principality in Anatolia
1356	Ottomans cross Dardanelles into Europe
1451–1481	Rule of Sultan Mehmed II, "the Conqueror"
1453	Fall of Constantinople to Mehmed the Conqueror
1512–1520	Rule of Selim I
1517	Ottoman conquest of Egypt, assumption of claim to Abbasid caliphal succession from Mamluks
1520–1566	Rule of Süleyman, "the Lawgiver"
1578	Death of Ottoman master architect, Sinan
1683	Ottoman siege of Vienna
1699	Treaty of Karlowitz, loss of Hungarian and other European territory
1774	Loss of Crimea to Russia; tsar becomes formal protector of Ottoman Orthodox Christians
1918	End of empire

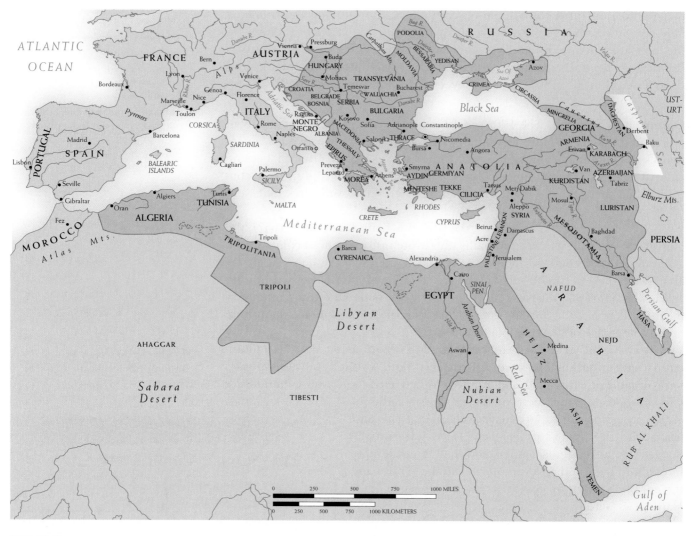

MAP 21–2

The Ottoman Empire at its Zenith, late 16th century. This large and multiethnic empire spanned three continents and lasted for more than 400 years.

WHAT WERE the strengths and weaknesses of the Ottoman Empire's geographical position?

THE DECLINE OF OTTOMAN MILITARY AND POLITICAL POWER

After the failure in 1683 of a second siege of Vienna, the Ottomans were driven out of Hungary and Belgrade and never again threatened Europe. The treaty of Karlowitz sealed the loss of Hungary to Austria (1699). Defeat by Russia cost the Ottomans the Crimea and made the tsar the protector of the Orthodox Christians within the Islamic empire (1774). The Ottoman economy had been based on conquest and control of land. Once expansion stopped, the sultans failed to adapt to the effects that European capitalism and industrialization were having on the world economy. Henceforth, the Ottomans were prey to the West. Outflanked by Russia to their north and by European sea power to the south and west, the Ottomans were also blocked in the east by Shi'ite foes in Iran. They never regained their earlier power and influence, and their empire collapsed in 1918.

THE SAFAVID SHI'ITE EMPIRE

ORIGINS

As noted in Chapter 13, Iranian history changed under the Safavid dynasty after 1500. The Safavids originated in the 14th century as hereditary Turkish spiritual leaders of a Sunni Sufi order in the northwestern Iranian province of Azerbaijan. In the 15th century, the Safavid order evolved a new, militant Shi'ite ideology. The Safavid spiritual masters (*shaykhs* and *pirs*) claimed descent from the seventh imam of the Twelver Shia (see Chapter 13), which made them the focus of Shi'ite religious allegiance.

The growing strength of the Safavids led to conflict with the dominant Sunni groups around Tabriz. The Safavids emerged victorious in 1501 under the leadership of the young Safavid master-designate Isma'il. By 1506, he had established sovereignty over the southern Caucasus, Azerbaijan, the Tigris-Euphrates valley, and western Iran. By 1512, the Safavids had taken eastern Iran from the Uzbek Turks. The Uzbeks, however, became implacable foes of the Safavids and throughout the ensuing century often forced them to fight a debilitating two-front war—Uzbeks in the east; Ottomans in the west.

Strong central rule now united Iran for the first time since the Abbasid caliphate. The regime adopted existing Persian bureaucratic institutions. Shah Isma'il enforced Shi'ite conformity on the Sunni majority, and Shi'ite conformity slowly took root across the realm—perhaps bolstered by Persian self-consciousness in the face of the Sunni Ottomans, Arabs, Uzbeks, and Mughals who surrounded Iran. He was determined to rule not merely as a leader of a Sufi religious movment but to govern as a restoration of the historic Iranian monarchy.

The Ottomans were determined that this Sufi-inspired Shi'ite monarchy not spread further into their territory. The better-armed army of Selim I defeated the Safavids in 1514, beginning a series of Ottoman-Safavid conflicts that continued for two centuries. The Ottomans took control of the Fertile Crescent and forced the Safavids to move their capital and their focus eastward to Isfahan.

SHAH ABBAS I

Tahmasp I (r. 1524–1576), Isma'il's successor, survived attacks by both Ottomans and Uzbeks. The strength of Shi'ite religious feeling and the allegiance of government bureaucrats preserved his regime. A few years later, the greatest Safavid ruler, Shah Abbas I (r. 1588–1629), pushed the Ottomans out of Azerbaijan and Iraq and turned back Uzbek invasions in Khorasan. He also sought alliances with the Ottomans' European enemies. This latter tactic, used by several Safavid rulers, reflects the division that the new militant Persian Shi'ism had brought to the Islamic world. Abbas also began to trade with the English and Dutch. The prosperity Iran enjoyed during his reign is reflected by the magnificent capital he built at Isfahan.

WHAT ROLE did Shi'ite ideology play in the Safavid Empire?

pirs Shi'ite holy men.

Worldly and Spiritual Drunkenness. This painting by the great 16th-century Safavid Iranian court painter Sultan Muhammad is from an illustrated copy of the *Diwan*, or collected works of the lyric and mystical poet Hafiz (1319–1389?). Hafiz appears himself as a drunken figure in the upper window. The entire picture plays the worldly drunkenness and debauchery of the characters in the center against the spiritual inebriation of the dancing Sufis in the garden and the angels on the roof. The angels, too, are shown drinking, a visual reference to the line of Hafiz at the top: "The angel of mercy took the cup of revelry."

Courtesy of the Metropolitan Museum of Art and Arthur M. Sackler Museum, Harvard University. Promised gift of Mr. and Mrs. Stuart Cary Welch, 1988; © 1989 Metropolitan Museum of Art.

The Safavid Empire

ca. 1500	Rise of Safavids under Shah Isma'il
1501–1512	Safavid conquest of greater Iran; Shi'ite state founded
1588–1629	Rule of Shah Abbas I
1722	Forced abdication of last Safavid ruler
1736–1747	Rule of the Sunni Afghan leader, Nadir Shah; revival of Sunni monarchy in Iran
1739	Nadir Shah sacks Delhi

12.5
The Safavid Shi'ite Empire of Persia

The Shah's Mosque (Masjid-i Shah) in Isfahan, Iran. During its heyday as the Safavid capital, Isfahan was given the lofty epithet "half of the world." Its elegant architecture and lavish use of ceramic tiles reflects the majestic Safavid self-image.

Corbis-Bettmann.

The most enduring feature of the Safavid consolidation of power in Iran was the replacement of Sunni Islam with Shi'ite Islam as the official religion. The Safavids discouraged pilgrimages to Mecca and urged visits to Karbala or to the shrine of Husayn, the grandson of the Prophet Muhammad.

SAFAVID DECLINE

After Shah Abbas, with the exception of Abbas II (1642–1666) and Husayn I (1694–1722), the empire never again found as able a leader. This led finally to its decline and collapse, the chief causes of which were (1) continued pressure from Ottoman and Uzbek armies, (2) economic decline, and (3) the power and bigotry of the Shi'ite ulama. The conservative ulama introduced Shi'ite legalism, emphasized their own authority over that of the Safavid monarch, persecuted religious minorities, and encouraged hatred of Sunni Muslims.

Shi'ite exclusivism inspired tribal revolts among the Sunni Afghans. In 1722, an Afghan leader took Qandahar (in modern Afghanistan) and then captured Isfahan and forced the abdication of Husayn I. Safavid princes managed to retake western Iran, but the empire's greatness was past. A revived, but officially Sunni, monarchy under Nadir Shah (r. 1736–1747) restored much of Iran's lost territories. However, his military ventures, which included the conquest of Delhi, sapped the empire's finances, and his despotic reign left a legacy of instability for Iran that continued for half a century.

CULTURE AND LEARNING

The most impressive achievement of the Safavid Era, besides the conversion of Iran to Shi'ism, was a cultural renaissance during the 16th and 17th centuries. Traditions of painting, originating with the powerful miniatures of the preceding century, were cultivated and modified. Portraiture and scenes from everyday life became popular. Among the most developed crafts were ceramic tiles, porcelain, and carpets. In architecture, the magnificent public squares, parks, palaces, hospitals, caravanserais, mosques, and other buildings of Isfahan constructed in Shah Abbas's time illustrate Safavid taste. Isfahan was the quintessential expression of the faith and imperial grandeur of Iran.

The Safavid age also saw a distinctively Shi'ite piety develop. It focused on commemorating the suffering of the imams and remaining loyal to the Shi'ite ulama, who alone (through knowledge of the Qur'an and traditions descending from Muhammad and the Imams) could provide guidance until the return of the hidden imam (see Chapter 11).

The Taj Mahal. Probably the most beautiful tomb in the world, the Taj was built from 1631 to 1653 by Shah Jahan for his beloved wife, Mumtaz Mahal. Located on the south bank of the Yamuna River at Agra, the Mughal capital, the Taj Mahal remains the jewel of Mughal architecture.
Michael Gotin.

THE MUGHALS

ORIGINS

In the early 16th century, invaders from the northwest, repeating an age-old pattern in Indian history, ended the political fragmentation that had, by 1500, reduced the Delhi sultanate to one among many Indian states. These invaders were descended from Timur (Tamerlane) and known to history as the **Mughals** (a Persianate form of *Mongol*). From 1525 to 1527, the founder of the Mughal dynasty, Babur, marched on India. By the time of his death in 1530, he ruled an empire stretching from the Himalaya to the Deccan. Akbar "the Great" (r. 1556–1605), however, was the real founder of the Mughal Empire, and the greatest Indian ruler since Ashoka (ca. 264–223 B.C.E.).

AKBAR'S REIGN

Akbar added North India and the northern Deccan to the Mughal dominions. Even more significant, however, were his governmental reforms, cultural patronage, and religious toleration. He reorganized government and rationalized the tax system. His marriages with Rajput princesses and his appointment of Hindus to power eased Muslim–Hindu tensions. So did his cancellation of the poll tax on non-Muslims (1564). Under his leadership, the Mughal Empire became a truly Indian empire.

WHAT ROLE did religious intolerance play in the decline of the Mughal Empire?

QUICK REVIEW

Akbar (r. 1556–1605)

- Added North India and the northern Deccan to Mughal Empire
- Carried out extensive governmental reforms
- Was interested in a variety of religious faiths

Mughals Descendants of the Mongols who established an Islamic empire in India in the 16th century with its capital at Delhi.

Akbar showed unusual interest in different religious traditions. He frequently brought together representatives of various faiths to discuss religion. Akbar tried to promulgate among his intimates a new monotheistic creed that subsumed Muslim, Hindu, and other viewpoints. However, his ideas died with him.

THE LAST GREAT MUGHALS

Akbar's three immediate successors were Jahangir (r. 1605–1627), Shah Jahan (r. 1628–1658), and Awrangzeb (r. 1658–1707). Although each left behind significant achievements, none matched Akbar. The problems of sustaining an Indian empire took their toll on Mughal power. The reigns of Jahangir and Shah Jahan were the golden age of Mughal culture. But the burdens imposed by military campaigns and the erosion of Akbar's administrative and tax reforms led to economic decline. Jahangir set a fateful precedent when he allowed English merchants to establish a trading post at Surat on the western coast in Gujarat. No less a burden on the treasury were Shah Jahan's elaborate building projects, the most magnificent of which was the Taj Mahal (built 1632–1653), the unparalleled tomb that he built for his beloved consort, Mumtaz.

With Shah Jahan, religious toleration began to fade, and under Awrangzeb, religious fanaticism reversed Akbar's earlier policies. The resulting disorder hastened the decline of Mughal power. Awrangzeb persecuted non-Muslims, destroying Hindu temples, reimposing the poll tax (1679), and alienating the Rajput leaders, whose forebears Akbar had cultivated. His intransigent policies coincided with the spread of the militant Sikh movement and the rise of Hindu Maratha nationalism.

India: The Mughals and Contemporary Indian Powers

1525–1527	Rule of Babur, founder of Indian Timurid state
1538	Death of Guru Nanak, founder of Sikh religious tradition
1556–1605	Rule of Akbar "the Great"
1605–1627	Rule of Jahangir
1628–1658	Rule of Shah Jahan, builder of the Taj Mahal
1646	Founding of Maratha Empire
1658–1707	Rule of Awrangzeb
1680	Death of Maratha leader, Shivaji
1708	Death of 10th and last Sikh guru, Gobind Singh
1724	Rise of Hyderabad state
1739	Iranian invasion of North India under Nadir Shah
1757	British East India Company victory over Bengali forces at Plassey

SIKHS AND MARATHAS

In the late 16th and early 17th centuries, the Sikhs, who trace their origins to the teachings of Guru Nanak (d. 1538), became a distinctive religious movement. Neither Muslim nor Hindu, they had their own scripture, ritual, and ideals. Awrangzeb was angered by their rejection of Islam, and he launched a persecution that earned him their lasting enmity. The Sikhs developed into a formidable military force, and Awrangzeb and his successors had to contend with repeated Sikh uprisings.

The Hindu Marathas, led by Shivaji (d. 1680) and driven by religious and nationalistic fervor, founded their own empire about 1646. By the time of Shivaji's death, the Maratha army had become the most disciplined military in India. After Awrangzeb's death, the Marathas created a confederation of the Deccan States under their leadership. While acknowledging Mughal sovereignty, the Marathas controlled far more of India after 1740 than did the Mughals.

POLITICAL DECLINE

In addition to these wars, other factors sealed the fate of the Mughal Empire after Awrangzeb's death in 1707: the rise in the Deccan of the powerful Islamic state of Hyderabad in 1724, the Persian invasion of North India by Nadir Shah in 1739, the invasions (1748–1761) by the Afghan tribal leader Ahmad Shah Durrani (r. 1747–1773), and the British

HISTORY'S VOICES

GURU ARJUN'S FAITH

These lines are from the pen of the fifth guru of the Sikh community, Arjun (d. 1606). In them he repeated the teaching of Kabir, a 15th-century Indian saint whose teachings are included with those of Guru Nanak and other religious poets in the Sikh holy scripture, the Adi Granth. This teaching focuses on the error of clinging to a doctrinaire communalist faith, be it that of the Hindus or of the Muslims.

WHY MIGHT syncretic teachings, such as those of the Sikhs, have been appealing in 17th-century India?

I practice not fasting, nor observe the [month of] Ramazan:
I serve Him who will preserve me at the last hour.

The one Lord of the earth is my God,
Who judgeth both Hindus and Muslims.
I go not on a pilgrimage to Mecca, nor worship at Hindu places of Pilgrimage.
I serve the one God and no other.
I neither worship as the Hindus, nor pray as the Muslims.
I take the Formless God into my heart, and there make obeisance unto Him.
I am neither a Hindu nor a Muslim.
The soul and the body belong to God whether He be called Allah or Ram.
Kabir hath delivered this lecture.
When I meet a true guru or pir, I recognize my own Master.

Source: Max Arthur Macauliffe, *The Sikh Religion*, 6 vols. (Oxford: Clarendon Press, 1909), p. 422.

victories over Bengali forces at Plassey in Bengal (1757) and over the French on the southeastern coast (1740–1763). By 1819, the dominance of the British East India Company had eclipsed Indian power, but the Mughal line did not officially end until 1858.

RELIGIOUS DEVELOPMENTS

The period from about 1500 to 1650 was of major importance for Indian religious life. In the 16th century, a number of religious figures preached a piety that transcended the legalism of both the ulama and the Brahmans and rejected caste distinctions. In these ideas, we can see both Muslim Sufi and Hindu *bhakti* influences at work. Guru Nanak, the spiritual father of the Sikh movement, preached faith and devotion to one loving and merciful God. He opposed narrow allegiance to particular creeds or rites and excessive pride in external religious observance. Dadu (d. 1603) preached a similar message. He was born a Muslim but strove to get people to transcend the division between Muslim and Hindu (see "Guru Arjun's Faith").

There was also a Hindu revival epitomized by Chaitanya (d. ca. 1533), who stressed total devotion to Lord Krishna. The forebears of present-day Hare Krishna devotees, his followers spread his ecstatic public praise of God and his message of the equality of all in God's sight. Tulasidas's (d. 1623) retelling of the *Ramayana* remains among the most popular works of Indian literature. Tulasidas used the story of Rama's adventures to present *bhakti* ideas that remain alive in Hindu life.

Muslim eclectic tendencies came primarily from the Sufis. By 1500, the Chishtiya Sufi order especially had won many converts to Islam. Such Sufis were,

The great central square of the Registan, in Samarkand. The 17th-century Shir Dar Madrasa is on the right and the 15th-century Ulugh Beg Madrasa is on the left. Samarkand and other major Central Asian cities were centers of Islamic culture and learning as well as political power.

Michel Gotin/Ouzebekistan.

WHAT WERE the most important Islamic states in central and southern Asia?

however, often opposed by the ulama, many of whom were royal advisers and judges responsible for upholding the religious law. The more intolerant side of the spirit of Awrangzeb's time eventually won the day. The possibilities for Hindu–Muslim rapprochement waned, presaging the communal strife that has recently so marred southern Asian history.

ISLAMIC ASIA

CENTRAL ASIA: ISLAMIZATION AND ISOLATION

Islam established a solid footing in Central Asia in the 15th century. Even in the preceding century, as the nomadic peoples of western Central Asia began to settle, the familiar pattern of Islamic diffusion from trading and urban centers had set in. Islamization slowed only in the late 16th century when Mongolia proper converted to Buddhism. In the region between the Aral and Caspian Seas, the most important states were founded by Uzbek and Chaghatay Turks.

UZBEKS AND CHAGHATAYS

During the 15th century, a new steppe khanate had been formed by the unification in 1428 of assorted clans of Turks and Mongols known as the Uzbeks. In time, an Uzbek leader who was descended from Genghis Khan, Muhammad Shaybani (d. 1510), invaded Transoxiana (1495–1500) and founded an Uzbek Islamic empire. Muhammad's line continued Uzbek rule in Transoxiana at Bukhara into the 18th century, while another Uzbek line ruled the khanate of Khiva in western Turkestan from 1512 to 1872.

OVERVIEW   MAJOR ISLAMIC STATES, CA. 1600

From the 15th century to the 18th century was the age of the last great Islamic empires. These states dominated the Islamic world, which stretched from Morocco on the Atlantic coast of North Africa across the Near East and along the eastern coast of Africa to the southeast Asian islands that today make up the Republic of Indonesia. Despite these political divisions and the religious divide between Sunni and Shi'ite Muslims, in many respects the Islamic world formed a single cultural unit.

State	Location	Islamic Tradition
Ottoman Empire	Balkans, Anatolia, North Africa, Syria, Iraq, Arabia	Sunni
Safavid Empire	Iran, Afghanistan Caucasus	Shi'ite
Mughal Empire	India	Sunni
Uzbeks	Central Asia: Kiva, Bokhara	Sunni
Chaghatays	Central Asia: Tukistan	Sunni
Acheh	Sumatra	Sunni

Hindus were the chief religious group the Muslims displaced. Islam never ousted the Indian Buddhist cultures of Burma, Thailand, and Indochina, but it did win most of Malaysia, Sumatra, Java, and the "Spice Islands" of the Moluccas. By the end of the 15th century, Islam had also spread along the East African coast.

Of the other Central Asian Islamic states after 1500, the most significant was established by the Chaghatay Turks. A revived Chaghatay state in eastern Turkestan lasted from about 1514 to 1678.

CONSEQUENCES OF THE SHI'ITE RIFT

On the surface, the Ottoman, Mughal, Safavid, and Central Asian were Islamic states that had much in common. Yet the deep religious division between the Shi'ite Safavids and their Sunni neighbors proved stronger than their common bonds. Shi'ite-Sunni political competition was sharpened by Safavid militancy, to which the Sunni states responded in kind. Both sought alliances with non-Muslim states. Although trade continued, the international flow of Islamic commerce was hurt by a militant Shi'ite state astride the overland trade routes of the larger Islamic world. The Safavid Shi'ite schism also ruptured the cultural traditions of the "abode of Islam." The militant Shi'ism of Iran isolated Central Asia from the rest of the Muslim world after 1500. However healthy Islam remained in this region, its ties to the Islamic heartlands diminished. Contact came primarily through pilgrims, Sufis, ulama, and students. Central Asian Islam mostly developed in isolation, peripheral to the Islamic mainstream.

POWER SHIFTS IN THE SOUTHERN SEAS

SOUTHERN-SEAS TRADE

The first half of the second millennium witnessed the spread of Islamic religion and culture along the southern rim of Asia, from the Red Sea and East Africa to the South China Sea. In port cities, Islamic traders established thriving

HOW DID the arrival of Europeans affect the control of the commerce in Southeast Asia?

communities that often became the dominant influence. Typically, this first stage of conversion in cities was followed by Islam's transmission to surrounding areas and inland regions of Hindu, Buddhist, or pagan culture. In this transmission, Sufi orders played the main role. However, conquest by Muslim coastal states quickened the process in Indonesia and East Africa.

CONTROL OF THE SOUTHERN SEAS

The Portuguese reached the East African coast in 1498. In the following three centuries, the history of the lands along the trade routes of the southern Asian seas was affected not only by Islamic networks but by the increasing influence of Christian Western Europe. The key attractions of these diverse lands for Europeans were their commercial and strategic possibilities.

In the 16th century, the Europeans began to displace by force the Muslims who dominated the maritime southern rim of Asia. They owed their success to support from their homelands and their superior warships. The effectiveness of this combination was evident along the west coast of India, where the Portuguese carved out a power base in the early 16th century at the expense of Muslim traders. They did so by employing their superior naval power, exploiting indigenous rivalries, and using terror.

However, Islamization continued apace, even in the face of Christian proselytizing and European power. The Muslims rarely abandoned their faith, which proved generally attractive to new peoples they encountered. The result was usually an Islamicized, but racially mixed, population.

The upshot of these developments was that while European imperialism had considerable military and economic success, European culture and Christian missionary work made little headway against Islam. Only in the Philippines did a substantial population become Christian.

The Southern Seas: Arrival of the Portuguese

1498	Portuguese come to the East African coast and to the west coast of India
1500–1512	Portuguese establish bases on west Indian coast, replace Muslims as Indian Ocean power
early 1500s	Muslim sultanates replace Hindu states in Java, Sumatra
1524–1910	State of Acheh in northwestern Sumatra
1600s	Major increase in Islamization and connected spread of Malay language in the archipelago
1641	Dutch conquest of Malacca
ca. 1800	Dutch replace Muslim states as main archipelago power
1873–1910	War between Holland and Acheh

THE INDIES: ACHEH

The history of the Indonesian archipelago has always revolved around the international demand for the spices it produces. By the 15th century, there were coastal Islamic states on the Malay Peninsula, the north shores of Sumatra and Java, and the Moluccas (the "Spice Islands"). Several Islamic sultanates developed in the 16th and 17th centuries, even as Europeans staked claims in the region. The most powerful of these sultanates was Acheh in northwestern Sumatra (ca. 1524–1910). It provided the only counterweight to the Portuguese presence across the straits in Malacca (Malaysia). Acheh dominated the pepper trade of Sumatra and thrived until the end of the 16th century. In the first half of the 17th century, the sultanate controlled both coasts of Sumatra and parts of the Malay peninsula. Meanwhile, the Dutch replaced the Portuguese, and in the early 20th century, they finally won full control of the region—after nearly 40 years of intermittent war with Acheh (1873–1910).

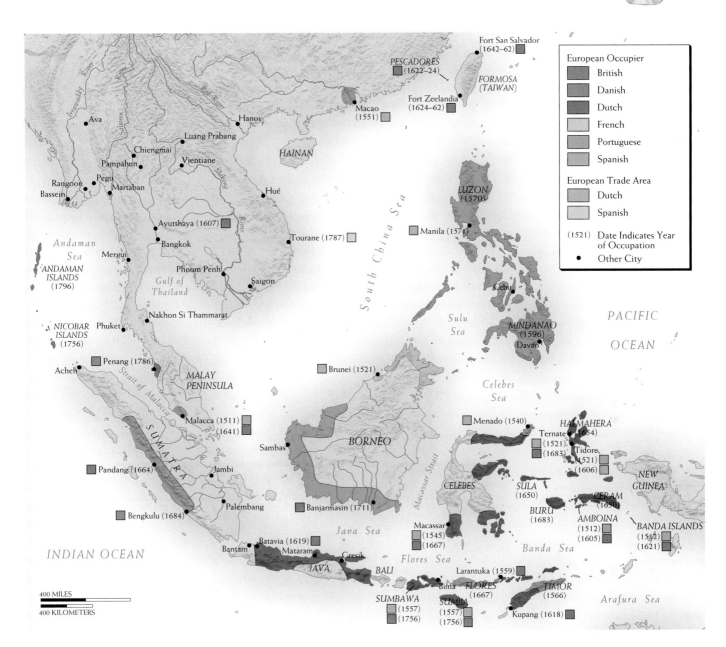

MAP 21–3
European Commercial Presence in Southeast Asia. Beginning with the Portuguese and Spanish in the 16th century, and then the Dutch in the 17th century, European powers established commercial bases throughout Southeast Asia, often cooperating with local rulers.

WHAT WERE the motives for European penetration of Southeast Asia?

SUMMARY

The Last Islamic Empires The period from 1500 to 1800 marks the cultural and political blossoming of the last Islamic empires and their sharp decline. The Islamic vitality in the first half of this period was exemplified in the Ottoman, Safavid, and Mughal Empires. All three built vast bureaucracies and arguably the greatest cities of their time. They patronized the arts. Yet they were conservative societies. Economically they remained tied to agricultural production and

IMAGE KEY

for pages 514–515

a. Emperor Jahangir seated on an hourglass conversing with a Muslim mystic.

b. Riaz Abbasi, Woman with a veil ca. 1590–95.

c. The Christ Church in Dutch Square, Melaka, Malaysia.

d. A whirling Dervish.

e. Topkapi Palace, Istanbul.

f. Suleyman the Lawyer giving advice to the Crown Prince, Mehmed Khan.

g. Samarcande, Place du Reghistan.

h. Ardabil carpet from Safavid dynasty in Iran.

i. Ottoman Sultan Mehmed II on a coin.

taxation based on land. They did not undergo the social or religious-political revolutions that rocked the West after 1500 or the sort of generative changes in material and intellectual life that the Western world experienced during the same period. There was no compelling challenge to traditional Islamic ideals, even though numerous Islamic movements of the 18th century called for reform.

Decline By the latter half of this period, all these empires were in economic, political, and military decline, even if they continued intellectually and artistically vigorous. It is not surprising, therefore, that European expansionism impinged during these three centuries on Africa, India, Indonesia, and the Islamic heartland, rather than the reverse. None of the Islamic states fared well in their encounters with Europeans during this age. Growing domination of the world's seas allowed Europeans to contain or bypass the major Islamic lands in their quest for commercial empires.

Industrial development joined economic wealth and political stability by the late 1700s to give the West global military supremacy for the first time. Before 1800, the Europeans were able to bring only minor Islamic states under colonial administrations. However, the footholds they gained in Africa, India, and Southeast Asia laid the groundwork for rapid colonial expansion after 1800. The age of the last great Muslim empires was the beginning of the first great modern European empires.

REVIEW QUESTIONS

1. What were the sources of the early Ottoman Empire's strength? What explains its later weakness?

2. What is the historical significance of the Safavid Empire in Iran?

3. What united all Islamic states? What began to divide them between 1500 and 1800?

4. What were Akbar's main policies toward the Hindu population? How did the Sikhs develop into a formidable military power?

5. How did outside powers affect the peoples of the South Seas lands?

KEY TERMS

devshirme (p. 518)   **millets** (p. 519)   *pirs* (p. 521)
Grand Mufti (p. 516)   **Mughals** (p. 523)   *Shari'a* (p. 516)
Janissaries (p. 518)

 For additional study resources for this chapter, go to:
www.prenhall.com/craig/chapter21

Visualizing The Past

The "Other" in the Early Modern Period

THE EARLY modern era (c. 1350–1750 c.e.) experienced increased trade and movements of peoples throughout the world. How did artists depict the strangers they encountered? Why do portrayals of the "other" reveal as much about the artist as the subject?

I n the West, the early modern period coincides with what is often called the "Age of Discovery," when Europeans "discovered" the New World and sailed for the first time to sub-Saharan Africa and Asia. Cultures also increased their encounters with peoples from other parts of the world. During this rich period of encounter, cultural prejudices influenced the way artists depicted people they had never seen before. Aspects and features most remarkable, strange, attractive, or repulsive were often emphasized.

◀ **Africans as Voyagers.** This superb painting of an Indian of African origin demonstrates that Africans were voyagers to other lands and that not all Africans who went elsewhere went as slaves. The man in this image is a merchant, probably a member of the Janjeera people, originally from Ethiopia. Janjeera merchants emigrated to India in the Middle Ages. Some remained there and during the 15th century they and their descendants obtained positions of power and authority in local governments. The sumptuous dress and dignified bearing of this man suggests wealth and influence.

K. L. Kamat.

Portuguese Trade with Africa. In the 16th and 17th centuries, the Portuguese explored the coast of West Africa, where they established trading outposts and forts, and the beginnings of the Atlantic slave trade. One of Africa's most important products was ivory, which African artisans carved into exquisite objects for the luxury trade. Saltcellars like the one depicted here, carved in Nigeria at the court of Benin in the 15th or 16th century, were popular in Portugal. African artists carving for a Portuguese audience often depicted Portuguese merchants, emphasizing those aspects of the Europeans that most impressed them: the heavy beards, the cross, heavy armor, and sword.

African, Nigeria, Edo peoples, court of Benin, Saltcellar: Portuguese Figure, 15th–16th century, Ivory; H. 7-1/8 in. (18.1 cm). The Metropolitan Museum of Art, Louis V. Bell and Rogers Funds, 1972.(972.63ab) Phoytograph by Stan Reis. Photograph © 1984 The Metropolitan Museum of Art.

Europeans in East Asia. This image shows a portion of a Namban screen from late 16th-century Japan. Europeans, beginning with the Portuguese, began arriving in Japan at this time. The Japanese found the strangely dressed Portuguese merchants and the African slaves, Indian pilots, and Catholic clerics who accompanied them fascinating.

De Young Memorial Museum/San Francisco/USA.

The Fall of the Aztecs. In Asia and Africa, early modern Europeans went as traders rather than as conquerors. In the New World, disease, superior weaponry, horses, and political disunity of the native peoples permitted Europeans to engage in conquest. This image from the Florentine codex depicts the fall of the Aztec capital Tenochtitlán. Note the Spanish soldiers

mounted on horses on the left. The Aztecs had never seen horses before they were greatly terrified by these strange creatures. The codex, produced in the 16th century by natives under the supervision of a Spaniard, Fray Bernardino de Sahagún, is the product of a blending of Spanish and Aztec culture and art styles.

Courtesy of the Library of Congress.

EUROPE

1756–1763	Seven Years' War
1762–1796	Catherine II "the Great" reigns in Russia
1763	Peace of Paris Seven Years' War
1772	First partition of Poland
1783	Peace of Paris
1789	French Revolution begins
1793 and 1795	Last partitions of Poland

Sir Isaac Newton ▶

◀ July 14, 1789,
Bastille prison, Paris

NEAR EAST/ INDIA

1757	British victory at Plassey, in Bengal
1761	English oust French from India
1772–1784	Warren Hastings' administration in India
1772–1833	Ram Mohan Roy, Hindu reformer in India
1794–1925	Qajar shahs in Iran
1805–1849	Muhammad Ali in Egypt

▲ Muhammad Ali

EAST ASIA

1753–1806	Kitagawa Utamaro, Tokugawa Era artist
1787–1793	Matsudaira Sadanobu's reforms in Japan
1789	White Lotus Rebellion in China
1823–1901	Li Hung-chang, powerful Chinese governor-general

◀ Utamaro
woodblock print

AFRICA

1754–1817	Usman Dan Fodio, founder of Sultanate in northern and central Nigeria
1762	End of Funj Sultanate in eastern Sudanic region

THE AMERICAS

1759–1788	Spain reorganizes government of its American Empire
1776	American Declaration of Independence
1791	First 10 amendments to U.S. Constitution (Bill of Rights) ratified
1791	Negro slave revolt in French Santo Domingo
1794	Canada Constitutional Act divides the country into Upper and Lower Canada

The "Boston Massacre" on ▶
March 5, 1770, by Paul Revere

1804–1814 Napoleon's empire
1814–1815 Congress of Vienna
1830–1848 Louis Philippe reigns in France
1832 First British Reform Act
1837–1901 Queen Victoria of England
1848 Revolutions across Europe

1835 Introduction of English education in India
ca. 1839–1880 Tanzimat reforms, Ottoman Empire
1839–1897 Muslim intellectual Jamal al-Din Al-Afghani
1845–1905 Muhammad Abduh

◄ *British colonial rule in India (1880)*

1835–1908 Empress Dowager Cixi
1839–1842 Opium War; 1842, Treaty of Nanjing grants Hong Kong to the British and allows them to trade in China
1844 Similar treaties made between China and France and the United States

Armed Chinese junk ►
during the
Opium War

1804 Fulani Jihad into Hausa lands
1806 British take Cape Colony from the Dutch
1817–1828 Zulu chief Shaka reigns
1830–1847 French invasion of Algeria
1830s Dutch settlers, the Boers, expand northward from Cape Colony
1848–1885 Sudanese Madhi, Muhammad Ahmad

◄ *Miners excavating diamonds in South Africa*

1804 Haitian independence
1808–1824 Wars of independence in Latin America
1822 Brazilian independence
1847 Mexican War

Simón Bolívar ►

22 The Age of European Enlightenment

CHAPTER HIGHLIGHTS

The Scientific Revolution The scientific ideas of the sixteenth and seventeenth centuries changed the way Western intellectuals thought about the world and humankind. Instead of a view of nature and humanity based on Scripture and divine revelation, Western thinkers came to rely on mathematical laws, empirical data, and experimentation. Copernicus, Kepler, and Galileo overturned the ancient idea that the Earth was the center of the universe and that the sun and the planets revolved around it. Francis Bacon urged the necessity for observation and experimentation. Newton showed the effects of gravity and established an enduring basis for physics. Locke argued that human beings were masters of their own destiny.

The Enlightenment The Enlightenment *philosophes* used reason as a basis for reform and to advocate progressive social, economic, and political movements. Voltaire attacked religious intolerance and advocated strong central government. Montesquieu and other *philosophes* argued for limited, constitutional government. Rousseau wished to reform society so that it focussed on virtue rather than material happiness. The spirit of the Enlightenment continues to pervade Western society.

Enlightened Absolutism Enlightened absolutism was a form of monarchical government dedicated to the rational strengthening of central government. Many of the reforms enlightened monarchs imposed were influenced by the ideas of the *philosophes*, but the chief goal of these rulers was to increase their own authority and military strength. The most important enlightened monarchs were Frederick II of Prussia, Joseph II of Austria, and Catherine the Great of Russia.

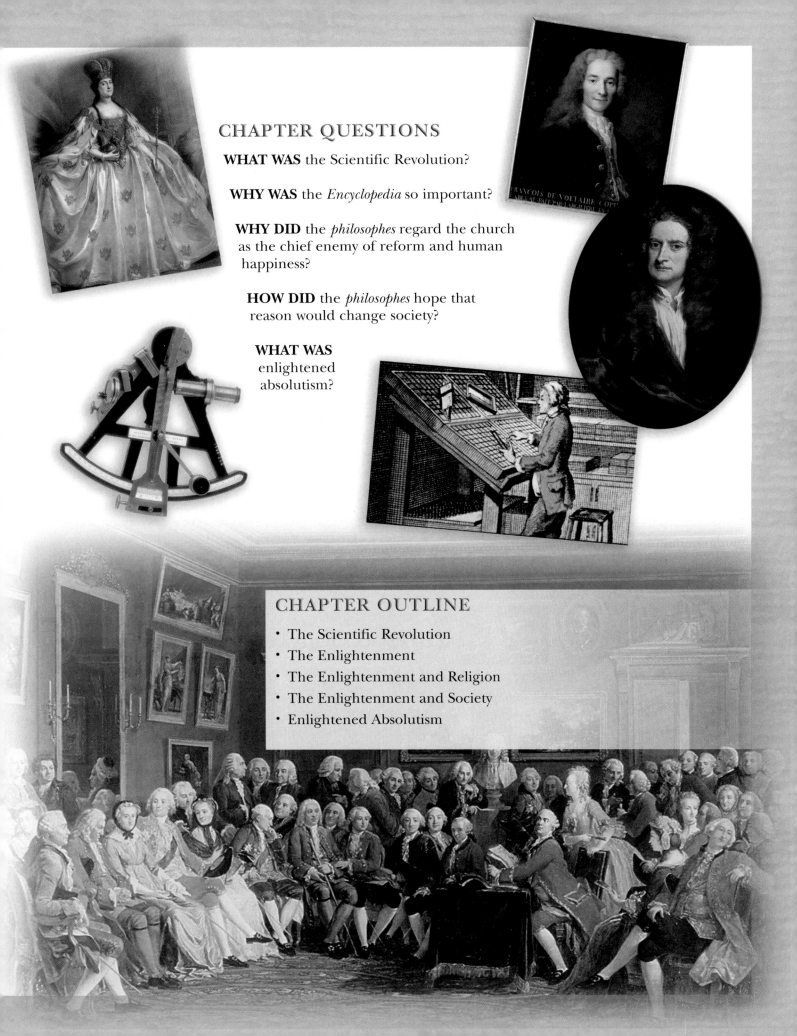

CHAPTER QUESTIONS

WHAT WAS the Scientific Revolution?

WHY WAS the *Encyclopedia* so important?

WHY DID the *philosophes* regard the church as the chief enemy of reform and human happiness?

HOW DID the *philosophes* hope that reason would change society?

WHAT WAS enlightened absolutism?

CHAPTER OUTLINE

- The Scientific Revolution
- The Enlightenment
- The Enlightenment and Religion
- The Enlightenment and Society
- Enlightened Absolutism

Enlightenment Eighteenth-century movement led by the philosophes that held that change and reform were both desirable through the application of reason and science.

No intellectual force of the past three centuries has so transformed the world as Western science and technology. Science today dominates human life, and scientific knowledge, which yields military advantages as well as medical and economic progress, is a goal of modern states. The impact of science could make itself felt first in Europe and then elsewhere only when the conviction spread that change and reform were possible and desirable. This attitude came into its own in Europe only after 1700. The movement that fostered it is called the **Enlightenment.** *It was an expression of confidence in the human mind and faith in the power of rational criticism to challenge tradition and revealed religion and discover truth. It promoted the spirit of innovation and quest for improvement that have come to characterize modern Western society. This has perhaps been Europe's most important cultural export to the rest of the world.*

WHAT WAS the Scientific Revolution?

THE SCIENTIFIC REVOLUTION

The 16th and 17th centuries witnessed a sweeping change in the way people viewed the universe. Initially being the center of the universe, the Earth came to be seen as only a planet orbiting the sun, which itself became one of millions of stars. This transformation led to a rethinking of ethics and religion as well as scientific theory, and science and the scientific method set a new standard for evaluating knowledge in the West.

The process by which this new view of scientific knowledge came to be established is termed the *Scientific Revolution*. Unlike most revolutions, it was a slow, complex movement that never involved more than a few hundred people. It entailed reappropriation of older knowledge as well as new discoveries, and it gradually achieved greater cultural authority in the Western world than any other form of intellectual activity. It has become one of the defining characteristics of modern Western civilization. Although workers in many fields contributed to it, the discipline that created the most early excitement about its potential was astronomy.

NICOLAUS COPERNICUS REJECTS AN EARTH-CENTERED UNIVERSE

The Ptolemaic System   Before Polish astronomer Copernicus (1473–1543) published *On the Revolutions of the Heavenly Spheres*, in which was his standard description of the Earth and the heavens, was a system proposed in Ptolemy's (ca. 90–168) *Almagest* (150 C.E.). The **Ptolemaic system** assumed that the Earth was the center of the universe. Surrounding the Earth was a series of crystalline spheres to which the heavenly bodies were attached. Aristotelian physics underlay the Ptolemaic systems. The heavy Earth provided a stable center, and the movement of the heavenly bodies was explained by their attachment to rotating crystalline spheres. The state of rest was assumed to be a natural condition and motion the exceptional thing that required explanation.

However, astronomers observed the planets moving in noncircular patterns around the Earth, and at times they appeared to go backward. The Ptolemaic system explained these strange motions by proposing the *epicycle*: a second revolution by a planet in an orbit tangent to its primary orbit around the Earth. The Ptolemaic explanations were effective as long as one accepted Aristotelian physics and the Christian belief that the Earth rested at the center of the created universe.

17.1
The Heliocentric Statement (ca. 1520) Nicolaus Copernicus

Scientific Revolution   Sweeping change in the scientific view of the universe that occurred in the West in the 16th and 17th centuries.

Ptolemaic system   Pre-Copernican explanation of the universe, which placed the Earth at the center of the universe.

Copernicus's Universe Copernicus challenged this picture in the most conservative manner possible. He suggested that if the Earth were assumed to move about the sun in a circle, there were fewer difficulties with the Ptolemaic system. With the sun at the center of the universe, mathematical astronomy would make more sense. The epicylces became smaller, and the retrograde motion of the planets could be explained as an optical illusion arising from an observer viewing the planets from a moving Earth. Except for the modification in the position of the Earth, most of Copernicus's book was Ptolemaic. It, however, prompted others who were discontented with the Ptolemaic system to think in new ways. Copernicus's combination of mathematics, empirical data, and observation established the model for scientific thinking.

TYCHO BRAHE AND JOHANNES KEPLER

The Danish astronomer Tycho Brahe (1546–1601) advocated a different kind of Earth-centered system in which the moon and the sun revolved around the Earth, and the other planets revolved around the sun. His critique of the Copernican model was supported by unprecedentedly accurate tables of astronomical observations made with the naked eye.

When Brahe died, these tables passed to Johannes Kepler (1571–1630), a German astronomer. Kepler was a convinced Copernican, but after much work he discovered that to keep the sun at the center of things, he must abandon Copernicus's circular orbits. The mathematical relationships that emerged from Brahe's observations suggested that the orbits of the planets were elliptical. Kepler published his findings in 1609. He had solved the problems of planetary orbits by using Copernicus's sun-centered universe and Brahe's empirical data, but the available theories could not explain why the planetary orbits were elliptical. The solution to that problem awaited Sir Isaac Newton.

GALILEO GALILEI

In 1609, the Italian scientist Galileo Galilei (1564–1642) first turned a telescope to the heavens. He saw stars where none had been known to exist, mountains on the moon, spots moving across the sun, and moons orbiting Jupiter. It suddenly became clear that the heavens were far more complex than anyone had suspected and that the Ptolemaic system could not accommodate these new phenomena.

Galileo publicized his findings and arguments for the Copernican system in his *Dialogues on the Two Chief Systems of the World* (1632). It was condemned by the Roman Catholic Church, which compelled him to recant his opinions. He did so, but reputedly muttered, "It [the Earth] still moves."

Galileo articulated the concept of a universe totally subject to mathematical laws. He believed that the smallest atom operated in consort with the same mathematical principles as the largest heavenly sphere. He championed the application of mathematics to scientific investigation with the objective of developing mathematical formulae that would explain all phenomena. The English philosopher Francis Bacon advocated a different method based solely on **empiricism**, but both empirical induction and mathematical analysis proved fundamental to scientific investigation.

FRANCIS BACON: EMPIRICAL METHOD

Francis Bacon (1561–1626) attacked the scholastic belief that most truth had already been discovered, as well as the scholastic reverence for tradition and the

empiricism Use of experiment and observation derived from sensory evidence to construct scientific theory or philosophy of knowledge.

17.4
Isaac Newton

Sir Isaac Newton. Newton discovered the mathematical and physical laws governing the force of gravity. Newton believed that religion and science were compatible and mutually supportive, and that the study of nature gave one a better understanding of the Creator. This portrait of Newton is by Sir Godfrey Kneller.

Sir Godfrey Kneller. Sir Isaac Newton. Bildarchiv Preussischer Kulturbesitz.

work of the ancients. He urged contemporaries to strike out on their own in search of a new understanding of nature.

Bacon was one of the first major European writers to champion innovation and change. Most people in Bacon's day thought that the best era of human history lay in antiquity. Bacon dissented from that view. He believed that human knowledge should produce useful results and that knowledge of nature should be used to improve the human condition. He anticipated a future of material improvement achieved through the empirical examination of nature. Although he did not make any major scientific discovery, his great achievement was to persuade others that scientific thought must proceed by means of empirical observation, not syllogistic reasoning or inference from assumptions.

ISAAC NEWTON DISCOVERS THE LAWS OF GRAVITATION

Isaac Newton (1642–1727) solved the major remaining problems of planetary motion and established a basis for physics that endured for more than two centuries. In 1687, he published *The Mathematical Principles of Natural Philosophy*, better known by its Latin title, *Principia Mathematica*. Newton was indebted to Galileo's argument that both motion and rest should be understood as givens that would continue (inertia) until something intervened to alter them. It was the cause of a change in these natural states that a scientist needed to explain. Galileo's mathematical bias also permeated Newton's thought. Newton reasoned that all physical objects exerted attractions, a force called gravity. Every object in the universe mutually attracted every other object, which explained why the planets moved in an orderly manner. Newton demonstrated the effect of gravity mathematically, but did not explain gravity itself.

Newton was a mathematical genius, but he also upheld the importance of empirical data and observation. The final test of any theory for him was whether it described what could actually be observed.

With the work of Newton, the natural universe became a realm governed by mechanistic laws. Spirits and divinities were no longer needed to explain it. This attitude helped to dispel belief in witchcraft and liberate human beings from the fear of a chaotic, inexplicable universe. Most scientists were devout and still found a place for God as the rational Creator of a rational, lawful nature. To study nature was to come to a better understanding of its Creator. Science and faith, they argued, were mutually supporting.

This approach to reconciling religion and science removed obstacles to the spread of the new physics and astronomy. Faith in a rational God also encouraged faith in the rationality of human beings and in their capacity to improve their lot. The Scientific Revolution convinced people of the desirability of change and critiquing inherited views.

WOMEN IN THE WORLD OF THE SCIENTIFIC REVOLUTION

Historians speculate about the relationship of women to the new science. Factors that had long excluded women from intellectual life continued during the Enlightenment to block their participation in the Scientific Revolution. The institutions of European intellectual life all but excluded women. With a few exceptions in Italy, women were not admitted to European universities until the end of the 19th century. Scientific academies spurned them, and there were no social spaces in which they might easily conduct scientific work.

A few isolated women—from both the nobility and the artisan class—did engage in scientific research, but only with the aid of men in their families.

Margaret Cavendish (1623-1673) had access to a circle of natural philosophers who gathered around her husband, the Duke of Newcastle. She published several books: *Observations upon Experimental Philosophy* (1666), *Grounds of Natural Philosophy* (1668), and *Descriptions of the New World, Called the Blazing World* (1666)—an introduction to science for women.

Artisan women had the advantage of always having been admitted to the crafts practiced by their families. In Germany, a number of women became astronomers by assisting astronomer fathers and husbands. Their discoveries were sometimes credited to men, and they were consistently refused posts and admission to learned academies. Although a few books were written to explain science to female readers, the dominant intellectual assumption of the 18th century was that differences between male and female minds made natural science a male vocation.

JOHN LOCKE

John Locke (1632–1704) attempted to discover laws governing the human mind similar to those which Newton had discovered as explanations for natural phenomena.

Major Publication Dates of the Enlightenment

1687	Newton's *Principia Mathematica*
1690	Locke's *Essay Concerning Human Understanding*
1733	Voltaire's *Letters on the English*
1738	Voltaire's *Elements of the Philosophy of Newton*
1748	Montesquieu's *Spirit of the Laws*
1750	Rousseau's *Discourse on the Moral Effects of the Arts and Sciences*
1751	First volume of the *Encyclopedia* edited by Diderot and d'Alembert
1755	Rousseau's *Discourse on the Origin of Inequality*
1762	Rousseau's *Social Contract*
1763	Voltaire's *Treatise on Toleration*
1776	Smith's *Wealth of Nations*
1779	Lessing's *Nathan the Wise*
1792	Wollstonecraft's *A Vindication of the Rights of Woman*

OVERVIEW   MAJOR FIGURES IN THE SCIENTIFIC REVOLUTION

The Scientific Revolution was a major turning point in Western culture. Although the Scientific Revolution never involved more than a few hundred people, the ideas they formulated and publicized gradually overturned the theological and religious modes of thought that were central to the medieval worldview. Humankind and life on Earth became the focus of Western thinking, and Western intellectuals developed more self-confidence in their capacity to shape the world and their own lives. Below is a list of the major scientific thinkers of the 16th and 17th centuries and their most important accomplishments.

Nicolaus Copernicus (1473–1543)	Argued that the Earth moved around the sun. His combination of mathematical astronomy with empirical observation and data became the model of scientific thought.
Tycho Brahe (1546–1601)	Compiled accurate tables of astronomical observations.
Johannes Kepler (1571–1630)	Used Brahe's data to argue that the orbits of the planets were elliptical.
Galileo Galilei (1564–1642)	First astronomer to use a telescope. Argued that mathematical laws governed the universe.
Francis Bacon (1561–1626)	Argued that scientific thought must conform to empirical evidence. Championed innovation and change.
Isaac Newton (1642–1727)	Explained the effect of gravity mathematically and established a theoretical basis for physics that endured until the late 19th century.
John Locke (1632–1704)	Argued that human nature was a blank slate that could be molded by modifying the environment. Human beings could thus take charge of their own destiny without divine aid.

Locke's *Essay Concerning Human Understanding* (1690) postulated that the human mind is blank at the time of birth. People, therefore, have no innate ideas. All their knowledge derives from sense experience. Each individual mind grows as it acquires information from the senses. Given that people's intellects are shaped by the interaction between their minds and the world, Locke argued that human nature can be molded by modifying the environment. Locke also rejected the Christian view that human beings were flawed by original sin. Human beings do not need to wait for divine aid; they can take charge of their own destinies.

Locke wrote *Two Treatises of Government* during the reign of Charles II (r. 1660–1685) in which he made a case against absolute monarchy. Nature's rational law, he argued, dictates that all human beings are equal and independent and that no one should harm another or disturb his property. People voluntarily relinquish some of their freedom and contract with their rulers for the protection and preservation of their natural rights. Rulers are, therefore, not absolute but bound by nature's laws. A monarch who does not comply can legitimately be overthrown. In *Letter Concerning Toleration*, Locke argued that governments existed to protect property and civil order. They should not legislate on religion, for the pursuit of salvation is the responsibility of the individual.

THE ENLIGHTENMENT

The movement known as the Enlightenment included writers living at different times in various countries. Its early exponents, the ***philosophes***, popularized the rationalism and scientific ideas of the 17th century. They exposed contemporary social and political abuses and argued that reform was necessary and possible. They confronted oppression and religious condemnation and by mid-century had brought enlightened ideas to the European public in a variety of formats.

VOLTAIRE

The most influential of the philosophes was François Marie Arouet, called Voltaire (1694–1778). During the 1720s, Voltaire offended the French authorities and was briefly imprisoned. In 1733, after visiting England, he published *Letters on the English,* which praised the intellectual and political freedom found in England and indirectly criticized French society. In 1738, he published *Elements of the Philosophy of Newton,* which popularized the thought of the great scientist. Both works enhanced his reputation.

Thereafter, Voltaire lived either in France or near Geneva, just across the French border where the royal authorities could not bother him. His essays, histories, plays, stories, and letters made him the literary dictator of Europe. He turned the venom of his satire against one evil after another in French and European life. In *Candide* (1759), he attacked war, religious persecution, and unwarranted optimism about the human condition. Like most philosophes, Voltaire believed that human society could and should be improved. But he was never certain that reform, if achieved, would be

---

WHY WAS the *Encyclopedia* so important?

philosophes Eighteenth-century writers and critics who forged the new attitudes favorable to change. They sought to apply reason and common sense to the institutions and societies of their day.

Voltaire. Philosopher, dramatist, poet, historian, and popularizer of scientific ideas, Voltaire (1694–1778) was the most famous and influential of the 18th-century philosophers. His sharp satire and criticism of religious institutions opened the way for a more general critique of the European political and social status quo.

Nicholas de Largilliere/Art Resource/Bildarchiv Preussischer Kulturbesitz.

permanent. Enlightenment optimism constituted a tempered hopefulness rather than a glib certainty. Pessimism can be found as an undercurrent in most Enlightenment works.

THE *ENCYCLOPEDIA*

The middle of the century witnessed the publication of the *Encyclopedia*, one of the greatest monuments of the Enlightenment. Under the leadership of Denis Diderot (1713–1784) and Jean le Rond d'Alembert (1717–1783), the first volume appeared in 1751. When completed in 1772, it numbered 17 volumes of text and 11 of plates. The *Encyclopedia* was the product of more than 100 authors, and its editors had solicited articles from all the major French philosophes. Attempts were made to censor it and halt its publication, but it was ultimately completed. The *Encyclopedia* made a plea for freedom of expression and set forth the most advanced critical ideas in religion, government, and philosophy. It also provided practical information in areas such as manufacturing, canal building, and agriculture.

The *Encyclopedia* had been designed to secularize learning, and the articles concentrated on humanity and its well-being. The encyclopedists looked to antiquity rather than to the Christian centuries for their inspiration, and they believed that the welfare of humankind lay not in the pursuit of revelation but in the application of reason to human relationships. The *Encyclopedia* diffused enlightened thought throughout the continent and drew German and Russian thinkers into the movement.

THE ENLIGHTENMENT AND RELIGION

*I*n the eyes of the philosophes, the chief enemy of the improvement and happiness of humankind was the church. They were especially critical of Roman Catholicism. But all the Christian churches advocated a religious rather than a scientific view of humankind and taught the idea that human beings were sinful and in need of divine grace. Religion turned attention away from this world and the solution to its problems to the world to come. The philosophes also indicted the churches for fostering intolerance and bigotry.

DEISM

The philosophes believed that religion should conform to reason and have as its primary goal the promotion of morality. Newton had convinced many that nature was a rational system. It seemed logical, therefore, that the God who had created it must also be rational. Lockean philosophy argued that all human knowledge derived from empirical experience. This cast doubt on the possibility of divine revelation and suggested that religion ought to be totally grounded on rational arguments. The rational religion of the Enlightenment is called *deism.*

There were two major points in the deists' creed. The first was a belief that God is a rational deity, which they thought could be supported by empirical observation of the rational laws God had established for the natural phenomena He created. If God is rational, then God must have established a rational basis for human morality. Because reason dictates that good must be rewarded and evil punished—and this does not inevitably happen in this life, there must be a life after death, when justice is done.

Deism was empirical, tolerant, reasonable, and capable of encouraging virtuous living. The deists hoped that rational religion would put an end to sectarian

Illustration from the *Encyclopedia*. The *Encyclopedia* included hundreds of illustrations of the work of skilled artisan. Here is illustrated the work of butchers in a slaughterhouse and the implements of their labors.
Corbis/Bettman.

WHY DID the *philosophes* regard the church as the chief enemy of reform and human happiness?

 **17.6**
On Universal Toleration: Voltaire

deism Belief in a rational God who had created the universe, but then allowed it to function without his interference according to the mechanisms of nature and a belief in rewards and punishments after death for human action.

divisions, religious persecution, and fanaticism. They also anticipated the disappearance of a priestly class, for rational individuals could come to an understanding of God by themselves without the need for dogma, ritual, or sacrament.

TOLERATION

The centuries immediately preceeding the Englightenment had been characterized by bloody religious wars, and philosophes hoped that the triumph of reason and science would end denominational hatred and establish religious toleration.

Voltaire championed this cause. In 1762, the French authorities ordered the execution of a Huguenot named Jean Calas (1698–1762) for having allegedly murdered his son to prevent him from converting to Roman Catholicism. Calas was tortured but died without confessing his guilt. Voltaire made the dead man's cause his own. In 1763, he published a *Treatise on Toleration*, and he continued to hound the authorities until in 1765 the decision against Calas was reversed. For Voltaire, the case illustrated the dangers of religious fanaticism and the need for rational judicial reform. In 1779, Gotthold Lessing's (1729–1781) play about a Jew, *Nathan the Wise*, broadened the plea for toleration beyond Christian sects to include all religious faiths. All of these calls for toleration argued that secular values were more important than religious ones.

ISLAM IN ENLIGHTENMENT THOUGHT

With the exception of the Balkans, there were few Muslims in Europe in the 18th century. European merchants traded with Islamic countries, but most of the information Europeans had about Islam came from hostile sources: histories, travel diaries, and books by Christian missionaries. They dismissed Islam as a false religion, a rival to Christianity that was characterized by carnality and sexual promiscuity.

Several European universities established chairs of Arabic studies in the 17th century, but the professors who held them tended to agree with the Christian theologians and to equate Islam with religious fanaticism. In 1742, Voltaire published a tragedy with the explicit title *Fanaticism, or Mohammed the Prophet*. Charles Louis de Secondat, baron de Montesquieu, claimed that Muslim countries were the prime examples of the dangers of religious despotism. Excessive influence of religious leaders, he insisted, prevented the Ottoman Empire from adapting itself to advances in science and technology.

John Toland, a deist advocate for religious toleration, was more generous in his assessment of Islam. He shocked many of his contemporaries by contending that Islam derived from early Christian writings and was a form of Christianity. The historian, Edward Gibbon, praised Muhammad's leadership and Islam's success in building a great empire. Lady Mary Wortley Montagu (1689–1762), who lived in Istanbul with her husband, the British ambassador, found much to praise about Ottoman society. Compared to the constraints on the lives of women in England, she insisted that upper-class Turkish women were remarkably free and well treated. She lamented the misinformation about the Muslim world that circulated through Europe.

The few European voices calling for fairness and empathy for Islam had little impact. But it must be acknowledged that Muslims, for their part, showed little curiosity about the West. The *ulama* maintained that Islam had superceded Christianity as a religion and, therefore, Muslims had little to learn from Europe's Christian culture.

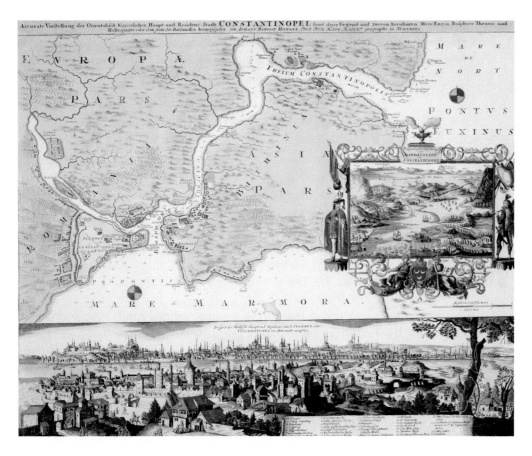

Map of Turkey and View of Constantinople. Few Europeans visited the Ottoman Empire. What little they know about it came from reports of travellers and from illustrations such as this view of Constantinople the empire's capital.

© Historical Picture Archive/Corbis.

THE ENLIGHTENMENT AND SOCIETY

*T*he philosophes believed that rational analysis of social behavior would reveal laws in human relationships similar to those found in natural phenomena. The discovery of social laws, they predicted, would end inhumane conduct, a byproduct of ignorance.

HOW DID the philosophes hope that reason would change society?

MONTESQUIEU AND *THE SPIRIT OF THE LAWS*

Charles Louis de Secondat, Baron de Montesquieu's (1689–1755) *The Spirit of the Laws* (1748) was perhaps the most influential book of the century. Montesquieu took an empirical approach to the study of law, passing his conclusions on legal texts from ancient as well as modern nations. He concluded that no single set of laws could apply to all peoples at all times and in all places. Only a careful examination and evaluation of many variables could reveal what mode of government would prove most beneficial for a given people.

The French, Montesquieu believed, would be best served by a monarchy whose power was limited by intermediary institutions: the aristocracy, the towns, the *parlements*, and other corporate bodies whose liberties the monarch had to respect. Their role was to preserve the liberty of subjects by restraining the power of their ruler. Montesquieu was a political conservative, but he believed that France's oppressive and inefficient monarchy was degrading life in France and it needed reform.

One of Montesquieu's most influential insights was the concept of the division of powers. He thought that Great Britain provided an excellent example of this principle in action. It vested executive power in its monarch, legislative power in its Parliament, and judicial power in its courts, and any two of these

Adam Smith (1723-1790)

- Advocated abolition of mercantile system
- Saw nature as set of physical resources to be exploited by human beings
- Was in favor of limited government activity in the economy

branches of government could check the power of the other. His perception of the 18th-century British constitution was incorrect, but his analysis made a strong case for limiting the power of rulers by constitutional means and relyinig on legislatures, not monarchs, to make laws. Montesquieu's ideas guided the West's subsequent experiments with liberal democracies.

ADAM SMITH ON ECONOMIC GROWTH AND SOCIAL PROGRESS

The most important Enlightenment exposition of economics was Adam Smith's (1723–1790) *An Inquiry into the Nature and Causes of the Wealth of Nations* (1776). Smith urged abolition of England's mercantile system. Mercantilists claimed that economic regulation by the state was needed to preserve the wealth of a nation as well as to increase wealth by taking it away from other nations. But Smith believed that such regulation constricted wealth and production. He believed that if individuals were unleashed to pursue their self-interest, the result would be economic expansion, for the rational demands of the marketplace would guide their productive activities.

Smith saw nature as a boundless expanse of material resources to be exploited for the benefit of humankind, and this idea came to dominate life in the West. At the time when Smith was writing, the population of the world was much smaller than it is today. Its people were poorer, and the quantity of undeveloped resources per capita was much greater than it is now. For people of the 18th century, the improvement of the human condition seemed to require the uninhibited exploitation of natural resources.

Smith is usually regarded as the founder of *laissez-faire* economics, the school that advocates a very limited role for government in economic life. However, Smith was not opposed to all government participation in the economy. He believed that the state should provide schools, armies, navies, and roads and undertake commercial ventures that were desirable but too risky for private enterprise. Smith, like most of the philosophes, was less doctrinaire than any brief summary of their thought suggests.

Smith's theories helped to justify Western imperialism. Smith endorsed a model popular with other social theorists of his day: the *four-stage theory*. It divided human societies into four categories according to their economic basis: hunting and gathering, pastoral or herding, agricultural, and commercial. Movement through these stages was assumed to be progress. This meant that economic development was the indicator of where a group fell on the continuum between barbarism and civilization. Smith's theory allowed Europeans to view their society as the pinnacle of human achievement and to justify their pursuit of imperial domination of the world as a civilizing mission.

ROUSSEAU

Jean-Jacques Rousseau (1712–1778) saw things differently. His *Discourse on the Moral Effects of the Arts and Sciences* (1750) contended that civilization and enlightenment had corrupted, not elevated, human nature. In a *Discourse on the Origin of Inequality* (1755), he agreed that economic problems were at the root of evil in the world, but the problem was maldistribution of property, not production. Rousseau felt that the purpose of society should be to nurture better, not wealthier, people. His vision of reform was much more radical than that of other philosophers.

The Social Contract (1762) outlines the kind of political structure that Rousseau believed would overcome the evils of contemporary society. Most 18th-century political thinkers regarded society as a collection of independent

laissez-faire French phrase meaning "allow to do." In economics, the doctrine of minimal government interference in the working of the economy.

Printing Shops.   Shops such as this were the productive centers for the book trade and newspaper publishing that spread the ideas of the Enlightenment.

The Granger Collection.

individuals pursuing selfish goals, and they advocated liberating these individuals from the undue bonds of government. Rousseau, however, claimed that society was more important than the individual, because individuals are what they are only because of their relationship to the larger community. Lone, independent human beings can achieve little, but in a community they become moral creatures capable of significant action. Rousseau, drawing on Plato and Calvin, claimed that true freedom was obedience to law—that is, rules determined by the general will. The general will, Rousseau believed, was the opinion of the majority of voting citizens who acted with adequate information and under the influence of virtuous customs and morals. This majority was always right, and to obey it was to be free. If a minority disagreed, it had (paradoxically) to be forced to be free. Radical direct democracy entailed collective action against individual citizens. Rousseau assaulted the 18th-century cult of the individual and selfishness and was at odds with the commercial spirit that was transforming his world.

ENLIGHTENED CRITICS OF EUROPEAN EMPIRE

Most of the Enlightenment's thinkers equated the expansion of Europe's empires with the spread of civilization and progress, but there were a few who disagreed. They were troubled, in particular, by the treatment of Native Americans and the enslavement of Africans. The leading critics of empire were: the philosophers Immanuel Kant (1724–1804) and Johann Gottfried Herder (1744–1803), and the encyclopedist Denis Diderot (1713–1784). They argued for a common humanity shared by all people that required recognition of their dignity and treatment of them with respect. They insisted that no single description of human nature could be exalted as an absolute standard and then used to dehumanize peoples who differed from it. Non-European cultures deserved respect and understanding and should not be destroyed on the assumption that they were inferior and, therefore, valueless. Humanity manifests itself, they believed, in different cultural forms that are too complex to be judged by a single standard. Herder went so far as to suggest that "European culture" itself was an abstraction that existed nowhere. The objections these men raised to slavery and abuse of native peoples (see "Denis Diderot Condemns European Empires") found a sympathetic hearing in some circles, but their criticisms of empire did not.

HISTORY'S VOICES

DENIS DIDEROT CONDEMNS EUROPEAN EMPIRES

Denis Diderot was one of the most prolific writers of the Enlightenment. He is most known for his role as editor of the Encyclopedia. Some of his writings were published without being directly attributed to him. Among these were his contributions to Abbé G. T. Raynal's History of the Two Indies, published in various changing editions after 1772. Diderot's contributions appear to have been made in 1780. The entire History was critical of the European colonial empires that had arisen since the Spanish encounter with the New World. Diderot was particularly concerned to condemn the inhumane treatment of the native populations of the Americas, the greed displayed by all Europeans, and the establishment of various forms of forced labor.

WHAT IS the basis for Diderot's view that Europeans have behaved tyrannically? How does he portray the behavior of Europeans once they have left their own native countries and find themselves in foreign areas? What are the specific social results he associates with European greed?

Let the European nations make their own judgment and give themselves the name they deserve . . . Their explorers arrive in a region of the New World unoccupied by anyone from the Ole World, and immediately bury a small strip of metal on which they have engraved these words: *This country belongs to us.* Any why does it belong to you? . . . You have no right to the natural products of the country where you land, and you claim a right over your fellow-men. Instead of recognizing this man as a brother you only see him as a slave, a beast of burden. Oh my fellow citizens! You think like that and you behave like that; and you have ideas of justice, a morality, a holy religion . . . in common with whose whom you treat so tyrannically. This reproach should especially be addressed to the Spaniards.

****

Beyond the Equator a man is neither English, Dutch, French, Spanish, nor Portuguese. He retains only those principles and prejudices of his native country which justify or excuse his conduct. He crawls when he is weak; he is violent when strong; he is in a hurry to acquire, in a hurry to enjoy, and capable of every crime which will lead him most quickly to his goals. He is a domestic tiger returning to the forest; the thirst for blood takes hold of him once more. This is how all the Europeans, every one of them, indistinctly, have appeared in the countries of the New World. There they have assumed a common frenzy—the thirst for gold.

****

The Spaniard, the first to be thrown up by the waves onto the shores of the New World, thought he had no duty to people who did not share his color, customs, or religion. He saw in them only tools for his greed, and he clapped them in irons. These weak men, not used to work, soon died in the foul air of the mines, or in other occupations which were virtually as lethal. Then people called for slaves from Africa. Their number has gone up as more land has been cultivated. The Portuguese, Dutch, English, French, Danes, all the nations, free or subjected, have without remorse sought to increase their fortune in the sweat, blood and despair of these unfortunates. What a horrible system!

Source: Denis Diderot, *Political Writings*, John Hope Mason and Robert Wokler, eds., (Cambridge: Cambridge University Press, 1998), pp. 177, 178, 186.

WOMEN IN THE THOUGHT AND PRACTICE OF THE ENLIGHTENMENT

Women, especially in France, helped to promote the careers of the philosophes. In Paris, the salons of women such as Marie-Thérèse Geoffrin (1699–1777), Julie de Lespinasse (1733–1776), and Claudine de Tencin (1689–1749) gave the philosophes a receptive forum for debating and publicizing their ideas. These women were well connected to political figures, and they were able to provide protection for philosophes whom the authorities might otherwise have silenced. The Marquise de Pompadour (1721–1764), the mistress of Louis XV, for example, helped defeat efforts to censor the *Encyclopedia*.

Despite their reliance on female patrons and general enthusiasm for reform, the philosophes advocated no radical changes in the social condition of women. Montesquieu, for example, believed that women were not naturally inferior to men and that they should play a greater role in society, but he also believed that men should dominate marriage and family. Furthermore, although he supported the right of women to divorce and opposed laws that oppressed them, he exalted chastity as the primary female virtue.

The salon of Mme. Marie-Thérèse Geoffrin (1699–1777). This was one of the most important gathering spots for Enlightenment writers during the mid-18th century. Well-connected women such as Mme. Geoffrin were instrumental in helping the philosophes they patronized to bring their ideas to the attention of influential people in French society and politics.

Giraudon/Art Resource, N.Y.

The *Encyclopedia*'s articles that dealt with women emphasized their physical inferiority, usually attributing it to menstruation or childbearing. Women, it was assumed, were reared to be frivolous and unconcerned with serious issues. The encyclopedists discussed women primarily in the context of the family, considered motherhood their most important occupation, and defended a double standard of sexual behavior. Despite the impression the articles give of women's relegation to the domestic sphere, the *Encyclopedia*'s illustrations show women, many of them lower and working class, involved in economically productive activities.

Rousseau urged women to embrace their traditional roles. In his novel *Émile* (1762), he declared that women should be educated to be subordinate to men and to center their lives on bearing and rearing children. He portrayed women as weaker and inferior to men, except perhaps for their capacity for feeling and giving love. He excluded them from public affairs and confined them to the domestic sphere.

Despite these views (and his ill treatment of his many children and the women who bore them), Rousseau won a vast following among women in the 18th century. They may have responded to the stress he put on women's emotions and subjective feelings in his various writings. By portraying domestic life and the roles of wife and mother as noble vocations, he gave middle- and upper-class women confidence that their lives had purpose.

In 1792, in *A Vindication of the Rights of Woman*, Mary Wollstonecraft (1759–1797) tested Rousseau's ideas against the philosophes' standards of reason and progressive enlightenment. She accused Rousseau and others who upheld traditional roles for women of attempting to narrow women's visions and limit their experiences. She argued that to confine women to the separate domestic sphere because of their supposed physiological limitations was to make them the sensual slaves of men and prevent them from achieving moral and intellectual identities of their own. Denying them good educations impeded human progress by squandering the talents of half the human species. Wollstonecraft demanded for women the kind of intellectual liberty that male writers of the Enlightenment insisted were the rights of men.

WHAT WAS enlightened absolutism?

ENLIGHTENED ABSOLUTISM

During the last third of the 18th century, several European rulers embraced many of the philosophes' reforms and experimented with a form of government called *enlightened absolutism*. Their goal was to rationalize administration by strengthening centralized government at the cost of local authorities. Frederick II of Prussia, Joseph II of Austria, and Catherine II of Russia were the major monarchs who were influenced by the Enlightenment, but they often found that political and social realities forced them to moderate the policies recommended by the philosophes with whom they corresponded or who were guests at their courts.

The relationship between these monarchs and the writers of the Enlightenment was complicated. Rulers were motivated to pursue rational economic and social integration of their realms less as an end in itself than as a means toward enhancing their military strength. They used "enlightened" reforms to pursue goals favored by the philosophes but also to further what the philosophes considered irrational militarism.

JOSEPH II OF AUSTRIA

No 18th-century ruler embodied rational, impersonal authority more than Emperor Joseph II of Austria, the son of Maria Theresa (r. 1740–1780). He prided himself on his narrow, passionless rationality, but he genuinely wanted to improve the lot of his people. However, his well-intentioned efforts prompted rebellions by both aristocrats and peasants from Hungary to the Austrian Netherlands.

The Habsburgs' empire was Europe's most diverse political entity. Its rulers never succeeded in creating a unified government or enlisting the loyalties of its various groups of aristocrats. Maria Theresa preserved the monarchy during the War of the Austrian Succession (1740–1748) by guaranteeing independence for aristocrats, especially the Hungarians. But after the conflict, she improved her position in Austria and Bohemia by imposing a more efficient system of tax collection. Even clergy and nobles were compelled to pay. She established central councils to deal with political problems. She expanded primary schooling, and she tried to redirect educational institutions to training officials for royal service. Concern for peasants and serfs (from whom she recruited her military manpower) led her to limit the services that landowners could demand from them..

Like his mother, Joseph believed that royal authority could promote prosperity and military power, but his reforms were more wide ranging than hers. His chief goal was to overcome the pluralism of the Habsburg domains by increasing the power of the central monarchy. In particular, he wanted to lessen Hungarian autonomy. He even refused to be crowned king of Hungary to avoid having to guarantee Hungarian privileges in a coronation oath. He reorganized local government in Hungary, increasing the authority of his own officials and imposing the use of German. The Magyar nobility, however, resisted, and in 1790 he rescinded most of his centralizing measures.

Joseph extended freedom of worship to Lutherans, Calvinists, and the Greek Orthodox. He gave Jews the right

Russia from Peter the Great Through Catherine the Great

1725	Death of Peter the Great
1741–1762	Elizabeth
1762	Peter III
1762	Catherine II (the Great) becomes empress
1767	Legislative Commission summoned
1768	War with Turkey
1771–1774	Pugachev's Rebellion
1772	First Partition of Poland
1774	Treaty of Kuchuk-Kainardji ends war with Turkey
1775	Reorganization of local government
1783	Russia annexes the Crimea
1785	Catherine issues the Charter of the Nobility
1793	Second Partition of Poland
1795	Third Partition of Poland
1796	Death of Catherine the Great

to worship privately and relieved them of certain taxes and signs of personal degradation. His empire was officially Roman Catholic, but he brought its church under royal control. He forbade his bishops to communication directly with the pope. He dissolved more than 600 monasteries and confiscated their lands, and he replaced traditional seminaries with eight general seminaries specializing in training men for parish duties. Joseph made Roman Catholic priests state employees and prevented the church from exercising much independent influence. His policies, known as *Josephinism*, prefigured those of the French Revolution.

Joseph believed that reducing traditional burdens would make the peasants more productive and industrious. He abolished serfdom and gave peasants more personal freedom. They were allowed to marry, engage in skilled work, and have their children trained in these skills without permission from their landlord. Manorial courts were reformed, and peasants were given right of appeal to royal officials. Joseph also encouraged landlords to change land leases so that it would be easier for peasants to inherit or transfer them.

In 1789, Joseph declared that all proprietors were to be taxed, regardless of social status. The aristocrats protested, and his death in 1790 ended attempts to put the system into effect. His policies created a legacy of turmoil for his heir, and his brother Leopold II (r. 1790–1792), although sympathetic to Joseph's goals, had to repeal many of his decrees.

CATHERINE THE GREAT OF RUSSIA

Joseph II never grasped the necessity of cultivating support for his policies, but Catherine II (r. 1762–1796) understood the fragility of her dynasty's power. After the death of Peter the Great in 1725, the court nobles and the army had chosen the heirs to Russia's throne. Peter's daughter Elizabeth (r. 1741–1762) was succeeded by Peter III, one of her nephews. He was weak and possibly insane, but his marriage in 1745 profoundly affected the future of his Romanov dynasty. His bride was the German princess, historically known as Catherine the Great. A few months into his reign, Peter III was deposed and murdered—with Catherine's approval, and she was proclaimed empress.

Catherine's familiarity with the Enlightenment and western Europe convinced her that Russia had to implement reforms if it hoped to remain a great power. Having acquired the throne by means of a palace coup, she well understood the necessity of recruiting support for whatever she tried to do. Consequently, in 1767 she summoned a Legislative Commission to advise her on reforms for Russia's government. More than 500 delegates represented all sectors of Russian life, and Catherine provided them with a set of *Instructions* drawn from the philosophes' theories. Catherine dismissed the commission before several of its key committees reported. It, however, gathered a vast amount of information about conditions in Russia, and its debates suggested that most Russians saw no alternative to an autocratic monarchy. Catherine herself had no intention of backing away from absolutism.

Catherine the Great. She ascended to the Russian throne after the murder of her husband. She tried initially to enact major reforms, but she never intended to abandon absolutism. She assured the nobility of their rights and by the end of her reign had imposed press censorship.

The Granger Collection.

Catherine carried out limited reforms on her own authority. In 1775, she reorganized local government to solve problems brought to light by the Legislative Commission. Instead of creating a royal bureaucracy, she gave most local offices to nobles. In 1785, she issued the Charter of the Nobility, which guaranteed the nobles certain rights and privileges. She issued a similar charter for townspeople. The empress had to rely on the nobles and urban classes, for she had too few educated subjects to establish an independent bureaucracy, and her treasury could not afford to sustain a professional army.

Catherine, like her predecessors, continued efforts to acquire warm-water ports. She fought the Turks from 1768 to 1774, and by the Treaty of Kuchuk-Kainardji won Russia a direct outlet on the Black Sea. In 1783, she annexed the Crimea (see Map 22–1).

MAP 22–1

Expansion of Russia, 1689–1796. The overriding territorial aim of the two most powerful Russian monarchs of the 18th century, Peter the Great (in the first quarter of the century) and Catherine the Great (in the last half of the century) was to secure navigable outlets to the sea in both the north and the south for Russia's vast empire; hence Peter's push to the Baltic Sea and Catherine's to the Black Sea. Russia also expanded into Central Asia and Siberia during this time period.

WHICH EMPIRE came into direct conflict with Russian expansion?

THE PARTITION OF POLAND

Russia's military successes made the other states of eastern Europe uneasy, but their anxieties were allayed by an agreement that led to the First Partition of Poland (see Map 22–2). Frederick the Great made a proposal to Russia and Austria that, by giving each something, would prevent conflict among them and save appearances. After complicated, secret negotiations among the three powers, the Polish state lost approximately one third of its territory. Two additional partitions of Poland in 1793 and 1795 removed Poland from the map of Europe entirely, and it was not restored until 1919. Without a strong central government, Poland's political weakness made the country ripe for plunder by the strong states that surrounded it.

MAP 22–2

Partitions of Poland, 1772, 1793, and 1795. The eradication of Poland from the map displayed 18th-century power politics at its most extreme.

WHY WAS Poland so easily destroyed in the 18th century?

IMAGE KEY

for pages 536–537

a. Astronomer Tycho Brahe from the *Atlas Major* by Joan Blaeu

b. Jean-Jacques Rousseau (1712–1778)

c. Catherine the Great as a young princess.

d. Catherine the Great after ascending to the Russian throne.

e. Voltaire (1694–1778).

f. Sir Isaac Newton (1642–1727).

g. One of Galileo's early telescopes.

h. The composing room of a print shop.

i. The salon of Mme. Marie-Therese Geoffrin

Summary

The Scientific Revolution The scientific ideas of the 16th and 17th centuries changed the way Western intellectuals thought about the world and humankind. Instead of a view of nature and humanity based on Scripture and divine revelation, Western thinkers came to rely on mathematical laws, empirical data, and experimentation. Copernicus, Kepler, and Galileo overturned the ancient idea, sanctioned by the Bible, that the Earth was the center of the universe and that the sun and the planets revolved around it. Galileo maintained that the world was governed by mathematical laws. Francis Bacon urged the necessity for observation and experimentation. Newton showed the effects of gravity and established an enduring basis for physics. Locke argued that human beings were masters of their own destiny.

The Enlightenment The Enlightenment philosophes used reason as a basis for reform and to advocate progressive social, economic, and political movements. Voltaire attacked religious intolerance and advocated a strong central government to impose rational solutions to social and political problems. Montesquieu and other philosophes argued for a limited, constitutional government. Rousseau wished to reform society to focus on virtue rather than material happiness. He maintained that in the pursuit of virtue the needs of society were more important than those of the individual. The spirit of the Enlightenment continues to pervade Western society.

Enlightened Absolutism Enlightened absolutism was a form of monarchical government dedicated to the rational strengthening of central government. Many of the reforms enlightened monarchs imposed were influenced by the ideas of the philosophes, but the chief goal of these rulers was to increase their own authority and military strength, as witnessed by the fate of Poland. The most important enlightened monarchs were Frederick II of Prussia, Joseph II of Austria, and Catherine the Great of Russia.

REVIEW QUESTIONS

1. What did Copernicus, Galileo, and Newton contribute to the Scientific Revolution? Is the Scientific Revolution accurately described as a revolution?

2. How did the Enlightenment change Western attitudes toward reform, faith, and reason?

3. Why were the philosophes opposed to organized religion? What did they prefer in its place?

4. What aspects of the Enlightenment did Rousseau oppose?

5. What kind of reforms did enlightened monarchs' implement? What was their purpose?

KEY TERMS

deism (p. 543)   *laissez-faire* (p. 546)   **Ptolemaic system** (p. 538)
empiricism (p. 539)   **philosophes** (p. 542)   **Scientific Revolution** (p. 538)
Enlightenment (p. 538)

 For additional study resources for this chapter, go to:
www.prenhall.com/craig/chapter22

23 Revolutions in the Transatlantic World

CHAPTER HIGHLIGHTS

The Transatlantic Revolutions The revolutions and the crusade against slavery that occurred throughout the transatlantic world between 1776 and the 1830s transformed three continents: North America, Europe, and South America. The foundations of modern liberal democracy were laid, and the largest republic since ancient times was established in North America. In France, written constitutions and elected legislatures became essential parts of government. In Latin America, republicanism triumphed everywhere except Brazil. Never again could government be undertaken in these regions without some form of participation by the governed.

Economic and Social Liberalization The expanding forms of political liberty found their counterparts in an economic life freed from the constraints of the old colonial empires and slavery. The new American republic constituted a vast free trade zone. And for the first time since the encounter with Europe, Latin America could trade freely among its own peoples and those of the rest of the world. In France and Europe, where the Napoleonic armies had carried the doctrines of the rights of man, economic life had been rationalized and freed from the domination of local authorities. National law formed the framework for economic activity. The movement to abolish slavery fostered a wage economy of free laborers which would generate its own set of problems, but it was nonetheless an economy of free human beings.

Nationalism Finally, the age of transatlantic revolutions saw the emergence of nationalism as a political force. The Americans saw themselves as forming a new kind of nation. The French had demonstrated the power of a nation mobilized for military purposes. In turn, the aggression of France had aroused national sentiment throughout Eurrope and the New World.

These various revolutions, their political doctrines, and their social and economic departures provided examples to peoples elsewhere in the world. But even more important, the transatlantic revolutions and eventual abolition of slavery meant that new political classes and independent nations would become actors on the world scene. Europeans would have to deal with a score of new nations in the Americas. The rest of the world confronted new nations freed from the direction and authority of European powers. The political changes in Europe meant that those nations and their relationships with the rest of the world would be directed by a broader range of groups than in the past.

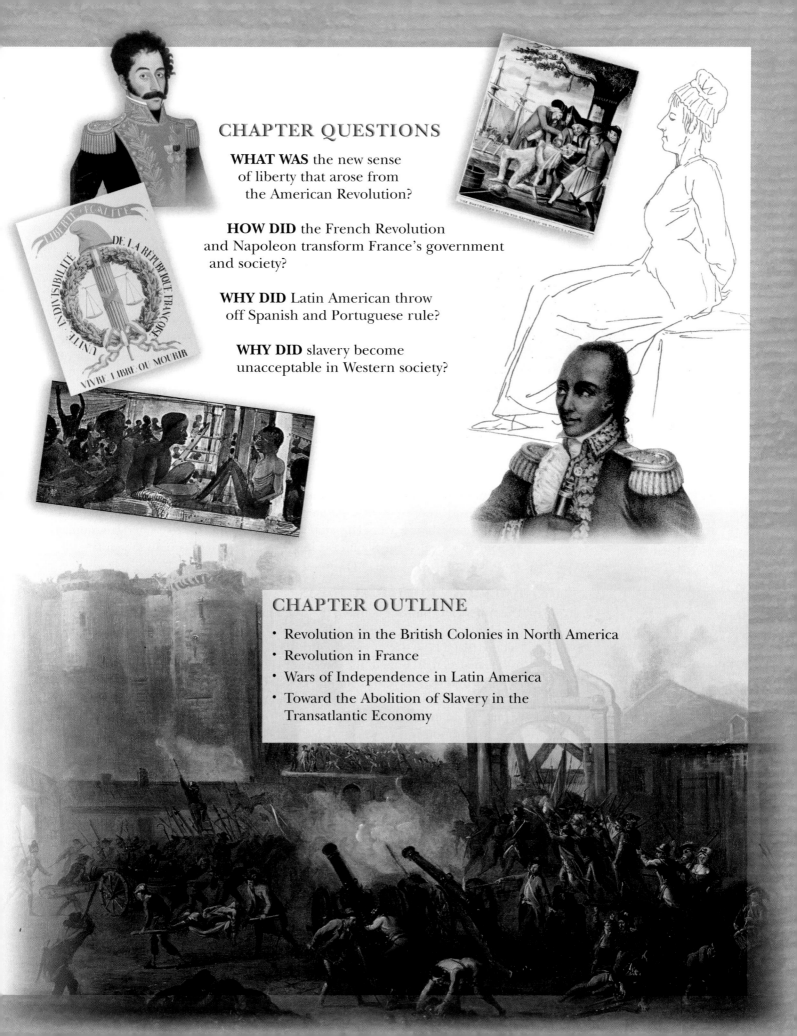

CHAPTER QUESTIONS

WHAT WAS the new sense of liberty that arose from the American Revolution?

HOW DID the French Revolution and Napoleon transform France's government and society?

WHY DID Latin American throw off Spanish and Portuguese rule?

WHY DID slavery become unacceptable in Western society?

CHAPTER OUTLINE

- Revolution in the British Colonies in North America
- Revolution in France
- Wars of Independence in Latin America
- Toward the Abolition of Slavery in the Transatlantic Economy

Between 1776 and 1824, a world-transforming series of revolutions occurred in France and the Americas. In a half century, the peoples of the two American continents established their independence of European political control, and in Europe, the French monarchy collapsed. The leaders of all the successful revolutions sought to establish new governments based largely on Enlightenment principles. The era also witnessed the commencement of an international crusade to abolish first the slave trade and then slavery throughout the transatlantic world.

WHAT WAS the new sense of liberty that arose from the American Revolution?

REVOLUTION IN THE BRITISH COLONIES IN NORTH AMERICA

RESISTANCE TO THE IMPERIAL SEARCH FOR REVENUE

After the Treaty of Paris in 1763 ended the Seven Years' War, the British government faced two problems. The first was the cost of defending the empire they had acquired. The second was the need to organize a vast new territory: all of North America east of the Mississippi (see Map 23–1).

The British drive for revenue began in 1764 with the Sugar Act. Britain hoped to enhance revenue from imports of sugar into the colonies by the rigorous collection of what was actually a reduced tax. Smugglers were to be tried in admiralty courts without juries. A year later, Parliament passed the Stamp Act, a tax on legal documents and other items. The British considered these taxes just because they had been approved by Parliament and because the revenue was to be spent in the colonies that paid them. The Americans, however, objected that they were not represented in Parliament and insisted that they alone had the right to tax themselves. Threatend with disorder in its American lands, Parliament repealed the Stamp Act in 1766 but asserted its right to legislate for the colonies.

AMERICAN POLITICAL IDEAS

The American colonists believed that the English Revolution of 1688 had established liberties that belonged to them as well as to the British. They claimed that George III (r. 1760–1820) and the British Parliament were dissolving the bonds of allegiance that united the two peoples by attacking those liberties. The colonists thus appealed to an argument that English aristocrats of an earlier generation had used to justify limiting the power of their king in order to support a popular revolution.

In addition to the works of John Locke (1632–1704), from which these ideas largely derived, Americans were reading British political writers called the *Commonwealthmen*. These authors held republican political ideas that stemmed from the radical branches of the Puritan revolution. They dismissed much parliamentary taxation as nothing more than a means for financing political corruption, and they feared standing armies as instruments of tyranny. The policy of Great Britain toward America after the Treaty of Paris made many colonists believe that the suspicions of the Commonwealthmen were correct.

CRISIS AND INDEPENDENCE

In May 1773, Parliament allowed the East India Company to import tea directly into the American colonies. Although the law lowered the price of tea, it levied a tax on it that was imposed without the colonists' consent. Protestors in Boston reacted by throwing a shipload of tea into the harbor, an event called the Boston Tea Party.

MAP EXPLORATION

Interactive map: To explore this map further, go to
http://www.prenhall.com/craig/map23.1

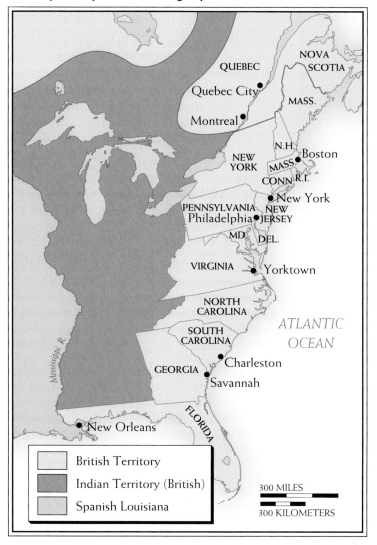

MAP 23–1

North America in 1763. In the year of the victory over France, the English colonies lay along the Atlantic seaboard. The difficulties of organizing authority over the previous French territory in Canada and west of the Appalachian Mountains would contribute to the coming of the American Revolution.

HOW DID westward expansion of the colonies lead to tensions with both the British and Indians?

The British ministry of Lord North (1732–1792) was determined to assert the authority of Parliament over the colonies. In 1774, Parliament closed the port of Boston, reorganized the government of Massachusetts, quartered troops in private homes, and transferred the trials of royal customs officials to England. Parliament also extended the boundaries of Quebec to include the Ohio River

18.4
Declaration of
Independence:
Revolutionary Declarations

"Boston Massacre." This view of the Boston Massacre of March 5, 1770 by Paul Revere owes more to propaganda than fact. There was no order to fire and the innocent citizens portrayed here were really an angry, violent mob.

The Granger Collection, New York.

The American Revolution

1760	George III becomes king
1763	Treaty of Paris concludes the Seven Years' War
1764	Sugar Act
1765	Stamp Act
1766	Stamp Act repealed and Declaratory Act passed
1770	Lord North becomes George III's chief minister
1773	Boston Tea Party
1774	First Continental Congress
1775	Second Continental Congress
1776	Declaration of Independence
1778	France enters the war on the side of America
1781	British forces surrender at Yorktown
1783	Treaty of Paris concludes War of the American Revolution

valley which the Americans regarded as an attempt to prevent them from spreading, with their political ideas, westward beyond the Appalachian Mountains.

During these years, committees of correspondence, composed of citizens critical of Britain, were established throughout the colonies, and in September 1774, these committees organized the First Continental Congress in Philadelphia. This body failed to persuade Parliament to abandon its attempt at direct supervision of colonial affairs. In 1775, the battles of Lexington, Concord, and Bunker Hill were fought, and the Second Continental Congress undertook to govern the colonies. In August 1775, George III declared the colonies in rebellion. During the winter, Thomas Paine's (1737–1809) pamphlet *Common Sense* galvanized public opinion in favor of separation from Great Britain. A colonial army and navy were organized, and on July 4, 1776, the Continental Congress adopted the Declaration of Independence. The War of the American Revolution continued until 1781, when the forces of George Washington (1732–1799) defeated those of Lord Cornwallis (1738–1805) at Yorktown. In 1778, however, the war had widened into a European conflict, for the French government supported the rebellion in the hope of weakening its traditional enemy, Great Britain. In 1779, Spain also came to the aid of the colonies. The 1783 Treaty of Paris concluded the conflict and recognized the independence of the 13 American colonies.

As the crisis with Britain unfolded, the American colonists first saw themselves as preserving traditional English liberties, but as the war went on, they developed a different understanding of what liberty meant. By the mid-1770s, they had rejected monarchy and embraced republican ideals. After the Constitution was adopted in 1788, a bill of rights was added to protect civil liberties. They rejected the aristocratic social hierarchy that had existed in the colonies and embraced democratic ideals. Although they limited the right to vote, they asserted the equality of white male citizens before the law and in social relations. They rejected social ranking based on birth and inheritance and asserted that all citizens had to have the opportunity to improve their social standing and economic lot by engaging in free commercial activity. Although the American Revolution did not free slaves or address the rights of women and Native Americans, it produced a society freer than any the world had seen—one in which political and social liberties would continue to increase. The American Revolution was a radical movement that spread its influence as Americans moved across their continent and as its success inspired other peoples to question traditional European governments. It inspired the Wars of Independence in Latin America and liberal and radical political movements in Europe.

REVOLUTION IN FRANCE

*T*he French monarchy emerged from the Seven Years' War defeated and deeply in debt, and the support it gave the American Revolution exacerbated its financial difficulties. Given France's economic vitality, the government's debt was not overly large, but the government could not enforce collection of sufficient taxes to service and repay its debt. Between 1786 and 1788, Louis XVI's (r. 1774–1792) ministers tried to persuade the aristocracy and the church to pay more taxes. The *parlement* of Paris insisted that only the Estates General could institute new taxes but failed. The Estates General had not met since 1614, but in July 1788, Louis agreed to convene it.

REVOLUTIONS OF 1789

The Estates General Becomes the National Assembly   The three "estates" that composed the Estates General were: the clergy (the First Estate), the nobility (the Second Estate), and everyone else (the **Third Estate**). The Estates General began to meet at Versailles in May 1789, and on June 1, the Third Estate, composed largely of local officials, professional men, and lawyers, invited the clergy and nobles to join it in organizing a new legislative body. A few of the lower clergy did so, and on June 17, that body declared itself the National Assembly.

Three days later, finding themselves accidentally locked out of their usual meeting place, the National Assembly moved to a nearby tennis court, where its members took the famous Tennis Court Oath. They vowed to remain in session until they had given France a constitution. Louis XVI ordered the National Assembly to desist, but this only encouraged most of the clergy and many nobles to support it. On June 27, the king capitulated, and the National Assembly reorganized as the National Constituent Assembly.

Fall of the Bastille   Two developments soon complicated the situation. First, Louis XVI tried to regain the initiative by mustering troops near Versailles and Paris. The National Constituent Assembly was beginning to demand a constitutional monarchy. Louis refused to consider their proposal and hoped that a show of military force would head off revolution.

The second development was the behavior of the people of Paris. The mustering of royal troops spread anxiety through the city, where there had already been several riots sparked by food shortages. By June, the Parisians were organizing by collecting arms and marshalling an army of their own, a citizen militia. On July 14, a crowd marched to the Bastille, a fortress in Paris that was sometimes used as a political prison, and demanded weapons for the militia. The royal troops in the Bastille fired into the crowd which then stormed the fortress, released the seven prisoners it held (none of whom was a politcal prisoner), and killed the governor. They found no weapons.

This was the first of many *journées*, or days when the populace of Paris would determine the course of the revolution. Similar disturbances took place in the provincial cities. Louis XVI came to Paris and recognized the legitimacy of its newly elected government and its National Guard.

The Great Fear and Surrender of Feudal Privileges   As disturbances erupted in various cities, the *Great Fear* swept across the French countryside. Peasants rose up to vent their anger at injustices and reclaim rights and property that they had

HOW DID the French Revolution and Napoleon transform France's government and society?

QUICK REVIEW

National Assembly
- June 17, 1789: Third Estate declares itself National Assembly
- Tennis Court Oath: Pledge to sit until France had a constitution
- June 27, 1789: King capitulates to National Assembly

18.8
Edmund Burke: Reflections on the Revolution in France

Third Estate   Branch of the French Estates General representing all of the kingdom outside the nobility and the clergy.

Storming of the Bastille. On July 14, 1789, crowds stormed the Bastille, a prison in Paris. This event, whose only practical effect was to free a few prisoners, marked the first time the populace of Paris redirected the course of the revolution.

Anonymous, France, 18th century. "Seige of the Bastille, 14 July, 1789." Obligatory mention of the following: Musee de la Ville de Paris, Musee Carnavalet, Paris, France. Bridgeman-Giraudon/Art Resource, N.Y.

18.7
Declaration of the Rights of Man and Citizen

lost during the aristocratic resurgence of the previous quarter century. Châteaux were burned, documents were destroyed; and peasants refused to pay feudal dues.

On the night of August 4, 1789, aristocrats in the assembly attempted to halt the disorder. By prearrangement, liberal nobles and churchmen "spontaneously" surrendered their hunting and fishing rights, judicial authority, tithes, and special exemptions. They were giving up what they had already lost and what they could not have regained without civil war. Many were subsequently compensated for their losses. Nonetheless, after August 4, France's laws applied equally to all its citizens.

Declaration of the Rights of Man and Citizen On August 27, 1789, the assembly issued the *Declaration of the Rights of Man and Citizen.* It proclaimed that all men were born free and equal with natural rights to liberty, property, and personal safety. Governments existed to protect those rights. All political sovereignty resided in the nation and its representatives. All citizens were to be equal before the law and to be equally eligible for public offices—as appropriate to their abilities and character. There was to be due process of law, and innocence was to be presumed until proof of guilt. Freedom of religion was affirmed. Taxation was to be apportioned equitably according to capacity to pay. Property rights were declared sacred.

When Louis XVI stalled before ratifying the declaration and the aristocrats' renunciation of their feudal privileges, his hesitation fanned suspicions that he might try to resort to force. Continuing bread shortages also angered the masses. On October 5, several thousand Parisian women marched to Versailles, demanding bread—one of several occasions when women played a major role in the revolution. The king agreed to sanction the decrees of the assembly, but the Parisians demanded more. They insisted that Louis and his family return to Paris. On October 6, 1789, the king and his family followed the crowd back to Paris and settled in the palace of the Tuileries. The assembly joined them. Things then remained relatively quiet until the summer of 1792.

RECONSTRUCTION OF FRANCE

The National Constituent Assembly set about reorganizing France. The assembly was determined to protect property but limit the political influence of small property owners and the unpropertied elements within the populace. While championing equality before the law, the assembly spurned social equality and extensive democracy. It thus charted a course that 19th-century liberals across Europe and in other areas of the world were to follow.

Political Reorganization   The Constitution of 1791 established a constitutional monarchy with a unicameral Legislative Assembly. The monarch could delay, but not halt, legislation. Voting was restricted to about 50,000 men. (France was home to about 26 million.)

The exclusion of women from voting and holding office did not pass unnoticed. In 1791, Olympe de Gouges (d. 1793), a butcher's daughter who became a radical in Paris, composed a *Declaration of the Rights of Woman*, which she ironically addressed to Queen Marie Antoinette (1755–1793). The document was fundamentally the *Declaration of the Rights of Man and Citizen* with the word *woman* strategically inserted. It demanded that women be regarded as citizens, not merely daughters, sisters, wives, and mothers of citizens. Olympe de Gouges further insisted that women be allowed to own property and that men be compelled

Women's March. The women of Paris marched to Versailles on October 5, 1789. The following day the royal family was forced to return to Paris with them. Henceforth, the French government would function under the constant threat of mob violence.

Anonymous, 18th century C.E. "To Versailles, to Versailles." The Women of Paris going to Versailles, 7 October, 1789. French, Musee de la Ville de Paris, Musee Carnavalet, Paris, France. Photograph copyright Bridgeman-Giraudon/Art Resource, N.Y.

a Versaille a Versaille. du 5 Octobre 1789.

to recognize the paternity of their children. She called for equality of the sexes in marriage and improved education for women. Her demands illustrated how the public listing of rights in the *Declaration of the Rights of Man and Citizen* created expectations even among those to whom it did not apply.

The National Constituent Assembly replaced France's former provinces with 83 departments *(départements)*. The ancient judicial courts, including the *parlements*, were replaced by uniform courts with elected judges and prosecutors. Legal procedures were simplified, and the most degrading punishments abolished.

Economic Policy The National Constituent Assembly suppressed the guilds, removed regulations on the grain trade, and established the metric system of uniform weights and measures. In 1790, it placed the burden of proof and the obligation to pay compensation on peasants who tried to rid themselves of residual feudal dues. In 1791, it enacted the Chapelier Law forbidding worker associations. This crushed efforts by urban workers to protect their wages. Peasants and laborers were to be left to the mercy of the free market.

The assembly decided to raise the money that was needed the pay the national debt by confiscating and selling the lands of the Roman Catholic Church. The assembly authorized the issuance of **assignats**, or government bonds, the value of which was guaranteed by the revenue generated from the sale of church property. When the *assignats* began to circulate as currency, the assembly succumbed to the temptation to issue larger quantities of them. This caused their value to fall, and fueled inflation that further stressed the urban poor.

Civil Constitution of the Clergy In July 1790, the assembly issued the Civil Constitution of the Clergy, which transformed the Roman Catholic Church into a branch of the government. The number of bishoprics was reduced, and the borders of dioceses were conformed to those of the new departments. Priests and bishops were to be elected and paid salaries by the state. The assembly consulted neither the pope nor the French clergy about these changes, and the king approved them reluctantly.

The Civil Constitution of the Clergy roused immense opposition from the French clergy. The assembly demanded that all clergy take an oath to support the Civil Constitution, but only about half complied. In reprisal, the assembly designated the clergy who had not taken the oath as "refractory" and ordered them to cease performing clerical functions. Refractory priests responded by celebrating mass.

In February 1791, the pope condemned not only the Civil Constitution of the Clergy but also the *Declaration of the Rights of Man and Citizen*. That condemnation marked the start of a Roman Catholic offensive against liberalism and revolution that continued for more than a century. The pope's action meant that many French people were torn between religious devotion and revolutionary loyalty. They divided between supporters of the constitutional priests and of the refractory clergy. Louis XVI favored the latter.

Counterrevolutionary Activity In the summer of 1791, the queen and some nobles persuaded Louis XVI to flee, but the royal family was caught and returned to Paris. The escapade had the unfortunate effect of persuading the leaders of the National Constituent Assembly that France's chief counterrevolutionary occupied its throne.

On August 27, 1791, Leopold II of Austria (r. 1790–1792), who was the brother of Marie Antoinette, and Frederick William II (r. 1786–1797) of Prussia

assignats Government bonds based on the value of confiscated church lands issued during the early French Revolution.

further endangered the royal family by issuing the Declaration of Pillnitz. They promised to intervene in France to protect the royal family if the other major European powers agreed that they could do so. The latter provision rendered the declaration meaningless for Great Britain would not consent. It had the effect, however, of convincing France's revolutionaries that they were surrounded by aristocratic and monarchical foes.

A SECOND REVOLUTION

In September 1791, a new Legislative Assembly was elected, and it convened on October 1 in an atmosphere that was becoming increasingly radical. Since the earliest days of the revolution, clubs of politically like-minded persons had sprung up in Paris. The best organized were the *Jacobins*, who had links with similar groups in the provinces. On April 20, 1792, the Legislative Assembly, led by a group of Jacobins known as the *Girondists* (because many came from the department of the Gironde), voted to declare war on Austria.

End of the Monarchy   The war went badly, and the looming threat to France radicalized the political environment. The result was a *second revolution*, which swept away the monarchy and established a republic.

Late in July, pressure from the working-class delivered the government of Paris into the hands of a committee, or commune, consisting of representatives from the municipal wards. On August 10, 1792, a mob invaded the Tuileries. Louis XVI and Marie Antoinette sought refuge with the Legislative Assembly. Royal guards and many Parisians were killed in the process. Thereafter, the royal family was imprisoned, and the king suspended from his political functions.

The Convention and the Role of Sans-Culottes   In early September, the Paris Commune killed about 1,200 people held in the city jails. Most were common criminals whom the crowd accused of being counterrevolutionaries. The Commune then compelled the Legislative Assembly to call for the election, by universal manhood suffrage, of a new assembly to write a democratic constitution. That body, the **Convention**, met on September 21, 1792, and declared France a republic.

The second revolution had been the work of radical Jacobins and of the people of Paris known as the *sans-culottes*, meaning "without breeches." (Working men wore long trousers instead of the knee breeches favored by aristocratic courtiers.) The sans-culottes were shopkeepers, artisans, wage earners, and a few factory workers. They had no political authority under the Old Regime, and the National Constituent Assembly had left them victims of unregulated free-market economy (see "A Pamphleteer Describes a Sans-Culotte").

The sans-culottes wanted price controls for food. They resented most forms of social inequality and were hostile to the aristocracy and the original leaders of the revolution. They advocated a community of small property owners. They were antimonarchical, republican, and suspicious of government. The Jacobins, by contrast, were republicans who favored representative government and an unregulated economy. However, once the Convention began its deliberations, the more extreme Jacobins, known as the Mountain, worked with the sans-culottes to pass revolutionary reforms and win the war.

In December 1792, Louis XVI was put on trial. He was convicted of conspiring against the state and was beheaded on January 21, 1793. The killing of a king shocked Europe, and France found itself isolated and at war with virtually everyone.

Jacobins Radical republican party during the French Revolution that displaced the Girondists.

Convention French radical legislative body from 1792 to 1794.

sans-culottes Meaning "without breeches." The lower-middle classes and artisans of Paris during the French Revolution.

HISTORY'S VOICES

A Pamphleteer Describes a Sans-Culotte

This document from 1793 describes a sans-culotte as a hardworking, useful, patriotic citizen who sacrifices himself to the war effort. It contrasts those virtues with the lazy and unproductive luxury of the noble and the self-interested plottings of the politician.

WHAT SOCIAL resentments appear in this description? How could these resentments create solidarity among the sans-culottes to defend the revolution? How does this document relate civic virtue to work? Where does this document suggest that the sans-culotte may need to confront enemies of the republic?

A sans-culotte you rogues? He is someone who always goes on foot, who has no millions as you would all like to have, no chateaux, no valets to serve him, and who lives simply with his wife and children, if he has any, on a fourth or fifth story.

He is useful, because he knows how to work in the field, to forge iron, to use a saw, to use a file, to roof a house, to make shoes, and to shed his last drop of blood for the safety of the Republic.

And because he works, you are sure not to meet his person in the Café de Chartres, or in the gaming houses where others conspire and game; nor at the National theatre . . . nor in the literary clubs . . . .

In the evening he goes to his section, not powdered or perfumed, or smartly booted in the hope of catching the eye of the citizenesses in the galleries, but ready to support good proposals with all his might, and to crush those which come from the abominable faction of politicians.

Finally, a sans-culotte always has his sabre sharp, to cut off the ears of all enemies of the Revolution; sometimes he even goes out with his pike; but at the first sound of the drum he is ready to leave for the Vendée, for the army of the Alps or for the army of the North . . . .

Source: "Reply to an Impertinent Question: What Is a Sans-Culotte?" April 1793. Reprinted in Walter Markov and Albert Soboul, eds., *Die Sansculotten von Paris*, and republished trans. by Clive Emsley in Merryn Williams, ed., *Revolutions: 1775–1830* (Baltimore, MD: Penguin Books, in association with the Open University, 1971), pp. 100–101.

Civil war broke out as well. In March 1793, aristocratic officers and priests raised a royalist revolt in western France and won local popular support.

THE REIGN OF TERROR AND ITS AFTERMATH

The **Reign of Terror** is the name given to a period, from autumn 1793 through mid-summer 1794, marked by thousands of quasi-judicial executions and murders. Two factors created the environment for the outbreak of the Terror: (1) the fear created by internal and external wars, and (2) the revolutionary aspirations of the Convention and the sans-culottes.

Committee of Public Safety In April 1793, the Convention established a Committee of Public Safety and charged it with responsibility for saving the revolution from enemies at home and abroad. It eventually assumed quasi-dictatorial power and generally enjoyed a working political relationship with the sans-culottes of Paris.

In June 1793, the Parisian sans-culottes invaded the Convention, drove out the Girondists, and gave the Mountain complete control. On August 23 the Convention decreed a *levée en masse*, or general military requisition of

Reign of Terror Period between the summer of 1793 and the end of July 1794 when the French revolutionary state used extensive executions and violence to defend the Revolution and suppress its alleged internal enemies.

levée en masse French revolutionary conscription (1792) of all males into the army and the harnessing of the economy for war production.

Execution of Louis XVI. On January 21, 1793, the Convention executed Louis XVI by guillotine.

Execution of Louis XVI. Aquatint. French, 18th century. Musée de la Ville de Paris, Musée Carnavalet, Paris. France. Giraudon/ Art Resource, N.Y.

population. It conscripted males into the army and mobilized economic production for military purposes. On September 29, price controls were imposed in accordance with sans-culottes' demands. During these same months, the armies of the revolution crushed many of the counterrevolutionary disturbances in the provinces.

The Society of Revolutionary Republican Women   In May 1793, Pauline Léon and Claire Lacombe founded the Society of Revolutionary Republican Women. Its members sought stricter price controls, worked to ferret out food hoarders, and brawled with market women it considered too insufficiently revolutionary. The women of the society also demanded the right to wear the revolutionary cap that male citizens had adopted. By October 1793, the Jacobins in the Convention had begun to fear the turmoil the increasingly radical Society was causing, and it banned all women's clubs and societies.

There were other examples of repression of women in 1793. When Olympe de Gouges spoke out against the Terror, she was tried and guillotined in November 1793. Women were excluded from the French army and from entering the galleries to watch the debates of the Convention.

The Republic of Virtue   The pressures of war made it relatively easy to excuse violations of the usual rules of due process. But the Convention and the Committee of Public Safety felt morally justified in doing so, for they saw themselves as creating something new in history: a republic devoted to eradicating aristocratic and monarchical corruption and promoting civic virtue.

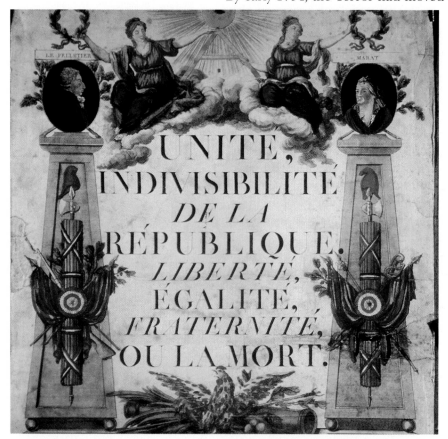

Revolutionary Calendar. To symbolize the beginning of a new era in human history, French revolutionary legislators established a new calendar. This calendar for Year Two (1794) proclaims the indivisible unity of the revolution and the goals of Liberty, Equality, and Fraternity.

Art Resource/Bildarchiv Preussischer Kulturbesitz.

Dechristianization　The revolutionaries associated the Christian religion with the repressive policies of the Old Regime and decided to abolish traditional theism in favor of an enlightened cult of reason. In October 1793, the Convention authorized a new, rationalized calendar dating from the first day of the French Republic. It featured 12 months of 30 days with names associated with the seasons and climate. In November 1793, the Convention renamed the Cathedral of Notre Dame the Temple of Reason. The legislature then sent trusted members as "deputies-on-mission" into the provinces to enforce dechristianization by closing churches and persecuting clergy and believers. This religious policy roused much opposition and alienated the provinces from the revolutionary government in Paris.

Progress of the Terror　During late 1793 and early 1794, Maximilien Robespierre (1758–1794) emerged as the chief figure on the Committee of Public Safety. The Jacobin Club provided his base of power, and he had the support of the sans-culottes of Paris. For political reasons, he considered dechristianization to be a strategic blunder.

The Reign of Terror was the work of a series of revolutionary tribunals established by the Convention during the summer of 1793. They were instituted to try the enemies of the republic, but the definition of enemy broadened as the months passed. Marie Antoinette, other members of the royal family, and many aristocrats were executed in October 1793. They were then followed by Girondist politicians. Robespierre gradually turned the Terror against republican political figures of the left and right and exterminated leaders who might have threatened his own position. On June 10, he secured a law that permitted the revolutionary tribunal to convict suspects without evidence. By early 1794, the Terror had moved to the provinces, where the deputies-on-mission presided over the execution of thousands of people.

In May 1794, at the height of his power, Robespierre concluded that the worship of reason was too abstract for most citizens. He replaced it with the Cult of the Supreme Being, but he did not long preside over this new religion. On July 27 (the Ninth of Thermidor), his opponents staged a coup. Members of the Convention, by prearrangement, shouted him down when he rose to speak and executed him the next day.

The Reign of Terror had claimed 40,000 victims. Most were peasants and sans-culottes who had rebelled against the revolutionary government. By the late summer of 1794, provincial uprisings had been crushed and the war against foreign enemies was going well. Those factors and the feeling that the revolution had consumed enough of its own children brought the Terror to an end.

The Thermidorian Reaction: End of the Terror and Establishment of the Directory   The tempering of the revolution, a phase called the **Thermidorian Reaction**, began in July 1794, with the establishment of a new constitutional regime. The influence of wealthy middle-class and professional people replaced that of the sans-culottes. Many of the people responsible for the Terror were removed from public life, and the Jacobin Club was closed.

The Thermidorian Constitution of the Year III was a conservative document that provided for bicameral legislative government dedicated to protecting the rights of property owners. Its executive branch was a five-person Directory elected by the upper legislative house.

True to their belief in an unregulated economy, the Thermidorians repealed the ceiling on prices. Rising prices led to food riots during the winter of 1794–1795, but the Convention suppressed them in an attempt to bring an end to the era of sans-culottes *journées*. When on October 5, 1795, a Paris mob rioted, a general named Napoleon Bonaparte (1769–1821) used artilery to disperse the crowd.

THE NAPOLEONIC ERA

Napoleon Bonaparte was born in 1769 to a poor noble family in Corsica. Because France had annexed Corsica in 1768, he was able to obtain a commission as a French artillery officer. At the start of his career, he was a fiery Jacobin. In 1793, he played a leading role in recovering the port of Toulon from the British. This won him promotion to the rank of brigadier general, and his defense of the Directory in 1794 won him a command in Italy. By October 1797, he had crushed the Austrians and concluded the Treaty of Campo Formio, which took Austria out of the war and left France dominant over Italy and Switzerland.

In November 1797, the triumphant Bonaparte returned to Paris to confront France's only remaining enemy, Britain. Judging it impossible to invade England, he decided to try to capture Egypt from the Ottoman Empire and cut off Britain's communication with India. However, Admiral Horatio Nelson (1758–1805) destroyed the French fleet and stranded the French army in Egypt. The Russians, Austrians, and Ottomans then joined Britain to form the Second Coalition, and in 1799, the Russian and Austrian armies defeated the French in Italy and Switzerland and threatened to invade France.

Bonaparte abandoned his men and returned to France in October 1799. On November 10, 1799 (19 Brumaire), he overthrew the Directory, and in December 1799, he issued the Constitution of the Year VII. It established him in power with the title First Consul. The constitution received approval from the electorate in a rigged plebiscite, and a government called the **Consulate** brought the revolution to an end.

The Consulate in France (1799–1804)   Bonaparte quickly won a peace for France. Russia had already left the Second Coalition, and in 1800, a French victory at Marengo in Italy took Austria out of the war. In 1802, Britain concluded the Treaty of Amiens, and all of Europe was at peace—at least temporarily.

Bonaparte also restored peace and order at home. In an effort to suppress political opposition, Bonaparte used generosity, flattery, and bribery to win over some of his enemies; issued a general amnesty; and employed people from all political factions. He set up a centralized administration in which all departments were managed by prefects appointed by the central government in Paris. Secret police helped him uncover and stamp out royalist rebellions and plots.

Thermidorean Reaction
Reaction against the radicalism of the French Revolution that began in July 1794. Associated with the end of terror and establishment of the Directory.

Consulate   French government dominated by Napoleon from 1799 to 1804.

The French Revolution

1789

May 5	Estates General opens at Versailles
June 17	Third Estate declares itself the National Assembly
June 20	National Assembly takes the Tennis Court Oath
July 14	Fall of the Bastille
July	Great Fear spreads in the countryside
August 4	Nobles surrender their feudal rights in a meeting of the National Constituent Assembly
August 27	*Declaration of the Rights of Man and Citizen*
October 5–6	Parisian women march to Versailles and force Louis XVI and his family to return to Paris

1790

July 12	Civil Constitution of the Clergy adopted
July 14	New constitution accepted by the king

1791

June 20–24	Louis XVI and his family attempt to flee France
August 27	Declaration of Pillnitz
October 1	Legislative Assembly meets

Napoleon placated French Catholics who had been angered by revolutionary attacks on religion. In 1801, he concluded a concordat with Pope Pius VII (r. 1800–1823). Both refractory and constitutional clergy were forced to resign. Their replacements received spiritual investiture from the pope, but the state named the bishops and paid their salaries and the salary of one priest in each parish. In return, the church gave up claims to its confiscated property, the clergy swore oaths of loyalty to the state, and the Organic Articles of 1802 established the supremacy of the state over the church. Similar laws applied to Protestant and Jewish religious organizations.

In 1802, another plebiscite ratified Bonaparte's appointment as consul for life, and he set about transforming the basic laws and institutions of France on the basis of both liberal principles derived from the Enlightenment and the revolution and conservative principles going back to the Old Regime and the spirit that had triumphed at Thermidor. This was especially true of the Civil Code of 1804, usually called the Napoleonic Code. It, however, stopped far short of the full equality advocated by liberal rationalists. Fathers were granted extensive control over their children and men over their wives. Labor unions were forbidden, and the rights of workers were subordinated to those of employers.

In 1804, Bonaparte used the fear created by a failed assassination attempt to strengthen his hold on power. Another new constitution, ratified by a plebiscite, designated Napoleon Emperor of the French. Napoleon summoned the pope to Notre Dame to take part in the coronation, but at the ceremony Napoleon crowned himself.

Napoleon's Empire (1804–1814)   Between his coronation as emperor and his final defeat at Waterloo (1815), Napoleon conquered most of Europe. France's victories ended the Old Regime and its feudal trappings in western Europe, and forced the eastern European states to reorganize themselves. Everywhere, opposition to Napoleon's advance unleashed the passions of nationalism.

Napoleon's military interventions led Britain to issue him an ultimatum and finally, in May 1803, to declare war. William Pitt the Younger (1759–1806) was returned to office as prime minister in 1804, and he persuaded Russia and Austria once again to try to block France's expansion. On October 21, 1805, Britain scored a major victory. Lord Nelson destroyed the French and Spanish fleets at the Battle of Trafalgar just off the Spanish coast. He was killed, but his victory guaranteed Britain control of the sea.

On land, however, between October 1805 and July 1807, Napoleon defeated the armies of Austria, Prussia, and Russia. He forced Austria to withdraw from northern Italy. He replaced the Holy Roman Empire with the Confederation of the Rhine, and Prussia and Russia were compelled to become his allies.

Napoleon could not be secure, however, until he had defeated Britain. Unable to compete with the British navy, he tried to cut off British trade with

Europe. This, he hoped, would cripple British commercial and financial power and drive the British from the war. This strategy, called the Continental System, harmed the European economies and roused opposition to Napoleon. The British economy, however, survived because of its access to the Americas and the eastern Mediterranean.

The Wars of Liberation   In 1807, a French army invaded the Iberian Peninsula to force Portugal to abandon its alliance with Britain. When a revolt broke out in Madrid in 1808, Napoleon deposed the Spanish Bourbons and placed his brother Joseph (1768–1844) on the Spanish throne. Napoleon's Spanish opponents launched a guerrilla war, and the British supported them by sending an army under Sir Arthur Wellesley (1769–1852), later the Duke of Wellington. This began a long campaign that played a critical role in Napoleon's ultimate defeat.

The Austrians renewed the war in 1809, but the French defeated them at the battle of Wagram. The resulting peace cost Austria territory containing 3.5 million subjects. Another spoil of victory was the Archduchess Marie Louise (1791–1847), Francis I's (r. 1792–1835) 18-year-old daughter. Napoleon married her in hopes of founding a dynasty. Bonaparte divorced his first empress, Josephine de Beauharnais (1763–1814), because she had borne him no children.

The Franco-Russian alliance began to falter. The Continental System had harmed the Russian economy, and Napoleon's establishment of a Polish state, the Grand Duchy of Warsaw, on Russia's doorstep angered Tsar Alexander I (r. 1800–1825). In 1810, Russia withdrew from the Continental System and began to prepare for war.

To stifle the Russian military threat, Napoleon amassed a so-called Grand Army of more than 600,000 men and invaded the country. Russia's generals decided to oppose him by retreating before his advance and stripping the countryside of supplies. Russia was too vast for Napoleon to maintain lines to supply, and his men could not live off the devastated land.

In September 1812, Russian public opinion forced the army to fight. At Borodino, the French lost 30,000 men and the Russians almost twice as many. The Russian army continued its advance, and occupied Moscow. In October, however, supply problems forced the Grand Army to begin a long, painful retreat. Perhaps only 100,000 lived to tell the tale.

In 1813, patriotic pressure and national ambition brought together the last and most powerful coalition against Napoleon. With British financing, the Russians drove westward to be joined by Prussia and Austria. From the west, Wellington marched his peninsular army into France. Napoleon waged a skillful campaign but met decisive defeat in October at Leipzig. At the end of March 1814, the allied army marched into Paris. Napoleon abdicated and went into exile on the island of Elba off the coast of Italy.

The French Revolution (*continued*)

1792		
	April 20	France declares war on Austria
	August 10	Tuileries palace stormed, and Louis XVI takes refuge with the Legislative Assembly
	September 2–7	September Massacres
	September 21	Convention meets, and monarchy abolished
1793		
	January 21	Louis XVI executed
	February 1	France declares war on Great Britain
	March	Counterrevolution breaks out
	April 6	Committee of Public Safety formed
	July	Robespierre enters Committee of Public Safety
	August 23	*Levée en masse* proclaimed
	September 29	Maximum prices set on food and other commodities
	October 16	Queen Marie Antoinette executed
	November 10	Cult of Reason proclaimed; revolutionary calendar
1794		
	May 7	Cult of the Supreme Being proclaimed
	July 27	Ninth of Thermidor and fall of Robespierre
	July 28	Robespierre executed
1795	August 22	Constitution of the Year III adopted, establishing the Directory

William Pitt and Napoleon. In this early 19th-century cartoon, England, personified by a caricature of William Pitt, and France, personified by a caricature of Napoleon, are carving out their areas of interest around the globe.

Cartoon by Gillray/Corbis-Bettmann.

Napoleonic Europe

1797	Napoleon concludes Treaty of Campo Formio
1799	Consulate established
1801	Concordat between France and papacy
1802	Treaty of Amiens
1803	War renewed between France and Britain
1804	Napoleonic Civil Code issued; Napoleon crowned emperor
1805	Nelson defeats French fleet at Trafalgar
1806	Continental System
1808	Beginning of Spanish resistance to Napoleonic domination
1809	Wagram; Napoleon marries Archduchess Marie Louise of Austria
1812	Invasion of Russia
1813	Leipzig (Battle of the Nations)
1814	Congress of Vienna convenes (September)
1815	Waterloo (June 18); Holy Alliance formed (September 26)
1821	Napoleon dies on Saint Helena; The Congress of Vienna and the European Settlement

THE CONGRESS OF VIENNA AND THE EUROPEAN SETTLEMENT

Once Napoleon was gone, the allies began to pursue their separate ambitions. The key leader was Viscount Castlereagh (1769–1822), the British foreign secretary. Even before the victorious allied armies entered Paris, he had negotiated the Treaty of Chaumont (March 9, 1814). It restored the Bourbons to the French throne and returned France to its 1792 frontiers. Remaining problems were left for a conference at Vienna.

The Congress of Vienna met from September 1814 until November 1815. The victors agreed that no single state should be allowed to dominate Europe. They constructed a series of states to prevent French expansion (see Map 23–2). They established the kingdom of the Netherlands in the north and added Genoa to Piedmont in the south. Prussia was given new territories in the west to deter French aggression along the Rhine River. Austria obtained control of northern Italy to prevent a repetition of Napoleon's conquests there. Most of Napoleon's arrangements in the rest of Germany were left untouched, and the Holy Roman Empire was not revived. The Congress established the rule of legitimate monarchs and rejected any compromise with the republican and democratic politics that had flowed from the French Revolution.

Eastern Europe created problems that divided the victors. Alexander I wanted Russia to govern all of Poland. Prussia wanted all of Saxony. Austria, however, refused to allow Prussia's power to grow and Russia to expand. The Polish-Saxon question gave France a chance to regain

MAP EXPLORATION

Interactive map: To explore this map further, go to **http://www.prenhall.com/craig/map23.2**

MAP 23–2

Europe 1815, after the Congress of Vienna. The Congress of Vienna achieved the post-Napoleonic territorial adjustments shown on the map. The most notable arrangements dealt with areas along France's borders (the Netherlands, Prussia, Switzerland, and Piedmont), in Poland, and northern Italy.

WHY DID the Congress of Vienna seek to place strong states on the borders of France?

influence in international affairs. The French Foreign Minister Talleyrand (1754–1838) negotiated a secret treaty with Britain and Austria. When the news leaked out, the tsar agreed to accept jurisdiction over a smaller Poland, and Prussia settled for part of Saxony. France was a major party to all future deliberations.

When Napoleon escaped from Elba and returned to France on March 1, 1815, the allies reunited and sent their armies to crush him. Wellington and the Prussians defeated him at Waterloo in Belgium on June 18, 1815. Napoleon was again exiled, this time to Saint Helena, a tiny island off the coast of Africa. He died there in 1821.

OVERVIEW THE VIENNA SETTLEMENT

The Congress of Vienna met from September 1814 to November 1815 to redraw the map of Europe after the defeat of Napoleon. With few exceptions, the borders the Congress agreed on remained in place until the 1850s. The statesmen at Vienna wanted to prevent another outbreak of the wars that had followed the French Revolution. The main principles behind their deliberations were a determination to confine France, which they saw as the home of revolution, within its traditional boundaries: legitimacy, by which they meant the restoration of Europe's traditional monarchs to their thrones; and compensation—the idea that the states that had defeated Napoleon deserved to be "compensated" for their expenditure of lives and treasure with new territory. Below is a summary of what the statesmen at Vienna achieved.

Britain	was compensated with a number of former French and Dutch colonies. It also became the dominant naval power in the Mediterranean by annexing Malta in the central Mediterranean and the Ionian Islands at the mouth of the Adriatic.
France	was reduced to its 1792 frontiers and ringed along its borders with a series of strengthened states to discourage French aggression. Thus, Prussia was given the Rhineland along France's eastern frontier; the Kingdom of the Netherlands was created to the north of France by combining Belgium and Holland; and the Kingdom of Sardinia on France's southern border was strengthened by the addition of the great port of Genoa.
Germany	The Holy Roman Empire was not revived. Instead, it was replaced by a loose Germanic confederation of mostly monarchical states under the presidency of Austria. Prussia was compensated by receiving two thirds of Saxony, which had been an ally of Napoleon.
Italy	Austria was compensated by becoming the dominant power in Italy and by being given Lombardy and Venetia. The Papal States were reconstituted, and the legitimate Italian rulers were restored to their thrones: the House of Savoy in Piedmont-Sardinia; the Bourbons in the Two Sicilies and Lucca; the Habsburgs in Tuscany, Modena, and Parma. Most of these rulers depended on Austrian support. The old republics of Venice and Genoa, which Napoleon had abolished, were not restored.
Poland	Poland was not restored as an independent state. It remained divided among Prussia, Austria, and Russia. Russia was compensated by being given the largest share of Poland.
Scandinavia	Denmark, another ally of Napoleon, had to cede Norway as compensation to Sweden, which had lost Finland to Russia.

The main outlines of the Vienna Settlement remained in place, and the alliance of England, Austria, Prussia, and Russia was renewed on November 20, 1815. It was to be a coalition for the maintenance of peace, and its existence and later operation represented an important departure in European affairs. The statesmen at Vienna, unlike their 18th-century counterparts, had seen the armies of the French Revolution change borders and overturn the political and social order of the continent. They were determined to prevent a recurrence of those upheavals. Their purpose was not to punish France but to establish a framework for future stability. The great powers, through the Vienna settlement, agreed to work together to defend the status quo and not, as in the 18th century, to use military force to change it.

The Congress of Vienna produced a long-lasting peace. Its work has been criticized for failing to recognize and provide for the great movements that would stir the 19th century—nationalism and democracy—but such criticism is unrealistic. The settlement, like all such agreements, was aimed at solving past ills, and in that it succeeded. It spared Europe a general war until 1914.

WARS OF INDEPENDENCE IN LATIN AMERICA

The French Revolution and the Napoleonic wars inspired movements for independence throughout Latin America. France was driven from Haiti, Portugal from Brazil, and Spain from all its American empire except for Cuba and Puerto Rico.

WHY DID Latin America throw off Spanish and Portuguese rule?

18TH-CENTURY DEVELOPMENTS

After Spain's defeat in the Seven Years' War in 1763, its king, Charles III (r. 1759–1788), decided that the American colonial system had to be changed. He abolished the monopolies of Seville and Cádiz, opened more South American and Caribbean ports to trade, and authorized direct trade between American ports. In 1776, he organized a fourth viceroyalty that encompassed much of present-day Argentina, Uruguay, Paraguay, and Bolivia. Charles III also tried to make tax collection more efficient and to eliminate bureaucratic corruption by appointing *intendents*, bureaucrats loyal only to the crown.

These reforms returned the empire to direct Spanish control. Many *peninsulares*, whites born in Spain, went to the New World to fill these new posts, depriving **Creoles**, whites born in America, of opportunity. Expanding trade brought more Spanish merchants to Latin America, where economic activity continued to be organized for the benefit of Spain.

peninsulares Native-born Spaniards who immigrated from Spain to settle in the Spanish colonies.

Creoles Persons of European descent who were born in the Spanish colonies.

FIRST MOVEMENTS TOWARD INDEPENDENCE

A slave revolt (1794–1804) led by Toussaint L'Ouverture (1746–1803) won Haiti independence from France. Haiti's revolution was the result of a popular uprising by a repressed social group. It proved to be the great exception in the Latin American wars for liberty from European masters. On the South American continent, it was the Creole elite who led the campaigns against Spain and Portugal. Few Indians, blacks, mestizos, mulattos, or slaves were involved or benefited from the end of Iberian rule. The Creoles were determined that political independence from Spain and Portugal should not entail the loss of their privileges. In this respect they were not unlike American revolutionaries in the southern colonies who wanted to reject British rule but keep their slaves—or the French revolutionaries who did not want to extend liberty to the French working class.

Creole complaints against Spain resembled those of the American colonists against Great Britain. Merchants wanted to trade more freely within their region and with North America and Europe. They wanted commercial regulations that would benefit them rather than Spain, and they resented Spanish policies and political patronage that favored peninsulares.

From the 1790s onward, Spain suffered reverses in the wars associated with the French Revolution and Napoleon. Military pressures forced the Spanish monarchy to resort to desperate measures to fill its treasury. Among these were increased taxation and the confiscation of property in the Americas that hurt the Creole elite.

Creole leaders had read the Enlightenment *philosophes* and believed that the political reforms the *philosophes* championed would benefit their region. They were also well aware of the political arguments that had justified the American

Toussaint L'Ouverture. L'Ouverture (1744–1803) began the revolt that led to Haitian independence in 1804.

Historical Pictures Collection/Stock Montage, Inc.

Revolution. The event that crystallized Creole discontent into revolt against Spain was Napoleon's overthow of the Portuguese monarchy in 1807 and the Spanish government in 1808. The Portuguese royal family fled to Brazil, but the Bourbon monarchy of Spain seemed vanquished. The Creole elite feared that a monarchy headed by Napoleon's brother in Spain would harm their economic and social interests and would drain the region of resources for Napoleon's wars. Creole juntas, or political committees, formed between 1808 and 1810 and claimed the right to govern regions of Latin America. Ten years of warfare ensued before Spain conceded Latin American independence.

SAN MARTÍN IN RÍO DE LA PLATA

The first region to assert its independence was the Río de la Plata, or modern Argentina. In 1810, the junta in Buenos Aires thrust off Spanish authority and sent soldiers to liberate Paraguay and Uruguay. They were defeated, but Paraguay asserted its own independence, and Brazil absorbed Uruguay.

The Buenos Aires government then attempted to liberate Peru, the greatest remaining stronghold of royalist power on the continent (see Map 23–3). In 1814, José de San Martin (1778–1850) led an army over the Andes Mountains. By early 1817, he had occupied Santiago in Chile and established Bernardo O'Higgins (1778–1842) as supreme dictator. In 1821, he drove royalist forces from Lima and assumed the title of Protector of Peru.

SIMÓN BOLÍVAR'S LIBERATION OF VENEZUELA

In 1810, Simón Bolívar (1783–1830), a firm advocate of independence and republicanism, had helped organize a liberating junta in Caracas, Venezuela. Between 1811 and 1814, civil war broke out as royalists, slaves, and cowboys challenged his republican government and drove him into exile. In 1819, with help from Haiti, he captured Bogotá, capital of New Granada (modern Colombia, Bolivia, and Ecuador) and established a base for attacking Venezuela. In 1821, his forces captured Caracas, and he was named president.

In July 1822, the armies of Bolívar and San Martín liberated the city of Quito, but the two leaders disagreed about the future political structure of Latin America. San Martín believed in monarchies; Bolívar favored republics. Shortly thereafter, San Martín retired from public life and moved to Europe. In 1823, Bolívar sent troops into Peru and on December 9, 1824, at the battle of Ayacucho, defeated the Spanish royalist forces. The battle marked the end of Spain's effort to retain its American empire.

INDEPENDENCE IN NEW SPAIN

The drive for independence in New Spain (modern Mexico, Texas, California, and the rest of the southwestern United States) illustrates how socially conservative the Latin American colonial revolutions were. As elsewhere, a local governing junta was organized. But before it had time to act, a Creole priest, Miguel Hidalgo y Costilla (1753–1811),

Simón Bolívar. Bolívar was the liberator of much of Latin America. He inclined toward a policy of political liberalism.

SuperStock Inc.

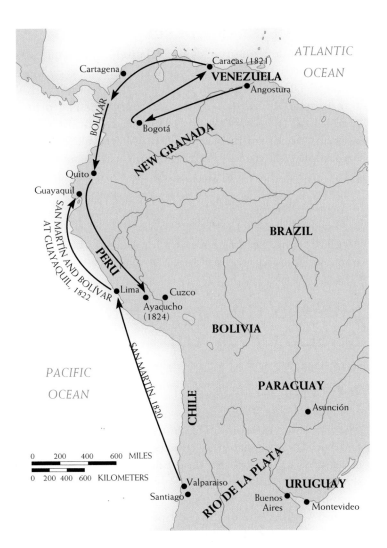

MAP 23–3
The Independence Campaigns of San Martín and Bolívar.

HOW DO the wars for independence in Latin America compare with the colonists' revolt against British rule in North America?

incited the Indians of his parish to rebel. They and other repressed groups responded to Father Hidalgo's call for social reform, and he soon had 80,000 followers. But in July 1811, he was captured and executed. Leadership of his movement then passed to José María Morelos y Pavón (1765–1815), a more radical mestizo priest. In 1815, he too was captured and executed.

In 1820, a revolution in Spain forced Ferdinand VII (r. 1813–1833) to accept a liberal constitution, and conservative Mexicans feared that a liberal Spanish monarchy would try to impose liberal reforms on Mexico. Therefore, for the most conservative of reasons, they declared Mexico independent under a government determined to resist social reform.

Great Britain supported the independence movements in Latin America, for independence opened the markets of the continent to British trade. In 1823, Britain accepted the Monroe Doctrine, the United States' insistence that there be no further intervention by European powers in America, and Britain soon recognized the Spanish colonies as independent states. Through the rest of the century, British commercial interests dominated Latin America.

The Wars of Latin American Independence

1759–1788	Charles III of Spain carries out imperial reforms
1794	Toussaint L'Ouverture leads slave revolt in Haiti
1804	Independence of Haiti
1807	Portuguese royal family flees to Brazil
1808	Spanish monarchy falls to Napoleon
1808–1810	Creole committees organized to govern much of Latin America
1810	Buenos Aires junta sends forces to liberate Paraguay and Uruguay
1811	Miguel Hidalgo y Costilla leads rebellion in New Spain and is executed
1811–1815	José María Morelos y Pavón leads rebellion in New Spain and is executed
1814	San Martín organizes army
1815	Brazil declared a kingdom
1817	San Martín occupies Santiago, Chile
1820	Revolution in Spain
1821	
February 24	New Spain declares independence
June 29	Bolívar captures Caracas, Venezuela
July 28	San Martín liberates Peru
1822	
July 26–27	San Martín goes into exile
September 7	Dom Pedro declares Brazilian independence
1824	Battle of Ayacucho—final Spanish defeat

WHY DID slavery become unacceptable in Western society?

BRAZILIAN INDEPENDENCE

Brazilian independence came relatively peacefully. As already noted, the Portuguese royal family and several thousand officials took refuge in Brazil in 1807, and their arrival transformed Rio de Janeiro into a court city. The prince regent Joao (r. 1816–1826) in 1815 declared Brazil a kingdom and no longer merely a colony of Portugal. In 1820, a revolution took place in Portugal, and its leaders offered the throne to Joao and demanded the return of Brazil to colonial status. Joao, who had become Joao VI in 1816, returned to Portugal and left his son Pedro (r. 1822–1831) as regent in Brazil. In 1822, Pedro asserted Brazil's independence and became emperor of Brazil. The country remained a monarchy until 1889.

TOWARD THE ABOLITION OF SLAVERY IN THE TRANSATLANTIC ECONOMY

*I*n 1750, few questioned the institution of slavery, but by 1888, slavery no longer existed in the transatlantic economy. This transformation of economic and social life occurred as the result of an international effort, first to abolish the slave trade and then to abolish slavery itself. No previous society in world history had attempted to abolish slavery. Its elimination in the transatlantic world is one of the most permanent achievements of the 18th-century Enlightenment and revolutions.

The 18th-century crusade against slavery originated among writers of the Enlightenment and religious critics. The era's movements championing political and social equality were inconsistent with the radical inequality of slavery, and the case Adam Smith made in *The Wealth of Nations* for free labor and free markets undermined economic defenses of slavery. Some *philosophes* also idealized native peoples as closer to nature and objected to slavers robbing Africans of their alleged original innocence. In such a climate, slavery grew to be regarded as unacceptable.

The slave system was a transatlantic affair, and so was the crusade against it. English Quakers began the protest against slavery, and Quaker communities in America quickly joined them in the fight. During the American Revolution, small groups of reformers, usually organized by Quakers, established an antislavery network, and emancipation gradually spread among the northern states. In 1787, the Continental Congress forbade slavery in the Northwest Territory north of the Ohio River.

Despite these American efforts, Great Britain was the true center for the antislavery movement. During the early 1780s, antislavery reformers in Britain decided that the best strategy was to work toward ending the slave trade rather than slavery itself. To many, the slave trade seemed worse than the holding of slaves, and attacking slavery raised complicating issues of property rights. If the trade were ended, it seemed likely as well that planters would have to treat their remaining slaves more humanely.

While the British reformers worked for the abolition of the slave trade, some slaves took matters into their own hands. The slave revolt in Haiti was a warning to slave owners throughout the West Indies. Other slave revolts occurred in Virginia, South Carolina, and British-controlled Demarra, but these were suppressed.

For economic reasons, some British West Indies planters decided that abolition of the slave trade might be in their best interest. They were experiencing soil exhaustion and increased competition from French planters. There was a glut of sugar on the market, and the price was falling. Without new slaves, the French would lack the labor they needed to exploit their islands.

By 1807, abolition sentiment was strong enough for Parliament to prohibit slave trading from any British port. Thereafter, the suppression of this trade became a major goal of 19th-century British foreign policy. The British navy maintained a squadron off West Africa to halt slave traders.

Sentiment to abolish slavery itself increased. In 1833, following the passage of the Reform Bill in Great Britain, Parliament abolished the right of British subjects to hold slaves, and in the British West Indies, 750,000 slaves were freed.

Leaders of the Latin American wars of independence were disposed by Enlightenment ideas to disapprove of slavery, and they sought the support of slaves by promises of emancipation. The newly independent nations slowly freed their slaves to maintain good relations with Britain, from whom they needed economic support. Slavery had disappeared from Latin America by the middle of the century, with the important exception of Brazil.

The other old colonial powers in the New World were slower to abolish slavery. Portugal did nothing about slavery in Brazil, and Brazil's independent government continued slavery. Portugal ended slavery elsewhere in its American possessions in 1836; the Swedes, in 1847; the Danes, in 1848; but the Dutch did not abolish the practice until 1863. France had a significant antislavery movement, but did not abolish slavery in its West Indian possessions until 1848.

Despite opposition, during the first 30 years of the 19th century, slavery expanded in parts of the transatlantic world: the lower south of the United States (for the cultivation of cotton), Brazil (for the cultivation of coffee), and Cuba (for the cultivation of sugar). World demand for the products of these regions made the slave system economically viable. Slavery ended in the United States only after the Civil War. In Cuba it persisted until 1886, and full emancipation did not occur in Brazil until 1888 (see Chapters 25, 26, and 27).

The emancipation crusade, like slave trading itself, drew Europeans into African affairs. In 1787, the British established a colony for free blacks from Britain in Sierra Leone. The French established a smaller experiment at Libreville in Gabon. The most famous and lasting attempt to settle former black slaves in Africa was the establishment of Liberia through the efforts of the American Colonization Society after 1817. Liberia became an independent republic in 1847. These efforts to move former slaves back to Africa had only modest success, but they had a profound influence on West Africa.

Other antislavery reformers were less interested in establishing outposts for settlement of former slaves than in transforming the African economy itself. These reformers attempted to spread both Christianity and free trade to Africa, hoping to exchange British manufactured goods for tropical goods produced by Africans. These commercial efforts of the antislavery movement marked the first serious intrusions of European powers into the heart of Africa.

The American Civil War finally halted any large-scale demand for slaves from Africa. Antislavery reformers then concentrated on ending the slave trade in East Africa and the Indian Ocean. This campaign against slavery and the slave trade in Africa itself became one of the rationales for the establishment of the late-19th-century European colonial empires.

IMAGE KEY
for pages 556–557

a. The Execution of Louis XVI, on January 21, 1793.

b. Marie Antoinette.

c. Napoleon.

d. *The Third of May, 1808*, Francisco de Goya, 1814–1815.

e. Simón Bolívar.

f. Bostonians Paying the Excise Man, or tarring & feathering.

g. Marie Antoinette, sketched from life by Jacques-Louis David.

h. A poster celebrating French liberation.

i. The slave quarters of a Spanish slave ship.

j. Francois Dominique Toussaint L'Ouverture.

k. Storming of the Bastille, July 14, 1789.

SUMMARY

The Transatlantic Revolutions The revolutions and the crusade against slavery that occurred throughout the transatlantic world between 1776 and the 1830s transformed three continents. In North America, in France and other parts of Europe, and in South America, political experiments challenged government by both monarchy and aristocracy. The foundations of modern liberal democracy were laid. The largest republic since ancient times had been established in North America. In France, written constitutions and elected legislatures remained essential parts of the government. In Latin America, republicanism triumphed everywhere except Brazil. Never again could government be undertaken in these regions without some form of participation by the governed.

Economic and Social Liberalization The expanding forms of political liberty found their counterparts in an economic life freed from the constraints of the old colonial empires and the slavery that marked their plantations. The new American republic constituted a vast free trade zone. Its commerce was open to the world. And for the first time since the encounter with Europe, Latin America could trade freely among its own peoples and those of the rest of the world. In France and Europe, where the Napoleonic armies had carried the doctrines of the rights of man, economic life had been rationalized and freed from the domination of local authorities and local weights and measures. National law formed the framework for economic activity. The movement to abolish slavery fostered a wage economy of free laborers. That kind of economy would generate its own set of problems and social dislocation, but it was nonetheless an economy of free human beings.

Nationalism Finally, the age of transatlantic revolutions saw the emergence of nationalism as a political force. All of the revolutions, because of their popular political base, had given power to the idea of nations defined by their own character and historical past rather than by dynastic rulers. The Americans saw themselves as forming a new kind of nation. The French had demonstrated the power of a nation mobilized for military purposes. In turn, the aggression of France had aroused national sentiment, especially in Great Britain, Spain, and Germany. The new nations of Latin America also sought to define themselves by their heritage and historical experience rather than by their past in the Spanish and Portuguese Empires.

These various revolutions, their political doctrines, and their social and economic departures provided examples to peoples elsewhere in the world. But even more important, the transatlantic revolutions and eventual abolition of slavery meant that new political classes and independent nations would become actors on the world scene. Europeans would have to deal with a score of new nations in the Americas. The rest of the world confronted new nations freed from the direction and authority of European powers. The political changes in Europe meant that those nations and their relationships with the rest of the world would be directed by a broader range of groups than in the past.

REVIEW QUESTIONS

1. What role did economic interests play in the American Revolution? What was the contribution of European ideas and political developments?

2. How did attempts to reform the French monarchy come to abolish it in favor of a republic?

3. What caused the Reign of Terror? Was it an inevitable outcome of the revolution or a violation of its principles?

4. How did Napoleon rise to power? What brought about his downfall? What did the Congress of Vienna achieve?

5. Did the revolutions that established the indepence of the Latin American countries differ from or follow the courses of the American and French revolutions?

6. What inspired the antislavery movement? What explains its success?

KEY TERMS

assignats (p. 564)   Jacobins (p. 565)   *sans-culottes* (p. 565)
Consulate (p. 569)   levée en masse (p. 566)   Thermidorean Reaction (p. 569)
Convention (p. 565)   *peninsulares* (p. 575)   Third Estate (p. 561)
Creoles (p. 575)   Reign of Terror (p. 566)

 For additional study resources for this chapter, go to:
www.prenhall.com/craig/chapter23

24 Political Consolidation in Nineteenth-Century Europe and North America, 1815–1880

PEOPLE'S MEETING!!

CITIZENS OF CHESTER COUNTY:—The time has arrived when it is necessary to make preparations for the next general election. In view of existing circumstances, it is proper that the citizens of this County

WITHOUT RESPECT TO PARTY

SLAVE POWER

OTHER SLAVE STATES TO THE UNION

NATURALIZATION LAWS

AMERICAN LABORER

CHAPTER HIGHLIGHTS

Nationalism Nationalism is the modern concept that people who share the same customs, culture, language, and history should also share the same government. It became the most powerful European political ideology of the nineteenth and early twentieth centuries.

Liberalism Politically, nineteenth-century liberals sought to establish constitutional governments that recognized civil liberties and made the executive responsible to a legislature elected by men of wealth and property. Economically, liberals wanted a laissez-faire economy with minimal government involvement.

Italian and German Unification With French assistance, most of the Italian peninsula was united by 1860.

German unification was achieved by Prussia between 1864 and 1871. Germany was henceforth the dominant power on the European continent.

North America In the United States, westward expansion brought vast new territories under the republic from the Mississippi River to the Pacific, but sectional conflict over economic issues and slavery led to the outbreak of the Civil War in 1861. Northern victory led to the abolition of slavery, the creation of a continent-wide free labor market, and enormous economic development that would make the United States the world's leading industrial power. Canada in these years achieved self-government from Britain and created a united Canadian federation in 1867.

Eastern Europe Nationalism created problems for the three eastern European empires: Germany, Russia, and Austria, but Habsburg Austria faced the greatest challenge from nationalism because it was a dynastic, not a national, state. Eleven different nationalities made up the Habsburg Monarchy, each with its own national aspirations. In 1867 the Habsburgs worked out the *Ausgleich*, or Compromise, with the Magyars, by which Hungary became an autonomous kingdom under the Habsburg emperor.

Racism and Anti-Semitism In the late nineteenth century, biological determinism, the concept that some peoples or races were inherently superior to others, took root in Western thought. In Germany, Austria, and France, some nationalists used the concept of race to blame the Jews for their countries' economic and political problems. Part of the Jewish response was the launching of the Zionist movement to found a separate Jewish state.

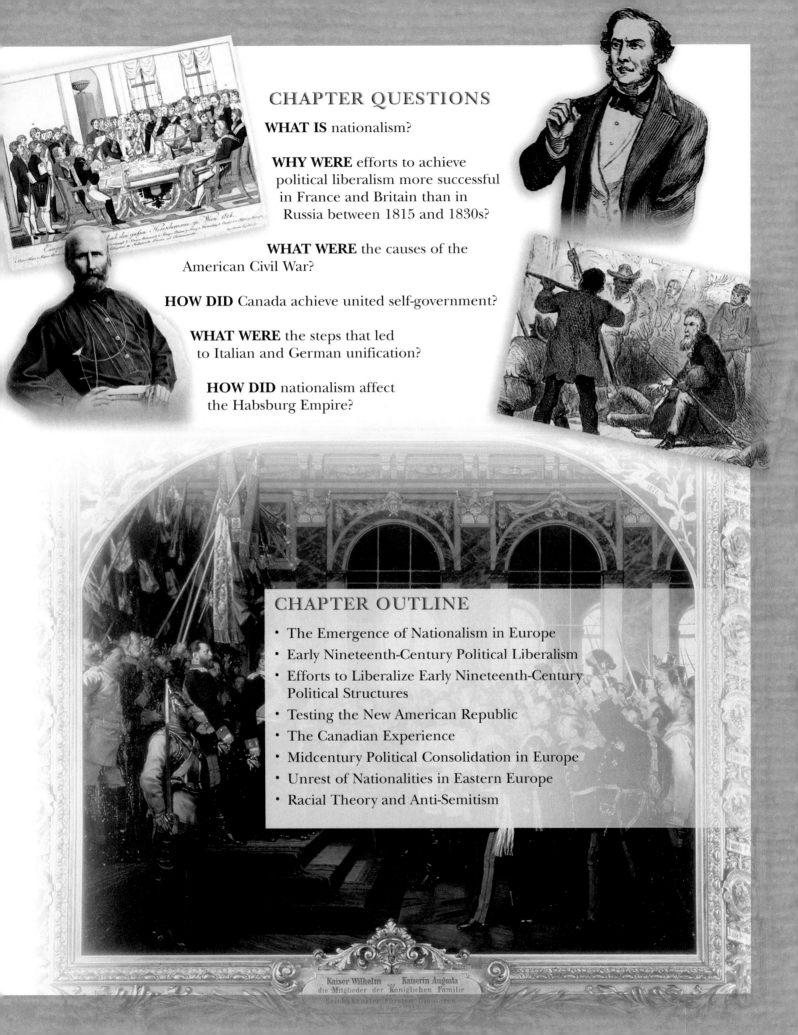

CHAPTER QUESTIONS

WHAT IS nationalism?

WHY WERE efforts to achieve political liberalism more successful in France and Britain than in Russia between 1815 and 1830s?

WHAT WERE the causes of the American Civil War?

HOW DID Canada achieve united self-government?

WHAT WERE the steps that led to Italian and German unification?

HOW DID nationalism affect the Habsburg Empire?

CHAPTER OUTLINE

- The Emergence of Nationalism in Europe
- Early Nineteenth-Century Political Liberalism
- Efforts to Liberalize Early Nineteenth-Century Political Structures
- Testing the New American Republic
- The Canadian Experience
- Midcentury Political Consolidation in Europe
- Unrest of Nationalities in Eastern Europe
- Racial Theory and Anti-Semitism

Kaiser Wilhelm   Kaiserin Augusta
die Mitglieder der Königlichen Familie

During the 19th century, two fundamental long-term developments occurred in the northern transatlantic world that would have a profound impact over the decades in every culture on the face of the Earth. First, in both Europe and North America a process of political consolidation took place that made the nation-states of that region the strongest of the period. Second, and directly contributing to that political strength, powerful, new industrial economies with a new kind of society no longer based primarily on the land emerged in Europe and North America. As a result of this political consolidation and industrialization, the nations of the northern transatlantic became the world's major military powers. By the close of the 19th century and well into the 20th, this political and military power allowed the nations of Europe and the United States to exert unprecedented political, military, and economic influence around the globe. On the basis of this power, many people in Europe and North America came to claim superiority to people dwelling in other cultures and other regions. Moreover, the manner in which Europeans and to a lesser extent Americans developed sets of ideas to explain what was happening politically and economically in their regions would later be used by people elsewhere in the world as they responded to the worldwide power that the northern transatlantic powers exerted.

This chapter will examine the process of political consolidation in the northern transatlantic world, while Chapter 25 will explore the social changes that occurred in the 19th century. Although we will consider the two processes separately, each contributed to the other.

THE EMERGENCE OF NATIONALISM IN EUROPE

WHAT IS nationalism?

Nationalism is based on the relatively modern concept that a nation is composed of people who are joined together by the bonds of common language, customs, culture, and history, and who, because of those bonds, should share the same government. That is to say, political and ethnic boundaries should coincide. This idea came into its own during the late 18th and early 19th centuries. Nationalists opposed the principle upheld at the Congress of Vienna that legitimate monarchies or dynasties should provide the basis for political unity. Nationalists rejected the concept of multinational states such as the Austrian or Russian Empires. They also objected to peoples of the same ethnic group, such as Germans and Italians, dwelling in political units smaller than that of the ethnic nation.

CREATING NATIONS

Nationalists created nations in the 19th century. During the first half of the century, writers spread *nationalistic* concepts. Many were historians who chronicled a people's past or literary scholars who established a national literature by collecting and publishing earlier writings in the people's language. In effect, they gave a people a sense of their past and a literature of their own, which schoolteachers spread.

The language to be used in schools and government was a point of contention for nationalists. In France and Italy, official versions of the national language were imposed in the schools. In eastern Europe, nationalists attempted to resurrect the national language. Often these resurrected languages were virtually invented by scholars. This process led to far more linguistic uniformity within European nations than had existed before the 19th century. Proficiency in the official language became a path to advancement. A uniform language helped to persuade people who had not thought of themselves as constituting a nation to believe that they were a nation. Yet even in 1850, less than half of the inhabitants of France, for example, spoke French.

nationalism Belief that one is part of a nation, defined as a community with its own language, traditions, customs, and history that distinguish it from other nations and make it the primary focus of a person's loyalty and sense of identity.

MEANING OF NATIONHOOD

Nationalists used a variety of arguments to express what they meant by nationhood. Some claimed that gathering Italians, for example, into a unified Italy would promote economic and administrative efficiency. Others insisted that nations, like biological species, were distinct creations of God.

A significant difficulty for nationalism was, and is, determining which ethnic groups should be considered nations with claims to territory and political autonomy. In theory, any of them could, but nationhood came to be associated with groups that were large enough to support an economy, that had a history of significant cultural association, that possessed a cultural elite who could nourish the national language, and that could conquer other peoples to protect their own independence. Many smaller ethnic groups claimed to fulfill these criteria but could not achieve either independence or recognition. They could and did, however, create unrest within the political units they inhabited. Such was the situation in Europe, and the American Civil War can be seen as having similar origins.

REGIONS OF NATIONALISTIC PRESSURE IN EUROPE

During the 19th century, nationalists challenged the political status quo in six major areas of Europe. Irish nationalists wanted independence from Britain or at least self-government. German nationalists wanted a single nation encompassing all German-speaking peoples, challenging the multinational Austrian Empire and pitting Prussia and Austria against each other. Italian nationalists sought to unify the peninsula and drive out the Austrians. Polish nationalists struggled, primarily against Russia, to restore Poland as an independent nation. In eastern Europe, Hungarians, Czechs, Slovenes, and others sought either autonomy or formal recognition within the Austrian Empire. Finally, in the Balkans, national groups sought independence from Ottoman and Russian control. In each area, nationalist activity ebbed and flowed. The dominant governments often thought they needed only to repress the activity or ride it out, but over the course of the century nationalists changed the map and political culture of Europe—as the Confederate States of America failed to do in the United States.

EARLY 19TH-CENTURY POLITICAL LIBERALISM

*T*he term *liberal* as used in present-day American political rhetoric has virtually no relationship to the kinds of ideologies that were described as liberal in the 19th century.

POLITICS

European **liberalism** derived from the Enlightenment, the example of English liberties, and the French *Declaration of the Rights of Man and Citizen.* Liberals favored legal equality, religious toleration, freedom of the press, and limits to the arbitrary power of governments. They believed that the legitimacy of government emanated from the freely given consent of the governed expressed through elected parliaments. Most important, free government required that state or crown ministers be responsible to the representatives of the nation rather than to the monarch.

These goals were limited. The people who espoused them tended to be those who were excluded from the existing political processes but whose wealth

20.3
Fustel de Coulanges, "What Is a Nation?" A Reply to Mr. Mommsen, Professor in Berlin

WHAT POLITICAL and economic goals did 19th-century liberals wish to achieve?

liberalism In the 19th century, support for representative government dominated by the propertied classes and minimal government interference in the economy.

and education made them feel that such exclusion was unjustified. Liberals were often academics, members of the learned professions, and people involved in commerce and manufacturing. They were products of career fields that admitted and rewarded people on the basis of talent. Monarchical and aristocratic regimes often failed to recognize their status and interests.

European liberals were not democrats. They despised the lower classes. Liberals transformed the 18th-century concept of aristocratic liberty into a new concept of privilege based on wealth and property. By the mid-century, this meant that throughout Europe, liberals had separated themselves from the working class. In the first half of the 19th century, political liberals generally did not support political rights for women, but liberal political principles provided women with strong arguments to use when agitating for rights.

ECONOMICS

The economic goals of the liberals furthered their separation from the working class. Liberal elements in the landed and commercial middle class, influenced by the Enlightenment and Adam Smith, wanted to be able to manufacture and sell goods freely. They favored the removal of barriers to trade and, from the 1830s onward, sought construction of rail networks for wide distribution of trade.

Economic liberals opposed the old paternalistic traditions in which governments of guilds passed legislation to fix wages and labor practices. They regarded labor simply as a commodity to be bought and sold freely. Liberals favored an open economy in which people were free to use their talents and property to enrich themselves. They contended that this would lead to more goods and services for everyone at lower prices.

The economic goals of European liberals found many followers outside Europe among groups who favored the expansion of free trade, new transport systems, and a free market in labor. In the United States, people with this outlook often attacked slavery as inefficient and paternalistic. In Latin America, political liberals sought to repeal legislation that had protected Native Americans under Spanish rule.

RELATIONSHIP OF NATIONALISM AND LIBERALISM

Liberalism and nationalism were often complementary. The idea that people should be free to pursue careers that rewarded their talents could be used to make a case for the liberation of suppressed national groups that were not free to realize their cultural or political potential. The efficient government and administration required by commerce and industry, which liberals favored, also necessitated joining small German and Italian states into larger political units. Nationalist movements could gain the sympathy of liberals by making representative government and political liberty one of the goals.

LIBERALISM AND NATIONALISM IN MODERN WORLD HISTORY

The French Revolution in Europe had demonstrated by the early 19th century that the ideals of political liberalism could easily cross dynastic borders. In time those liberal ideals as well as those of nationalism would spread around the globe. Thus, what began as a European development is also important for global history. The concept of the "rights of man and citizen" was used during the Wars of Independence in Latin America to challenge Spanish government. By the close of the 19th century, those same ideals had been turned

---

QUICK REVIEW

Liberal Economics

• Embraced the theories of Adam Smith

• Wanted free markets with limited governmental interference

• Perceived labor as a commodity to be bought and sold

against the colonial governments that Europeans imposed on Africa and Asia. Furthermore, the belief that people should have the right to govern themselves inspired the settlers who spread across both the United States and Canada as well as those who settled in Australia and New Zealand. Similarly, the belief that individual ethnic groups should constitute independent nations became a major political conviction that led peoples living under European colonial government during the late 19th century and, even more importantly, the 20th century to challenge the right of Europeans and later Americans to govern them or dominate their lives through economic power. Political developments in Europe during the early 19th century profoundly affected global politics during the 20th century.

A CONVENTION OF HEMMERS AND STITCHERS HELD AT LYNN, FEB. 28, FOR ADOPTING A LIST OF PRICES; MRS. E. HALL, PRESIDING.—(See page 284.)

Female Activism. Women's gatherings, like the first women's rights convention in Seneca Falls in 1848 and this meeting of strikers in Lynn in 1860, were indicators of widespread efforts to liberalize 19th-century European and American political structures.
Lynn Museum.

WHY WERE efforts to achieve political liberalism more successful in France and Britain than in Russia between 1815 and the 1830s?

Efforts to Liberalize Early 19th-Century European Political Structures

European nations did not move toward liberal political structures rapidly or without considerable conflict. Indeed, after the Congress of Vienna, most conservatives hoped that they had established blocks to liberal advances. The following examples indicate the kinds of situations that confronted European liberals early in the 19th century.

Russia: The Decembrist Revolt of 1825 and the Autocracy of Nicholas I

In the process of driving Napoleon's army across Europe and then occupying defeated France, many officers in the Russian army were introduced to the ideas of the French Revolution and the Enlightenment. They realized how economically backward and politically stifled Russia was, and groups within the officer corps began to form secret societies. These societies were small and divided in their goals; they agreed only that the government of Russia must change. In 1825, they decided to stage a coup d'état the following year.

Events intervened. In late November 1825, Tsar Alexander I suddenly and unexpectedly died. His death created two crises. The first was a dynastic one: Alexander had no direct heir. His brother, Constantine, was next in line to be tsar, but Constantine, who commanded Russian forces in Poland, had renounced any claim to the throne. Secret instructions left by Alexander and made public only after his death named the tsar's younger brother, Nicholas (r. 1825–1855), his successor, but the legality of Alexander's orders was uncertain. Constantine acknowledged Nicholas as tsar, and Nicholas acknowledged Constantine. This family muddle continued for about three weeks, during which Russia actually had no ruler. Then, in early December, the army command reported to Nicholas the existence of a conspiracy among certain officers. Nicholas concluded that he could not delay and had himself declared tsar.

The second crisis now unfolded—a plot by junior officers to rally the troops under their command to compel reform. On December 26, 1825, the army was to take the oath of allegiance to Nicholas, who was less popular than Constantine and was regarded as more conservative. Nearly all of the regiments did so, but the Moscow regiment refused. Its chief officers, surprisingly, were not secret society members, but they supported Constantine and wanted a constitution. Attempts to settle the situation peacefully failed, and late in the afternoon Nicholas ordered cavalry and artillery to attack the insurgents. Five of the plotters were executed, and more than 100 other officers were exiled to Siberia.

The revolt had the effect of ending liberalism as even a moderate political influence in Russia. It also made Nicholas I the conservative policeman of Europe, ready to provide troops to suppress liberal and nationalist movements wherever they appeared. Except for a modest experiment early in the 20th century, tsarist Russia was never to know a genuinely liberal political reform.

REVOLUTION IN FRANCE (1830)

In 1824, Louis XVIII (r. 1814–1824), the Bourbon restored to the throne of France by the Congress of Vienna, died. He was succeeded by his brother, Charles X (r. 1824–1830). The new king considered himself a monarch by divine right. He wanted to restore lands that the French aristocrats had lost during the revolution and pressed other conservative measures through the Chamber of Deputies. Opposition soon developed. After elections in 1827, Charles moderated his conservatism, but French liberals pressed for a constitutional regime. Matters came to a head in 1829 when Charles abandoned efforts to accommodate liberals and appointed an ultra-royalist ministry. This backfired.

In 1830, Charles X called for new elections, and the liberals scored a stunning victory. Instead of attempting to accommodate the new Chamber of Deputies, the king and his ministers decided to attempt a royalist seizure of power. In June and July 1830, the ministry sent a naval expedition against Algeria. On July 9, reports of its victory, the start of a French empire in North Africa, reached Paris. On July 25, 1830, Charles X, euphoric in victory, issued the Four Ordinances. They restricted freedom of the press, dissolved the

Vive La France. *Liberty Leading the People* by Eugene Delacroix is a famous evocation of the Revolution of 1830.

Giraudon/Art Resource, N.Y.

recently elected Chamber of Deputies, called for new elections, and limited the franchise to the wealthiest people in the country.

Liberal newspapers immediately called on the nation to reject the monarch's actions. The laboring populace of Paris, suffering since 1827 from the effects of an economic downturn, took to the streets and erected barricades. The king called out troops, and more than 1,800 people died during the ensuing battles in the city. On August 2, Charles X abdicated and left France for exile in England. The liberals in the Chamber of Deputies named a new ministry composed of constitutional monarchists. They proclaimed Louis Philippe (r. 1830–1848), the Duke of Orléans and the head of the liberal branch of the royal family, the new monarch. In the so-called **July Monarchy**, Louis Philippe reigned as king of the French rather than of France. He had to cooperate with the Chamber of Deputies, and he could not dispense with laws on his own authority. The revolutionary tricolor replaced the white flag of the Bourbons. The Charter, or constitution, was regarded as embodying the natural rights of the people rather than a concession of privileges granted them by the monarch. Catholicism was recognized only as the religion of the majority of the people, not the official religion. Censorship was abolished. The franchise, though still restricted, was extended.

Socially, the Revolution of 1830 proved quite conservative. The landed oligarchy retained its economic, political, and social influence. Money became the path to power and influence in the government, resulting in much corruption. Most revealing, the liberal monarchy displayed scant sympathy for the lower and working classes.

The Great Reform Bill in Britain (1832)

The passage of the **Great Reform Bill**, which became law in 1832, was the result of events different from those that occurred on the continent. In Britain, the forces of conservatism and reform compromised with each other. As a result, during the century Great Britain was regarded as the exemplary liberal state not only of Europe but of the world.

English determination to maintain union with Ireland began the reform process. England's relationship to Ireland was not unlike that of Russia's to Poland or Austria's to Hungary. The Act of Union in 1800 between England and Ireland had suppressed the separate Irish parliament and seated Irish representatives in the British parliament at Westminster. Only Protestant Irishmen, however, could be elected to represent what was an overwhelmingly Catholic country.

During the 1820s, under the leadership of Daniel O'Connell (1775–1847), Irish nationalists organized the Catholic Association to agitate for **Catholic emancipation**, as the movement for legal rights for Roman Catholics was known. In 1828, O'Connell was elected to Parliament but could not legally take his seat. The British ministry of the Duke of Wellington (1769–1852) realized that henceforth Ireland might elect a predominantly Catholic delegation to Parliament, and if they were not seated, civil war might erupt. Consequently, in 1829, Wellington and Robert Peel (1788–1850) steered the Catholic Emancipation Act through Parliament. Roman Catholics could now become members of Parliament. This measure, together with the repeal in 1828 of restrictions against Protestant nonconformists, ended the monopoly held by members of the Church of England on British political life.

Catholic emancipation alienated many of Wellington's Tory supporters. In the election of 1830, many supporters of parliamentary reform were returned to

July Monarchy French regime set up after the overthrow of the Bourbons in July 1830.

Great Reform Bill (1832) Limited reform of the British House of Commons and expansion of the electorate to include a wider variety of the propertied classes. It laid the groundwork for further orderly reforms within the British constitutional system.

Catholic emancipation Grant of full political rights to Roman Catholics in Britain in 1829.

Parliament. Some Tories thought that parliamentary reform was necessary because they believed that Catholic emancipation could have been passed only by a corrupt House of Commons. The Wellington ministry soon fell. The Tories were badly divided, and King William IV (r. 1830–1837) turned to the Whigs under the leadership of Earl Grey (1764–1845) to form a government.

The Whig ministry authored a major reform bill that had two broad goals. The first was to replace "rotten" boroughs, which had few voters, with representatives for the previously unrepresented and populous manufacturing districts and cities. The second was to increase the number of voters in England and Wales. In 1831, the House of Commons narrowly defeated the bill. Grey called for a new election in which a majority in favor of the bill was returned to the Commons. The House of Commons passed the reform bill, but the House of Lords rejected it. Mass meetings were held throughout the country, and riots broke out in several cities. Finally, William IV agreed to create enough new peers to give a third reform bill a majority in the House of Lords. Under this pressure, the measure became law in 1832.

The Great Reform Act expanded the size of the English electorate, but it was not a democratic measure. The electorate was increased by more than 200,000 persons, or by almost 50 percent. The basis of voting, however, remained a property qualification, and some working-class voters actually lost the vote when their old franchise rights were abolished. New urban boroughs gave the growing cities a voice in the House of Commons. Yet the passage of the Reform Act did not, as it was once thought, constitute the triumph of the middle-class interest in England. For every new urban electoral district, a new rural district was also created. It was expected that the aristocracy would dominate the rural elections.

Although passed with much turmoil and conflict, the Great Reform Act established the foundation for long-term political stability in Britain. During the 1840s, a major working-class political movement known as **Chartism** brought the demands of industrial workers into the political process. Despite the tensions created by Chartism, British political structures survived intact. Throughout the second half of the 19th century, Great Britain continued to symbolize the confident liberal state. A large body of ideas emphasizing competition and individualism was accepted by the members of all classes. Even the leaders of trade unions during these years asked only to receive some of the fruits of prosperity and a chance to prove their social respectability. Parliament absorbed new groups and interests into the existing political processes.

The most important example of the opening of parliamentary processes was the Second Reform Act passed by a Conservative government in 1867. By increasing the number of voters from approximately 1,430,000 to 2,470,000, it advanced Britain toward democracy. Benjamin Disraeli (1804–1881), who led the conservatives in the House of Commons, thought significant portions of the working class would eventually support conservative candidates who responded to social issues. He also thought the growing suburban middle class would become more conservative.

Chartism First large-scale European working-class political movement. It sought political reforms that would favor the interests of skilled British workers in the 1830s and 1840s.

Gladstone and Disraeli The election of 1868, which followed the Second Reform Act, dashed Disraeli's hopes. William Gladstone (1809–1898) became the new prime minister, and his ministry (1868–1874) witnessed the culmination of classical British liberalism. Gladstone introduced competitive examinations into the civil service, abolished the purchase of army officers' commissions, and introduced the secret ballot. He opened Oxford and Cambridge universities to students of all religious denominations and, by the Education Act of 1870, made the British government responsible for establishing and running elementary schools, which previously had been maintained by the various churches.

The liberal policy of creating popular support for the nation by extending political liberty and reforming abuses had its conservative counterpart in concern about social reform. Disraeli succeeded Gladstone as prime minister in 1874. Whereas Gladstone looked to individualism, free trade, and competition to solve social problems, Disraeli believed the state should protect its weaker citizens and that paternalistic legislation would alleviate class antagonism. His most important measures were the Public Health Act of 1875, which consolidated and extended previous sanitary legislation, and the Artisans Dwelling Act of 1875, through which the government became involved in providing housing for the working class.

The Irish Question   Ireland remained a major issue for the British government. From the late 1860s onward, Irish nationalists had sought to achieve home rule for Ireland, by which they meant more Irish control of local government. What they demanded from the British government resembled what Hungarians first and then Czechs demanded from the Habsburg government (discussed later in this chapter). The Irish, like the Hungarians and Czechs in the Habsburg Empire, were a profoundly disruptive force in British politics.

The leader of the Irish movement for **home rule** was Charles Stewart Parnell (1846–1891). By 1885, Parnell had organized 85 Irish members of the House of Commons into a tightly disciplined party that often voted as a bloc. After the election of 1885, the Irish Party held the balance of power in a house divided between the English liberals and conservatives. The Irish could decide which party would take office, and in December 1885, Gladstone won their votes by announcing his support for home rule for Ireland. However, the issue split Gladstone's Liberal Party. In 1886, a group known as the Liberal Unionists

QUICK REVIEW

William Gladstone (1809–1898)
* Became prime minister in election of 1868
* His ministry witnessed the culmination of classical British liberalism
* Carried out reforms of governmental abuses and extended political liberty

home rule   Advocacy of a large measure of administrative autonomy for Ireland within the British Empire between the 1880s and 1914.

A House of Commons Debate. William Ewart Gladstone, standing on the right, is attacking Benjamin Disraeli, who sits with legs crossed and arms folded. Gladstone served in the British Parliament from the 1830s through the 1890s. Four times the Liberal Party prime minister, he was responsible for guiding major reforms through Parliament. Disraeli, regarded as the founder of modern British conservatism, served as prime minister from 1874 to 1880.
Mary Evans Picture Library.

20.2
Irish National Identity
and Destiny: Three Views

joined with the conservatives to defeat Gladstone's Home Rule Bill. Gladstone called for a new election, which the liberals lost. They remained permanently divided. The new conservative ministry of Lord Salisbury (1830–1903) attempted to reconcile the Irish to the English government through public works and administrative reform, but he had only marginal success.

In 1892, Gladstone returned to power and sponsored a second Home Rule Bill that passed the House of Commons but was defeated in the House of Lords. With the failure of this bill, further action on the Irish question was suspended until a liberal ministry passed the third Home Rule Bill in the summer of 1914. However, the implementation of home rule was then suspended for the duration of World War I.

As already noted, the Irish question affected British politics much the way that the nationalities problem affected Austria. Normal British domestic issues could not be adequately addressed because of the political divisions created by Ireland. The split of the Liberal Party hurt the cause of further social and political reform. The people who could agree about reforms could not agree on Ireland, and Ireland seemed more important. Because the two traditional parties failed to deal with the social questions, by the turn of the century a newly organized Labour Party appeared to fill the vacuum.

1848: YEAR OF REVOLUTIONS IN EUROPE

In 1848, a series of liberal and nationalistic revolutions and revolts spread across Europe (see Map 24–1). No single factor caused this general revolutionary groundswell, but similar conditions existed in several countries. Severe food shortages had prevailed since 1846 due to poor harvests. The commercial and industrial economy was in recession, resulting in widespread unemployment. However, the pressure for change in 1848 originated not with the working classes but with the political liberals, who were generally drawn from the middle classes. Throughout the continent, liberals were pushing for more representative governments, civil liberty, and free and unregulated economies.

To put additional pressure on their governments, the liberals began to appeal for support from the urban working classes, even though the goals of the two groups were different. The working classes wanted more jobs and better working conditions rather than political reform for its own sake. By refusing to follow political revolution with social reform, the liberals separated themselves from their temporary working-class allies. Without potential mass support, the liberal revolutions were easy prey for the armies of reactionary governments. Consequently, the revolutions of 1848 failed to establish genuinely liberal or national states.

The revolutions of 1848 were confined to the continent, and their results were important for individual nation-states. In France, the monarchy of Louis Philippe was overthrown and briefly replaced by a republic. In 1851, the republic was in turn overthrown in a military coup led by Louis Napoleon, a nephew of Napoleon I. Thereafter, Louis Napoleon created the Second Empire and took the title of Napoleon III. In Prussia and the Austrian Empire, short-lived revolutions brought political liberals and nationalists to the fore, but in each case the revolutions were suppressed by the military. The same was true of efforts by Italian nationalists to thrust off Austrian rule of Italy.

From the standpoint of world history, the chief importance of the failed liberal and national revolutions of 1848 was the emergence on the European continent of strongly conservative governments that would dominate the scene for the next quarter century. The turmoil of 1848 through 1850 ended the era of

QUICK REVIEW

Factors Leading to Revolutions

- Food shortages due to bad harvests
- Recession and widespread unemployement
- Pressure from continental liberals for change

MAP 24–1

Centers of Revolution in 1848–1849. The revolution that toppled the July Monarchy in Paris in 1848 soon spread to Austria and many of the German and Italian states. Yet by the end of 1849, most of these uprisings had been suppressed.

WHICH REGIONS were most affected by the uprisings of 1848 and 1849?

liberal revolution that had begun in 1789. Liberals and nationalists had discovered that rational argument and local insurrections would not help them to achieve their goals. The working class also adopted new tactics and organization. The era of the riot and urban insurrection was ending. In the future, workers would turn to trade unions and political parties to achieve their political and social goals. Finally, after the revolutions of 1848, the political initiative in Europe passed for a time to the conservative political groups.

The defeat of liberal political forces in 1848 and the triumph of conservative powers also influenced the modernization of Japan. Within a few years,

Japan was to emerge from its long, self-imposed isolation. After the Meiji Restoration, the new leaders of Japan looked to Europe for examples of successful modern nations. The nation they would most clearly copy was the conservative, militaristic Germany that emerged after the defeat of the liberals of 1848.

TESTING THE NEW AMERICAN REPUBLIC

TOWARD SECTIONAL CONFLICT

WHAT WERE the causes of the American Civil War?

While the nations of Western Europe very slowly embraced political liberalism, the United States of America was continuing its bold republican political experiment. By the first quarter of the century, however, serious sectional tensions had arisen, the most important of which concerned the institution of slavery in the southern states.

The issue had come up at the Constitutional Convention of 1788, which debated what proportion of the slave population, if any, should be counted in determining how many seats the southern states would have in the House of Representatives. A compromise allowed the slave-holding states to count three-fifths of their slaves when calculating their population for representation in Congress. The Constitution also forbade any federal attempt to prevent the importation of slaves until 1808. Between 1788 and 1808, thousands of slaves were brought into the United States.

The opening of the western territories to settlement revived debates over slavery. The Ordinance of 1787, passed by Congress under the Articles of Confederation, had prohibited slavery in the Northwest Territory (the future states of Illinois, Indiana, Michigan, Ohio, and Wisconsin). Territory south of the Ohio River and beyond the Mississippi River was, however, open to slavery. By 1820, the number of slave and free states was evenly divided, and there was, therefore, an equal number of senators from slave and free states. That year, Missouri was admitted as a slave state and Maine as a free one. The Missouri Compromise temporarily ended congressional debate over slavery by decreeing that no slave states would be carved out of land north of the southern border of Missouri. However, problems loomed, for the economies of the North and the South were rapidly diverging.

Northern Economic Development   The North's economy featured family farms, free labor, commerce, and early industrialization in textiles. Northern farmers tended primarily to produce foodstuffs for local markets. Their farms were relatively small and worked by family members and free hired laborers. Workers in the towns, on the ships, and in the factories of the North were also free. The political spokesmen for the North tended to favor tariffs to protect their young industries from cheaper foreign competition. Many Americans whose political views otherwise resembled European liberals differed from their European counterparts in their support for tariffs.

The North was the site of the earliest textile factories in the United States. Samuel Slater had established the first textile mill in Rhode Island in 1790. He had learned how to manufacture textiles in the new mills of industrializing Great Britain. His transfer of that technology to America illustrates how important British and European advances were transported to the United States. Much of the early industrialization of the United States depended on such technological transfers. By the second decade of the 19th century, the North had hundreds of cotton factories. These mills used cotton that was produced in the South, but most southern cotton was sold overseas, mainly to the growing British textile industry.

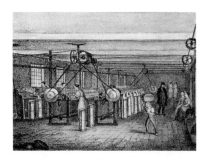

Textile Mill. In New England, as in Europe, textile manufacturing was the first of the highly mechanized industries. American and European textile mills closely resembled each other because those in America had been copied from European and most particularly English technology.

The Granger Collection, N.Y.

During the second quarter of the century, innovations in transportation led to the fuller integration of different parts of the Northern economy (see Map 24–2). Canals were built to link the major rivers with manufacturing and agricultural markets. The most famous was the Erie Canal, which connected the Hudson River to the Great Lakes. Other canals linked the Great Lakes to the Ohio River. Major efforts were undertaken to make the Ohio, Mississippi, and Missouri Rivers navigable so that steamboats could transport goods. But by the late 1840s, in America as in Europe, railroads were becoming the future of transportation. Most of the railways linked the Northeast and the West and fostered the commercial agriculture of the Midwest. Its products were sold in the Northeast and exported from Northern ports. The development of east–west railways weakened ties between the North and the South by undermining the older north–south river-based trade routes of the Ohio and Mississippi. The building of the early railways also aided the development of the Northern coal and iron industries. The expansion of railways at mid-century caused new sectional tensions, as it became clear that they were opening vast territories for settlement and reigniting a national debate over the future of slavery.

Rivers, canals, and railways allowed the upper Midwest to develop into a rich area for agriculture. Consequently, much of the northern economy was as rural and agricultural as the southern. What most distinguished the two regions was free versus slave labor. The southern economy depended on slavery and could expand only if slavery were allowed to spread as well (see Map 24–2).

The Southern Economy The overwhelmingly rural economy of the American South was dependent on cotton and slavery. In this respect, the Southern economy resembled those of many Latin American countries, which used slave labor to produce a specialized crop or exploit a natural resource for export. The South had to export goods, especially raw cotton, either to the North or to Europe, primarily to Great Britain, to maintain its standard of living.

The invention of the cotton gin by Eli Whitney (1765–1825) in 1793 made cotton cultivation much more profitable because the seed no longer had to be laboriously picked out of the raw cotton by hand. The industrial revolution in textiles kept cotton prices high, and the expansion in world population kept the demand for cotton cloth steady. The South profited from growing the cotton, New England profited from shipping it, and other parts of the North profited from supplying the manufactured goods the South needed. The South had virtually no incentive to diversify its agriculture.

Slavery in the American South Slavery had been abolished in the North by the early 19th century. This was a response to the egalitarian principles of the American Revolution and a recognition of the fact that slavery had never been fundamental to the northern economy. But in the South, the growth of a cotton-producing empire in the Mississippi Delta in the early 19th century gave slavery a new lease on life. Although most southern families never owned any slaves and relatively few slave owners possessed more than a few, the institution of slavery survived for many reasons. For one, it was economically viable, and no one could find a way that was politically or socially acceptable to white southerners to abolish it. No less important was the strong commitment to the protection of private property, which included slaves, throughout American society in both the North and the South. Perhaps the most basic reason for the endurance of slavery after the early 19th century, however, was racist thinking that saw Blacks as fundamentally inferior to Whites. Such thinking was not

Cotton fields. Slaves harvest cotton under the watchful eyes of an overseer, mid 19th-century.

MAP EXPLORATION

Interactive map: To explore this map further, go to **http://www.prenhall.com/craig/map24.2**

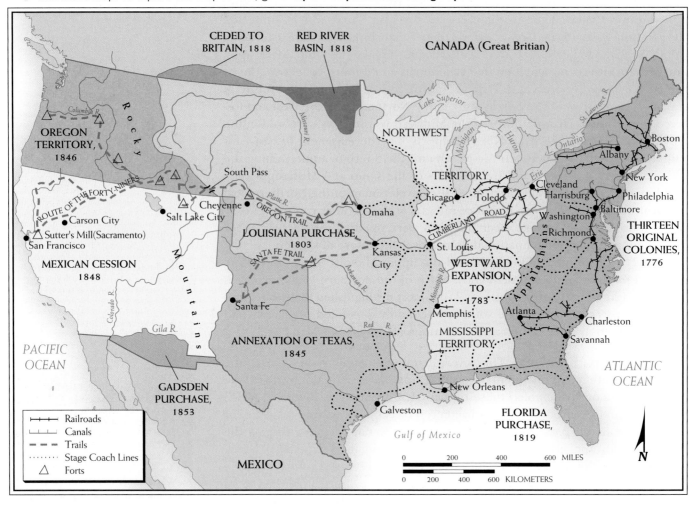

MAP 24-2

19th-Century North America. During the 19th century the United States expanded across the entire North American continent. The revolutionary settlement had provided most of the land east of the Mississippi. The single largest addition thereafter was the Louisiana Purchase of 1803. The annexation of Texas, and later the Mexican Cession following the Mexican War, added the major southwestern territories. The borders of the Oregon Territory were settled through long, difficult negotiations with Great Britain.

HOW DID the westward expansion of the United States help cause the Civil War?

peculiar to the South, but it functioned there to bolster arguments against abolishing slavery.

All American slaves were non-White, the descendants of Africans who had been forcibly captured and shipped in the most wretched of conditions to the United States (see Chapter 17). Despite much miscegenation among Africans and their White slave owners and Native Americans, the various slave codes defined as Black virtually anyone who had any African antecedents. Slaves were regarded as chattel property; that is, they could be sold, given away, or gambled away like any other piece of property. They had no recourse to law or constitutional protections and could be, and often were, treated badly by their masters. Whipping and beating were permitted. State laws protected slaves from extreme violence, but were laxly enforced; slaves had no serious protection from the law or legal authorities. Their standard of living was generally poor. Although owners wanted to see their slave investments reproduce themselves, slaves suffered from overwork and diseases associated with poor nutrition, sanitation, and housing.

Slaves worked primarily in the fields, where they plowed, hoed, and harvested cotton, rice, sugar, tobacco, or corn. They were usually organized into work gangs supervised by White overseers. This work was, like all farming, seasonal; but during planting or harvest seasons, people labored from sunrise to sunset. Children also worked in the fields. Older or more privileged slaves might be employed in their owner's house, cleaning, cooking, or taking care of his children.

Recent scholarship has emphasized how the slave communities helped to preserve family life and inner personalities of the slaves. Some elements of African culture persisted; African legends were passed on orally. Religion proved extraordinarily important. Slaves, for instance, found special meaning in the Old Testament stories of the Jews' liberation from Egypt, and they combined elements of African religion with evangelical Protestantism. Their efforts to preserve a sense of community and family had to contend with the fact that their marriages and family ties were not legally recognized. The integrity of the slave family could be violated at the master's whim or as a result of changing economic circumstances. White men often sexually exploited Black slave women. Because slaves were property, they could be sold for profit or transported when the owner moved to a different region. Consequently, families could be, and were, separated by sale or after an owner's death. Many young children were reared and cared for by other slaves to whom they were not related. In a world of White dominance, the institutions, customs, and religions of the slave community were the only means Black slaves had to protect the autonomy of their own personalities.

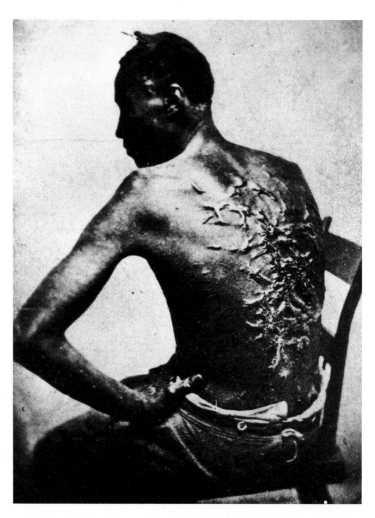

Scars of Slavery. This Louisiana slave named Gordon was photographed in 1863 after he had escaped to Union lines during the Civil War. He bears the permanent scars of the violence that lay at the heart of the slave system. Few slaves were so brutally marked, but all lived with the threat of beatings if they failed to obey.

Corbis/Bettmann.

THE ABOLITIONIST MOVEMENT

During the 1830s, a militant antislavery movement emerged in the North. Its leaders and followers refused to accept what they regarded as the moral compromise of living in a nation that tolerated slavery. Abolitionists, such as William Lloyd Garrison, editor of *The Liberator*, condemned the Union and the Constitution as structures that perpetuated slavery. Former slaves who had escaped slavery such as Frederick Douglass and Sojourner Truth, and freeborn Black Americans such as Daniel A. Payne, also joined the cause. The antislavery movement, which was initially only one of many American reform movements, gained adherents as the question of extending slavery into the new territories came to the fore toward the end of the Mexican War (1846–1848). This military victory added significant new territory in the Southwest and California, in addition to Texas, which had been annexed in 1845. Through negotiations with Britain, the United States also acquired the vast Oregon Territory in the Northwest in 1846.

Southerners feared that the changing climate of national feeling about slavery and the opening of territories where slavery might be prohibited would eventually make them a minority in the country and render them impotent to defend their political position and social institutions. Northerners, for their part, came to believe that proslavery factions had somehow conspired to win control of the federal government. The Compromise of 1850 temporarily restored political calm and reassured the South. But many Northerners thought that the compromise only demonstrated the strength of the slave-power conspiracy in Washington.

The introduction of the Kansas-Nebraska Bill in 1854 renewed the formal national political debate over slavery and galvanized the antislavery forces. The bill, which was introduced by Stephen A. Douglas (1813–1861), proposed popular sovereignty: Each new territory was to decide by popular vote whether slavery was to be permitted within its borders. This involved repealing the Missouri Compromise, which had prohibited slavery in most of the Louisiana Territory. It also meant that every newly organized territory would have to debate slavery. In 1854, opposition to the Kansas-Nebraska Bill inspired the formation of the new Republican Party. Some of the bill's opponents did more than debate it: John Brown went to Kansas, where armed conflict had already broken out, to wage virtual guerrilla warfare against slaveholding settlers. In 1854, civil war was already being waged in "Bleeding Kansas."

In 1857, in the Dred Scott decision, the Supreme Court effectively repealed the Missouri Compromise by declaring that Congress could not prohibit slavery in the territories. The decision further declared that slaves did not become free by living in free states and that slaves did not have rights that others were bound to respect. For radical antislavery Northerners, the decision raised the most serious questions about the morality of the Union itself, and it seemed once again to be evidence for a southern conspiracy to protect slavery. Thereafter, slavery dominated national political debate.

Abraham Lincoln. The election of Lincoln in 1860 sparked the secession crisis that started the Civil War. This picture shows Lincoln as he was when elected, without the famous beard that he grew later.

Preston Butler/Library of Congress.

In 1859, John Brown seized the federal arsenal at Harpers Ferry, Virginia, as part of an effort to foment a slave rebellion. He was captured, tried, and hanged, further increasing sectional polarization. Radical Southerners feared more than ever a northern conspiracy to attack the institution of slavery, while northern radicals feared that the South would use the federal government to protect slavery. Thus the politics of both sections became radicalized.

The Republican Party had become the party that opposed slavery, although most Republicans did not favor outright abolition. In 1858, Abraham Lincoln (1809–1865) ran against Stephen Douglas for the U.S. Senate in Illinois. Lincoln lost, but he made a national reputation for himself in the debates leading up to the election. In 1860, Lincoln, the Republican candidate, was elected president. Neither he nor the Republican Party had campaigned for the abolition of slavery. Nonetheless, Southerners perceived his election as the victory of a party and a president dedicated to the eradication of slavery. In December 1860, southern states began to secede and formed the Confederate States of

America. Attempts at political compromise to maintain the Union failed, and when Confederate forces fired on Fort Sumter in Charleston harbor in April 1861, the most destructive war in U.S. history began.

The Civil War lasted almost four years, and it transformed the nation. In 1863, Lincoln emancipated the slaves in the rebel states. The Emancipation Proclamation made the North's fight a campaign to extend liberty, not just to suppress a southern rebellion. By the time the Confederacy was defeated in 1865, the South was occupied by northern armies, its farms were often fallow, its transportation network disrupted, and many of its cities in ruins. Southern political leaders had virtually no impact on the immediate postwar decisions. The Thirteenth, Fourteenth, and Fifteenth Amendments to the Constitution largely recast the character of the Union. The Thirteenth abolished slavery, the Fourteenth granted citizenship to the former slaves, and the Fifteenth allowed them to vote. The Fourteenth Amendment also limited political activity by people who had taken up arms against the Union. These amendments resolved the issues of slavery and the relative roles of the state and federal governments.

The Civil War and the Reconstruction Era that followed overturned the antebellum social and political structures of the South. Slaves were freed and for a time participated broadly and actively in the politics of the southern states. For more than 10 years, federal troops occupied parts of the South. Many of the antebellum southern leaders abandoned politics. Attempts to bring manufacturing into the South met with limited success. Economically, the South remained largely rural and dependent on cotton, but for the first time since its earliest colonial era, its work force was free. Many of the freed slaves and poor Whites who tilled the land remained hopelessly in debt to wealthier landowners, and rampant racism hindered economic development. For the rest of the century, the South remained in a semicolonial relationship to the North. More than ever, to pay for the goods and services it needed, the South had to export raw materials or partially finished goods to the North, according to economic rules set by northern manufacturers and financiers. Poverty was the norm throughout the rural South.

Within the context of world history, the American Civil War is important for several reasons. With the exception of the Taiping Rebellion in China (1851–1864), it was the greatest war that occurred anywhere in the world between the defeat of Napoleon in 1815 and the onset of World War I in 1914. It resulted in the establishment of a continent-wide free labor market, even though freed Blacks lived in great poverty and an economic dependence not unlike that of the rural classes of Latin America. The free labor market, purged of slavery, helped to open the entire North American continent to economic development. The war also allowed American political and economic interests to develop without the distraction of the debates over states' rights and the morality of slavery. Thereafter, free labor became the American norm, and the debates over the role of industrial labor in the United States resembled those in Europe (see the next chapter).

THE CANADIAN EXPERIENCE

Under the Treaty of Paris of 1763, all of Canada came under the control of Great Britain. Canada then, as now, included both an English-speaking and a French-speaking population—the latter concentrated primarily in Quebec. The Quebec Act of 1774 made the Roman Catholic Church the established church in Quebec. During the American Revolution approximately 30,000 English loyalists fled the colonies and settled in Canada. They strengthened English influences and were staunchly loyal to the British Crown.

HOW DID Canada achieve united self-government?

Tension between the French and English populations led, in part, to the Constitutional Act of 1791, which divided the colony into Upper Canada (primarily English) and Lower Canada (primarily French). Each section had its own legislature, and a governor-general presided over the two provinces on behalf of the British Crown. Cape Breton Island, New Brunswick, Newfoundland, Nova Scotia, and Prince Edward Island remained separate colonies.

In the early 19th century, relations with the United States were often tense. There were local disputes over the fur trade and fear that the United States would dominate Canada. That apprehension, along with the Anglo-French ethnic divisions, constitute two of the major themes of Canadian history.

By the late 1830s, political tensions in Canada were beginning to generate considerable internal pressure. Long-established families with powerful economic interests in both Upper and Lower Canada were at odds with new settlers seeking opportunities to prosper, and there were quarrels over the influence of the British Crown in local affairs. In 1837, rebellions occurred in both Upper and Lower Canada. Although there were relatively few casualties, Great Britain realized that the situation needed to be resolved.

ROAD TO SELF-GOVERNMENT

The British government, operating in the more liberal political climate following the first Reform Act (1832), was determined to avoid another North American revolution. Consequently, it sent the Earl of Durham (1792–1840) to Canada with extensive authority to implement reforms. In 1839, his *Report on the Affairs of British North America* advocated extensive self-government for Canada. He recommended that most Canadian affairs be left in the hands of a Canadian legislature and that only foreign policy and defense remain under British control. Durham also proposed that the two Canadian provinces be united. He thought that political unification would eventually promote English culture throughout Canada and overwhelm the French influence in Quebec. In effect, Durham wanted Canadians to govern themselves so that English culture would dominate. The Canada Act of 1840 accepted his recommendations and established a single legislature composed of two houses as Canada's government.

Durham's report established the political pattern that the British government would, to a greater or lesser extent, follow with its other English-speaking colonies during the 19th century. Britain sought to foster responsible self-government in Australia, New Zealand, and South Africa. The Canadian experience thus had a considerable impact throughout the world. But, until well into the 20th century, the British government, like other Western imperial powers, also generally believed that non-White peoples such as those of India required direct British colonial administration.

KEEPING A DISTINCTIVE CULTURE

Canadians learned to exercise self-government, but distinct English and French cultures survived to complicate that task. Within the legislature there were almost always tradeoffs between the eastern and western sections of the nation. Furthermore, during the American Civil War fears arose that the American republic might seek to invade or dominate Canada. One response to this fear was an attempt to unite the Maritime Provinces in 1862. Those discussions led to broader considerations of the desirability for a stronger federation among all the parts of Canada.

The result of those debates and discussions was the British North America Act of 1867, which created a Canadian federation. Canadians hoped to avoid what they saw as flaws in the U.S. Constitution. The Canadian system of government was to be federal, but with much less emphasis on states' rights than in the United States. Canadians established a parliamentary mode of government, but also chose to retain allegiance to the British monarchy represented by a governor-general as head of state. The person most responsible for establishing this new government and for leading it between 1867 and 1891 was John A. MacDonald (1815–1891).

MID-CENTURY POLITICAL CONSOLIDATION IN EUROPE

While the United States and Canada were establishing themselves as strong unified political entities in North America, major political consolidation occurred in Europe that would have an enormous impact on the rest of the world. As has so often been true in modern European history, war made change possible. In this case, a conflict disrupted the international balance that had prevailed since 1815 and unleashed forces that upset the internal political situation in several of the involved states. The war itself was in some respects less important than the political consequences that flowed from it during the next decade.

THE CRIMEAN WAR

The Crimean War (1854–1856), named after the Black Sea peninsula on which it was largely fought, originated from a long-standing rivalry between Russia and

WHAT WERE the steps that led to Italian and German unification?

Florence Nightingale. During the Crimean War, Florence Nightingale of Great Britain organized nursing care for the wounded.

Corbis-Bettmann Archive.

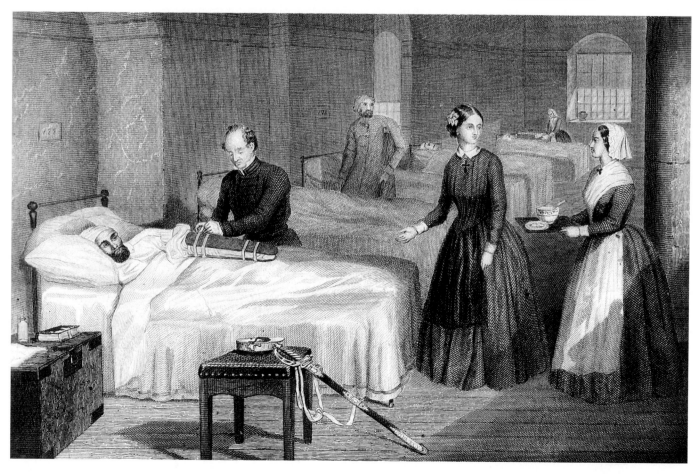

the Ottoman Empire. Russia wanted to extend its influence over the Ottoman provinces of Moldavia and Walachia (now in Romania). In 1853, Russia went to war against the Ottomans on the pretext that the Ottomans had given Roman Catholic France, instead of Orthodox Russia, the right to protect Christians and Christian shrines in the Holy Land. The next year France and Great Britain supported the Ottoman Empire to protect their interests in the eastern Mediterranean. Austria and Prussia remained neutral. The war quickly bogged down after the French and the British invaded the Crimea. In March 1856, a peace conference convened in Paris and eventually concluded a treaty highly unfavorable to Russia.

The Crimean War shattered the image of an invincible Russia that had prevailed since the close of the Napoleonic Wars. It also shattered the power of the Concert of Europe to settle international disputes on the continent. The major European powers were no longer willing to cooperate to maintain the existing borders between themselves and their neighbors. For the next 25 years, instability prevailed in European affairs, allowing a largely unchecked adventurism in foreign policy.

ITALIAN UNIFICATION

Italian nationalists had long wanted to unite the small absolutist principalities of the peninsula into a single state but could not agree on how to do it. Romantic republicans, such as Giuseppe Mazzini (1805–1872) and Giuseppe Garibaldi (1807–1882), sought to drive out the Austrians by popular military force and to establish a republic. They not only failed but also frightened more moderate Italians. The person who eventually achieved unification was Count Camillo Cavour (1810–1861), the prime minister of Piedmont.

Piedmont (the "Kingdom of Sardinia"), in northwestern Italy, was the most independent state on the peninsula (see Map 24–3). It had unsuccessfully fought against Austria in 1848 and 1849. Following the second defeat, King Charles Albert (r. 1831–1849) abdicated in favor of his son, Victor Emmanuel II (r. 1849–1878). In 1852, the new monarch chose Cavour—a moderate liberal in economics and a strong monarchist who rejected republicanism—as his prime minister.

Cavour believed that if Italians proved themselves to be efficient and economically progressive, the great powers might decide that Italy could govern itself. He worked for free trade, railway construction, credit expansion, and agricultural improvement. He also fostered the Nationalist Society, which established chapters in other Italian states to press for unification under the leadership of Piedmont. Cavour also believed that Italy could be unified only with the aid of France.

Cavour supported the French and British in the Crimean War so as to have a seat at the peace conference, where he raised the question of Italian unification. He won nothing specific, but Napoleon III (r. 1852–1870) of France expressed sympathy for his cause. In 1858, Cavour and the French emperor met to plot war with Austria.

During the winter and spring of 1859, tension grew between Austria and Piedmont as the latter mobilized its army. In late April, when war erupted, France came to Piedmont's aid. On June 4, the Austrians were defeated at Magenta, and on June 24, at Solferino in Lombardy. Fearing too extensive a Piedmontese victory, Napoleon III concluded a separate peace with Austria at Villafranca on

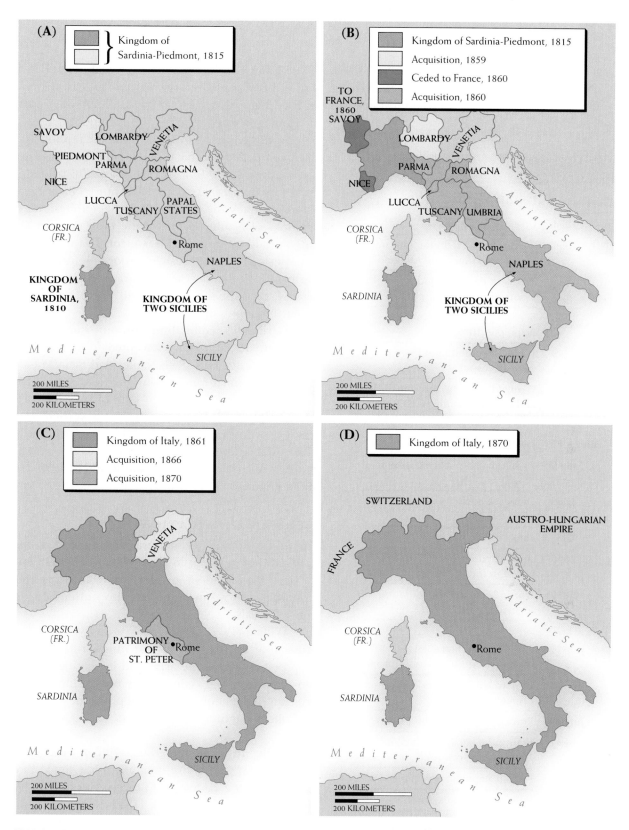

MAP 24–3

The Unification of Italy.   Beginning with the association of Sardinia and Piedmont by the Congress of Vienna in 1815, unification was achieved through the expansion of Piedmont between 1859 and 1870. Both Cavour's statesmanship and the campaigns of ardent nationalists played large roles.

WHAT WERE the stages of Italian unification between 1815 and 1870?

July 11. Piedmont received Lombardy, but the Veneto remained under Austrian control. Cavour felt betrayed by France, but the war had at least driven Austria from most of northern Italy. Later that summer Parma, Modena, Tuscany, and the Romagna voted to unite with Piedmont.

At this point the forces of romantic republican nationalism compelled Cavour to pursue unification of northern and southern Italy. In May 1860, Garibaldi landed in Sicily with more than 1,000 troops. He captured Palermo and prepared to attack the mainland. By September, the city and kingdom of Naples, probably the most corrupt absolutist state in Italy, were under his control. To forestall a republican victory Cavour rushed troops south to confront Garibaldi. On the way Cavour's troops conquered the Papal States except for the area around Rome, which remained under the pope's direct control.

Garibaldi's nationalism won out over his republicanism, and he unhappily accepted domination by the Piedmontese. In late 1860, Naples and Sicily voted to join Piedmont's northern union. In March 1861, Victor Emmanuel II was proclaimed king of Italy. Three months later Cavour died. The new state was governed by the conservative constitution promulgated in 1848 by Charles Albert. Italy gained the Veneto in 1866 as a result of the war between Austria and Prussia, and Rome in 1870 as a result of the Franco-Prussian War.

GERMAN UNIFICATION

The unification of Germany was the single most important political development in Europe between 1848 and 1914. It was spearheaded by Prussia's conservative army, monarch, and prime minister, who outflanked the kingdom's liberals.

William I's (r. 1861–1888) primary concern was the Prussian army. In 1860, his war minister and chief of staff proposed enlarging the army and increasing the service of conscripts from two to three years, but the liberal-dominated Prussian parliament refused to approve the necessary taxes. A deadlock continued for two years.

Bismarck   In September 1862, William I turned for help to the person who, more than any other single individual, determined the course of European history for the next 30 years: Otto von Bismarck (1815–1898). Bismarck came from Junker stock, and his outlook was deeply informed by the most traditional Prussian values: admiration for the monarchy, the nobility, and the army. After being appointed prime minister and foreign minister in 1862, Bismarck immediately moved against the liberal parliament. He contended that further parliamentary votes on taxes were not required, for the Prussian constitution

German and Italian Unification

	1854	Crimean War opens
	1855	Cavour leads Piedmont into war on side of France and England
July 20, 1856		Treaty of Paris concludes Crimean War
	1858	Secret conference between Napoleon III and Cavour
	1859	War of Piedmont and France against Austria
	1860	Garibaldi lands his forces in Sicily and conquers southern Italy
1861		
	March 17	Death of Cavour
	June 6	Proclamation of the Kingdom of Italy;
	1862	Bismarck becomes prime minister of Prussia
	1864	Danish War
	1866	Austro-Prussian War; Veneto ceded to Italy
	1867	North German Confederation formed
1870		
	July 12	Crisis over Hohenzollern candidacy for the Spanish throne
	July 13	Bismarck publishes edited press dispatch
	July 19	France declares war on Prussia
	September 1	France defeated at Sedan and Napoleon III captured
	September 4	French Republic proclaimed
	October 2	Italian state annexes Rome
1871		
	January 18	Proclamation of the German Empire at Versailles
	March 18–May 28	Paris Commune
	May 10	Treaty of Frankfurt between France and Germany

permitted the government to function on the basis of taxes that had already been approved. The army and most of the bureaucracy backed his interpretation of the constitution, but new elections in 1863 sustained the liberal majority in the parliament. Bismarck sought a cause that would draw popular support away from the liberals and toward the monarchy and the army. His tactic was to use foreign affairs to divert public attention from domestic matters by having Prussia assume leadership of the effort to unify Germany.

Bismarck favored what was known as the *kleindeutsch*, or small German, solution to unification. It excluded Austria. To promote his plan, he fought two brief wars. In 1864, he went to war with Denmark over the status of the duchies of Schleswig and Holstein, German-speaking areas that had long been administered by the Danish monarchy (see Map 24–4). The Austrians helped defeat Denmark and joined Prussia in jointly administering the two duchies. Bismarck then concluded various alliances with France and Italy to gain their support against Austria, and in the summer of 1866, decisively defeated Austria in the Seven Weeks' War. The consequent Treaty of Prague excluded the Habsburgs from German affairs and left Prussia the only major power among the German states.

In 1867, Hanover, Hesse, Nassau, and the city of Frankfurt, all of which had supported Austria during the war, were annexed by Prussia, and their rulers deposed. Prussia and these newly incorporated territories, plus Schleswig and Holstein and the rest of the German states north of the Main River, constituted the North German Confederation. Prussia was its undisputed leader.

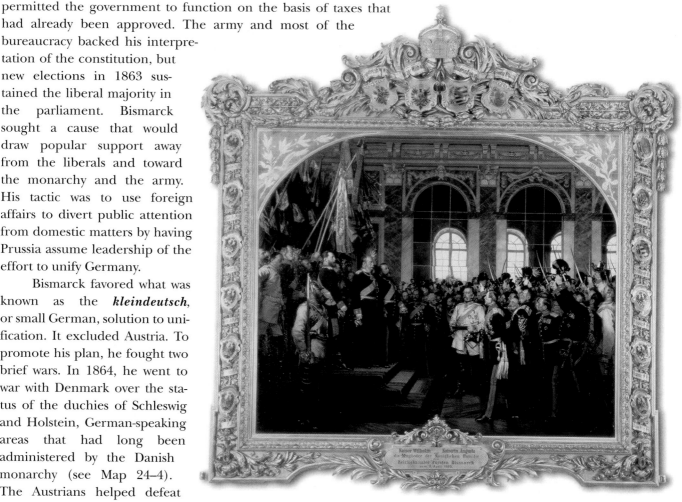

Creating a Nation. The proclamation of the German Empire in the Hall of Mirrors at Versailles, January 18, 1871, after the defeat of France in the Franco-Prussian War. Kaiser Wilhelm I is standing at the top of the steps under the flags; Bismarck is in the center in a white uniform.

Bildarchiv Preussicher Kulturbesitz/Original: Friedrichsruher Fassung, Bismarck-Museum.

THE FRANCO-PRUSSIAN WAR AND THE GERMAN EMPIRE

Bismarck next looked for an opportunity to bring the states of southern Germany into the confederation. It appeared during complex diplomatic negotiations surrounding the possibility that a cousin of William I of Prussia might become king of Spain. France opposed this, for it did not want a second state on its borders ruled by a Hohenzollern. Bismarck personally edited a press dispatch about these negotiations to make it appear that William I had insulted the French ambassador, even though the king had not done so. Bismarck's intention was to goad France into war, and he succeeded. On July 19, France

kleindeutsch Meaning "small German." Argument that the German-speaking portions of the Habsburg Empire should be excluded from a united Germany.

OVERVIEW   ITALIAN AND GERMAN UNIFICATION

The unifications of Italy and Germany, which took place between 1859 and 1871, were the two most important political developments that occurred in Europe between the end of the Napoleonic Wars in 1815 and the outbreak of World War I in 1914. Creation of the Kingdom of Italy in 1860 and of the German Empire in 1871 were the most significant nationalist triumphs of the 19th century. Moreover, the formation of these two states permanently changed the balance of power in Europe. Austria lost its historic role as the dominant power in Italian and German affairs, and Germany replaced France as continental Europe's most powerful nation. Below are the steps by which Italy and Germany achieved unification.

Italy	1855	Piedmont enters the Crimean War on the side of France and Britain.
	1858	Napoleon III of France and Count Cavour of Piedmont secretly discuss a war against Austria in Italy.
	1859	France and Piedmont defeat Austria. Austria cedes Lombardy to Piedmont. Tuscany, Parma, Modena and the Romagna revolt against their pro-Austrian rulers and vote to join Piedmont.
	1860	Garibaldi conquers Sicily and Naples. Cavour sends troops to occupy southern Italy and the Papal States except for Rome.
	1861	Proclamation of the Kingdom of Italy.
	1866	Italy receives Venetia in return for siding with Prussia against Austria in the Austro-Prussian War.
	1870	Italy occupies Rome when the French garrison is withdrawn to fight in the Franco-Prussian War.
Germany	1862	Otto von Bismarck becomes prime minister of Prussia.
	1864	Prussia and Austria defeat Denmark and occupy Schleswig-Holstein.
	1866	Prussia defeats Austria and forms the North German Confederation. Prussia annexes Hanover, Hesse, Nassau, and Frankfurt. The Habsburgs are excluded from German affairs.
	1870	Prussia defeats France in the Franco-Prussian War. The southern German states of Bavaria, Wurtemberg, Baden, and Hesse Darmstadt fight alongside Prussia.
	1871	Proclamation of the German Empire. France cedes Alsace-Lorraine to Germany.

declared war. Napoleon III hoped that victory would increase popular support for his regime. The states of southern Germany supported Prussia against France, and on September 1, at Sedan, the Germans defeated the French army and captured Napoleon III. By late September, Paris was besieged. It capitulated on January 28, 1871. Ten days earlier, in the Hall of Mirrors at the Palace of Versailles, the German Empire had been proclaimed. The rulers of the states of south Germany had requested William I to accept the imperial title—allowing them to retain their kingly titles and thrones.

The unification of Germany established a strong, coherent state in the middle of Europe. It had been forged by the Prussian army and monarchy and would be dominated by Prussian institutions. It possessed enormous economic resources and nationalistic ambitions. For the next 80 years, Europe had to come to grips with this new political reality both on the continent and abroad. For some, the unification of Italy and Germany implied that nationalistic aspirations could only be fulfilled by armed force. France, in the wake of its defeat by Prussia, again became a republic—the Third Republic—governed by a chamber of deputies, a senate, and a president.

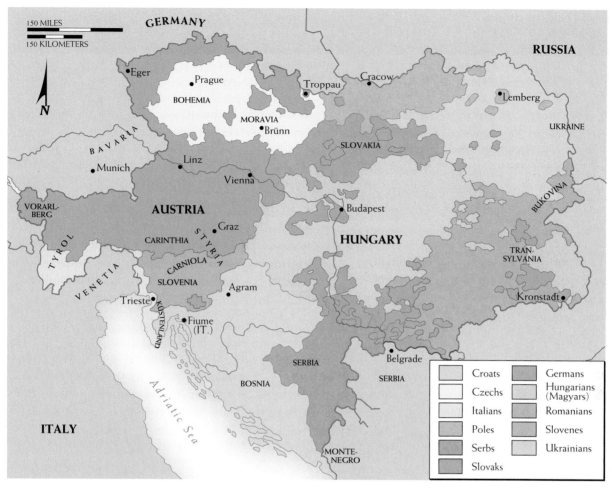

MAP 24–4

Nationalities within the Habsburg Empire. The patchwork appearance reflects the unusual problem of the numerous ethnic groups that the Habsburgs could not, of course, meld into a modern national state. Only the Magyars were recognized in 1867, leaving nationalist Czechs, Slovaks, and the others chronically dissatisfied.

HOW DID the Compromise of 1867 affect the Habsburg Empire?

UNREST OF NATIONALITIES IN EASTERN EUROPE

HOW DID nationalism affect the Habsburg Empire?

In an age increasingly characterized by national states, liberal institutions, and industrialism, the Habsburg domains remained dynastic, absolutist, and agrarian. Following the revolutions of 1848, Emperor Francis Joseph (r. 1848–1916) and his ministers attempted to impose a centralized administration on the multinational empire. The system amounted to a military and bureaucratic government dominated by German-speaking Austrians. This especially annoyed the Hungarians. The defeats in 1859 and 1866 and the exclusion of Austria from Italy and from German affairs compelled Francis Joseph to come to terms with the Hungarian nobles. The subsequent **Ausgleich**, or Compromise, of 1867 transformed the Habsburg Empire into a dual monarchy. Francis Joseph was crowned king of Hungary in Budapest. Except for the common monarch, foreign policy, and army, Austria and Hungary functioned almost as separate states (see Map 24–4).

ausgleich Meaning "compromise." Agreement between the Habsburg emperor and the Hungarians to give Hungary considerable administrative autonomy in 1867. It created the Dual Monarchy, or Austria-Hungary.

HISTORY'S VOICES

LORD ACTON CONDEMNS NATIONALISM

Lord Acton (1834–1902) was a major 19th-century English historian and commentator on contemporary religious and political events. In all his writings, he was deeply concerned with the character and preservation of liberty. His was one of the earliest voices to warn against the political dangers of nationalism.

WHY DOES Acton see the principle of nationality as dangerous to liberty? Why does he see nationalism as a threat to minority groups? Why does he see nationalism as a threat to democracy?

The greatest adversary of the rights of nationality is the modern theory of nationality. By making the State and the nation commensurate with each other in theory, it reduces practically to a subject condition all other nationalities that may be within the boundary. It cannot admit them to an equality with the ruling nation which constitutes the State, because the State would then cease to be national, which would be a contradiction of the principle of its existence. According, therefore, to the degree of humanity and civilization in that dominant body which claims all the rights of the community, the inferior races are exterminated, or reduced to servitude, or outlawed, or put in a condition of dependence.

If we take the establishment of liberty for the realization of moral duties to be the end of civil society, we must conclude that those states are substantially the most perfect which, like the British and Austrian Empires, include various distinct nationalities without oppressing them. Those in which no mixture of races has occurred are imperfect; and those in which its effects have disappeared are decrepit. A State which is incompetent to satisfy different races condemns itself; a State which labors to neutralize, to absorb, or to expel them, destroys its own vitality; a State which does not include them is destitute of the chief basis of self-government. The theory of nationality, therefore, is a retrograde step in history . . . .

[N]ationality does not aim either at liberty or prosperity, both of which it sacrifices to the imperative necessity of making the nation the mold and measure of the State. Its course will be marked with material as well as moral ruin, in order that a new invention may prevail over the works of God and the interests of mankind. There is no principle of change, no phrase of political speculation conceivable, more comprehensive, more subversive, or more arbitrary than this. It is a confutation of democracy, because it sets limits to the exercise of the popular will, and substitutes for it a higher principle.

Source: John Emerich Edward Dalbert-Acton, *First Baron Acton, Essays in the History of Liberty*, ed. by J. Rufus Fears (Indianapolis IN: Liberty Classics, 1985), pp. 431–433.

Many of the other national groups within the empire—including the Czechs, Ruthenians, Romanians, and Serbo-Croatians—opposed the compromise because it permitted the German-speaking Austrians and the Hungarian Magyars to dominate the other nationalities in their respective states. The Czechs of Bohemia were the most vocal group. For more than 20 years, they were conciliated by generous Austrian patronage and posts in the bureaucracy, but by the turn of the century they were becoming restive. They and German-speaking groups in the Austrian Reichsrat disrupted the Parliament rather than permit a compromise on language issues. This ended constitutional government, for the emperor ruled thereafter by imperial decree with the support of the bureaucracy. Constitutionalism survived in Hungary, but only because the Magyars used it to dominate competing national groups.

Nationalist unrest within the Habsburg Empire, in addition to causing internal political difficulties, constituted one of the major sources of political instability for all of central and eastern Europe. Virtually all the nationality problems had a foreign policy as well as a domestic political dimension. Both the Serbo-Croatians and the Poles believed they deserved a wholly independent state in union with their fellow nationals who lived outside the empire. Other national groups, such as Ukrainians, Romanians, and Bosnians, saw themselves as potentially linked to Russia, Romania, Serbia, or a larger, yet-to-be-established Slavic state. Many of these nationalities looked to Russia for protection. Out of these nationalistic tensions emerged much of the turmoil that would spark World War I. The dominant German population of Austria proper was generally loyal to the emperor. However, a significant segment of the Austrian German population was strongly nationalistic and yearned to be part of the united German state being established by Bismarck. These nationalistic Germans in the Austrian Empire often hated the non-German national groups, particularly the Jews. Such attitudes would influence Adolf Hitler (1889–1945) in his youth and would shape his political opinions.

Nationality problems touched each of the three great central and eastern European empires—the German, the Russian, and the Austrian. All had Polish populations. Each shared at least two other major national groups. Each nationality regarded its own aspirations and discontents as more important than the larger good or even survival of the empire they inhabited. The stirrings of nationalism affected the fate of all three empires from the 1860s through the outbreak of World War I. The government of each would be overturned during the war, and the Austrian Empire would disappear. These same unresolved problems of central and eastern European nationalism would then lead directly to World War II. During more recent years they have led to civil war in what was formerly Yugoslavia and to the breakup of what used to be called Czechoslovakia. (See "Lord Acton Condemns Nationalism.")

RACIAL THEORY AND ANTI-SEMITISM

Theories about race were a new source of late-century nationalistic unrest. Racial thinking, or **racism**, had long existed in Europe. Renaissance explorers had displayed considerable prejudice against non-Whites. Since at least the 18th century, biologists and anthropologists had classified human beings according to the color of their skin, their language, and their stage of civilization. Late 18th-century linguistic scholars, who had observed similarities between many of the European languages and Sanskrit, had postulated the existence of an ancient race called the Aryans, speakers of the original language from which the rest derived. During the Romantic period, writers had called the different cultures of Europe *races*. The debates over slavery in the European colonies and the United States had given further opportunity for the development of racial theory. And finally, in the late 19th century, the concept of race emerged as a single dominant explanation for the history and the character of large groups of people.

Arthur de Gobineau (1816–1882), a reactionary French diplomat, enunciated the first important theory of race as the major determinant of human history. In his four-volume *Essay on the Inequality of the Human Races* (1853–1854), Gobineau argued that the problems of Western civilization stemmed from the

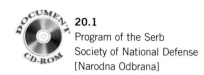

20.1
Program of the Serb Society of National Defense [Narodna Odbrana]

WHY DID anti-Semitism arise in the late 19th century?

racism Pseudoscientific theory that biological features of race determine human character and worth.

slow degeneration of its original white Aryan race. Aryans, he theorized, had unwisely intermarried with inferior yellow and Black races and diluted the greatness and ability conveyed by their blood. Gobineau saw no way to reverse their degeneration.

Gobineau's essay remained relatively obscure for years. Houston Stewart Chamberlain (1855–1927), an Englishman who settled in Germany, put racial theory on an alleged scientific basis in his widely read two-volume work, *Foundations of the Nineteenth Century* (1899). He championed the concept of biological determinism through race. Chamberlain, relying on modern genetic theory, argued, in opposition to Gobineau, that the human race could be improved and that a superior race could be developed. Furthermore, he fingered the Jews as the major obstacle to European racial regeneration. Chamberlain's book and the lesser works on which it drew aided the spread of **anti-Semitism**.

ANTI-SEMITISM AND THE BIRTH OF ZIONISM

The tragic anti-Semitic campaigns, which cast such dark shadows across the 20th century, emerged in part from the racial theorizing of the late 19th century. Religious anti-Semitism dated from at least the Middle Ages, but following the French Revolution, Western European Jews had gradually gained entry into civil society in Austria, Britain, France, and Germany. Popular anti-Semitism, which identified the Jewish community with money and banking interests, persisted. During the last third of the century, as finance capitalism changed the economic structure of Europe, people who suffered from the changes focused their anger on the Jewish community. In Austria, France, and Germany various political leaders and parties used their anti-Semitism to considerable political advantage.

To this already ugly situation, racial thought contributed the belief that no matter how well Jews assimilated to the culture and even the religions of the countries they inhabited, their Jewishness—and thus their alleged danger to the society—remained. The problem of race was not in the character of Jews, but in their blood.

An important Jewish response to the rabid outbreak of this new form of anti-Semitism was the launching in 1896 of the Zionist movement: a campaign to found a separate Jewish state in Palestine. Its founder was an Austro-Hungarian, Theodor Herzl (1860–1904). The growth of political anti-Semitism, especially in Austria and France, as well as Herzl's personal experiences with discrimination, convinced him that liberal politics and the institutions of the liberal state could not protect the Jews in Europe or ensure that they would be treated justly. In 1896, Herzl published *The Jewish State*, in which he called for a separate state in which the Jews of the world might be assured of those rights and liberties that they should be enjoying in the liberal states of Europe. Herzl followed the tactics of late-century mass democratic politics by directing his appeal in particular to

Theodor Herzl. Herzl's visions of a Jewish state would eventually lead to the creation of Israel in 1948.

BBC Hulton/Corbis-Bettmann.

anti-Semitism Prejudice, hostility, or legal discrimination against Jews.

the impoverished Jews who lived in the ghettos of eastern Europe and the slums of Western Europe. The original call to **Zionism** thus combined a rejection of the anti-Semitism of Europe with a desire to establish some of the ideals of both liberalism and socialism in a state outside Europe.

Racial thinking and revived anti-Semitism were part of a wider late-century aggressive nationalism. Previously, nationalism had been a literary and liberal movement. From the 1870s onward, however, nationalism became a movement with mass support, well-financed organizations, and political parties. The new nationalism tended to redefine nationality in terms of race and blood, and it opposed the internationalism of both liberalism and socialism. National loyalty was proposed as a means for overcoming divisions of class, religion, and geography. Nationalistic patriotism sometimes became a secular religion in the hands of state schoolteachers, who were replacing the clergy as the instructors of youth. Aggressive and racist, nationalism would become the most powerful ideology of the early 20th century.

Zionism Movement to create a Jewish state in Palestine (the Biblical Zion).

Summary

Nationalism Nationalism is the modern concept that people who share the same customs, culture, language, and history should also share the same government. It became the most powerful European political ideology of the 19th and early 20th centuries. Nationalists challenged both the domestic and the international order of the Vienna settlement in the decades after 1815.

Liberalism Politically, 19th-century liberals sought to establish constitutional governments that recognized civil liberties and made the executive responsible to a legislature elected by men of wealth and property. Economically, liberals wanted a laissez-faire economy with minimal government involvement. They thought that people should be free to use their talents and property to enrich themselves without the state intervening to protect the working classes or the poor. Liberals often supported nationalists' efforts to create a single national state that could function as a more efficient economic unit. Although efforts to liberalize tsarist Russia failed, liberalism largely triumphed in France after the revolution of 1830 and in Britain after the passage of the Great Reform Bill. The British were, however, unable to resolve the problem of Irish nationalism in the 19th century.

Italian and German Unification With French assistance, Piedmont and its premier Count Camillo Cavour managed to unite most of the Italian peninsula by 1860. The new Kingdom of Italy was formed from the northern Italian duchies, Austrian Lombardy, the Papal States, and the Kingdom of the Two Sicilies. Austrian Venetia was added in 1866, and Italy occupied Papal Rome in 1870.

German unification was achieved by Prussia under the leadership of Otto von Bismarck between 1864 and 1871. In three victorious wars against Denmark, Austria, and France, Bismarck forged the German states into a German Empire dominated by Prussia. Germany was henceforth the dominant power on the European continent.

IMAGE KEY

for pages 582–583

a. Transylvanian revolutionaries revolt against Russian rule, 1848.

b. A pro-slavery poster warns of "the Slave Power."

c. A Louisiana slave named Gordon after escaping to Union lines during the Civil War, 1863.

d. The leaders of Europe in debate during the Congress of Vienna.

e. Gladstone.

f. Italian Nationalist General Garibaldi.

g. John Brown and his men, trapped by U.S. Marine fire.

h. The proclamation of the German Empire in the Hall of Mirrors at Versailles, January 18, 1871.

North America In the United States, westward expansion and war against Mexico brought vast new territories under the republic from the Mississippi River to the Pacific, but sectional conflict between North and South over economic issues and slavery culminated in the outbreak of the Civil War in 1861. Northern victory led to the abolition of slavery, the creation of a continent-wide free labor market, and enormous economic development that would make the United States the world's leading industrial power in the 20th century.

Canada achieved self-government from Britain and created a united Canadian federation in 1867. However, Canada remained part of the British Empire and retained its connection with the British monarchy.

Eastern Europe Nationalism created problems for the three eastern European empires: Germany, Russia, and Austria, but Habsburg Austria faced the greatest challenge from nationalism because it was a dynastic, not a national, state. Eleven different nationalities made up the Habsburg monarchy, each with its own national aspirations. In 1867, the Habsburgs worked out the *Ausgleich*, or Compromise, with the Magyars, by which Hungary became an autonomous kingdom under the Habsburg emperor. Thereafter the Habsburg monarchy became known as Austria-Hungary. However, Czechs, Croats, and other Slavs in the monarchy became increasingly dissatisfied.

Racism and Anti-Semitism In the late 19th century, biological determinism, the concept that some peoples or races were inherently superior to others, took root in Western thought. In Austria, France, and Germany, some nationalists used the concept of race to blame the Jews for their countries' economic and political problems. Part of the Jewish response was the launching of the Zionist movement to found a separate Jewish state.

REVIEW QUESTIONS

1. What is nationalism? Where did significant nationalist movements develop between 1815 and 1830? Which were successful and which were unsuccessful?

2. What were the characteristics of 19th-century liberalism? How did they differ from conservatives? What relationship did liberalism have to nationalism?

3. Why did the American North and the South diverge and become distinctively different regions? How did the debate over slavery evolve?

4. Why was it so difficult to unify Italy?

5. How was Germany unified? How did its unification affect European politics?

6. How did racial theory evolve in the modern era?

KEY TERMS

anti-Semitism (p. 610)	**Great Reform Bill** (p. 589)	**liberalism** (p. 585)
ausgleich (p. 607)	**home rule** (p. 591)	**nationalism** (p. 584)
Catholic Emancipation (p. 589)	**July Monarchy** (p. 589)	**racism** (p. 609)
Chartism (p. 590)	*kleindeutsch* (p. 605)	**Zionism** (p. 611)

 For additional study resources for this chapter, go to:
www.prenhall.com/craig/chapter24

Visualizing The Past

Imagining Women in the Eighteenth and Nineteenth Centuries

WHAT DOES the artistic depictions of women in the eighteenth and nineteenth centuries tell us about the ways in which modern societies have imagined the roles of women in society?

Although the roles of many women changed significantly in the eighteenth and nineteenth centuries, in part due to the new demands and opportunities brought about by industrialization, the themes of sexuality, spirituality, docility, and maternal caring that characterized artists' imaginations of women in earlier eras also appear in the art of this period. Since most artists until the 20th century were male, depictions of women and gender roles often derive from a male perspective on the *proper* roles of women in a society, and not necessarily on the reality of women's lives.

Suzuki Harunobu, "Geisha as Daruma Crossing the Sea." Edo period, mid-eighteenth century. In this color woodcut we see a geisha, a woman whose profession was to entertain men, in a pose mirroring that of a famous Zen Buddhist master, Daruma. Her clothing, highly feminine, with hints of her delicate body beneath it, contrast with the Zen spirituality her pose suggests.

Suzuki Harunobu, "Geisha as Daruma Crossing the Sea", Edo period, mid-18th century. Color woodcut, 10 7/8 × 8 1/4" (27.6 × 21 cm). Philadelphia Museum of Art. Gift of Mrs. Emile Geyelin, in memory of Anne Hampton Barnes.

**Eugene Delacroix, "The Women of ▶
Algiers in Their Apartment," 1834.**
Delacroix, the leading French
Romantic painter, spent six months in
North Africa in 1832. In the painting
shown here Delacroix depicts a
common theme in eighteenth and
nineteenth-century depictions of the
"Orient": the position of women in
Islamic society in general, and the
harem in particular. Western commentators often described Islamic society
as barbaric because of its perceived
marginalization and exploitation of
women. Note the passivity of the light-
skinned women in contrast to the
dominant pose of the black servant.
Delacroix, Eugene (1798–1863). *The Women of
Algiers in Their Apartment.* Oil on canvas,
180 × 229 cm. Louvre, Paris, France.

◀ **Veiled Women.** This nineteenth-century print
of a veiled woman in traditional costume from
Tartarstan in Central Asia shows another aspect
of how women were imagined. Note how the
veils and layers of clothing are used to hide
femininity in the interests of modesty. Unlike
men's clothing, the woman's costume does not
reveal any sort of professional identity. Gender,
rather than economic activities, continued to
define women's identity in the modern world.
©Dorling Kindersley

Europeans in New Zealand. This postcard from late ▶
nineteenth-century New Zealand depicts a group of people
bathing on the seaside. Here we see another recurring theme
in modern images of gender: women as wives and mothers.
The point here is that the beach and, by implication New
Zealand itself, which many Europeans still viewed as an exotic
and somewhat dangerous destination, was safe and
"family-friendly." The wilderness of New Zealand, once home
to the dangerous Maori, has now been tamed by European
gentility and domesticity, so that it has become a suitable destination even for European women and children.
©Dorling Kindersley

PART SIX · INTO THE MODERN WORLD

EUROPE

1852–1870	The Second French Empire, under Napoleon III
1854–1856	The Crimean War
1861	Italy unified
1861	Emancipation of Russian serfs
1866	Austro-Prussian War; creation of Dual Monarchy of Austria-Hungary in 1867
1870–1871	Franco-Prussian War; German Empire proclaimed in 1871
1873	Three Emperors League

◀ Karl Marx

▲ German Empire proclaimed

NEAR EAST / INDIA

1857–1858	Sepoy Rebellion: India placed directly under the authority of the British government in 1858
1869	Suez Canal completed; 1875, British purchase controlling interest
1869–1948	Mohandas (Mahatma) Gandhi
1876–1949	Muhammad Ali Jinnah, "founder of Pakistan"

"Mahatma" Gandhi ▶

EAST ASIA

1850–1873	Taiping and other rebellions
1853–1854	Commodore Perry "opens" Japan to the West, ending seclusion policy
1859	French seize Saigon
1860s	Establishment of treaty ports in China
1864	French protectorate over Cambodia
1868	Meiji Restoration in Japan
1870s	Civilization and Enlightenment movement in Japan
1870s–1890s	Self-Strengthening movement in China

The empress ▶
dowager Tz'u-hsi

AFRICA

1856–1884	King Mutasa of Buganda reigns
1870	British protectorate in Zanzibar
1879–1880	Henry M. Stanley gains the Congo for Belgium
1880s	Mahdist revival and uprising in Sudan
1880	French protectorate in Tunisia and the Ivory Coast

THE AMERICAS

1854	Kansas-Nebraska Act
1856	Dred Scott Decision
1859	Raid on Harper's Ferry
1860	Abraham Lincoln elected U.S. president
1861–1865	U.S. Civil War
1862–1867	French invasion of Mexico
1863	Emancipation Proclamation in United States
1865–1877	Reconstruction
1865–1870	Paraguayan War
1879–1880	Argentinian conquest of the desert

George Caleb Bingham, "Fur Traders ▶
Descending the Missouri" ca. 1845

1882	Triple Alliance
1890	Bismarck dismissed by Kaiser Wilhelm II
1902	Entente Cordiale
1905	January 22, "Bloody Sunday"
1905	Revolution in Russia
1914	War begins in Europe

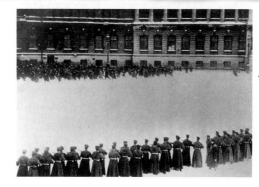

◀ *"Bloody Sunday," Russia*

1882	English occupation of Egypt
1886	India National Congress formed
1889–1964	Jawaharlal Nehru
1899	Ottoman sultan Abdulhamid II grants concession to Kaiser Wilhelm II to extend railway to Baghdad ("Berlin-to-Baghdad" Railway)
1908	"Young Turk" Revolt

1889	Meiji Constitution in Japan
1894–1895	Sino-Japanese War; Japan gets Taiwan as colony
1898–1900	Boxer Rebellion in China
1904–1905	Russo-Japanese War
1910	Japan annexes Korea
1911	Republican Revolution begins in China; Ch'ing dynasty overthrown

Promulgation ▶ of the Meiji Constitution

1884–1885	International Conference in Berlin to prepare rules for further acquisition of African territory; the Congo Free State declared
1884	German Southwest Africa
1885	British control Nigeria and British East Africa
1894	French annex Dahomey
1899	German East Africa; British in Sudan
1899–1902	Boer War
1900	Nigeria a British Crown colony
1907	Orange Free State and the Transvaal join with Natal and Cape Colony to form the Union of South Africa
1911	Liberia becomes a virtual U.S. protectorate
1914	Ethiopia the only independent state in Africa

◀ *Three carved wooden African figures of colonial officials*

1880s	Slavery eliminated in Cuba and Brazil
1898	Spanish-American War
1901	Theodore Roosevelt elected U.S. president
1910–1917	Mexican Revolution
1912	Woodrow Wilson elected U.S. president

◀ *Slavery in Brazil*

25 Northern Transatlantic Economy and Society, 1815–1914

CHAPTER HIGHLIGHTS

Workers After 1850, European workers underwent a process of proletarianization as the process of industrialization spread across the continent. To protect their interests, European workers joined trade unions and socialist parties, such as the Labour Party in Britain. The Marxist critique of modern capitalism strongly influenced European socialism when the German Social Democratic Party adopted the thought of Karl Marx. In Russia, Lenin founded the Bolsheviks as an elite Marxist party that advocated the overthrow of the tsarist regime through a revolution of workers and peasants.

Urban Reform European cities grew rapidly after 1850. The growth of industry and the influx of new workers led to slums and a host of urban health and social problems. In response, middle-class reformers redesigned cities and improved sanitation, housing, and water and sewer systems.

Women Nineteenth-century women were divided along class lines. Unlike working-class women, most women of the upper and middle classes adopted a cult of domesticity and did not work outside the home. Most jobs available to women were low paying and insecure. Women of all classes faced social, political, and legal disabilities that were only gradually improved in the late nineteenth and early twentieth centuries. Before World War I, only Norway allowed women to vote, and few women could earn university degrees or enter the professions.

Jewish Emancipation With the exception of Russia, European countries had abolished their legal restrictions on Jews by the mid-nineteenth century. Jews became more fully integrated into European political and economic life. After 1880, however, anti-Semitism increased as Jews were blamed for economic and social problems.

The United States By 1914, the United States had become the world's leading industrial power. However, despite the creation of a mass industrial work force, socialism did not take root in the United States. Under presidents Theodore Roosevelt and Woodrow Wilson, the Progressive Movement enacted a number of social and political reforms. The United States also embarked on a more aggressive foreign policy with the Spanish-American War, the acquisition of a colonial empire, interventions in Latin America, and, under Wilson, participation in World War I.

CHAPTER QUESTIONS

WHAT DOES the term *proletarianization* mean?

WHAT SOCIAL AND LEGAL disabilities did European women confront in the nineteenth century?

HOW DID emancipation affect Jewish participation in European social and political life outside of Russia?

WHY DID Marxism become so influential among European socialists?

HOW DID industrialization in the United States differ from industrialization in Europe?

CHAPTER OUTLINE

- European Factory Workers and Urban Artisans
- Nineteenth-Century European Women
- Jewish Emancipation
- European Labor, Socialism, and Politics to World War I
- North America and the New Industrial Economy
- The Emergence of Modern European Thought
- Islam and Late Nineteenth-Century European Thought

During the 19th century, northwestern Europe and the United States developed major industrial economies. These economies produced more goods and services than ever before in world history. This economic achievement undergirded the enormous international political power exerted by the industrial nations of the West from that time to the present.

The first half of the 19th century witnessed in Europe and to a lesser extent in the United States the emergence of a new kind of industrial labor force. Laborers worked in factories rather than in their homes or in small artisan workshops. More often than not the new industrial working class dwelled in cities. The presence and growth of this new labor force were the most important social developments of the century and would produce a vast influence on European and American political life. It was out of the social and political experience of this work force that the political movement known as socialism arose.

During the second half of the 19th century, European and American political, economic, and social life assumed many characteristics of our present-day world. In Europe nation-states with large electorates, political parties, centralized bureaucracies, and universal military service emerged. In the United States the politics associated with the Progressive movement brought the presidency to the center of American political life. On both sides of the North Atlantic, business adopted large-scale corporate structures, and the labor force organized itself into trade unions. The number of white-collar laborers grew as urban life became predominant throughout western Europe. But even as new vast cities arose in the United States, farming continued to spread across the central Midwest and upper Southwest. During this period, too, women began to assert new political awareness and to become politically active in both Europe and America.

During these same years Europe quietly became dependent on the resources and markets of the rest of the world. Farms in the United States, Canada, Latin America, Australia, and New Zealand supplied food to much of the world. Consequently, climate changes in Kansas, Argentina, or New Zealand might now affect the European economy. However, before World War I the dependence was concealed by Europe's industrial, military, and financial supremacy. At the time Europeans assumed their supremacy to be natural, but the 20th century would reveal it to have been temporary. Nevertheless, while it prevailed, Europeans dominated most of the other peoples of the world and displayed extreme self-confidence. Toward the close of the 19th century, the United States, having achieved the status of a major industrial power as well as an agricultural supplier, now entered the world stage as a military power, defeating Spain in the Spanish-American War in 1898. With that victory, the United States also acquired its first colonial territories.

During these same decades a number of major new ideas arose: theories of evolution in biology, relativity in physics, the irrational in philosophy, and psychoanalysis. These concepts shaped the intellectual outlook for the rest of the century.

WHAT DOES the term *proletarianization* mean?

19.1
Sybil (1845)
Benjamin Disraeli

EUROPEAN FACTORY WORKERS AND URBAN ARTISANS

Although the seeds of industrial production had been sown in the 18th century, it was only in the 19th century that much of Europe headed toward a more fully industrial society. By 1830, only Great Britain had attained that status, but new factories and railways were beginning to be constructed elsewhere in Europe. However, what characterized the second quarter of the century was less the triumph of industrialism than the final gasps of those economic groups that opposed it and were displaced by it. Intellectually, the period saw the formulation of the major creeds supporting and criticizing the new society.

The specter of poor harvests haunted Europe. The worst was the failure of potato crops that produced the Irish famine from 1845 to 1847. Half a million Irish peasants starved to death; hundreds of thousands emigrated. Many moved to urban areas to find work in factories.

In much of northern Europe both artisans and factory workers underwent a process of *proletarianization*. This term indicates the entry of workers into a wage economy and their gradual loss of significant ownership of the means of production, such as tools and equipment, and of control over the conduct of their own trades. The process occurred rapidly wherever the factory system arose. The factory owner provided the financial capital to construct the factory, purchase the machinery, and secure the raw materials. Factory workers contributed their labor for a wage. Those workers also submitted to factory discipline, which meant that work conditions became largely determined by the demands for smooth operation of the machines. Closing of factory gates to late workers, fines for lateness, dismissal for drunkenness, and public scolding of faulty laborers constituted attempts to enforce regularity on humans that would match the regularity of cables, wheels, and pistons. Factory workers had no direct say over the quality of the product or its price. For all their difficulties, factory conditions were often better than those of textile workers who resisted the factory mode of production. In particular, English hand-loom weavers, who continued to work in their homes, experienced decades of declining trade and growing poverty in their unsuccessful competition with power looms.

Urban artisans in the 19th century experienced proletarianization more slowly than factory workers, and machinery had little to do with the process. The emergence of factories in itself did not harm urban artisans. Many even prospered from the development. For example, the construction and maintenance of the new machines generated demand for metal workers, who consequently did well. The actual erection of factories and the expansion of cities benefited all craftsmen in the building trades, such as carpenters, roofers, joiners, and masons. Lower prices for machine-made textiles aided artisans involved in the making of clothing, such as tailors and hatters, by reducing the costs of their raw materials. Where the urban artisans encountered difficulty and found their skills and livelihood threatened was in the organization of production.

In the 18th century, a European town or city workplace usually consisted of a few artisans laboring for a master, first as apprentices and then as journeymen, according to established guild regulations and practices. The master owned the workshop and the larger equipment, and the apprentices and journeymen owned their tools. The journeyman could expect to become a master. This guild system had allowed considerable worker control over labor recruitment and training, production pace, product quality, and price.

Industrial Labor and Pro-Slavery Arguments. The condition of European industrial workers entered the political debates on both sides of the Atlantic. This 1841 proslavery cartoon from the United States contrasts allegedly healthy, well-cared-for African-American slaves with unemployed British factory workers living in poverty. American proslavery advocates also frequently made the comparison between supposed contented southern slaves and miserable northern "wages slaves."

Courtesy of the Library of Congress.

QUICK REVIEW

Factory Work
- Proletarianization: loss of ownership of the means of production
- Factory work demanded submission to new kind of work discipline
- Factory workers were better off than the hand-loom workers who competed with them

proletarianization Process whereby independent artisans and factory workers lose control of the means of production and of the conduct of their own trades to the owners of capital.

OVERVIEW   MAJOR EUROPEAN CITIES IN 1914

Between 1850 and the outbreak of World War I, European cities from Britain to Russia grew rapidly as rural populations moved to the cities in search of jobs, stimulation, and social opportunities. The tables below show the growth of seven major European cities between 1850 and 1910 and list 14 other European cities whose populations had grown to exceed 500,000 by 1914.

Growth of Major Cities	1850	1880	1914
Berlin	419,000	1,122,000	2,071,000
Birmingham	233,000	437,000	840,000
Frankfurt	65,000	137,000	415,000
London	2,685,000	4,470,000	7,256,000
Madrid	281,000	398,000	600,000
Paris	1,053,000	2,269,000	2,888,000
Vienna	444,000	1,104,000	2,031,000

Cities with More than 500,000 People, 1914

Amsterdam	Hamburg	Munich
Barcelona	Istanbul	Naples
Brussels	Liverpool	St. Petersburg
Budapest	Manchester	Warsaw
Glasgow	Moscow	

QUICK REVIEW

Improved Conditions in Cities

- Cholera epidemics spurred action
- New awareness of the value of modern water and sewer systems
- Expanded involvement of government in public health

In the 19th century, the situation of the urban artisan changed. It became increasingly difficult for artisans to exercise corporate or guild direction and control over their trades. The French Revolution had outlawed such organizations in France. Across Europe, political and economic liberals disapproved of labor and guild organizations and attempted to make them illegal.

Other destructive forces were also at work. The masters often found themselves under increased competitive pressure from larger, more heavily capitalized establishments or from the possibility of the introduction of machine production into a previously craft-dominated industry. In many workshops masters began to follow a practice, known in France as *confection*, whereby goods such as shoes, clothing, and furniture were produced in standard sizes and styles rather than by special orders for individual customers. This practice increased the division of labor in the workshop. Each artisan produced a smaller part of the uniform final product. Consequently, less skill was required of each artisan, and the particular skills possessed by a worker became less valuable. Masters also attempted to increase production and reduce their costs for piecework. Those attempts often led to work stoppages or strikes. Migrants from the countryside or small towns into the cities created, in some cases, a surplus of relatively unskilled workers who were willing to work for lower wages or under less favorable and protected conditions than traditional artisans. The dilution of skills and lower wages, caused not by machinery but by changes in the organization of artisan production, made it much more difficult for urban journeymen to become masters with their own workshops where they would be in charge. Increasingly, these artisans became lifetime wage laborers whose skills were simply bought and sold in the marketplace.

In the United States defenders of slavery frequently compared what they claimed to be the protected situation of slaves living on plantations with the plight of factory workers in Europe and the northern United States. They argued that a free market in wage labor left workers worse off than slaves. But the situation in the European labor market as in the American North was much more complicated than the defenders of slavery contended.

19TH-CENTURY EUROPEAN WOMEN

WOMEN IN THE EARLY INDUSTRIAL REVOLUTION

The industrial economy ultimately produced an immense impact on the home and the family life of women. First, it took virtually all productive work out of the home and allowed many families to live on the wages of the male spouse alone. That transformation prepared the way for a new concept of gender-determined roles in the home and in general domestic life. Women came to be associated with domestic duties such as housekeeping, food preparation, child rearing and nurturing, and household management. Men were associated almost exclusively with breadwinning. Children were reared to match these gender patterns. Previously, this domestic division of labor had prevailed only among the relatively small middle and gentry classes. During the 19th century, it came to characterize the working class as well. Second, industrialization created new modes of employment that allowed many young women to earn enough money to marry or, if necessary, to support themselves independently. Third, industrialism, although fostering more employment for women, lowered the skills required of them.

Because the Industrial Revolution had begun in textile production, women and their labor were deeply involved from the start. While both spinning and weaving were still domestic industries, women usually worked in all stages of production. Hand spinning was virtually always a woman's task. When spinning was moved into factories and involved large machines, however, men displaced women. The higher wages commanded by male cotton-factory workers allowed many women to stop working or to work only to supplement their husbands' wages.

With the next generation of machines in the 1820s, unmarried women rapidly became employed in the factories. However, their jobs tended to require less skill than most work done by men and less skill than women had previously exercised in the home production of textiles. There was thus a certain paradox in the impact of the factory on women. Many new jobs opened to them, but those jobs were less skilled than what had been available to them before. Moreover, the women in the factories were almost always young and single or widows. At marriage or perhaps at the birth of the first child, a woman usually found that her husband earned enough money for her to leave the factory. Factory owners also disliked employing married women because of the likelihood of pregnancy, the influence of husbands, and the duties of child rearing.

In Britain and elsewhere by mid-century, industrial factory work accounted for less than half of all employment for women. The largest group of employed women in France continued to work on the land. In England they were domestic servants. Domestic industries, such as lace glove and garment making and other kinds of needlework, employed many women. Their conditions of labor were almost always harsh, whether they worked in their homes or in sweated workshops. Generally all work done by women commanded low wages and involved

WHAT SOCIAL and legal disabilities did European women confront in the 19th century?

 **19.3**
Sadler Report: Child Labor

Working-class women. Although new opportunities opened to them in the late 19th century, many working-class women, like these women ironing in a laundry, remained in traditional occupations. As the wine bottle suggests, alcoholism was a problem for women as well as men engaged in tedious work. The painting is by Edgar Degas.
Photo R.M.N./Senice Photographique des Muses Nationaux, Paris.

Women in Textile Factories. As textile production became increasingly automated in the 19th century, textile factories required fewer skilled workers and more unskilled attendants. To fill these unskilled positions, factory owners turned increasingly to unmarried women and widows, who worked for lower wages than men and were less likely to form labor organizations.

Bildarchiv Preussischer Kulturbesitz.

low skills. They had virtually no way to protect themselves from exploitation. The cleaning lady, with mop and bucket, was a common sight across the continent and symbolized the plight of working women.

One of the most serious problems facing working women was the uncertainty of employment. Because they almost always found themselves in the least skilled jobs and trades, their employment was never secure. Much of their work was seasonal. Many working-class women feared they might be compelled to turn to prostitution. On the other hand, cities and the more complex economy did allow a greater variety of jobs. Movement to cities and entrance into the wage economy also gave women wider opportunities for marriage. Cohabitation before marriage seems to have been common. Parents did not arrange marriages as frequently as in the past. Marriage also generally meant that a woman would leave the work force to live on her husband's earnings. If all went well, that arrangement might improve her situation, but if the husband became ill or died, or deserted her, she would have to reenter the market for unskilled labor at a more advanced age.

Nonetheless, many of the traditional practices associated with the family economy survived into the industrial era. As a young woman came of age, both family needs and her desire to marry still directed what she would do with her life. The most likely early occupation for a young woman was domestic service. A girl born in the country usually migrated to a nearby town or city for such employment, often living initially with a relative. As in the past, she would attempt to earn enough in wages to give herself a dowry so that she might marry and establish her own household. If she became a factory worker, she would probably live in a supervised dormitory. By convincing parents that their daughters would be safe, these factory owners attracted young women workers. The lives of young women in the cities were more precarious than it had been earlier. There were fewer family and community ties and more available young men. These men, who worked for wages rather than in the older apprenticeship structures, were more mobile, so relationships between men and women were often fleeting. In any case, illegitimate births increased. That is to say, fewer women who became pregnant before marriage found the father willing to marry them.

Marriage in the wage industrial economy was also different. It still involved the starting of a separate household, but the structure of gender relationships within the household was different. Marriage was less an economic partnership: The husband might be able to support the entire family. The wage economy and the industrialization that separated workplace and home made it difficult for women to combine domestic duties with work. When married women worked, it was usually in the nonindustrial sector of the economy. More often than not children rather than the wife were sent to work, which may help explain the increase of fertility within marriages, since children in the wage economy tended to be an economic asset. Married women worked outside the home only when family needs or illness or the death of a spouse really required them to do so.

Within the home, the domestic duties of working-class women were an essential factor in the family wage economy. Homemaking came to the fore when a life at home had to be organized that was separate from the place of work. Wives were primarily concerned with food and cooking, but they often were also in charge of the family's finances. The role of the mother expanded when the children still living at home became wage earners. She was then providing home support for her entire wage-earning family. She created the environment to which the family members returned after work. The longer period of home life of working children may also have strengthened the affection between those children and their hardworking, homebound mothers.

SOCIAL DISABILITIES CONFRONTED BY ALL WOMEN

During the early 19th century, virtually all European women faced social and legal disabilities in property rights, family law, and education. By the close of the century, each area had shown improvement. In this period European women, like European men, led lives that reflected their social rank. Yet within each rank, the experience of women was distinct from that of men. Women remained, generally speaking, economically dependent and legally inferior, whatever their social class. Their position thus resembled that of women around the world in that all women found their lives circumscribed by traditional social customs and expectations.

Women and Property   Until the last quarter of the century, in most European countries no married woman, whatever their social class, could own property. In effect, upon marriage women lost to their husbands' control any property they owned or that they might inherit or earn by their own labor. Their legal identities were subsumed into their husbands' and they had no independent standing before the law. The courts saw the theft of a woman's purse as a theft of her husband's property. Because European society was based on private property and wage earning, these disabilities put married women at a great disadvantage, limiting their freedom to work, save, and relocate.

Reform of women's property rights came slowly. By 1882, Great Britain allowed married women to own property in their own right. In France, however, a married woman could not even open a savings account in her own name until 1895, and not until 1907 were married women granted possession of their own wages. In 1900, Germany allowed women to take jobs without their husbands' permission, but a German husband retained control of most of his wife's property except for her wages. Similar laws prevailed elsewhere in Europe.

Family Law   European family law also worked to the disadvantage of women. Legal codes required wives to obey their husbands. The Napoleonic Code and the remnants of Roman law made women legal minors throughout Europe. Divorce was difficult for most of the century. Until 1857, divorce required an act of Parliament in England. Most nations did not permit divorce by mutual consent. French law forbade divorce between 1816 and 1884. Thereafter the chief recognized legal cause for divorce was cruelty and injury, which had to be proven in court. In Great Britain adultery was the usual cause for divorce, but a woman had to prove her husband's adultery as well as other offenses, whereas a man only had to prove his wife's adultery. In Germany only adultery or serious maltreatment was recognized as grounds for divorce. Across Europe extramarital sexual relations by husbands were more tolerated than those of wives. Everywhere, divorce required legal hearings and proof, making the process expensive and all the more difficult for women who did not control their own property.

The authority of husbands also extended to children. A husband could take children away from their mother and give them to someone else to rear. Only the husband, in most countries, could permit his daughter to marry. In some countries he could virtually force his daughter to marry the man of his

Middle-Class Family. Family was central to the middle-class conception of a stable and respectable social life. This portrait of the Bellelli family is by Degas. Notice that the husband and father sits at his desk, suggesting his association with business and the world outside the home, whereas the wife and mother stands with their children, suggesting her domestic role.

Edgar Degas (1834–1917), "The Bellelli Family" c. 1858–60. Musee d'Orsay, Paris, France. Photograph Copyright Bridgeman-Giraudon/Art Resource, N.Y.

choice. In cases of divorce and separation, the husband normally assumed authority over children no matter how he had treated them previously.

The sexual and reproductive rights of women, which have been so widely debated in recent years, could hardly be discussed in the 19th century. Both contraception and abortion were illegal. The law on rape normally worked against women. Wherever they turned—whether to physicians or lawyers—women confronted an official or legal world populated and controlled by men.

Educational Barriers Throughout the 19th century, women had less access to education than men, and what was available to them was inferior. Not surprisingly, the percentage of illiterate women exceeded that of men. Most women were educated only enough for the domestic careers they were expected to follow.

University and professional education remained reserved for men until at least the third quarter of the century. The University of Zurich opened its doors to women in the 1860s. The University of London admitted women for degrees in 1878. Women were not awarded degrees at Oxford until 1920 or at Cambridge until 1921. They could not attend Sorbonne lectures until 1880. Just before the turn of the century, universities and medical schools in the Austrian Empire allowed women to matriculate, but Prussian universities did not until after 1900. Russian women did not attend universities before 1914, but other institutions that awarded degrees were open to them. Italian universities were more open to both women students and women instructors than similar institutions elsewhere in Europe.

The absence of a system of private or public secondary education for women prevented most of them from gaining the qualifications they needed to enter a university whether or not the university prohibited them. Considerable evidence suggests that educated, professional men feared the competition of women. Women who attended universities and medical schools were sometimes labeled political radicals.

By 1900, men in the educated elite also feared the challenge educated women posed to traditional gender roles in the home and workplace. Restricting their access to secondary and university education helped bar women from social and economic advancement. Women would benefit only marginally from the expansion of professional employment that occurred during the late 19th and early 20th centuries. Although a few women did enter the professions, especially medicine, most nations prevented women from becoming lawyers until after World War I.

Schoolteaching at the elementary level, which was seen as a female job because of its association with the nurturing of children, became a professional haven for women. Trained at institutions that were equivalent to normal schools, women schoolteachers were regarded as educated, but not as university educated. Secondary education remained largely the province of men.

The few women who pioneered in the professions and on government commissions and school boards or who dispersed birth control information faced grave social obstacles, personal humiliation, and often outright bigotry. These women and their male supporters were challenging that clear separation of life into male and female spheres that had emerged in middle-class European society during the 19th century. Women themselves often hesitated to support feminist causes or expanded opportunities for themselves because they had been so thoroughly acculturated into the recently stereotyped roles. Many women saw a real conflict between family responsibilities and feminism.

Major Dates in Late 19th-Century and Early 20th-Century Women's History

1857	Revised English divorce law
1865	University of Zurich admits women for degrees
1869	*The Subjection of Women* by John Stuart Mill and Harriet Taylor
1878	University of London admits women as candidates for degrees
1882	English Married Woman's Property Act
1894	Union of German Women's Organizations founded
1901	National Council of French Women founded
1903	British Women's Social and Political Union founded
1907	Norway permits women to vote on national issues
1910	British suffragettes adopt radical tactics
1918	Vote extended to some British women
1918	Weimar constitution allows German women to vote
1920–1921	Oxford and Cambridge Universities award degrees to women
1922	French Senate defeats bill extending vote to women
1928	Britain extends vote to women on same basis as men

New Employment Patterns for Women

During the late 19th century, two major developments affected the economic lives of women. The first was an expansion in the variety of jobs available outside the better-paying learned professions. The second was a withdrawal of married women from the work force. These two seemingly contradictory developments require explanation.

Availability of New Jobs   The expansion of governmental bureaucracies, the emergence of corporations and other large-scale businesses, and the expansion of retail stores opened many new employment opportunities for women. The need for elementary schoolteachers, usually women, grew with compulsory education laws. Technological inventions and innovations, such as the typewriter and eventually the telephone, also fostered female employment. Women by the

Women Working at a Telephone Exchange.
The invention of the telephone
opened new employment opportunities
for women.

Mary Evans Picture Library.

thousands became secretaries and clerks for governments and private businesses. Even more became shop assistants.

Although these jobs did open new and often better employment opportunities for women, they nonetheless required low-level skills and involved minimal training. They were occupied primarily by unmarried women or widows. Few women had prominent positions.

Employers continued to pay women low wages because they assumed, often knowing better, that a woman did not need to support herself independently but could expect additional financial support from her father or husband. Consequently, a woman who did need to support herself independently could rarely find a job paying an adequate income or a position that paid as well as one held by a man who was supporting himself independently.

Withdrawal from the Labor Force Most of the women filling these new service positions were young and unmarried. After marriage, or certainly after the birth of her first child, a woman normally withdrew from the labor force. She either did not work or she worked at home. This pattern was not new, but it had become more common by the end of the 19th century. The industrial occupations that women had filled in the mid-19th century, especially textile and garment making, were shrinking. Those industries thus offered fewer jobs for either married or unmarried women. Employers in offices and retail stores preferred young, unmarried women whose family responsibilities would not interfere with their work. The decline in the number of births also meant that fewer married women were needed to look after other women's children.

The wages paid to male workers increased during this period, thus reducing families' need for a second income. Also, thanks to improving health conditions, men lived longer than before, so wives were less likely to be thrust into the work force by an emergency. Smaller families also lowered the need for supplementary wages. Working children stayed longer at home and continued to contribute to the family's wage pool.

Finally, the cultural dominance of the middle class, with its generally idle wives, established a pattern of social expectations. The more prosperous a working-class family became, the less involved in employment its women were supposed to be. Indeed, the less income-producing work a wife did, the more prosperous and stable the family was considered.

Yet behind these generalities stands the enormous variety of social and economic experience late 19th-century women actually encountered. As might be expected, social class largely determined these individual experiences.

LATE 19TH-CENTURY WORKING-CLASS WOMEN

Although less dominant than earlier in the century, the textile and garment-making industries continued to employ many women. The German clothing-making trades illustrate the kind of vulnerable economic situation that women could encounter as a result of their limited skills and the organization of the trade. The manufacture of mass-made clothes in Germany was designed to require minimal capital investment by manufacturers and to protect them from significant risk. A major manufacturer would arrange to produce clothing through a putting-out system. He would purchase the material and then put it out for tailoring. The clothing was made not in a factory but usually in independently owned, small sweatshops or by workers in their homes.

In 1896, there were more than 80,000 garment workers, mostly women, in Berlin. When business was good, employment for these women was high. If business became poor, however, less work was put out, idling many of them. In effect, the workers who actually sewed the clothing carried much of the risk of the enterprise. Some women did work in factories, but they, too, were subject to layoffs. Furthermore, women in the clothing trade were nearly always in positions less skilled than those of the male tailors or the middlemen who owned the workshops.

The expectation of separate social and economic spheres for men and women and the definition of women's chief work as pertaining to the home contributed heavily to the exploitation of women workers outside the home. Because their wages were regarded merely as supplementing their husbands', they became particularly vulnerable to the economic exploitation that characterized the German putting-out system for clothing production. Women were nearly always treated as casual workers in Europe.

THE RISE OF POLITICAL FEMINISM

As can be seen from the previous discussion, liberal society and its values neither automatically nor inevitably improved the lot of women. In particular, it did not give them the right to vote or access to political activity. Male liberals feared that granting the vote to women would benefit political conservatives because women were thought to be unduly controlled by the clergy. Consequently, anticlerical liberals often had difficulty working with feminists.

Obstacles to Achieving Equality Women also were often reluctant to support feminist causes. Political issues relating to gender were only one of several priorities for many women. Some were sensitive to their class and economic interests. Others subordinated feminist political issues to national unity and nationalistic patriotism. Still others would not support particular feminist organizations because of differences over tactics. The various social and tactical differences among women often led to sharp divisions within the feminists' own ranks. Except in England, it was often difficult for working-class and middle-class women to cooperate. Roman Catholic feminists were uncomfortable with radical secularist feminists.

Although liberal society and law presented women with many obstacles, they also provided feminists with many of their intellectual and political tools. As early as 1792 in Britain, Mary Wollstonecraft (1759–1797), in *The Vindication of the Rights of Women*, applied the revolutionary doctrines of the rights of man to the predicament of the members of her own sex (see Chapter 22). John Stuart Mill (1806–1873), with his wife Harriet Taylor (1804–1858), applied the logic of liberal freedom to the position of women in *The Subjection of Women* (1869). The arguments for utility and efficiency so dear to middle-class liberals could be used to expose the human and social waste implicit in the inferior role assigned to women.

Furthermore, the socialist criticism of capitalist society often, though by no means always, included a harsh indictment of the social and economic position to which women had been relegated. The earliest statements of feminism arose from critics of the existing order and were often associated with people who had unorthodox opinions about sexuality, family life, and property. This hardened resistance to the feminist message, especially on the continent.

These difficulties prevented continental feminists from raising the kind of massive public support or mounting the large demonstrations that feminists in Great Britain and the United States could. Everywhere in Europe, however, including Britain, the feminist cause was badly divided over both goals and tactics.

Women's Suffrage. The creator of this poster cleverly reveals the hypocrisy and foolishness of denying the vote to women.

Private collection/Bridgeman Art Library.

Votes for Women in Britain

Europe's most advanced women's movement was in Great Britain. There, Millicent Fawcett (1847–1929) led the moderate National Union of Women's Suffrage Societies. She believed Parliament would grant women the vote only when convinced that women would be respectable and responsible in their political activity. In 1908, this organization could rally almost half a million women in London. Fawcett was the wife of a former Liberal Party cabinet minister and economist. Her tactics were those of English liberals.

Emmeline Pankhurst (1858–1928) led a different and much more radical branch of British feminists. Pankhurst's husband had been active in both labor and Irish nationalist politics. Irish nationalists had developed numerous disruptive political tactics. Early labor politicians also occasionally had confrontations with police over the right to hold meetings. In 1903, Pankhurst and her daughters founded the Women's Social and Political Union. For several years they and their followers, known derisively as **suffragettes**, lobbied publicly and privately for women's suffrage. By 1910, having failed to move the government, they turned to the violent tactics of arson, window breaking, and sabotage of postal boxes. They marched en masse on Parliament. The liberal government of Herbert Asquith (1852–1928), prime minister from 1908 to 1916, imprisoned many of the demonstrators and force-fed those who went on hunger strikes in jail. The government refused to extend the franchise. Only in 1918, and then as a result of their contribution to the war effort, did some British women receive the vote.

Political Feminism on the Continent

The contrast of France and Germany shows how advanced the British women's movement was. In France, when Hubertine Auclert (1848–1914) began campaigning for the vote in the 1880s, she stood virtually alone. During the 1890s, several women's organizations emerged. In 1901, the National Council of French Women (CNFF) was organized among upper-middle-class women, but it did not support the vote for women for several years. French Roman Catholic feminists, such as Marie Mauguet (1844–1928), supported the franchise. Almost all French feminists,

suffragettes British women who lobbied and agitated for the right to vote in the early 20th century.

however, rejected violence. They also were never able to organize mass rallies. The leaders of French feminism believed that the vote could be achieved through careful legalism. In 1919, the French Chamber of Deputies granted the vote to women, but in 1922 the French Senate defeated the bill. French women did not receive the right to vote until 1944, at the end of World War II.

In Germany feminist awareness and action were even more underdeveloped. German law actually forbade German women from political activity. Because no group in the German Empire enjoyed extensive political rights, women were not certain that they would benefit from demanding them. Any such demand would be regarded as subversive of both the state and society.

In 1894, the Union of German Women's Organizations (BDFK) was founded. By 1902, it was calling for the right to vote. But it was largely concerned with improving women's social conditions, their access to education, and their right to other protections. The group also worked to see women admitted to political or civic activity on the municipal level. Their work usually included education, child welfare, charity, and public health. The German Social Democratic Party supported women's suffrage, but that Socialist Party was so disdained by the German authorities and German Roman Catholics that this support only made suffrage more suspect in their eyes. Women received the vote in Germany only in 1918 under the constitution of the Weimar Republic. Before World War I, only in Norway (1907) could women vote on national issues.

JEWISH EMANCIPATION

One of the most important social changes to occur throughout Europe during the 19th century was the emancipation of European Jews from the narrow life of the ghetto into a world of equal or nearly equal citizenship and social status. This transformation represented one of the major social impacts of political liberalism on European life.

EARLY STEPS TO EQUAL CITIZENSHIP

Emancipation, slow and never fully completed, began in the late 18th century and continued throughout the 19th century. It moved at different paces in different countries. In 1782, Joseph II (r. 1765–1790), the Habsburg emperor, issued a decree that placed the Jews of his empire under more or less the same laws as Christians. In France, the National Assembly recognized Jews as French citizens in 1789. During the Napoleonic Wars, Jewish communities in Italy and Germany were allowed to mix on a generally equal footing with the Christian population.

These various steps toward political emancipation were frequently limited or partially repealed with changes in rulers or governments. Even in countries that granted them political rights, Jews could not own land and could be subject to discriminatory taxes. Nonetheless, by the first half of the 19th century, Jews in western Europe and to a much lesser extent in central and eastern Europe had begun to acquire equal or nearly equal citizenship.

In Russia, however, the traditional modes of prejudice and discrimination continued unabated until World War I. Jews were treated as aliens under Russian rule. The government undermined Jewish community life, limited publication of Jewish books, restricted areas where Jews might live, required internal passports from Jews, and banned them from many forms of state service and many institutions of higher education. The police and others were allowed to conduct **pogroms**—organized riots—against Jewish neighborhoods and villages.

HOW DID emanicipation affect Jewish participation in European social and political life outside of Russia?

pogroms Organized riots against Jews in the Russian Empire.

BROADENED OPPORTUNITIES

After the Revolutions of 1848, and especially in western Europe, the situation of European Jews improved for several decades. Throughout Germany, Italy, the Low Countries, and Scandinavia, Jews were allowed full rights of citizenship. After 1858, Jews in Great Britain could sit in Parliament. In Austria-Hungary, full legal rights were extended to Jews in 1867. From approximately 1850 to 1880, there was relatively little organized or overt prejudice toward Jews. They entered the professions and other occupations once closed to them. They participated fully in the literary and cultural life of their nations. They were active in the arts and music. They became leaders in science and education. Jews intermarried freely with non-Jews as legal prohibitions against such marriages were repealed during the last quarter of the century.

Outside of Russia, Jewish political figures served in the highest offices of the state. Politically they tended to be aligned with liberal parties because such groups had championed equal rights. Later in the century, especially in eastern Europe, many Jews became associated with the Socialist parties.

The prejudice that had been associated with religious attitudes toward Jews seemed to have dissipated, although it still appeared in rural Russia and eastern Europe. From these regions, hundreds of thousands of European Jews immigrated to the United States. Almost anywhere in Europe Jews might encounter prejudice on a personal level. But in western Europe, including England, France, Italy, Germany, and the Low Countries, the Jewish populations seem to have felt relatively secure from the old dangers of legalized persecution and discrimination.

Feelings toward Jews began to change during the last two decades of the 19th century. In the 1870s, anti-Semitic sentiments attributing the economic stagnation of the decade to Jewish bankers and financial interests began to be voiced. In the 1880s, organized anti-Semitism erupted in Germany as it did in France in the 1890s. As described in Chapter 24, those developments gave birth to Zionism, the movement to establish a Jewish state in Palestine. However, Zionism was initially a minority movement within the Jewish community. Most Jewish leaders believed the attacks on Jewish life to be temporary recurrences of older prejudice; they felt that their communities would remain safe under the legal protections that had been extended during the century. That analysis would be proved disastrously wrong during the 1930s and 1940s.

WHY DID Marxism become so influential among European socialists?

EUROPEAN LABOR, SOCIALISM, AND POLITICS TO WORLD WAR I

THE WORKING CLASSES IN THE LATE 19TH CENTURY

After 1848, European workers ceased taking to the streets and rioting to voice their grievances. They also stopped trying to revive the old paternalistic guilds. They accepted the inevitability of modern industrial production and sought a share of the benefits it produced. They looked to new organizations and ideologies to defend their interests: trade unions, democratic political parties, and socialism.

Trade Union Trade unionism came of age as legal protections were extended to unions throughout the second half of the century. Unions became fully legal in Great Britain in 1871 and were allowed to picket in 1875. In France, the Third Republic fully legalized unions in 1884. After 1890, they could function in

Germany with little disturbance. Initially, most trade unions were slow to enter the political process directly. As long as the traditional governing classes looked after labor interests, members of the working class rarely sought office themselves.

The mid-century organizational efforts of the unions aimed to improve the wages and working conditions of skilled workers. By the close of the century, large industrial unions for unskilled workers were also being organized. They confronted extensive opposition from employers, and were often recognized only after long strikes. In the decade before 1914, strikes were common throughout Europe as unions attempted to raise wages to keep up with inflation. However, despite the advances of unions and the growth of their membership in 1910 to approximately 3 million in Britain, 2 million in Germany, and 977,000 in France, they never included a majority of the industrial labor force. Unions did represent a new collective fashion in which workers could associate to confront the economic difficulties of their lives and attain better security.

Democracy and Political Parties   The democratic franchise gave workers direct political influence, which meant they could no longer be ignored. Except for Russia, all the major European states adopted broad-based, if not perfectly democratic, electoral systems. Democracy brought new modes of popular pressure to bear on all governments. Discontented groups could now voice their grievances and advocate their programs within government rather than from outside it.

The advent of democracy witnessed the formation for the first time in Europe of organized mass political parties, such as had existed throughout the 19th century in the United States. In the liberal European states with narrow electoral bases, most voters had been men of property who understood what they had at stake in politics. Organization had been minimal. The expansion of the electorate brought into the political processes many people whose level of political consciousness and interest was low. This electorate had to be organized and taught the nature of power and influence in the liberal democratic state. The organized political party—with its workers, newspapers, offices, social life, and discipline—was the vehicle that mobilized the new voters. The largest single group in these mass electorates was the working class. The democratization of politics presented the Socialists with opportunities and required the traditional ruling class to vie with them for the support of the new voters.

MARXIST CRITIQUE OF THE INDUSTRIAL ORDER

During the 1840s, Karl Marx (1818–1883) produced the most influential of all critiques of the newly emerged industrial order. His analysis became so important because later in the century it was adopted by the leading Socialist political party in Germany, which in turn influenced most other European Socialist parties including a small group of exiled Russian Socialists led by V. I. Lenin. Marx was born in the Rhineland. His Jewish middle-class parents sent him to the University of Berlin, where he became deeply involved in radical politics. During 1842 and 1843, he edited the radical *Rhineland Gazette*. Soon the German

Major Dates in the Development of Socialism

1864	International Working Men's Association (the First International) founded
1875	German Social Democratic Party founded
1876	First International dissolved
1878	German antisocialist laws passed
1884	British Fabian Society founded
1889	Second International founded
1891	German antisocialist laws permitted to expire
1891	German Social Democratic Party's Erfurt Program
1895	French *Confédération Générale du Travail* founded
1899	Eduard Bernstein's *Evolutionary Socialism*
1902	Formation of the British Labour party
1902	Lenin's *What Is to Be Done?*
1903	Bolshevik-Menshevik split

Karl Marx. Marx's Socialist philosophy eventually triumphed over most alternative versions of socialism in Europe, but his monumental work has been subject to varying interpretations, criticisms, and revisions that continue to this day.

Bildarchiv Preussischer Kulturbesitz.

19.8
Karl Marx and
Friedrich Engels

authorities drove him into exile—first in Paris; then in Brussels; and finally, after 1849, in London.

In 1844, Marx met Friedrich Engels (1820–1895), another young middle-class German, whose father owned a textile factory in Manchester, England. The next year, Engels published *The Condition of the Working Class in England*, which presented a devastating picture of industrial life. The two men became fast friends. Late in 1847, they were asked to write a pamphlet for a newly organized and ultimately short-lived secret Communist league. *The Communist Manifesto*, published in German, appeared early in 1848. Marx, Engels, and the league had adopted the name *Communist* because the term was more self-consciously radical than *Socialist*. *Communism* implied the outright abolition of private property rather than some less extensive rearrangement of society. The *Manifesto* itself was a work of fewer than 50 pages. It would become the most influential political document of modern European history, but that development lay in the future. At the time it was simply one more political tract. Moreover, neither Marx nor his thought had any effect on the revolutionary events of 1848.

In *The Communist Manifesto*, Marx and Engels contended that human history must be understood rationally and as a whole. According to their analysis, history is the record of humankind's coming to grips with physical nature to produce the goods necessary for survival. That basic productive process determines the structures, values, and ideas of a society. Historically, the organization of the means of production has always involved conflict between the classes who owned and controlled the means of production and those classes who worked for them. That necessary conflict has provided the engine for historical development; it is not an accidental byproduct of mismanagement or bad intentions. Consequently, only a radical social transformation, not piecemeal reforms, can eliminate the social and economic evils inherent in the very structures of production. Such a revolution will occur as the inevitable outcome of the development of capitalism.

In Marx's and Engels's eyes, the class conflict that had characterized previous Western history had become a struggle between the bourgeoisie and the proletariat, or between the middle class and the workers in the 19th century. The character of capitalism ensured the sharpening of the struggle. Capitalist production and competition would steadily increase the size of the unpropertied proletariat. Large-scale mechanical production crushed both traditional and smaller industrial producers into the ranks of the proletariat. As the business structures grew larger and larger, smaller middle-class units would be squeezed out by the competitive pressures. Competition among the few remaining gigantic concerns would lead to more intense suffering by the proletariat. As the workers suffered increasingly from the competition among the ever-enlarging firms, they would foment revolution and finally overthrow the few remaining owners of the means of production. For a time the workers would organize the means of production through a dictatorship of the proletariat, which would eventually give way to a propertyless and classless communist society.

This proletarian revolution was inevitable, according to Marx and Engels. The structure of capitalism required competition and consolidation of enterprise.

Although the class conflict involved in the contemporary process resembled that of the past, it differed in one major respect. The struggle between the capitalistic bourgeoisie and the industrial proletariat would culminate in a wholly new society that would be free of class conflict. The victorious proletariat, by its very nature, they contended, could not be a new oppressor class: "The proletarian movement is the self-conscious, independent movement of the immense majority, in the interest of the immense majority."[1] The result of the proletarian victory would be "an association, in which the free development of each is the condition for the free development of all."[2] The victory of the proletariat over the bourgeoisie represented the culmination of human history. For the first time, one group of people would not be oppressing another. Marx's analysis was conditioned by his own economic environment. The 1840s had seen much unemployment and deprivation. Capitalism, however, did not collapse as he predicted, nor did the middle class during the rest of the century or later become proletarianized. Rather, more and more people came to benefit from the industrial system. Nonetheless, within a generation Marxism had captured the imagination of many Socialists and large segments of the working class. Its doctrines were allegedly based on the empirical evidence of hard economic fact. This much proclaimed scientific aspect of **Marxism** helped the ideology, as science became more influential during the second half of the century. Marx had made the ultimate victory of socialism seem certain. His works also suggested that the path to socialism lay with revolution rather than reform. As Marxist thought permeated the international Socialist movement during the next 75 years, it would provide the ideological basis for some of the most momentous and ultimately repressive political movements in the history of virtually the entire modern world.

GERMANY: SOCIAL DEMOCRATS AND REVISIONISM

Karl Marx's ideas ultimately came to exercise such vast influence, as they were being adopted by the German Social Democratic Party (SPD). Founded in 1875, the SPD suffered 12 years of persecution by Otto von Bismarck (1815–1898), who believed socialism would undermine German politics and society. In 1878, there was an attempt to assassinate Emperor William I (r. 1861–1888). Bismarck unfairly blamed the Socialists and steered antisocialist laws through the Reichstag, the German Parliament. These measures suppressed the organization, meetings, newspapers, and other public activities of the SPD. Nonetheless, the SPD steadily polled more votes in elections to the Reichstag.

Repression having failed, Bismarck enacted social welfare legislation to wean German workers from socialist loyalties. These measures provided health insurance, accident insurance, and old age and disability pensions. The German state itself thus organized a system of social security that did not change the system of property holding or politics.

In 1891, after forcing Bismarck's resignation, Emperor William II (r. 1888–1918) allowed the antisocialist legislation to expire. The SPD then had to decide how to operate as a legalized party. Their new direction was announced in the Erfurt Program of 1891. In good Marxist fashion, the program declared the imminent doom of capitalism and the necessity of socialist ownership of the means of production. However, these goals were to be achieved by legal political participation rather than by revolutionary activity. Since the revolution was inevitable, it was argued, the immediate task of Socialists was to improve workers'

Marxism Theory of Karl Marx (1818–1883) and Friedrich Engels (1820–1895) that history is the result of class conflict, which will end in the inevitable triumph of the industrial proletariat over the bourgeoisie and the abolition of private property and social class.

[1] Robert C. Tucker, ed., *The Marx-Engels Reader* (New York: W. W. Norton, 1972), p. 353.
[2] Ibid.

Fabians   British Socialists in the late 19th and early 20th centuries who sought to achieve socialism through gradual, peaceful, and democratic means.

revisionism   Advocacy among 19th-century German Socialists of achieving a humane socialist society through the evolution of democratic institutions, not revolution.

Trade Union Membership Certificate.
Trade unions continued to grow in late-century Great Britain. The effort to curb the unions eventually led to the formation of the Labour Party. The British unions often had quite elaborate membership certificates, such as this one for the National Union of Gas Workers and General Labourers of Great Britain and Ireland.
The Granger Collection.

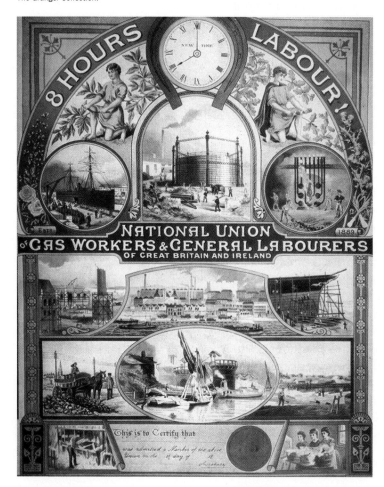

lives. In theory, the SPD was vehemently hostile to the German Empire, but in practice the party functioned within its institutions.

This situation of the SPD, however, generated the most important internal socialist challenge to the orthodox Marxist analysis of capitalism and the socialist revolution. Eduard Bernstein (1850–1932) wrote what was regarded as his socialist heresy. Bernstein, who was familiar with the British **Fabians**, questioned whether Marx and his later orthodox followers had been correct in their pessimistic appraisal of capitalism and the necessity of revolution. In *Evolutionary Socialism* (1899), Bernstein pointed to the rising standard of living in Europe, the ongoing power of the middle class, and the opening of the franchise to the working class. He argued that a humane socialist society required not revolution but more democracy and social reform. Bernstein's doctrines, known as *revisionism*, were widely debated among German Socialists and were finally condemned as theory, although the party actually pursued a peaceful, reformist program. His critics argued that evolution toward social democracy might be possible in liberal, parliamentary Britain but not in authoritarian, militaristic Germany with its basically powerless Reichstag. Therefore, the German SPD continued to advocate revolution.

The German debate over revisionism became important for the later history of Marxist socialism. The German SPD was, as noted, the most successful prewar Socialist party. Its rejection of an ideology of reform socialism in favor of revolutionary socialism influenced all Socialists who looked to the German example. Most significant, Lenin adopted this position, as did the other leaders of the Russian Revolution. Thereafter, wherever Soviet Marxism was influential, the goal of its efforts would be revolution rather than reform.

GREAT BRITAIN: THE LABOUR PARTY AND FABIANISM

No form of socialism made significant progress in Great Britain, the most advanced industrial society of the day. Members of the growing trade unions normally supported Liberal Party candidates. The "new unionism" of the late 1880s and the 1890s organized the dock workers, the gas workers, and similar unskilled groups. Employer resistance to unions heightened class antagonism. In 1892, Keir Hardie (1856–1915) became the first independent worker elected to Parliament. In 1893, the Socialist Independent Labour Party was founded, but it remained ineffective.

In 1901, however, a decision by the House of Lords (Britain's supreme court) removed the legal protection previously accorded union funds. The Trades Union Congress responded by launching the Labour Party, which sent 29 members to Parliament in the election of 1906. Their goals did not yet encompass socialism. The British labor movement also became more militant. In scores of strikes, workers fought for wages to meet the rising cost of living. The government intervened to mediate these strikes, which in 1911 and 1912 involved the railways, the docks, and the mines.

British socialism itself remained primarily the preserve of intellectuals. The Socialists who exerted the most influence were from the Fabian Society, founded in 1884. The society took its name from Q. Fabius Maximus (d. 203 B.C.E.), the Roman general who defeated Hannibal by waiting before attacking. Its name thus indicated a gradualist approach to social reform. Its leading members were Sydney Webb (1859–1947), Beatrice Webb (1858–1943), H. G. Wells (1866–1946), and George Bernard Shaw (1856–1950). Many of the Fabians were civil servants who believed that the problems of industry, the expansion of ownership, and the state direction of production could be solved and achieved gradually, peacefully, and democratically. They sought to educate the country to the rational wisdom of socialism. They were particularly interested in collective ownership on the municipal level, or so-called gas-and-water socialism.

RUSSIA: INDUSTRIAL DEVELOPMENT AND THE BIRTH OF BOLSHEVISM

Following its defeat in the Crimean War, the tsarist government in Russia had undertaken a series of major internal reforms. The most important of these was the emancipation of the serfs in 1861. That measure was extremely complicated and in effect required serfs to pay for their land. The poverty of the emancipated serfs became a political cause for groups of urban revolutionaries in Russia who succeeded in assassinating Tsar Alexander II (r. 1855–1881) in 1881. Thereafter, the government pursued a policy of general political repression.

At the same time in the late 19th century, the tsarist government was determined to make Russia an industrial power. It favored the growth of heavy industries, such as railways, iron, and steel. A small but significant industrial proletariat arose. By 1900, Russia had approximately 3 million factory workers. Their working and living conditions were bad by any standard.

New political departures accompanied this economic development. In 1901, the Social Revolutionary Party was founded. It opposed industrialism and looked to the communal life of rural Russia as a model for the economic future. In 1903, the Constitutional Democratic Party, or Cadets, was formed. Liberal in outlook, the Cadets were drawn from people who participated in the *zemstvos* (local governments). They wanted a parliamentary regime with responsible ministries, civil liberties, and economic progress. The Cadets hoped to model themselves on the liberal parties of western Europe.

Lenin's Early Thought and Career   The situation for Russian Socialists differed radically from that in other major European countries. Russia had no representative political institutions and only a small working class. Compromises and accommodations achieved elsewhere were meaningless in Russia, where socialism in both theory and practice had to be revolutionary. The Russian Social Democratic Party had been established in 1898. It was Marxist, and its members greatly admired the German SPD, but tsarist repression meant that it had to function in exile.

The leading late-19th-century Russian Marxist was Georgii Plekhanov (1857–1918), based in Switzerland. His chief disciple was Vladimir Ilyich Ulyanov (1870–1924), who took the name of Lenin. The future leader of the communist revolution was the son of a high bureaucrat. His older brother had been executed in 1887 for participating in a plot against Alexander III (r. 1881–1894).

Marxist revolutionary Vladimir Ilyich Lenin. Lenin sits alone at a desk littered with papers and books.

Corbis/Bettman.

Bolsheviks Meaning the "majority." Term Lenin applied to his faction of the Russian Social Democratic Party. It became the Communist Party of the Soviet Union after the Russian Revolution.

Mensheviks Meaning the "minority." Term Lenin applied to the majority moderate faction of the Russian Social Democratic Party opposed to him and the Bolsheviks.

In 1893, Lenin moved to St. Petersburg, where he briefly practiced law. Soon he, too, was drawn to the revolutionary groups among the factory workers. In 1895, he was exiled to Siberia. After his release in 1900, Lenin spent most of the next 17 years in Switzerland.

In Switzerland, Lenin became deeply involved in the organizational and policy disputes of the exiled Russian Social Democrats. They all considered themselves Marxists, but quarreled about the proper nature of a Marxist revolution in primarily rural Russia and the structure of their own party. The Social Democrats were modernizers who favored further industrial development. Most believed that Russia must develop a large proletariat before the revolution could come. This same majority hoped to mold a mass political party like the German SPD.

Lenin dissented from both positions. In *What Is to Be Done?* (1902), he condemned any accommodations. He also criticized a trade unionism that settled for short-term gains rather than true revolutionary change for the working class. Lenin further rejected the concept of a mass party composed of workers. Revolutionary consciousness would not arise spontaneously from the working class. It must be carried to them by a small, elite party, "people who make revolutionary activity their profession."[3]

The guiding principle of that party should be "the strictest secrecy, the strictest selection of members, and the training of professional revolutionaries."[4]

Establishment of the Bolsheviks In 1903, at the London Congress of the Russian Social Democratic Party, Lenin split the party ranks. Although it lost most of the votes during the congress, Lenin's group mustered a slim majority near the close. Thereafter, his faction assumed the name *Bolsheviks*, meaning "majority," and the other, more moderate, democratic revolutionary faction became known as the *Mensheviks*, or "minority." There was, of course, a considerable public relations advantage to the name *Bolshevik*. (In 1912, the Bolsheviks organized separately from other Social Democrats.) In 1905, Lenin complemented his organizational theory with a program for revolution in Russia. His *Two Tactics of Social Democracy in the Bourgeois-Democratic Revolution* urged that the socialist revolution unite the proletariat and the peasants. He grasped better than any other revolutionary the profound discontent in the Russian countryside. He knew that an alliance of workers and peasants in rebellion probably could not be suppressed. Lenin's two principles of an elite party and a dual social revolution allowed the Bolsheviks, in late 1917, to capture the leadership of the Russian Revolution and to transform the political face of the modern world.

The Revolution of 1905 and Its Aftermath The quarrels among the Russian Socialists had no immediate influence within Russia itself. In 1904, Russia went to war with Japan, but the result was defeat and political crisis. The Japanese captured Port Arthur, Russia's base on the eastern coast of China, early in 1905. A few days later, on January 22, a priest named Father Gapon (1870–1906) led thousands of workers to petition the tsar for improvements in industrial conditions. As the petitioners approached the Winter Palace in Saint

---

[3]Quoted in Albert Fried and Ronald Sanders, eds. *Socialist Thought: A Documentary History* (Garden City, NY: Anchor Doubleday, 1964), p. 459.
[4]Ibid., p. 468.

Petersburg, troops opened fire. About 100 people were killed, and many more were wounded.

Revolutionary disturbances spread throughout Russia: Sailors mutinied, peasants revolted, and property was attacked. An uncle of the tsar was assassinated. Liberal Constitutional Democratic leaders from the *zemstvos* demanded political reform. University students went on strike. In early October 1905, strikes broke out in Saint Petersburg, and worker groups, called *soviets*, virtually controlled the city. Tsar Nicholas II (r. 1894–1917) promised Russia constitutional government.

Early in 1906, the tsar announced the election of a parliament, the **Duma**, with two chambers. However, he reserved for himself ministerial appointments, financial policy, and military and foreign affairs. Nicholas named as his chief minister P. A. Stolypin (1862–1911). Neither the tsar nor his minister was sympathetic to the Duma. It would meet, disagreements would occur, and it would be dismissed. In 1906, however, the government canceled any redemptive payments the peasants still owed from the emancipation of the serfs in 1861. Thereafter Stolypin repressed rural discontent.

After Stolypin's assassination in 1911 by a social revolutionary, the tsarist government simply muddled along. But the imperial family became surrounded by scandal over the influence of Grigori Rasputin (1871?–1916), who seemed able to heal the tsar's hemophilic son, the heir to the throne. The undue influence of this strange and uncouth man, the continued social discontent, and the conservative resistance to liberal reforms rendered the position and policy of the tsar uncertain after 1911.

EUROPEAN SOCIALISM IN WORLD HISTORY

The debates among late 19th- and early 20th-century European Socialists were complicated and in some respects obscure. They proved, however, significant not only for European politics but for political developments around the world. The impact arose for two reasons. First, Europeans who immigrated to North and South America carried many of these socialist ideas and quarrels with them. They continued to debate the issues in their new homelands. Second, by the end of the 19th century, numerous students from different parts of the European empires in Africa and Asia traveled to Europe for education. There they confronted these debates among European Socialists. Many of those students later returned home to become leaders of anticolonial political movements and carried with them the ideas and quarrels about methods, theory, and tactics they had encountered among European Socialists.

Major Dates in Turn-of-the-Century Russian History

	1895	Lenin arrested and sent to Siberia
	1897	Eleven-and-a-half-hour workday established
	1898	Russian Social Democratic Party founded
	1900	Lenin leaves Russia for western Europe
	1901	Social Revolutionary Party founded
	1903	Constitutional Democratic Party (Cadets) founded
	1903	Bolshevik-Menshevik split
	1904	Russo-Japanese War begins
1905		
	January	Japan defeats Russia
	January 22	Revolution breaks out in Saint Petersburg after Bloody Sunday massacre
	October 20	General strike
	October 26	*October Manifesto* establishes constitutional government
1906		
	May 10	Meeting of first Duma
	June	Stolypin appointed prime minister
	July 21	Dissolution of first Duma
	November	Land redemption payments canceled for peasants
1907		
	March 5–June 16	Second Duma seated and dismissed
	1907	Franchise changed and a third Duma elected, which sits until 1912
	1911	Stolypin assassinated by a social revolutionary
	1912	Fourth Duma elected
	1914	World War I breaks out

soviets Workers' and soldiers' councils formed in Russia during the revolution.

Duma Russian parliament, after the revolution of 1905.

HOW DID industrialization in the United States differ from industrialization in Europe?

NORTH AMERICA AND THE NEW INDUSTRIAL ECONOMY

The full industrialization of the United States followed a pattern not unlike that of 19th-century Europe. The first industry to become thoroughly mechanized was textile manufacture, followed by growth in the iron and steel industries. There were certain significant differences, however. The United States industrialized considerably later than Great Britain. Its major expansion in iron and steel took place after the Civil War and was thus approximately contemporary to the economic rise of the newly united Germany. In the United States, there had always been enormous social respect for entrepreneurial enterprise. American manufacturers and commercial developers thus encountered little of the prejudice against trade and commerce that existed among the European aristocracy. Wealthy American businessmen had considerable political influence. The United States possessed an immense internal market that functioned without trade restraints for the shipment of unprocessed goods to factories or of finished products to their markets. Much of the capital for American industrial expansion came from British bankers who saw the United States as an area of secure investment. Finally, the United States had a relative shortage of labor and consequently relatively high wages—factors that attracted so many immigrants to the industrial sector during the second half of the century.

In America as in Europe, however, the railways spurred the most intense industrial growth. The number of railway miles increased from approximately 50,000 in the mid-1860s to almost 200,000 by 1900. Much of the construction was made possible by vast European investments in the United States. The railways created enormous demand for iron, steel, coal, and lumber. They also stimulated settlement, vastly expanded markets, and helped to knit the country together.

EUROPEAN IMMIGRATION TO THE UNITED STATES

The same conditions that made American life so difficult for Blacks and Native Americans (see Chapter 23) turned the United States into a land of vast opportunity for White European immigrants. These immigrants faced religious and ethnic discrimination as well as frequent poverty in the United States; however, for many of them and their children, the social and economic structures of the United States allowed for assimilation and remarkable upward social mobility. This was especially true of those immigrants, mostly from northern and western Europe, who arrived approximately between 1840 and 1890—the great period of German, English, Welsh, Scottish, and Irish immigration. Among this group, the Irish undoubtedly encountered the most difficulties and resistance.

Toward the end of the century and well into the next—in what is sometimes known as the New Immigration—millions of people arrived from the Mediterranean, eastern Europe, and the Balkans (see Map 25–1). Most of these peoples left economically depressed areas, and financed their immigration themselves. However, some American companies did send ships to Italy for immigrants to work in American factories and mines.

These new immigrants, who generally came to work in the growing industrial cities, were perceived as fundamentally different from those who had come before them. They were seen and treated as of a lower class and inherently more difficult to assimilate than earlier immigrants. Predominately Roman Catholic, Orthodox, and Jewish, they encountered much intolerance. The same kind of racial theory that spread through Europe during these years was present in the

Emigration from Europe
Emigration from Japan
Emigration from China
Emigration from India
Migration from European Russia

Number of Immigrants

From Asia		700,000
Main groups		
Chinese	370,000	
Japanese	275,000	
From Canada		2,200,000
From Europe		30,000,000
Main groups		
Germans	5,000,000	
Irish	4,500,000	
Italians	4,500,000	
Poles	2,600,000	
English	2,600,000	
Jews	2,000,000	
From Latin America		900,000

MAP 25–1
Patterns of Global Migration, 1840–1900. Emigration was a global process by the late 19th century, yet more immigrants went to the United States than to all the other nations combined.

HOW DID global migration alter societies of the late 19th century?

United States. These new immigrants were often regarded as being from less desirable racial stocks. As a result, turn-of-the-century immigrants often encountered serious prejudice and endured lives of enormous poverty. They also often settled into communities of people from their own ethnic background. What ultimately held them together were various private organizations, such as churches and synagogues, clubs, newspapers in their own languages, and social agencies they organized for themselves.

Although none of these immigrants faced the same legal discrimination as did American Blacks, the Jews encountered restricted covenants on real estate, obstacles to joining private clubs, and quotas for admission to many schools and universities. Asian immigrants to the U.S. West Coast faced harsher prejudice.

UNIONS: ORGANIZATION OF LABOR

The expansion of industrialism led to various attempts to organize labor unions. In America as in Europe, workers faced great resistance from employers and those who feared that labor unions might lead to socialism. Another difficulty arose from the social situation of the labor force itself. White laborers would not organize alongside Blacks. Different ethnic minorities would not cooperate. The ongoing flood of immigration ensured a supply of workers willing to work for low wages. Business owners more often than not could divide and conquer the sprawling, ethnically mixed labor force.

The first effort at labor organization occurred in the 1870s with the National Labor Union and railroad unions. In 1881, the American Federation of Labor (AFL) was founded. In contrast to earlier organizations and the advanced European socialist movement, such as that in Germany, it did not seek to transform the life of workers in a radical fashion but rather focused on higher wages and better working conditions. The AFL concentrated on organizing skilled

Ellis Island. In 1892, the federal government opened the immigration station on Ellis Island, located in New York City's harbor, where about 80 percent of the immigrants to the United States landed. As many as 5,000 passengers per day reported to federal immigration officers for questions about their background and for physical examinations, such as this eye exam. Only about 1 percent were quarantined or turned away for health problems.

Brown Brothers.

workers; it did not seek to organize whole industries. Among its most effective leaders was Samuel Gompers (1850–1924). Other unions, such as the United Mine Workers and the Railway Brotherhoods, organized workers by industry.

The industrialization of the United States—again, like that of Europe—saw major periods of business crisis or downturn. Serious depressions occurred in both the 1870s and the 1890s. There was no government relief. What little relief there was came from local authorities and private charities. This pattern would continue until the Great Depression of the 1930s. The economic turmoil of the 1880s and 1890s spawned violent strikes. Perhaps the most famous of these incidents was the breaking of the Pullman strike in Chicago in 1894 by federal troops. The major goal of labor thereafter was to achieve the full legal right to organize. Although the Clayton Act of 1914 moved in that direction, the clear right to organize with the protection of the federal government was achieved only through the legislation of Franklin Roosevelt's (1882–1945) New Deal in the 1930s.

Socialism was a path not taken by American labor and one not allowed to be taken. Leaders of the conservative unions worked against the Socialists, and spokesmen for business did everything possible to block their influence. Federal and state governments actively sought to repress socialist activities wherever they appeared. After the Bolshevik Revolution of 1917, virtually all American Socialists were persecuted as Bolshevists during the 1920s and beyond. The United States thus became the land where many social issues tended to be addressed by trade unions rather than by socialist parties. Furthermore, although many conservative American political and business leaders disliked them, unions were not legally attacked in the United States as they were in Britain, which led to the founding of the British Labour Party after the turn of the century.

In many European countries, socialist parties, or ministers like Bismarck who attempted to outflank the Socialists, had pressed their governments to pass legislation providing social security and other social services. As with so many other policies favorable to labor, no significant legislation of this kind was passed in the United States, at either the federal or state level, until the New Deal.

THE PROGRESSIVES

Much of the power in American politics in the decades after the Civil War, especially in cities, often lay in the hands of political bosses. This system depended on patronage at every level of government. In return for jobs, contracts, licenses, favors, and sometimes actual services, the boss expected and received political support. Government was a vehicle for distributing spoils. The point of boss politics was not merely venality; it was also a way, however crude and unattractive, of organizing the disorderly social and economic forces of the great cities. It was a way of managing cities that were growing as never before with highly diverse populations.

Toward the close of the century, reform-minded political figures began to emerge on the city and state levels. These reformers feared that people such as themselves from the White upper-middle classes might soon lose political and social influence. Deeply disturbed by the corruption of much of political life, these reformers found the urban environment with its slums an unacceptable picture of disorder. They wanted to see more efficient and less corrupt government. They also wanted the government to become a direct agent of change and reform. Pursuing these goals, they ushered in what has been called the *Progressive Era*, which lasted from approximately 1890 through 1914. Although the Progressives were reformers, they were not always liberal by later standards. For example, Progressives in the South often disenfranchised Blacks and poor Whites by imposing literacy tests and similar devices.

Bandits' Roost. The Progressive photographer Jacob Riis documented the squalor, poverty, and despair of New York City's slums at the turn of the century, including this famous 1888 shot of " Bandits' Roost" near Mulberry Street.

The Progressives began their reform work on the local level, especially in the cities, before they launched into national politics. The disorder and extreme disparity of wealth and poverty in the cities disturbed them. Urban reformers believed that the politics of bosses and patronage robbed cities of the money needed to make them livable places. In place of patronage, they demanded social and municipal services to clean up the cities. They repeatedly attacked special interests who blocked reform. Progressive mayors called for lower utility rates and streetcar fares and also attacked police corruption.

SOCIAL REFORM

Not only politicians joined the progressive crusade. Churches began to address the question of social reform. It was in this era that the "Social Gospel" was first preached, with its message that Christianity involved civic action. Young men and women began to work in settlement houses in the slums. The most famous was Chicago's Hull House, led by Jane Addams (1860–1935). Other young persons from the middle class became active in housing and health reform, education, and charities. They conducted extensive surveys of the poorest parts of the great cities. These people believed that the urban environment could be cleaned up and social order made to prevail. Their vision of such social order was that of the White middle class.

Beginning in the mid-1890s, progressivism began to affect state governments. There the impulse toward reform involved various attempts to protect whole classes of persons who were perceived as unable to protect themselves against exploitation, especially children and women working under unwholesome conditions for low wages. Other aspects of progressivism at the state level involved the civil-service requirements and the regulation of railways. Virtually all of these reformers partook of the cult of science that was so influential in the late 19th century. They believed that the problems of society were susceptible to scientific, rational management. The general public interest should replace special interests.

THE PROGRESSIVE PRESIDENCY

Roosevelt Theodore Roosevelt became president in 1901 after the assassination of William McKinley (1843–1901). Roosevelt had been police commissioner of New York City and later a reforming governor of New York State. Roosevelt, in effect, created the modern American presidency. By force of personality and intelligence, he began to make the presidency the most important and powerful branch of government. As president, he began to set the agenda for national affairs and to define the problems that the federal government was to address. He surrounded himself with strong advisers and Cabinet members. He used his own knowledge of party patronage to beat the bosses at their own game.

In domestic policy, Roosevelt was determined to control the powerful business trusts. No centers of economic power should, through their organization, be stronger than the federal government. He successfully moved against some of the most powerful financiers in the country, such as J. P. Morgan and John D. Rockefeller. Through legislation associated with the term "Square Deal," Roosevelt attempted to assert the public interest over that of the various powerful special interests. He was not opposed to big business in itself, but he wanted it to operate according to rules established by the government for the public good.

In 1902, Roosevelt brought the moral power of the presidency to the aid of mine workers who were on strike. He appointed a commission to arbitrate the dispute. This was a major intrusion of the federal government into the economic system. It reversed the policies that had prevailed a decade earlier, when the government had used federal troops to break strikes. Roosevelt sought to make the presidency and the federal government the guarantor of fairness in economic relations. Thus he fostered the passage of the Pure Food and Drug Act and the Meat Packing Act in 1906, which protected the public against adulterated foodstuffs. Here again, the regulatory principle came to the fore. His conservation policies ensured that millions of acres of national forests came under the care of the federal government.

Roosevelt was associated with a vigorous, imperialistic foreign policy that had roots in the 1890s. In 1898, McKinley had led the nation into the Spanish-American War, and the United States had emerged as an imperial power with control of Cuba, Puerto Rico, Guam, and the Philippines. Roosevelt believed that the United States should be a major world power, and he sent a war fleet around the world. In Latin America, naval intervention assured the success of the Panamanian revolt of 1903 against Colombia. A treaty with the new Panamanian government allowed the United States to construct and control a canal across the Isthmus of Panama. The United States was following the model of the European great powers, which had been intervening in Africa and Asia. Like the other great powers, the imperialist policies of the United States were built on a conviction of racial superiority.

Roosevelt was succeeded in 1909 by William Howard Taft (1857–1930), his hand-picked successor. Taft disappointed Roosevelt, and in 1912 the election was a three-way contest among Taft, Roosevelt (running as a third-party candidate), and Woodrow Wilson. The Democrat Wilson won and brought a different concept of progressivism to the White House.

Wilson Woodrow Wilson (1856–1924) was a former president of Princeton University and a reforming governor of New Jersey, where he had battled the bosses. While still an academic, he had criticized the weak presidency of the late 19th century. Wilson, like Roosevelt, accepted a modern industrialized nation. However, unlike Roosevelt, Wilson disliked big business almost in and of itself. He believed in economic competition in which the weak would receive protection from the government. Wilson termed his attitude and policy the New Freedom. Although he had pressed this idea during the campaign, in office he followed a policy of moderate regulation of business.

Wilson also had a different view of the presidency. He saw the office as responsible for leading Congress to legislative decisions. Wilson was the first American president since 1800 to deliver the State of the Union address to Congress in person. He presented Congress with a vast agenda of legislation and then worked carefully with the Democratic leadership to see that it was passed. Although Wilson appeared to be an advanced reformer, he retained many beliefs that have disappointed his later admirers. For example, he reinstated racial segregation in the federal civil service and opposed female suffrage.

Wilson had long seen his real goals in terms of domestic reform. But war broke out in Europe in August 1914. Although Wilson was reelected in 1916 on the slogan "He Kept Us Out of War," in April 1917, he led the nation into the European conflict. The expertise that he and other Progressives had brought to the task of efficient domestic government was then turned to making the nation an effective military force. These two impulses—the first toward domestic reform, the second toward a strong international role—had long marked the Progressive movement and would shape American history in the years after the war.

The American Progressives resembled political leaders of their generation in Great Britain. The Conservative Benjamin Disraeli (1804–1881) and liberals

Theodore Roosevelt. This 1905 cartoon portraying President Theodore Roosevelt, "The World's Constable," appeared in *Judge* magazine. In depicting the president as a strong but benevolent policeman bringing order in a contentious world, the artist Louis Dalrymple drew on familiar imagery from Roosevelt's earlier days as a New York City police commissioner.

The Granger Collection.

William Gladstone (1809–1898) and David Lloyd-George (1863–1945) had supported various measures of social reforms. Elsewhere in Europe political leaders in France and Germany had undertaken reforms in housing and urban life to forestall the advance of socialism and to address the problems of industrialization and urbanization. These leaders had favored unprecedented use of central government authority and the establishment of stronger governments.

THE EMERGENCE OF MODERN EUROPEAN THOUGHT

HOW DID science transform European thinking in the late 19th century?

natural selection According to Darwin, the process in nature by which only the organisms best adapted to their environment tend to survive and transmit their genes, while those less adapted tend to be eliminated.

Natural Selection. Theories about the evolution of humankind from the higher primates aroused enormous controversy. This caricature shows Darwin with a monkey's body holding a mirror to an apelike creature.

National History Museum, London, UK/Bridgeman Art Library.

At mid-century, learned persons viewed the world much as Newton had described it: as rational, mechanical, and dependable. Its laws could be discovered objectively through experiment and observation, and scientists could describe physical nature as it really existed. Science had become a recognized discipline at universities, and the word *scientist* was coined in the early 1830s. In the last quarter of the 19th century and the first decade of the 20th century, Western intellectuals began to portray physical reality, human nature, and society in ways different from those of the past. The vast change in thinking commenced in the realm of biology.

DARWIN'S THEORY OF NATURAL SELECTION

In 1859, Charles Darwin's (1809–1882) *On the Origin of Species* carried the mechanical interpretation of physical nature into the world of living things (see "Darwin Defends a Mechanistic View of Nature"). Darwin did not originate the concept of evolution, which had been discussed widely before he wrote the essay. What he and Alfred Russel Wallace (1823–1913) did, working independently, was to formulate the principle of natural selection, which explained how species change or evolve over time.

The two scientists contended that more living organisms come into existence than can survive in their environment. Those organisms with a marginal advantage in the struggle for existence (the "fittest") produce more surviving offspring and repopulate their species. This principle of survival of the fittest Darwin called **natural selection**. What neither Darwin nor anyone else in his day could explain was the origin of those chance variations that provided some living things with the new traits. Only after 1900, when the work on heredity of the Austrian monk Gregor Mendel (1822–1884) received public attention, did the mystery of those variations begin to be unraveled.

Darwin and Wallace's mechanistic theory removed the idea of preconceived divine purpose from organic nature. Thus it not only contradicted the biblical narrative of the Creation, but also undermined both the deistic argument for the existence of God from the design of the universe and the belief that the universe was a fixed, stable system. If the world of nature was in flux, it implied that society, values, customs, and beliefs might also be changeable.

In 1871, in *The Descent of Man*, Darwin applied the principle of evolution by natural selection to human beings. Darwin contended that humankind's moral nature and religious sentiments, as well as its physical frame, had evolved in response to the requirements of survival. Neither the origin nor the character of humankind required postulating a deity to explain their existence. Not since Copernicus had removed the Earth from the center of the universe had human pride received so sharp a blow.

THE REVOLUTION IN PHYSICS

By the late 1870s, many physical scientists were questioning whether mechanistic models, solid atoms, and absolute time and space truly described the real universe. In 1883, Ernst Mach (1838–1916) published *The Science of Mechanics,* in which he urged that scientists consider their concepts descriptive not of the physical world in itself, but of the sensations of the scientific observer. Similarly, the French scientist Henri Poincaré (1854–1912) urged that the theories of scientists be regarded as hypothetical constructs of the human mind rather than as true descriptions of nature. By World War I, few scientists believed they could portray the "truth" about physical reality.

X Rays and Radiation   Discoveries in the laboratory supported the view that nature was more complex than Newton had imagined. In December 1895, Wilhelm Roentgen (1845–1923) published a paper on his discovery of X rays, a form of energy that penetrated various opaque materials. Major steps in the exploration of radioactivity followed within months of the publication of his paper. In 1896, Henri Becquerel (1852–1908) discovered that uranium emitted a similar form of energy. The next year, J. J. Thomson (1856–1940), at Cambridge University, formulated the theory of the electron, and the interior world of the atom became a new realm for human exploration. In 1902, Ernest Rutherford (1871–1937) explained radiation as the disintegration of atoms of radioactive materials.

Theories of Quantum Energy, Relativity, and Uncertainty   The discovery of radioactivity and discontent with Newtonian mechanical models led to revolutionary theories in physics. In 1900, Max Planck (1858–1947) pioneered the quantum theory of energy, according to which energy is a series of discrete quantities, or packets, rather than a continuous stream. In 1905, Albert Einstein (1879–1955) published his first epoch-making papers on **relativity** in which he contended that time and space form a continuum and that measurement of time and space depends on the observer as well as on the entities being observed. In 1927, Werner Heisenberg (1901–1976) set forth his uncertainty principle. It states that the behavior of subatomic particles can only be inferred by statistical probability rather than observed as an outcome of cause and effect.

The mathematical complexity of 20th-century physics meant that science would rarely again be intelligible to the masses—although it was starting to affect daily life more than ever. Scientists from the late 19th century onward won the financial support of governments and private institutions for their work, and they have altered modern life more significantly than any other intellectuals.

FRIEDRICH NIETZSCHE AND THE REVOLT AGAINST REASON

During the second half of the century, philosophers, such as the German philosopher Friedrich Nietzsche (1844–1900), began to question the adequacy of rational thinking to address the human situation. Nietzsche was wholly at odds with the values of his era. He attacked Christianity, democracy, nationalism, rationality, science, and progress. He was less interested in changing values than in discovering their sources. He wanted to tear away the masks of respectable life and find out how human beings made such masks.

His first important work was *The Birth of Tragedy* (1872) in which he urged that the nonrational aspects of human nature are as important and noble as reason itself. He insisted that instinct and ecstasy had important functions and that to limit humankind to rational behavior was to impoverish human life. In

Marie and Pierre Curie. The Curies were two of the most important figures in the advance of physics and chemistry. Marie was born in Poland in 1869 but worked for most of her life in France. She is credited with the discovery of radium, for which she was awarded the Nobel Prize in 1911.

relativity   Theory of physics, first expounded by Albert Einstein in 1905, in which time and space exist not separately, but rather as a combined continuum.

HISTORY'S VOICES

DARWIN DEFENDS A MECHANISTIC VIEW OF NATURE

In the closing paragraphs of On the Origin of Species *(1859), Charles Darwin contrasted the view of nature he championed with that of his opponents. He argued that an interpretation of organic nature based on mechanistic laws was actually nobler than an interpretation based on divine creation. In the second edition, however, Darwin added the term* Creator *to these paragraphs.*

WHY DOES Darwin believe a mechanistic creation suggests no less dignity than creation by God? How does the insertion of the term Creator change this passage? What is the grandeur that Darwin finds in his view of life?

Authors of the highest eminence seem to be fully satisfied with the view that each species has been independently created. To my mind it accords better with what we know of the laws impressed on matter by the Creator, that the production and extinction of the past and present inhabitants of the world should have been due to secondary causes, like those determining the birth and death of the individual. When I view all beings not as special creations, but as the lineal descendants of some few beings which lived long before the first bed of the Cambrian [geological] system was deposited, they seem to me to become ennobled. . . .

It is interesting to contemplate a tangled bank, clothed with many plants of many kinds, with birds singing on the bushes, with various insects flitting about, and with worms crawling through the damp earth, and to reflect that these elaborately constructed forms, so different from each other, and dependent upon each other in so complex a manner, have all been produced by laws acting around us. These laws, taken in the largest sense, being Growth with Reproduction; Inheritance which is almost implied by reproduction; Variability from the indirect and direct action of the conditions of life, and from use and disuse: a Ratio of Increase so high as to lead to a Struggle for Life, and as a consequence to Natural Selection, entailing Divergence of Character and the Extinction of less-improved forms. Thus, from the war of nature, from famine and death, the most exalted object which we are capable of conceiving, namely the production of the higher animals, directly follows. There is grandeur in this view of life, with its several powers, having been originally breathed by the Creator into a few forms or into one; and that, whilst this planet has gone cycling on according to the fixed law of gravity, from so simple a beginning endless forms most beautiful and most wonderful have been, and are being evolved.

Source: Charles Darwin, *On the Origin of Species and the Descent of Man* (New York: Modern Library, n.d.), pp. 373–374.

Nietzsche's view, the strength to live heroically and achieve great art derived from sources beyond rationality.

In later works, such as the prose poem *Thus Spake Zarathustra* (1883), Nietzsche criticized democracy and Christianity, claiming that they promoted mediocrity and sheepish behavior. He announced the death of God and proclaimed the coming of the *Overman* (Übermensch). The term was frequently interpreted as referring to a superman or superrace, but Nietzsche had in mind the kind of heroism that Homer had described and that had motivated the ancient Greeks. He thought the values of Christianity and of bourgeois morality prevented humankind from realizing its heroic potential.

In two of Nietzsche's most profound works, *Beyond Good and Evil* (1886) and *The Genealogy of Morals* (1887), he sought to uncover the social and psychological sources of judgments of good and evil. He claimed that morality was only a human convention and that when people realized this, they were freed to create new life-affirming values. Christianity and middle-class respectability could be replaced by a new moral order that glorified pride, assertiveness, and strength rather than meekness, humility, and weakness.

THE BIRTH OF PSYCHOANALYSIS

The major figures of late 19th-century science, art, and philosophy shared a determination to probe beneath surface appearances. They sought to discern the undercurrents, tensions, and complexities within atoms, families, rationality, and social relationships. This was particularly true of Sigmund Freud (1856–1939).

Development of Freud's Early Theories   In 1886, Freud, an Austrian Jew, opened a medical practice in Vienna, where he lived until driven out by the Nazis in 1938. His earliest medical interests were psychic disorders. In late 1885, he had studied in Paris with Jean-Martin Charcot (1825–1893), who used hypnosis to treat cases of hysteria.

In the mid-1890s, Freud abandoned hypnosis and began to urge his patients to talk freely and spontaneously about themselves. He found that they associated their particular neurotic symptoms with a chain of experiences going back to childhood. He also noted that sex was significant in his patients' problems. For a time, he thought that perhaps sexual incidents during childhood accounted for their illnesses. But by 1897, he had replaced that idea with a theory of infantile sexuality. He suggested that infants have sexual drives and energy and that these things do not simply emerge at puberty. He thus questioned the concept of childhood innocence and made sexuality one of the bases of mental order and disorder.

Freud's Concern with Dreams   During the same decade, Freud also examined the psychic phenomena of dreams. He believed that the seemingly irrational content of dreams must have a reasonable, scientific explanation. He concluded that dreams allow unconscious wishes, desires, and drives that had been excluded from everyday conscious life to enjoy freer play in the mind. During waking hours, the mind represses or censors certain wishes, which are as important to the individual's psychological makeup as conscious thought is. In fact, Freud argued, unconscious drives and desires contribute to conscious behavior. Freud developed these ideas in his most important book, *The Interpretation of Dreams* (1900).

Freud's Later Thought   In later books and essays, Freud developed a new model of the of the mind as an arena in which three entities struggle: the id, the superego, and the ego. The **id** consists of amoral, irrational, driving instincts for sexual gratification, aggression, and general physical and sensual pleasure. The **superego** embodies the external moral imperatives and expectations imposed on the personality by society and culture. The **ego**, by mediating between the impulses of the id and the standards of the superego, helps the personality cope with the inner and outer demands of its existence.

Freud was a realist who wanted human beings to live free of fear and illusion by rationally understanding themselves and their world. However, he understood the immense sacrifice of instinctual drives required for rational civilized behavior. It is a grave misreading of Freud to see him as urging humankind to thrust off all repression. He believed that excessive repression could lead to mental disorder, but he also believed that civilization and the survival of humankind required some repression of sexuality and aggression. Freud thought the sacrifice and struggle were worthwhile, but he was pessimistic about the future of civilization in the West.

HOW DID Muslim thinkers respond to Western science?

QUICK REVIEW

Islam and the West

- European thinkers applied the same scientific critique to Islam as they did to Christianity and Islam
- European racism shaped attitudes towards Arabs
- Response to Western ideas and technology varied in the Islamic world

ISLAM AND LATE 19TH-CENTURY EUROPEAN THOUGHT

The few late 19th-century European thinkers who wrote about Islam interpreted it, consistent with the contemporary scientific outlook, as a historical phenomenon that, like the other great world religions, was only a product of a particular culture. The influential French writer Ernest Renan (1823–1892) and sociologists such as the German Max Weber, saw Muslim religion and cultures as incapable of developing science and closed to new ideas. Their views, however, were opposed by Jamal al-din Al-Afghani (1839–1897), an Egyptian intellectual, who argued that, given time, Islam (which was, afterall, 600 years younger than Christianity) would eventually produce cultures as modern as those in Europe.

European racial and cultural outlooks that denigrated non-White peoples framed concepts of the Arab world. Christian missionaries reinforced this by blaming Islam for Arab economic backwardness, for mistreating women, and for condoning slavery. Because the penalty for abjuring Islam is death, missionaries made few converts among Muslims. So they turned their efforts to founding schools and hospitals, hoping these Christian foundations would eventually lead some Muslims to Christianity. Few Muslims converted, but these institutions taught young Arabs Western science and medicine, and many of their students became leaders in the Middle East.

Within the Islamic world, political leaders who championed Western scientific education and technology confronted a variety of responses from religious thinkers. Some of these thinkers (the Salafi or the salafiyya movement, for example) believed there was no inherent contradiction between science and Islam. They believed that Muhammad had addressed the issues of his day and that similarly a reformed Islamic faith could modernize itself without imitating the West. This outlook, which had originally sought to reconcile Islam with the modern world, eventually led many Muslims in the 20th century to oppose Western influence.

Other Islamic religious leaders simply rejected the West and modern thought. They included the Mahdist movement in Sudan, the Sanussiya in Libya, and the Wahhabi movement in the Arabian peninsula (see Chapter 27). Religiously based opposition was strongest in those portions of the Middle East where the European presence was least direct—outside of Algeria, Egypt, Morocco, and Tunisia (which for all intents and purposes were under the control of Western powers by 1900), and Turkey, where Ottoman leaders had long been deeply involved with the West.

SUMMARY

Workers   During the course of the 19th century, European workers underwent a process of proletarianization as the process of industrialization spread across the continent. To protect their interests, European workers joined trade unions and socialist parties, such as the Labour Party in Britain. The Marxist critique of modern capitalism strongly influenced European socialism when the German Social Democratic Party adopted the thought of Karl Marx. In Russia, Lenin founded the Bolsheviks as an elite Marxist party that advocated the overthrow of the tsarist regime through a revolution of workers and peasants.

Women   In the 19th century, women were divided along class lines. Unlike working-class women, most women of the upper and middle classes adopted a cult of domesticity and did not work outside the home. Most jobs available to women were low paying and insecure. Women of all classes faced social, political, and legal disabilities that were only gradually improved in the late 19th and early 20th centuries.

Jewish Emancipation With the exception of Russia, European countries had abolished their legal restrictions on Jews by the mid-19th century. After 1880, however, anti-Semitism increased as Jews were blamed for economic and social problems.

The United States By 1914, the United States had become the world's leading industrial power. Despite the creation of a mass industrial work force, socialism did not take root in the United States. The United States also embarked on a more aggressive foreign policy.

Modern European Thought By the first decades of the 20th century, philosophers, scientists, psychologists, and artists began to portray physical reality, human nature, and society in ways that seem familiar to us today. Physicists probed the mysteries of the atom. Theories of evolutionary biology contended that human nature is part of the order of nature, traditional morality and the primacy of reason were challenged by Nietzsche and Freud. Within the Islamic world, modern European thought produced a variety of often conflicting responses.

REVIEW QUESTIONS

1. What accounts for the proletarianization of the European labor force?

2. How did industrialization affect working-class women? What were the social factors that limited the opportunities of women?

3. How did the ideas of Karl Marx come to dominate so much late 19th-century European socialism? Why did socialism not emerge as a major political force in the United States?

4. What caused the rise of trade unions and mass political parties?

5. Why were the debates of "opportunism" and "revisionism" important to the socialist parties? Why were there so many disputes among Socialists?

6. What were the major changes in science in the late 19th century?

IMAGE KEY
for pages 618–619

a. A Bull Moose Party campaign button.

b. Women laundry workers in the late 19th century, as painted by Edgar Degas (1834–1917).

c. *A Sunday on La Grande Jatte–1884*, by George Seurat (1859–1891).

d. Workmen repairing a sewer of London.

e. A crowd of Italian socialists depicted by Giuseppe Pellizza da Volpedo, *Il Quatro Stato*, 1901.

f. The Great Railroad Strike of 1877.

g. Jean Juares.

h. Textile production.

i. Factories spewing smoke over the English landscape.

j. Women working as operators at a telephone exchange.

KEY TERMS

Bolsheviks (p. 638)
Duma (p. 639)
ego (p. 649)
Fabians (p. 636)
id (p. 649)

Marxism (p. 635)
Mensheviks (p. 638)
natural selection (p. 646)
pogroms (p. 631)
proletarianization (p. 621)

relativity (p. 647)
revisionism (p. 636)
soviets (p. 639)
suffragettes (p. 630)
superego (p. 649)

 For additional study resources for this chapter, go to:
www.prenhall.com/craig/chapter25

26 Latin America from Independence to the 1940s

LEAL INTERPRETE DE LOS "DESCAMISADOS"

CHAPTER HIGHLIGHTS

Economic Dependence   In the 1820s, Latin America threw off Spanish and Portuguese rule. But the traditional elites remained in control. A series of strongmen called *caudillos* dominated most Latin American republics. Nor did independence bring economic prosperity. Because Latin American economies remained dependent on producing agricultural commodities for export, foreign nations dominated Latin American economic life. When commodity prices collapsed during the Great Depression, Latin American economies were devastated.

Argentina   After independence, Buenos Aires came to dominate Argentina economically and politically. Agricultural exports, the growth of industry, and large-scale European immigration contributed to a strong export economy. However, urban social discontent and the growth of nationalism in the 1930s led to military intervention in politics and the dictatorship of Juan Perón from 1946 to 1956.

Mexico   In the first decades after independence, Mexico was politically and economically unstable. Mexico lost half its territory to the United States, and it was invaded by France in the 1860s. The long-lasting dictatorship of Porfirio Díaz brought political stability but led to increasing discontent. The Mexican Revolution that began in 1911 produced cautious social and economic reform under the one-party rule of the PRI, the Institutional Revolutionary Party, which remained in power until the end of the century.

Brazil   Brazil was a stable constitutional monarchy after independence until 1889. It also retained slavery until 1888. The establishment of a republic did not change Brazil's economic dependence on coffee exports, however, and the collapse of coffee prices in 1929 led to the dictatorship of Getulio Vargas. Although politically repressive, Vargas instituted social reforms and promoted industrial development, which continued to expand in the decade after his death in 1954.

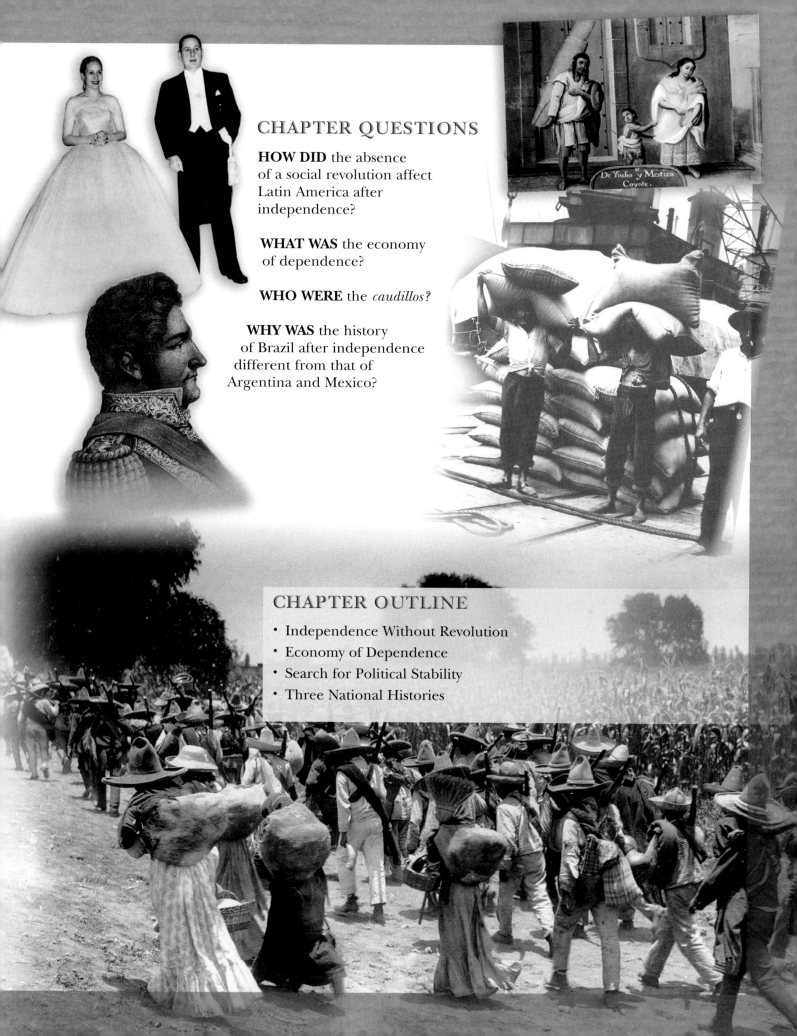

CHAPTER QUESTIONS

HOW DID the absence of a social revolution affect Latin America after independence?

WHAT WAS the economy of dependence?

WHO WERE the *caudillos?*

WHY WAS the history of Brazil after independence different from that of Argentina and Mexico?

CHAPTER OUTLINE

- Independence Without Revolution
- Economy of Dependence
- Search for Political Stability
- Three National Histories

By the mid-1820s, Latin Americans had driven out their colonial rulers and broken the colonial trade monopolies. Although rich in natural resources, the region did not achieve widespread prosperity and political stability for more than a century after independence.

The explanations for why Latin America has been less stable and prosperous than Europe and North America lie in the role it played in the integrated global economic system that began to develop when it achieved political independence. This system prevented Latin Americans from achieving economic independence. The region's leaders thought their nations could prosper by providing raw materials to the world economy. Most Latin American nations developed export economies devoted to raw materials or semifinished goods. This decision made their export products vulnerable to worldwide fluctuations in demand. They were also susceptible to influence from foreign business interests and interference by U.S. and European governments.

Latin America had much in common with Africa and Asia during the 19th and early 20th centuries. In all three regions, areas would specialize by filling a niche to supply a particular raw product to the increasingly integrated world economy. While this economic strategy might bring initial prosperity, it provided too narrow a base for sustained economic well-being. In contrast, the economic advance of the United States and Europe was largely due to their ability to dominate and exploit niche economies around the globe.

INDEPENDENCE WITHOUT REVOLUTION

IMMEDIATE CONSEQUENCES OF LATIN AMERICAN INDEPENDENCE

HOW DID the absence of a social revolution affect Latin America after independence?

The wars of independence liberated Latin America from direct European control but left it economically exhausted and politically unstable (see Map 26–1). Only Brazil tended to prosper immediately after independence. In contrast, the new republics of the former Spanish Empire felt themselves vulnerable. Because the wars of independence had been civil wars, the new governments realized that many of their populations might welcome their collapse. Economic life contracted: In 1830, overall production was lower than in 1800. Rugged terrain over vast distances made interregional trade difficult. The old patterns of overseas trade had been disrupted. There was an absence of funds for investment. Many wealthy *peninsulares* departed. Consequently, Latin American governments and businesses looked to Britain for protection, markets, and investment.

Independence also created new sources of discontent. There was much disagreement about the character of the future government. Institutions, such as the Roman Catholic Church, sought to maintain their privileges. Indian communities found themselves subject to new exploitation. Quarrels arose between the **Creole** elites of different regions of the new nations. The agricultural hinterlands resented the predominance of the port cities. Investors or merchants from one Latin American nation found themselves in conflict with those of others over tariffs or mining regulations. Civilians became rivals of the military.

ABSENCE OF SOCIAL CHANGE

Yet all the elites opposed social reform. The Creole victors in the wars of independence granted equal rights to all persons and, except for Brazil, had abolished slavery by 1855. However, the right to vote depended on a property qualification, and peasants remained subservient to their landlords. Colonial racial codes disappeared, but not racial prejudice. Persons of white or nearly white complexion tended to constitute the elite of Latin America. Most important, there were no major changes in landholding; the ruling classes protected the interests of landholders.

Creole A person of European descent born in Latin America or the Caribbean.

MAP 26–1

Latin America In 1830. By 1830 most of Latin America had been liberated from Europe. This map shows the initial borders of the states of the region with the dates of their independence. The United Provinces of La Plata formed the nucleus of what later became Argentina.

HOW DID Brazil become a monarchy after independence?

Except for Mexico in 1910, no Latin American nation until the 1950s experienced a revolution that overthrew the social and economic structures dating from the colonial period. The absence of such social revolution is perhaps the most important factor in Latin American history during the first century of independence. The rise and fall of political regimes represented quarrels among the elite. Everyday life for most of the population did not change. Throughout the social structure, there was no mutual trust or allegiance to the political system.

CONTROL OF THE LAND

Most Latin Americans during the 19th century lived in the countryside. Agriculture was dominated by large *haciendas*, or plantations. The landowners ruled these estates as small domains. The *latifundia* (the large rural estates) grew larger during the 19th century from confiscated church lands and conquered Indian territories. Work was labor intensive because little machinery was available. For some products—salted meats, for example—there was a limited manufacturing stage in Latin America. Most crops, including grains, tobacco, sugar, coffee, and cacao, were exported.

Landowners constituted a society of their own. They sometimes formed family alliances with the wealthy urban classes who were involved in export commerce or the law. Younger sons might enter the army or the church. Landowners served in the national parliaments. Their wealth, literacy, and social connections made them the rulers of the countryside, and the army would protect them from any social uprising.

The rural work force was socially and economically dependent on the landowners. In Brazil, slavery persisted until 1888. In other rural areas, many people lived as virtual slaves. **Debt peonage** was widespread and often tied a peasant to the land like a serf. Later in the 19th century, the new lands that were opened were generally organized as large holdings with tenants rather than as small land holdings with independent farmers. This was different from both the United States and Canada. Poor transportation made internal travel difficult and kept many people on the land. Little effort was made to provide education, leaving Latin American peasants ignorant, lacking technological skills, and incapable of improving their condition.

The second half of the 19th century witnessed a remarkable growth in Latin American urban life. There was some movement from the countryside to the city and an influx of European and even Asian immigrants. Throughout this period there arose a political and social trade-off between the urban and rural elites. Each permitted the other to pursue its economic self-interest and repress discontent. Nonetheless, the growth of the urban centers shifted political influence to the cities and gave rise to an urban working class and the social discontents associated with many poor people working in difficult situations. Urban growth in Latin America created difficulties not unlike those that arose in Europe and the United States at about the same time.

SUBMISSIVE POLITICAL PHILOSOPHIES

The political philosophies embraced by the Creole elites also discouraged challenges to the social order. The political ideas associated with European liberalism, which flourished in Latin America after independence, supported republican government but limited the franchise to property holders. Thus in Latin America, as in Europe, liberalism protected property and tended to ignore the social problems of the poor. The Creole elite also exhibited racial prejudice toward non-Whites.

debt peonage System that forces agricultural laborers (peons) to work and live on large estates until they repaid their debts to the estate's owner.

Economic liberalism and the need for British investment led to free trade. After independence, Latin America exported less than it had under colonial rule and achieved a trade balance only by exporting precious metals. The general economic view was that Latin America would produce raw materials for export in exchange for manufactured goods imported from Europe, especially from Britain.

For most of the 19th century, the landed sector of the economy dominated because cheap imports and a shortage of local capital discouraged indigenous industrialism. Latin American liberals championed the great landed estates and the social dependence associated with them. The produce of the new land could contribute export goods to pay for the import of finished goods. Liberals thus favored confiscating land owned by the church and the Indians, because they did not exploit their lands in a progressive manner, according to the liberals.

During the second half of the century, **positivism**, the ideas of French philosopher Auguste Comte (1798–1857), swept across Latin America. Comte and his followers had advocated the cult of technological progress. This undemocratic outlook suggested that either technocrats or authoritarians could best achieve modernization. It was popular among military officers and influenced the ongoing Latin American struggle between civilian and military elites. The great slogan of Latin American positivism, emblazoned on the flag of the Brazilian republic, was "Order and Progress." Groups that challenged the existing social order were viewed as unprogressive.

Toward the close of the century, the officer corps was often the most important educated elite in a country. Their education and attachment to the army gave them influence, generally conservative.

Finally, European theories of "scientific" racism were used to preserve the Latin American social status quo. Racial theory could attribute the economic backwardness of the region to its vast non-white or mixed-blood population. This explanation shifted responsibility for the economic difficulties of Latin America away from the mostly white governing elites toward Indians, blacks, **mestizos**, and **mulattos**, who had long been exploited or repressed.

This conservative intellectual heritage affected 20th-century political thought. First, it can be seen in the tendency of military groups in Latin America to view themselves as the guarantors of order. They were ready to seize control from civilians to thwart social change. Second, it can be seen in the way the political elites of Latin America opposed communism after the Russian Revolution. Governments used the fear of communism to resist political movements—communist or not—that advocated social reform or questioned property arrangements. Communism would become an even more powerful issue after the Cuban Revolution of 1957 installed a communist state in Latin America.

A Chilean Cattle Estate. The great landowners of Latin America ruled their huge estates as small domains.

Sergio Larrain/Magnum Photos Inc.

positivism Philosophy of Auguste Comte that science is the final, or positive, stage of human intellectual development because it involves exact descriptions of phenomena, without recourse to unobservable operative principles, such as gods or spirits.

mestizos Persons of mixed Native American and European descent.

mulattos Persons of mixed African and European descent.

ECONOMY OF DEPENDENCE

*T*he wars of independence destroyed the colonial trade monopolies. But Latin America remained dependent on non-Latin American economies. Trade was free and the nations were independent, but other nations continued to shape Latin American economic life.

One of the chief reasons for this dependence was the absence of large internal markets. Trade after independence flowed in the same direction that it had flowed before independence because Europe remained the source of imports of finished goods. Furthermore, then as now, geographical barriers

WHAT WAS the economy of dependence?

hindered internal trade, and European and American investments in railways facilitated exports.

NEW EXPLOITATION OF RESOURCES

The wars of independence disrupted the Latin American economy. Mines were flooded; machinery was in disrepair; labor was dispersed. Agricultural production was also disrupted. To restore old industries such as mining, and gain access to steamships and railroads, Latin Americans had to turn to Europe and North America. For decades, Britain economically dominated Latin America. The desire to pour manufactured goods into Latin America led Britain and other nations to discourage the development of manufacturing industries there.

To pay for foreign imports, Latin American nations produced agricultural commodities. Production for the export market led governments to expand into unsettled territory and to confiscate the lands of the church.

After 1850, the Latin American republics became relatively more prosperous. Chile exported copper and nitrates as well as wheat. Peru exported guano for fertilizer. Coffee was becoming king in Venezuela, Brazil, Colombia, and Central America. Sugar continued to be produced in the West Indies and Cuba, which remained under Spanish control. Argentina supplied hides and tallow. But this limited prosperity was based on the export of agricultural commodities or raw materials and the importation of finished goods. Yet the export economy seemed to foster genuine economic growth.

Both the trading patterns for these goods and internal improvements in Latin American production linked the economy of the region to Europe and, after 1900, to the United States. Europeans and North Americans provided capital and the technological skills to build bridges, roads, railroads, steam lines, and mines. But whenever the economy of Europe or the United States floundered, Latin America was hurt. The region could not control its own economic destiny.

INCREASED FOREIGN OWNERSHIP AND INFLUENCE

During the late 19th century, the relative prosperity of the export sector increased the degree of dependence. The growing European demand gave Latin Americans a false sense of security. The vast profits to be made through mining and agricultural exports discouraged investment in local industry. Foreigners saw no reason to capitalize local industry that might replace imported goods. By late in the century, the wealthy in Latin America had, in effect, lost control of valuable sectors of their economy. For example, in 1901 British and other foreign investors owned approximately 80 percent of the Chilean nitrate industry.

Foreign powers also used their political and military influence to protect their economic interests. Britain, as the dominant power until the turn of the century, was frequently involved in the political affairs of the Latin American nations. From the Spanish-American War of 1898 onward, the United States began

20.7
Francisco Garcia
Calderón, "The North
American Peril"

Brazilian Coffee. This photograph shows Brazilian coffee being loaded onto a British ship. Most Latin American countries developed an export economy based on the exchange of agricultural products, raw materials, and semifinished goods for finished goods and services from abroad. Until recently, the coffee industry dominated both the political and economic life of Brazil.
Corbis-Bettmann.

to exercise more direct influence in the region. In 1903, to facilitate its plans to build a canal across Panama, the United States participated in the rebellion that allowed Panama to separate from Colombia. The U.S. military intervened in the Caribbean and Central America. By the 1920s, the United States had replaced Britain as the dominant trading partner of Latin America.

U.S. interventions were one cost of Latin America's dependent economy. More significant costs, however, arose from fundamental shifts in world trade that were brought on by World War I and continued through the 1920s. First, the amount of trade carried on by European countries decreased. Second, during the 1920s, world prices of agricultural commodities dropped. Latin American nations had to produce more goods to pay for their imports. Third, synthetic products manufactured in Europe or North America replaced the natural products supplied by Latin America. Finally, petroleum began to replace other natural products as an absolute percentage of world trade. This shift meant that petroleum-exporting countries, such as Mexico, gained a greater share of export income.

ECONOMIC CRISES AND NEW DIRECTIONS

The Great Depression produced a crisis in this **neocolonial economy**. Commodity prices collapsed. The republics of Latin America could not repay their debts to foreign banks. The Depression led to the beginning of a new economic era in Latin America after the conclusion of World War II. It was marked by economic nationalism and a determination to create national economies that were not wholly dependent on foreign events and wealth.

With the Depression, it became necessary to substitute domestic manufactured goods for those imported from abroad. Various nations pursued policies called **import substitution**, and by the mid-1940s there were three varieties of manufacturing in Latin America. First, there were industries that, as in the past, transformed raw materials for export, such as food processing, mining, and petroleum refining. Second, there were industries addressing local demands, such as power plants and machine shops. Third, there were industries, basically assembly plants, that transformed imported materials to take advantage of cheap labor. None of this manufacturing involved heavy industry.

SEARCH FOR POLITICAL STABILITY

*T*he new states of independent Latin America had no experience in self-government. The Spanish Empire had been ruled directly by the monarchy and by Spanish-born bureaucrats. This monarchical or paternalistic heritage survived in the proclivity of the Latin American political elites to tolerate or support strong executives. The early republic constitutions were frequently suspended or rewritten, so that a strong leader could consolidate his power. Such figures were called *caudillos*. They usually came from the officer corps or enjoyed strong ties to the army. The real basis of their rule was force. Caudillos might support conservative causes, such as protection of the church or

United States and Latin America. U.S. influence and investments in Latin America grew rapidly after 1900 and surpassed those of Britain by the 1920s. As this cartoon illustrates, the United States tended to regard its southern neighbors as at best junior and dependent partners.

Corbis-Bettmann.

neocolonial economy
Economic relationship between a former colonial state and countries with more developed economies in which the former colony exports raw materials to and imports manufactured goods from the more developed nations.

import substitution
Replacement of imported goods with those manufactured domestically.

WHO WERE the *caudillos?*

caudillo Latin American strongman, or dictator, usually with close ties to the military.

strong central government, or they might pursue liberal policies, such as the confiscation of church land, the extension of landed estates, and the development of education.

Even when caudillos were forced from office and parliamentary government was restored, the regimes that replaced them were neither genuinely liberal nor democratic. Parliamentary governments usually ruled by courtesy of the military and in the interest of the elites. No matter who ruled, the lives of most of the population changed little. Except for the Mexican Revolution of 1910, Latin American politics was run by and for the elite.

THREE NATIONAL HISTORIES

WHY WAS the history of Brazil after independence different from that of Argentina and Mexico?

rgentina, Mexico, and Brazil possess more than 50 percent of the land, people, and wealth of the region. Their histories illustrate the general themes of Latin American history.

ARGENTINA

Argentine history from independence to World War II can be divided into three eras. From the rebellion against Spain in 1810 until mid-century, the question of which region of the nation would be dominant was foremost. From 1853 until 1916, Argentina experienced economic expansion and large-scale immigration from Europe, which transformed its society and its world position. From 1916 to 1943, Argentines failed to establish a democratic state and struggled with an economy they did not control.

Buenos Aires versus the Provinces   In 1810, the junta in Buenos Aires overturned Spanish government. However, the other regions of the viceroyalty of Río de la Plata refused to accept its leadership. Paraguay, Uruguay, and Bolivia went their separate ways. Conflicts between Buenos Aires and the remaining provinces dominated the first 70 years of Argentine history. Eventually, Buenos Aires established its primacy because it dominated trade on the Río de la Plata.

A commercial treaty in 1823 established Great Britain as a dominant trading partner. Thus began a deep intermeshing of trade and finance between the two nations that would continue for more than a century. In 1831, the caudillo of the province of Buenos Aires, Juan Manuel de Rosas (1793–1877), negotiated the Pact of the Littoral, whereby Buenos Aires was put in charge of foreign relations and trade while the other provinces ran their own internal affairs. Within Buenos Aires, Rosas set up dictatorial rule. His major policies were expansion of trade and agriculture, suppression of the Indians, and nationalism.

Expansion and Growth of the Republic   Rosas's success in strengthening Buenos Aires bred resentment in other provinces. In 1852, Rosas was overthrown. The next year a federal constitution was promulgated for the Argentine Republic, but Buenos Aires remained economically and politically dominant.

The Argentine economy was agricultural, the chief exports at mid-century being animal products. Internal

Argentina

1810	Junta in Buenos Aires overthrows Spanish government
1827–1852	Era of Rosas's dictatorial government
1876	Ship refrigeration makes possible export of beef around the world
1879–1880	Conquest of the Desert against the Indian population
1914–1918	Argentina remains neutral in World War I
1930s	Period of strong influence of nationalist military
1943–1956	Era of Juan and Eva Perón

transportation was poor and the country was sparsely populated. Technological advances changed this situation during the last quarter of the century. In 1876, the first refrigerator ship steamed into Buenos Aires. Henceforth, it would be possible to transport Argentine beef to Europe. Furthermore, it became clear that wheat could be farmed throughout the pampas. In 1879 and 1880, the army carried out a major campaign against the Indian population. The British soon began to construct and manage railways to carry wheat to the coast, where it would be loaded on British and other foreign steamships. Government policy made the purchase of land by wealthy Argentines simple and cheap. The owners, in turn, rented the land to tenants. The predominance both of large landowners and of foreign business interests thus continued throughout the most significant economic transformation in Argentine history.

The vastly increased production of beef and wheat made Argentina one of the wealthiest nations of Latin America and an agricultural rival of the United States. The opening of land, even if only for tenant farming and not ownership, encouraged many Europeans, particularly from Spain and Italy, to emigrate to Argentina. The immigrants also provided workers for the food-processing, service, and transportation industries in Buenos Aires. By 1900, Argentina had become much more urbanized and industrialized. More people had reason to be politically discontent. Moreover, the children of the immigrants often became the strongest Argentine nationalists during the 20th century.

Prosperity quieted political opposition for a time. The conservative landed oligarchy governed under presidents who perpetuated a strong export economy. Like similar groups elsewhere, they ignored the social questions raised by urbanization and industrialization.

However, the urban middle and professional classes wanted a greater share in political life and an end to corruption. In 1890, these groups founded the Radical Party. Its leader, Hipólito Irigoyen (1850–1933), was elected president in 1916. Without significant support in the legislature, his presidency brought few changes. In World War I, Argentina traded with both sides. Nonetheless, the war put pressure on the economy, and labor agitation resulted. Irigoyen used troops against strikers. Thereafter, the Radical Party pursued policies that benefited landowners and urban business interests. This was possible because of the close relationship between agricultural producers and processors and because both the landed and the middle classes resisted concessions to the working classes.

The Military in Ascendence   By the end of the 1920s, the Radical Party had become corrupt and directionless. The worldwide commodity depression hurt exports. In 1930, the military staged a coup. The officers returned power to conservative civilians, and Argentina remained dependent on the British export market.

In the 1930s, a right-wing nationalistic movement, *nacionalismo*, arose among writers, journalists, and a few politicians. It resembled the fascist political movements then active in Europe. Its supporters equated British and American domination of the economy with imperialism. They rejected liberalism, detested communism, were anti-Semitic, and supported the Roman Catholic Church. Nacionalismo advocated social reforms that recognized the needs of workers and the poor, but that also sought to promote social harmony rather than communist revolution or socialist reconstruction of the economy. In effect, these groups were anti-imperialistic, socially concerned, authoritarian, and sympathetic to the

nacionalismo Right-wing Argentine nationalist movement that arose in the 1930s and resembled European fascism.

Eva and Juan Perón. Eva was as influential as her husband during his years in power in the late 1940s and early 1950s. She was especially effective in attracting popular support for his government. They are shown here in a reception line in 1951.

Corbis-Bettmann.

Perónism Authoritarian, nationalist movement founded in Argentina in the 1940s by the dictator Juan Perón.

La Reforma The 19th-century Mexican liberal reform movement that opposed Santa Ana's dictatorship and sought to foster economic progress, civilian rule, and political stability. It was strongly anticlerical.

rule of a modern caudillo. World War II gave these attitudes and their supporters new influence.

The war closed most of Europe to Argentine exports, creating an economic crisis. In 1943, the military again seized control. Many of the officers were fiercely nationalistic children of immigrants. Some had become impressed by the fascist and Nazi movements and were hostile to Britain. They contended that the government must address social questions, industrialize the country, and liberate it from foreign economic control. In these respects, they echoed the *nacionalistas*.

Between 1943 and 1946, Juan Perón (1895–1974), one of the colonels involved in the 1943 coup, forged this social discontent and authoritarianism into a political movement known as **Perónism**. It was authoritarian, anticommunist, and socially progressive. Perón understood that political power could be exerted by appeals to the Argentine working class. He gained the support of the trade unions that were opposed to communism. In 1946, he made himself the voice of working-class democracy, even though he created an authoritarian regime that only marginally addressed industrial problems. He was aided by his wife, the former actress Eva Duarte (1919–1952), who enjoyed charismatic support among the working class.

Perón was the supreme 20th-century embodiment of the caudillo. His power and appeal were rooted in the antiliberal attitudes that had been fostered by the corruption and aimlessness of Argentine politics during the Depression. He was ousted in 1956, but stability would continue to elude Argentine politics.

MEXICO

For the first century of Mexican independence, conservative forces held sway, but in 1910, the Mexican people launched the most far-reaching revolution in Latin American history.

Turmoil Follows Independence   The years from 1820 to 1876 were a time of turmoil, economic floundering, and humiliation. Independent Mexico attempted no liberal political experiments. Its first ruler was Agustín de Iturbide (1783–1824), who ruled until 1823 as an emperor. Thereafter, Mexico was governed by a succession of caudillo presidents, who depended on the army for support. The strongest of these figures was Antonio López de Santa Anna (1795–1863), a general and political opportunist who was finally exiled in 1855.

The mid-century movement against Santa Anna's autocracy was called *La Reforma*. In theory, its supporters were liberal, but Mexican liberalism was associated with anticlericalism, confiscation of church lands, and opposition to military influence on national life and politics. La Reforma aimed to produce political stability and civilian rule and attract foreign capital and immigrants. Its attack on the church led to further civil war. In January 1861, Benito Juárez (1806–1872) entered Mexico City as the temporary victor.

Political instability was matched by economic stagnation. The mines that had produced Mexico's colonial wealth were in poor condition, and the country could not repair them. The hacienda system left farming in a backward condition. Cheap imports of manufactured goods stifled domestic industries. Transportation was primitive. The government's remedy was massive foreign borrowing; as a result, interest payments consumed the national budget.

Foreign Intervention   Political weakness and economic disarray invited foreign intervention. The territorial ambitions of the United States led to war with Mexico in 1846 and the U. S. Army occupation of Mexico City. Mexico lost a vast portion of its territory, including what is now New Mexico, Arizona, and California.

Further foreign intervention occurred as a result of Juárez's liberal victory in 1861. Mexican conservatives and clerics invited the Austrian Archduke Maximilian (1832–1867) to become the emperor of Mexico. Napoleon III (r. 1852–1870) of France, who portrayed himself as a defender of the Roman Catholic Church, provided support for this venture. In May 1862, French troops invaded Mexico. Maximilian became emperor, but was unable to gain support from much of the population. In 1867, Juárez captured the unhappy emperor and executed him.

Díaz and Dictatorship   The liberal leaders continued their measures against the church but also failed to rally popular support. In 1876, Porfirio Díaz (1830–1915), a liberal general, seized power and retained it until 1911. He maintained one of the most successful dictatorships in Latin American history by giving almost every political sector something it wanted. He allowed landowners to purchase public land cheaply; he cultivated the army; and he made peace with the church. He used repression against opponents and bribery to cement the loyalty of his supporters. Wealthy Mexicans grew even richer, and Mexico became a respectable member of the international financial community. Foreign capital, especially from the United States, flooded the nation.

Yet problems remained. The peasants wanted land. Many Mexicans were malnourished. Labor unrest afflicted the textile and mining industries. Real wages for the working class declined. The Panic of 1907 in the United States disrupted the Mexican economy. By 1910, the *Pax Porfiriana* was unravelling.

Revolution   In 1911, Francisco Madero (d. 1913), a wealthy landowner and moderate liberal, led an insurrection that drove Díaz into exile. Shortly thereafter, Madero was elected president. He recognized the right of unions to strike, but was unwilling to undertake agrarian reform that might have changed the pattern of landholding. More radical leaders called for social change. Pancho Villa (1874–1923) in the north and Emiliano Zapata (1879–1919) in the south rallied mass followings of peasants who demanded fundamental changes in rural landholding. In late 1911,

Benito Juarez.   Juarez led *La Reforma*, a mid-19th-century movement opposed to the autocracy of Santa Anna. He is portrayed with the tools of an engineer in front of a background of railway building to suggest his dedication to economic progress and modernization in Mexico.

Portrait of Benito Juarez. Oil on canvas, 1941. Presidential collection of portraits of Mexican Presidents. Corbis-Bettmann.

Mexico

1820–1823	Agustín de Iturbide rules as emperor
1833–1855	Santa Anna dominates Mexican political scene
1846–1848	Mexico defeated by United States and loses considerable territory
1861	Victory of liberal forces under Juárez
1862–1867	French troops led by Archduke Maximilian of Austria invade Mexico
1876–1911	Era of Porfirio Díaz
1911	Beginning of Mexican Revolution Zapata proclaims Plan of Ayala
1917	Forces of Carranza proclaim constitution
1929	Institutional Revolutionary Party (PRI) organized

The Mexican Revolution. The forces of Emiliano Zapata march on Xochimilco in 1914. Women fought alongside men and played other prominent roles during the Mexican Revolution.

UPI/Corbis-Bettman.

Zapata proclaimed his Plan of Ayala, which set forth a program of large-scale peasant confiscation of land. Much of the struggle during the next 10 years would be between supporters and opponents of such agrarian reform. (See Document: Emiliano Zapata Issues the Plan of Ayala.)

Madero was squeezed between conservatives and the radical peasant revolutionaries. No one trusted him. In early 1913, he was overthrown by General Victoriano Huerta (1854–1916), who had help from the United States. In the meantime, Venustiano Carranza (1859–1920), a wealthy landowner, put himself at the head of a large army that initially received the support of both Zapata and Villa. On August 15, 1914, Carranza's forces entered Mexico City. Thereafter, disputes between Carranza, Villa, and Zapata arose both from political rivalry and from Carranza's refusal to embrace radical agrarian reform. Carranza eventually won out.

Carranza's political skills helped him build a broad base and edge out Villa and Zapata as the chief leader of the revolution. He separated the concerns of urban industrial workers from the land hunger of rural peasants, and thus doomed the effort to implement an agrarian revolution.

In early 1915, Carranza's army attacked Villa and Zapata. The peasant leaders still commanded regional support but could not win control of the nation. During 1916, Carranza confronted U.S. military intervention along the border that continued until early 1917, when the United States became

HISTORY'S VOICES

EMILIANO ZAPATA ISSUES THE PLAN OF AYALA

By November 1911, the Díaz regime had fallen in Mexico, and Francisco Madero was attempting to establish a moderately liberal government. He was confronted by a major popular peasant revolution led in the valley of Morelos by Emiliano Zapata. On November 28, the rebel leader set forth his opposition to Madero and announced sweeping goals of land reform. Zapata never took dominant control of the Mexican Revolution, but the radical economic demands of his Plan of Ayala would influence the course of Mexican social development for the next 30 years.

WHY DID Zapata place so much emphasis on collective ownership of natural resources? What is Zapata's vision of future economic life? Who would be the winners and losers from his proposed policies?

. . . be it known: that the lands, woods, and water usurped by the *hacendados* [great landowners] . . . henceforth belong to the towns or citizens in possession of the deeds concerning these properties of which they were despoiled through the devious action of our oppressors. The possession of said properties shall be kept at all costs, arms in hand. The usurpers who think they have right to said goods may state their claims before special tribunals to be established upon the triumph of the Revolution.

. . . the immense majority of Mexico's villages and citizens own only the ground on which they stand. They suffer the horrors of poverty without being able to better their social status in any respect, or without being able to dedicate themselves to industry or agriculture due to the fact that the lands, woods, and water are monopolized by a few. For this reason, through prior compensation, one-third of such monopolies will be expropriated from their powerful owners in order that the villages and citizens of Mexico may obtain *ejidos* [agricultural communities], colonies, town sites, and rural properties for sowing or tilling, and in order that the welfare and prosperity of the Mexican people will be promoted in every way.

The property of those *hacendados* . . . who directly or indirectly oppose the present plan shall be nationalized, and two-thirds of their remaining property shall be designated for war indemnities—pensions for the widows and orphans of the victims that succumb in the struggle for this plan.

Source: James W. Wilkie and Albert L. Michaels, eds., *Revolution in Mexico: Years of Upheaval, 1910–1940.* Copyright © 1969 by Alfred A. Knopf, p. 46.

involved in World War I in Europe. Throughout the turmoil in Mexico, the U.S. government attempted to protect American interests through diplomacy and military intervention.

By 1917, after years of civil war, Carranza's forces wrote a constitution. Although the Constitution of 1917 set forth a program for ongoing social revolution—and political reform, it was never pursued with vigor. Years would pass before all the provisions of the constitution could be enforced, but it provided the goals and ideals toward which Mexican governments were expected to strive.

Carranza and his subordinates recognized the agrarian problem but were cautious about addressing it. They admired the economic development they had seen in California and were determined to modernize Mexican political life and attract capital investment; Mexican leaders would share these goals from that time onward. Thus, despite the radical rhetoric and the upheaval among peasants that the revolution involved, the Mexican revolution saw the victory of a middle-class elite who would attempt to govern through enlightened paternalism.

The decade after 1917 witnessed both confusion and consolidation. In 1919, Zapata was killed. Carranza was assassinated in 1920; Villa in 1923. In this turmoil, Carranza's generals provided stability. During the 1920s, they served as presidents. They moved cautiously and hesitated to press land redistribution but were opposed by the Roman Catholic Church. In 1929, Plutarco Elías Calles (1877–1945) organized the **PRI**, the Institutional Revolutionary Party, which remained in power for the rest of the century.

In 1934, Lázaro Cárdenas (1895–1970) was elected president and moved to fulfill the promises of 1917. He turned tens of millions of acres of land over to peasant villages and nationalized the oil industry.

With the election of Manuel Ávila Camacho (1897–1955) in 1940, the era of revolutionary politics ended. Thereafter, the major issues in Mexico were those associated with postwar economic development. But unlike other Latin American nations, Mexico, because of its revolution, could confront those issues with a democratic perspective and a sense of social responsibility.

BRAZIL

Postcolonial Brazil differed from other newly independent nations in the region. Its language and heritage were Portuguese, not Spanish. For the first 67 years of its independence, it had a stable monarchical government. And it retained slavery until 1888.

Brazil became an independent empire in 1822. The first emperor, Pedro I (r. 1822–1831), while serving as regent for his father, the king of Portugal, had put himself at the head of the independence movement. Although he granted Brazil a constitution in 1823, Pedro's high-handed rule led to his abdication in 1831. Brazilians then took hold of their own destinies.

His 15-year-old son, Pedro II (r. 1831–1889), assumed power in 1840 and governed Brazil until 1889. Pedro II established a reputation as a constitutional monarch by asking leaders of both the conservative and the liberal political parties to form ministries. Consequently, Brazil enjoyed political stability.

The Slavery Issue   The great divisive issue in Brazil was slavery. Sugar production remained the mainstay of the economy until the 1850s, when coffee cultivation began to dominate Brazilian agriculture. Like sugar planters, coffee producers also used slave labor, but their profits were much larger than those of the sugar producers, so a transition to free labor would have been easier for them. Coffee planters also tended to see themselves as economic progressives. Hence, people investing in coffee were more open to emancipation than those who had invested in sugar, which depended on slave labor to be profitable.

By 1850, Brazil had virtually ceased importing slaves. The end of slave imports doomed the institution of slavery because the slave population could not reproduce itself. It was nonetheless one issue to face this inevitability and another to abolish slavery.

The Paraguayan War of 1865–1870 postponed consideration of the slave question. This conflict pitted Brazil, Argentina, and Uruguay against Paraguay. The dictator of Paraguay, Francisco Solano López (1827–1870), fought a war

PRI   The Institutional Revolutionary Party, which emerged from the Mexican revolution of 1911 and governed Mexico until the end of the 20th century.

Antislavery Print. Slavery lasted longer in Brazil than in any other nation in North or South America. Antislavery groups circulated prints such as this one published in France to illustrate the brutality of slave life in Brazil.

The Granger Collection, N.Y.

of attrition. His death in battle ended the war, but only after more than half of the adult male population of Paraguay had been killed.

The end of the war returned slavery to the forefront of Brazilian politics. Brazil and the Spanish colonies of Puerto Rico and Cuba were now the only slaveholding countries in the hemisphere. The emperor favored gradual emancipation. A law in 1871 freed slaves owned by the crown and decreed legal freedom for future children of slaves, but it required them to work on plantations until the age of 21. However, throughout the 1870s and 1880s, the abolition movement grew in Brazil. In 1888, Pedro II was in Europe and his daughter was regent. She favored abolition and signed a law abolishing slavery without compensation to the slave owners. Thus ended slavery in Brazil.

A Republic Replaces Monarchy The law that abolished slavery also brought to a head other issues that in 1889 ended the monarchy. Planters who received no financial compensation for their slaves were resentful. Roman Catholic clerics were disaffected by disputes with the emperor over education. Pedro II was unwell; his daughter, the heir to the throne, was unpopular. The officer corps of the army wanted more political influence. In November 1889, the army sent Pedro II into exile.

The Brazilian republic lasted from 1891 to 1930. Like the monarchy, it was dominated by a small group of wealthy persons. The political arrangement that allowed the republic to function smoothly was an agreement among the state governors. The president was to be chosen alternately from the states of São Paulo and Minas Gerais. In turn, the other 18 governors had local political control. Fixed elections and patronage kept the system going. Literacy tests left few people qualified to vote. There was little organized opposition.

From the 1890s onward, the coffee industry dominated the nation. Around 1900, Brazil was producing more than three-fourths of the world's coffee. The crop's success led to overproduction. To meet this problem, the government subsidized prices with loans from foreign banks and taxes on the rest of the economy, which felt exploited by the coffee interests. Throughout the life of the republic, Brazil produced essentially a single product for export and few goods for internal consumption.

Economic Problems and Military Coups The end of slavery, the expansion of coffee production, and the beginning of urban industry attracted foreign immigrants. They tended to settle in the cities and constituted the core of the early industrial labor force. In Brazil, as elsewhere, World War I caused major economic disruption. Urban labor discontent appeared. The failure to address urban and industrial social problems and the political corruption led to attempted military coups. The revolts demonstrated that segments of the military wanted a modern nation that was not dependent on a single exportable product and a political system that recognized interests besides those of the coffee planters.

Brazil

1822	Brazil becomes an independent empire
1840	Pedro II assumes personal rule
1840s and 1850s	Spread of coffee cultivation
1865–1870	Paraguayan War
1871	First law curbing slavery
1888	Slavery abolished
1889	Fall of the monarchy
1929	Collapse of coffee prices
1930–1945	Vargas Era
1957	Construction of Brasília begins
1964	Military takes control of the government

QUICK REVIEW

The Brazilian Republic
- 1889: Pedro III sent into exile
- Brazilian republic (1891–1930) controlled by small group of wealthy persons
- Coffee production dominated the Brazilian economy

Coffee had ruled as the economic "king" of the Brazilian republic, and its collapse brought the republic down with it. In 1929, coffee prices hit record lows, and the economic structure of the republic lay in shambles. In October 1930, a military coup installed Getulio Vargas (1883–1954) in the presidency. Vargas governed Brazil until 1945.

The Vargas years represent a major turning point in Brazilian history. Vargas was initially supported by the reform elements in the military, middle-class groups, and urban workers. In office, he was a pragmatist who wanted to hold on to power and modernize Brazil. Vargas recognized the new social and economic groups shaping Brazilian political life. First with constitutionalism and then with dictatorship, he attempted to allow the government to act on behalf of those groups without allowing them to influence or direct the government in a democratic manner. However, he did not form his own political party or movement as Perón would later do in Argentina. Vargas rather attempted to function like a ringmaster directing the various forces in Brazilian life. His failure to establish a genuinely stable institutional political framework for a Brazil that included many interest groups besides the coffee planters still influences Brazil.

Vargas and his supporters sought to lessen dependence on coffee by fostering industries that would produce domestically goods that had previously been imported from abroad. The policy succeeded, and by the mid-1930s, domestic manufacturing was increasing. Vargas also established a legal framework for labor relations that included an eight-hour work day and a minimum wage.

In the Brazilian context, these measures appeared reformist, if not necessarily liberal. However, in the late 1930s, Vargas confronted major political opposition and assumed dictatorial power in 1937. His regime thereafter was repressive. He claimed to have established an *Estado Novo* ("new state"). He presented himself as the protector of national stability against factions that would foster instability and of the national interest against international opponents.

Like the European dictators of the same era, Vargas used censorship, secret police, and torture. He also diversified and modernized the economy. In 1940, a five-year plan provided more state direction for the economy. His government favored the production of goods from heavy industry that would be used in Brazil itself. To maintain the support of trade unions, the state issued a progressive labor code. Siding with the Allies in World War II, Brazil built up large reserves of foreign currency through the export of foodstuffs. This economic activity and imposed political stability allowed the government to secure foreign loans for further economic development. By the end of the war, Brazil was becoming the major Latin American industrial power.

Participation in World War II on the side of the Allies had led many in Brazil to believe that they should not remain under a dictatorship. This attitude was widespread in the military, which had fought in Europe and established close contact with the United States. In 1945, the military carried out a coup, and Vargas retired temporarily from political life.

The new regime, which was democratic, continued the policy of economic development through foreign-financed industrialization. When in 1950 Vargas was elected president, his return to office was anticlimactic. He was elderly and past his prime. When a member of his staff became involved in the assassination of a journalist, the military demanded that Vargas resign. Instead, he took his own life in 1954.

In the decade after Vargas's death, Brazil remained a democracy, although an unstable one. The government began to undertake vast projects such as the

Estado Novo "New state" based on political stability and economic and social progress supposedly established by the dictator Getulio Vargas after 1937.

OVERVIEW   LATIN AMERICA'S DEPENDENT ECONOMY

After independence, most Latin American nations relied on export economies that sold raw materials or semifinished goods, such as animal hides and leather, to the world's economy. Most manufactured goods were imported, primarily from Britain. This created a dependent economy in which Latin American prosperity depended on other nations to pay high prices for its raw materials. What made this dependence even more precarious was that most Latin American nations relied on one or two products for their export earnings. When prices for these products fell or collapsed, as they did during the Great Depression of the 1930s, Latin America had little else to trade, and its prosperity plummeted. The table below shows the main products of the principal Latin American countries between the 1820s and 1930.

Argentina	animal products (meat, leather, wool), grain
Bolivia	tin, silver
Brazil	coffee, sugar, rubber
Chile	copper
Colombia	coffee, cattle
Ecuador	bananas
Mexico	silver, cattle, oil
Peru	nitrates, silver
Uruguay	animal products (meat, leather)
Venezuela	coffee, cattle

costly construction of the new capital of Brasília, begun in 1957. The rapid growth of cities and the expansion of a working class radicalized political life. The political system could not readily accommodate itself to the concerns of workers and the urban poor. Poverty and illiteracy plagued both the cities and the countryside.

By the early 1960s, when President João Goulert (1918–1977) took office, Brazilian political life was in turmoil. Goulert's predecessors, including Vargas, had attempted to balance interests and political forces. However, Goulert committed himself to the left. In 1964, he announced his support for land reform, which was anathema to conservatives. Goulert also questioned the authority of the military hierarchy. In March 1964, the military, claiming to protect Brazil from communism, seized control of the government, ending its post–World War II experiment with democracy.

SUMMARY

Economic Dependence In the 1820s, Latin America threw off Spanish and Portuguese rule. But the traditional elites—landowners, military officers, the church—remained in control. A series of strongmen called caudillos dominated most Latin American republics. Nor did independence bring economic prosperity. Because Latin American economies remained dependent on producing agricultural commodities for export, foreign nations, particularly

IMAGE KEY

for pages 652–653

a. A Mexican felt hat.

b. Eva Perón

c. Coffee beans.

d. *Orgy-Night of the Rich*, 1926, by Diego Rivera.

e. El Toro, a black bull.

f. Juan and Eva Perón in 1951.

g. *De Indio y Mestiza Nace Coyote*; South American painting.

h. General Juan Manuel de Rosas.

i. Porters carrying bags of coffee beans.

j. Mexico's civil war leader Emiliano Zapata's forces are seen here marching to Xochimico.

Britain, dominated Latin American economic life. When commodity prices collapsed during the Great Depression, Latin American economies were devastated. The crisis did, however, lead to the beginnings of manufacturing in many Latin American countries in an effort to avoid dependence on imports.

Argentina After independence, Buenos Aires came to dominate Argentina economically and politically. Agricultural exports, the growth of industry, and large-scale European immigration contributed to a strong export economy. However, urban social discontent and the growth of nationalism in the 1930s led to military intervention in politics and the corporatist dictatorship of Juan Perón from 1946 to 1956.

Mexico In the first decades after independence, Mexico was politically and economically unstable. Mexico lost half its territory to the United States and was invaded by France in the 1860s. The long-lasting dictatorship of Porfirio Díaz brought political stability but led to increasing discontent. The Mexican Revolution that began in 1911 produced cautious social and economic reform under the one-party rule of the PRI, the Institutional Revolutionary Party.

Brazil Brazil was a stable constitutional monarchy after independence until 1889. It also retained slavery until 1888. The establishment of a republic did not change Brazil's economic dependence on coffee exports, however, and the collapse of coffee prices in 1929 led to the dictatorship of Getulio Vargas. Although politically repressive, Vargas instituted social reforms and promoted industrial development.

REVIEW QUESTIONS

1. What was the condition of the Latin American economies after independence? What role did their economies play in the worldwide economy that developed in the 19th century?

2. Did the structure of Latin American societies change after independence? What role did the traditional elites play in the economic and political life of their nations? What was the condition of the mass of the population?

3. How did European and U.S. investments affect Latin America?

4. Why did Latin American nations find it difficult to develop stable regimes? What role did the military play?

5. How did European immigration affect Argentina? Why was Juan Perón able to hold power?

6. How did the Vargas regime change the Brazilian economy? Why did Brazilian democracy end in a military coup in 1964?

KEY TERMS

caudillo (p. 659)

Creole (p. 654)

debt peonage (p. 656)

Estado Novo (p. 668)

import substitution (p. 659)

La Reforma (p. 662)

mestizos (p. 657)

mulattos (p. 657)

nacionalismo (p. 661)

neo-colonial economy (p. 659)

Perónism (p. 662)

positivism (p. 657)

PRI (p. 666)

 For additional study resources for this chapter, go to:
www.prenhall.com/craig/chapter26

27 India, the Islamic Heartlands, and Africa
The Challenge of Modernity (1800–1945)

CHAPTER HIGHLIGHTS

Western Encroachment The century and a half following the French Revolution was a bleak one for the Indian subcontinent, Africa, and the Islamic societies. For centuries there had been a rough balance among the major cultural regions of the world. Suddenly, over the span of 150 years, Europe came to dominate the globe.

The Middle East, Africa, Iran, Central Asia, India, and Indonesia-Malaysia, along with Central and South America—what is today referred to as "the Third World" of "developing nations"—were most drastically affected by European imperialism and colonialism. Regardless of indigenous developments in these regions, the decisive development of this era was unprecedented domination by the west.

Reactions of Native Peoples The vitality of so many of the cultures and traditions that bore the brunt of the Western onslaught has been striking. Arab, Iranian, Indian, African, and other encounters with Western material and intellectual domination produced different responses and initiatives. These have borne full fruit in political, economic, and intellectual independence only since 1945; however, most began much earlier, some even well before 1800. The imperial-colonial experiences of the Third World nations may well prove to have been not only ones of misery and reversal, but also of transition to positive development and resurgence, despite the looming economic, educational, and demographic problems that plague many of them.

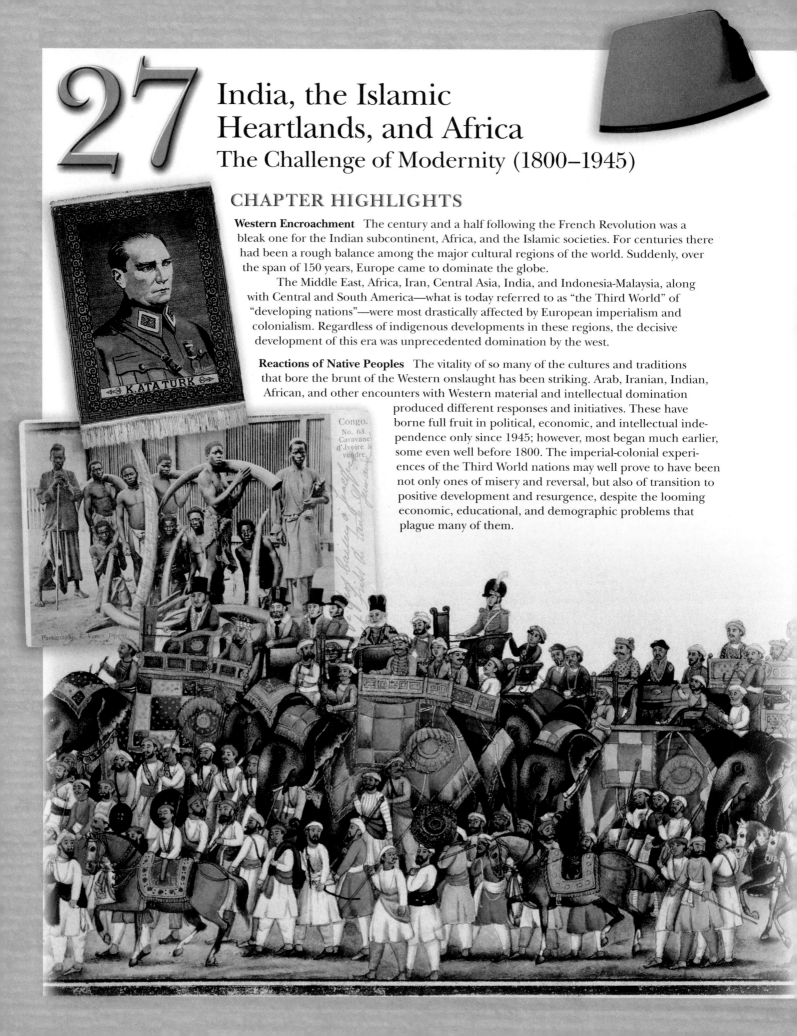

K. ATATURK

Congo.
No. 63.
Caravane
d'Ivoire à
vendre.

CHAPTER QUESTIONS

HOW DID British rule affect India?

WHAT ROLE did Gandhi play in ending British rule in India?

WHY DID Islamic reform movements arise during the eighteenth century?

WHAT WERE the three typical Islamic reactions to Western encroachment?

WHAT WERE the main Islamic reform movements in nineteenth-century Africa?

HOW DID Africans react to European colonialism?

CHAPTER OUTLINE

THE INDIAN EXPERIENCE

- British Dominance and Colonial Rule
- From the Raj to Independence

THE ISLAMIC EXPERIENCE

- Islamic Responses to Declining Power and Independence
- Western Political and Economic Encroachment
- The Western Impact
- Islamic Responses to Foreign Encroachment

THE AFRICAN EXPERIENCE

- New States and Power Centers
- Islamic Reform Movements
- Increasing European Involvement
- African Resistance to Colonialism: The Rise of Nationalism

The encroachment of the European nations on the rest of the world from the late 15th century onward brought radical changes. In the West itself, spiritual and material disruption accompanied the Renaissance, the Reformation, the Enlightenment, and the Industrial and Scientific revolutions. The effects of these watershed European developments on the Indian, Asian, and African worlds came more rapidly, in greater concentration, and with less preparation than they had in the West.

To call these complex processes of "modernization" does not reflect the acute differences between the relatively lengthy and gradual processes of change in Western Europe and the more rapid and disruptive changes that European imperialism and colonialism brought to other parts of the world. The very concept of "modernity" has been appropriated by the West. Western dominance has led it to a specific and novel notion of modernity: namely, as a special set of ideas and institutions that evolved in Europe between the Renaissance and the early 20th century and was then gradually exported to, or imposed on, other societies. The expression "__the impact of modernity__" refers to how the introduction of "modern" Western civilization affected traditional cultures.

The consequences of the spread of Western culture have been so massive that today non-Western peoples are often merely its passive recipients. The American or European view of the world often portrays the West as the active, creative, dominant force in recent history, as though the rest of the world were some monolithic, archaic entity.

As parochial as such chauvinistic generalizations are, the impingement of the West has been a major element in the recent history of African, Asian, and Indian civilizations. Yet in all of these "Third World" areas, Western modernity entered cultures that had ancient and highly developed traditions of their own. These traditions did not simply melt away on the arrival of the Westerners. Rather, a profound transformation took place that sought to balance the challenges of modernity with tradition.

impact of modernity Effect of western political, economic, and social ideas and institutions on traditional societies.

HOW DID British rule affect India?

THE INDIAN EXPERIENCE

BRITISH DOMINANCE AND COLONIAL RULE

*I*n the 18th century, Britain became the dominant naval and commercial power in the southern seas. In India by the early 19th century, the British had built the largest European colonial empire in the Afro-Asian world. India was the "jewel in the crown" of that empire.

BUILDING THE EMPIRE: THE FIRST HALF OF THE 19TH CENTURY

It was no simple undertaking for Britain to penetrate multiethnic, multilingual, multiconfessional India. To do so, the British had to convince various stratas of Indian society and various ethnic groups that cooperation with Britain's imperial enterprise was in their best interests.

A half century before the British Crown asserted direct rule over India in 1858, the British wielded effective imperial control through the East India Company. Those areas not annexed were recognized as independent princely states. They retained their status only so long as they remained faithful to Britain. The India that resulted was a polyglot mixture of tributary states and provinces that the British administered directly.

The economic impact of company rule was extensive. The need for ever higher revenues squeezed peasants. In addition, demand for Indian indigo, cotton, and opium in the China and British trade also decreased in the 1830s, and famines brought widespread suffering.

Company rule also affected the physical face of India. Company policies encouraged settled agriculture and small commodity production at the expense of the nomadic and pastoralist cultures of North and central India. British "pacification" involved the clearing of land to deny natural cover to military enemies and the often-forced settlement of peasants in new regions. Early in the 19th century, European loggers caused extensive deforestation as, after 1840, did the tracts leveled for tea and coffee plantations in Assam and the Bengal hills. This ecological destruction was part of the transformation of India into a more homogeneous peasant farming society that provided a better base for colonial administration.

The Indians were by no means passive in the face of this exploitation. The first half of the 19th century saw almost constant revolt in one place or another. The revolts included peasant movements of noncooperation, Muslim farm workers' attacks on British and Hindu estate owners, grain riots, tribal revolts, and other actions. They culminated in the Indian Revolt of 1857.

The immediate trigger of the Indian Revolt was the concern among Bengal troops that animal grease on newly issued rifles exposed them to ritual pollution, a violation of the rules of their religion. Behind this issue, however, lay other grievances, including the addition of Sikhs, Gurkhas, and lower-caste soldiers to the army; deteriorating economic conditions; outrage at excessive tax rates; and anger at the 1856 British annexation of the princely state of Awadh. Another contributing factor to the revolt was the desire to rebuild a pre-British political order in North India. The revolt was not an all-India affair. It centered on Delhi, where the last Mughal emperor joined in the rebel cause.

The British eventually won the day. With their forces augmented by Sikhs from the Panjab and Gurkhas from Bengal, they overcame the divided Indian opposition. By the end of 1857, the revolt was broken, often with great brutality. In 1858, the East India Company was dissolved, and India came under direct rule of the British Crown.

The "Mutiny" of 1857 was not a nationalist revolution, but a series of antiforeigner, anti-British spontaneous uprisings. Still, it highlighted resentment of the burdens of foreign domination that were to grow increasingly oppressive for Indians of all regions and religions during the ensuing 90 years of crown rule, known as the **raj**.

BRITISH–INDIAN RELATIONS

The overall impact of British presence on the Indian masses was brutal but impersonal and largely economic. India was effectively integrated into Britain's economy, becoming a market for British goods, providing Britain with raw materials and other products, and helping Britain maintain a healthy balance of trade.

British cultural imperialism was never a major nor even an official policy of the East India Company. Nonetheless, the British–Indian relationship had a paternalistic and patronizing dimension, both before and after the events of 1857. The ethos of the British rulers included the understanding that they had the task of governing an inferior "race" that could not handle the job by itself. Even Indians whose university degrees or army training were impeccable by British standards were never accepted as equals. From army to civil-service ranks, the upper echelon of command was British.

Despite this unequal relationship, British ideas influenced a small but powerful Indian elite in both their business and political life and their manners and

20.4
Lord William Bentinck, Comments on Ritual Murder and the Limits of Religious Toleration

raj The years from 1858 to 1947 during which India was governed directly by the British Crown.

The Indian Mutiny of 1857. The mutinous Sepoy cavalry attacking a British infantry division at the 1857 battle of Cawpore. Although the uprising was suppressed, it was not easily forgotten. In its aftermath the British reorganized the government of India.

The Granger Collection, New York.

customs. Conversion to Christianity was rare, but Christian and secular values associated with the European Enlightenment influenced Hindu and Muslim educated classes.

In the 19th century, probably the most influential member of the Indian elite to engage the British on their own ground was Ram Mohan Roy (1772–1833). Roy, a Bengali Hindu, rose to the top of the native ranks of East India Company service and became a strong voice for reform, both of Hindu life and of British colonial policy. Roy was a modernist who wanted to meld the best of European-Christian morality and thought with the best of Hindu piety and thought. He opposed autocratic and unfair British legal and commercial practices and campaigned in India and England to reform the company's India policies. He studied the Christian scriptures and the great thinkers of European civilization and drew on these sources in his Hindu reform efforts. His public campaigns for education, political involvement, and social progress against the "backward" practices and ideas of many of his Hindu compatriots alienated most of the leading Hindu thinkers of his age, but 20th-century Indians have often seen him as a visionary.

While many Indians sought to acquire British ways and join the British in business and administration, many more resented their subordinate status. The antiimperial sentiment that blossomed into the nationalist movement at the end of the 19th century extended to the grass-roots level—among tribal groups, peasant farmers, and workers. Whatever their status, the distrust and animosity most Indians felt continued to grow.

FROM THE RAJ TO INDEPENDENCE

THE BURDEN OF CROWN RULE

The Revolt of 1857 had numerous consequences beyond the transfer of the administration of India to the British Crown. The bloody conflict exacerbated mutual fear and hatred. Before the revolt, the British had maintained a largely native army under British officers. After the revolt, they tried to maintain a ratio of at least one British to three Indian soldiers. The army was financed by Indian, not British, revenues. This imposed a huge economic burden on India, diverting one third of its annual revenues to pay for its own occupation.

British economic policies and accelerating population growth put great strains on India's poor. Cheap British goods were exchanged for Indian raw materials and the products of its home industries, harming Indian craft industries and forcing multitudes into poverty or onto the land. Industrialization, which might have provided work for India's unemployed masses, was avoided. Finally, many peasants lost their hereditary lands because of other British policies, forcing thousands to emigrate to Britain's dominions in South Africa, where they worked as indentured servants.

The Revolt of 1857 also created a poisonous distrust of Indians within the British colonial administration. **Cantonments** segregating White masters from natives became the rule in Indian cities. Despite the intentions expressed in royal statements and the opening of the civil service to Indian candidates, at least nominally, the raj discouraged equality between Indian and Britisher.

INDIAN RESISTANCE

Indians soon took up political activism. Late in the 19th century, they founded the institutions that would help overcome regionalism, build national feeling, and end colonial rule. In 1885, Indian modernists formed the Indian National Congress. The Muslim league developed as a counterbalance to the Hindu-dominated Congress. The league ultimately worked for, and gained, a separate independent Muslim state, Pakistan. Erratic British policies strengthened the desire for independence.

Besides the British themselves, Indian internal divisions were the major obstacle to independence. These divisions included the many language groups and subject princely states of the subcontinent. These, however, were not even the most critical divisions. For much of British rule, every Indian politician was first a representative of his own region or state and second an Indian nationalist. Furthermore, the Indian elite had little in common with the masses beyond antagonism to foreign rule, making unified resistance difficult. Conflict among Hindus, Muslims, Sikhs, and Jains also impeded concerted political action.

Yet a nationalist movement took root. Three principal elements within the independence movement led to the creation of India and Pakistan in 1947.

WHAT ROLE did Gandhi play in ending British rule in India?

27.2
Gandhi and Nehru: "Two Utterly Different Standpoints": Jawaharal Nehru

cantonments Segregation of areas in which Europeans lived in British-ruled India from those areas inhabited by native Indians.

Faces of the Raj. A tennis party at the Residency, Kapurkala, Punjab, ca. 1894.

Hulton/Corbis-Bettman.

India

1772–1833	Ram Mohan Roy, Hindu reformer
1857–1858	Indian Revolt of 1857, followed by direct crown rule as a British colony
1885	Indian National Congress formed
1869–1948	Mohandas K. Gandhi
1873–1938	Muhammad Iqbal
1876–1949	Muhammad Ali Jinnah
1889–1964	Jawaharlal Nehru
1947	Independence and partition

"Mahatma" Mohandas K. Gandhi. Also known as the "Great Soul," Gandhi is honored as the father of the modern state of India.

UPI/Corbis-Corbis-Bettmann.

The first element consisted of those in the National Congress who sought gradual reform and progress toward Indian self-governance, or *svarāj*. This position did not preclude opposition to the British, but it did mean trying to change the system from within. Among the proponents of this approach were the spiritual and political genius Mohandas K. Gandhi (1869–1948) and his follower Jawaharlal Nehru (1889–1964). Nehru became the first prime minister of India. Gandhi was the principal Indian leader after World War I and directed the all-India drive that finally forced out the British. An English-trained lawyer, Gandhi drew not only on his own Hindu (and Jain and Buddhist) heritage, but also on the ideas of Western liberal and Christian thinkers. In the end, Gandhi became a world figure.

The second element consisted of the militant Hindu nationalists, whose leader, the extremist B. G. Tilak (1856–1920), stressed the use of Indian languages and a revival of Hindu culture and learning. Tilak also subscribed to an anti-Muslim, Hindu communalist vision of Indian self-governance. The Hindu extremists looked to a return to traditional Indian values and self-sufficiency. Their ideas still influence Indian political life, as the resurgence of Hindu extremist groups in recent years and communal strife, especially with Muslims, are unhappy testimony.

Muslims made up the third element. The subcontinent held many divergent regional and sectarian Muslim constituencies. Their leaders could be brought to make common cause only by the fear that, as a minority, Muslims stood to lose what power they had in a Hindu-majority, all-India state. Muslims had been slower than the Hindus to take up British ideas and education and thus lagged behind the Hindu intelligentsia in numbers and influence with the British or other Indians.

HINDU–MUSLIM FRICTION ON THE ROAD TO INDEPENDENCE

In the 20th century, the rift between Muslims and Hindus in the subcontinent grew wider. In the end, the great Indo-Muslim poet and thinker, Muhammad Iqbal (1873–1938), and the "founder of Pakistan," Muhammad Ali Jinnah (1876–1949), helped move Muslims to separatism.

The independence of India and Pakistan from Western domination was only achieved with violence. Blood was spilled in the long battle with the British, in communal violence between Hindus and Muslims that accompanied partition in 1947, and in the ongoing dispute over Kashmir between India and Pakistan. Still, the victory of 1947 gave the people of the subcontinent, Indians and Pakistanis, at last a sense of participation in the world of nations on their own terms instead of on those dictated by a foreign power. The British left a legacy of unity and egalitarian and democratic ideals that Indian nationalists turned to their own uses.

THE ISLAMIC EXPERIENCE

ISLAMIC RESPONSES TO DECLINING POWER AND INDEPENDENCE

WHY DID Islamic reform movements arise during the 18th century?

*T*he 18th century saw the weakening of the great Muslim empires and the increasing ascendancy of the West. The diverse Islamic peoples and states were thrust into a struggle for survival. The decline of Islamic preeminence was also the result of internal problems.

By the 18th century, the largest Muslim empires had declined from their heydays in the 16th and 17th centuries. They had grown decentralized, were less stable economically and politically, and were increasingly dominated by entrenched hereditary elites. For millennia, the Middle East had prospered by providing the trade link between Europe and Asia, but modern sea routes made the region more peripheral to a world economy centered on Western Europe. The Middle East, however, became enmeshed in the European imperial competition for its industrial resources, particularly oil. As the Western powers asserted dominance over the region, conflict ensured. But Muslim intellectuals also began to study the basis for European ascendancy and to question whether European values, education, and technology could be used to revitalize the Islamic world without totally secularizing it.

During the 18th century, reform movements sought to revive Islam as a comprehensive guide for living and to purify it from the more stultifying developments in Islamic societies during the preceding centuries. In major urban areas, reformers sought to reenginer the armies, institutions and soceities of the Middle East to conform to the reality of European domination. As they sought to adapt to contemporary society, they emphasized the malleability of Islam. However, in rural areas less touched by European influence, reformers rejected the more flexible forms of Islam and Western models.

The most famous of these movements was that of the **Wahhabis**, the followers of Ibn Abd al-Wahhab (1703–1792) in Arabia. It sought to combat excesses of popular and Sufi piety to break the stranglehold of the *ulama*'s conformist interpretations of legal and religious issues. The only authorities were to be the Qur'an and the traditions of the Prophet. Allied with a local Arab prince, Sa'ud, the Wahhabi movement swept much of the Arabian peninsula. It was crushed in the early 19th century by the Ottomans. It finally saw victory under a descendant of Sa'ud at the onset of the 20th century and has become the guiding ideology of Saudi Arabia.

Other Muslim reform movements reflected similar revivalist and even militantly pietist responses to Islamic decadence and decline. This call continues to rally movements from Africa to Indonesia. In Islamic societies everywhere in recent times, it has provided a response to the challenge of Western-style "modernity" and a model for cultural and religious life.

The Founding Father of Pakistan. Muhammad Ali Jinnah was the president of India's Muslim League. In the 1930s, he advanced the "two nations" theory and made the first formal demand for a separate Muslim homeland. His ideas led to the establishment of Pakistan.

AP Wide World Photos.

Linking Asia and Europe. The opening of the Suez Canal in 1869 was a major engineering achievement. It also became a major international waterway benefiting all maritime states, reducing the distance from London to Bombay by half.

Index Stock Imagery, Inc.

WHY WAS it easy for Western powers to encroach on the Islamic world during the 19th century?

WESTERN POLITICAL AND ECONOMIC ENCROACHMENT

From the late 1700s until World War II, the political fortunes of Islamic states were increasingly dictated by Western powers. Western governments extracted capitulations favorable to their own interests from indigenous governments in exchange for promises of military protection or other considerations. These capitulations took the form of treaty clauses granting commercial concessions, special protection, and "extraterritorial" legal status to European merchant enclaves. Such concessions had originally been reciprocal and had served the commercial purposes of Muslim rulers and some merchants as well as Western traders. However, they eventually provided Western powers with pretexts for direct intervention in Ottoman, Iranian, Indian, and African affairs. The Ottoman Empire suffered from internal disunity; its provincial rulers, or *pashas,* were virtually independent. This, combined with the economic problems facing all the agrarian societies of Asia and Africa, made it easy for the Western powers—with their industrializing economies and militaries—to take control. Repeated Ottoman diplomatic and military defeats made that once great imperial power "the sick man of Europe" after 1800; similar weaknesses allowed Westerners to control Indian and Iranian states.

Napoleon Bonaparte's (1769–1821) unsuccessful invasion of Egypt in 1798 heralded a new era of European imperialism and colonialism in the region. By this date, the British had already wrested control over India and the Persian Gulf from the French; they now became the preeminent European power in the eastern Mediterranean as well. The Russians presented the most serious 19th-century challenge to Britain's colonial empire. Russia sought to gain as much territory and influence in the Iranian and Central Asian regions as possible. Afghanistan, an independent kingdom established by Ahmad Shah Durrani (r. 1737–1773), acted as a buffer that prevented Russia from penetrating southwestward into British India. In the Iranian and Ottoman regions, however, Russia and Britain—with French involvement—struggled with each other for supremacy. The Crimean War of 1854–1856 (see Chapter 24) was one result of this conflict.

THE WESTERN IMPACT

HOW DID Iran react to the West during the 19th century?

Beyond the overt political and commercial impact of the West, Western political ideology, culture, and technology proved critical factors for change in Islamic societies. Outside of India, this effect was most strongly felt in Egypt, Lebanon, North Africa, and Turkey. The Islamic states least and last affected by Western "modernity" were Iran, Afghanistan, and the Central Asian khanates.

Iran The rulers of Iran from 1794 to 1925 were the Qajar shahs, whose absolutist reign was not unlike that of the Safavids. However, the Qajars did not claim, as had the Safavids, to descent from the Shi'ite *imams.* Under Qajar rule, the *ulama* of the Shi'ite community became less strongly connected with the state apparatus. This period also saw the emergence of a Shi'ite traditionalist doctrine that encouraged all Shi'ites to choose a ***mujtahid***—a qualified scholarly guide— from among the *ulama* and follow his religious/legal interpretations. As a result, the *ulama* were often the chief critics of the government (not least for attempts to admit Western influences) and exponents of the people's grievances.

mujtahid Shi'ite religious-legal scholar.

A demonstration of *ulama* power occurred in 1890 when the Qajar Shah granted a 50-year monopoly on tobacco sales to the British. In 1891, the *ulama* decreed a tobacco boycott to protest the concession. This popular action was supported by modernist-nationalist opponents of the Qajar regime who had strong connections to Iran's commercial, or **bazaari**, middle classes. The Shah was forced to rescind the concession, resulting in a stunning victory for opponents of the spread of Western commercial interests. Ironically, though, it only made Iran more dependent on Western capital. The government was forced to pay exorbitant compensation to British interests, and it incurred its first foreign debt.

Subject as it was to the machinations of outsiders, such as Russia, Britain, and France, Iran felt the impact of Western ideas, especially in the latter half of the century, when younger Iranian intellectuals began to warm to Western liberalism. As in other Islamic countries, the seeds of secular nationalism were being sown where religious sentiments had held sway. It worked with a desire among larger sectors of the populace for a voice in government. An uneasy alliance of Iranian modernists with conservative *ulama* proved, on occasion, an effective counterforce to Qajar absolutism, as in the tobacco boycott and in the early stages of the effort to force the Qajars to accept a constitution in 1906–1911. Yet such alliances did not bridge the inherent ideological divisions of the two groups.

ISLAMIC RESPONSES TO FOREIGN ENCROACHMENT

*A*s the Iranian case shows, Western impingement on the Islamic world in the 19th and 20th centuries elicited varied responses. Every people or state had a different experience. Yet we can point to at least three typical styles of reaction: (1) a tendency to emulate and adopt Western ideas and institutions; (2) the attempt to join Western innovations with traditional Islamic institutions; and (3) a traditionalist rejection of Western influence in favor of either the status quo or return to a purified Islamic community.

EMULATION OF THE WEST

A strategy of emulation is exemplified in the career of the virtually independent Ottoman viceroy Muhammad Ali (ca. 1769–1849), pasha of Egypt from 1805 to 1849. He set out to rejuvenate Egypt's agriculture, to introduce modern industry, to modernize the army with European help, and to introduce European education and culture in government schools. Although he did not bring Egypt to a position of power equal to the European states, and his successors' financial and political catastrophes led the British to occupy Egypt (1882–1922), Muhammad Ali did set his country on the path to becoming a modern national state. Hence he is rightly called "the father of modern Egypt."

Efforts to appropriate Western experience and success were made by several Ottoman sultans and viziers after the defeat of the Turks by Russia in 1774. Most notable were the reforms of Selim III (r. 1762–1808), Mahmud II (r. 1808–1839), and the so-called Tanzimat, or beneficial "legislation" era from about 1839 to 1880. Selim made serious attempts at economic as well as

bazaari Iranian commercial middle class.

WHAT WERE the three typical Islamic reactions to Western encroachment?

Islamic Lands

1703–1792	Ibn Abd al-Wahhab
1737–1773	Rule of Ahmad Shah Durrani, founder of modern Afghanistan
1794–1925	Qajar shahs of Iran
1798	Invasion of Egypt by Napoleon Bonaparte
1805–1849	Rule of Muhammad Ali in Egypt
ca. 1839–1880	Era of the Tanzimat reforms of the Ottoman Empire
1839–1897	Jamal al-Din al-Afghani
1845–1905	Muhammad Abduh
1882–1922	British occupation of Egypt
1908	"Young Turk" revolution
1922–1938	Mustafa Kemal, "Atatürk" in power

Kemal Atatürk. This 1928 photograph shows Atatürk (right) giving instruction in the Latin alphabet. It reflects the personal engagement of Mustafa Kemal in the many reform efforts he instituted.

Historical Pictures Collection/Stock Montage Inc.

administrative and military reform. Mahmud's reforms were much like those of Muhammad Ali. Most important were his destruction of the Janissary corps, his tax and bureaucratic reforms, and his encouragement of Western military and educational methods. Like Muhammad Ali, he was less interested in promoting European enlightenment ideas about citizen rights and equity and more interested in building a stronger, more modern government.

The Tanzimat reforms, introduced by several liberal Ottoman ministers of state, continued the efforts of Selim and Mahmud. They were intended to bring the Ottoman state into line with ideals espoused by the European states, to give European powers less cause to intervene in Ottoman affairs, and to regenerate confidence in the state.

The 19th-century Ottoman reforms failed to save the empire. Nevertheless, they paved the way for the rise of Turkish nationalism, the "Young Turk" revolution of 1908, and the nationalist revolution of the 1920s that produced modern Turkey.

The creation of the Turkish republic out of the ashes of the Ottoman state after World War I is probably the most extreme example of an effort to modernize and nationalize an Islamic state on a Western model. This state was largely the child of Mustafa Kemal (1881–1938), known as "Atatürk" ("father of the Turks"), its first president (1922–1938). Atatürk's major reforms ranged from the introduction of a European-style code of civil law to the abolition of the caliphate, Sufi orders, Arabic script, and the Arabic call to prayer. These changes constituted a radical attempt to secularize an Islamic state and to separate religious from political and social institutions. Nothing quite like it has ever been repeated. Despite some adjustments and even reversals of Atatürk's measures, Turkey has maintained its independence, reaffirmed its commitment to democratic government, and emerged with a unique but still distinctly Islamic identity.

INTEGRATION OF WESTERN AND ISLAMIC IDEAS

The attempt to join modernization with traditional Islamic institutions and ideas is exemplified in the thought of famous Muslim intellectuals, such as Jamal al-Din al-Afghani (1839–1897), and Muhammad Abduh (1845–1905). These thinkers argued for a progressive Islam rather than a materialist Western secularism as the best answer to life in the modern world.

Afghani is best known for his emphasis on the unity of the Islamic world, or **pan-Islamism**, and on a populist, constitutionalist approach to political order.

WOMEN AND REFORM IN THE MIDDLE EAST

Though the discussion of reform, religion, and modernity in the Middle East was dominated by men, some of the region's women raised the issue of woman's role in modern society. Most important were those women who demanded political rights. Some Iranian women confronted their fathers and brothers in the Iranian Parliament in December 1911, concerned that the men might capitulate to the Russian-British demands to remove the American reforming administrator,

pan-Islamism Movement that advocates that the entire Muslim world should form a unified political and cultural entity.

Morgan Schuster. The wives of some Egyptian diplomats, after returning from Paris in 1919, discarded the veil. In 1929, some Palestinian women convened a Women's Congress of Palestine to address the political issues that ensued after the Wailing Wall riots of the same year. In the late 19th and early 20th centuries, a number of journals and magazines devoted to women's concerns appeared. These mainly focused on traditional issues such as cooking, parenting, and fashion, but some stressed that women were an essential part of society and should not be excluded from participation in commerce and politics. The Egyptian Feminist Union was founded in 1923 by Huda Sha'rawi (1879–1947) to fight for women's suffrage, reform of marriage laws, and equal access to education. In a well-publicized gesture, Sha'rawi and her colleague Saize Nabrawi removed their veils in the midst of the crowd at Cairo's train station. For them the veil symbolized the inadequate public status of women in Middle Eastern countries. Many Middle Eastern feminists stress, however, that women's inequality is rooted in wide-ranging cultural, political, and economicial structures that need to be addressed long before the issue of the veil.

PURIFICATION AND REVIVAL OF ISLAM

A third Muslim reaction to Western domination has focused on recourse to Islamic values and ideals to the exclusion of "outside" forces. This approach includes reformist revivalism like Wahhabism and the kind of conservatism often associated with Sunni or Shi'ite "establishment" *ulama*, as in Iran since 1979. The conservative spirit has often been the target of revivalist reformers who see in it the worst legacy of medieval Islam. Still, both conservative and revivalist Muslim thinkers look for answers to the questions facing Muslims in the modern world within, not outside, the Islamic tradition.

NATIONALISM

Nationalism is a product of modern history. Nationalist movements in the Islamic world have been either stimulated by Western models or produced in reaction to Western exploitation and colonial occupation. During the late 19th century, many intellectuals in Asia or Africa grappled with the question of identity and whether their ethnic or linguistic group constituted a distinct nation or whether they were part of a larger whole. The often arbitrary or artificial division of the colonial world by European administrators demanded an answer to this question in Asia and Africa. In the European capitals, new "nations" were drawn on the map to reflect the realities and interests of imperialism rather than the facts on the ground. In due time, these borders took on an aura of legitimacy. However, forging nations from artificial parameters has proven to be a difficult and sometimes violent process.

THE AFRICAN EXPERIENCE

Between 1800 and 1945, virtually every part of Africa changed, but nowhere more than sub-Saharan Africa. With the exception of South Africa below the Transvaal, tropical and southern Africa came under major influence and finally colonial control from outside only after

Southern Africa

ca. 1800–1818	Dingiswayo, Nguni Zulu king, forms new military state
1800–1825	The *mfecane* among the Bantu of southeastern Africa
1795	British take Cape Colony from the Dutch
ca. 1818–1828	Shaka's reign as head of the Nguni state; major warfare, destruction, and expansion
ca. 1825–1870	Sotho kingdom of King Mosheshwe in Lesotho region
1835–1843	Great Trek of Boers into Natal and north onto the high veld beyond the Orange River
1843	British annexation of Natal province
1852–1860	Creation of the Orange Free State and the South African Republic

1880. Before then, internal developments—demographic and power shifts and then the rise of Islamic reform movements—overshadowed the European presence in the continent.

NEW STATES AND POWER CENTERS

SOUTHERN AFRICA

In the south, below the Limpopo River, the first quarter of the 19th century saw devastating internal warfare, depopulation, and forced migrations of many Bantu peoples in what is known as the *mfecane*, or "crushing" era. Likely brought on by a population explosion and economic competition, the mfecane was marked by the rise of military states among the northern Nguni-speaking Bantu. Its result was a period of warfare and chaos; depopulation; and the creation of multitribal, multilingual Bantu states in modern Malawi, Mozambique, Tanzania, Zambia, and Zimbabwe.

The Nguni warrior-king Dingiswayo formed the first of the new military states between about 1800 and 1818. The most important state was formed by his successor, Shaka, leader of the Nguni-speaking Zulu nation and kingdom (ca. 1818–1828). Shaka's brutal military tactics led to the Zulu conquest of a vast dominion in southeastern Africa and the depopulation of some 15,000 square miles. Refugees fled north into Sotho-speaking Bantu territory or south to put increasing pressure on the southern Nguni peoples. Chaos ensued north and south of Zululand and even in the high veld above the Orange River.

The net result was the creation of diverse states. Some people tried to imitate the military state of Shaka; others fled to the mountains; others even went west into the Kalahari. The most famous of these was Lesotho, the Sotho kingdom of King Mosheshwe, which survived as long as he lived (from the 1820s until 1870). Mosheshwe defended his people from the Zulu and held off the Afrikaners, missionaries, and British. After his death, the latter groups became Lesotho's chief predators.

The new state-building spawned by the mfecane was nullified by Boer expansion and British annexation of the Natal province (1843). These developments stemmed from the **Great Trek** of Boer *voortrekers*, which took place between 1835 and 1843. This migration brought about 6,000 Afrikaners from the eastern Cape Colony northeastward into the more fertile regions of southern Africa, Natal, and the high veld above the Orange River. It resulted in the creation after 1850 of two Afrikaner republics: the Orange Free State between the Orange and Vaal Rivers and the South African Republic north of the Vaal.

EAST AND CENTRAL AFRICA

In East and east-central Africa, external trade resulted in the formation of strong states. In the Lakes region, peoples such as the Nyamwezi to the east of Lake Tanganyika and the Baganda west of Lake Victoria gained regional power from as early as the late 18th century through trade with the Arab-Swahili eastern coast and the eastern Congo to the west. This east–west commerce involved slaves; ivory; copper; and, from the outside, Indian cloth, firearms, and manufactured goods.

WEST AFRICA

In West Africa, the slave trade was replaced by European demand for palm oil and gum arabic by the 1820s. In the first half of the century, *jihad* (holy struggle) movements of the Fulbe (or Fulani) and others shattered the stability of the western savannah and forest regions from modern Senegal and Ghana through

---

WHAT NEW states arose in Africa during the early 19th century?

mfecane Period of widespread warfare and chaos among Bantu peoples in east-central Africa during the early 19th century.

Great Trek Migration between 1835 and 1847 of Boer pioneers (called *voortrekkers*) north from British-ruled Cape Colony to establish their own independent republics.

The Kingdom of Lesotho. Mosheshwe, king and founder of Lesotho. Not all of the Bantu peoples followed the militaristic example of Shaka. Mosheshwe, prince of a subtribe of the Sotho Bantus, fought off Zulu attacks and led his people to a mountain stronghold in southern Africa, where, through diplomacy and determination, he founded a small nation that has endured to the present. The kingdom became the British protectorate of Basutoland in 1868. In 1966 it achieved independence as the kingdom of Lesotho under Mosheshwe's great-grandson, King Mosheshwe II.
Courtesy of the Library of Congress.

southern Nigeria. Wars and dislocation resulted in the rise of regional kingdoms, such as those of Asante and Dahomey (modern Benin). These eventually succumbed to internal dissension and the colonial activities of Britain and France later in the century.

ISLAMIC REFORM MOVEMENTS

*T*he vitality of Islam was a significant agent of change in sub-Saharan Africa before the European rush for colonies in the 1880s. It is still a factor. In 1800, Islam was already well established from West Africa across the Sudan to the Red Sea and along the East African coast. Islam was the law of the land in states such as the sultanate of Zanzibar on the eastern coast and the waning Funj sultanate on the Blue Nile in the eastern Sudan. But in many African "Islamic" states, the rural populace were still partly, if not wholly, pagan, and even the urban elites were only nominally Muslim.

The 19th century is notable for the militant Islamic revivalist and reform movements of jihad, which fixed and spread Islam as a lasting part of the African scene. The most important jihad movement was led by a Fulbe Muslim scholar from Hausa territory in the central Sahel. Usman Dan Fodio (1754–1817) was influenced by the reformist ideas that spread throughout the Muslim world in the 18th century. Shortly after 1804, he gathered an army and conquered most of the Hausa lands of northern and central Nigeria, bringing an explicitly Islamic order to the area. Dan Fodio left behind a sultanate centered on the new capital of Sokoto and governed by one of his sons, Muhammad Bello, until 1837. The Fulbe became the ruling class in the Hausa regions, and Islam spread into the countryside, where it still predominates (see "Usman Dan Fodio on Evil and Good Government").

Other 19th-century reform movements had similar success in spreading a revivalist, reformist Islamic message among the masses. Most notable were the Sanusi of Libya and the eastern Sahara (after about 1840) and the Mahdist uprising of the eastern Sudan (1880s and 1890s). The Libyan movement provided the focus for resistance to the Italian invasion of 1911. The Sudanese Muhammad Ahmad (1848–1885) condemned the corruption of basic Muslim ideals and declared himself the awaited deliverer, or Mahdi, in 1881. He led the northern Sudan in rebellion against Ottoman-Egyptian control. His successor governed the Sudan until the British destroyed the young Islamic state in 1899. In the Caucasus, Islamic reform movements merged into resistance against Russian expansion.

INCREASING EUROPEAN INVOLVEMENT

*M*uslim reform movements were not the only important developments in Africa during the 19th century. Another was the growing involvement of Europe, which led to European domination of the continent. Before the mid-1800s, the penetration of White outsiders had been limited largely to coastal areas, although their slave trade had had significant effects inland (see Chapter 17 and Map 27–1). This changed as trading companies, explorers, missionaries, and then colonial troops and governments moved into Africa. Ironically, the elimination of the slave trade (primarily through Britain's efforts) was accompanied by increased European exploration and Christian missionizing, which ushered in imperial and colonial ventures that were to have even more disastrous consequences than slaving.

Challenging Russia. A Muslin separatist movement led by Imam Shamil established an independent state in 1834 that lasted for 25 years in the Caucasus region of Dagestan.

Getty Images Inc. – Hulton Archive Photos.

WHAT WERE the main Islamic reform movements in 19th-century Africa?

WHAT WAS the "scramble for Africa?"

HISTORY'S VOICES

USMAN DAN FODIO ON EVIL AND GOOD GOVERNMENT

Following in the tradition of the Wahhabis in Arabia and virtually all previous Islamic reform movements, Dan Fodio (1754–1817) stressed adherence to Muslim norms as expressed in the Shari'a, the Divine Law. In the two excerpts that follow, he enumerated some of the evils of the previous Hausa rulers and their "law," and then listed five principles of proper Islamic government.

WHAT DOES the first principle of good government, that "authority shall not be given to one who seeks it," mean? What abuses by government listed by Dan Fodio might be most appalling to the average Muslim? Why?

One of the ways of their government [that is, of the Hausa or Habe kings] is succession to the emirate by hereditary right and by force to the exclusion of consultation. And one of the ways of their government is the building of their sovereignty upon three things: the people's persons, their honour, and their possessions; and whomsoever they wish to kill or exile or violate his honour or devour his wealth they do so in pursuit of their lusts, without any right in the Shari'a. One of the ways of their government is their imposing on the people monies not laid down by the Shari'a, being those which they call janghali and kurdin ghari and kurdin salla. One of the ways of their governments is their intentionally eating whatever food they wish, whether it is religiously permitted or forbidden, and wearing whatever clothes they wish, whether religiously permitted or forbidden, and drinking what

beverages [ta'am] they wish, whether religiously permitted or forbidden, and riding whatever riding beasts they wish, whether religiously permitted or forbidden, and taking what women they wish without marriage contract, and living in decorated palaces, whether religiously permitted or forbidden, and spreading soft (decorated) carpets as they wish, whether religiously permitted or forbidden. . . .

And I say—and help is with God—the foundations of government are five things: the first is that authority shall not be given to one who seeks it. The second is the necessity for consultation. The third is the abandoning of harshness. The fourth is justice. The fifth is good works. And as for its ministers, they are four. (The First) is a trustworthy wazir to wake the ruler if he sleeps, to make him see if he is blind, and to remind him if he forgets, and the greatest misfortune for the government and the subjects is that they should be denied honest wazirs. And among the conditions pertaining to the wazir is that he should be steadfast in compassion to the people, and merciful towards them. The second of the ministers of government is a judge whom the blame of a blamer cannot overtake concerning the affairs of God. The third is a chief of police who shall obtain justice for the weak from the strong. The fourth is a tax collector who shall discharge his duties and not oppress the subjects. . . .

From translation of Usman Dan Fodio's *Kitab al-Farq* by M. Hiskett, *Bulletin of the School of Oriental and African Studies*, London, 1960, Part 3, p. 558. Reprinted by permission of Oxford University Press, Oxford, Great Britain.

EXPLORATION

The 19th-century European explorers—mostly English, French, and German—uncovered for Westerners the "secrets" of Africa: sources and courses of the Niger, Nile, Zambezi, and Congo Rivers; natural wonders such as Mount Kilimanjaro and Lake Tanganyika; and fabled places like Timbuktu, the once, great Berber trading gateway and center of Islamic learning. The history of European exploration is one of fortune hunting, self-promotion, violence, and mistakes, but also of patience and perseverance, bravery and dedication.

MAP EXPLORATION

Interactive map: To explore this map further, go to **http://www.prenhall.com/craig/map27.1**

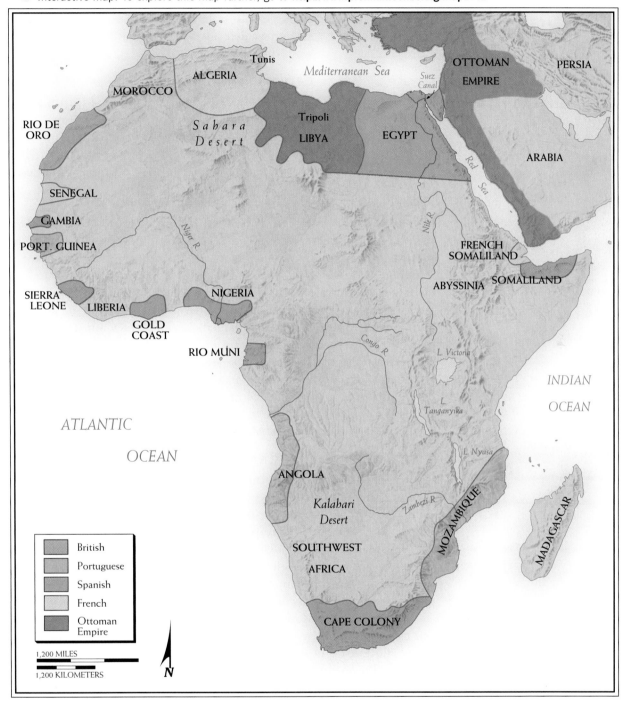

MAP 27–1

Imperial Expansion in Africa up to 1880.   Until the 1880s, only a few European countries held colonies in Africa, mostly on the fringes of the continent. A comparison of this map with Map 27–2 shows how rapidly the situation changed.

WHICH EUROPEAN country held the most African possessions at this time?

Central Africa

1754–1817	Usman Dan Fodio, Fulbe leader of major Islamic jihad
1810	Dan Fodio founds Islamic sultanate in lands of former Hausa states of northern and central Nigeria
1817–1837	Reign at Sokoto of Muhammad Bello, son of Dan Fodio

QUICK REVIEW

Key Factors in "Scramble for Africa"

- Popular and commercial interests in Africa spurred by exploration
- Intra-European competition for power and prestige
- Technological and material superiority of Europe

The explorers stimulated European interest and opened the way for traders, missionaries, and finally soldiers and governors from the Christian West. One of the greatest explorers was Dr. David Livingstone (1813–1873), who was a missionary dedicated to Africa and its peoples as few other Westerners have been.

CHRISTIAN MISSIONS

The late 19th century saw an influx of Christian missionaries, both Protestant and Catholic (by 1900, perhaps as many as 10,000). The missionaries came to know the African peoples far better than did the explorers. Their accounts of Africa contained chauvinistic and misleading descriptions of the "degraded" state of African culture and religion, but they brought real knowledge of and interest in Africa to Europe. Their schools also brought some alphabetic culture and literacy to the African tribal world. Although their settlements, often in remote areas, provided European governments with convenient pretexts for intervention, the missionaries themselves were more often idealists than opportunists. Many who went into the tropical regions succumbed to diseases, such as malaria, yellow fever, and sleeping sickness. If they were often paternalistic and instruments of the imperialism of their home countries, they also sought to provide Africans with medicine and education. Through the ideals of their faith, the missionaries provided Africans—sometimes inadvertently—with a weapon of principle to use against their European exploiters. African Christian churches, for example, played a leading role in resisting apartheid in South Africa, despite White Christian oppression and collusion with racism in that country and elsewhere in Africa (see Chapter 35). The role of Africans in the European domination of Africa was neither simple nor wholly positive.

THE COLONIAL "SCRAMBLE FOR AFRICA"

Before 1850, the only significant European attempts to take African territory were in South Africa and Algeria. In South Africa, as we have noted, the Boers came into conflict with Bantu tribes on their Great Trek. The French invaded Algeria in 1830, settled Europeans on choice farmlands, and waged war on native resistance fighters (1830–1847). Over most of the continent, however, the European presence was felt with real force only from the 1880s. Yet by World War I, all of Africa except Ethiopia and Liberia was divided arbitrarily into a patchwork of European colonial administrations (see Map 27–2).

This takeover was supported by mounting European popular and commercial interests fueled by the publicity given African exploration and missionary work. The European desire for the markets and resources of Africa, together with intra-European competition for power and prestige, pushed one European state after another to lay claim to whatever segments of Africa they could.

This wholesale takeover was made possible by the superior power the West commanded. In particular, European technical expertise opened up the interior of the continent. Except for the Nile and the Niger, the great African rivers have impassible waterfalls near the sea. Steamboats above the falls and railroads around them provided access to the African interior and opened its riches to exploitation.

Britain and France were the colonial vanguards. The British had the largest involvement. On one axis, it ranged from their South African holdings (begun

when they took the Cape Colony from the Dutch in 1795) to their protectorate in Egypt (from 1882). On another axis, it extended from trading interests in West Africa to colonies such as Sierra Leone and Gambia, to protectorate rule, as in the Niger districts after 1885, and to a Zanzibar-based sphere of influence in East Africa.

The British preferred "indirect" to "direct" colonial administration. Their rule was only slightly more enlightened than that of the French, who carved out a colonial empire under their direct control. The French had long had government-supported trading outposts in West Africa. Tunisia and the Ivory Coast became French protectorates in the 1880s; Dahomey was bloodily annexed in 1894; and the colony of French Equatorial Africa was proclaimed in 1910.

Beginning in the mid-1880s, the European powers began to seek mutual agreement to their claims on segments of Africa. Leopold II of Belgium (r. 1865–1909) and Otto von Bismarck (1815–1898) in Germany established their claims to parts of South, Central, and East Africa. France and England set about consolidating their African interests. Italy took African colonial territory in Eritrea, Somaliland, and Libya. But the Italian design on Ethiopia was thwarted when Ethiopia defeated an Italian invasion in 1896. The Italians eventually conquered Ethiopia in 1935. The **"scramble for Africa"** was over by the outbreak of World War I. In the aftermath of the war, Germany lost its African possessions to other colonial powers. Europe's colonies in Africa did not gain independence (see Chapters 33 and 35) until after World War II in the 1950s.

European colonial rule in Africa is one of the uglier chapters of modern history. The paternalistic attitudes of late-19th-century Europe and America amounted to racism when applied in Africa. The regions with large-scale White settlement produced the worst exploitation at

20.6
Rudyard Kipling

scramble for Africa Late 19th-century takeover of most of Africa by European powers.

Colonial Africa

1830	French invasion of Algeria
1890	British protectorate in Zanzibar
ca. 1880	French protectorate in Tunisia and Ivory Coast
1880s–1890s	Mahdist uprising in eastern Sudan
1882	British protectorate in Egypt
1894	French annexation of Dahomey
1910	French colony of Equatorial Africa

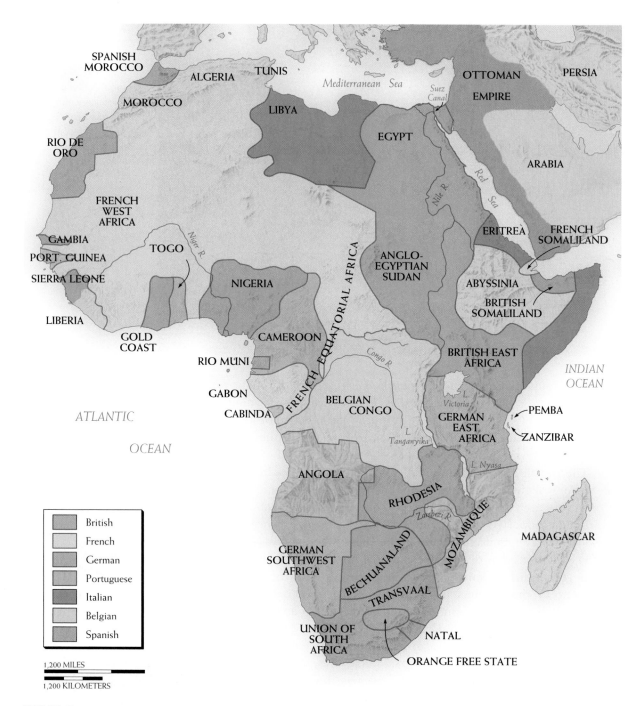

MAP 27–2

Partition of Africa, 1880–1914. By 1914, the only countries in Africa that remained independent were Liberia and Abyssinia (Ethiopia). The occupying powers included most large European states.

COMPARE THIS map to Map 27–1. Which new European countries have entered the "scramble for Africa"?

the expense of vastly greater native populations. The worst legacy of the European presence was the White racist state of modern South Africa, which only ended in 1994. No Western nation can have a clear conscience about its involvement in Africa.

OVERVIEW   COLONIALISM, 1815–1914

Between the end of the Napoleonic Wars and the outbreak of World War I, European powers, the United States, and Japan extended their rule over much of the Near East, Africa, Asia, and the Pacific. The imposition of foreign rule was often the result of conquest, but it also occurred through purchase or the imposition of a "protectorate" in which a local ruler kept his title but ceded real power, especially over foreign affairs, defense, and finances, to colonial advisors or officials. By 1914, except for the Latin American republics, only Liberia and Abyssinia (Ethiopia) in Africa, the Ottoman Empire in the Near East, and Iran, Afghanistan, Thailand, and China had escaped some form of colonial rule. The table below lists the countries and territories that the Western powers and Japan acquired or dominated as protectorates (in which a local ruler keeps his title but cedes real power to a foreign country) between 1815 and 1914. In addition, older possessions, such as British India and the Portuguese colonies of Angola and Mozambique, were also increased during these hundred years.

NEAR EAST AND NORTH AFRICA

Britain	Aden (in Yemen), Bahrain, Cyprus, Egypt, Kuwait, Oman, Qatar, United Emirates
France	Algeria, Morocco, Tunisia
Italy	Libya, Rhodes

AFRICA

Belgium	Congo (Zaire)
Britain	Botswana, Ghana, Kenya, Lesotho, Malawi, Nigeria, Somaliland, Sudan, Swaziland, Uganda, Zambia, Zanzibar, Zimbabwe, Zululand (in South Africa)
France	Benin, Burkina Faso, Central African Republic, Chad, Congo, Djibouti, Ivory Coast, Madagascar, Mali, Mauretania, Niger
Germany	Burundi, Cameroons, Namibia, Rwanda, Tanganyika (Tanzania), Togo
Italy	Eritrea, Somalia

ASIA

Britain	Brunei, Hong Kong, Malaysia, Myanmar (Burma), Nepal, Papua, Singapore
France	Cambodia, Laos, Vietnam
Germany	New Guiana, Tientsin (in China)
Japan	Korea, Okinawa, Taiwan
Netherlands	Acheh
Russia	Amur Territories (from China), Central Asia, Chechnya
United States	Philippines

PACIFIC

Britain	Fiji, Tonga, Solomons
France	New Caledonia, Tahiti
Germany	Carolines, Marianas
United States	Guam, Hawaii, Midway, Wake

Mutesa of Bugand and His Court. Noted for his cunning and diplomatic skill and for his autocratic and often cruel conduct, Mutesa was one of the few African rulers who was able to maintain a powerful and successful army and court, which enabled him to deal effectively with Egyptian and British efforts to encroach on his sphere of influence.

Brown Brothers.

AFRICAN RESISTANCE TO COLONIALISM: THE RISE OF NATIONALISM

African states were not, however, passive objects of European manipulation. Astute native rulers sought to use the European presence to their own advantage. Some, like the Bagandan king Mutesa in the 1870s (in what is today Uganda), succeeded for some time. Direct armed resistance was doomed (even Ethiopia's) because of European technological superiority. Nevertheless, such resistance was widespread. In the end, however, other factors brought an end to most foreign rule on African soil.

The most prominent factor was the rise of nationalism across Africa, especially after World War I. However little the colonial partition of Africa reflected native divisions, it still influenced nationalist movements and the eventual shape of African states. The "national" consciousness of the diverse peoples of a given colonial unit was fueled by common opposition to foreign rule, use of a common European tongue, and the assimilation of European thought and culture by an educated native elite. These elites were educated in mission schools and foreign universities. Their ranks increased in the early 20th century. From them came the leaders of Africa's nationalist movements between the two world wars and of Africa's independent nations after World War II.

The severest indigenous critiques of the Western treatment of Africa often drew on Western religious and political ideals. The process culminated in the creation of more than 40 self-governing African nations after 1945. African independence movements were based on modern nationalist models from Europe and America rather than ancient ones derived from native tradition. The nationalist and independence movements sought to eject the colonial intruders, not to return to an earlier status quo. Their aim was to take over and run for themselves the Western institutions that colonialism had introduced. This legacy from the West is still visible today.

SUMMARY

Western Encroachment The century and a half following the French Revolution was a bleak one for the Indian subcontinent, Africa, and the Islamic societies. For centuries there had been a rough balance in material and intellectual culture, commerce, and political stability among the major cultural regions of the world. Suddenly, during the course of 150 years, the European sector of the global community came to dominate the rest of the world.

The Middle East, Africa, Iran, Central Asia, India, and Indonesia-Malaysia, along with Central and South America—what is today referred to as the "Third World" of "developing nations"—were most drastically affected by European imperialism and colonialism. Regardless of indigenous developments in these regions, the decisive development of this era was unprecedented domination by a single segment of the global community. Western dominance, sometimes positive, often sordid and ugly, was by no means synonymous with "progress," as Westerners have often liked to think.

Indigenous Reactions The vitality of so many of the cultures and traditions that bore the brunt of the Western onslaught has been striking. Arab, Iranian, Indian, African, and other encounters with Western material and intellectual domination produced different responses and initiatives. These have borne full fruit in political, economic, and intellectual independence only since 1945; however, most began much earlier, some even well before 1800.

One result of the imperial-colonial experience almost everywhere has been the sharpening of cultural self-consciousness and self-confidence among those peoples most negatively affected by Western dominance. The imperial-colonial experiences of the Third World nations may well prove to have been not only ones of misery and reversal, but also of transition to positive development and resurgence, despite the looming economic, educational, and demographic problems that plague many of them.

REVIEW QUESTIONS

1. What kind of policies did the British follow in India? What were the kinds of political activism against British rule were there in India after 1800?

2. How was the Islamic world internally divided after 1800? How did those divisions influence the coming of European powers?

3. How did nationalism affect European control in south Asia, Africa, and the Middle East?

4. What was the role of African nationalism in resisting foreign control?

IMAGE KEY
for pages 672–673

a. A fez.
b. Kemal Ataturk.
c. ivory for sale, congo.
d. An Imperial procession, or *durbar*.
e. Mahatma Ghandi.
f. Bungandan Kabaka Mutesa I and members of his court.
g. A page from a 19th-century Moroccan Koran.
h. Imam Shamil of Dagestan.
i. Sepoy cavalry attacking British infantry at the Battle of Cawpore in 1857.

KEY TERMS

bazaari (p. 681)
cantonments (p. 677)
Great Trek (p. 684)

mfecane (p. 684)
mujtahid (p. 680)
pan-Islamism (p. 682)

raj (p. 675)
scramble for Africa (p. 689)
Wahhabis (p. 679)

  For additional study resources for this chapter, go to:
www.prenhall.com/craig/chapter27

ISLAM

The Islamic tradition is one of the youngest major world religions. Since its inception during the lifetime of the Prophet Muhammad (632 B.C.E.) it has grown, like the Christian and Buddhist traditions, into a worldwide community not limited by national boundaries or defined in racial or ethnic terms. It began among the Arabs but spread widely. Islam's historical heartlands are those Arabic-, Turkic-, and Persian-speaking lands of the Near East between Egypt and Afghanistan. However, today more than half of its faithful live in Asia east of Karachi, Pakistan; and more Muslims live in sub-Saharan Africa than in all of the other Arab lands. There are also growing Muslim minorities in the United States and Europe.

The central vision of Islam is a just and peaceful society where people can freely worship God. It focuses on a human community of worshippers who recognize the absolute sovereignty and oneness of God and strive to do God's will. Muslims believe that divine will is found first in his revealed word, the Qur'an; then as elaborated and specified in the actions and words of his final prophet, Muhammad; and finally as interpreted and extended in the scriptural exegesis and legal traditions of the Muslim community during the past 13½ centuries.

Muslim vision thus centers on one God who has guided humankind throughout history by means of prophets or apostles and repeated revelations. God is the Creator of all, and in the end all will return to God. God's majesty would seem to make him a distant, threatening deity of absolute justice; there is such an element in the Muslim understanding of the wide chasm between the human and the Divine. Still, there is an immanent as well as a transcendent side to the Divine in the Muslim view. Indeed, Muslims have given us some of the greatest images of God's closeness to his faithful worshipper, images that have a special place in the thought of the Muslim mystics, who are known as *Sufis* (taken originally from *suf*, "wool," because of the early Muslim ascetics' use of simple wool dress).

Muslims understand God's word in the Qur'an and the elaboration of that word by tradition to be a complete prescription for human life. Thus Islamic law is not law in the Western sense of civil, criminal, or international systems. Rather, it is a comprehensive set of standards for the moral, ritual, social, political, economic, aesthetic, and even hygienic and dietary dimensions of life. By being faithful to God's law, the Muslim hopes to gain salvation on the Last Day, when human history shall end and all of God's creatures who have ever lived will be resurrected and called to account for their thoughts and actions during their lives on earth. Some will be saved, but others will be eternally damned.

Thus *Islam*, which means "submission [to God]," has been given as a name to the religiously defined system of life that Muslims have sought to institute wherever they have lived. Muslims have striven to organize their societies and political realities around the ideals represented in the traditional picture of the Prophet's community in Medina and Mecca. This approach necessitated compromise in which power was given to temporal rulers and accepted by Muslim religious

Muhammad and Ali. This 16th-century Persian miniature shows the prophet Muhammad and his kinsman Ali purifying the Ka'ba in Mecca of pagan idols. The Ka'ba is the geographical point toward which all Muslims face when performing ritual prayer.

Art Resource/Bildarchiv Preussischer Kulturbesitz.

Friday Congregational Worship. Every Friday at the noon hour of daily worship, Muslims are enjoined to gather in as large a congregation as possible to worship together and listen to a weekly preaching in the major mosque in their town or city. Here at a mosque in Jakarta, Indonesian Muslims are seen in the midst of worship rites. More Muslims live in Indonesia than in any other country.

Getty Images, Inc. — Photodisc.

from fighting Muslim states it regards as un-Islamic to opposing what it considers the U.S. intrusion into the Arab Islamic world and its unpopular foreign policy in the region. While mainstream Muslims everywhere reject bin Laden's extremism, Wahhabi zealotry has adherents on the fringes of Islamic communities around the world. In this respect, Islam is not unlike Christianity, Judaism, Hinduism, or other major religions, each of which has over its history spawned literalists, zealots, and extremists, who have urged violence in the name of their version of their parent faith.

The major sectarian, or minority, groups among Muslims are those of the Shi'ites, who have held out for an ideal of a temporal ruler who is also the spiritual heir of Muhammad and God's designated deputy on earth. Most Shi'ites, notably those of Iran, hold that after 11 designated blood descendants of the prophets had each failed to be recognized by the majority of Muslims as the rightful leader, or *Imam*, the 12th disappeared and remains to this day physically absent from the world, although not dead. He will come again at the end of time to vindicate his faithful followers.

Muslim piety takes many forms. Common duties of Muslims are central for Muslims everywhere: faith in God and trust in his Prophet; regular performance of ritual worship (*Salat*); fasting during daylight hours for 30 days in Ramadan (the ninth month of the lunar year); giving one's wealth to the needy (*zakat*); and at least once in a lifetime, if able, making the pilgrimage to Mecca and its environs (*Hajj*). Other more regional or popular, but ubiquitous, practices are also important. Celebration of the Prophet's birthday indicates the exalted popular status of Muhammad, even though any divine status for him is strongly rejected theologically. Recitation of the Qur'an permeates all Muslim practice, from daily worship to celebrations of all kinds. Visitation of saints' tombs is a prominent form of popular devotion. Sufi chanting or even ecstatic dancing are also practiced by Muslims around the world.

Muslims vary enormously in their physical environment, language, ethnic background, and cultural allegiances. What binds them now as in the past are not political allegiances but religious affinities and a shared heritage of religious faith and culture. How these allegiances and sensibilities will fare in the face of global challenges will be an important factor in shaping the world of the 21st century.

leaders as long as those rulers protected God's Law, the *Shari'ah*. The ideal of a single international Muslim community, or *Umma*, has never fully been realized politically, but it remains an ideal.

Many movements of reform over the centuries have called for greater adherence to rigorist interpretations of Islamic law and greater dominance of piety and religious values in sociopolitical as well as individual life. The most famous of these movements, that of the Wahhabis in 18th-century Arabia, remains influential in much of the Muslim world, including Saudi Arabia. The Wahhabis' puritanical zeal in fighting what they consider "innovations" in many regional Islamic contexts, such as Shi'ism, Sufi traditions, and all more liberal forms of Islamic practice, continues to the present day. Wahhabism has had considerable success in the past half century and was apparently the spawning ground of the extremist views of Osama bin Laden's al-Qaeda terrorist movement, which is largely Arab in its ethnic makeup and has turned

- How has the ideal of a single, international Muslim community influenced Islamic history? World history?

- What impact have reform movements had on Islam since its inception? What impact do they have today?

28 Modern East Asia

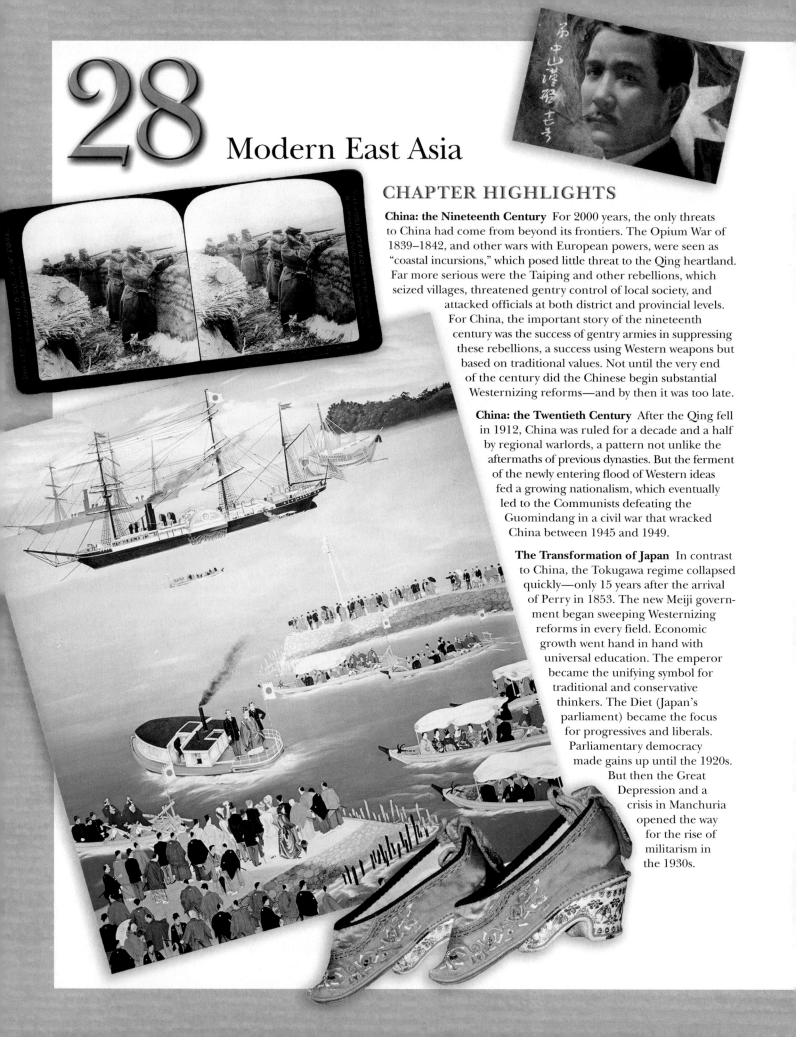

CHAPTER HIGHLIGHTS

China: the Nineteenth Century For 2000 years, the only threats to China had come from beyond its frontiers. The Opium War of 1839–1842, and other wars with European powers, were seen as "coastal incursions," which posed little threat to the Qing heartland. Far more serious were the Taiping and other rebellions, which seized villages, threatened gentry control of local society, and attacked officials at both district and provincial levels. For China, the important story of the nineteenth century was the success of gentry armies in suppressing these rebellions, a success using Western weapons but based on traditional values. Not until the very end of the century did the Chinese begin substantial Westernizing reforms—and by then it was too late.

China: the Twentieth Century After the Qing fell in 1912, China was ruled for a decade and a half by regional warlords, a pattern not unlike the aftermaths of previous dynasties. But the ferment of the newly entering flood of Western ideas fed a growing nationalism, which eventually led to the Communists defeating the Guomindang in a civil war that wracked China between 1945 and 1949.

The Transformation of Japan In contrast to China, the Tokugawa regime collapsed quickly—only 15 years after the arrival of Perry in 1853. The new Meiji government began sweeping Westernizing reforms in every field. Economic growth went hand in hand with universal education. The emperor became the unifying symbol for traditional and conservative thinkers. The Diet (Japan's parliament) became the focus for progressives and liberals. Parliamentary democracy made gains up until the 1920s. But then the Great Depression and a crisis in Manchuria opened the way for the rise of militarism in the 1930s.

CHAPTER QUESTIONS

WHAT WERE the most serious threats to Manchu rule in the nineteenth century?

WHO WERE the key figures in the revolution of 1911?

WHY DID the communists win the Chinese Civil War?

WHAT ROLE did the Chōshū and Satsuma play in the overthrow of Tokugawa rule?

WHAT POWERS did the Meiji Constitution give to the emperor?

WHY DID Japan set out to build a modern economy?

CHAPTER OUTLINE

MODERN CHINA (1839–1949)

- Close of Manchu Rule
- From Dynasty to Warlordism (1895–1926)
- Cultural and Ideological Ferment: The May Fourth Movement
- Nationalist China

MODERN JAPAN (1853–1945)

- Overthrow of the Tokugawa Bakufu (1853–1868)
- Building the Meiji State (1868–1890)
- Growth of a Modern Economy
- The Politics of Imperial Japan (1890–1945)
- Japanese Militarism and German Nazism

In the mid-19th century, the West was the expanding, aggressive, imperialistic force in world history; it was the trigger for change throughout the world. But the response to the Western impact depended on internal forces in each country. Japan and China were both relatively successful in their responses, for neither became a colony.

The two countries' governing elites were educated in Confucianism, which was just secular enough to crumble in the face of the more powerful secularism of 19th-century science and the doctrines associated with it. In both countries, one of the "breakdown products" of the Confucian sociopolitical identity was a strong new nationalism.

But in most other respects, modern Japan and China could hardly be more different. The coming of Commodore Matthew Perry (1794–1858) in 1853 and 1854 precipitated rapid change in Japan. The old Tokugawa regime collapsed, and the Japanese built a modern state. Economic growth followed. By 1900, Japan had defeated China and was about to defeat Russia. After the Great Depression, Japan, like Italy and Germany, became an aggressive and militarized state and was defeated in World War II. But after the war, Japan reemerged more stable and productive, and with a stronger parliamentary government than ever before.

In contrast, the hold of tradition in China was remarkable. But in one sense, its strength was China's weakness, for only after the overthrow of Manchu rule in 1911 was China willing to begin the modernization that Japan had started in 1868. Even then it was unsuccessful. Along with warlordism, new ills arose from the rending of the very fabric of the dynastic pattern. That China "failed" during this modern century is the view held by the Chinese themselves.

Modern China (1839–1949)

China's modern century was not the century in which it became modern, but the one in which it encountered the modern West. Its first phase, from the Opium War to the fall of the Qing or Manchu dynasty (1911), was little affected by Western impact. Only during the decade before 1911 did the Confucian tradition begin to be discarded in favor of new ideas from the West. The second phase, from 1911 to the establishment of a communist state in 1949, was a time of turmoil: decades of warlord rule, war with Japan, and then four years of civil war.

Close of Manchu Rule

The Opium War

WHAT WERE the most serious threats to Manchu rule in the 19th century?

The 18th-century three-country trade—British goods to India, Indian cotton to China, and Chinese tea to Britain—was in China's favor. Then the British replaced cotton with Indian opium, and by the 1820s, the balance of trade was reversed.

To check the evil of opium and the outflow of silver, the Chinese government banned opium in 1836. In 1839, the government sent Lin Zexu (1785–1850) to Guangzhou (Canton) to superintend the ban. He destroyed a six-month supply of opium belonging to foreign merchants, leading to a confrontation with the British.

War broke out in November 1839. For the next two years, the British fought battles and attempted negotiations. The Chinese troops were ineffective. The war was finally ended in August 1842 by the Treaty of Nanjing, the first of the **"unequal treaties."**

"unequal treaties"
Agreements imposed on China in the 19th century by European powers, the United States, and Japan that granted their citizens special legal and economic privileges on Chinese soil.

The treaty gave Britain the island of Hong Kong and a huge indemnity. It also opened five ports: Fuzhou, Guangzhou, Ningpo, Shanghai, and Xiamen

(Amoy). British merchants and their families could reside in the ports and engage in trade; Britain could appoint a consul for each city; and British residents within China were subject to British, not Chinese, law. In 1844, similar treaties followed with the United States and France.

After the signing of the British treaty, Chinese imports of opium increased, but other kinds of trade did not grow as much as had been hoped. Western merchants blamed the lack of growth on Chinese officials. They also complained that Guangzhou remained closed to trade. Chinese authorities were incensed by the export of coolies to work in Cuba and Peru. A second war broke out in 1856, and the British captured Beijing in 1860. New treaties provided for indemnities, the opening of 11 new ports, the stationing of foreign diplomats in Beijing, the propagation of Christianity anywhere in China, and the legalization of the opium trade.

Meanwhile, the Russians were encroaching on China's northern frontier. In 1858, China ceded the north bank of the Amur to Russia, and in 1860, China gave Russia the Maritime Province between the Ussuri River and the Pacific.

REBELLIONS AGAINST THE MANCHU

More serious threats to Manchu rule were the Nian, Muslim, and **Taiping rebellions** that convulsed China between 1850 and 1873. The torment and suffering caused by these events were unparalleled in world history. China's population dropped by 60 million.

The Taipings were begun by Hong Xiuquan (1814–1864), a schoolteacher from the southern province of Kwangtung. Influenced by Protestant tracts, Hong announced that he was the younger brother of Jesus and that God had told him to rid China of Manchus, Confucians, Daoists, and Buddhists. Like earlier rebels, the Taipings combined moral reform, religious fervor, and a vision of egalitarian society. The Taipings were soon joined by peasants, miners, and workers. Fighting spread until the Taipings controlled most of the Yangzi basin and had entered 16 of the 18 Chinese provinces. Their army numbered close to a million.

The other rebellions were of lesser note. The Nian were located north of the Taipings along the Huai River. They were organized in secret societies and raided the countryside. Eventually they built an army, collected taxes, and ruled 100,000 square miles. A longer revolt was of Muslims against Chinese in the southwest and the northwest. These rebellions took advantage of the weakened state of the dynasty and occurred in areas that had few officials and no Qing military units.

Against the rebellions, the imperial forces proved helpless: In 1852, the court sent Zeng Guofan (1811–1872) to south-central China to organize a local army. Zeng, a product of the Confucian examination system, saw the Manchu government, of which he was an elite member, as the upholder of morality and the social order, and Chinese rebels as would-be destroyers of that order. He recruited members of the gentry as officers. They were Confucian, and as landlords had the most to lose from rebel rule. They recruited soldiers from their local areas and stopped the Taipings' advance.

In 1860, when the British and French occupied Beijing, a reform government began internal changes, adopted a policy of cooperation with Western powers, and put Zeng in charge of suppressing all the rebellions. Zeng appointed able officials to raise regional armies. Foreigners and Shanghai merchants gave their support. The Taipings collapsed when Nanjing was captured in 1864. The Nian were suppressed by 1868 and the Muslim rebellion was put down five years later. Scholar-officials, relying on local gentry, had saved the dynasty.

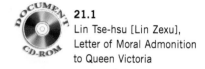

21.1
Lin Tse-hsu [Lin Zexu], Letter of Moral Admonition to Queen Victoria

---

QUICK REVIEW

Rebellions

- Taiping: Led by Hung Hsiu-ch'uan (1814–1864), the Taiping assembled an army of close to a million men
- Nien: Located along the Huai River, the Nien came to control a 100,000-square-mile area
- Muslim rebellions: Muslim revolt against Chinese in southwest and northwest, areas where China had few officials and little military presence

---

Taiping rebellion A 19th-century revolt against China's Manchu dynasty that was inspired by quasi-Christian ideas and that led to enormous suffering and destruction before its collapse in 1868.

Empress Dowager. Tz'u-hsi, the empress dowager (1835–1908), manipulated the levers of power at the Manchu court in Peking.

Hulton Picture Library/Corbis-Bettmann.

SELF-STRENGTHENING AND DECLINE (1874–1895)

In view of the dynasty's advanced stage of administrative decentralization, the Chinese resiliency and capacity to rebuild in the two decades after the suppression of the rebellions were impressive. But if we ask how effective China's response was to the West, or if we compare China's progress with that of Japan, then China during the same decades looks almost moribund. Historians often call these years the period of "self-strengthening," yet China was relatively weaker at the end of the period than at the start.

The Court at Beijing China's inability to act effectively is explained partly by the situation at the court. Prince Gong (1833–1898) and the empress dowager (1835–1908) were coregents for the young emperor. Prince Gong was a man of ideas. In 1861, he established a new office to handle the court's relations with foreign diplomats in Beijing. The following year, he established a school to train Chinese in foreign languages. However, outmaneuvered by the empress dowager, he was ousted in 1884.

The empress dowager had produced the only male child of the former emperor. She had no conception of how to reform China; her single goal was power. She acquired it by forging a political machine of conservative bureaucrats, military commanders, and eunuchs, and by maintaining a balance between the court and the regional governor-generals. The result was a court just able to survive but too weak to govern effectively.

Regional Governments The most vital figures during these decades were a handful of able governors-general. Each had an army and was in charge of two or three provinces. They were loyal to the dynasty that they had restored in the face of almost certain collapse and were allowed great autonomy.

Their first task was reconstruction. Millions were hungry or homeless. The leaders' response was massive and effective. Just as they had mobilized the gentry to suppress the rebellions, now they obtained their cooperation in rebuilding. They set up refugee centers, reduced taxes in the devastated Yangzi valley, reclaimed lands gone to waste, began water-control projects, and built granaries. By the early 1890s, well-being had been restored to Chinese society.

Their second task was self-strengthening—the adoption of Western arms and technology. The Chinese built arsenals and shipyards, a telegraph company, railways, and cotton mills. The formula applied in running these enterprises was "official supervision and merchant operation." Major decisions were made by scholar-officials, but day-to-day operations were left to the merchants.

treaty ports Chinese ports ruled by foreign consuls where foreigners enjoyed commercial privileges and immunity from Chinese laws.

Treaty Ports The **treaty ports**, of which there were 14 by the 1860s, were little islands of privilege and security, under the rule of foreign consuls, where capital was safe from confiscation, trade was free, and "squeeze" (extortion by officials) was the exception. Foreign companies naturally located in the ports, as did Chinese merchants who were also attracted by these conditions. Well into the 20th century, the foreign concessions (treaty-port lands leased in perpetuity by foreigners) remained the vital sector of China's modern economy.

The effects of the treaty ports and of Western imperialism on China were largely negative. Under the low tariffs mandated by the treaties, Chinese industries had little protection from imports. Native cotton spinning was almost destroyed by imports of yarn. Chinese tea lost ground to Indian tea and Chinese silk to Japanese silk. China found few products to export. The level of foreign trade stayed low, and China's interior markets were affected only slightly.

By the 1870s, foreign powers had reached an accommodation with China. They counted on the court to uphold the treaties; in return, they became a prop for the dynasty. By 1900, for example, the court's revenues from customs fees were larger than those from any other source. The fees were collected by the Maritime Customs Service, an efficient and honest treaty-port institution headed by an Irishman. In 1895, the Maritime Customs Service had 700 Western and 3,500 Chinese employees.

THE BORDERLANDS: THE NORTHWEST, VIETNAM, AND KOREA

China's other foreign relations were with fringe lands that China claimed by right of past conquest or as tributaries. The tributaries were the mirrors in which China saw reflected its own self-image as a universal empire. During the late 19th century, this image was strengthened in the northwest but dealt a fatal blow in Vietnam and Korea.

The Northwest   In the northwest, China confronted imperial Russia. Caught between them, the independent nomadic tribes were rendered impotent. By 1878, China had reconquered Chinese Turkestan, which was renamed Xinjang, or the "New Territories." A treaty signed with Russia in 1881 restored most of the Ili region in western Mongolia to Chinese control. The victories strengthened court conservatives who wished to take a stronger stance toward the West.

Vietnam   Vietnam, which had retained its independence from China since 935, saw itself as an independent state but used the Chinese writing system, modeled its laws and government on those of China, and traded with China. China simply saw Vietnam as a tributary.

During the 1840s, the second emperor of the Nguyen dynasty, which had begun in 1802, moved to reduce French influences and suppress Christianity. Thousands were killed, including French and Vietnamese priests. The French responded by seizing Saigon and Cochin China in 1859, establishing a protectorate over Cambodia in 1864, and taking Hanoi in 1882. China in 1883 sent troops to aid its tributary, but after a two-year war with France, in 1885 China was forced to abandon its claims to Vietnam. By 1893, France had brought together Vietnam, Cambodia, and Laos to form the Federation of Indochina, which remained a French colony until 1940.

Korea   Unlike Vietnam, Korea saw itself as a tributary of China on Chinese terms. The Korean ruler styled himself as a king and not an emperor.

During the last decades of the long (1392–1910) Choson dynasty, the Korean state was weak. It hung on to power in part by enforcing a policy of seclusion almost as total as that of Tokugawa Japan, winning it the name of the Hermit Kingdom. Its only foreign ties were with China and Japan. In 1876, Japan "opened" Korea to international relations, using much the same tactics that Perry had used against Japan. Japan then contended with China for influence in Korea.

QUICK REVIEW

Korea in the Late 19th Century
- Tributary of China
- The Korean state was weak in the last decades of the 19th century
- After 1876, Japan contended with China for influence in Korea

In 1893, a popular religious sect unleashed a rebellion against the Seoul government. When the government requested Chinese help to suppress the rebellion, China sent troops, but Japan sent more, and in 1894, war broke out between China and Japan. Taiwan became Japan's first colony. The defeat convinced many in China that basic changes were inevitable.

FROM DYNASTY TO WARLORDISM (1895–1926)

WHO WERE the key figures in the revolution of 1911?

China was ruled by officials who had mastered the Confucian classics. This intellectual formation was resistant to change. For most officials living in China's interior, the foreign crises of the 19th century were "coastal phenomena," soon forgotten. Few officials realized the magnitude of the foreign threat.

China's defeat by Japan in 1895 came as a shock. The response within China was a new wave of reform proposals. The most influential thinker was Kang Youwei (1858–1927), who described China as "enfeebled" and blamed the "conservatives." They did not understand, Kang argued, that Confucius himself had been a reformer who had invented the idea of a golden age to persuade the rulers of his own age to adopt his ideas. History was evolutionary—a march forward from absolute monarchy to constitutional monarchy to democracy. Kang's reinterpretation of Confucianism removed a major barrier to the entry of Western ideas into China.

In 1898, the emperor himself became sympathetic to Kang's ideas and launched "one hundred days of reform." He took as his models Peter the Great (r. 1682–1725) and the Japanese Meiji Emperor (r. 1867–1912). Edicts were issued to reform China's schools, railroads, police, laws, military, bureaucracy, post offices, and examination system. But conservative resistance was nationwide. At court, the empress dowager regained control and ended the reforms. Kang fled to Japan. One reformer was executed.

Boxers Nationalistic Chinese religious society that attacked foreigners and their encroachments on China in the late 19th century.

"Open Door" Cartoon. An American view of the "open door." The combination of high self-esteem and negative attitudes toward foreigners at the turn of the century was not a Chinese monopoly.

Corbis-Bettmann.

The response of the Western powers to China's 1895 defeat was to define spheres of interest, which usually consisted of a leasehold along with railway rights and commercial privileges. Russia gained a leasehold at Port Arthur; Germany acquired one in Shandung. Britain got the New Territories adjoining Jiulong (Kowloon) at Hong Kong. New ports and cities were opened to foreign trade. The United States was in a weaker position, so it enunciated an "open-door" policy: equal commercial opportunities for all powers and the preservation of the territorial integrity of China.

At this time there was a religious society in China known as the **Boxers** (in Chinese, literally the "Righteous and Harmonius Fists"). They rebelled first in Shandung in 1898, and, gaining court support, entered Beijing in 1900. There followed a two-month siege of the foreign legation quarter. The rebellion was fueled by pent-up resentments against decades of foreign encroachments. Eventually an international force captured Beijing, and the Russians occupied Manchuria.

The defeat of the Boxers convinced even conservative Chinese leaders of the futility of clinging to old ways. A more powerful reform movement began, with the empress dowager in its vanguard. But the dynasty could not control the movement and eventually was bypassed.

Educational reforms began in 1901. Women were admitted to newly formed schools. In place of Confucianism, instructors taught science, mathematics, geography, and an antiimperialist version of Chinese history. Western doctrines, such as classical economics, liberalism, socialism, anarchism, and social Darwinism, were introduced into China. By 1906, there were 8,000 Chinese students in Japan, which became a hotbed of Chinese reformist and revolutionary societies.

Military reforms were begun by Yuan Shikai (1859–1916), whose New Army drew on Japanese and Western models. Young men from gentry families, spurred by patriotism, joined the New Army as officers. Their loyalty was to their commanders and their country, not to the dynasty.

In 1905, the examination system was abolished; officials were to be recruited directly from the schools and those who had studied abroad. Provincial assemblies were formed in 1909, and a consultative assembly was established in Beijing in 1910.

These changes sparked the 1911 revolution. It began with an uprising in Sichuan province against a government plan to nationalize the main railways. The key figures were:

1. Gentry who stood to lose their investments in the railways.

2. Qing military commanders, who declared their provinces independent.

3. Sun Zhongshan (or Sun Yat-sen) (1866–1925), a republican revolutionary. He organized the Revolutionary Alliance in Tokyo in 1905 and was associated with the Nationalist Party (Guomindang) formed in 1912.

4. Yuan Shikai, who arranged for the last child emperor to abdicate, for Sun to step aside, and for himself to become president of the new Republic of China.

The nationalists won an election called in 1913, but Yuan routed them and proclaimed a new dynasty with himself as emperor. The idea of another dynasty, however, met opposition from all quarters. Yuan died in June 1916. China then fell into the hands of warlord armies. The years until the late 1920s were a time of agony for the Chinese people. Yet they were also in a time of intense intellectual ferment.

Execution of Boxers. The rebels, arms bound behind, lie headless. Chinese soldiers watch. In the 1900 siege of the foreign legations in Bejing, 76 foreigners were killed by the Boxers. Twelve years later, the dynasty fell.

Neg./Transparency no. 336289. (Photo Copied by P. Goldberg). Courtesy Dept. of Library Services, American Museum of Natural History.

CULTURAL AND IDEOLOGICAL FERMENT: THE MAY FOURTH MOVEMENT

WHAT WAS the May Fourth Movement?

A period of freedom and vigorous experimentation with new doctrines began in 1914 and extended into the 1920s. It is called the May Fourth Movement after an incident in Beijing in 1919 in which thousands of students protested the settlement at Versailles that awarded former German possessions in Shandung to Japan. The nationalist fervor that led the students to demonstrate in the streets changed the complexion of Chinese thought. Leading thinkers began to judge ideas in terms of their value in solving China's problems.

During the May Fourth era, the center of advanced thought was Beijing. Ideas propounded there quickly spread to the rest of China, especially to its urban centers. Protest demonstrations against imperialist privilege broke out in Guangzhou, Shanghai, and Wuhan, as they had in the capital. Nationalism and antiimperialist sentiment were stronger than liberalism, although most thinkers spoke of democracy. Only members of an older generation of reformers, appalled by the slaughter of World War I and what they saw as Western materialism, advocated a return to traditional philosophies.

After the Russian Revolution of 1917, Marxism-Leninism entered China. The Leninist definition of imperialism as the last crisis stage of capitalism put the blame for China's ills on the West and offered "feudal" China the possibility of leapfrogging over capitalism to socialism. Marxist study groups formed in Beijing and other cities. In 1919, a student from Hunan, Mao Zedong, who had worked in the Beijing University library, returned to Changsha to form a study group. The Chinese Communist Party was formed in Shanghai in 1921; Zhou Enlai (1898–1976) formed a similar group in Paris the same year.

NATIONALIST CHINA

GUOMINDANG UNIFICATION OF CHINA AND THE NANJING DECADE (1927–1937)

WHY DID the communists win the Chinese Civil War?

Sun Zhongshan had fled to Japan during the 1913–1916 rule by Yuan Shikai. He returned to Guangzhou in 1916, but he was a poor organizer, and his **Guomindang (GMD)**—or Nationalist Party—made little headway. From 1923, Sun began to receive Soviet support. He reorganized his party on the Leninist model, with an executive committee on top of a national party congress, provincial and county organizations, and local party cells.

Since 1905, Sun had enunciated his "three principles of the people": nationality, livelihood, and rights. Sun's nationalism was now directed against Western imperialism. The principle of people's livelihood was defined in terms of equalizing land holdings and nationalizing major industries. By "people's rights" Sun meant democracy, although he argued that it must be preceded by a preparatory period of single-party dictatorship. Sun sent his loyal lieutenant Jiang Jieshi (Chiang Kai-shek) (1887–1975) to the Soviet Union for study. Jiang returned after four months with a cadre of Russian advisers and established a military academy at Huangpu south of Guangzhou in 1924. Sun died in 1925. By 1926, the Huangpu Academy had graduated several thousand officers, and the GMD army numbered almost 100,000. The GMD had become the major political force in China.

The growth of the party was spurred by changes within Chinese society. Industries arose in the cities. Labor unions were organized. New ventures were begun outside the treaty ports. A politically conscious middle class developed.

The quicksilver element in cities was the several million students. In May 1925, students demonstrated in Shanghai. Police in the international settlement fired on the demonstrators. The incident inflamed national and antiimperialist feelings. Strikes and boycotts of foreign goods were called throughout China.

Under these conditions the Chinese Communist Party (CCP) also grew and was influential in student organizations, labor unions, and even within the GMD. Sun had permitted CCP members to join the GMD as individuals, but had

Guomindang (GMT) China's Nationalist Party, founded by Sun Zhongshan.

enjoined them from organizing CCP cells within it. Moscow approved of this policy. It felt that the CCP was too small to accomplish anything on its own.

By 1926, Jiang Jieshi felt ready to march against the warlords. He worried about the growing communist strength, however, and before setting off he ousted the Soviet advisers and CCP members from the GMD offices in Guangzhou. The march north began in July. By the spring of 1927, Jiang's army had reached the Yangzi, defeating warlord armies as it advanced.

After entering Shanghai in April 1927, Jiang carried out a sweeping purge of the CCP. Many were killed. The surviving CCP members fled to the mountainous border region of Hunan and Jiangxi to the southwest and established the "Jiangxi Soviet." Jiang's army took Beijing and gained the nominal submission of most northern Chinese warlords during 1928. Most foreign powers recognized the GMD regime as the government of China.

Jiang Jieshi was the key figure in the government. He believed in military force. He was unimaginative, strict, and incorruptible. Jiang venerated Sun Zhongshan and his three "people's principles." But where Sun was a revolutionary, Jiang was conservative and, though a Methodist, often appealed to Confucian values. The New Life Movement begun by Jiang in 1934 was an attempt to revitalize these values.

Jiang's power rested on the army, the party, and the bureaucracy. The army was dominated by the Huangpu clique, which was loyal to Jiang, and by officers trained in Japan. After 1927, German advisers reorganized Jiang's army along German lines with a general staff system. The larger part of GMD revenues went to the military, which was expanded into a modernized force of 300,000. Huangpu graduates also controlled the secret military police and used it against communists and any others who opposed the government. The GMD was a dictatorship under a central committee. Jiang became president of the party in 1938.

The densely populated central and lower Yangzi provinces were the area of GMD strength. The party, however, was unable to control the outlying areas occupied by warlords, communists, and the Japanese. Warlords ruled some areas until 1949. In 1931, Jiang attacked the Jiangxi Soviet. In 1934, the communists were forced to flee to the southwest and then to Shaanxi province in northwestern China in the epic "**Long March.**" During this march Mao Zedong wrested control of the CCP from the Moscow-trained, urban-oriented leaders and established his unorthodox view that a Leninist party could base itself on the peasantry.

The Japanese had held special rights in Manchuria since the Russo-Japanese War of 1905. When Jiang's march north and Chinese nationalism threatened the Japanese position, Japan's army engineered a military coup in 1931, and in 1932 it established a puppet state and proclaimed the independence of Manchuria. In the years that followed, Japanese forces moved south as far as the Great Wall. Chinese nationalism demanded that Jiang resist. Jiang, well aware of the disparity between his

Long March Flight of the Chinese communists from their nationalist foes to northwest China in 1934.

Modern China

1839–1842	Opium War
1850–1873	Taiping and other rebellions
1870s–1880s	Self-strengthening movement
1894–1895	Sino-Japanese War
1898	One hundred days of reform
1898–1900	Boxer Rebellion
1911	Republican revolution overthrows Qing dynasty
1912–1916	Yuan Shikai president of Republic of China
1916–1928	Warlord era
1919	May Fourth incident
1924	Founding of Huangpu Military Academy
1926–1928	March north and Guomindang reunification of China
1934–1935	Chinese Communists' Long March to Yan'an
1937–1945	War with Japan
1945–1949	Civil war and the establishment of the People's Republic of China

armies and those of Japan, said that the internal unification of China must take precedence. In 1937, however, a full-scale war with Japan broke out, and China's situation changed.

WAR AND REVOLUTION (1937–1949)

The war with Japan began in July 1937 as an unplanned clash at Beijing and then quickly spread. Beijing and Tianjin fell to Japan within a month, Shanghai was attacked in August, and Nanjing fell in December. During the following year, the Japanese took Guangzhou and set up puppet regimes in Beijing and Nanjing. In 1940, the leader of the left wing of the GMD and many of his associates joined the Japanese puppet government. Japan proclaimed its "New Order in East Asia." It expected Jiang to submit. Instead, in 1938 he relocated his capital to Chongqing, far to the west, and was joined by thousands of Chinese.

Jiang's stubborn resistance won admiration from all sides. But the withdrawal to Chongqing cut the GMD off from most of the Chinese population; programs for modernization ended; and the GMD's former tax revenues were lost. Inflation increased geometrically and exacerbated the already widespread corruption.

The United States sent advisers and military equipment to strengthen Jiang's forces after the start of the Pacific War. However, Jiang wanted not to fight the Japanese but to husband his forces for a postwar confrontation with the communists. Within his own army a gap appeared between officers and men. Conditions in the camps were primitive, food poor, and medical supplies inadequate. The young saw conscription almost as a death sentence. Jiang's unwillingness to commit his troops against the Japanese also meant that the surge of anti-Japanese patriotism was not converted to popular support for the GMD.

For the communists, the Japanese occupation was an opportunity. Headquartered at Yan'an, they began campaigns to promote literacy and self-sufficiency. Soldiers farmed so as not to burden the peasants. The CCP abandoned its earlier policy of expropriating lands in favor of reductions in rents and interest. They took only those offices needed to ensure their control and shared the rest with the GMD and other parties. They expanded village councils to include tenants. But they also strengthened their party internally.

Party membership expanded from 40,000 in 1937 to 1.2 million in 1945. Schools were established in Yan'an to train party cadres. Orthodoxy was maintained by a rectification campaign. Those tainted by impure tendencies were made to repent at public meetings. Mao's thought was supreme. To the Chinese at large, Mao represented himself as the successor to Sun Zhongshan, but within the Communist Party he presented himself as a theoretician in the line of Marx (1818–1883), Engels (1820–1895), Lenin (1870–1924), and Stalin (1879–1953).

The communists learned to operate at the grass-roots level. They infiltrated Japanese-controlled areas and GMD organizations and military units. CCP armies were built up from 90,000 in 1937 to 900,000 in 1945. These armies were supplemented by

Mao Zedong. Photographed at his cave headquarters in Shaanxi province during World War II, Mao Zedong (1893–1976) wears a padded winter jacket and writes with a Chinese brush.

Getty Images, Inc. – Taxi.

a rural people's militia and by guerrilla forces. The Yan'an leadership and its party, army, and mass organizations possessed cohesion, determination, and morale that were lacking in Chongqing.

But the strength of the Chinese communists as of 1945 should not be overstated. When the war in the Pacific ended in 1945, China's future was unclear. Even the Soviet Union recognized the GMD as the government of China and expected it to win the postwar struggle. The Allies directed Japanese armies to surrender to the GMD forces in 1945. The United States flew Jiang's troops to key eastern cities. His armies were by then three times the size of the communists' and far better equipped.

A civil war broke out immediately. Efforts by U.S. General George Marshall (1880–1959) to mediate were futile. Until the summer of 1947, GMD armies were victorious—even capturing Yan'an. But the tide turned in July as CCP armies went on the offensive in north China. In January 1949, Beijing and Tianjin fell. A few months later all of China was in communist hands. Many Chinese fled with Jiang to Taiwan or escaped to Hong Kong. In China, apprehension was mixed with anticipation. The feeling was widespread that the future of China was once again in the hands of the Chinese.

MODERN JAPAN (1853–1945)

OVERTHROW OF THE TOKUGAWA BAKUFU (1853–1868)

From the 17th century into the 19th century, the natural isolation of the islands of Japan was augmented by the country's policy of seclusion, making Japan into a little world of its own. The 260-odd domains were the states of this world, the bakufu in Edo was its hegemon, and the imperial court in Kyoto provided a religious sanction for the bakufu-domain system. Then at mid-century, the American ships of Commodore Perry came and forced Japan to sign a treaty, opening it to foreign intercourse. Fourteen years later, the entire bakufu-domain system collapsed, and a group of talented leaders seized power. Seclusion, like the case of a watch, had been necessary to preserve the Tokugawa political mechanism. With the case removed, the inner workings flew apart.

Little changed during the first four years after Perry. The break came in 1858 when the bakufu, ignoring the imperial court's disapproval, was persuaded to sign a commercial treaty with the United States. Some daimyo, who wanted a voice in national policy, criticized the treaty as contravening the hallowed policy of seclusion. Younger samurai, frustrated by their exclusion from office, started a movement to "honor the emperor." The bakufu, in turn, responded with a purge. But in 1860, the head of the bakufu council was assassinated by extremist samurai. His successors lacked the nerve to continue his tough policies.

In 1861, two domains, Chōshū and Satsuma, emerged to heal the breach between the bakufu and the court. First, Chōshū officials proposed a policy that favored the bakufu but made concessions to the court. Next, Satsuma advocated a policy that made further concessions and ousted Chōshū as "the friend of the court." In response, the moderate reformist government of Chōshū adopted the proemperor policy of its extremist faction and, in turn, ousted Satsuma. Satsuma then seized the court in 1863 in a military coup.

DOCUMENT CD-ROM

24.6
"From the Countryside to the City" (May 1949): Mao Zedong

WHAT ROLE did the Chōshū and Satsuma play in the overthrow of Tokugawa rule?

Several points are of note about the 1861–1863 diplomatic phase of domain action:

1. Even after 250 years of bakufu rule, several domains could still act when the opportunity occurred.

2. The two domains that acted first and most of the others that followed had many samurai and substantial financial resources.

3. Both Satsuma and Chōshū had fought against the Tokugawa in 1600 and remembered an earlier independence.

4. By 1861–1863, the new politics had opened decision making to middle-ranking samurai officials in a way that would have been impossible before 1853.

The 1863 Satsuma coup at the Kyoto court initiated a military phase of politics in which battles would determine every turning point. As long as Satsuma and Chōshū remained enemies, politics stalemated and the bakufu continued as hegemon. But when the two domains became allies in 1866, the bakufu was overthrown in less than two years.

One factor contributing to this process was the movement for a "union of court and camp"; daimyo campaigned for a new conciliar rule in which they

Commodore Matthew Perry Meeting Japanese Officials at Kurigahama in 1853. At the right are two emissaries of the bakufu; at the left is Perry's Chinese translator, who speaks English and communicates with the Japanese in written Chinese. Perry's ships are visible in the background, along with smaller Japanese craft.

U.S. Naval Academy Museum.

HISTORY'S VOICES

A JAPANESE VIEW OF THE INVENTIVENESS OF THE WEST

Serious Japanese thinkers reacted to their country's weakness with proposals to adopt Western science and industry. But the "Civilization and Enlightenment Movement" of the 1870s had its lighter side as well. In 1871, the novelist Kanagaki Robun wrote a satire about a man with an umbrella, a watch, and eau de cologne on his hair, eating with a friend in a new beef restaurant. Before the Restoration, Buddhism had banned beef eating as a defilement. The comic hero, however, wonders "why we in Japan haven't eaten such a clean thing before." He then goes on to rhapsodize about Western inventions.

WHAT DO pickled onions have to do with the marvels of Western technology?

In the West they're free of superstitions. There it's the custom to do everything scientifically, and that's why they've invented amazing things like the steamship and the steam engine. Did you know that they engrave the plates for printing newspapers with telegraphic needles? And that they bring down wind from the sky with balloons? Aren't they wonderful inventions! Of course, there are good reasons behind these inventions. If you look at a map of the world you'll see some countries marked "tropical," which means that's where the sun shines closest. The people in those countries are all burnt black by the sun. The king of that part of the world tried all kinds of schemes before he hit on what is called a balloon. That's a big round bag they fill with air high up in the sky. They bring the bag down and open it, causing the cooling air inside the bag to spread out all over the country. That's a great invention. On the other hand, in Russia, which is a cold country where the snow falls even in summer and the ice is so thick that people can't move, they invented the steam engine. You've got to admire them for it. I understand that they modeled the steam engine after the flaming chariot of hell, but anyway, what they do is to load a crowd of people on a wagon and light a fire in a pipe underneath. They keep feeding the fire inside the pipe with coal, so that the people riding on top can travel a great distance completely oblivious to the cold. Those people in the West can think up inventions like that, one after the other . . . You say you must be going? Well, good-bye. Waitress! Another small bottle of *sake*. And some pickled onions to go with it!

Source: *Modern Japanese Literature*, D. Keene, ed. and trans. pp. 32–33. Copyright © 1956 Grove Press. Reprinted by permission of Grove/Atlantic, Inc.

---

would participate together with the emperor and withdrew support from the bakufu. A second feature of the years between 1863 and 1868 was antiforeignism. Extremists assassinated foreigners as well as bakufu officials; one of their slogans was "expel the barbarians." A third was the formation of new rifle units, commanded mostly by lower samurai. These units transformed political power in Japan. A fourth development during 1867 and 1868 was a cultural shift in the way Japanese saw themselves. During the Tokugawa era, the Japanese saw themselves as civilized Confucians and much of the rest of the world as barbarians. But in the face of Western gunboats, this view seemed hollow. Turning the traditional view on its head, the West, with its technology, science, and humane laws, was now seen as "civilized and enlightened;" China, Japan, and countries like Turkey were seen as half civilized; and other areas were dismissed as barbarian. Moreover, influential scholars claimed that technology was not detachable, but grew out of the Western legal, political, economic, and educational stystems (see "A Japanese View of the Inventiveness of the West").

WHAT POWERS did the Meiji
Constitution give to the emperor?

BUILDING THE MEIJI STATE (1868–1890)

The idea of a "developing nation" did not exist in the mid-19th century. Yet Japan, after the 1868 **Meiji restoration**, was just such a nation. (The years from 1868 to 1912 are referred to as the Meiji period, after the name of the emperor.) It was committed to progress, which meant achieving wealth and power of the kind possessed by Western industrial nations. There was no blueprint for progress. The government advanced by trial and error. It also demanded that the Japanese people make sacrifices for the sake of the future.

The announcement of the restoration of rule by an emperor was made on January 3, 1868. In the battles that followed, Chōshū and Satsuma troops defeated those of the bakufu. Edo surrendered and was renamed Tokyo, the "eastern capital." Edo castle became the imperial palace. A year later, the last bakufu holdouts surrendered. At the start the Meiji government was made up of only a small group of samurai leaders from Chōshū, Satsuma, and a few other domains. They have been described, only half humorously, as 12 bureaucrats in search of a bureaucracy. But their vision defined the goals of the new government.

CENTRALIZATION OF POWER

Their immediate goal was to centralize political power. By 1871, the young leaders had replaced the domains with prefectures controlled from Tokyo. To ensure a break with the past, each new prefectural governor was chosen from samurai of other regions.

Having centralized political authority, about half of the most important Meiji leaders went abroad for a year and a half to study the West. On their return to Japan in 1872, they discovered that officials were planning war with Korea. They quashed the plan, insisting that priority be given to domestic development.

The second goal or task of the Meiji leaders was to stabilize government revenues that, because the land tax was collected mostly in grain, fluctuated with the price of rice. The government converted the grain tax to a money tax. But a third of the revenues still went to pay for samurai stipends, so in 1873 the government raised a conscript army and abolished the samurai class. The samurai were paid off in government bonds; but as the bonds fell during the inflation of the 1870s, most former samurai became impoverished. What had begun as a reform of government finance ended as a social revolution.

Some samurai rebelled. The last and greatest uprising was in 1877. When it was suppressed in 1878, the Meiji government became militarily secure.

POLITICAL PARTIES

Other samurai opposed the government by forming political parties and campaigning for popular rights, elections, and a constitution. They drew heavily on liberal Western models. National assemblies, they argued, were the means used by advanced societies to tap the energies of their peoples. Parties in a national assembly would unite the emperor and the people, thereby curbing the Satsuma-Chōshū clique. Samurai were the mainstay of the early party movement, despite its doctrines proclaiming all classes to be equal. In 1881, the government promised a constitution and a national assembly within 10 years. As the date for national elections approached, the parties gained strength, and the ties between party notables and local men of influence grew closer.

Meiji restoration Overthrow of the Tokugawa *bakufu* in Japan in 1868 and the transfer, or "restoration," of power to the imperial government under the Emperor Meiji.

The Constitution

The government viewed the party movement with distaste but was not sure how to counter it. Itō Hirobumi (1841–1909), originally from Chōshū, went abroad to shop for a constitution that would serve the needs of the Meiji government. He brought home a German jurist to help adapt the conservative Prussian constitution of 1850 to Japanese uses. As promulgated in 1889, the Meiji constitution granted extensive powers to the emperor and severely limited the powers of the lower house in the **Diet** (the English term for Japan's bicameral national assembly).

The emperor was sovereign. According to the constitution, he was "sacred and inviolable," and in Itō's commentaries this was defined in Shinto terms. The emperor was given direct command of the armed forces. Yamagata Aritomo (1838–1922) had set up a German-type general staff system in 1878. The emperor had the right to name the prime minister and to appoint the cabinet. He could dissolve the lower house of the Diet and issue imperial ordinances when the Diet was not in session. The Imperial Household Ministry, which was outside the cabinet, administered the great wealth given to the imperial family during the 1880s—so that the emperor would never have to ask the Diet for funds. It was understood that the Meiji leaders would act for the emperor in all of these matters. Finally, the constitution itself was presented as a gift from the emperor to his subjects.

The lower house of the Diet was given the authority only to approve budgets and pass laws, and both of these powers were hedged. The previous year's budget would remain in effect if a new budget was not approved. The appointive House of Peers, the upper house of the Diet, had to approve any bill to become law. Furthermore, the vote was given only to adult males paying 15 yen or more in taxes. In 1890, this was about 5 percent of the adult male population. In sum, Itō's intention was to create not a parliamentary system, but a constitutional system that included a parliament as one of its parts.

Diet   Bicameral Japanese parliament.

The Promulgation of the Meiji Constitution in 1889.   The emperor standing under the canopy, was declared "sacred and inviolable." Seated on the throne, at the left, is the empress.

Shosai Ginko (Japanese, act. 1874–1897). View of the Issuance of the State Constitution in the State Chamber of the New Imperial Palace, March 2, 1889 (Meiji 22), Ink and color on paper, 14 1/8 × 28 3/8 in. "The Metropolitan Museum of Art, Gift of Lincoln Kirstein, 1959 (JP3233-3235) Photograph © The Metropolitan Museum of Art.

WHY DID Japan set out to build a modern economy?

During the 1880s, the government also created institutions to limit the future influence of the political parties. In 1884, it created a new nobility with which to stock the future House of Peers. The nobility was composed of ex-nobles and the Meiji leaders themselves. Itō, born a lowly foot soldier, ended as a prince. In 1885, he established a cabinet system and became the first prime minister. In 1887, Itō established a Privy Council, with himself as its head, to approve the constitution he had written. In 1888, laws were passed and civil service examinations instituted to insulate the imperial bureaucracy from the tawdry concerns of politicians.

GROWTH OF A MODERN ECONOMY

The late Tokugawa economy was not markedly different from the economies of other East Asian countries. Almost 80 percent of the population lived in the countryside at close to a subsistence level. Taxes were high, and two-thirds of the land tax was paid in kind. Money had only partially penetrated the rural economy. Japan had not developed factory production with machinery, steam power, or large accumulations of capital.

Early Meiji reforms unshackled the late Tokugawa economy. Occupations were freed, which meant that farmers could trade and samurai could farm. Barriers on roads were abolished, as were the monopolistic guilds. The abolition of domains threw open regional economies and a groundswell of new commercial ventures and traditional, agriculturally based industries followed.

Silk was the wonder crop. The government introduced mechanical reeling, enabling Japan to win markets previously held by the hand-reeled silk of China. Silk production rose from 2.3 million pounds in the post-Restoration era to 93 million pounds in 1929.

A parallel unshackling occurred on the land. The land tax reform of the 1870s created an incentive for growth by giving farmers a clear title to their land and by fixing the tax in money. The freedom to buy and sell land led to a rise in tenancy from perhaps 25 percent in 1868 to about 44 percent at the turn of the century. Progressive landlords bought fertilizer and farm equipment. Rice production rose from 149 million bushels a year during 1880–1884 to 316 million during 1935–1937. More food, combined with a drop in the death rate—the result of better hygiene—led to population growth: from about 30 million in 1868 to 45 million in 1900 to 73 million in 1940. Because the farm population remained constant, the extra hands were available for factory and other urban jobs.

FIRST PHASE: MODEL INDUSTRIES

The modern sector of the economy was the government's greatest concern. It developed in four phases. The first was the era of model industries, which lasted until 1881. With military strength as a major goal, the Meiji government expanded arsenals and shipyards, built telegraph lines, made a start on railroads, developed mines, and established factories. The quantitative output of these early industries was insignificant, however. They were pilot-plant operations that doubled as "schools" for technologists and labor.

Just as important to economic development were banks, post offices, ports, roads, commercial laws, a system of primary and secondary schools, a government university, and so on. They were patterned after European and American examples.

A Model Industry. A silk factory, late 1800s. Note the male foreman, whose western-style dress contrasts with the traditional attire of the female workers.

SECOND PHASE: 1880S–1890S

More substantial growth in the modern sector took place during the 1880s and 1890s. It was marked by the appearance of what would later become the great industrial combines known as *zaibatsu*. One of the first industries to benefit was cotton textiles. By 1896, the production of yarn had reached 17 million pounds, and by 1913 it was more than 10 times that amount. Production of cotton cloth rose from 22 million square yards in 1900 to 2.7 billion in 1936.

Another area of growth was railroads. Railroads gave Japan an internal circulatory system, opening up hitherto isolated regions. In 1872, Japan had 18 miles of track; in 1894, 2,100 miles; and by 1934, 14,500 miles.

Cotton textiles and railroads were followed during the 1890s by cement, bricks, matches, glass, beer, chemicals, and other private industries. The government created a favorable climate for growth: The society and the polity were stable, the yen was sound, capital was safe, and taxes on industry were low. In every respect, the conditions enjoyed by Japan's budding entrepreneurs differed from those of China.

THIRD PHASE: 1905–1929

Economic growth spurted ahead during World War I. But an economic slump followed the war, and the economy grew slowly during the 1920s. One factor was renewed competition from a Europe at peace; another was the earthquake that destroyed Tokyo in 1923. Agricultural productivity also leveled off during the 1920s: It became cheaper to import food from the colonies than to invest in new agricultural technology at home.

By the 1920s, Japanese society, especially in the cities, was becoming modern. The Japanese were healthier and lived longer. Personal savings rose with the standard of living. Even factory workers drank beer, went to movies, and read newspapers. By 1925, primary school education was universal. Japan had done what no other non-Western nation had even attempted: It had achieved universal literacy. Nevertheless, an immense cultural and social gap remained between the majority who had only a primary school education and the 3 percent who attended university. This gap was a basic weakness in the political democracy of the 1920s.

The costs of growth were sometimes high. Because textiles played a large role in the early phase of Japan's modern economic growth, well into the 20th century more than half of the industrial labor force was women. They went to the mills after leaving primary school and returned to their villages before marrying. Their working hours were long, their dormitories crowded, and their movements restricted. Some contracted tuberculosis, the plague of late-19th- and early-20th-century Japan, and were sent back to their villages to die.

FOURTH PHASE: DEPRESSION AND RECOVERY

A Japanese bank crisis in 1927, followed by the worldwide Great Depression in 1929, plunged Japan into unemployment and suffering. The political consequences were enormous. Yet most of Japan recovered by 1933, more rapidly than any other industrial nation.

The recovery was fueled by an export boom and military procurements. During the 1930s, the production of pig iron, raw steel, and chemicals doubled. By 1937, Japan had a merchant fleet of 4.5 million tons, the third largest and the newest in the world. The quality of Japan's manufacturers also rose. The outcry in the West against Japanese exports at this time was not so much

QUICK REVIEW

Development of the Japanese Economy

- First Phase (–1881): Development of model industries
- Second Phase (1880s–1890s): Emergence of the zaibatsu and growth of the railroads
- Third Phase (1905–1929): Slow economic growth and modernization of Japanese society
- Fourth Phase (1929–1937): Depression and recovery

zaibatsu Large industrial combines that came to dominate Japanese industry in the late 19th century.

because of volume—a modest 3.6 percent of world exports in 1936—but because Japanese products had become competitive in terms of quality.

WHY DID Japan join the imperialist scramble for colonies?

THE POLITICS OF IMPERIAL JAPAN (1890–1945)

*P*arliaments began in the West and have worked better there than in the rest of the world. Even so cautious a constitution as that of Meiji had no precedent outside the West at the time. How are we then to view the Japanese political experience after 1890?

One view is that because Japanese society was not ready for constitutional government, the militarism of the 1930s was inevitable. From the perspective of an ideal democracy, Japanese society had many weaknesses: a small middle class, weak trade unions, an independent military under the emperor, a strong emperor-centered nationalism, and so on. But these weaknesses did not prevent the Diet from growing in importance, nor did they block the transfer of power from the bureaucratic Meiji leaders to the political party leaders. The transfer fell short of full parliamentary government. However, had it not been derailed by the Great Depression and other events, the advance toward parliamentary government might well have continued.

FROM CONFRONTATION TO THE FOUNDING OF THE SEIYŪ KAI (1890–1900)

In 1890, the Meiji leaders—sometimes called *oligarchs*, the few who rule—were concerned with nation building, not politics. They saw the cabinet as serving the emperor and nation above the ruck of partisan interests. They viewed the political parties as ineffective and irresponsible. They saw the lower house of the Diet as a place to let off steam without interfering in the government's work of building a new Japan. But the oligarchs had miscalculated: The authority of the lower house to approve or turn down the budget made it more powerful than they had intended. This involved the oligarchs, willy-nilly, in the political struggles.

The first act of the parties in the new 1890 Diet was to slash the government's budget. Prime Minister Yamagata had to make concessions to get part of the cut restored. This pattern continued for 10 years. Rising costs meant that the previous year's budget was never enough. The government tried to intimidate and bribe the parties, but failed. Opposing political parties maintained their control of the lower house. They also had the support of the voters, mostly well-to-do landowners, who opposed the government's heavy land tax.

In 1900, Itō Hirobumi formed a new party, called the Rikken Seiyū kai, or "Friends of Constitutional Government." It was composed of ex-bureaucrats associated with Itō and of politicians from the Liberal Party that Itagaki Taisuke (1837–1919) had formed in 1881. For most of the next 20 years, it was the most important party in Japan, providing parliamentary support for successive governments through its control of the lower house. This arrangement was satisfactory to both sides: Prime ministers got the Diet support necessary for the government to function smoothly, and party politicians got cabinet posts and pork barrel legislation with which to reward their supporters.

THE GOLDEN YEARS OF MEIJI

The years before and after the turn of the century represented the culmination of what the government had striven for since 1868. Economic development was under way. Japan got rid of extraterritoriality in 1899 and regained control of its own tariffs in 1911. However, it was international events that won Japan recognition as a world power.

The first event was a war with China in 1894–1895 over Korea. From its victory, Japan secured Taiwan, the Pescadores Islands, the Kwantung Peninsula in southern Manchuria, an indemnity, and a treaty giving it the same privileges in China as those enjoyed by the Western powers (see Map 28–1.). Russia, however, with French and German support, forced Japan to give up the Kwantung Peninsula, which included Port Arthur. Three years later, Russia took Kwantung for itself.

The second event was Japan's participation in 1900 in the international force that relieved the Boxers' siege of the foreign legations in Beijing. A third

24.2
Japanese Imperialism

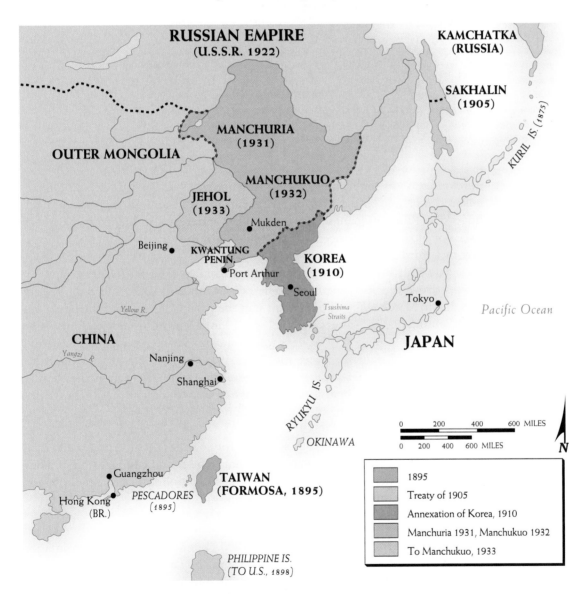

MAP 28–1
Formation of the Japanese Empire.   The Japanese Empire grew in three stages: the Sino-Japanese War of 1894–1895, the Russo-Japanese War of 1904–1905, and Japanese conquests in Manchuria and nothern China after 1931.

WHAT WERE the reasons behind Japan's desire for an empire on the Asian mainland?

Russo-Japanese War. Japanese soldiers with flag and bayonets charge across a smoky field to engage Russian troops in the 1904–1905 Russo-Japanese War. Victory over Russia gave Korea to Japan and a new international standing. The popularity of postcards, such as this one, reflected the new nationalism of Japan.

Corbis-Bettmann.

development was the Anglo-Japanese Alliance of 1902. For Britain, this alliance ensured Japanese support for its East Asian interests and warded off the likelihood of a Russian-Japanese agreement over spheres of influence in Northeast Asia. For Japan, the alliance meant it could fight Russia without fear of intervention by a third party.

The fourth event was the war with Russia that began in 1904. Japanese armies drove the Russians from their railway zones in Manchuria and seized Mukden in March 1905. The Russians sent their Baltic fleet to join the battle, but it was annihilated by Admiral Tōgō (1847–1934) at the Straits of Tsushima. After months of war, both countries were worn out, and Russia was plagued by revolution. President Theodore Roosevelt (1858–1919) proposed a peace conference in Portsmouth, New Hampshire. The resulting treaty gave Japan the Russian lease in the Liaotung Peninsula, the Russian railway in south Manchuria, the southern half of Sakhalin, and a recognition of Japan's "paramount interest" in Korea, which was annexed in 1910.

Japan joined the imperialist scramble for colonies because it wanted equality with the great Western powers, and military power and colonies were the best credentials. Enthusiasm for empire was shared by political party leaders, most liberal thinkers, and conservative leaders alike.

RISE OF THE PARTIES TO POWER

The founding of the Seiyū kai by Itō in 1900 ended a decade of confrontation between the Diet and the government. The aging oligarch Itō found it intolerable to deal with party politicians, who, unlike the bureaucrats, neither obeyed him nor paid him the respect that he thought was his due. In 1903, he relinquished the presidency of the party to Saionji Kinmochi (1849–1940), who passed the post to Hara Takashi (1856–1921) in 1914. With Hara, the office found the man.

Hara was an outsider. Born a generation after the founding fathers of the Meiji state, he helped Itō to found the Seiyū kai and was the most able politician in Japan. His goals for Japan centered on the expansion of national wealth and power and were no different from those of Itō or Yamagata. But he felt that they should be achieved by party government, not oligarchic rule, and worked to expand the power of his party. The years between 1905 and 1921 were marked by the struggle between these two alternative conceptions of government.

The struggle can be represented as a rising curve of party strength and a descending curve of oligarchic influence. The rising curve had two vectors: a buildup of the Seiyū kai party machine that enabled it to win elections and maintain itself as the majority (or plurality) party in the Diet, and the strengthening of the Diet vis-á-vis other elites within the government in Tokyo. For the former, Hara obtained campaign funds from moneyed interests. He also promoted pork barrel legislation. Constituencies that supported Seiyū kai candidates got new schools, bridges, dams, roads, or even railroad lines. Hara was even willing to call on the police and local officials to aid Seiyū kai election campaigns.

In co-opting other governmental elites, the Seiyū kai had mixed success. The party increased its representation in the cabinet and gained some patronage appointments in the bureaucracy, although most bureaucrats remained professionals and resisted the intrusion of political appointees. The House of Peers and the Privy Council, which ratified treaties, remained independent bodies. The Seiyū kai had no success in penetrating the military services.

The descending curve of weakening oligarchic control reflected the aging of the "men of Meiji." In 1900, Itō was the last oligarch to become prime minister. From 1901 to 1912, Katsura Tarō (1847–1913), a Chōshū general and Yamagata's protégé, and Saionji, Itō's protégé, took turns in the post. Both had Seiyū kai support. The oligarchs were also weakened by changes within the elites. A younger generation of officers in the military services chafed at the continuing domination by the old cliques. In the civil bureaucracy, younger officials who had graduated from the Law Faculty of Tokyo Imperial University were achieving positions of responsibility. They saw the bureaucracy as an independent service and resisted oligarchic control almost as much as they resisted that of the parties.

The oligarchs maintained their power to act for the emperor in appointing prime ministers. With the deaths of Itō in 1909 and Yamagata in 1922, this vital function was taken over by Saionji and, later, by ex-prime ministers.

As the rising and descending curves approached each other, the political parties advanced. Several turning points were critical. One came in 1912. When the army's demands for a larger budget were refused, it withdrew its minister, causing Saionji's cabinet to collapse. Katsura tried to govern using imperial decrees in place of Diet support. This infuriated the parties, and even the Seiyū kai withdrew its support. Massive popular demonstrations broke out. Katsura was forced to resign in 1913. The lower house had defeated an oligarchic prime minister.

The curves finally crossed in 1918 when Hara became prime minister. It was the first time a politician who was not a Meiji founding father or a protégé of one had obtained the post. He enacted reforms but did nothing to remedy the parliamentary shortcomings of the Meiji constitution.

A third development was the wave of liberalism that began during World War I and culminated in the period of party governments from 1924 to 1932. Joining the Allies in World War I, Japan had been influenced by democratic thought from England and America. Scholars discussed revising the Meiji constitution. Labor unions were organized, at first liberal and often Christian, and later Marxist. A social movement was launched to improve conditions in Japan's industrial slums and to pass social and labor legislation. Japan's second political party, the Kenseikai, which had been out of power since 1916, steadily grew more liberal and adopted several of the new social causes as its own, such as universal manhood suffrage. When Hara cut the tax qualification for voting from 10 to 3 yen—a considerable extension of the franchise—the Kenseikai criticized the change as insufficient.

In 1924, the Kenseikai and the Seiyū kai formed a coalition government. For the next eight years, the presidents of one or the other of the two major parties were appointed as prime ministers.

The cabinets (1924–1926) of Katō Kōmei are considered the peak of parliamentarianism in prewar Japan. Blunt, cold, and haughty, Katō was respected, if not liked. He was an Anglophile who advocated a British model of government. His ministry passed universal manhood suffrage, increased academic appointments to the House of Peers, and cut the military budget. He also enacted social and labor legislation. In effect, he legalized the moderate socialist movement and outlawed revolutionary socialism. Katō's cabinet brought Japan close to a true parliamentary government.

MILITARISM AND WAR (1927–1945)

The future of Japan's parliamentary coalition seemed assured during the mid-1920s. The economy was growing, society was stable, and the party leaders were experienced. Japan's international position was secure. By a decade later, however, the party leaders had lost the gains of 35 years. By 1945, Japan had been defeated in a devastating war and was occupied by foreign troops for the first time in its history. How did this come about?

Simply put, a small shift in the balance of power among the governmental elites established by the Meiji constitution had produced a major change in Japan's foreign policy. The parties had been the obstreperous elite between 1890 and 1926 and had advanced by forcing the other elites to compromise. From the late 1920s, the military became the obstreperous elite and did the same. Beginning in 1932, military men replaced party presidents as prime ministers. In 1937, Japan went to war with China; and by the end of 1941, Japan was allied with Germany and Italy and had gone to war with the United States.

From their inception, the military services in Japan had been constructed on different principles from Japan's civilian society. Soldiers were not samurai. Universal conscription had put the new military on a changed footing. But the armed services had their own schools, which inculcated the values of discipline, bravery, loyalty, and obedience. The military saw themselves as the heirs of those who had founded the modern Japanese state and the guardians of Japanese tradition. They contrasted their loyalty to the emperor and their concern for all Japanese with the pandering to special interests by the political parties.

They resented their diminished national stature during the 1920s, when military budgets were cut and the prestige of a military career declined. But even during the liberal 1920s there had been no change in the constitutional position of the services. The general staffs remained directly responsible to the emperor. With the passing of the Meiji oligarchs, this meant they were responsible to no one but themselves.

A Crisis in Manchuria   The new multilateral treaties (the 1924 Washington Conference and the 1930 London Conference) that replaced the earlier system of bilateral treaties (such as the Anglo-Japanese Alliance) recognized the existing colonies of the victors in World War I but opposed new colonial ventures.

Japan's position in Manchuria was ambiguous. Because Japan maintained its rule through a tame Chinese warlord, Manchuria was not, strictly speaking, a colony. But because Japan had gained its special position in Manchuria at the cost of 100,000 lives in the 1905 Russo-Japanese War, it saw its claim to Manchuria as similar to that of Western nations to their colonies.

From the late 1920s, the Guomindang unification of China and the blossoming of Chinese nationalism threatened Japan's special position. Japanese army units tried to block the march north and murdered the Manchurian warlord when he showed signs of independence. In this crisis, the party government in Tokyo equivocated, hoping to preserve a status quo that was crumbling before its eyes. The army saw Manchuria as a buffer between the Soviet Union and the Japanese colony of Korea. In 1931, the army provoked a crisis, took over Manchuria, and proclaimed it an independent state in 1932. When the League of Nations condemned this action, Japan withdrew from the league in 1933.

The Great Depression Japan's government acted effectively to counter the Great Depression, as noted earlier, but the recovery came too late to help the political parties. By 1936, political trends that had begun during the worst years of the depression had become irreversible.

The depression galvanized the political left and right. The political left was composed mainly of socialist moderates, who won 8 Diet seats in 1928 and 37 in 1937. Supported by unionists and white-collar workers, they would reemerge as an even stronger force after World War II. The radical left consisted of many little Marxist parties led by intellectuals and of the Japanese Communist Party. Although small and subject to governmental repression, the radical parties were influential in intellectual and literary circles during the 1920s and 1930s.

The Radical Right and the Military The political right in pre–World War II Japan is difficult to define. Most Japanese, even socialists, were imbued with an emperor-centered nationalism. During the 1930s, however, a new array of right-wing organizations went beyond the usual nationalism to challenge the status quo. Civilian ultranationalists used Shinto myths and Confucian values to attack Western liberalism in Japan's urban society. Some bureaucrats looked to the example of Nazi Germany and argued for the exclusion of party politicians from government. Military officers envisioned a "defense state" guided by themselves. They argued for military expansion and an autarchic colonial empire insulated from the uncertainties of the world economy. Young officers of the revolutionary right advocated "direct action" against the elites of the parliamentary coalition. They called for a second restoration of imperial power.

Modern Japan

Overthrow of Tokugawa Bakufu

1853–1854	Perry obtains Treaty of Friendship
1858	Bakufu signs commercial treaty
1861–1863	Chōshū and Satsuma mediate
1866	Chōshū defeats bakufu army
1868	Meiji restoration

Nation Building

1868–1871	Shaping a new state
1873–1878	Social revolution from above
1877–1878	Satsuma rebellion
1889	Meiji Constitution promulgated
1890	First Diet session

Imperial Japan

1894–1895	Sino-Japanese War
1900	Seiyū kai formed
1904–1905	Russo-Japanese War
1910	Korea annexed

Era of Party Government

1918	Hara becomes prime minister
1924	Katō becomes prime minister, universal manhood suffrage passed

Militarism

1931	Japan takes Manchuria
1937	War with China
1941	Japan attacks Pearl Harbor
1945	Japan surrenders

Tōjō Hideki. Prime minister at the time of the attack on Pearl Harbor in 1941, Tōjō Hideki (1884–1948) was one of the chief figures in the rise of Japanese militarism.

Corbis-Bettmann.

The last group precipitated political change. On May 15, 1932, junior army and navy officers attacked the Seiyū kai offices, the Bank of Japan, and the Tokyo police headquarters, and murdered Prime Minister Inukai. The attack occurred at the peak of right-wing agitation and the pit of the depression. Saionji decided that it would be unwise to appoint another party president as the new prime minister; and chose instead a moderate admiral. For the next four years, cabinets were led by moderate military men, but with party participation. These cabinets satisfied neither the parties nor the radical young officers.

During 1936 and 1937, Japanese politics continued to drift to the right. In the election of February 1936, the opposition overturned the Seiyū kai-dominated Diet with the slogan, "What shall it be, parliamentary government or Fascism?" A week later, young officers attempted a coup in Tokyo. They killed cabinet ministers and occupied the Diet and other government buildings. They wanted their army superiors to form a new government. Saionji and other men about the emperor stood firm; the navy opposed the rebellion; and within three days it was suppressed. It was the last "direct action" by the radical right in prewar Japan. The ringleaders were tried and executed, and generals sympathetic to them were retired. The officers in charge of the purge within the army were tough-minded elitist technocrats. They included General Tōjō Hideki (1884–1948), who would lead Japan into World War II.

But the services interfered more than ever in the formation of cabinets. From 1936 on, moderate prime ministers gave way to more outspokenly militaristic figures.

Opposition to militarism remained substantial nonetheless. In the 1937 election, the two major centrist parties, which had joined in opposition to the government, won 354 Diet seats. The Japanese people were more level-headed than their leaders. But the centrists' victory proved hollow. The Diet could not oppose a government in wartime, and by summer, Japan was at war in China.

The Road to Pearl Harbor Three critical junctures occurred between the outbreak of the war with China and World War II in the Pacific. The first was the decision in January 1938 to strike a knockout blow at the Nationalist Party (GMD) government. The war had begun as an unplanned skirmish between Chinese and Japanese troops in the Beijing area but had quickly spread. The Japanese army's leaders disagreed on whether to continue. Many held that the only threat to Japanese interests in Korea and Manchuria was the Soviet Union, and that a long war in China was foolish. But as the Japanese armies advanced, the general staff argued that the only way to end the war was to convince the nationalists that fighting was hopeless. The army occupied most of the cities and railroads of eastern China, but Jiang Jieshi refused to give in. A stalemate ensued that lasted until 1945. China was never a major theater of the war in the Pacific.

The second critical decision was the signing of the **Tripartite Pact** with Germany and Italy in September 1940. Japan had long admired Germany. In

Tripartite Pact Alliance between Japan and Nazi Germany and Fascist Italy that was signed in 1940.

1936, it had joined Germany in the Anti-Comintern Pact directed against international communism. It also wanted an alliance with Germany against the Soviet Union. Germany insisted, however, that any alliance would also have to be directed against the United States and Britain. The Japanese disagreed. The Japanese navy saw the American Pacific fleet as its only potential enemy and was not willing to risk being dragged into a German war. When Japanese troops battled Russian troops in an undeclared mini-war from May to September 1939 on the Mongolian border, sentiment rose in favor of an alliance with Germany, but then Germany "betrayed" Japan by signing a nonaggression pact with the Soviet Union. For a time Japan decided to improve its relations with the United States, but America insisted that Japan get out of China. By the late spring of 1940, German victories in Europe—the fall of Britain appeared imminent—again led military leaders in Japan to favor an alliance with Germany.

When Japan signed the Tripartite Pact, it had three objectives: to isolate the United States, to inherit the Southeast Asian colonies of the countries defeated by Germany in Europe, and to improve its relations with the Soviet Union through the good offices of Germany. The last objective was reached when Japan signed a neutrality pact with the Soviet Union in April 1941. Two months later, Germany attacked the Soviet Union without consulting its ally, Japan. It compounded this second "betrayal" by asking Japan to attack the Soviet Union in the east. Japan waited and watched. When the German advance was stopped short of Moscow, Japan decided to honor the neutrality pact and turn south. This decision marked, in effect, the end of Japan's participation in the Axis. Thereafter, it fought its own war in Asia. Yet instead of deflecting American criticism as intended, the pact, by linking Japan to Germany, led to a hardening of America's position on China.

The third and fatal decision was to go to war with the United States. In June 1940, following Germany's defeat of France, Japanese troops had moved into northern French Indochina. The United States retaliated by limiting strategic exports to Japan. When Japanese troops took southern Indochina in July 1941, the United States embargoed all exports to Japan; this cut Japanese oil imports by 90 percent. The navy's general staff argued that oil reserves would last only two years; after that the navy would lose its capability to fight. Its general staff pressed for the capture of the oil-rich Dutch East Indies. But it was too dangerous to move against Dutch and British colonies in Southeast Asia with the United States on its flank in the Philippines. The navy, therefore, planned a preemptive strike against the United States, and on December 7, 1941, it bombed Pearl Harbor. The Japanese decision for war wagered Japan's land-based air power, shorter supply lines, and what it saw as greater will power against American productivity. The navy's chief of staff compared the war with the United States to a dangerous operation that might save the life of a critically ill patient. In the end, the war left Japan defeated and in ruins.

JAPANESE MILITARISM AND GERMAN NAZISM

*T*he growths of militarism in Japan and Nazi German had some similarities. Both countries were late developers with elitist, academic bureaucracies and strong military traditions. Both had patriarchal family traditions and relatively new parliamentary systems. Both tried to solve the economic problems created by the Great Depression with territorial expansion. Both persecuted socialists and liberals. Both had modernized their military services, schools,

WHAT ARE the differences and similarities between the rise of militarism in Japan and Germany?

governments, and communications to support authoritarian regimes, but their values were not sufficiently modern or democratic to resist antiparliamentary forces.

There were differences between the two countries. Japan was more homogeneous than Germany. It had no Catholic-Protestant split, no *Junker* class, and no significant socialist movement. In Germany, parliament ruled, and the Nazis had to win an election to come to power. Japan's Diet was weaker. Control of the government was taken away from the Seiyūkai and Minseitō even while they continued to win elections.

The process by which the two countries went to war was also different. The Nazis created a mass party and a totalitarian state and then declared war. In Japan, there was neither a mass party nor a single group of leaders in continuous control of the government. It was not the totalitarian state that made war as much as it was war that made the state totalitarian—creating a nationalism so intense that university students became suicide *(kamikaze)* pilots after the outbreak of hostilities.

The Allies compared General Tōjō, Japan's prime minister, with Hitler. However, while Nazi authority survived until Hitler died in a Berlin bunker, General Tōjō was removed from office when American planes began to bomb Japan in 1944. The military continued to prosecute the war. But when the Imperial Conference on August 14, 1945, divided three-to-three over the Allied ultimatum demanding unconditional surrender, the emperor broke the deadlock, saying that the unendurable must be endured. It was the only important decision that he had ever been allowed to make.

SUMMARY

China: The 19th Century China's bureaucracy centered on the imperial court in Beijing. The court was concerned about governing China and, then, to protecting its land frontiers. For 2,000 years, the only threats to China had come from beyond those frontiers. The expansion of imperial Russia reinforced this orientation. In the east, China was protected by the ocean. Even the Sino-Japanese pirates of the 16th century had been more a nuisance than a serious threat, and Europeans were initially viewed in the same light. The Opium War was fought in 1839–1842, and other wars with European powers thereafter, but these were seen as "coastal incursions," which posed little threat to the Qing heartland. Far more serious were the Taiping and other rebellions, which seized villages, threatened gentry control of local society, and attacked officials at both district and provincial levels. For China, the important story of the 19th century was the success of gentry armies in suppressing these rebellions, a success using Western weapons but based on traditional values. Not until the very end of the century after Japan's defeat of China in 1895 and its defeat of Russia in 1905 did the Chinese begin substantial Westernizing reforms—and by then it was too late for the dynasty.

China: The 20th Century After the Qing fell in 1912, China was ruled for a decade and a half by regional warlords, a pattern not unlike the aftermaths of previous dynasties. But the ferment of the newly entering flood of Western ideas fed a growing nationalism. This nationalism permeated the Huangpu Military Academy that trained the officers of the Guomindang (or Nationalist) army; it lent legitimacy to the army's march north and to the establishment of the Nanjing government. By 1934, the Guomindang was winning; communists were forced to abandon bases in south China and flee to the arid northwest. But then

Japan invaded and occupied just those areas on which the Guomindang had depended. The communists built up their army, extended their influence into "occupied China," and won the civil war that wracked China between 1945 and 1949.

The Transformation of Japan In contrast to China, the Tokugawa regime collapsed quickly—only 15 years after the arrival of Perry in 1853. With its collapse, an elaborate structure of vested interests was destroyed. Leon Trotsky once spoke of dislocations in history produced by modern weapons in countries with less advanced technologies. Traditional vested interests in Japan—represented by samurai rebellions using old-fashioned weapons—attempted to fight against the new reformist government in the decade after 1868, but they lost every battle. The new Meiji government began sweeping Westernizing reforms in every field. Economic growth went hand in hand with universal education. The emperor became the unifying symbol for traditional and conservative thinkers. The Diet (Japan's parliament) became the focus for progressives and liberals. A shifting balance between conservatives and liberals ensued, with parliamentary democracy making gains into the 1920s. But then the Great Depression and a crisis in Manchuria opened the way for the rise of militarism in the 1930s. One thing led to another and Japan went to war with the United States in 1941.

IMAGE KEY

for pages 696–697

a. Chinese president Sun Yat Sen.

b. A duotype of Field Marshall Oyama's infantrymen confront Russian troops.

c. Japan's first foreign mission headed by Prince Iwakura.

d. Shoes designed for bound feet.

e. The dowager empress Tz'u-hsi.

f. Picture of steam engine traffic at Shiodome, 1872.

g. The Comodore Perry expedition to Japan.

h. Imperial Japanese national flag.

REVIEW QUESTIONS

1. Which had the greater impact on China, the Opium War or the Taiping rebellions?

2. How did the Qing (or Manchu) dynasty recover from the Taiping rebellions? Why did the recovery not prevent the overthrow of the dynasty in 1911?

3. Did the May Fourth Movement prepare the way for the nationalist revolution and communist revolutions?

4. After the Meiji restoration, what steps did Japan's leaders take to achieve their goal of "wealth and power"?

5. What were the strengths and weaknesses of Japan's prewar parliamentary institutions? What led to the sudden rise of militarism during the 1930s?

KEY TERMS

Boxers (p. 702)

Diet (p. 711)

Guomindang (GMD) (p. 704)

Long March (p. 705)

Meiji restoration (p. 710)

Taiping rebellions (p. 699)

treaty ports (p. 700)

Tripartite Pact (p. 720)

unequal treaties (p. 698)

zaibat (p. 713)

 For additional study resources for this chapter, go to:
www.prenhall.com/craig/chapter28

Visualizing The Past...

Industrialization

HOW DID the advent of industrialization in the 19th and early 20th centuries shape the art of those countries that industrialized? Did artists view industrialization as a negative or a positive force?

The Industrial Revolution began in Britain in the 18th century. By the mid-19th century factories, coal-fired machines, and railroads had spread throughout Western Europe, and also the eastern portion of the United States. By the later 19th-century industrialization and railroad building advanced in the United States, and also in Japan, which had become the most industrialized non-Western power in the world by the 1930s. Industry was understood to be about power, not only the power machines generated and artists celebrated, but also the power of political and military domination.

◄ **Power Loom Weaving of cotton cloth in a textile mill; colored engraving, 1834.** Industrialization began in the cloth industry because cloth was the most important manufactured product in the world from ancient times to the dawn of the modern era. Early factory owners often employed women, whose labor came cheaper than that of men. Factory women worked long hours and were subject to close supervision designed to ensure that their morals would not suffer in the factory setting.
The Granger Collection.

Shōsai Ikkei, "Picture of Steam Engine Traffic at Shiodome," 1872. In stark contrast to China, Japan's strategy for dealing with Western imperialism in 19th-century Asia was to compete with it head on as an industrial power. To do this, Japan imported, copied, and ultimately improved on Western technology. In this image we see in the foreground the great symbol of 19th-century technology, the railroad, as well as modern, Western-style buildings and, in the distance, steamships in the harbor.

Courtesy of the Library of Congress. Gift of Mrs E. Crane Chadbourne; 1930.

Diego Rivera, "Detroit Industry," Mural, North Wall, 1933. As industrialization spread from the cloth industry to all forms of manufacture, it became increasingly dominated by men, both because it became a mainstay of male employment in the West but also because its association with power and war meant that it was imagined as largely masculine. In this image we see strong, upright American men at work manufacturing the premier symbol of American industry—the automobile.

Diego Rivera (1886–1957). "Detroit Industry". North Wall, 1933. © 2003 Banco de Mexico Diego Rivera & Frida Kahlo Museums Trust. Av. Cinco de Mayo No. 2, Col. Centro, Del. Cuauhtemoc 06059, Mexico, D.F. Reproduction authorized by the Instituto Nacional de Bellas Artes y Literatura. Photograph © 2001 The Detroit Institute of Art/Bridgeman Art Library.

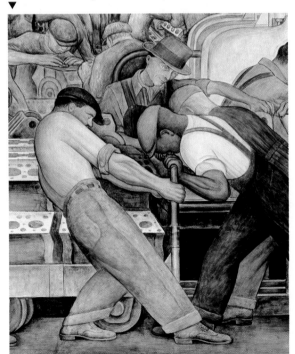

Kazimir Malevich, "The Knife Grinder," 1912. To those who experienced industrialization, technology seemed to speed up life to a dizzying rate. Although some found the new emphasis on speed and motion disorienting, many celebrated it—none more than the futurists, a group of painters active in the first decades of the twentieth century. In the painting shown here, the distinction between the knife grinder and his work dissolves into a dizzying blur of geometric shapes.

PART SEVEN · GLOBAL CONFLICT AND CHANGE

EUROPE

1914–1918	World War I
1917	Bolsheviks seize power, Russia
1919	Versailles Settlement
1922	Mussolini seizes power, Italy
1925	Locarno Pact
1933	Hitler comes to power
1936	Spanish Civil War begins
1938	Munich Conference
1939	World War II begins

▲ *American World War II poster*

1944	D-Day
1945	World War II ends
1948	Berlin blockade and airlift
1949	NATO treaty; Russia detonates atomic bomb
1953	Death of Stalin
1955	Warsaw Pact
1956	Soviets crush Hungarian revolt
1957	EEC founded
1958	Charles de Gaulle comes to power in France

◄ Guernica, *Pablo Picasso, 1937*

NEAR EAST / INDIA

1922	British leave Egypt
1922–1938	Mustafa Kemal first president of Turkey
1928	The Muslim Brotherhood founded by Hasan Al-Banna

1947	Indian Independence; creation of Pakistan
1948	Assassination of Mahatma Gandhi
1949	State of Israel founded
1953	Mosaddeq overthrown in Iran
1954–1970	Abdel Nasser leads Egypt
1956	Suez Crisis

EAST ASIA

Mao Zedong ►
with Nikita Khrushchev

1916–1928	Warlord Era in China
1919	May 4th Movement in China
1925	Universal male suffrage in Japan
1928–1937	Nationalist government in China at Nanking
1931	Japan occupies Manchuria
1937–1945	Japan at war with China

1941	Japan attacks Pearl Harbor
1945	Japan surrenders after U.S. atomic bombs
1945–1949	Civil War in China; People's Republic founded
1950	N. Korea invades S. Korea
1952	U.S. ends occupation of Japan
1953–1972	Double-digit growth in Japan
1955	Liberal-Democratic Party formed in Japan
1959–1960	Sino-Soviet split

AFRICA

1919	W.E.B. DuBois holds first Pan-African Congress in Paris
1935	Mussolini invades Ethiopia

1942–1945	World War II engulfs North Africa
1955–1962	Wars of independence in French Algeria
1956	Sudan gains independence from Britain and Egypt
1956	Morocco and Tunisia gain independence from France
1957	Ghana an independent state under Kwame Nkrumah

THE AMERICAS

1917	U.S. enters World War I
1929	Wall Street crash; the Great Depression begins
1930–1945	Vargas dictatorship in Brazil
1932	F.D. Roosevelt elected U.S. president
1938	Mexico nationalizes oil

1941	U.S. enters World War II
1945	Death of F.D. Roosevelt
1946	Perón elected president in Argentina
1954	U.S. Supreme Court outlaws segregation
1955	Perón overthrown
1956	Montgomery bus boycott
1959	Fidel Castro comes to power in Cuba

◄ *Fidel Castro*

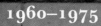
1960	Paris Summit Conference collapses after U-2 incident	**1977**	Brezhnev president of USSR	**1989**	Berlin Wall demolished
1961	Berlin Wall erected	**1979**	Margaret Thatcher becomes British prime minister	**1990**	Germany unified
1964	Khrushchev replaced as Soviet prime minister by Kosygin; replaced as party secretary by Brezhnev	**1980**	Solidarity Movement in Poland	**1991**	Failed coup in Soviet Union; Yeltsin emerges as leader of Russia
1968	Soviets invade Czechoslovakia	**1981**	Crackdown against Solidarity	**1991**	Major replaces Thatcher as England's prime minister
1972	British Impose direct rule on Northern Ireland	**1984–1985**	Bitter strikes by miners in England	**1993**	Czechoslovakia divides into two republics
1972	Israeli Olympic athletes killed by Arab terrorists	**1984**	Mikhail Gorbachev introduces *glasnost* in USSR	**1995**	Dayton Peace Accords end war in Bosnia
1974	End of military rule in Greece			**1999**	NATO military campaign against Serbia
1974	Portuguese dictatorship deposed; democratic reforms begin			**2000**	Putin elected president of Russia; overthrow of Milŏsevic in Yugoslavia

▲ *Opening of the Berlin Wall, 1989*

1966	Indira Gandhi becomes prime minister of India	**1977**	Menachem Begin becomes prime minister of Israel	**1989**	Soviets leave Afghanistan
1967	Israeli-Arab June War	**1978**	Iranian revolution under Khomeini's leadership	**1989**	Death of Khomeini
1969	Golda Meir becomes prime minister of Israel	**1979**	Egyptian-Israeli Peace Treaty	**1990**	Central Asian States become independent on fall of USSR
1969	Arafat elected P.L.O. chairman	**1979**	Iran takes U.S. hostages	**1990–1991**	Gulf War
1971	India-USSR friendship treaty	**1979**	Soviets invade Afghanistan	**1991**	Indian prime minister Rajiv Ghandi assassinated
1973	Arab-Israeli October War	**1980–1988**	Iran-Iraq War		
1972	Independence for Bangladesh	**1981**	Hostages released in Iran		
1973	OPEC oil embargo	**1981**	Egypt's Sadat assassinated; succeeded by Hosni Mubarak		
		1982	Israel invades Lebanon		
		1984	Indira Gandhi assassinated		

Oil wells left burning ▶ by Iraqi troops in Kuwait

1959–1975	Vietnam War	**1976**	Death of Mao Tse-tung	**1988**	Japan's GNP second in world
1965–1976	Cultural Revolution devastates China	**1978–1989**	New Economic policies of Teng Hsiao-p'ing in China	**1989**	Vietnam pledges to withdraw from Cambodia
1968	Death of Ho Chi Minh, president of North Vietnam	**1978–1989**	Vietnam occupies Cambodia	**1989**	China crushes pro-democracy demonstrations in Beijing
1971	Lin Piao killed in China	**1980s**	Double-digit economic growth in South Korea and Taiwan	**1991–1992**	Political scandals and plummeting stock market in Japan
1972	President Nixon visits China			**1992**	Kim Young Sam, civilian party leader, elected S. Korean president
1973	Economic growth slows in Japan				

▲ *The Cultural Revolution, China*

Tienanmen Square ▶

1960	Belgian Congo granted independence as Zaire			**1989**	Conservative Botha government resigns in South Africa; DeKlerk becomes president
1963	Kenya becomes an independent republic			**1992**	Nelson Mandela freed from prison in South Africa
1964	Zanzibar, the Congo, and Northern Rhodesia (Zambia) become independent republics	**1980**	Southern Rhodesia (Zimbabwe) gains independence from Britain	**1994**	Nelson Mandela elected president of South Africa
1965	Revolution in Kenya	**1984**	Bishop Desmond Tutu awarded Nobel Peace Prize		
1967–1970	Nigerian Civil War	**1985**	U.S. economic sanctions against South Africa result in more repression		
1974	Drought and famine in Africa				
1974	Emperor Haile Selassie of Ethiopia is deposed				
1974–1975	Portugal grants independence to Guinea, Angola, Mozambique, Cape Verde				

Nelson Mandela ▶

1960	Kennedy elected president	**1979**	Revolution in Nicaragua and El Salvador		
1962	Cuban Missile Crisis	**1980**	Iran hostage crisis		
1963	Kennedy assassinated	**1980**	Reagan elected president	**1991**	Gulf War
1964	Passage of Civil Rights Act	**1982**	War between Argentina and Great Britain over Islas Malvinas (Falkland Islands)	**1992**	Clinton elected president
1965	U.S. expands Vietnam commitment			**1994**	Revolt in Chiapas, Mexico
1968	Martin Luther King and Robert Kennedy assassinated; campus unrest	**1983**	Argentine military government overthrown; elected government restored	**1998**	Pope visits Cuba
1968	Nixon elected	**1983**	End of Mexican oil boom	**2001**	Terrorists attacks on the World Trade Center in New York City and the Pentagon in Washington, D.C.
1970	Allende elected in Chile	**1988**	Major arms agreement between U.S. and USSR		
1972	Nixon visits China and USSR; is reelected president				
1973	Watergate scandal breaks				
1973	Perón reelected, Argentina				
1973	Chile's Allende overthrown				
1974	Nixon resigns presidency				

29

Imperialism and World War I

CHAPTER HIGHLIGHTS

The New Imperialism European imperialism in the last part of the nineteenth century brought the Western countries into contact with most of the world. By 1914, European nations had divided Africa among themselves and controlled large parts of Asia and the islands of the Pacific. Much of the Middle East was under the nominal control of the Ottoman Empire, which was in its death throes and under European influence. The Monroe Doctrine made Latin America a protectorate of the United States. Japan had become an imperial power at the expense of China and Korea.

World War I The emergence of a new, powerful German state at the center of Europe upset the old balance of power. The German emperor, William II, sought more power and influence for his country. The result was a system of alliances that divided Europe into two armed camps. What began as yet another Balkan War involving the European powers became a world war that influenced the rest of the world. As the terrible war of 1914–1918 dragged on, the real motives that had driven the European powers to fight gave way to public affirmations of the principles of nationalism and self-determination.

The Peace Settlement The peoples under colonial rule took these statements seriously and sought to win their own independence and nationhood. For the most part they were disappointed by the peace settlement. However, the old imperial nations, especially Britain and France, had paid an enormous price in lives, money, and will for their victory in the war. Colonial peoples pressed for the rights that were proclaimed as universal by the West but denied to their colonies. Tension between colonies and their ruling nations was a cause of instability in the world created by the Paris treaties of 1919.

CHAPTER QUESTIONS

WHAT WAS the New Imperialism?

WHAT WERE the two alliance systems that faced each other in Europe before 1914?

WHAT CAUSED the outbreak of World War I in 1914?

WHY WERE the Bolsheviks able to seize power in Russia ?

WHY DID the Versailles settlement leave Germany bitter?

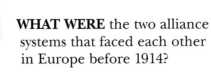

CHAPTER OUTLINE

- Expansion of European Power and the "New Imperialism"
- Emergence of the German Empire
- World War I
- The Russian Revolution
- End of World War I

During the second half of the 19th century, Europe exercised unprecedented control over the rest of the world. The Americas, Australia, and New Zealand almost became part of the European world as streams of European immigrants populated these areas. Africa was divided among European nations (see Chapter 27), and Europe imposed its power across Asia (see Map 29–1 and Chapter 28). By 1900, European dominance had brought every part of the globe into a single world economy.

But these developments helped to foster competition and hostility among the great powers of Europe and to bring on a terrible war. The frenzy for imperial expansion that seized Europeans in the late 19th century did much to destroy its peace, prosperity, and dominant place in the world.

WHAT WAS the
New Imperialism?

EXPANSION OF EUROPEAN POWER AND THE "NEW IMPERIALISM"

xplosive developments in 19th-century science, technology, industry, agriculture, transportation, communication, and military weapons enabled a few Europeans (and Americans) to impose their will on other peoples many times their number. Westerners had institutional as well as material advantages—particularly the mobilizing power of national states and a belief in the superiority of their civilization.

By the mid-19th century, only Great Britain retained extensive overseas holdings, and there was general hostility to territorial expansion. The dominant doctrine of free trade opposed political interference in other lands. But after 1870, European states swiftly exerted control over about a fifth of the world's land area and a tenth of its population in a movement called the **New Imperialism** (see Map 29–1).

THE NEW IMPERIALISM

Imperialism can be defined as extending a nation's influence by some form of power over foreign peoples. The usual pattern of the New Imperialism was for the European nation to invest capital in the "backward" country and thereby to transform its economy and culture. To guarantee their investments, European states would establish different degrees of political control ranging from full annexation as a colony, to protectorate status (whereby the local ruler was controlled by the dominant European state), to "spheres-of-influence" status (whereby the European state received special privileges without direct political involvement).

MOTIVES FOR THE NEW IMPERIALISM: ECONOMIC INTERPRETATION

There is still no agreement about the motives for the New Imperialism. The most widespread interpretation has been economic. Lenin saw imperialism as the final stage in capitalism's development—the pursuit of monopoly. He claimed that as capitalists exhausted opportunities of investment in their home countries, they persuaded their governments to acquire colonies. The facts, however, do not support this thesis. Only a small part of European investments overseas went to the colonies acquired by the new imperialism. Most of it went to older, established areas like the United States, Canada, and Australia. Colonies were not usually important markets for the great imperial nations, and

New Imperialism Extension in the late 19th and early 20th centuries of Western political and economic dominance to Asia, the Middle East, and Africa.

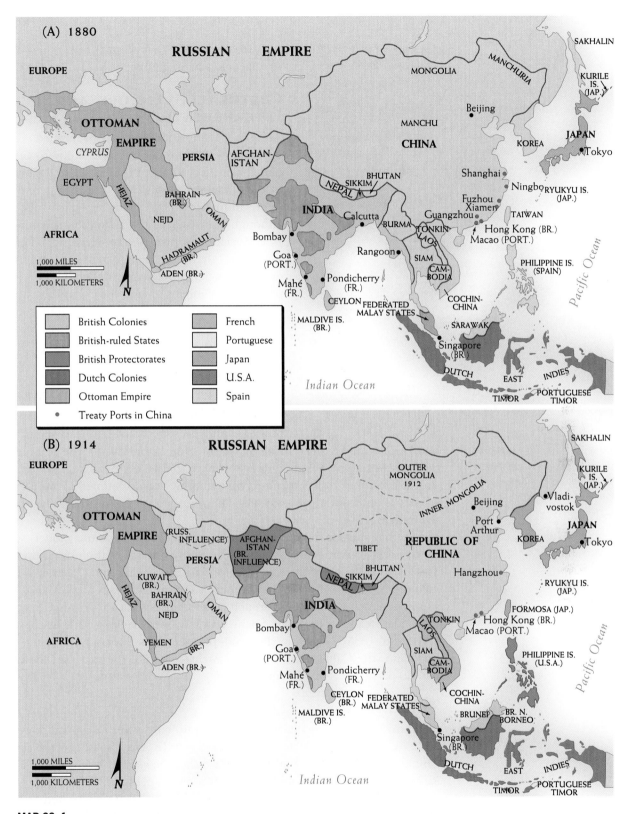

MAP 29–1

Asia 1880–1914. As in Africa (see Maps 27–1 and 27–2), the late 19th century saw imperialism spread widely and rapidly in Asia. Two new powers, Japan and the United States, joined the British, French, and Dutch in extending control throughout south and southeast Asia and in exploiting an enfeebled China.

HOW DID the new Japanese empire affect the balance of power in Asia?

THE DEVILFISH IN EGYPTIAN WATERS.

John Bull. An American cartoonist in 1888 depicted John Bull (England) as the octopus of imperialism, grabbing land on every continent. Notice the hand at the left poised to grab Egypt.

The Granger Collection, N.Y.

it is not even clear that control of the new colonies was particularly profitable.

CULTURAL, RELIGIOUS, AND SOCIAL INTERPRETATIONS

Some advocates of imperialism argued that the European nations had a responsibility to bring the benefits of their superior civilization and Christianity to the people of "backward" lands, but few people were influenced by such arrogant arguments, although many shared the assumptions behind them (see "Social Darwinism and Imperialism"). Politicians suggested that imperial expansion might solve domestic social problems by deflecting public attention from problems at home or providing an outlet for surplus population. The new colonies, however, attracted few European emigrants. Most went to the Americas and Australia.

STRATEGIC AND POLITICAL INTERPRETATIONS: THE SCRAMBLE FOR AFRICA

Strategic and prestige considerations seem to have been more important in bringing on the New Imperialism. The completion of the Suez Canal in 1869 made Egypt vital to the British because it sat astride the shortest route to India. When Egypt's stability was threatened in the 1880s, the British established a protectorate. Then, to protect Egypt, they advanced into the Sudan.

Other European nations equated status (Britain was the model) with the possession of colonies and sought colonies as evidence of their own importance. This explains much of the scramble for Africa (see Chapter 27). France became involved in North Africa in 1830, when it sent a naval expedition to Algeria to suppress piracy. By 1882, the French controlled Algeria and Tunisia. Soon lesser states like Belgium, Portugal, Spain, and Italy were seeking African colonies. In 1884 and 1885, Germany declared protectorates over southwestern Africa, Togoland, the Cameroons, and East Africa—despite the fact that these places had no particular strategic importance.

THE IRRATIONAL ELEMENT

Germany's annexations started a wild scramble by other European powers, and by 1890, almost all of Africa was parceled out. In Asia, Japan exerted claims on China and Korea that frightened the other powers with interests in China. Russia, France, and Germany applied diplomatic pressure to contain Japan, and all pressed feverishly for concessions in China. In 1899, the United States proposed the "open door policy," which opposed annexations in China and allowed all nations to trade there on equal terms. Victory in the Spanish-American War of 1898 had won the United States control over Cuba and Puerto Rico, and the Americans then purchased the Philippines and Guam from Spain. In 1898, the United States annexed Hawaii. By 1900, most of the world had come under the control of the industrialized West.

HISTORY'S VOICES

SOCIAL DARWINISM AND IMPERIALISM

One of the intellectual foundations of the New Imperialism was the doctrine of social Darwinism, a pseudoscientific application of Darwin's ideas about biology to nations and races. The impact of social Darwinism was substantial. In the selection that follows, an Englishman, Karl Pearson (1857–1936), attempts to connect concepts from evolutionary theory—the struggle for survival and the survival of the fittest—to the development of human societies.

HOW DOES the author connect Darwin's ideas to the concept of human progress? Is it reasonable to equate biological species with human societies, races, or nations? How do the author's ideas justify imperial expansion? What arguments can you make against the author's assertions?

History shows me one way, and one way only, in which a state of civilisation has been produced, namely, the struggle of race with race, and the survival of the physically and mentally fitter race. This dependence of progress on the survival of the fitter race, terribly black as it may seem to some of you, gives the struggle for existence its redeeming features; it is the fiery crucible out of which comes the finer metal. You may hope for a time when the sword shall be turned into the ploughshare, when American and German and English traders shall no longer compete in the markets of the world for raw materials, for their food supply, when the white man and the dark shall share the soil between them, and each till it as he lists. But, believe me, when that day comes mankind will no longer progress; there will be nothing to check the fertility of inferior stock; the relentless law of heredity will not be controlled and guided by natural selection. Man will stagnate. . . . The path of progress is strewn with the wreck of nations; traces are everywhere to be seen of the hecatombs of inferior races, and of victims who found not the narrow way to the greater perfection. Yet these dead peoples are, in very truth, the stepping stones on which mankind has arisen to the higher intellectual and deeper emotional life of today.

Source: Karl Pearson, *National Life from the Standpoint of Science*, 2nd ed. (Cambridge, UK: Cambridge University Press, 1907), pp. 21, 26–27, 64.

EMERGENCE OF THE GERMAN EMPIRE

FORMATION OF THE TRIPLE ALLIANCE (1873–1890)

Prussia's victories over Austria and France and its creation of the German Empire in 1871 revolutionized European diplomacy. The sudden appearance of a powerful new state posed problems.

The balance of power created at the Congress of Vienna was altered radically. Britain and Russia retained their position. Austria, however, had lost ground and was threatened by nationalism within the Austro-Hungarian Empire. French power and prestige were badly damaged by the Franco-Prussian War and the German annexation of Alsace-Lorraine. The French were both afraid of Germany and resentful of their loss of territory and of France's traditional dominance in western Europe.

BISMARCK'S LEADERSHIP (1873–1890)

Until 1890, Otto von Bismarck (1815–1898) continued to guide German policy. He insisted after 1871 that Germany wanted no further territorial gains, and he

WHAT WERE the two alliance systems that faced each other in Europe before 1914?

QUICK REVIEW

Bismarck's Goals
- No additional German territorial expansion
- Tried to cultivate friendship with France
- Sought to prevent alliance between France and any other European power that would threaten Germany on two fronts

meant it. He wanted to avoid a war that might undo his achievement. He tried to assuage France by cultivating friendly relations and supporting its colonial aspirations. He also prepared for the worst. If France could not be conciliated, it must be isolated. Bismarck sought to prevent an alliance between France and any European power—especially Austria or Russia—that would threaten Germany with a war on two fronts.

War in the Balkans Bismarck's first move was to establish the Three Emperors' League in 1873. The league brought together the three great conservative empires of Germany, Austria, and Russia. It collapsed when Russia went to war with Turkey in 1877. The tottering Ottoman Empire was preserved chiefly by the competing aims of those powers who awaited its demise. Ottoman weakness encouraged its Slavic subjects in the Balkans to rebel.

When Russia entered the fray, it created an international crisis. The Russians hoped to gain control of Constantinople. Russian intervention also reflected the influence of the **Pan-Slavic movement**, which sought to bring all the Slavs, even those under Austrian or Ottoman rule, under the protection of Holy Mother Russia.

The Ottoman Empire was forced to sue for peace. The Treaty of San Stefano of March 1878 was a Russian triumph. The Slavic states in the Balkans were freed of Ottoman rule, and Russia obtained territory and an indemnity. But the terms of the Russian victory alarmed the other great powers. Austria feared that the new Slav states and the increase in Russian influence would threaten its own Balkan provinces. The British were alarmed by the possible Russian control of Constantinople. Disraeli (1804–1881) was determined to resist, and British public opinion supported him.

Congress of Berlin Disraeli sent a fleet to Constantinople, and Britain and Austria forced Russia to agree to an international conference at which the provisions of San Stefano would be reviewed by the other great powers. The resulting Congress of Berlin met in June and July of 1878 under the presidency of Bismarck.

The decisions of the Congress were a blow to Russian ambitions. Bulgaria lost two thirds of its territory. Austria-Hungary was given Bosnia and Herzegovina to "occupy and administer" under formal Ottoman rule. Britain received Cyprus, and France gained permission to occupy Tunisia. These were compensations for the gains that Russia was permitted to keep. Germany asked for nothing, but the Russians were angry. The Three Emperors' League was dead.

The south Slavic states of Serbia and Montenegro resented the Austrian occupation of Bosnia and Herzegovina. The south Slavic question, no less than the estrangement between Russia and Germany, was a threat to the peace of Europe.

German Alliances with Russia and Austria Bismarck could ignore the Balkans, but not Russia. He concluded a secret treaty with Austria in 1879. This Dual Alliance provided that if either Germany or Austria were attacked by Russia, the ally would help the attacked party. If either was attacked by another country, each promised at least to maintain neutrality. The treaty was renewed every five years until 1918.

Bismarck never allowed the alliance to drag Germany into Austria's Balkan quarrels. He made it clear to the Austrians that Germany would never attack Russia. Bismarck expected the Austro-German negotiations to frighten Russia into seeking closer relations with Germany, and he was right. By 1881, he had renewed the Three Emperors' League on a firmer basis.

Pan-Slavic movement Effort to create a nation or federation that would embrace all the Slavic peoples of Eastern Europe.

Bismarck and the young Kaiser William II meet in 1888. The two disagreed over many issues, and in 1890 William dismissed the aged chancellor.
German Information Center.

The Triple Alliance   In 1882, Italy, annoyed by the French preemption of Tunisia, asked to join the Dual Alliance. Bismarck was now allied with three of the great powers and friendly with Great Britain, which held aloof from all alliances. France was isolated. Although the Three Emperors' League was allowed to lapse, the Triple Alliance (Germany, Austria, and Italy) was renewed for another five years in 1887. To restore German relations with Russia, Bismarck negotiated the Reinsurance Treaty that same year, in which both powers promised to remain neutral if either was attacked. However, a change in the German monarchy overturned Bismarck's system.

In 1888, William II (r. 1888–1918) came to the German throne. Like many Germans of his generation, he was filled with a sense of Germany's destiny as the leading power of Europe. To achieve a "place in the sun," he wanted a navy and colonies like Britain's. These aims, of course, ran counter to Bismarck's policy. In 1890, William dismissed Bismarck.

During Bismarck's time, Germany was a force for European peace. This position would not have been possible without its great military power. But it also required a statesman who could exercise restraint and understand what his country needed and what was possible.

FORGING THE TRIPLE ENTENTE (1890–1907)

Franco-Russian Alliance   After Bismarck's retirement, his system of alliances collapsed. General Leo von Caprivi refused the Russian request to renew the Reinsurance Treaty, which he considered incompatible with the Austrian alliance. Political isolation and the need for foreign capital drove the Russians toward France. The French, who were even more isolated, were glad to pour capital into Russia if it would help produce security against Germany. In 1894, the Franco-Russian alliance was signed.

Britain and Germany   Britain now became the key to the international situation. Colonial rivalries pitted the British against the Russians in Central Asia and against the French in Africa. Traditionally, Britain had also opposed Russian control of Constantinople and French control of the Low Countries. There was no reason to think that Britain would soon become friendly to its traditional rivals or abandon its friendliness toward the Germans. Yet within a decade of William II's accession, Germany had become the enemy in the minds of the British. The problem lay in Germany's foreign and naval policies.

At first Germany tried to win over the British to the Triple Alliance, but when Britain clung to "splendid isolation," Germany sought to demonstrate its worth as an ally by making trouble for Britain. The Germans began to exert pressure against Britain in Africa by barring British attempts to build a railroad from Capetown to Cairo. They also openly sympathized with the Boers of South Africa in their resistance to British expansion.

In 1898, William's dream of a German navy began to achieve reality with the passage of a naval law providing for 19 battleships. In 1900, a second law doubled that figure. The architect of the new navy, Admiral Alfred von Tirpitz (1849–1930), proclaimed that Germany's naval policy was aimed at Britain. As the German navy grew and German policies seemed more threatening, the British abandoned their traditional policies.

Entente Cordiale   In 1902, Britain concluded an alliance with Japan to help defend British interests in the Far East against Russia. Next, Britain in 1904 made a series of agreements with the French, collectively called the Entente Cordiale. It

was not a formal treaty and had no military provisions, but it settled all outstanding colonial differences between the two nations. The Entente Cordiale went far toward aligning the British with Germany's great potential enemy.

First Moroccan Crisis   In March 1905, William II landed at Tangier and challenged the French predominance there in a speech in favor of Moroccan independence. Germany's chancellor, Prince Bernhard von Bülow (1849–1929), intended to show France how weak it was and how little it could expect from Britain; he also hoped to gain colonial concessions.

The Germans might have achieved their aims, but they demanded an international conference to exhibit their power. The conference met in 1906 at Algeciras in Spain. Austria sided with its German ally, but Spain, Italy, and the United States voted with Britain and France. The French were confirmed in their position in Morocco, and German bullying had driven Britain and France closer together. Sir Edward Grey (1862–1933), the British foreign secretary, without making a firm commitment, authorized conversations between the British and French general staffs. By 1914, French and British military and naval plans were so mutually dependent that the two countries were effectively, if not formally, allies.

British Agreement with Russia   Hardly anyone believed that Britain and Russia could ever be allies. The Russo-Japanese War of 1904–1905 made such a development seem even less likely because Britain was allied with Russia's enemy. But defeat and the Russian Revolution of 1905 left Russia weak and reduced British apprehensions. The British were also concerned that Russia might drift into the German orbit.

With French support, in 1907 an agreement settled Russo-British quarrels in Central Asia and Persia and opened the door for wider cooperation. The Triple Entente, an informal but powerful association of Britain, France, and Russia, was now ranged against the Triple Alliance. Because Italy was unreliable, Germany and Austria-Hungary stood surrounded by two great land powers and Great Britain.

William II and his ministers had turned Bismarck's nightmare of the prospect of a two-front war with France and Russia into a reality and had added Britain to the hostile coalition. Bismarck's alliance system had been intended to maintain peace, but the new one increased the risk of war and made the Balkans, where Austrian and Russian ambitions clashed, a likely spot for it.

QUICK REVIEW

First Moroccan Crisis
- March 1905: William II implies Germany has a role in furthering Moroccan independence
- Germany hoped to weaken relationship between France and Great Britain
- 1906: Conference in Algeciras confirms France's claims in Morocco

WORLD WAR I

THE ROAD TO WAR (1908–1914)

WHAT CAUSED the outbreak of World War I in 1914?

Except for the Greeks and the Romanians, most of the inhabitants of the Balkans were Slavs and felt a kinship with one another and with Russia. For centuries they had been ruled by Austrians, Hungarians, or Turks, and the nationalism that characterized late-19th-century Europe made many Slavs eager for liberty or at least autonomy. The more radical among them longed for a union of the south Slavic, or Yugoslav, peoples in a single nation led by independent Serbia. They hoped to detach all the Slavic provinces (especially Bosnia, which bordered on Serbia) from Austria. Serbia was to unite the Slavs at the expense of Austria, as Piedmont had united the Italians and Prussia the Germans.

The Bosnian Crisis   In 1908, modernizing reformers called the Young Turks overthrew the Ottoman government. This threatened to revive the empire and precipitated a series of Balkan crises that would lead to world war. Austria and Russia decided to act before Turkey became stronger. They agreed to call an international conference in which each of them would support the other's demands. Russia would agree to the Austrian annexation of Bosnia and Herzegovina, and Austria would support Russia's request to open the Dardanelles to Russian warships.

Austria, however, declared the annexation unilaterally before any conference was called. The British, concerned about their own position in the Mediterranean, rejected the Russian demand. The Russians were furious. The Serbs were enraged by the annexation of Bosnia. The Russians were too weak to do anything but accept the new situation. The Germans were unhappy because Austria's action threatened their relations with Russia. But Germany felt so dependent on the Dual Alliance that it assured Austria of its support. To an extent, German policy was being made in Vienna. It was a dangerous precedent. At the same time, the failure of Britain and France to support Russia strained the Triple Entente and made it harder for them to oppose Russian interests again if they wanted to retain Russian friendship.

Second Moroccan Crisis   The second Moroccan crisis, in 1911, emphasized the French and British need for mutual support. When France sent an army to Morocco to put down a rebellion, Germany took the opportunity to extort colonial concessions in the French Congo by sending the gunboat *Panther* to the port of Agadir in Morocco, allegedly to protect German citizens there. As in 1905, the Germans went too far.

Anglo-German relations had already been deteriorating, chiefly because of the naval race. The British now mistakenly believed that the Germans meant to turn Agadir into a naval base on the Atlantic. The crisis passed when France yielded bits of the Congo and Germany withdrew from Morocco. The main result was to draw Britain closer to France. Plans were formulated for a British expeditionary force to help defend France against German attack, and the British and French navies agreed to cooperate.

The Balkan Wars   After the second Moroccan crisis, Italy feared that France would move into Ottoman Libya. Consequently, in 1911 Italy attacked the Ottoman Empire to forestall the French, and obtained Libya and the Dodecanese Islands in the Aegean. The Italian victory encouraged the Balkan states to try their luck. In 1912, Bulgaria, Greece, Montenegro, and Serbia attacked the Ottoman Empire and won easily. The Serbs and the Bulgarians then quarreled about the division of Macedonia, and in 1913, Turkey and Romania joined Greece and Serbia against Bulgaria, which lost much of what it had gained since 1878.

The Austrians were determined to limit Serbian gains and prevent the Serbs from obtaining a port in Albania on the Adriatic. An international conference sponsored by Britain in early 1913 resolved the matter in Austria's favor and called for an independent kingdom of Albania. But Austria felt humiliated by the public airing of Serbian demands and in October unilaterally forced Serbia to withdraw from Albania. Russia again let Austria have its way.

The lessons learned from this affair influenced behavior in the final crisis of 1914. The Russians had, as in 1908, been embarrassed by their passivity, and their allies were now more reluctant to restrain them. The Austrians were determined not to accept an international conference again. They and their German allies had seen that better results might be obtained from a threat of force.

QUICK REVIEW

Second Moroccan Crisis

- 1911: France sends an army to Morocco and Germany sends gunboat to Moroccan port of Agadir

- British overreaction leads to naval arms race between Germany and Britain

- Chief effects of the crisis were to increase suspicion between Germany and Britain and to drawn France and Britain closer together

SARAJEVO AND THE OUTBREAK OF WAR (JUNE–AUGUST 1914)

The Assassination　On June 28, 1914, a Bosnian nationalist killed the Austrian Archduke Francis Ferdinand (1863–1914), heir to the throne, and his wife in the Bosnian capital of Sarajevo. The assassin was a member of a conspiracy hatched by a political terrorist society. The chief of intelligence of the Serbian army had helped plan the crime. Even though his role was unknown at the time, it was generally believed that Serbian officials were involved.

Germany and Austria's Response　The assassination was condemned throughout Europe. To those Austrians who had long favored an attack on Serbia as a solution to the empire's Slavic problem, the opportunity seemed irresistible. But Count Stefan Tisza (1861–1918), speaking for Hungary, resisted. Count Leopold Berchtold (1863–1942), the Austro-Hungarian foreign minister, knew that German support would be required if Russia should decide to protect Serbia and to persuade the Hungarians to accept a war. The question of peace or war, therefore, had to be answered in Berlin.

William II and Chancellor Theobald von Bethmann-Hollweg (1856–1921) promised German support for an attack on Serbia. They urged the Austrians to move swiftly, while the other powers were still angry at Serbia. They also indicated that a failure to act would be evidence of Austria-Hungary's uselessness as an ally. Therefore, the Austrians planned to attack Serbia. They hoped, with the protection of Germany, to avoid a general European conflict, but were prepared to risk one. The Germans also knew that they risked a general war, but hoped to "localize" the fight between Austria and Serbia.

These calculations proved to be incorrect. Bethmann-Hollweg hoped that the Austrians would strike while the outrage of the assassination was still fresh. He also hoped that German support would deter Russian involvement. Failing that, he was prepared for a continental war that would bring rapid victory over France and allow a full-scale attack on the Russians, who were always slow to bring their strength into action. The German chancellor convinced himself that the British would stand aloof.

However, the Austrians were slow to act. They did not even deliver their deliberately unacceptable ultimatum to Serbia until July 24, when the general hostility toward Serbia had begun to subside. Serbia returned a conciliatory answer, but the Austrians were determined not to turn back. On July 28, they declared war on Serbia, even though they could not field an army until mid-August.

The Triple Entente's Response　The Russians responded angrily to the Austrian demands on

Assassination of the Archduke.

Above: The Austrian Archduke Franz Ferdinand and his wife in Sarajevo on June 28, 1914. Later in the day the royal couple were assassinated by young revolutionaries trained and supplied in Serbia, igniting the crisis that led to World War I. Below: Moments after the assassination the Austrian police captured one of the assassins.

Brown Brothers.

Serbia. The government ordered partial mobilization to pressure Austria to hold back its attack on Serbia.

Mobilization of any kind, however, was generally understood to be equivalent to an act of war. It was especially alarming to General Helmuth von Moltke (1848–1916), head of the German general staff. Russian mobilization could upset the delicate timing of Germany's battle plan—the **Schlieffen Plan**, which required an attack on France first—and would endanger Germany. From this point on, Moltke pressed for war. The pressure of military necessity became irresistible.

The western European powers were not eager for war. But the French gave the Russians the same assurances that Germany had given its ally. The British worked hard for another conference of the powers, but Austria would not hear of it. The Germans privately supported the Austrians but were publicly conciliatory in the hope of keeping the British neutral.

When Bethmann-Hollweg realized that if Germany attacked France, Britain would fight, he tried to persuade the Austrians to negotiate, but the Austrians could not retreat without losing their own self-respect and that of the Germans. On July 30, Austria ordered mobilization against Russia. Russia and Germany then ordered general mobilization. The Schlieffen Plan went into effect. The Germans invaded Belgium on August 3, which violated the treaty of 1839, in which the British had guaranteed Belgian neutrality. This undermined sentiment in Britain for neutrality and united the nation against Germany. Germany then invaded France. On August 4, Britain declared war on Germany. Europe would never be the same.

STRATEGIES AND STALEMATE (1914–1917)

Throughout Europe jubilation greeted the outbreak of war. No general war had been fought since Napoleon, and the horrors of modern warfare were not yet understood. The dominant memory was of Bismarck's swift and decisive campaigns, in which costs and casualties were light and the rewards great.

Both sides expected to take the offensive and win a quick victory. The Triple Entente powers—or the Allies, as they came to be called—had superior numbers and financial resources as well as command of the sea. Germany and Austria, the Central Powers, had the advantages of internal lines of communication and of having launched their attack first.

The War in the West   After 1905, Germany's war plan was the one developed by Count Alfred von Schlieffen (1833–1913), chief of the German general staff from 1891 to 1906. It aimed to sweep through Belgium to the English Channel, then wheel to the south and east to envelop the French and crush them against the German fortresses in Lorraine. In the east, the Germans planned to stand on the defensive against Russia until France had been beaten, a task they thought would take only six weeks.

Coming of World War I

1871	End of the Franco-Prussian War; creation of the German Empire; German annexation of Alsace-Lorraine
1873	Three Emperors' League (Germany, Russia, and Austria-Hungary)
1877	Russo-Turkish War
1878	Congress of Berlin
1879	Dual Alliance between Germany and Austria
1881	Three Emperors' League is renewed
1882	Italy joins Germany and Austria in Triple Alliance
1888	William II becomes German emperor
1890	Bismarck dismissed
1894	Franco-Russian alliance
1898	Germany begins to build battleship navy
1902	British alliance with Japan
1904	Entente Cordiale between Britain and France
1904–1905	Russo-Japanese War
1905	First Moroccan crisis
1907	British agreement with Russia
1908–1909	Bosnian crisis
1911	Second Moroccan crisis; Italy attacks Turkey
1912–1913	First and Second Balkan wars
1914	Outbreak of World War I

22.4
The Perversion of Technology: War in "No Man's Land"

Schlieffen Plan   Germany's plan for achieving a quick victory in the West at the outbreak of World War I by invading France through Belgium and Luxembourg.

The Western Front. French troops advancing on the Western Front. This picture of trench warfare characterizes the 20th century's first great international conflict. Trenches were protected by barbed wire and machine guns, which gave defenders the advantage.

Hulton/Corbis-Bettmann.

Italia Irredenta Meaning "unredeemed Italy." Italian-speaking areas that had been left under Austrian rule at the time of the unification of Italy.

Women Munitions Workers in England. The World War I demanded more from the civilian populations than had previous wars, resulting in important social changes. Demands of the munitions industries and a shortage of men (so many of whom were in uniform) brought many women out of traditional roles at home and into factories and other war work.

Hulton Getty Picture Collection/Tony Stone Images.

The execution of his plan, however, was left to Helmuth von Moltke, a gloomy and nervous man, who made enough tactical mistakes to cause it to fail by a narrow margin. As a result, the French and British were able to stop the Germans at the Battle of the Marne in September 1914. Thereafter, the war in the West became one of position. Both sides dug in behind a wall of trenches protected by barbed wire that stretched from the North Sea to Switzerland. Machine-gun nests made assaults dangerous. Both sides, nonetheless, attempted massive attacks initiated by artillery bombardments of unprecedented force and duration. Still, the defense always prevented a breakthrough.

The War in the East In the East, the Russians advanced into Austrian territory and inflicted heavy casualties, but Russian incompetence and German energy soon reversed the situation. General Erich Ludendorff (1865–1937), under the command of the elderly Paul von Hindenburg (1847–1934), destroyed or captured an entire Russian army at the Battle of Tannenberg. In 1915, the Central Powers drove into the Baltic states and western Russia, inflicting more than 2 million casualties. Russian confidence was shaken (see Map 29–2).

Both sides sought new allies. Turkey and Bulgaria joined the Central Powers. Italy joined the Allies in 1915, after they agreed to give it *Italia Irredenta* (i.e., the Trentino, the South Tyrol, Trieste, and some of the Dalmatian Islands) from Austria after victory. Romania joined the Allies in 1916 but was quickly defeated and driven from the war. In the Far East, Japan honored its alliance with Britain and overran the German colonies in China and the Pacific.

In 1915, the Allies undertook to break the deadlock in the fighting by going around it. The idea came chiefly from Winston Churchill (1874–1965), First Lord of the British Admiralty. He proposed to attack the Dardanelles and capture Constantinople. This policy would knock Turkey from the war and ease communication with Russia. Success depended on daring leadership, but the attack was inept. Before the campaign was abandoned, the Allies lost almost 150,000 men.

Return to the West Both sides turned back to the West in 1916. Erich von Falkenhayn (1861–1922), who had succeeded Moltke in September 1914, sought success by an attack on the French stronghold of Verdun. It failed. The Allies, in turn, launched a major offensive along the River Somme in July, resulting in enormous casualties on both sides (see Map 29–3).

The War at Sea As the war continued, control of the sea became more important. The British imposed a strict blockade to starve out the enemy, regardless of international law. The Germans responded with submarine warfare to destroy British shipping and starve the British. They declared the waters around the British Isles a war zone, where

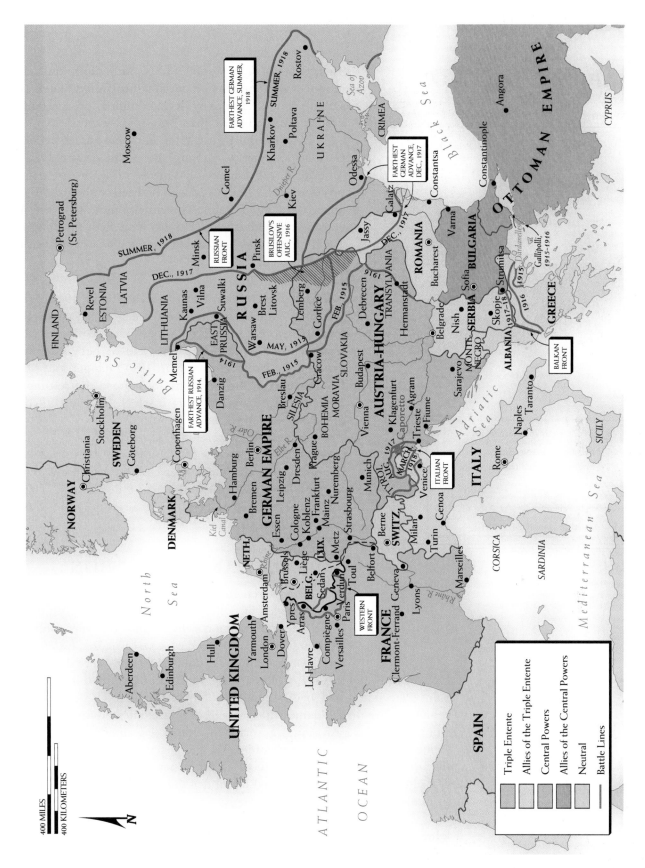

MAP 29–2

World War I in Europe. Despite the importance of military action in Asia, in the Middle East, and at sea, the main theaters of activity in World War I were in the European areas shown here.

WHICH REGIONS were most affected by military action?

MAP EXPLORATION

Interactive map: To explore this map further, go to
http://www.prenhall.com/craig/map29.3

MAP 29–3
The Western Front 1914–1918. This map shows the crucial Western Front in detail.

IF THE Germans had captured Paris, what effect would this have had on the war?

WHY WERE the Bolsheviks able to seize power in Russia?

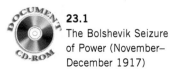

23.1
The Bolshevik Seizure of Power (November–December 1917)

even neutral ships would not be safe. Both policies were unwelcome to neutrals, especially the United States. But the sinking of neutral ships by German submarines was both more dramatic and offensive than Britain's blockade.

In 1915, the British liner *Lusitania* was torpedoed by a German submarine. Among the 1,200 drowned were 118 Americans. President Woodrow Wilson (1856–1924) protested, and the Germans desisted rather than further anger the United States. This development gave the Allies a considerable advantage. The German fleet that had cost so much money and had caused so much trouble played no significant part in the war.

America Enters the War In December 1916, President Wilson attempted to bring about a negotiated peace. But neither side would give up its hopes for total victory. The war seemed likely to continue until one or both sides reached exhaustion. Two events early in 1917 changed the situation. On February 1, the Germans announced the resumption of unrestricted submarine warfare, which led the United States to declare war on Germany on April 6.

One of the deterrents to an earlier American intervention had been the presence of autocratic tsarist Russia among the Allies. Wilson could conceive of the war only as an idealistic crusade "to make the world safe for democracy." That problem was resolved in March 1917 by a revolution in Russia that overthrew the tsarist government.

THE RUSSIAN REVOLUTION

The March Revolution in Russia was neither planned nor led by political faction. It was the result of the collapse of the monarchy's ability to govern. Military and domestic failures produced massive casualties, hunger, strikes, and disorganization. All political factions were discontented.

In early March 1917, strikes and demonstrations erupted in Petrograd, as Saint Petersburg had been renamed. The ill-disciplined troops in the city refused to fire on the demonstrators, and the tsar abdicated on March 15. The Duma formed a provisional government composed chiefly of Constitutional Democrats with Western sympathies. Various socialists also began to organize the workers into councils called *soviets*. They became estranged as the Constitutional Democrats failed to control the army or purge "reactionaries" from the government.

The provisional government decided to continue the war against Germany, but a new offensive in the summer of 1917 collapsed. Disillusionment with the war, shortages of food and other necessities, and the demand for land reform undermined the government, even after its leadership had been taken over by the moderate socialist Alexander Kerensky (1881–1970).

Since April the Bolsheviks had been working against the provisional government. The Germans had rushed V. I. Lenin (1870–1924) in a sealed train from his exile in Switzerland to Petrograd in the hope that he would cause trouble for the revolutionary government. The Bolsheviks demanded that all political power go to the soviets, which they controlled. They attempted a coup, but it failed. Lenin fled to Finland, and his chief collaborator, Leon Trotsky (1877–1940), was imprisoned.

An abortive right-wing counter-coup gave the Bolsheviks another chance. Trotsky, released from prison, led the powerful Petrograd Soviet. Lenin returned in October and insisted that the time was ripe to take power. On November 6, the Bolsheviks seized power.

The victors moved to fulfill their promises and to assure their own security. The provisional government had decreed an election for late November to select a Constituent Assembly. The Social Revolutionaries won a large majority over the Bolsheviks. When the assembly gathered in January, the Red Army, controlled by the Bolsheviks, dispersed it. All other political parties ceased to function in any meaningful fashion. The Bolshevik government nationalized the land and turned it over to its peasant proprietors. Factory workers were put in charge of their plants. Banks were seized for the state, and the debt of the tsarist government was repudiated. The property of the church was also seized.

The Bolsheviks signed an armistice with Germany in December 1917. On March 3, 1918, they accepted the Treaty of Brest-Litovsk, by which Russia yielded Finland, Poland, the Baltic states, and the Ukraine. Some territory in the Transcaucasus region went to Turkey. The Bolsheviks also agreed to pay an indemnity. These terms were a high price to pay for peace, but the Bolsheviks needed time to impose their rule on Russia.

Until 1921, the Bolsheviks confronted massive domestic resistance. A civil war erupted between the "Red" Russians supporting the revolution and the **"White" Russians**, who opposed the Bolsheviks and received aid from the Allies. In the summer of 1918, the tsar and his family were murdered. However, led by Trotsky, the Red Army overcame the opposition. By, 1921, Lenin and his supporters were in firm control.

Petrograd Munitions Workers Demonstrating in 1917. The barely-legible slogan at the top of the banner reads, "Victory to the Petrograd Workers!"

RIa-Novosti/Sovfoto/Eastfoto.

White Russians Russians who opposed the Bolsheviks (the "Reds") in the Russian Civil War of 1918–1921.

END OF WORLD WAR I

MILITARY RESOLUTION

The Treaty of Brest-Litovsk brought Germany to the peak of its success. In 1918, it decided to gamble everything on a last offensive. But the German army could not get beyond the Marne. Germany was exhausted. The Allies, on the other hand, were bolstered by the arrival of American troops in ever-increasing numbers. They launched a counteroffensive that was irresistible. As the Austrian fronts in the Balkans and Italy collapsed, the German high command knew that the end was imminent but wanted peace to be made before the army could be thoroughly defeated in the field, so that the responsibility should fall on civilians.

WHY DID the Versailles settlement leave Germany bitter?

The army therefore allowed a new government to be established on democratic principles to seek peace. The new government, under Prince Max of Baden (1867–1928), asked for peace on the basis of the **Fourteen Points** that President Wilson had declared as the American war aims. These were idealistic principles, but Wilson insisted that he would deal only with a democratic German government that spoke for the German people.

The disintegration of the German army forced William II to abdicate on November 9, 1918. The Social Democratic Party proclaimed a republic to prevent the establishment of a soviet government under the control of its Leninist wing. Two days later this republican, socialist-led government signed an armistice and accepted German defeat. The German people were, in general, unaware that their army had been defeated. No foreign soldier stood on German soil. Many Germans expected a mild settlement. The real peace embittered the German people, many of whom came to believe that Germany had been stabbed in the back by republicans and socialists at home.

Casualties on all sides came to about 10 million dead and twice as many wounded. The financial resources of the European states were badly strained. The victorious Allies, formerly creditors to the world, became debtors to the new American colossus.

The old international order, moreover, was dead. Russia was ruled by a Bolshevik dictatorship that preached world revolution. Germany was in chaos. Austria-Hungary had disintegrated. These changes stirred the colonial empires ruled by the European powers; they would never again be as secure as they had seemed before the war. Europe was no longer the center of the world, free to interfere when it wished or to ignore the outer regions if it chose. Its easy confidence in progress was shattered by four years of horrible war. The memory of that war shook the nerve of the victorious Western powers in the postwar world.

SETTLEMENT AT PARIS

The Peacemakers   Representatives of the victorious states gathered at Versailles and other Parisian suburbs in the first half of 1919. Wilson speaking for the United States, David Lloyd George (1863–1945) for Britain, Georges Clemenceau (1841–1929) for France, and Vittorio Emanuele Orlando (1860–1952) for Italy made up the Big Four. Japan also had an important part in the discussions.

Wilson's idealism came into conflict with the war aims of the victorious powers and with the secret treaties that had been made before and during the war. The British and French people had been told that Germany would be made to pay for the war. Romania had been promised Transylvania at the expense of Hungary. Italy and Serbia had competing claims in the Adriatic. During the war, the British had encouraged Arab hopes of an independent Arab state carved out of the Ottoman Empire; those plans conflicted with the Balfour Declaration (1917), in which the British also seemed to accept Zionism and to promise the Jews a national home in Palestine. Both of these plans conflicted with an Anglo-French agreement to divide the Near East between themselves.

The national goals of the victors presented further obstacles to an idealistic "peace without victors." France was eager to achieve a settlement that would permanently weaken Germany and preserve French political and military superiority. Italy sought to acquire *Italia Irredenta*; Britain looked to its imperial interests; Japan pursued its own advantage in Asia; and the United States insisted on

22.6
The Balfour Declaration

Fourteen Points   President Woodrow Wilson's (1856–1924) idealistic war aims.

OVERVIEW   CASUALTIES OF THE MAJOR BELLIGERENTS IN WORLD WAR 1

Country	Killed	Wounded	Total Killed as Percentage of Population
Austria-Hungary	1.1 million	3.62 million	1.9%
Belgium	38,000	44,000	0.5%
Britain	723,000	1.16 million	1.6%
Bulgaria	88,000	152,000	1.9%
France	1.4 million	2 million	3.4%
Germany	2 million	4.2 million	3.0%
Italy	578,000	947,000	1.6%
Romania	250,000	120,000	3.3%
Russia	1.8 million	1.45 million	1.1%
Serbia	278,000	138,000	5.7%
Turkey	804,000	400,000	3.7%
United States	114,000	205,000	0.1%

freedom of the seas, which favored American commerce, and on its right to maintain the Monroe Doctrine.

Finally, the peacemakers of 1919 faced a world in turmoil. The greatest immediate threat appeared to be Bolshevism. While Lenin and his colleagues were distracted by civil war, the Allies landed small armies in Russia to help overthrow the Bolshevik regime. Communist governments were established in Bavaria and Hungary. Berlin also experienced an abortive communist uprising. The Allies were so worried that they supported the suppression of these communist movements by right-wing forces. They even permitted an army of German volunteers to fight the Bolsheviks in the Baltic states. But fear of Germany remained the chief concern for France, and traditional interests governed the policies of the other Allies.

The Peace   The Paris settlement consisted of five separate treaties between the victors and the defeated powers. The Soviet Union (as Russia was now called) and Germany were excluded from the peace conference. The Germans were simply presented with a treaty and compelled to accept it. The principle of national self-determination was violated often, as it was unavoidable. The undeserved adulation accorded Wilson on his arrival turned into equally undeserved scorn. He had not abandoned his ideals but had given way to the irresistible force of reality.

The League of Nations   Wilson put great faith in the new **League of Nations**. Its covenant was an essential part of the peace treaty. The league was not intended as an international government but as a body of sovereign states that agreed to pursue common policies. If war threatened, the members promised to submit the matter to an international court or the League Council. Refusal to abide by this

League of Nations Association of sovereign states set up after World War I to pursue common policies and avert international aggression.

Peacemakers. The Allies promoted Arab efforts to secure independence from Turkey in an effort to remove Turkey from the war. Delegates to the peace conference of 1919 in Paris included British Colonel T. E. Lawrence, who helped lead the rebellion against Turkey, and representatives from the Middle East. Prince Feisal, the third son of King Hussein, stands in the foreground of this picture; Lawrence is in the middle row, second from the right; and Brigadier General Nuri Pasha Said of Baghdad is second from the left.

Corbis-Bettmann.

agreement would justify league intervention in the form of economic or military sanctions.

But the league was to have no armed forces. Action would require the unanimous consent of its council, which was to consist of Britain, France, Italy, the United States, Japan, and four other states with temporary seats. The league was generally seen as a device to ensure the security of the victorious powers, and the exclusion of Germany and the Soviet Union undermined the league's claim to evenhandedness.

Provisions of the covenant that dealt with colonial areas and disarmament were ineffective. Members of the league remained fully sovereign and pursued their national interests.

Germany In the West, the main territorial issue was the fate of Germany. The French would have liked to set up the Rhineland as a buffer state, but Lloyd George and Wilson would not permit that. But France did receive Alsace-Lorraine and the right to work the coal mines of the Saar for 15 years. Germany west of the Rhine, and 50 kilometers east of it, was to be a demilitarized zone; Allied troops could stay on the west bank for 15 years. The treaty also provided that Britain and the United States would guarantee to aid France if it were attacked by Germany. Such an attack was made more unlikely by the permanent disarmament of Germany. Its army was limited to 100,000 men; its fleet was all but eliminated; and it was forbidden to have war planes, submarines, tanks, heavy artillery, or poison gas. As long as these provisions were observed, France would be safe (see Map 29–4).

The East The settlement in the East ratified the collapse of the empires that had ruled it for centuries. Germany lost part of Silesia, and East Prussia was cut off from the rest of Germany by a corridor carved out to give the revived state of Poland access to the sea. The Austro-Hungarian Empire disappeared. Most of its German-speaking people in the small Republic of Austria were forbidden to unite with Germany. The Magyars occupied the much-reduced kingdom of Hungary.

The Czechs of Bohemia and Moravia joined with the Slovaks and Ruthenians to form Czechoslovakia, which also included several million unhappy Germans. The southern Slavs were united in the kingdom of Serbs, Croats, and Slovenes, or Yugoslavia. Italy gained the Trentino and Trieste. Romania gained Transylvania from Hungary and Bessarabia from Russia. Bulgaria lost territory to Greece and Yugoslavia. Finland, Estonia, Latvia, and Lithuania became independent states, and much of Poland was carved out of formerly Russian soil. In the Caucasus, the new nations of Georgia, Armenia, and Azerbaijan took advantage of the turmoil following the Russian revolution to enjoy a period of independence (1918–1921). Ukraine and Russia were also autonomous during this brief period.

MAP 29–4

World War I Peace Settlement in Europe and the Middle East. The map of central and eastern Europe, as well as that of the Middle East, underwent drastic revision after World War I. The enormous territorial losses suffered by Germany, Austria-Hungary, the Ottoman Empire, Bulgaria, and Russia were the other side of the coin represented by gains for France, Italy, Greece, and Romania and by the appearance, or reappearance, of at least eight new independent states from Finland in the north to Yugoslavia in the south, to Georgia in the east. The mandate system for former Ottoman territories outside Turkey proper laid foundations for several new, mostly Arab, states in the Middle East.

HOW DID the creation of new countries in central and eastern Europe set the stage for future conflicts?

The old Ottoman Empire also disappeared. The new republic of Turkey was limited to little more than Constantinople and Asia Minor. Palestine and Iraq came under British control and Syria and Lebanon under French control as mandates under the purely theoretical authority of the League of Nations. Germany's former colonies in Africa and the Pacific were divided among the victors.

Reparations Before the armistice, the Germans promised to pay compensation "for all damages done to the civilian population of the Allies and their property." However, France and Britain were eager to have Germany pay the full cost of the war. No sum was fixed at the conference. Germany was to pay $5 billion annually until 1921, when a final figure would be set, which Germany would have to pay within 30 years. The French calculated that either Germany would be bled into impotence or refuse to pay and justify French intervention.

To justify these huge reparation payments, the Allies inserted the notorious **war guilt clause** into the treaty, which placed the responsibility for the war solely on Germany. The Germans bitterly resented the charges but had to accept the treaty as it was written by the victors without negotiation. The German government led by the Social Democrats and the Catholic Center Party signed the treaty. These parties formed the backbone of the German Republic, but they never overcame the stigma of accepting the treaty.

EVALUATION OF THE PEACE

Few peace settlements have been more attacked than the Treaty of Versailles, but many of the attacks on it are unjustified. Germany was neither dismembered nor ruined. Reparations were scaled down, and until the Great Depression of the 1930s, the German economy recovered. The attempt at achieving self-determination for nationalities was less than perfect, but it was the best Europe had ever accomplished.

The peace, nevertheless, was unsatisfactory. The elimination of the Austro-Hungarian Empire, however inevitable, created serious problems. Economically it was disastrous, for it separated raw materials from manufacturing areas and producers from their markets. Poland and especially Czechoslovakia contained unhappy German minorities. Disputes over territories in eastern Europe promoted further tension. The peace also rested on a defeat that Germany did not admit. The Germans believed they had been cheated, not defeated.

Finally, the peace failed to accept reality. Germany and Russia must inevitably play an important part in European affairs, yet they were excluded from the settlement and from the League of Nations. Given the many discontented parties, the peace was not self-enforcing; yet no satisfactory machinery for enforcing it was established. The league was never a serious force for this purpose. It was left to France, with no guarantee of support from Britain and no hope of help from the United States, to defend the new arrangements. France was simply not strong enough for the task if Germany were to rearm. The Treaty of Versailles was neither conciliatory enough to remove the desire for change, nor harsh enough to make another war impossible.

war guilt clause Clause of the Versailles Treaty, which assigned responsibility for World War I solely to Germany.

SUMMARY

The New Imperialism European imperialism in the last part of the 19th century brought the Western countries into contact with most of the world. By 1914, European nations had divided Africa among themselves and controlled large parts of Asia and the islands of the Pacific. Much of the Middle East was under the nominal control of the Ottoman Empire, which was in its death throes and under European influence. The Monroe Doctrine made Latin America a protectorate of the United States. Japan had become an imperial power at the expense of China and Korea.

World War I   The emergence of a new, powerful German state at the center of Europe upset the old balance of power. Bismarck, however, preserved the peace for as long as he remained in power. The new German emperor, William II, abandoned the policy of restraint and sought more power and influence for his country. The result was a system of alliances that divided Europe into two armed camps. What began as yet another Balkan War involving the European powers became a global war. As the terrible war of 1914–1918 dragged on, the motives that had driven the European powers to fight gave way to public affirmations of the principles of nationalism and self-determination.

The Peace Settlement   The peoples under colonial rule took these statements seriously and sought to win their own independence and nationhood. For the most part they were disappointed by the peace settlement. The British and French Empires were larger than ever. The United States added to the islands it controlled in the Pacific. Japan was rewarded at the expense of China.

However, the old imperial nations, especially Britain and France, had paid an enormous price in lives, money, and will for their victory in the war. Colonial peoples pressed for the rights that were proclaimed as universal by the West but denied to their colonies; influential minorities in the countries that ruled them sympathized with colonial aspirations for independence. Tension between colonies and their ruling nations would be a cause of world instability.

REVIEW QUESTIONS

1. What was the New Imperialism?

2. What role did Bismarck expect the new Germany to play after 1871? Was he wise to tie Germany to Austria-Hungary?

3. Why did Britain abandon "splendid isolation"?

4. How did developments in the Balkans lead to the outbreak of World War I? Did Germany want a general war?

5. Why did Germany lose World War I? Was Versailles too harsh or too conciliatory? How might it have been improved?

6. Why was Lenin successful in establishing Bolshevik rule in Russia? Was it wise policy for him to take Russia out of the war?

IMAGE KEY

for pages 728–729

a. Dice showing the flags of Russia, Japan, Belgium, and the United Kingdom.

b. *The New York Times* announces the sinking of the Lusitania, May 8, 1915.

c. A map of the British empire in 1886.

d. Shells containing poison gas.

e. Lenin at the Tribune, 1930, by Alexander Gerasimov.

f. A red triplane with the German Iron Cross.

g. A British biplane.

h. American cartoon, 1882, depicting John Bull (England) as the octopus of imperialism.

i. A Renault tank, 1917.

j. English and Belgian uniform styles.

KEY TERMS

Fourteen Points   (p. 744)
Italia Irredenta   (p. 740)
League of Nations   (p. 745)

New Imperialism   (p. 730)
Pan-Slavic movement   (p. 734)
Schlieffen Plan   (p. 739)

war guilt clause   (p. 748)
White Russians   (p. 743)

 For additional study resources for this chapter, go to:
www.prenhall.com/craig/chapter29

30

Depression, European Dictators, and the American New Deal

CHAPTER HIGHLIGHTS

Postwar Problems The Versailles settlement left much of Europe dissatisfied. In the 1920s there were endless wrangles over reparations between Germany and the Allied powers. After World War I, Europe never recovered its prewar prosperity or stability. The onset of the Great Depression in 1929 caused severe problems in both Europe and the United States and led to the Nazi seizure of power in Germany and FDR's New Deal in the United States.

The Soviet Union The Bolsheviks had expected communist revolutions to break out across Europe. When that did not happen, they were forced to consolidate their regime within Russia. Lenin's New Economic Policy gave the state control over heavy industry, transportation, and international commerce but allowed for small-scale private enterprise and peasant farms. Stalin abandoned this policy to push for rapid industrialization. He abolished private enterprise, collectivized agriculture, and eliminated his opponents in a series of purges.

Fascist Italy Benito Mussolini came to power in Italy in 1922, promising order and a strong state. Although he achieved power by legal means, he soon transformed Italy into a single-party dictatorship.

Nazi Germany The postwar Weimar Republic in Germany was buffeted by social, political, and financial instability. Rampant inflation destroyed the savings of the middle class. The Great Depression brought financial collapse and massive unemployment. Many Germans looked to Adolf Hitler and the Nazi Party for solutions. Once Hitler came to power in 1933, he quickly established a one-party dictatorship based on police terror, propaganda, and the cult of himself as supreme leader. The Jews, in particular, were persecuted. Hitler also formed an alliance with the German army and began a program of rapid rearmament.

The United States The United States emerged from World War I as a world power, but retreated into isolation during the 1920s. The prosperity of the 1920s ended in the Great Depression. Franklin Delano Roosevelt's New Deal greatly expanded the power of the federal government in social and economic affairs and preserved capitalism in a democratic setting.

CHAPTER QUESTIONS

WHAT FACTORS made the Great Depression so severe and longlasting?

HOW DID Stalin gain and keep power in the Soviet Union?

WHY DID the Fascists achieve power in Italy?

WHAT ROLE did terror play in Nazi Germany?

HOW DID FDR's policies affect the role of the federal government?

In the two decades that followed the Paris settlement, the Western world saw a number of experiments in politics and economic life. Two broad factors accounted for these experiments. First, the war, the Russian Revolution, and the peace treaty had transformed the political face of Europe. The new regimes that emerged in the wake of the collapse of the monarchies of Germany, Austria-Hungary, and Russia faced economic dislocation and nationalistic resentments.

Second, the Great Depression caused political instability and economic crisis. In Europe this often produced authoritarian regimes. In the United States it led to an increased role for the federal government.

AFTER VERSAILLES: DEMANDS FOR REVISION AND ENFORCEMENT

WHAT FACTORS made the Great Depression so severe and longlasting?

The Paris settlement fostered resentments that counted among the chief political factors in Europe for the next two decades. The arrangements for reparations led to endless haggling. National groups in eastern Europe felt that injustice had been done to them and demanded border adjustments. The victorious powers, especially France, often believed that the treaty was being inadequately enforced. Too many political figures were willing to fish in these troubled international waters for domestic votes.

TOWARD THE GREAT DEPRESSION IN EUROPE

Three factors combined to bring about the severity and the extended length of the **Great Depression**. First, a financial crisis stemmed directly from the war and the peace settlement. In addition, a crisis erupted in the production and distribution of goods in the world market. Finally, these difficulties were exacerbated because no major western European country or the United States provided responsible economic leadership.

FINANCIAL TAILSPIN

France was determined to collect reparations from Germany. The United States was no less determined that its allies repay the wartime loans it had extended to them. German reparations were to provide the means of repaying these debts.

The quest for payment of German reparations caused one of the major diplomatic crises of the 1920s; the crisis itself resulted in further economic upheaval. In early 1923, the Allies—and France in particular—declared Germany to be in default of its reparation payments. On January 11, French troops occupied the Ruhr mining and manufacturing district. The **Weimar Republic** ordered passive resistance. Confronted with this tactic, the French ran the German mines and railroads. The Germans paid, but Britain became more sympathetic to Germany. The cost of the Ruhr occupation, moreover, damaged the French economy.

The political and economic turmoil of the Ruhr invasion led to international attempts to ease German payment of reparations. The most famous were the Dawes Plan of 1924 and the Young Plan of 1929, both devised by Americans. At the same time, American investment capital was pouring into Europe. However, the crash of Wall Street in October 1929—the result of unregulated speculation—saw the loss of large amounts of money. Thereafter, little American capital was available for investment in Europe.

Great Depression Prolonged worldwide economic downturn that began in 1929 with the collapse of the New York Stock Exchange.

Weimar Republic German democratic regime that existed between the end of World War I and Hitler's coming to power in 1933.

In May 1931, the Kreditanstalt—a primary lending institution for much of central and eastern Europe—collapsed. The German banking system then came under severe pressure. As German difficulties increased, U.S. President Herbert Hoover (1874–1964) announced in June 1931 a one-year moratorium on all payments of international debts. The Hoover moratorium was a prelude to the end of reparations. In the summer of 1932, the Lausanne Conference, in effect, ended the era of reparations.

PROBLEMS IN AGRICULTURAL COMMODITIES

The 1920s witnessed a contraction in the market demand for European goods. The difficulty arose from agriculture. Better methods of farming and more extensive transport facilities all over the globe vastly increased the quantity of grain. Wheat prices fell to record lows, decreasing the income of European farmers, while increasing the cost of the industrial goods they used. Consequently, farmers had great difficulty paying off their debts. These problems were especially acute in central and eastern Europe and abetted farmers' disillusionment with liberal politics.

Outside Europe similar problems affected wheat, sugar, coffee, rubber, wool, and lard producers. The people who produced these goods in underdeveloped nations could no longer make enough money to buy finished goods from industrial Europe. Commodity production had outstripped world demand.

The result was stagnation and depression for European industry. Coal, iron, and textiles had depended largely on international markets. Unemployment spread from these industries to those producing consumer goods. Unemployment in Britain and Germany during the 1920s had created "soft" domestic markets. The policies of reduced spending, with which the governments confronted the depression, further weakened domestic demand. By the early 1930s, the depression was feeding on itself.

DEPRESSION AND GOVERNMENT POLICY

The depression did not mean absolute economic decline or total unemployment. However, the economic downturn made people insecure. Even the employed often seemed to make no progress, and their anxieties created discontent.

Governments of the late 1920s and the early 1930s were not well suited to confront these problems. The electorates demanded action. Government response depended largely on the severity of the depression in a particular country and on the self-confidence of its political system.

Great Britain and France undertook moderate political experiments. In 1924, the Labour Party in Great Britain established itself as a viable governing entity. Under the pressure of the depression, Labour prime minister Ramsay MacDonald (1866–1937) organized a National Government, which was a coalition of the Labour, Conservative, and Liberal parties. It remained in power until 1935, when a Conservative ministry led by Stanley Baldwin (1867–1947) replaced it.

The most important French political experiment was the **Popular Front** Ministry, which came to office in 1936. This government was composed of socialists,

Human Casualties. One of the last American soldiers killed on the Western Front in November 1918. The carnage of World War I was one of the main causes of European weakness and instability in the 1920s and 1930s.
American Stock/Archive Photos.

Popular Front Government of all left-wing parties that took power in France in 1936 to enact social and economic reforms.

radicals, and communists—the first time that socialists and communists had cooperated in a ministry. The Popular Front addressed major labor problems in the French economy, but by 1938 it was at an end.

The political experiments of the 1920s and 1930s that reshaped world history involved a Soviet government in Russia, a Fascist regime in Italy, and a Nazi dictatorship in Germany.

THE SOVIET EXPERIMENT

HOW DID Stalin gain and keep power in the Soviet Union?

*T*he Bolshevik Revolution in Russia led to the most durable of all 20th-century authoritarian governments. The Communist Party of the Soviet Union retained power from 1917 until the end of 1991, and it influenced the history of much of the world like no other single factor. Unlike the Italian Fascists or the German National Socialists, the Bolsheviks seized power violently through revolution. Their leaders long felt insecure about their hold on the country. The Communist Party was not a mass party nor a nationalistic one. The Bolsheviks confronted a much less industrialized economy than that in Italy or Germany. They believed in and practiced the collectivization of economic life attacked by right-wing dictatorships. The Marxist-Leninist ideology was broader than the nationalism of the Fascists and the racism of the Nazis. Communism was an exportable commodity. Communists regarded their government and their revolution as epoch-making events in the development of humanity. Fear of communism and determination to stop its spread were leading political forces in Western Europe and the United States for most of the rest of the century and would influence their relationships to much of the rest of the world.

WAR COMMUNISM

Within months of the revolution, a new secret police, known as *Cheka*, appeared. Throughout the Russian civil war Lenin had declared that the Bolshevik Party, as the vanguard of the revolution, was imposing the dictatorship of the proletariat. Under the economic policy of "**War Communism**," the revolutionary government confiscated banks, transport facilities, and heavy industry. The state also requisitioned grain and shipped it from the countryside to feed the army and the cities.

War Communism helped the Red Army defeat its opponents. The revolution had survived and triumphed. The policy, however, generated domestic opposition. Many Russians were no longer willing to make the sacrifices demanded by central party bureaucrats. In 1920 and 1921, strikes occurred. Peasants resisted the requisition of grain. In March 1921, the navy mutinied. Each of these incidents suggested that the proletariat itself was opposing the dictatorship of the proletariat. Also, by late 1920, it had become clear that revolution would not sweep across the rest of Europe. The Soviet Union was a vast island of revolutionary socialism in a sea of worldwide capitalism.

War Communism Economic policy adopted by the Bolsheviks during the Russian civil war to seize the banks, heavy industry, railroads, and grain.

New Economic Policy (NEP) Limited revival of capitalism, especially in light industry and agriculture, introduced by Lenin in 1921 to repair the damage inflicted on the Russian economy by the civil war and War Communism.

THE NEW ECONOMIC POLICY

Lenin made a strategic retreat. In March 1921, he outlined the **New Economic Policy**, or NEP. Apart from "the commanding heights" of banking, heavy industry, transportation, and international commerce, private economic enterprise was allowed and peasants could farm for a profit. The countryside became more stable, and a secure food supply seemed assured for the cities. Similar free enterprise flourished within light industry and retail trade. The revolution seemed to have transformed Russia into a land of small farms and private shops and businesses.

STALIN VERSUS TROTSKY

The NEP had caused sharp disputes within the Politburo, the highest governing committee of the Communist Party. These frictions increased when Lenin suffered a stroke in 1922 and died in 1924. An intense struggle for leadership of the party commenced. Two factions emerged. One was led by Trotsky; the other by Joseph Stalin (1879–1953), who had become general secretary of the party in 1922.

The power struggle was fought over the question of Russia's path toward industrialization and the future of the Communist revolutionary movement. Trotsky, speaking for what became known as the left wing, urged rapid industrialization and looked to voluntary collectivization of farming by poor peasants as a means of increasing agricultural production. Trotsky further argued that the revolution in Russia could succeed only if new revolutions took place elsewhere.

A right-wing faction manipulated by Stalin opposed Trotsky. This group pressed for the continuation of Lenin's NEP. Stalin was the ultimate victor. His power lay in his command of bureaucratic and administrative methods. He mastered the crucial details of party structure, including admission and promotion. He had the support of the lower levels of the party when he clashed with other leaders.

In 1924, Stalin enunciated, in opposition to Trotsky, the doctrine of "socialism in one country." Russian success did not depend on the fate of the revolution elsewhere. Stalin thus nationalized the previously international scope of the Marxist revolution. By 1927, Trotsky had been ousted from the party. In 1929, he was expelled from Russia and was eventually murdered in 1940 by one of Stalin's agents. With the removal of Trotsky, Stalin was firmly in control of the Soviet state.

DECISION FOR RAPID INDUSTRIALIZATION

During the depression, the Soviet Union registered tremendous industrial advance. As usual in Russia, the direction and impetus came from the top. Stalin far exceeded the tsars in the coercion and terror he brought to the task. Russia achieved its economic growth during the 1930s only at the cost of millions of human lives.

Through 1928, Lenin's NEP steered Soviet economic development. A few farmers, the *kulaks*, became prosperous. During 1928 and 1929, the kulaks and other farmers withheld grain from the market because prices were too low. Food shortages in the cities caused unrest. Stalin came to a momentous decision. Russia must industrialize rapidly to match the power of the West. Agriculture must be collectivized to produce sufficient grain for food and export and to free peasant labor for the factories. This program, which basically embraced Trotsky's earlier economic position, unleashed a second Russian revolution.

Agricultural Policy In 1929, Stalin ordered party agents to confiscate hoarded wheat. As part of the general plan to collectivize farming, the government undertook to eliminate the kulaks as a class. A kulak, however, soon came to mean any peasant who opposed Stalin's policy. In the countryside, peasants at all levels of wealth resisted stubbornly. They wreaked their vengeance on the policy of **collectivization** by slaughtering more than 100 million horses and cattle between 1929 and 1933. The situation in the countryside amounted to open warfare.

As many as 10 million peasants were killed, and millions of others were sent to labor camps. Because of the turmoil, famine persisted in 1932 and 1933. Yet Stalin persevered. Peasants had their lands incorporated into large collective farms. The state controlled the machinery for these units.

Lenin. Anxiety over the spread of the Bolshevik Revolution was a fundamental factor of European politics during the 1920s and 1930s. Images like this Soviet portrait of Lenin as a heroic revolutionary conjured fears among people in the rest of Europe of a political force determined to overturn their social, political, and economic institutions.

Gemalde von A. M. Gerassimow, "Lenin as Agitator"/Bildarchiv Preussischer Kulturbesitz.

QUICK REVIEW

Stalin's Rise to Power
- Sided with the opposition to Trotsky in the 1920s
- Used control of the Central Committee to marginalize Trotsky and his supporters
- Emerged from struggle with Trotsky with unchallenged control of the Soviet state

collectivization Bedrock of Stalinist agriculture, which forced Russian peasants to give up their private farms and work as members of collectives, large agricultural units controlled by the state.

Soviet Communist Party Meeting. By the mid-1930s Stalin's purges had eliminated many leaders and other members from the Soviet Communist Party. This photograph of a meeting of a party congress in 1936 shows a number of the surviving leaders with Stalin, who sits fourth from the right in the front row. To his left is Vyacheslav Molotov, long-time foreign minister. The first person on the left in the front row is Nikita Khrushchev, who headed the Soviet Union in the late 1950s and early 1960s.

Itar-Tass/Sovfoto/Eastfoto.

The government now had primary direction over the food supply. Peasants could no longer determine whether there would be stability or unrest in the cities. Stalin and the Communist Party had won the battle of the wheat fields, but the problem of producing enough grain still plagues the former Soviet Union.

Five-Year Plans The revolution in agriculture had been undertaken for the sake of industrialization. The increased grain supply was to feed the labor force and provide exports to finance the imports required for industrial development. The industrial achievement of the Soviet Union between 1928 and World War II was one of the most striking accomplishments of the 20th century. Russia made a more rapid advance toward economic growth than any other nation in the Western world has ever achieved during a similar period of time. Soviet industrial production rose approximately 400 percent between 1928 and 1940. Few consumer goods were produced. Labor for this development was supplied internally. Capital was raised from the export of grain, even at the cost of internal shortage. Technology was borrowed from industrialized nations.

The organizational vehicle for industrialization was a series of five-year plans that began in 1928. The State Planning Commission, or Gosplan, set goals of production and organized the economy to meet them. Coordinating all facets of production was difficult and complicated. A vast program of propaganda was undertaken to sell the five-year plans to the Russian people. The industrial labor force became subject to regimentation similar to that being imposed on the peasants. The accomplishment of the three five-year plans probably allowed the Soviet Union to survive the German invasion.

Many non-Russian contemporaries looked at the Soviet economic experiment uncritically. While the capitalist world lay in the throes of the depression, the Soviet economy had grown at an unprecedented pace. These observers seemed to have had little idea of the social cost of the Soviet achievement. Millions had been killed or uprooted. The suffering and human loss during those years will probably never be known; it far exceeded anything described by Marx and Engels in relation to 19th-century industrialization in Western Europe.

THE PURGES

Stalin's decisions to industrialize rapidly and to move against the peasants aroused internal political opposition because they were departures from the policies of Lenin. In 1933, Stalin began to fear that he would lose control over the party apparatus. These fears were probably paranoid. Nevertheless, they resulted in the **Great Purges**, among the most mysterious and horrendous political events of this century.

On December 1, 1934, Sergei Kirov (1888–1934), the popular party chief of Leningrad (formerly Saint Petersburg), was assassinated. In the wake of the shooting, thousands of people were arrested, and still more were expelled from the party and sent to labor camps. It now seems certain that Stalin himself authorized Kirov's assassination to forestall any threat from him.

Great Purges Imprisonment and execution of millions of Soviet citizens by Stalin between 1934 and 1939.

The purges after Kirov's death were just the beginning. Between 1936 and 1938, spectacular show trials were held in Moscow. Previous high Soviet leaders publicly confessed political crimes and were executed. Their confessions were palpably false. Other leaders and party members were tried in private and shot. Thousands of people received no trial at all. It is inexplicable why some were executed, others sent to labor camps, and still others left unmolested. After the civilian party members had been purged, important officers, including heroes of the civil war, were killed. The exact numbers of executions and imprisonments are unknown but ran into the millions.

The scale of the political turmoil was unprecedented. The Russians themselves did not comprehend what was occurring. The only rational explanation is found in Stalin's concern for his own power. The purges created a new party structure absolutely loyal to him.

Despite the violence and repression, the Soviet experiment found many sympathizers. The Soviet Union after the Bolshevik seizure of power had fostered Communist parties subservient to Moscow throughout the world. Others who were not members of these parties sympathized with what they believed were the goals of the Soviet Union. During at least the first 50 years of its existence, the Soviet Union managed to capture the imagination of some intellectuals around the globe who hoped for a utopian egalitarian transformation of society. During much of the 1930s, the Soviet Union also appeared as an enemy to the fascist experiments in Italy and Germany. The Marxist ideology championed by the Soviet Union appeared to many people living in the European colonial empires as a vehicle for freeing themselves. The Soviet Union welcomed and trained many such anti-colonial leaders. With what is now known about Soviet repression, it is difficult to understand the power its presence exercised over many people's political imaginations, but that attraction was a factor in world politics from the 1920s through at least the early 1970s.

THE FASCIST EXPERIMENT IN ITALY

The first authoritarian political experiment in western Europe that arose in part from fears of the spread of bolshevism occurred in Italy. The general term *fascist,* which has been used to describe the various right-wing dictatorships that arose between the wars, was derived from the Italian fascist movement of Benito Mussolini (1883–1945).

Governments regarded as fascist were antidemocratic, anti-Marxist, antiparliamentary, and frequently anti-Semitic. They hoped to hold back the spread of Bolshevism, which seemed a real threat at the time. They sought a world that would be safe for the middle class and small farmers. **Fascism** rejected the political ideas of the French Revolution and of liberalism. Facist adherents believed that parliamentary politics and parties sacrificed national greatness to petty party disputes. They wanted to overcome the class conflict of Marxism and the party conflict of liberalism by consolidating all classes within the nation for great national purposes. Fascist governments were usually single-party dictatorships rooted in mass political parties and characterized by terrorism and police surveillance.

RISE OF MUSSOLINI

The Italian *Fasci di Combattimento* ("Band of Combat") was founded in 1919 in Milan. Most of its members were veterans who felt that the sacrifices of World War I had been in vain. They resented Italy's failure to gain the city of Fiume at the Paris conference. They feared socialism, inflation, and labor unrest.

23.4
Nadezhda Mandelstam, Hope Against Hope

WHY DID the Fascists achieve power in Italy?

fascism Political movements that tend to be antidemocratic, anti-Marxist, antiparliamentary, and often anti-Semitic. Fascists were invariably nationalists and exhalted the nation over the individual. They supported the interests of the middle class and rejected the ideas of the French Revolution and 19th-century liberalism. The first fascist regime was founded by Benito Mussolini (1883–1945) in Italy in the 1920s.

Mussolini and the Black Shirts.
Mussolini poses with supporters the day after the Black Shirt March on Rome intimidated the king of Italy into making him prime minister.

Bildarchiv Preussischer Kutturbesitz.

Their leader, or **Duce**, Benito Mussolini, had been active in Italian socialist politics but broke with the socialists in 1914 and supported Italian entry into the war. He then established his own paper, *Il Popolo d'Italia*, and was wounded in the army. As a politician, Mussolini was an opportunist. He could change his ideas and principles to suit any occasion. Action for him was always more important than thought. His goal was political survival.

Many Italians were dissatisfied with the parliamentary system. They felt that Italy had not been treated as a great power at the peace conference and had not received the territories it deserved. The main spokesman for this discontent was the extreme nationalist writer Gabriele D'Annunzio (1863–1938). In 1919, he captured Fiume with a force of patriotic Italians. The Italian army drove him out, but this made the parliamentary ministry seem unpatriotic.

Between 1919 and 1921, Italy was also wracked by social turmoil. Numerous strikes occurred, and workers occupied factories. Peasants seized land. Parliamentary government seemed incapable of dealing with this unrest. Many Italians believed that a Communist revolution might break out.

Mussolini first supported the factory occupations and land seizures, but soon reversed himself. He had discovered that many upper- and middle-class Italians who were pressured by inflation and feared property loss had no sympathy for the workers or peasants. They wanted order. Consequently, Mussolini and his Fascists took direct action in the face of the government inaction. They terrorized Socialist supporters, attacked strikers and farm workers, and protected strikebreakers. Conservative land and factory owners were grateful. The government ignored these crimes. By early 1922, the Fascists controlled the local government in much of northern Italy.

In 1921, Mussolini and 34 of his followers had been elected to the Chamber of Deputies. The Fascist movement now had hundreds of thousands of supporters. In October 1922, the Fascists, dressed in their characteristic black shirts, began a march on Rome. King Victor Emmanuel III (r. 1900–1946) refused to authorize using the army against them, which ensured a Fascist seizure of power. The cabinet resigned. On October 29, the king telegraphed Mussolini in Milan and asked him to become prime minister. The next day Mussolini arrived in Rome by train and, as head of the government, greeted his followers when they entered the city.

Technically, Mussolini had come into office by legal means. The monarch had the power to appoint the prime minister. Mussolini, however, had no majority in the Chamber of Deputies. Behind the legal facade lay the months of terrorist intimidation and the threat of the Fascists' October march.

THE FASCISTS IN POWER

Duce Meaning "leader." Mussolini's title as head of the Fascist Party.

Mussolini, who had not expected to be appointed prime minister, succeeded because of the impotence of his rivals, his use of his office, his power over the masses, and his ruthlessness. On November 23, 1922, the king and Parliament granted Mussolini dictatorial authority for one year to restore order. Wherever possible, Mussolini appointed Fascists to office. In 1924, Parliament changed the election law so that the party that gained the largest popular vote (with at least 25 percent) received two-thirds of the seats in the chamber. Coalition government, with all its compromises and hesitations, would no longer be necessary. In the election of 1924, the Fascists won complete control of the Chamber of Deputies. They used that majority to end legitimate parliamentary life. Laws permitted Mussolini to rule by decree. In 1926, Italy was transformed into a single-party, dictatorial state.

One domestic initiative brought Mussolini significant political dividends and respectability. Through the Lateran Accord of February 1929, the Roman Catholic Church and the Italian state made peace with each other. The agreement recognized the pope as the temporal ruler of Vatican City. The Italian government agreed to pay an indemnity to the papacy for confiscated land. The state also recognized Catholicism as the religion of the nation, exempted church property from taxes, and allowed church law to govern marriage.

23.5
The Rise of Benito Mussolini

GERMAN DEMOCRACY AND DICTATORSHIP

THE WEIMAR REPUBLIC

The Weimar Republic was born from the defeat of the imperial army, the revolution of 1918, and the hopes of German Liberals and Social Democrats. Its name derived from the city of Weimar where its constitution was written in August 1919. While the constitution was being debated, the republic, headed by the Social Democrats, accepted the hated Versailles Treaty. Although its officials had signed only under duress, the republic was permanently associated with the national disgrace. Throughout the 1920s, the government was required to fulfill the economic and military provisions imposed by the Paris settlement. Nationalists and military figures whose policies had brought on the tragedy and defeat of the war blamed the young republic and the socialists for its results. In Germany, the desire to revise the treaty was related to a desire to change the form of government.

The Weimar Constitution was an enlightened document. It guaranteed civil liberties and provided for direct election, by universal suffrage, of the **Reichstag** and the president. It also, however, contained structural flaws that eventually allowed it to be overthrown. A complicated system of proportional representation made it relatively easy for small political parties to gain seats in the Reichstag, which resulted in instability. The president appointed and removed the chancellor, the head of the cabinet. Article 48 allowed the president, in an emergency, to rule by decree. This permitted a possible presidential dictatorship.

In March 1920, a right-wing putsch, or armed insurrection, erupted in Berlin. It failed, but only after government officials had fled the city. In the same month, strikes took place in the Ruhr, and the government sent in troops. Such extremism from both the left and the right would haunt the republic. In May 1921, the Allies presented a reparations bill for 132 billion gold marks. The German government accepted this preposterous demand only after new Allied threats. Throughout the early 1920s, there were assassinations or attempted assassinations of republican leaders. Violence was the hallmark of the first five years of the republic.

Invasion of the Ruhr and Inflation   Inflation brought on the major crisis of this period. The war and postwar deficit spending generated an immense rise in prices. The value of German currency fell. By early 1921, the German mark traded against

WHAT ROLE did terror play in Nazi Germany?

Reichstag German parliament, which existed in various forms, until 1945.

23.6
Adolf Hitler, *Mein Kampf*

Major Political Events of the 1920s and 1930s

1919		
	August	Constitution of the Weimar Republic promulgated
	1920	Putsch in Berlin
1921		
	March	Lenin initiates his New Economic Policy
1922		
	October	Fascist march on Rome leads to Mussolini's assumption of power
1923		
	January	France invades the Ruhr
	November	Hitler's Beer Hall Putsch
	1924	Death of Lenin
	1925	Locarno Agreements
	1928	Kellogg-Briand Pact; first five-year plan launched in USSR
1929		
	January	Trotsky expelled from USSR
	February	Lateran Accord between the Vatican and the Italian state
	October	New York stock market crash
	November	Stalin's power affirmed

the American dollar at a ratio of 64 to 1, compared with a ratio of 4.2 to 1 in 1914. The German financial community contended that the mark could not be stabilized until the reparations issue had been solved. Meanwhile, the government kept issuing paper money, which it used to redeem government bonds.

The French invasion of the Ruhr in January 1923, to secure the payment of reparations, and the German response of passive economic resistance produced cataclysmic inflation. Unemployment spread, creating a drain on the treasury and reducing tax revenues. The printing presses had difficulty providing enough paper currency to keep up with the daily rise in prices. Money was literally not worth the paper it was printed on. Stores were unwilling to exchange goods for the worthless currency, and farmers hoarded produce.

The values of thrift and prudence were undermined. Middle-class savings, pensions, insurance policies, and investments in government bonds were wiped out. Debts and mortgages could not be paid off. Speculators made fortunes, but to the middle and lower-middle classes, inflation was another trauma coming hard on the heels of military defeat and the peace treaty. This social and economic upheaval was behind the later German desire for order and security at almost any cost.

Hitler's Early Career In 1923, Adolf Hitler (1889–1945) made his first significant appearance on the German political scene. The son of a minor Austrian customs official, his hopes of becoming an artist had been dashed in Vienna. Hitler absorbed the rabid German nationalism and extreme anti-Semitism that flourished there. He came to hate Marxism, which he associated with Jews. During World War I, Hitler fought in the German army, was wounded, rose to the rank of corporal, and won the Iron Cross for bravery. The war gave him his first sense of purpose.

After the conflict, Hitler settled in Munich and became associated with a small nationalistic, anti-Semitic party that in 1920 adopted the name of National Socialist German Workers Party, better known as the Nazis. The group paraded under a red banner with a black swastika. Its program called for the repudiation of the Versailles Treaty, the unification of Austria and Germany, the exclusion of Jews from German citizenship, agrarian reform, the prohibition of land speculation, the confiscation of war profits, state administration of the giant cartels, and the replacement of department stores with small retail shops.

The "socialism" that Hitler and the Nazis had in mind had nothing to do with traditional German socialism. It meant not state ownership of the means of production but the subordination of all economic enterprise to the welfare of the nation. It often implied protection for small economic enterprises. The Nazis discovered that their social appeal was to the lower-middle class, which found itself squeezed between big business and socialist labor unions. The Nazis tailored their message to this troubled economic group.

Nazi stormtroopers, or SA *(Sturm Abteilung)*, were organized under the leadership of Captain Ernst Roehm (1887–1934). The stormtroopers were the chief Nazi instrument for terror and intimidation before the party controlled the government. The existence of such a private party army was a sign of the potential for violence in the Weimar Republic and of contempt for the republic.

The social and economic turmoil following the French occupation of the Ruhr and the German inflation gave the Nazis an opportunity for direct action against the Weimar Republic. By this time, Hitler dominated the Nazi Party. On November 9, 1923, Hitler and a band of followers, accompanied by General Erich Ludendorff (1865–1937), attempted an unsuccessful putsch at a beer hall in Munich. Local authorities crushed the rising, and 16 Nazis were killed. Hitler and Ludendorff were tried for treason. The general was acquitted. Hitler made himself into a national figure. In his defense, he condemned the republic, the Versailles Treaty, and the Jews. He was sentenced to five years in prison but spent only a few months in jail before being paroled. During this time, he dictated *Mein Kampf* ("My Struggle"). Another result of the brief imprisonment was his decision to seize political power by legal methods.

The Stresemann Years   Gustav Stresemann (1878–1929) was primarily responsible for the reconstruction of the republic and its achievement of a sense of self-confidence. Stresemann abandoned the policy of passive resistance in the Ruhr. With the aid of banker Hjalmar Schacht (1877–1970), he introduced a new German currency. The rate of exchange was 1 trillion of the old German marks for one new Rentenmark. Stresemann also moved against challenges from both the left and the right. He supported the crushing of both Hitler's abortive putsch and smaller communist disturbances. In late November 1923, after four months as chancellor, he became foreign minister, a post he held until his death in 1929.

In 1924, the Weimar Republic and the Allies renegotiated the reparation payments. French troops left the Ruhr in 1925. The same year, Field Marshal Paul von Hindenburg (1847–1934), a military hero and a conservative monarchist, was elected president and governed in strict accordance with the constitution. The prosperity of the latter 1920s seemed to reconcile conservative Germans to the republic. Foreign capital flowed into Germany, and employment improved smartly. Giant industrial combines spread.

In foreign affairs, Stresemann pursued a conciliatory course. He fulfilled the provisions of the Versailles Treaty but attempted to revise it by diplomacy. He accepted the settlement in the west but aimed to recover German-speaking territories lost to Poland and Czechoslovakia and possibly to unite with Austria, chiefly by diplomatic means.

Locarno   These developments gave rise to the Locarno Agreements of October 1925. Foreign ministers Austen Chamberlain (1863–1937) for Britain and Aristide Briand (1862–1932) for France accepted Stresemann's proposal for a fresh start. France and Germany accepted the western

Major Political Events of the 1920s and 1930s (*continued*)

1930		
March	Brüning government begins in Germany	
September	Nazis capture 107 seats in German Reichstag	
1931		
August	National Government formed in Britain	
1932		
March 13	Hindenberg defeats Hitler for German presidency	
May 31	Franz von Papen forms German cabinet	
July 31	German Reichstag election	
November 6	German Reichstag election	
December 2	Kurt von Schleicher forms German cabinet	
1933		
January 30	Hitler made German chancellor	
February 27	Reichstag Fire	
March 5	Reichstag election	
March 23	Enabling Act consolidates Nazi power	
1934		
June 30	Blood purge of the Nazi Party	
August 2	Death of Hindenburg	
December 1	Assassination of Kirov leads to the beginning of Stalin's purges	
1936		
May	Popular Front government in France	
July–August	Most famous of public purge trials in Russia	

frontier established at Versailles. Britain and Italy agreed to intervene against the aggressor if either side violated the frontier or if Germany sent troops into the demilitarized Rhineland. No such agreement was made about Germany's eastern frontier, but the Germans made arbitration treaties with Poland and Czechoslovakia, and France strengthened its alliances with those countries. France supported German membership in the League of Nations and agreed to withdraw its occupation troops from the Rhineland in 1930, five years earlier than specified at Versailles.

The Locarno Agreements brought new hope to Europe. Chamberlain, Briand, and Stresemann received the Nobel Peace Prize. The spirit of Locarno was carried even further when the leading European states, Japan, and the United States signed the Kellogg-Briand Pact in 1928, renouncing "war as an instrument of national policy." The joy and optimism were not justified. France had merely recognized its inability to coerce Germany without help. Britain had shown its unwillingness to uphold the settlement in the east. Germany was not reconciled to the eastern settlement.

In both France and Germany, moreover, the conciliatory politicians represented only a part of the nation. In Germany especially, most people continued to reject Versailles and regarded Locarno as only an extension of it. Despite these problems, war was by no means inevitable. Europe, aided by American loans, was returning to prosperity. German leaders like Stresemann would certainly have continued to press for change, but not through force, much less a general war. Continued prosperity and diplomatic success might have won the loyalty of the German people for the Weimar Republic and moderate revisionism, but the Great Depression of the 1930s brought new forces to power.

DEPRESSION AND POLITICAL DEADLOCK

The outflow of foreign, and especially American, capital from Germany that began in 1928 undermined the prosperity of the Weimar Republic. The resulting economic crisis brought parliamentary government to a halt. In 1928, a coalition of center parties and the Social Democrats governed. When the depression struck, the coalition partners differed sharply on economic policy, and the coalition dissolved in March 1930. President von Hindenburg appointed Heinrich Brüning (1885–1970) as chancellor. Lacking a majority in the Reichstag, the new chancellor governed through emergency presidential decrees. The Weimar Republic had become a presidential dictatorship.

German unemployment rose from 2,258,000 in March 1930 to more than 6,000,000 in March 1932. The economic downturn and the parliamentary deadlock worked to the advantage of extremists. In the election of 1928, the Nazis had won only 12 seats in the Reichstag and the Communists won 54. In the election of 1930, the Nazis won 107 seats and the Communists won 77.

The power of the Nazis in the streets also rose. Unemployment fed thousands of men into the stormtroopers, which had almost 1 million members in 1933. The SA attacked Communists and Social Democrats. For the Nazis, politics meant the capture of power through terror and intimidation as well as through elections. Decency and civility in political life vanished. Nazi rallies resembled religious revivals. They paraded through the streets and the countryside. They gained powerful supporters in the business, military, and newspaper communities. Some intellectuals were also sympathetic. The Nazis transformed this discipline and enthusiasm born of economic despair and nationalistic frustration into electoral results.

European Turmoil. In this painting, which reflects the mood of social and political disillusionment that prevailed in much of Europe in the 1920s, George Grosz satirized conservative and right-wing groups in Weimar Germany, including the army, the courts, the newspapers, and the Nazi Party.

Bildarchiv Preussischer Kulturbesitz.

HITLER COMES TO POWER

For two years, Brüning governed with the confidence of Hindenburg. The economy did not improve, and the political situation deteriorated. In 1932, the 83-year-old president stood for reelection. Hitler ran against him and Hindenburg won. But Hitler got 36.8 percent of the final vote. The vote convinced Hindenburg that Brüning had lost the confidence of conservative Germans. In May 1932, he appointed Franz von Papen (1878–1969) chancellor. Papen was one of a small group of extremely conservative advisers on whom Hindenburg had become dependent. With the continued paralysis in the Reichstag, the advisers' influence over the president amounted to control of the government.

Hitler. Hitler's mastery of the techniques of mass politics and propaganda—including huge staged rallies like this one in 1938—was an important factor in his rise to power.

Bildarchlv Preussischer Kulturbesitz.

Papen and the circle around the president wanted to draw the Nazis into cooperation with them without giving Hitler effective power. The government needed the popular support on the right that only the Nazis seemed able to generate. The Hindenburg circle decided to convince Hitler that the Nazis could not come to power on their own. Papen removed the ban on Nazi meetings that Brüning had imposed and called a Reichstag election for July 1932. The Nazis won 230 seats and polled 37.2 percent of the vote. Hitler would only enter the cabinet if he were made chancellor. Hindenburg refused. Another election was called in November. The Nazis gained only 196 seats, and their percentage of the popular vote dipped to 33.1 percent.

In early December 1932, Papen resigned, and General Kurt von Schleicher (1882–1934) became chancellor. People were now afraid of civil war between the extreme left and the far right. Schleicher tried to fashion a coalition of conservatives and trade unionists. The Hindenburg circle did not trust Schleicher's motives, which have never been clear. They persuaded Hindenburg to appoint Hitler chancellor. To control him, Papen was named vice chancellor, and other traditional conservatives were appointed to the cabinet. On January 30, 1933, Adolf Hitler became the chancellor of Germany.

Hitler had come into office by legal means. The proper procedures had been observed. This permitted the civil service, courts, and other government agencies to support him in good conscience. He had forged a rigidly disciplined party structure and had mastered the techniques of mass politics and propaganda. His support appears to have come from across the social spectrum. Pockets of resistance appeared among Roman Catholic voters in the country and small towns. Otherwise, support for Hitler was strong among farmers, veterans, and the young, who had suffered from the insecurity of the 1920s and the depression. Hitler promised them security, effective government in place of petty politics, and a strong, restored Germany.

There is little evidence that business contributions made any crucial difference to the Nazis' success. Hitler's supporters were frequently suspicious of business and

Anti-Jewish Policies. Soon after seizing power, the Nazi government began harassing German Jewish businesses. Non-Jewish German citizens were urged not to buy merchandise from shops owned by Jews.

Bildarchiv Preussischer Kulturbesitz.

giant capitalism. They wanted a simpler world in which small property would be safe from both socialism and large-scale capitalist consolidation. These people looked to Hitler and the Nazis rather than to the Social Democrats because the latter never appeared sufficiently nationalistic. The Nazis won out over other conservative nationalistic parties because, unlike those conservatives, the Nazis addressed the problem of social insecurities.

HITLER'S CONSOLIDATION OF POWER

Once in office, Hitler moved swiftly to consolidate his control. This process had three facets: the capture of full legal authority, the crushing of alternative political groups, and the purging of rivals within the Nazi Party itself. On February 27, 1933, a mentally ill Dutch Communist set fire to the Reichstag building in Berlin. The Nazis turned the incident to their own advantage by claiming that the fire proved the existence of a Communist threat to the government. To the public, this seemed plausible. Under Article 48, Hitler suspended civil liberties and arrested Communists or alleged Communists. This decree was not revoked for as long as Hitler ruled Germany.

In early March, another Reichstag election took place. The Nazis still received only 43.9 percent of the vote. However, the arrest of Communist deputies and the fear aroused by the fire meant that Hitler could control the Reichstag. On March 23, 1933, the Reichstag passed an Enabling Act, which permitted Hitler to rule by decree. Thereafter, there were no legal limits on his power. The Weimar Constitution was never formally repealed.

Hitler understood that he and his party had come to power because his potential opponents had stood divided between 1929 and 1933. To prevent them from regrouping, Hitler outlawed or undermined any German institutions that might have served as rallying points for opposition. By the close of 1933, all major institutions of potential opposition—trade unions, other political parties, the federal state governments—had been eliminated.

The final element in Hitler's personal consolidation of power involved the Nazi Party itself. Ernst Roehm, the commander of the SA, was a possible rival to Hitler. The German officer corps, whom Hitler needed to rebuild the army, were jealous of the SA. To protect his own position and to shore up support with the army, Hitler ordered the murder of key SA officers, including Roehm. Between June 30 and July 2, 1934, more than 800 people were killed, including the former chancellor Kurt von Schleicher and his wife. The German army, which might have prevented the murders, did nothing. On August 2, 1934, President Hindenburg died, and the offices of chancellor and president were combined. Hitler was now the sole ruler, or *Führer*, of Germany and of the Nazi Party.

THE POLICE STATE

Terror and intimidation had helped propel the Nazis to office. As Hitler consolidated his power, he oversaw the organization of a police state. The chief vehicle of police surveillance was the SS *(Schutzstaffel)*, or security units, commanded by Heinrich Himmler (1900–1945). This group was a more elite paramilitary organization than the larger SA. In 1933, the SS had approximately 52,000 members. It was the instrument that carried out the blood purges of the party in 1934. By 1936, Himmler had become head of all police matters in Germany.

Führer Meaning "leader." Title taken by Hitler when he became dictator of Germany.

The police character of the Nazi regime was all-pervasive, but the people who most consistently experienced its terror were the Jews. Anti-Semitism had been a key plank of the Nazi program—anti-Semitism based on biological racial theories stemming from late-19th-century thought rather than from religious discrimination. Before World War II, the Nazi attack on the Jews went through three stages. In 1933, the Nazis excluded Jews from the civil service and attempted to enforce boycotts of Jewish businesses. The boycotts won little public support. In 1935, the Nuremberg Laws robbed German Jews of their citizenship. All persons with at least one Jewish grandparent were defined as Jews. The professions and major occupations were closed to Jews. Marriage and sexual intercourse between Jews and non-Jews were prohibited. Legal exclusion and humiliation of the Jews became the norm (see "The Nazis Pass Their Racial Legislation").

The persecution of the Jews increased again in 1938. In November, under orders from the Nazi Party, thousands of Jewish stores and synagogues were destroyed. The Jewish community itself had to pay for the damage that occurred on this **Kristallnacht** because the government confiscated the insurance money. In both large and petty ways, the German Jews were harassed. This persecution allowed the Nazis to inculcate the rest of the population with the concept of a master race of pure German "Aryans" and also to display their own contempt for civil liberties.

After the war broke out, Hitler decided in 1942 to destroy the Jews in Europe. It is thought that more than 6 million Jews, mostly from eastern Europe, died as a result of that decision, unprecedented in its scope and implementation.

WOMEN IN NAZI GERMANY

The Nazis believed in separate social spheres for men and women. Men belonged in the world of action, women in the home. The two spheres should not mix. Respect for women should arise from their function as wives and mothers.

These attitudes conflicted with the social changes that German women, like women elsewhere in Europe, had experienced during the first three decades of

Kristallnacht Meaning "crystal night" because of the broken glass that littered German streets after the looting and destruction of Jewish homes, businesses, and synagogues across Germany on the orders of the Nazi Party in November 1938.

OVERVIEW   POLITICAL TYRANNY OF THE 1920S AND 1930S

Although political tyranny was not new to Europe, several factors in the 1920s and 1930s combined to give dictators of the right and the left unique power. The regimes set up by Mussolini in Italy, Stalin in Russia, and Hitler in Germany shared the following characteristics:

1. Well-organized political parties

2. Nationalism

3. Programs that promised to cure social, political, and economic frustrations and end the pettiness of everyday politics

4. A monopoly over mass communications and propaganda

5. Highly effective instruments of terror and police power

6. Real or imagined national, class, or racial enemies who could be demonized to whip up mass support

7. Command over modern technology and its capacity for immense destruction

HISTORY'S VOICES

THE NAZIS PASS THEIR RACIAL LEGISLATION

nti-Semitism was a fundamental tenet of the Nazi Party and became a major policy of the Nazi government. This comprehensive legislation of September 15, 1935, carried anti-Semitism into all areas of public life and into some of the most personal areas of private life as well. It was characteristically titled the Law for the Protection of German Blood and Honor. Hardly any aspect of Nazi thought and action shocked the non-German world as much as this policy toward the Jews.

HOW WOULD this legislation have affected the normal daily interaction between Jews and non-Jews in Germany? Why are there specific prohibitions against mixed marriages and sexual relations between Jews and non-Jews? How does this legislation separate German Jews from the symbols of German national life?

Imbued with the knowledge that the purity of German blood is the necessary prerequisite for the existence of the German nation, and inspired by an inflexible will to maintain the existence of the German nation for all future times, the Reichstag has unanimously adopted the following law, which is now enacted:

Article I: (1) Any marriages between Jews and citizens of German or kindred blood are herewith forbidden. Marriages entered into despite this law are invalid, even if they are arranged abroad as a means of circumventing this law.

(2) Annulment proceedings for marriages may be initiated only by the Public Prosecutor.

Article II: Extramarital relations between Jews and citizens of German or kindred blood are herewith forbidden.

Article III: Jews are forbidden to employ as servants to their households female subjects of German or kindred blood who are under the age of forty-five years.

Article IV: (1) Jews are prohibited from displaying the Reich and national flag and from showing the national colors.

(2) However, they may display the Jewish colors. The exercise of this right is under state protection.

Article V: (1) Anyone who acts contrary to the prohibition noted in Article I renders himself liable to penal servitude.

(2) The man who acts contrary to the prohibition of Article II will be punished by sentence to either a jail or penitentiary.

(3) Anyone who acts contrary to the provisions of Articles III or IV will be punished with a jail sentence up to a year and with a fine, or with one of these penalties.

Article VI: The Reich Minister of Interior, in conjunction with the Deputy to the Führer and the Reich Minister of Justice, will issue the required legal and administrative decrees for the implementation and amplification of this law.

Article VII: This law shall go into effect on the day following its promulgation, with the exception of Article III, which shall go into effect on January 1, 1936.

Source: *Documents of German History*, Louis L. Snyder, ed. and trans. Copyright © 1938 Rutgers the State University, pp. 427–428. Reprinted by permission of Rutgers University Press.

the 20th century. German women had become much more active and assertive. They worked in factories or were independently employed, and had begun to enter the professions. Under the Weimar Constitution, they voted. Throughout the Weimar period, there was also a lively discussion of women's emancipation. For the Nazis, these developments were signs of cultural weakness.

The Nazis' point of view was supported by women of a conservative outlook and women who followed traditional roles as housewives. In a period of high unemployment, the Nazi attitude also appealed to many men because it discouraged women from competing with them in the workplace. Such competition had begun during World War I, and many Nazis considered it symptomatic of the social confusion that had followed the German defeat.

The Nazi discussion of the role of women was also rooted in Nazi racism. It was the special task of German mothers to preserve racial purity. Hitler championed this view of women. They were to breed strong sons and daughters for the German nation. Nazi journalists often compared the role of women in childbirth to that of men in battle. Each served the state in particular gender roles. In both cases, the good of the nation was superior to that of the individual.

The Nazis also attacked feminist outlooks. Women were encouraged to bear many children, because the Nazis believed the declining German birth rate was the result of emancipated women who had spurned their natural roles as mothers. The Nazis sponsored schools that taught women how to rear children.

The Nazis also saw women as educators of the young and thus the protectors of German cultural values. Through cooking, dress, music, and stories, mothers were to instill a love for the nation. As consumers for the home, women were to buy German goods and avoid Jewish merchants.

The Nazis realized that in the midst of the depression many women would need to work, but the party urged them to pursue employment that the Nazis considered natural to their character. These tasks included agriculture, teaching, nursing, social work, and domestic service. Nonetheless, the percentage of women employed in Germany changed little from the Weimar to the Hitler years: 37 percent in 1928 and in 1939. Thereafter, because of the war, many more women were recruited into the German work force.

THE GREAT DEPRESSION AND THE NEW DEAL IN THE UNITED STATES

HOW DID FDR's policies affect the role of the federal government?

*T*he United States emerged from World War I as a world power. However, it retreated from that role when the Senate refused to ratify the Versailles Treaty and failed to join the League of Nations. In 1920, Warren Harding (1865–1923) became president and urged a return to what he termed "normalcy," which meant minimal involvement abroad and conservative economic policies at home. Business interests remained in the ascendent, and the federal government took a relatively inactive role in national life, especially under Harding's successor, Calvin Coolidge (1872–1933).

The first seven or eight years of the decade witnessed remarkable American prosperity. New electrical appliances such as the radio, phonograph, washing machine, and vacuum cleaner appeared on the market. Real wages rose for many workers. Industry grew at a robust rate. Automobile manufacturers assumed a major role in national economic life. Factories became mechanized. Engineers and efficiency experts were the heroes of the business world. The stock market boomed. This activity stood in marked contrast to the economic dislocations of Europe.

The material prosperity appeared, however, in a divided society. Segregation remained a basic fact of life for Black Americans. The Ku Klux Klan, which sought to terrorize Blacks, Roman Catholics, and Jews, enjoyed a resurgence. The Prohibition Amendment of 1919 (repealed in 1933) forbade the manufacture and transport of alcoholic beverages. In the wake of this divisive national policy, major criminal operations arose to supply liquor and disrupt civic life. Many immigrants came from Mexico and Puerto Rico. They

Assembly line. Ford Motor Company assembly-line workers on the job in 1928 in Dearborn, Michigan.
© Hulton Getty/Archive Photos.

settled in cities where their labor was desired but where they were often not welcomed or assimilated. Finally, the wealth of the nation was concentrated in too few hands.

ECONOMIC COLLAPSE

In March 1929, Herbert Hoover became president, the third Republican in as many elections. On October 29, 1929, the New York Stock Exchange crashed. Other financial markets also went into a tailspin. During the next year the stock market continued to fall. Banks that had loaned people money with which to speculate in the market suffered great losses.

The financial collapse of 1929 triggered the Great Depression in America, although there were other underlying domestic causes. Manufacturing firms had not made sufficient capital investment. The disproportionate amount of profits going to about 5 percent of the U.S. population undermined the purchasing power of other consumers. Agriculture was in trouble. Finally, the economic difficulties in Europe and Latin America, which predated those in the United States, meant foreigners were less able to purchase American products.

The most pervasive problem of the Great Depression was unemployment. Joblessness hit unskilled workers first but then worked its way up the job ladder to touch factory and white-collar workers. As unemployment spread, small retail businesses suffered. In the major American manufacturing cities, hundreds of thousands of workers could not find jobs. The price of corn fell so low in some areas that it was not profitable to harvest it. By the early 1930s, banks began to fail, and people lost their savings.

The federal government was not equipped to address the emergency. There was no tradition of federal action to alleviate economic distress. President Hoover organized economic conferences and encouraged the Federal Reserve to make borrowing easier. He supported the ill-advised Hawley-Smoot Tariff Act of 1930, which hoped to protect American industry by a high tariff barrier. Hoover believed relief was a matter for local government and voluntary organizations; however, many local relief agencies had run out of money by 1931.

NEW ROLE FOR GOVERNMENT

The election of 1932 was one of the most crucial in American history. The Democratic Party's candidate, Franklin Delano Roosevelt (1882–1945), promised "a new deal for the American people." He overwhelmingly defeated Hoover, and quickly redirected federal policy toward the depression.

Roosevelt had been born into a moderately wealthy New York family and was a distant cousin of Theodore Roosevelt (1858–1919). After serving in World War I as Assistant Secretary of the Navy, in 1920 he ran as the Democratic vice presidential candidate. The next year, however, he was struck with polio and his legs became paralyzed, but he went on to be elected governor of New York in 1928. As president, he attempted to convey to the nation the same kind of optimistic spirit that had informed his own struggle of the 1920s.

Roosevelt's first goal was to give the nation a sense that the federal government was meeting the economic challenge. The first hundred days of his administration became legendary. He immediately closed all the banks and permitted only sound institutions to reopen. Congress rapidly passed a new banking act and then enacted the Agricultural Adjustment Act and the Farm Credit Act to aid farmers. To provide jobs, Roosevelt sponsored the Civilian

Conservation Corps. The Federal Emergency Relief Act funded state and local relief agencies. To restore confidence, Roosevelt began making speeches, known as "fireside chats," to the American people.

Roosevelt's most ambitious program was the National Industrial Recovery Act (NIRA), which established the National Recovery Administration (NRA). This agency attempted to foster codes written by various industries to regulate wages and prices to monitor competition and thus protect jobs and assure production.

The NIRA and other New Deal legislation, such as the Wagner Act of 1935, which established the National Labor Relations Board and the Fair Labor Standards Act of 1938, provided a larger role in the American economy for organized labor. It became easier for unions to organize. Union membership grew, and American unionism took on a new character. Most unions had been organized by craft and were affiliated with the American Federation of Labor (AFL). In the 1930s, however, whole industries composed of workers in various crafts were organized in a single union. The most important of these organizations were the United Mine Workers and United Automobile Workers. These new unions organized themselves into the Congress of Industrial Organizations (CIO). The CIO and the AFL merged in the 1950s. These strong industrial labor organizations introduced a new force into the American economic scene.

In 1935, the U.S. Supreme Court declared the NRA unconstitutional. Thereafter, Roosevelt deemphasized centralized economic planning. The number of federal agencies increased, but they operated in general independence from each other.

Through New Deal legislation, the federal government was far more active in the economy than it had ever been. The government itself attempted to provide relief for the unemployed in the industrial sector. The major institution of the relief effort was the **Works Progress Administration**. Created in 1935, the WPA began a massive program of public works.

Programs of the New Deal years also involved the federal government directly in economic development rather than turning such development over to private enterprise. Through the Tennessee Valley Authority (TVA), the government became directly involved in the economy of the four states of the Tennessee River valley. The TVA built dams and then produced and sold hydroelectricity. Never had the government undertaken so extensive an economic role. Another major new function for the government was providing security for the elderly, through the establishment of the Social Security Administration in 1935.

In one area of American life after another, it was decided that the government must provide personal economic security. These actions established a mixed economy in the United States—one in which the federal government would play an active role alongside the private sector.

The Works Progress Administration. This economic relief effort agency was one of the chief New Deal organizations designed to create public works projects that would generate employment, as with this group repairing a street.

Corbis/Bettmann.

Works Progress Administration New Deal program created by the Roosevelt administration in 1935 that provided relief for the unemployed in the industrial sector during the Great Depression in the United States.

Yet the New Deal did not solve the unemployment problem. In the late 1930s, the economy began to falter again. Only the entry of the nation into World War II brought the U.S. economy to full employment.

The experience of the United States under the New Deal stood in marked contrast to the economic and political experiments in Europe. Many business-people found Roosevelt too liberal and his policies too activist. Nonetheless, the New Deal preserved capitalism in a democratic setting, where, again in contrast to Europe, there was free political debate—much of it critical of the administration. The United States had demonstrated that a nation with a vast industrial economy could confront its gravest economic crisis and still preserve democracy.

IMAGE KEY

for pages 750–751

a. Poster glorifying work, Soviet Union, 1930s.

b. Hitler salutes from an open car at a rally in 1938.

c. A Works Progress Administration (WPA) poster.

d. Il Duce, Benito Mussolini.

e. A George Grosz painting satirizing conservative and right-wing groups in Weimar Germany.

f. Works Progress Administration (WPA) workers.

g. A Soviet propoganda poster.

h. A Volkswagen on a German Reich postage stamp, 1939.

i. Unemployed workers outside the Municipal Lodging House in New York City during the Great Depression, 1930.

SUMMARY

Postwar Problems The Versailles settlement left much of Europe dissatisfied. The 1920s saw endless wrangles over reparations between Germany and the Allied powers. After World War I, Europe never recovered its prewar prosperity or stability. The onset of the Great Depression in 1929 caused severe problems in both Europe and the United States and led to the Nazi seizure of power in Germany and Roosevelt's New Deal in the United States.

The Soviet Union The Bolsheviks had expected Communist revolutions to break out across Europe. When that did not happen, they were forced to consolidate their regime within Russia. Lenin's New Economic Policy gave the state control over heavy industry, transportation, and international commerce but allowed for small-scale private enterprise and peasant farms. Stalin abandoned this policy. He abolished private enterprise, collectivized agriculture, and eliminated his opponents in a series of purges. Despite this, Marxist parties around the world were subservient to the Soviet Union as the world's only Communist state and the enemy of fascism.

Fascist Italy Benito Mussolini came to power in Italy in 1922. Many Italians were dissatisfied with the terms of the Versailles Treaty and frightened by the social unrest that followed World War I. Mussolini promised order and a strong state. Although he achieved power by legal means, he soon transformed Italy into a single-party dictatorship. In 1929, he came to terms with the Catholic Church by negotiating the Lateran Accord, which recognized the pope as the independent ruler of Vatican City.

Nazi Germany The postwar Weimar Republic in Germany was buffeted by social, political, and financial instability. Many Germans refused to accept Germany's defeat in World War I or the terms of the Versailles Treaty. Rampant inflation destroyed the savings of the middle class. The Great Depression brought financial collapse and massive unemployment. Many Germans looked to Adolf Hitler and the Nazi Party for solutions. Once Hitler came to power in 1933, he quickly established a one-party dictatorship based on police terror, propaganda, and the cult of himself as supreme leader. The Jews, in particular, were persecuted.

The United States The United States emerged from World War I as a world power, but retreated into isolation during the 1920s. The shallow prosperity of the 1920s ended in the Great Depression. Franklin Delano Roosevelt's New Deal greatly expanded the power of the federal government in social and economic affairs and preserved capitalism in a democratic setting.

REVIEW QUESTIONS

1. How did Stalin achieve supreme power in the Soviet Union? Why did he decide that Russia had to industrialize rapidly and collectivize agriculture? Did these policies succeed? How did they affect the Russian people? What were the causes of the Great Purges?

2. How did Mussolini achieve power? What were the characteristics of the Fascist state?

3. Why did Weimar Republic collapse? How did Hitler come to power?

4. Why did the U.S. economy collapse in 1929? How did Roosevelt combat the depression?

KEY TERMS

collectivization (p. 755)

Duce (p. 758)

fascism (p. 757)

Führer (p. 764)

Great Depression (p. 752)

Great Purges (p. 756)

Kristallnacht (p. 765)

Mein Kampf (p. 761)

New Economic Policy
   (NEP) (p. 754)

Popular Front (p. 753)

Reichstag (p. 759)

War Communism (p. 754)

Weimar Republic (p. 752)

Works Progress
   Administration (p. 769)

  For additional study resources for this chapter, go to:
www.prenhall.com/craig/chapter30

31 World War II

CHAPTER HIGHLIGHTS

The Coming of War The second great war of the twentieth century (1939–1945) grew out of the unsatisfactory resolution of the first war. Whatever the flaws of the treaties of Paris, the world suffered an even more terrible war than the first as a result of failures of judgment and will on the part of the victorious democratic powers. The United States disarmed almost entirely and withdrew into foolish isolation; it could play no important part in restraining the ambitious dictators who would bring on the war. Britain and France refused to face the threat posed by the Axis powers until the most deadly war in history was required to put it down.

World War II The second war itself was plainly a world war. The Japanese occupation of Manchuria in 1931 was a precursor. Italy attacked Ethiopia in 1935. Italy, Germany, and the Soviet Union intervened in the Spanish Civil War (1936–1939). Japan attacked China in 1937. The formation of the Axis among Germany, Italy, and Japan guaranteed that the war would be fought around the world. The use of atomic weapons brought the struggle to a close, but what are called conventional weapons did almost all the damage. The survival of civilization was threatened even without the use of nuclear devices.

The world quickly split into two unfriendly camps: the Western, led by the United States, and the Eastern, led by the Soviet Union. This division hastened the liberation of former colonial territories.

CHAPTER QUESTIONS

WHAT WERE the main events between 1933 and 1939 that led to World War II?

WHY WAS 1943 the turning point in World War II?

HOW DID war affect civilians in Germany, France, Britain, and the Soviet Union?

WHY DID cooperation between the Soviet Union and the Western powers break down in 1945?

CHAPTER OUTLINE

- Again the Road to War (1933–1939)
- World War II
- The Domestic Fronts
- Preparations for Peace

This is Nazi brutality

The more idealistic survivors of World War I, especially in the United States and Britain, thought of it as "the war to end all wars" and "a war to make the world safe for democracy." Only thus could they justify the slaughter, expense, and upheaval. Yet only 20 years after the peace treaties, a second great war broke out that was more global than the first. In this war, the democracies would be fighting for their lives against militaristic, nationalistic, authoritarian, and totalitarian states in Europe and Asia. Britain and the United States would be allied with the Communist Soviet Union. The defeat of the militarists and dictators would lead to a Cold War in which the European states became second-class powers, subordinate to the Soviet Union and the United States.

AGAIN THE ROAD TO WAR (1933–1939)

WHAT WERE the mains events between 1933 and 1939 that led to World War II?

*I*n light of the world depression of the 1930s, the Versailles Treaty that ended World War I took on a special meaning for Germans. The reparations demanded by the Allies had contributed to ruinous inflation in Germany, and many Germans blamed their economic troubles on the treaty. Adolf Hitler and the Nazi Party had long denounced the treaty as the source of Germany's problems, and the economic woes of the the early 1930s seemed to bear them out. This, in addition to Nazi party discipline and a message of fervent nationalism, helped Hitler overthrow the Weimar Republic and take control of Germany.

HITLER'S GOALS

The Nazi destruction of political opposition meant that German foreign policy lay in Hitler's hands. From first to last, Hitler's racial theories and goals were central in his thought. He intended to bring the entire German people (*Volk*), understood as a racial group, together into a single nation. The new Germany would include all the Germanic parts of the old Habsburg Empire, including Austria. This virile nation would need more space to live (**Lebensraum**), which would be taken from the Slavs, a lesser race. The new Germany would be purified by the removal of the Jews, the most inferior race in Nazi theory. The plan required the conquest of Poland and the Ukraine to settle Germans and provide badly needed food. However, neither *Mein Kampf* nor later statements of policy were blueprints for action. Hitler exploited opportunities as they arose. But he never lost sight of his goals, which would almost certainly require a major war (see "Hitler Describes His Goals").

DESTRUCTION OF VERSAILLES

When Hitler came to power, Germany was weak. The first problem was to shake off the fetters of Versailles and make Germany a formidable military power. In October 1933, Germany withdrew from an international disarmament conference and from the League of Nations. These acts were merely symbolic, but in March 1935, Hitler renounced the disarmament provisions of the Versailles Treaty with the formation of a German air force. Soon he reinstated conscription, which aimed at an army of half a million men.

His path was made easier because the League of Nations was ineffective. In September 1931, Japan occupied Manchuria. China appealed to the league, which condemned the Japanese for resorting to force. But the powers would not impose sanctions. Japan withdrew from the league and kept Manchuria.

The league condemned Hitler's decision to rearm Germany, but took no steps to prevent it. France and Britain met with Mussolini in June 1935 to form the so-called Stresa Front and agreed to maintain the status quo in Europe by force if

Lebensraum "Living space," Nazi plan to colonize and exploit eastern Europe.

HISTORY'S VOICES

HITLER DESCRIBES HIS GOALS

From his early career, Hitler had certain long-term general views and goals. They were set forth in his Mein Kampf, *which appeared in 1925, and included consolidation of the German Volk ("people"), provision of more land for the Germans, and contempt for such "races" as Slavs and Jews. Here are some of Hitler's views.*

WHAT IS the basic principle on which Hitler's policy is founded? How does he justify his plans for expansion? What reasons does he give for hostility to France and Russia? What is the basis for Hitler's claim of a right of every man to own farmland? Was that a practical goal for Germany in the 1930s? Was there any way for Hitler to achieve his goals without a major war?

The National Socialist movement must strive to eliminate the disproportion between our population and our area—viewing this latter as a source of food as well as a basis for power politics—between our historical past and the hopelessness of our present impotence. . . .

The demand for restoration of the frontiers of 1914 is a political absurdity of such proportions and consequences as to make it seem a crime. Quite aside from the fact that the Reich's frontiers in 1914 were anything but logical. For in reality they were neither complete in the sense of embracing the people of German nationality, nor sensible with regard to geo-military expediency. . . .

As opposed to this, we National Socialists must hold unflinchingly to our aim in foreign policy, namely, to secure for the German people the land and soil to which they are entitled on this earth. . . .

. . . The soil on which some day German generations of peasants can beget powerful sons will sanction the investment of the sons of today, and will some day acquit the responsible statesmen of blood-guilt and sacrifice of the people, even if they are persecuted by their contemporaries. . . .

Much as all of us today recognize the necessity of a reckoning with France, it would remain ineffectual in the long run if it represented the whole of our aim in foreign policy. It can and will achieve meaning only if it offers the rear cover for an enlargement of our people's living space in Europe. . . .

If we speak of soil in Europe today, we can primarily have in mind only Russia and her vassal border states. . . .

. . . See to it that the strength of our nation is founded, not on colonies, but on the soil of our European homeland. Never regard the Reich as secure unless for centuries to come it can give every scion of our people his own parcel of soil. Never forget that the most sacred right on this earth is a man's right to have earth to till with his own hands, and the most sacred sacrifice the blood that a man sheds for this earth.

Excerpts from Adolf Hitler, *Mein Kampf,* trans. by Ralph Manheim. Published by Pimlico. Copyright © 1943, renewed 1971 by Houghton Mifflin Company. Reprinted by permission of Houghton Mifflin Company, the Estate of Ralph Manheim, and Random House UK Limited. All rights reserved.

necessary. But Britain was desperate to maintain superiority at sea. Contrary to the Stresa accords, Britain soon made a separate naval agreement with Hitler, allowing him to rebuild the German fleet to 35 percent of the British navy.

ITALY ATTACKS ETHIOPIA

The Italian attack on Ethiopia in October 1935 made the impotence of the League of Nations and the timidity of the Allies even clearer. Using a border incident as an excuse, Mussolini's intent was to avenge a humiliating defeat that the Italians had suffered in 1896 and perhaps to divert Italians from Fascist corruption and Italy's economic troubles.

The League of Nations voted economic sanctions and imposed an arms embargo. But Britain and France were afraid of alienating Mussolini, so they refused to place an embargo on oil, the one economic sanction that could have prevented Italian victory. Nor did the British prevent the movement of Italian troops and munitions through the Suez Canal. This wavering policy was disastrous. The League of Nations and collective security were discredited, and Mussolini turned to Germany.

REMILITARIZATION OF THE RHINELAND

On March 7, 1936, Hitler took his greatest risk yet, sending a small armed force into the demilitarized Rhineland. This was a breach of the Versailles Treaty and of the Locarno Agreements. It also removed an important element of French security. Yet Britain and France made only a feeble protest.

A Germany that was rapidly rearming and had a defensible western frontier presented a new problem to the Western powers. Their response was the policy of **appeasement**. It was based on the assumption that Germany had real grievances, that Hitler's goals were limited, and that the wise thing to do was to make concessions before a crisis could lead to war. Behind this approach was the horror of another war. As Germany armed, the French huddled behind their defensive wall, the Maginot Line, and the British hoped for the best.

THE SPANISH CIVIL WAR

The new European alignment that found the Western democracies on one side and the Fascist states on the other was made clearer by the Spanish Civil War, which broke out in July 1936. In 1931, the Spaniards had established a republic. Elections in February 1936 brought to power a government of the left. The defeated groups, especially the Falangists, the Spanish version of Fascists, would not accept defeat at the polls. In July, General Francisco Franco (1892–1975) led an army against the republic.

Thus began a civil war that lasted almost three years. Germany and Italy aided Franco with troops and supplies. The Soviet Union sent equipment and advisers to the republicans. Leftists from Europe and America volunteered to fight against fascism.

The civil war, fought on ideological lines, brought Germany and Italy closer together, leading to the Rome-Berlin **Axis** Pact in 1936. They were joined in the same year by Japan in the Anti-Comintern Pact, ostensibly against communism. In western Europe, the appeasement mentality reigned. By early 1939, the Fascists had won control of Spain.

AUSTRIA AND CZECHOSLOVAKIA

In 1934, Mussolini, not yet allied with Hitler, frustrated a Nazi coup in Austria by threatening military intervention. In March 1938, the new diplomatic situation encouraged Hitler to try again. Mussolini made no objection, and Hitler marched into Vienna to the cheers of his Austrian sympathizers.

The *Anschluss*, or union of Germany and Austria, had great strategic significance. Czechoslovakia was now surrounded by Germany on three sides. It was allied both to France and the Soviet Union but contained about 3.5 million ethnic Germans who lived in the Sudetenland, a portion of Czechoslovakia near the German border. Supported by Hitler, they agitated for privileges and autonomy within the Czech state. The Czechs made concessions; but Hitler's true intent was to destroy Czechoslovakia.

appeasement Anglo-French policy of making concessions to Germany in the 1930s to avoid a crisis that would lead to war. It assumed that Germany had real grievances and Hitler's aims were limited and ultimately acceptable.

Axis Alliance between Nazi Germany and Fascist Italy. Also called the Pact of Steel.

Anschluss Meaning "union." Annexation of Austria by Germany in March 1938.

The French, as usual, deferred to British leadership. The British prime minister Neville Chamberlain (1869–1940) was determined not to allow Britain to go to war again. In September 1938, German intervention seemed imminent. Chamberlain sought to appease Hitler by compelling the Czechs to grant the Sudetenland separate status. But Hitler then increased his demands and insisted on immediate German military occupation of the Sudetenland (see Map 31–1).

MUNICH

France and Britain prepared for war. At the last moment, Mussolini proposed a conference of Germany, Italy, France, and Britain. The group met on September 29 at Munich. Hitler received almost everything he had demanded. The Sudetenland became part of Germany, thus depriving the Czechs of any chance of self-defense. In return, the rest of Czechoslovakia was spared. Hitler promised, "I have no more territorial demands to make in Europe." Chamberlain told a cheering crowd, "I believe it is peace for our time."

MAP EXPLORATION

Interactive map: To explore this map further, go to **http://www.prenhall.com/craig/map31.1**

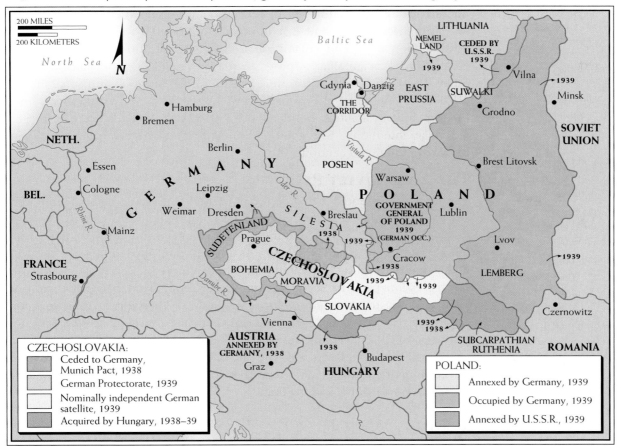

MAP 31–1

Partitions of Czechoslovakia and Poland, 1938–1939. The immediate background of World War II is found in the complex international drama unfolding on Germany's eastern frontier in 1938 and 1939. Germany's expansion inevitably meant the victimization of Austria, Czechoslovakia, and Poland. With the failure of the Western powers' appeasement policy and the signing of a German-Soviet pact, the stage for the war was set.

HOW DID the failure of appeasement lead to war?

Agreement at Munich. On September 29–30, 1938, Hitler met with the leaders of Britain and France at Munich to decide the fate of Czechoslovakia. Allied leaders abandoned the small democratic nation in a vain attempt to appease Hitler and avoid war. Hitler sits in the center of the picture. To his right is British Prime Minister Neville Chamberlain.

Ullstein Bilderdienst.

25.1
Adolf Hitler, The Obersalzberg Speech

WHY WAS 1943 the turning point in World War II?

Soon, however, Poland and Hungary tore bits of territory from Czechoslovakia, and the Slovaks demanded autonomy. Finally, on March 15, 1939, Hitler broke his promise and occupied Prague, putting an end to Czech independence. Munich remains an example of short-sighted policy that helped bring on a war in disadvantageous circumstances as a result of the very fear of war and the failure to prepare for it.

Hitler's occupation of Prague discredited appeasement in Britain. Poland was the next target of German expansion. In the spring of 1939, the Germans put pressure on Poland to restore the formerly German city of Danzig and allow a railroad and a highway through the Polish corridor to connect East Prussia with the rest of Germany. When the Poles would not yield, the pressure mounted. On March 31, Chamberlain announced a Franco-British guarantee of Polish independence. Hitler did not take the guarantee seriously. He knew that both countries were unprepared for war and that much of their populations opposed war for Poland.

Moreover, France and Britain could not get effective help to the Poles. The only way to defend Poland was to bring Russia into the alliance against Hitler, but a Russian alliance posed problems. Each side was suspicious of the other. The French and British were hostile to communism, and since Stalin's (1879-1953) purge of the officer corps of the Red Army, they questioned Russia's military abilities. Besides, both Poland and Romania were suspicious of Russian intentions—with good reason. As a result, Western negotiations with Russia were slow and cautious.

THE NAZI-SOVIET PACT

The Russians resented being left out of the Munich agreement and were annoyed by the low priority that the West seemed to give to negotiations with Russia. They feared, rightly, that the Western powers meant for them to bear the burden of the war against Germany. As a result, they opened negotiations with Hitler, and on August 23, 1939, the world was shocked to learn of a Nazi-Soviet nonaggression pact. Its secret provisions divided Poland between them and allowed Russia to annex the Baltic states and take Bessarabia from Romania. Communist parties in the West changed their line overnight from advocating resistance to Hitler to a policy of peace and quiet.

The Nazi-Soviet Pact sealed the fate of Poland. On September 1, 1939, the Germans invaded Poland. Two days later, Britain and France declared war on Germany. World War II had begun.

WORLD WAR II (1939–1945)

GERMAN CONQUEST OF EUROPE

The speed of the German victory over Poland astonished everyone, and the Russians hastened to collect their share of the booty before Hitler could deprive them of it. On September 17, Russia invaded Poland from the east, dividing the country with the Germans. The Russians then absorbed Estonia, Latvia, and Lithuania. In November 1940, the Russians invaded Finland, but the Finns fought back and retained their independence.

Meanwhile, the western front was quiet. The French remained behind the Maginot Line. Britain imposed the traditional naval blockade. Cynics in the west called it the phony war, but in April 1940, the Germans invaded Denmark and Norway. A month later, a combined land and air attack struck the Low Countries. The Dutch surrendered in a few days, and the Belgians less than two weeks later. British and French armies in Belgium were forced to flee to the English Channel to seek escape from the beaches of Dunkirk. More than 200,000 British and 100,000 French soldiers were saved, but valuable equipment was abandoned.

The Maginot Line ran from Switzerland to the Belgian frontier. Hitler's swift advance through Belgium therefore circumvented France's main line of defense. The French army, poorly led, collapsed. Mussolini attacked France on June 10, though without success. Less than a week later, the French government, under the ancient hero of Verdun, Henri Philippe Pétain (1856–1951), asked for an armistice.

The terms of the armistice, signed on June 22, 1940, allowed the Germans to occupy more than half of France, including the Atlantic and English Channel coasts. To prevent the French from fleeing to North Africa to continue the fight, Hitler left southern France unoccupied. Pétain set up a dictatorial regime at the resort city of Vichy and collaborated with the Germans to preserve as much autonomy as possible. The French were too stunned to resist. Many thought that Hitler's victory was certain and saw no alternative to collaboration. A few, notably General Charles de Gaulle (1890–1969), fled to Britain and organized the French National Committee of Liberation, or "Free French." As expectations of a quick German victory faded, French resistance arose.

Coming of World War II

1919 June	Versailles Treaty
1923 January	France occupies the Ruhr
1925 October	Locarno Agreements
1931 Spring	Onset of Great Depression in Europe
1933 January	Hitler comes to power
October	Germany withdraws from League of Nations
1935 March	Hitler renounces disarmament, starts an air force, and begins conscription
October	Mussolini attacks Ethiopia
1936 March	Germany reoccupies and remilitarizes the Rhineland
July	Outbreak of Spanish Civil War
October	Formation of the Rome-Berlin Axis
1938 March	Anschluss with Austria
September	Munich Conference and partition of Czechoslovakia
1939 March	Hitler occupies Prague; France and Great Britain guarantee Polish independence
August	Nazi-Soviet pact
September 1	Germany invades Poland
September 3	Britain and France declare war on Germany

BATTLE OF BRITAIN

Hitler expected the British to come to terms. Any chance that the British would consider terms disappeared when Winston Churchill (1874–1965) replaced Chamberlain as prime minister in May 1940.

Churchill established a close relationship with the U.S. President Franklin D. Roosevelt. In 1940 and 1941, before the United States was at war, America sent military supplies and even convoyed ships across the Atlantic to help the British survive.

As Britain remained defiant, Hitler was forced to contemplate an invasion, which required control of the air. The German air force (**Luftwaffe**) destroyed much of London, and about 15,000 people were killed. But the Royal Air Force (RAF), aided by the newly developed technology of radar, inflicted heavy losses on the *Luftwaffe*. Hitler was forced to abandon his plans for invasion.

GERMAN ATTACK ON RUSSIA

Operation Barbarossa, the code name for the invasion of Russia, was aimed at knocking Russia out of the war before winter could set in. Success depended in

Luftwaffe German air force in World War II.

Churchill and Roosevelt. The close cooperation between Prime Minister Winston Churchill of Britain and President Franklin Roosevelt of the United States helped to assure the effective alliance of their two countries in World War II.

UPI/Corbis-Bettmann.

QUICK REVIEW

Operation Barbarossa

- June 22, 1941: Surprise invasion of Soviet Union by Germany (Operation Barbarossa) launched
- Germany advanced rapidly in the early stages of the campaign
- German failure to deliver a decisive blow delayed victory until winter set in, turning the tide in the Soviet's favor

---

Blitzkrieg Meaning "war by lightening strokes." German tactic early in World War II of employing fast-moving, massed armored columns supported by air power to overwhelm the enemy.

part on an early start, but here Hitler's Italian alliance proved costly. Mussolini had launched an attack against the British in Egypt and also invaded Greece. But in North Africa the British counterattacked and drove into Libya, and the Greeks repulsed the Italians. In March 1941, the British sent help to the Greeks, and Hitler was forced to divert his attention to the Balkans and to Africa. General Erwin Rommel (1891–1944) soon drove the British back into Egypt. In the Balkans, the German army occupied Yugoslavia and crushed Greek resistance, but the price was a delay of six weeks for Barbarossa. This proved to be costly the following winter.

Operation Barbarossa was launched against Russia on June 22, 1941, and it almost succeeded. Stalin panicked. By November, the German army stood at the gates of Leningrad, on the outskirts of Moscow, and on the Don River. Of the 4.5 million troops with which the Russians had begun the fighting, they had lost 2.5 million; of their 15,000 tanks, only 700 were left.

A German victory seemed imminent, but Hitler at that point diverted significant forces to the south. By the time he decided to march on Moscow, winter was setting in. The German army lacked appropriate equipment, and Stalin had reorganized, fortified the city, and brought in troops from Siberia. In November and December, the Russians counterattacked. Hitler's *Blitzkrieg* ("war by lightening strokes") turned into a war of attrition.

HITLER'S EUROPE

The demands of war and Hitler's defeat prevented him from fully carrying out his plans, so no one can be sure precisely what he intended. But the measures he took before his death suggest a regime unmatched in history for planned terror and inhumanity. Hitler regarded the conquered lands merely as a source of plunder and slave labor. He stripped them of entire industries and their peoples of basic necessities. He intended ultimately to displace their inhabitants and appropriate their lands to provide Lebensraum for Germans. Regions such as Scandinavia and the Low Lands, inhabited by people racially akin to the Germans, were to be absorbed into Germany.

RACISM AND THE HOLOCAUST

The most horrible aspect of the Nazi rule in Europe arose from the inhumanity inherent in Hitler's racial doctrines. He considered the Slavs *Untermenschen*, subhuman creatures like beasts. In Poland, the upper and professional classes were jailed, deported, or killed, and harsh living conditions were imposed. In Russia, the situation was even worse. Hitler spoke of his Russian campaign as a war of extermination. The SS formed extermination squads to eliminate 30 million Slavs to make room for the Germans. Some 6 million Russian prisoners of war and civilians may have died under Nazi rule.

Hitler meant to make Europe *Judenrein* ("free of Jews"). Eventually he decided on the "final solution of the Jewish problem": extermination. The Nazis built extermination camps in Germany and Poland and killed millions of men, women, and children just because they were Jews (see Map 31–2). Before the war was over, 6 million Jews had died in what is called the **Holocaust**. Only about a million survived, mostly in pitiable condition.

THE ROAD TO PEARL HARBOR

The war took on truly global proportions in December 1941. In January 1938, Japan had invaded China to overthrow the Chinese Nationalist Party government in Nanjing. They occupied most of the cities and railroads of eastern China, killing more than 300,000 people and brutally raping 7,000 women. Jiang Jieshi (Chiang Kai-shek) refused to surrender, however, and a stalemate ensued until the end of the global conflict in 1945.

In September 1940, Japan signed the Tripartite Pact with Germany and Italy. Germany's European victories in late spring 1940 seemed a prelude to German victory, and Japan hoped that the pact would help it achieve three objectives: to isolate the United States (which was demanding that Japan withdraw from China); to take over the Southeast Asian colonies of Britain, France, and the Netherlands; and to improve its relations with the Soviet Union with Germany's help. Japan remained neutral when Germany attacked the Soviet Union and ceased at that point to work with the Axis powers. But its association with them hardened America's demands that it leave China.

In June 1941, when Japan occupied northern French Indochina, the United States retaliated by limiting strategic exports to Japan, and when Japanese troops took southern Indochina a month later, the United States embargoed all exports to Japan, cutting Japanese oil imports by 90 percent. The Japanese navy urged seizure of the oil-rich Dutch East Indies, but this was dangerous so long as the United States held the Philippines. Japan's navy, therefore, planned a preemptive strike against the United States.

AMERICA'S ENTRY INTO THE WAR

On Sunday morning, December 7, 1941, even while Japanese representatives were negotiating in Washington, Japan launched an air attack on Pearl Harbor, Hawaii, the chief American naval base in the Pacific. The next day, the United

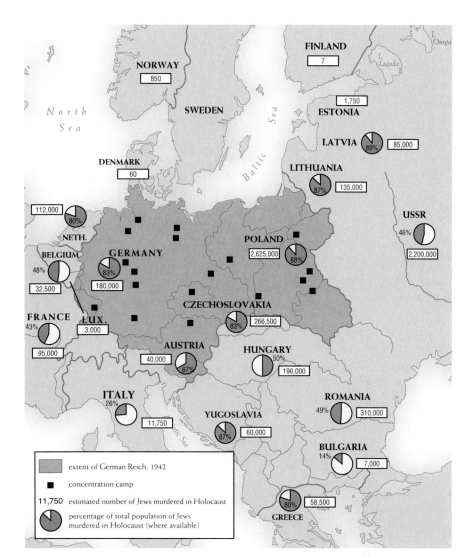

MAP 31–2

The Holocaust. The Nazi policy of ethnic cleansing—targeting Jews, gypsies, political dissidents, and "social deviants"—began with imprisoning them in concentration camps, but by 1943 the *Endlösung*, or Final Solution, called for the systematic extermination of "undersirables."

WHICH COUNTRIES were most severely affected by the Holocaust?

Holocaust Nazi extermination of millions of European Jews between 1940 and 1945. Also called the "final solution to the Jewish problem."

MAP 31–3

Axis Europe 1941. On the eve of the German invasion of the Soviet Union, the Germany-Italy Axis bestrode most of Western Europe by annexation, occupation, or alliance—from Norway and Finland in the north to Greece in the south and from Poland to France. Britain, the Soviets, a number of insurgent groups, and, finally, the United States had before them the long struggle of conquering this Axis "fortress Europe."

WHAT WERE the strengths and weaknesses of Germany's territorial position in 1941?

States and Britain declared war on Japan. Three days later, Germany and Italy declared war on the United States.

THE TIDE TURNS

Although its potential power was enormous, America was ill-prepared for war. The U.S. Army was tiny, inexperienced, and poorly supplied. American industry was not ready for war. By the summer of 1942, the Japanese Empire stretched

Pearl Harbor. The successful Japanese attack on the American base at Pearl Harbor in Hawaii on December 7, 1941, together with simultaneous attacks on other Pacific bases, brought the United States into war against the Axis powers. For Japan, it was the opening phase of a campaign to capture European and American colonies in Southeast Asia.

U.S. Army Photograph.

from the Aleutian Islands south almost to Australia, and from Burma east to the Gilbert Islands in the mid-Pacific (see Map 31–4).

In the same year, the Germans almost reached the Caspian Sea. In Africa, Rommel drove the British back toward the Suez Canal. Relations between the democracies and their Soviet ally were not close; German submarines were threatening British supplies.

The tide turned at the Battle of Midway in June 1942. American planes destroyed four Japanese aircraft carriers. Soon U.S. Marines landed on Guadalcanal in the Solomon Islands and began to reverse the momentum of the war. Japan was checked sufficiently to allow the Allies to concentrate their efforts first in the West.

Allied Landings in Africa, Sicily, and Italy   In November 1942, an Allied force landed in French North Africa. Even before that landing, the British Field Marshal Bernard Montgomery (1887–1976), after stopping Rommel at El Alamein, had begun a drive to the west. The American general Dwight D. Eisenhower (1890–1969) pushed eastward through Morocco and Algeria. The German army was trapped in Tunisia and crushed. In July and August 1943, the Allies took Sicily. Mussolini was driven from power, the Allies landed in Italy, and Marshal Pietro Badoglio (1871–1956), leader of the new Italian government, declared war on Germany. German resistance in Italy was tough and determined, but the need to defend it further strained the Germans' energy and resources.

Battle of Stalingrad   The Russian campaign became especially demanding. In the summer of 1942, the Germans resumed the offensive. Their goal was the oil fields near the Caspian Sea, and they got as far as Stalingrad on the Volga. Hitler was determined to take the city and Stalin to hold it. The Battle of Stalingrad

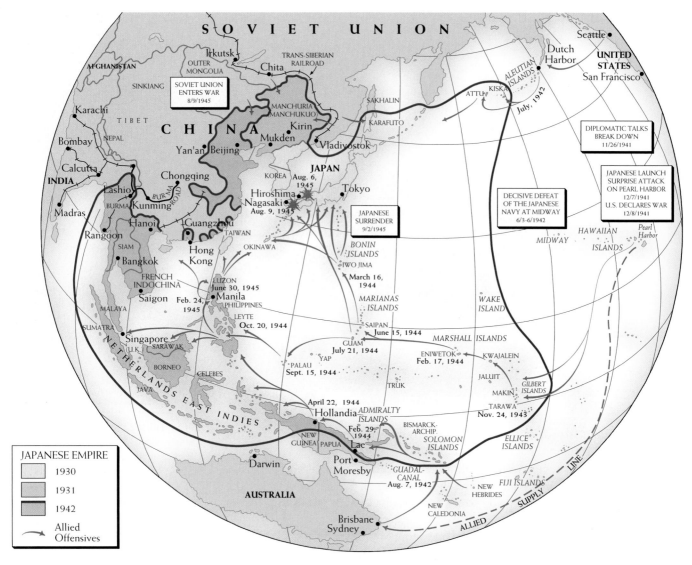

MAP 31–4

The War in the Pacific. As in Europe, the Allies initially had trouble recapturing areas that the Japanese had quickly seized early in the war. The map shows the initial expansion of the Japanese and the long struggle of the Allies to push them back to their homeland and defeat them.

WHAT WAS the American strategy for defeating Japan in World War II?

raged for months. The Russians lost more men than the Americans lost in combat during the entire war, but their defenses prevailed. Hitler overruled his generals and would not allow a retreat. An entire German army was lost.

Stalingrad marked the turning point of the Russian campaign. Thereafter, as German resources dwindled, the Russians advanced westward inexorably.

Strategic Bombing   In 1943, the Allies also gained ground in production and logistics. The industrial might of the United States came into play. New technology and tactics began eliminating the submarine menace. In the same year, the American and British air forces began massive bombardments of Germany by night and day. In 1944, the Americans introduced long-range fighters that could protect the bombers and allow accurate missions by day. By 1945, the Allies could bomb at will.

DEFEAT OF NAZI GERMANY

On June 6, 1944 (D-Day), Allied troops landed in Normandy (see Map 31–5). By September, France had been liberated. In December, the Germans launched a counterattack called the Battle of the Bulge through the Forest of Ardennes. It was their last gasp. The Allies recovered and crossed the Rhine in March 1945. German resistance crumbled. There could be no doubt that the Germans had lost the war on the battlefield.

In the east, the Russians were within reach of Berlin by March 1945. Because the Allies insisted on unconditional surrender, the Germans fought until May. Hitler committed suicide in an underground hideaway in Berlin on May 1, 1945. The Russians occupied Berlin. The Third Reich had lasted only a dozen years.

QUICK REVIEW

Key Battles

- June 6, 1944 (D Day): Allied forces land in Normandy
- December 1944: Germans inflict heavy losses at the Battle of the Bulge but fail to halt Allies advance
- May 1945: Soviet troops capture Berlin

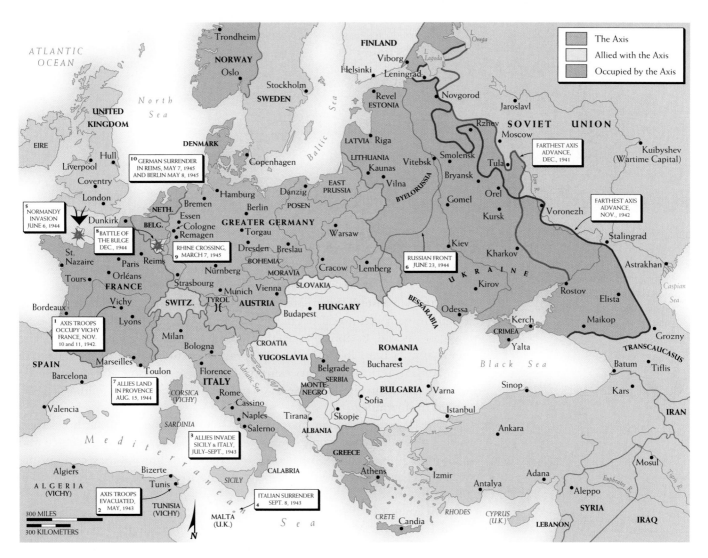

MAP 31–5

Defeat of the Axis in Europe, 1942–1945.   Here we see some major steps in the progress toward Allied victory against Axis Europe. From the south through Italy, the west through France, and the east through Russia, the Allies gradually conquered the continent to bring the war in Europe to a close.

WHY WAS it important for the Allies to force the Germans to fight on more than one front?

D-Day. Allied troops landed in Normandy on D-Day, June 6, 1944. This photograph, taken two days later, shows long lines of men and equipment moving inland from the beach to reinforce the troops leading the invasion.

Archive Photos.

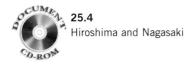
25.4
Hiroshima and Nagasaki

FALL OF THE JAPANESE EMPIRE

The war in Europe ended on May 8, 1945. By then victory over Japan was in sight. The Japanese attack on the United States had been a calculated risk. The longer the war lasted, the greater the impact of American superiority in industry and human resources. Beginning in 1943, American forces began a campaign of "island hopping," selecting places strategically located along the enemy supply line. Relentlessly, they moved northeast toward the Japanese homeland. American bombers destroyed Japanese industry and disabled the Japanese navy. But the Japanese government, dominated by a military clique, refused to surrender.

The Americans made plans for an assault on the Japanese homeland, which, they calculated, would cost huge casualties. At this point, science and technology presented the Americans with another choice. Since early in the war a secret program group had been working to use atomic energy for military purposes.

On August 6, 1945, an American plane dropped an atomic bomb on the city of Hiroshima. More than 70,000 of its 200,000 residents were killed. Two days later, the Soviet Union declared war on Japan and invaded Manchuria. The next day, a second atomic bomb fell on Nagasaki. The Japanese were still prepared to face an invasion, but Emperor Hirohito (r. 1926–1989) forced the government to surrender on August 14. Even then, the U.S. cabinet made the condition that Japan could keep its emperor. President Harry S. Truman

(1884–1972), who had come to office on April 12, 1945, on the death of Franklin D. Roosevelt, accepted the condition. Peace was formally signed on September 2, 1945.

THE COST OF WAR

World War II was the most terrible war in history. Military deaths are estimated at 15 million, and at least as many civilians were killed. If deaths linked indirectly to the war are included, 40 million people may have died. Most of Europe and parts of Asia were devastated. Yet the end of the war brought little opportunity for relaxation. The dawn of the Atomic Age made people conscious that another major war might destroy humanity. Everything depended on the conclusion of a stable peace, but the victors soon quarreled.

Hiroshima. This photo, taken a few days after the atomic bomb was dropped, poignantly captures the total devastation wreaked on the city.
Corbis-Bettmann.

THE DOMESTIC FRONTS

*W*orld War II represented an effort of total war by all the belligerents. One result was the carnage that occurred in the fighting. Another was an unprecedented organization of civilians on the various home fronts. Each domestic effort and experience was different, but few escaped the impact of the conflict. Shortages, propaganda, and new political developments were ubiquitous.

HOW DID war affect civilians in Germany, France, Britain, and the Soviet Union?

GERMANY: FROM APPARENT VICTORY TO DEFEAT

Hitler had expected the strategy of *Blitzkrieg* to win the war so quickly that Germany's society and economy would not be adversely affected. During the first two years of the war, Hitler demanded few sacrifices from the German people. Spending on domestic projects continued; food was plentiful; the economy was not on a full wartime footing. Failure to knock out the Soviet Union changed everything. Germany had to mobilize for total war, and the government demanded major sacrifices.

A great expansion of army and military production began in 1942. Albert Speer (1905–1981) guided the economy, and Germany met its military needs instead of making consumer goods. German businesses aided the growth of wartime production. Between 1942 and late 1944, the output of military products tripled; but as the war went on, the army absorbed more men from industry, hurting the production of even military goods.

Beginning in 1942, everyday products became scarce. The standard of living fell. Food rationing began in April 1942, and shortages were severe until the Nazi government seized food from occupied Europe. To preserve their own home front, the Nazis passed on the suffering to their defeated neighbors.

By 1943, there were serious labor shortages. The Nazis required German teenagers and the elderly to work in the factories, and many women joined them. To achieve total mobilization, the Germans closed retail businesses, made more women do compulsory service, shifted non-German domestic workers to wartime industry, moved artists and entertainers into military service, closed theaters, and reduced basic public services. Finally, the Nazis forced thousands of people from conquered lands to labor in Germany.

Hitler assigned women a special place in the war effort. The celebration of motherhood continued, with an emphasis on the mothers of military figures. Films portrayed ordinary women who became brave and patriotic during the war and remained faithful to their soldier husbands. Government portrayed other wartime activities of women as the natural fulfillment of their maternal roles. As air raid wardens, they protected their families; as workers in munitions plants, they aided their sons on the front lines. Women working on farms were feeding their soldier sons and husbands; as housewives they were helping to win the war by managing their households frugally. Finally, by their faithful chastity, German women were protecting racial purity.

The war years also saw an intensification of political propaganda. The Nazis believed that weak domestic support had led to Germany's defeat in World War I, and they were determined that this would not happen again. Propaganda Minister Josef Goebbels (1897–1945) used radio and films to boost the Nazi cause. Movies demonstrated German military might. As the German armies were checked on the battlefield, especially in Russia, propaganda became a substitute for victory. The propaganda also aimed to frighten the German population about the consequences of defeat.

After May 1943, when the Allies began their major bombing offensive over Germany, one German city after another endured bombing, fires, and destruction. But the bombing did not undermine German morale—on the contrary, it may have confirmed the fear of defeat by such savage opponents and increased German resistance.

World War II brought increased power to the Nazi Party. Every area of the economy and society came under its influence or control. The Nazis were determined that they, rather than the German officer corps, would profit from the new authority flowing to the central government because of the war effort. Throughout the war years there was little serious opposition to Hitler or his ministers. In 1944, a small group of army officers attempted to assassinate Hitler; they failed, and had no significant popular support.

The war brought great changes to Germany, but what transformed the country afterward was the experience of defeat accompanied by destruction, invasion, and occupation. A new state with new political structures emerged.

FRANCE: DEFEAT, COLLABORATION AND RESISTANCE

In France, the Vichy government cooperated with the Germans for a variety of reasons. Some collaborators believed that the Germans were sure to win. A few sympathized with the ideas and plans of the Nazis. Many conservatives regarded the French defeat as a judgment on what they saw as the corrupt Third Republic. But most of the French were not active collaborators and remained demoralized by defeat.

Youth rally. Members of the Nazi German Women's Youth Movement perform calisthenics.

Getty Images Inc. – Hulton Archive Photos.

Many conservatives and extreme rightists saw the Vichy government as a device to reshape the French national character and halt the decadence they associated with liberalism. The Roman Catholic clergy gained status under Vichy. The church supported Pétain; his government supported religious education. Vichy adopted the church's views of the importance of family and spiritual values. Divorce was made difficult; large families were rewarded.

The Vichy regime embraced a chauvinistic nationalism. It persecuted foreigners who were not regarded as genuinely French. The chief victims were French Jews. Anti-Semitism was not new in France. Even before Germany undertook Hitler's "final solution" in 1942, the French had begun to remove Jews from government, education, and publishing. In 1941, the Germans began to intern Jews living in occupied France. In 1942, they began deporting Jews, ultimately more than 60,000, to extermination camps. The Vichy government made no protest, and its own anti-Semitic policies facilitated the process.

Serious internal resistance to the German occupiers and the Vichy government developed only late in 1942. The Germans attempted to force young French people to work in German factories; some fled and joined the Resistance, but the total number of resisters was small. Many were deterred by fear. Some disliked the violence that resistance entailed. So long as it appeared that the Germans would win the war, moreover, resistance seemed imprudent and futile. In all, less than 5 percent of the adult French population appear to have been involved.

By early 1944, an Allied victory appeared inevitable, and the Vichy government was clearly doomed. Only then did an active resistance assert itself. From Algiers on August 9, 1944, the Committee of National Liberation declared the authority of Vichy illegitimate. French soldiers joined in the liberation of Paris and established a government for Free France. On October 21, 1945, France voted to adopt a new constitution as the basis of the Fourth Republic.

GREAT BRITAIN: ORGANIZATION FOR VICTORY

On May 22, 1940, Parliament gave the government emergency powers. The government could institute compulsory military service, food rationing, and economic controls.

Churchill and the British war cabinet mobilized the nation. By the end of 1941, British production had already surpassed Germany's. Factory hours were extended, and women were brought into the work force in great numbers. Unemployment disappeared, and the working classes had more money to spend than they had enjoyed for many years.

The bombing "blitz" conducted by the *Luftwaffe* against British cities from 1940 to 1941 was the most immediate and dramatic experience of the war for the British people. Many homes were destroyed; families removed their children to the countryside; more than 30,000 people were killed. This toll was much smaller than the number of Germans killed by Allied bombing. In England as in Germany, however, the bombing seems to have made the people more determined.

Churchill cheered and encouraged the British people. They had to make many sacrifices: Transportation facilities were strained; food, clothing, and gasoline for civilians were in short supply.

The British established their own propaganda machine. The British Broadcasting Company (BBC) sent programs to every country in Europe to encourage resistance. At home the government used the radio to unify the nation. Soldiers heard the same programs as their families.

We Can Do It! A World War II poster encourages American women to show their strength and go to work for the war effort.

For most of the population the standard of living actually improved during the war, as did the general health of the nation. These gains should not be exaggerated, but many connected them with the active involvement of the government in the economy and the lives of the citizens. This wartime experience may have contributed to the Labour Party's victory in 1945; many feared that conservative rule would revive the economic misery of the 1930s.

THE UNITED STATES: AMERICAN WOMEN AND AFRICAN AMERICANS IN THE WAR EFFORT

The induction of millions of American men into the armed forces created a demand for workers that was filled, in part, by women. The Great Depression had already increased the numbers of female workers, despite lingering and widespread hostility to the idea of women working outside their homes. America's entry into the war changed that quickly. The need for vast amounts of equipment to wage the war opened the way to employment for them and another disadvantaged group—African Americans. Blacks from the South migrated to northern and western cities to seek well-paying jobs. Popular songs celebrated the woman "behind the man behind the gun" as well as "Rosie the Riveter," a young woman building aircraft to protect her boyfriend in the Marines.

THE SOVIET UNION: "THE GREAT PATRIOTIC WAR"

No nation suffered more deaths or destruction during World War II than the Soviet Union. Perhaps 16 million people were killed. Hundreds of cities and towns and more than half of the industrial and transportation facilities of the country were devastated.

In the decade before the war, Stalin had already made the Soviet Union a highly centralized nation. The country was on what amounted to a wartime footing long before the conflict erupted, and the induction of millions of citizens into the army did not increase the military's influence at the expense of the Communist Party—that is, Stalin.

Soviet propaganda differed from that of other nations. Because the Soviet government distrusted the loyalty of its citizens, it confiscated radios. Instead, loudspeakers broadcast to the people. Soviet propaganda emphasized Russian patriotism: The struggle was called "The Great Patriotic War."

Stalin even made peace with the Russian Orthodox Church. He hoped that this would give him more support at home and make the Soviet Union more popular in eastern Europe where the Orthodox church predominated.

Within occupied portions of the Soviet Union, resistance arose against the Germans. The swiftness of the German invasion had stranded thousands of Soviet troops, some of whom escaped and carried on irregular warfare behind enemy lines. Stalin supported partisan forces for two reasons: He wanted to cause difficulty for the Germans; and the Soviet-sponsored resistance reminded the peasants in the conquered regions that the Soviet government had not disappeared. Stalin feared that the peasants' hatred of the Communist government might lead them to collaborate with the invaders.

As the Soviet armies reclaimed the occupied areas and then moved across eastern and central Europe, the Soviet Union established itself as a world power second only to the United States. Stalin had been a reluctant belligerent, but he emerged a major victor. The war and the extraordinary patriotic effort and sacrifice it generated consolidated the power of Stalin and the party more effectively than had the political and social policies of the 1930s.

PREPARATIONS FOR PEACE

The split that followed the war between the Soviet Union and its wartime allies should cause no surprise. As the self-proclaimed center of world communism, the Soviet Union was dedicated to the overthrow of the capitalist nations. The Western allies were no less open about their hostility to communism and its chief purveyor, the Soviet Union.

Although cooperation against a common enemy and strenuous propaganda helped improve Western feeling toward the Soviet ally, Stalin remained suspicious and critical of the Western war effort. Likewise, Churchill never ceased planning to contain the Soviet advance into Europe. Roosevelt seems to have hoped that the Allies could continue to work together after the war. But even he was losing faith by 1945. Differences in historical development and ideology, as well as traditional conflicts over power and influence, dashed hopes of a satisfactory peace settlement and continued cooperation.

WHY DID cooperation between the Soviet Union and the Western powers break down in 1945?

THE ATLANTIC CHARTER

In August 1941, even before America entered the war, Roosevelt and Churchill agreed to the Atlantic Charter. A broad set of principles in the spirit of Wilson's Fourteen Points, it provided a theoretical basis for the peace they sought. When Russia and the United States joined Britain in the war, the three powers entered a military alliance, leaving political questions aside. In Moscow in October 1943, their foreign ministers reaffirmed earlier agreements to fight on until the enemy surrendered unconditionally and to continue cooperating after the war in a united-nations organization.

TEHRAN

The first meeting of the three leaders took place at Tehran, the capital of Iran, in 1943. Western promises to open a second front in France the next summer (1944) and Stalin's agreement to join in the war against Japan (when Germany was defeated) created an atmosphere of goodwill in which to discuss a postwar settlement. Stalin wanted to retain what he had gained in his pact with Hitler and to dismember Germany. Roosevelt and Churchill made no firm commitments. The most important decision was for the Western allies to attack Germany from Europe's west coast. This decision meant, in retrospect, that Soviet forces would occupy eastern Europe and control its destiny. At Tehran in 1943, the Western allies did not foresee this clearly, for the Russians were still fighting deep within their own frontiers.

But by August 1944, Soviet armies were in sight of Warsaw, which had risen in expectation of liberation. But the Russians allowed the Polish rebels to be annihilated. The Russians also gained control of Romania and Hungary. Alarmed by these developments, Churchill went to Moscow and met with Stalin in October. They agreed to share power in the Balkans on the basis of Soviet predominance in Romania and Bulgaria, western predominance in Greece, and equality of influence in Yugoslavia and Hungary. But the Americans were hostile to such un-Wilsonian devices as "spheres of influence."

The three powers agreed on Germany's disarmament and denazification and on its division into four zones of occupation by France and the Big Three (the USSR, Britain, and the United States). Churchill, however, began to balk at Stalin's plan to dismember Germany and to his demands for $20 billion in reparations and forced labor. These matters caused dissension in the future.

Eastern Europe remained a problem. Everyone agreed that the Soviet Union deserved neighboring governments that were friendly, but the West

Big Three at Potsdam. This photograph shows the "Big Three" at Potsdam. By the summer of 1945 only Stalin remained of the original leaders of the major Allies. Roosevelt and Churchill had been replaced by Harry Truman and Clement Attlee, respectively.

Corbis-Bettmann.

25.6
The Charter of the United Nations

insisted that they also be independent and democratic. However, Stalin knew that freely elected governments in Poland and Romania would not be safely friendly to Russia. He had already established a subservient government in Poland. Under pressure, Stalin agreed to include some Poles friendly to the West. He also promised self-determination and free democratic elections. He probably thought it worth endorsing some meaningless principles as the price of continued harmony. In any case, he soon violated these agreements.

YALTA

The next meeting of the Big Three was at Yalta in the Crimea in February 1945. The Western armies had not yet crossed the Rhine. The war with Japan continued, and no atomic explosion had yet taken place. Roosevelt, faced with an invasion of Japan and heavy losses, was eager to bring the Russians into the Pacific war.

As a true Wilsonian, Roosevelt also suspected Churchill's determination to maintain the British Empire. The Americans thought that Churchill's plan to set up British spheres of influence in Europe would encourage the Russians to do the same and lead to another war. To encourage Russian participation in the war against Japan, Roosevelt and Churchill made extensive concessions to Russia in Asia. Again in the tradition of Wilson, Roosevelt wanted a United Nations. Soviet agreement on these points seemed well worth concessions elsewhere.

POTSDAM

The Big Three met for the last time in the Berlin suburb of Potsdam in July 1945. Much had changed. Germany was defeated, and news of a successful atomic weapon reached the American president during the meetings. President Truman had replaced Roosevelt; and Clement Attlee (1883–1967), leader of the Labour Party, replaced Churchill during the conference. Progress on undecided questions was slow.

Russia's western frontier was moved far into what had been Poland and German East Prussia. In compensation, Poland was moved about a hundred miles west, at the expense of Germany. The Allies agreed that Germany would be divided into occupation zones until the final peace treaty was signed, and the country remained divided until the end of the Cold War more than 40 years later.

A Council of Foreign Ministers was established to draft peace treaties for Germany's allies. Disagreements made the job difficult, and it was not until February 1947 that Bulgaria, Finland, Hungary, Italy, and Romania signed treaties. The Russians signed their own agreements with the Japanese in 1956.

SUMMARY

The Coming of War The second great war of the 20th century (1939–1945) grew out of the unsatisfactory resolution of the first. In retrospect, the two wars appear to some people to be one continuous conflict, with the two main periods of fighting separated by an uneasy truce. To others, that point of view distorts the situation by implying that the second war was the inevitable result of the first and its inadequate peace treaties.

The latter opinion seems more sound. Whatever the flaws of the treaties of Paris, the world suffered an even more terrible war than the first as a result of failures of judgment and will on the part of the victorious democratic powers. The United States, which had become the wealthiest and potentially the strongest nation in the world, disarmed almost entirely and withdrew into foolish isolation; it could play no important part in restraining the ambitious dictators who would bring on the war. Britain and France refused to face the threat posed by the Axis powers until the most deadly war in history was required to put it down. If the victorious democracies had remained strong, responsible, and realistic, they could have remedied whatever injustices or mistakes arose from the treaties without endangering the peace.

World War II   The second war itself was plainly a world war. The Japanese occupation of Manchuria in 1931 was a precursor. Italy attacked Ethiopia in 1935. Italy, Germany, and the Soviet Union intervened in the Spanish Civil War (1936–1939). Japan attacked China in 1937. These developments revealed that aggressive forces were on the march across the globe and that the defenders of the world order lacked the will to stop them. The formation of the Axis among Germany, Italy, and Japan guaranteed that the war would be fought around the world. There was fighting and suffering in Asia, Africa, the islands of the Pacific, and Europe. The use of atomic weapons brought the struggle to a close, but conventional weapons did almost all the damage. The survival of civilization was threatened even without the use of nuclear devices.

This was ended not with unsatisfactory peace treaties but with no treaty at all in the European area where it had begun. The world quickly split into two unfriendly camps: the West led by the United States, and the East led by the Soviet Union. This division hastened the liberation of former colonial territories.

IMAGE KEY
for pages 772–773

a. An Allied war poster, World War II.

b. Jews were rounded up in Warsaw for deportation to concentration "death" camps.

c. A Nazi party membership book, with a photograph of the member.

d. The Big Three Conference—Winston Churchill, Franklin Delano Roosevelt, and Josef Stalin.

e. An American propaganda poster, World War II.

f. An atomic bomb explosion like that in Hiroshima, Japan.

g. A refugee Jewish girl.

h. An Imperial Japanese war bond.

REVIEW QUESTIONS

1. What were Hitler's foreign policy aims?

2. Why did Britain and France adopt a policy of appeasement in the 1930s? Strategically, was the policy a good or bad move?

3. Why did Hitler invade Russia? Why did the invasion fail?

4. What were Hitler's racial beliefs? What policies did they inspire?

5. How did America become involved in the war? What was the significance of its intervention? Why did it drop atomic bombs on Japan?

KEY TERMS

Anschluss (p. 776)   *Blitzkrieg* (p. 780)   *Lebensraum* (p. 774)
appeasement (p. 776)   **Holocaust** (p. 781)   *Luftwaffe* (p. 779)
Axis (p. 776)

  For additional study resources for this chapter, go to:
www.prenhall.com/craig/chapter31

32

The West Since World War II

CHAPTER HIGHLIGHTS

The Cold War U.S.–Soviet cooperation did not survive World War II. After 1945 Europe was divided into a Soviet-dominated zone in the East (the Warsaw Pact) and a U.S.-led zone in the West (NATO). U.S.–Soviet rivalry played itself out around the world from the 1950s to the 1980s, although gradually a spirit of détente arose between the two powers, especially under President Ronald Reagan and Soviet leader Mikhail Gorbachev. The Cold War ended with the collapse of Communist rule in Eastern Europe in 1989 and the disappearance of the Soviet Union in 1991.

Postwar European Society Since World War II, European society has been marked by a rise in prosperity and consumerism, more rights and opportunities for women, moves toward political and economic unification symbolized by the adoption of a common currency, the euro, in 2002 and the publication of a draft constitution for a united Europe in 2003.

The United States The major themes in postwar American history were opposition to Communism at home and abroad, the expansion of civil rights to African Americans, and economic prosperity. Politically, the relatively liberal years from the late 1950s through the 1970s were succeeded by a growing conservatism especially under the presidencies of Ronald Reagan, George Bush, and George W. Bush. Even the Democratic President Bill Clinton was more a centrist than a liberal. After the terrorist attacks of September 11, 2001, the United States embarked on a war on terrorism that led to wars in Afghanistan and Iraq.

Eastern Europe The failure of the Communist regimes in Eastern Europe and the Soviet Union to produce economic prosperity or political liberalization led to their growing unpopularity. Soviet economic difficulties led Mikhail Gorbachev to institute liberal reforms that led to the collapse of the communist rule first in Eastern Europe, then in the Soviet Union itself. The disappearance of the Soviet Union led to independence for much of the former Soviet empire. Russia itself has experienced social, economic, and political turmoil under presidents Boris Yeltsin and Vladimir Putin.

In the former Yugoslavia, the end of Communist rule led to disintegration and civil war. In the 1990s the NATO powers, led by the United States, intervened to halt the fighting and end a pattern of ethnic atrocities.

CHAPTER QUESTIONS

WHAT WERE the causes of the Cold War?

WHAT MAJOR trends have marked European society since World War II?

WHAT ARE the main themes that have characterized postwar America?

WHY DID communist regimes collapse so easily in Eastern Europe in 1989?

HOW DID the West respond to the collapse of Yugoslavia?

WHAT PROBLEMS has Europe faced since the fall of Communism?

CHAPTER OUTLINE

- The Cold War Era
- European Society in the Second Half of the Twentieth Century and Beyond
- American Domestic Scene Since World War II
- The Soviet Union to 1989
- 1989: Year of Revolutions in Eastern Europe
- The Collapse of the Soviet Union
- The Collapse of Yugoslavia and Civil War
- Challenges to the Atlantic Alliance

*Since the conclusion of World War II, Europe's influence on the world has been transformed. The destruction of the war itself left Europe incapable of exercising the kind of power it had formerly exerted. The **Cold War** between the United States and the Soviet Union made Europe a divided and contested territory. Furthermore, Europeans soon began to lose control of their overseas empires.*

The decision by the United States to take an activist role in world affairs touched every aspect of the postwar world. American domestic politics and foreign policy became intertwined as in no previous period of American history.

Like virtually every other part of the world, Europe experienced the impact of American culture through military alliances, trade, tourism, and popular entertainment. Europeans also began to build structures for greater economic cooperation.

While Western Europe enjoyed increased democratization and unprecedented prosperity, Eastern Europe experienced economic stagnation and Soviet domination. Yet from the late 1970s onward, there were political stirrings in the East. These culminated in 1989 with revolutions throughout Eastern Europe and in 1991 with the collapse of Communist government in the Soviet Union itself. Since then, Europeans have sought new political direction. The movement toward unification, particularly economic, continues in Western Europe. Political confusion and economic stagnation afflict some of the nations that emerged from the Soviet Union, and the attacks of September 11, 2001, on the United States led to events that have challenged the post-World War II Western alliance.

THE COLD WAR ERA

INITIAL CAUSES

The tense relationship between the United States and the Soviet Union that dominated world history during the second half of the 20th century originated in the closing months of World War II.

The split arose from basic differences of ideology and interest. The Soviet Union's attempt to extend its control westward into Europe and southward into the Middle East was a continuation of the policy of tsarist Russia. It had been Britain's traditional role to restrain Russian expansion into these areas; the United States inherited that task as Britain's power waned. The alternative was to permit a major increase in power by a huge, traditionally hostile state. That state, dedicated in its official ideology to the overthrow of nations like the United States, was governed by Stalin (1879–1953), an absolute dictator with a proven record for horrible cruelties. Few nations would take such risks.

However, the United States made no attempt to roll back Soviet power where it already existed, even though American military forces were the greatest in its history, American industrial power was unmatched, and America had a monopoly on atomic weapons. In less than a year from the war's end, the United States reduced its forces in Europe from 3.5 million to half a million. The speedy withdrawal was in accord with America's peacetime goals. These goals included support for self-determination, autonomy, and democracy in the political sphere; and free trade, freedom of the seas, no barriers to investment, and the Open Door in the economic sphere. As the strongest, richest nation in the world, the United States would benefit from an international order based on such goals.

However, the Soviets saw American resistance to its expansion as a threat to its security and legitimate aims. American objections over Poland and other states were seen as attempts to undermine regimes friendly to Russia and encircle the Soviet Union with hostile neighbors.

WHAT WERE the causes of the Cold War?

26.1
The Soviet Victory: Capitalism versus Communism (February 1946): Joseph Stalin

Cold War Ideological and geographical struggle between the United States and its allies and the USSR and its allies that began after World War II and lasted until the dissolution of the USSR in 1989.

The growth in France and Italy of Communist parties taking orders from Moscow led the Americans to believe that Stalin was engaged in a worldwide plot to subvert capitalism and democracy. We do not know for certain if these suspicions were justified, but most people in the West considered them plausible.

AREAS OF EARLY COLD WAR CONFLICT

The new mood of hostility among the former allies appeared quickly. In February 1946, both Stalin and his foreign minister, Vyacheslav Molotov (1890–1986), publicly spoke of the Western democracies as enemies. A month later, Churchill (1874–1965) delivered a speech in Fulton, Missouri, in which he spoke of an Iron Curtain dividing a free and democratic West from an East under totalitarian rule. In this atmosphere, difficulties grew.

The attempt to deal cooperatively with the problem of atomic energy was an early victim of the Cold War. The United States continued to develop its own atomic weapons in secrecy, and the Russians did the same. By 1949, the Soviet Union had exploded its own atomic bomb, and the race for nuclear weapons was on.

The resistance of Westerners to what they perceived as Soviet intransigence and Communist subversion took clearer form in 1947. Since 1944, civil war had been raging in Greece between the royalist government restored by Britain and insurgents supported by the Communist countries. In 1947, Britain informed the United States that it was financially no longer able to support the Greeks. On March 12, President Truman (1884–1972) asked Congress to provide funds to support Greece and Turkey, which was also under Soviet pressure. Congress complied. In what became known as the Truman Doctrine, the American president advocated a policy of supporting "free people who are resisting attempted subjugation by armed minorities or by outside pressures," by implication anywhere in the world.

For Western Europe, where the menacing growth of Communist parties was fueled by postwar poverty and hunger, the Americans devised the European Recovery Program. Named the **Marshall Plan** after George C. Marshall (1880–1959), the secretary of state who introduced it, this program provided broad economic aid to European states only on condition that they work together. The Soviet Union forbade its satellites to take part.

The Marshall Plan helped restore prosperity to Western Europe and set the stage for its unprecedented economic growth. The plan also led to the establishment there of solid democratic regimes.

Stalin's answer was to replace all multiparty governments behind the Iron Curtain with thoroughly Communist regimes under his control. He also organized in 1947 the Communist Information Bureau (Cominform), dedicated to spreading revolutionary communism throughout the world.

In February 1948, a brutal display of Stalin's policy took place in Prague. The Communists expelled the democratic members of what had been a coalition government and murdered the foreign minister. Czechoslovakia was brought fully under Soviet rule.

These Soviet actions increased America's determination to make its own arrangements in Germany. The Russians dismantled German industry in the eastern zone, but the Americans tried to make Germany self-sufficient, which meant restoring its industrial capacity. To the Soviets the restoration of a powerful industrial Germany was unacceptable.

When the Western powers agreed to go forward with a separate constitution for the western sectors of Germany in February 1948, the Soviets walked out

26.2
"An Iron Curtain Has Descended Across the Continent" (March 1946): Sir Winston Churchill

Marshall Plan U.S. program, named after Secretary of State George C. Marshall, that provided economic aid to Europe after World War II.

The Berlin Airlift. Every day for almost a year Western planes supplied the city until Stalin lifted the Berlin blockade in May 1949.

Bildarchiv Preussischer Kulturbesitz.

of the joint Allied Control Commission. Berlin, although well within the Soviet zone, was governed by all four powers. The Soviets sealed off the city by closing all railroads and highways to West Germany. Their purpose was to drive the Western powers out of Berlin.

The Western allies responded to the Berlin Blockade with an airlift of supplies that lasted almost a year. In May 1949, the Russians were forced to reopen access to Berlin. The incident hastened the separation of Germany into two states, which prevailed for 40 years. West Germany became the German Federal Republic in September 1949, and the eastern region became the German Democratic Republic a month later.

NATO AND THE WARSAW PACT

Meanwhile, Western Europe was coming closer together. The Marshall Plan encouraged international cooperation. In April 1949, Belgium, Britain, Denmark, France, Iceland, Italy, Luxembourg, the Netherlands, Norway, and Portugal signed a treaty with Canada and the United States that formed the North Atlantic Treaty Organization (NATO) for mutual assistance in case of attack. NATO formed the West into a bloc. A few years later Greece, Turkey, and West Germany joined the alliance (see Map 32–1).

Unlike the NATO states, the states of Eastern Europe were under direct Soviet domination through local Communist parties controlled from Moscow and overawed by the Red Army. The Warsaw Pact of May 1955, which included Albania, Bulgaria, Czechoslovakia, East Germany, Hungary, Poland, Romania, and the Soviet Union, merely gave formal recognition to a system that already existed. Europe stood divided into two unfriendly blocs.

CRISES OF 1956

The events of 1956 had considerable significance both for the Cold War and for what they implied about the realities of European power in the postwar era.

Suez In July 1956, President Gamal Abdel Nasser (1918–1970) of Egypt nationalized the Suez Canal. Britain and France feared that this action would imperil their supplies of oil in the Persian Gulf. In October 1956, war broke out between Egypt and Israel. The British and French intervened; however, the United States refused to support them. The Soviet Union protested vehemently. The Anglo-French forces had to be withdrawn, and control of the canal remained with Egypt. The Suez intervention proved that without the support of the United States, the nations of Western Europe could no longer impose their will on the rest of the world.

Poland Developments in Eastern Europe demonstrated similar limitations on independent action among the Soviet bloc nations. When the prime minister of Poland died, the Polish Communist Party refused to choose a successor

Major Dates in the Era of the Cold War

1948–1949	Berlin Blockade
1949	Formation of the North Atlantic Treaty Organization (NATO)
1950	Outbreak of the Korean War
1953	Death of Stalin
1956	
July	Egypt seizes the Suez Canal
October	Anglo-French attack on the Suez Canal; Hungarian Revolution
1957	Treaty of Rome establishes the European Economic Community (EEC)
1960	Paris Summit Conference collapses
1961	Berlin Wall erected
1962	Cuban missile crisis
1963	Russian-American Nuclear Test Ban Treaty
1968	Russian invasion of Czechoslovakia
1975	Helsinki Accords
1979	Russian invasion of Afghanistan
1981	Military crackdown on Solidarity Movement in Poland
1985	Reagan-Gorbachev summit
1987	Major American-Soviet Arms Limitation Treaty
1989	Berlin Wall comes down
1991	Soviet Union dissolves

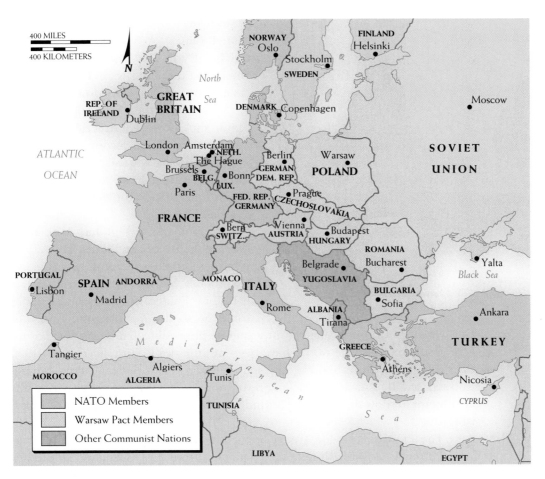

MAP 32–1
Major Cold War European Alliance Systems.   The North Atlantic Treaty Organization, which includes both Canada and the United States, stretches as far east as Turkey. By contrast, the Warsaw Pact nations were the contiguous Communist states of Eastern Europe, with the Soviet Union as the dominant member.

WHY DID NATO and the Warsaw Pact emerge and become rivals after World War II?

selected by Moscow. Considerable tension developed. In the end, Wladyslaw Gomulka (1905–1982) emerged as the new communist leader of Poland. He proved acceptable to the Soviets because he promised to keep Poland in the Warsaw Pact. However, he halted the collectivization of Polish agriculture and improved relations with the Polish Roman Catholic Church.

Uprising in Hungary   Hungary provided the second trouble spot for the Soviet Union. In late October, fighting erupted in Budapest. A new ministry headed by Imre Nagy (1896–1958) was installed. Nagy was a Communist who sought an independent position for Hungary. Unlike Gomulka, he called for Hungarian withdrawal from the Warsaw Pact. Soviet troops deposed Nagy, who was later executed, and imposed Janos Kadar (1912–1989) as premier.

THE COLD WAR INTENSIFIED

The events of 1956 ended the era of fully autonomous action by the European nation-states. The two superpowers had demonstrated the new political realities. After 1956, the Soviet Union began to talk about "peaceful coexistence" with the United States. In 1959, tensions relaxed sufficiently for Soviet Premier Nikita

QUICK REVIEW

Polish–Soviet Relations

- 1956: Wladyslaw Gomulka comes to power in Poland

- Gomulka confirmed Poland's membership in Warsaw Pact, promised an end to collectivization, and improved relations with the Catholic Church

- Compromise prompted Hungary to seek greater autonomy

Soviet Invasion of Czechoslovakia. In the summer of 1968 Soviet tanks rolled into Czechoslovakia, ending that country's experiment in liberalized communism, known as the Prague spring. This picture shows defiant, flag-waving Czechs passing a Soviet tank in the immediate aftermath of the invasion.

Hulton Archive Photos/Getty Images, Inc.

QUICK REVIEW

The Cuban Missile Crisis

• 1959: Fidel Castro comes to power as a result of the Cuban revolution

• 1962: Khrushchev orders construction of missile bases in Cuba

• Tense negotiations resulted in the Soviets backing down and removing the missiles

Khrushchev (1894–1971) to tour the United States. A summit meeting was scheduled for May 1960 in Paris, and American President Dwight D. Eisenhower (1890–1969) was to go to Moscow.

Just before the gathering, the Soviet Union shot down an American U-2 aircraft that was flying reconnaissance over Soviet territory. Khrushchev refused to take part in the summit conference, and Eisenhower's trip to the Soviet Union was canceled.

In fact, the Soviets had long been aware of the American flights. They chose to protest at this time for two reasons. Khrushchev had hoped that the leaders of Britain, France, and the United States would be so divided over the future of Germany that a united Allied front would be impossible. The divisions did not arise, so the conference would have been of little use to him. Second, by 1960 the Communist world had become split between the Soviets and the Chinese, who accused the Russians of lacking revolutionary zeal. Khrushchev's action was an attempt to show the hard-line attitude of the Soviet Union toward the capitalist world.

The abortive Paris conference opened the most difficult period of the Cold War. Throughout 1961, thousands of refugees from East Germany had fled to West Berlin. To stop this outflow, in August 1961 the East Germans erected a concrete wall along the border between East and West Berlin that remained until November 1989.

A year later, the Cuban missile crisis brought the most dangerous days of the Cold War. The Soviet Union placed missiles in Cuba, a nation friendly to Soviet aims. The missiles were placed less than a hundred miles from the United States. The United States blockaded Cuba, halted the shipment of new missiles, and demanded the removal of existing installations. After a tense week, the Soviets backed down and the crisis ended.

DÉTENTE AND AFTERWARD

In 1963, the two powers concluded a Nuclear Test Ban Treaty. This agreement marked the start of a detente, or lessening in tensions, between the United States and the Soviet Union that intensified during the presidency of Richard Nixon (1913–1994). This policy involved trade agreements and mutual reduction of strategic armaments. But the Soviet invasion of Afghanistan in 1979 hardened relations between Washington and Moscow, and the U.S. Senate refused to ratify the Strategic Arms Limitation Treaty of 1979.

However, President Ronald Reagan (b. 1911) and Soviet leader Mikhail S. Gorbachev (b. 1931) held a friendly summit meeting in 1985, the first East–West summit in six years. Other meetings followed. In December 1987, the United States and the Soviet Union agreed to dismantle more than 2,000 medium- and shorter-range missiles. The treaty provided for mutual inspection. This action represented the most significant agreement since World War II between the two superpowers.

Thereafter, the political upheavals in Eastern Europe and the Soviet Union overwhelmed the issues of the Cold War. The Soviet Union abandoned its support for Communist governments in Eastern Europe. By the close of 1991, the Soviet Union itself had collapsed. The Cold War was over.

EUROPEAN SOCIETY IN THE SECOND HALF OF THE 20TH CENTURY AND BEYOND

*T*he sharp division of Europe into a democratic West and Communist East for most of the second half of the 20th century makes generalizations about social and economic developments difficult. Prosperity in the West contrasted with shortages in the Eastern economies, which were managed to benefit the Soviet Union. Most of the developments discussed in this chapter have taken place in Western Europe.

TOWARD WESTERN EUROPEAN UNIFICATION

Since 1945, the nations of Western Europe have taken unprecedented steps toward economic cooperation. The process is not completed. The collapse of the Soviet Union and the emergence of new free governments in Eastern Europe have further complicated the process.

The Marshall Plan and NATO gave the involved countries new experience in working with each other and demonstrated the gains from cooperative action. In 1950, Belgium, France, Italy, Luxembourg, the Netherlands, and West Germany organized the European Coal and Steel Community. Its success reduced suspicions about the concept of coordination and economic integration.

In 1957, through the Treaty of Rome, the six members of the Coal and Steel Community agreed to form a new organization: the **European Economic Community (EEC)**, or Common Market. The members sought to achieve the eventual elimination of tariffs, a free flow of capital and labor, and similar wage and social benefits in all the participating countries. The chief institution of the EEC was a High Commission composed of technocrats.

The Common Market was a stunning success. By 1968, all tariffs among the six members had been abolished. Trade and labor migration among the members grew steadily. Moreover, nonmember states began to seek membership. In 1973, Denmark, Great Britain, and Ireland became members, and Austria, Finland, Greece, Portugal, Spain, and Sweden were eventually admitted.

In 1988, the leaders of the EEC decided to create a virtual free-trade zone throughout the member community. In 1991, the Treaty of Maastricht called for a unified currency and a strong central bank. The European Community was renamed the **European Union (EU)**.

However, as the prospect of unity becomes imminent, the people of Europe have begun to raise issues about the democratic nature of the emerging political entity they are being asked to join. They are clearly in favor of closer cooperation, but they are unwilling to see it set forth only by politicians and bureaucrats. They want a wider European market to be genuinely free and not overregulated.

The most striking element of the expanding momentum of economic cooperation is the common currency, called the **euro**. In 1999, the currencies of Austria, Belgium, Finland, France, Germany, Ireland, Italy, Luxembourg, the Netherlands, Portugal, and Spain were fixed according to the value of the euro. In 2002, their

WHAT MAJOR trends have marked European society since World War II?

European Economic Community Economic association formed by France, Germany, Italy, Belgium, the Netherlands, and Luxembourg in 1957. Also known as the Common Market.

European Union New name given to the EEC in 1993. It included most of the states of Western Europe.

euro Common currency created by the EEC in the late 1990s.

President Ronald Reagan and Premier Mikhail Gorbachev. The two world leaders confer at a summit meeting in December 1989.
AP/Wide World Photos.

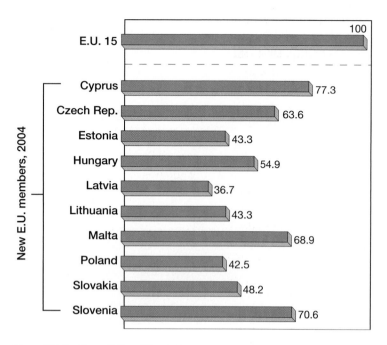

Figure 32–1. Gross National Product of Existing EU Members Compared to New Member States, 2004. The cost of absorbing new EU members, many of which have standards of living that are far lower, is high but the economic potential is great.

QUICK REVIEW

Western Europe's Consumer Society

• Western Europe's economy emphasized consumer goods in the second half of the 20th century

• Soviet bloc economies focused on capital investments and the military

• Discrepancy in Western and Eastern European standards of living caused resentment in the East

---

national currencies and that of Greece were replaced by new coins and notes denominated in the euro. Such a widespread common currency is unprecedented in European history.

In 2004, the EU accepted 10 new members. This expansion poses enormous challenges, because the economies of the new members (mostly former states from the Eastern Soviet bloc) are much less developed than those of the former members.

STUDENTS AND POPULAR MUSIC

Nothing so characterized both student and youth culture in the second half of the 20th century as rock music, which first emerged in the 1950s. The lyrics of the Beatles, the British rock group that became wildly popular on both sides of the Atlantic in the 1960s, may have become the most widely dispersed poetry in history. Rock appealed across national and cultural borders and did much to create a more uniform European culture.

It also offered a critique of contemporary society. Many lyrics emphasized the need for love, the anguish of isolation, a desire for sexual liberation, and hopes for community and peace. During the 1960s, rock music in the West promoted antiwar movements, student rebellions that rocked both Europe and the United States, and discontent with the older generation. In the 1970s and 1980s, rock music emerged as a major vehicle for cultural and political protest in Eastern Europe and the Soviet Union.

THE MOVEMENT OF PEOPLES

Many people have migrated from, to, and within Europe during the past half century.

External Migration   In the decade and a half after 1945, approximately a half million Europeans each year settled elsewhere in the world. Many of these migrants were educated city dwellers.

Decolonization in the postwar period contributed to an inward flow of European colonials and non-European inhabitants of the former colonies to Europe. This influx has caused social tension and conflict. In Great Britain, for example, during the 1980s clashes arose between the police and non-European immigrants. France has had similar difficulties. Moreover, large Islamic populations now exist in several European nations and have become political factors in France and Germany.

Internal Migration   The major motivation for internal migration from the late 1950s onward was economic opportunity. The prosperous nations of northern and Western Europe offered jobs that paid good wages and provided excellent benefits. Thus, there was a flow of workers from the poorer countries of Greece, Italy, Portugal, Spain, Turkey, and Yugoslavia into the wealthier countries of the Benelux nations, France, Switzerland, and West Germany. The establishment of the EEC in 1957 facilitated this movement.

The migration of workers into northern Europe snowballed after 1960. Several hundred thousand workers would enter France and Germany each year. They were usually welcomed during years of prosperity, and resented when economies began to slow in the mid-1980s. In Germany during the early 1990s, they were attacked.

In the late 1980s, politics again became a major factor in European migration. With the collapse of the Communist governments of Eastern Europe in 1988 and 1989, people from all over Eastern Europe have migrated to the West. The civil war in the former Yugoslavia has also created many refugees. However, the new migrants are generating resentment. Several nations have taken steps to restrict migration.

THE NEW MUSLIM POPULATION

Well into the 20th century, Europeans encountered Muslims, if at all, as subjects in their colonies. With the exception of a few minority communities in the Balkans and the former Soviet Empire, Europeans saw themselves and their national cultures as Christian or secular.

European indifference to Islam began to change in the 1960s as a sizable Muslim population settled in Europe. Two factors encouraged Muslim emigration to Western Europe: Europe's economic growth and decolonization. As Western economies recovered in the wake of World War II, a labor shortage developed in Europe, and laborers ("guest workers"), many of whom came from Muslim nations, were imported to fill it. The aftermath of decolonization and the quest for a better life led Muslims from East Africa and the Indian subcontinent to Great Britain and others from North Africa to France. Smaller but significant numbers settled in Denmark, Italy, the Netherlands, Spain, and Sweden—nations that had always had homogeneous populations.

These Muslim immigrant communities share some characteristics. Many Muslims came to Europe expecting eventually to return to their homelands, an expectation their host countries shared. Unlike the United States, few European countries had any experience in dealing with large-scale immigration, and the various Muslim communities have largely remained unassimilated. Most of the Muslim immigrants to Europe were neither highly skilled nor professionally educated, and many of the unskilled jobs that they originally filled have disappeared. As European economic growth has slowed, Muslims have become a target blamed for a host of problems from crime to unemployment.

The radicalization of parts of the Islamic world has also affected Europe's Muslim communities. Muslims in both Germany and Great Britain have been involved in radical Islamic groups, and some belonged to organizations involved in the September 11, 2001, attack on the United States. The French government has exerted more control over its Muslim community. Despite the fact that Europe's Muslims are not a homogeneous group, their communities are often plagued by poverty and unemployment and are a major concern for Europeans, who disagree on how to deal with them.

NEW PATTERNS IN THE WORK AND EXPECTATIONS OF WOMEN

Since World War II, the work patterns and social expectations of women have changed markedly. In all social ranks, women have begun to assume larger economic and political roles. They have entered the professions and are filling major managerial positions.

Feminism   Enormous gains were made during the second half of the 20th century, but gender inequality remained a major characteristic of European societies at the start of the 21st century. After World War II, European feminism developed a

Muslim Women Wearing Headscarves, France. The presence of foreign-born Muslims whose labor is necessary for the prosperity of the European economy is a major issue in contemporary Europe. Many of these Muslims, such as these women, live in self-contained communities.

Figaro Magazine/Torregano/Getty Images, Inc.

HISTORY'S VOICES

SIMONE DE BEAUVOIR URGES ECONOMIC FREEDOM FOR WOMEN

Simone de Beauvoir was the single most important feminist voice of mid-20th-century Europe. In The Second Sex, published in France in 1949, she explored the experience of women coming of age in a world of ideas, institutions, and social expectations shaped historically by men. Much of the book discusses the psychological strategies that modern European women had developed to deal with their status as "the second sex." Toward the end of her book, de Beauvoir argues strongly that economic freedom and advancement for women are fundamental to their personal fulfillment.

WHY DOES de Beauvoir argue that the achievement of civic rights must be accompanied by economic freedom for women? Why does the example of the small number of professional women illustrate issues for European women in general? How does de Beauvoir indicate that even professional women must overcome a culture in which the experience of women is fundamentally different from that of men? Do her comments seem relevant for women at the opening of the 21st century?

According to French law, obedience is no longer included among the duties of a wife, and each woman citizen has the right to vote; but these civil liberties remain theoretical as long as they are unaccompanied by economic freedom. . . . It is through gainful employment that woman has traversed most of the distance that separated her from the male; and nothing else can guarantee her liberty in practice. Once she ceases to be a parasite, the system based on her dependence crumbles; between her and the universe there is no longer any need for a masculine mediator. . . .

When she is productive, active, she regains her transcendence; in her projects she concretely affirms her status as subject; in connection with the aims she pursues, with the money and the rights she takes possession of, she makes trial of and senses her responsibility. . . .

There are . . . a fairly large number of privileged women who find in their professions a means of economic and social autonomy. These come to mind when one considers woman's possibilities and her future . . . [E]ven though they constitute as yet only a minority; they continue to be the subject of debate between feminists and antifeminists. The latter assert that the emancipated women of today succeed in doing nothing of importance in the world and that furthermore they have difficulty in achieving their own inner equilibrium. The former exaggerate the results obtained by professional women and are blind to their inner confusion. There is no good reason . . . to say they are on the wrong road; and still it is certain that they are not tranquilly installed in their new realm: as yet they are only halfway there. The woman who is economically emancipated from man is not for all that in a moral, social, and psychological situation identical with that of man. The way she carried on her profession and her devotion to it depends on the context supplied by the total pattern of her life. For when she begins her adult life she does not have behind her the same past as does a boy; she is not viewed by society in the same way; the universe presents itself to her in a different perspective. The fact of being a woman today poses peculiar problems for an independent human individual.

Source: Simone de Beauvoir, *The Second Sex*, trans. by H. M. Parshley. Copyright 1952 and renewed 1980 by Alfred A. Knopf, Inc. Reprinted by permission of Alfred A. Knopf, a division of Random House Inc.

new agenda. Simone de Beauvoir's (1908-1986) book, *The Second Sex* (1949), was a major influence (see "Simone de Beauvoir Urges Economic Freedom for Women"). She and other feminists documented the social, legal, and economic disadvantages of their gender, challenged discrimination against women in family law, and called attention to social problems such as spousal abuse.

More Married Women in the Work Force   Both middle- and working-class women have increasingly sought employment outside the home, and the number of married women in the work force has risen sharply. Some employers adjust hours to accommodate them, and consumer conveniences and child care made it easier for them to work. Given that 20th-century children were compelled to spend much of their time in school, they are no longer expected to contribute to the support of their families. If additional income is needed, their mothers work outside the home. But even when there is no financial necessity, both parents are now likely to pursue careers.

New Work Patterns   In the late 20th century, the work pattern of European women displayed much more continuity than it did in the 19th century. Single women enter the work force after their schooling and continue to work after marriage. The number of married women in the work force has risen sharply. Both middle- and working-class married women have sought jobs outside the home. They might withdraw from the work force to care for young children but return when the children begin school.

Several factors created this new pattern, but women's increasing life expectancy is one of the most important. The lengthening life span has meant that child rearing occupies much less of women's lives. Women throughout the Western world have new concerns about how they will spend those years when they are not rearing children. The age at which women have decided to bear children has risen. In urban areas, childbearing occurs later and the birthrate is lower than elsewhere.

Many women have begun to limit the number of children they bear or to forgo childbearing altogether. Both men and women continue to expect to marry. But the new careers open to women and the desire of couples for a higher standard of living have contributed to a declining birthrate.

Women in the New Eastern Europe   Many paradoxes surround the situation of women in Eastern Europe now that it is no longer governed by Communists. Under communism women generally enjoyed social equality as well as a broad spectrum of government benefits. Well over 50 percent of women worked in these societies both because they could and because it was expected of them. There were, however, no significant women's movements since they, like all independent associations, were frowned on.

The new governments of the region are free, but have shown little concern toward women's issues. Economic difficulties may endanger the funding of various health and welfare programs that benefit women and children, like the extensive maternity benefits they used to enjoy. Moreover, the high proportion of women in the work force could leave them more vulnerable than men to the region's economic troubles.

Simone de Beauvoir. Depicted here with her companion, philosopher Jean Paul Sartre, de Beauvoir was the major feminist writer in postwar Europe.

Getty Images Inc./Hulton Archive Photos.

American Domestic Scene Since World War II

*T*hree major themes have characterized the postwar American experience—opposition to the spread of communism, expansion of civil rights to Blacks and other minorities at home, and a determination to achieve economic growth.

WHAT ARE the main themes that have characterized postwar America?

TRUMAN AND EISENHOWER ADMINISTRATIONS

The foreign policy of President Harry Truman was directed against Communist expansion in Europe and East Asia. Domestically, the Truman administration tried to continue the New Deal. However, Truman encountered opposition from conservative Republicans, who in 1947 passed the Taft-Hartley Act, which limited labor-union activity. Truman won the 1948 election against great odds. Through policies he termed the Fair Deal, he sought to extend economic security.

Those efforts, however, were frustrated by fears of a domestic Communist menace fanned by Senator Joseph McCarthy (1909–1957) of Wisconsin. That development, a frustration with the war in Korea, and perhaps the natural weariness of the electorate after 20 years of Democratic Party government, led to the election of war hero Dwight Eisenhower in 1952.

The Eisenhower years now seem a period of calm. Eisenhower ended the Korean War. The country was generally prosperous. The president was less activist than either Roosevelt or Truman had been.

Beneath the apparent quiet, however, stirred forces that would lead to the disruptions of the 1960s.

CIVIL RIGHTS

In 1954, the U.S. Supreme Court, in *Brown v. Board of Education of Topeka,* declared racial segregation unconstitutional. Shortly thereafter, the court ordered the desegregation of schools. In 1957, President Eisenhower had to send troops into Little Rock, Arkansas, to integrate the schools, and for the next 10 years, the struggle over school integration and civil rights for Black Americans stirred the nation. Southern states attempted to resist desegregation. American Blacks began to protest it. In 1955, Reverend Martin Luther King, Jr. (1929–1968) organized a boycott in Montgomery, Alabama, against segregated buses that marked the beginning of the use of civil disobedience to fight racial discrimination in the United States. The civil rights struggle continued well into the 1960s. The greatest achievements of the movement were the Civil Rights Act of 1964, which desegregated public accommodations, and the Voting Rights Act of 1965, which cleared the way for Blacks to vote. Black citizens were brought nearer to the mainstream of American life than they had ever been.

However, much remained undone. In 1967, race riots occurred in American cities. Those riots, followed by the assassination of Martin Luther King, Jr., in 1968, weakened the civil rights movement. Not until the late 1980s did a new leader emerge in the person of the Reverend Jesse Jackson (b. 1941). He spearheaded a move to register Black voters, but progress on race relations has been slow. In 1992, a court decision involving treatment of Black Americans by police sparked one of the most destructive riots in American history in Los Angeles. Furthermore, as other groups, particularly Latino Americans, began to raise issues on behalf of their own communities, racial relations became more complicated. Black Americans and other minorities continue to lag behind White Americans economically.

NEW SOCIAL PROGRAMS

The advance of the civil rights movement in the late 1950s and early 1960s represented the cutting edge of a new advance of political liberalism. In 1960, John F. Kennedy (1917–1963) narrowly won the presidential election. He attempted unsuccessfully to expand medical care under the Social Security program, but the reaction to his assassination in 1963 allowed his successor, Lyndon Johnson

(1908–1973), to press for activist legislation. Johnson's domestic program, known as the War on Poverty, established major federal programs to create jobs and provide job training. It also added new entitlements to the Social Security program, including Medicare, which provides medical services for the elderly and disabled. Johnson's drive for what he termed the Great Society ended the era of major federal initiatives that had begun under Franklin Roosevelt. By the late 1960s, the electorate had become more conservative.

THE VIETNAM WAR AND DOMESTIC TURMOIL

Johnson's activist domestic vision was overshadowed by the U.S. involvement in Vietnam (see Chapter 33). By 1965, Johnson had decided to send American troops to Vietnam. This policy led to the longest of American wars. At home, the war and the military draft provoked large-scale protests on the streets and on college campuses. The Vietnam War divided the nation as had no conflict since the Civil War.

Lyndon Johnson decided not to seek reelection in 1968. Richard Nixon led the Republicans to victory. His election marked the beginning of an era of American politics dominated by conservative policies. Perhaps the most important act of his administration was to establish diplomatic relations with the People's Republic of China. Although half of the casualties in the Vietnam War occurred under Nixon's administration, he concluded the war in 1972. That same year he was reelected, but the Watergate scandal began to erode his administration.

THE WATERGATE SCANDAL

On the surface, the Watergate scandal involved only the burglary of the Democratic Party national headquarters by White House operatives in 1972. The deeper issues related to presidential authority and the right of the government to intrude into the lives of citizens. In 1973, Congress established a committee to investigate the scandal. Testimony revealed that President Nixon had recorded conversations in the White House. In the summer of 1974, the newly released tapes showed that Nixon had ordered federal agencies to try to cover up White House participation in the burglary. After this revelation, Nixon resigned, becoming the first American president to resign from office.

The Watergate scandal further shook public confidence in the government. It was also a distraction from the major problems facing the country, especially inflation, which had resulted from fighting the war in Vietnam while expanding federal domestic expenditures. The administrations of Gerald Ford (1974–1977; b. 1913) and Jimmy Carter (1977–1981; b. 1924) battled inflation and high interest rates without success.

THE TRIUMPH OF POLITICAL CONSERVATISM

In 1980, Ronald Reagan was elected president by a large majority and reelected four years later. Reagan was the first fully ideological conservative to be elected in the postwar era. He sought to reduce the role of the federal government in

Kent State Protest. The clash between protesting students and the Ohio National Guard at Kent State University was the most violent moment in the protests against the U.S. involvement in Vietnam.

AP/Wide World Photos.

Farewell. President Richard M. Nixon flashes his trademark "V" gesture one last time before boarding a helicopter after his resignation.

American life through major tax cuts. This plus vastly increased defense spending produced the largest fiscal deficit in American history, but inflation was controlled, and the economy expanded.

In 1988, George H. W. Bush (b. 1924) was elected to succeed Reagan. In the summer of 1990, in response to the invasion of Kuwait by Iraq, he initiated the largest mobilization of American troops since the Vietnam War and forged a worldwide coalition, which forced Iraq out of Kuwait in 1991.

But Bush stumbled in the face of serious economic problems. In 1992, the Democratic nominee, Governor William (Bill) Clinton (b. 1946) of Arkansas, won the election.

In 1994, the Republic Party won majorities in both houses of Congress in an election that marked a major conservative departure in American political life. This Congress continued the conservative redirection of federal policy that had begun under Reagan.

President Clinton and a Republican-dominated Congress were reelected in 1996, but scandals plagued both parties. Because of a personal sexual scandal and allegations of perjury, President Clinton was impeached in 1998 but acquitted in early 1999 by the Senate. In terms of policy, Clinton was seen as moving the Democractic Party into a more conservative stance.

The presidential election of 2000 between Texas governor George W. Bush (son of the former president) and Vice President Al Gore was the closest in modern American history. Gore won a majority of the popular vote, but failed to win a majority in the electoral college. The pivotal electoral votes depended on which candidate carried Florida, where the final vote count was disputed for more than a month after the November election. After complicated legal disputes over how, or indeed whether, to recount the Florida vote, the U.S. Supreme Court voted 5 to 4 to halt the recount, which resulted in Bush being declared the winner in Florida and thus in the presidential election as well.

On September 11, 2001, surprise terrorist attacks on New York City and Washington, D.C., transformed the political life of the United States. In October 2001, the United States began a war against terrorism. U.S. forces overran the forces of the extremist Islamic Taliban regime in Afghanistan, which had tolerated the presence of Islamic terrorists. In 2003, as a second step in the response to the terrorist threat, the United States invaded Iraq (see Chapter 34).

In 2004, President Bush overcame Democratic challenger John Kerry and was reelected, this time with a popular and electoral college majority vote. This strengthened his hand in pursuing his conservative legislative agenda and foreign policy.

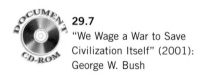

29.7
"We Wage a War to Save Civilization Itself" (2001): George W. Bush

WHY DID Gorbachev seek to change the Soviet Union?

THE SOVIET UNION TO 1989

The major themes of Soviet history after 1945 were the rivalry with the United States for world leadership, the rivalry with China for leadership of Communist nations, the effort to sustain Soviet domination of Eastern Europe, and a series of unsuccessful attempts to reform the Stalinist state, which ended in 1991 with the collapse of the Soviet Union.

The Soviet Union emerged from World War II as a major world power, but Stalin did not modify the repressive regime he had fostered. The central bureaucracy grew. Heavy industry was still favored at the expense of consumer goods. Agriculture remained troubled. Stalin's authority was unchallenged. He solidified Soviet control over Eastern Europe.

THE KHRUSHCHEV YEARS

Stalin died on March 6, 1953. No single leader immediately replaced him, but by 1956, Nikita Khrushchev (1894–1971) became premier, but without the extraordinary powers of Stalin.

In 1956, at the Twentieth Congress of the Communist Party, Khrushchev denounced Stalin and his crimes. The speech shocked party circles and opened the way for limited internal criticism of the Soviet government. Under Khrushchev, intellectuals were somewhat freer to express their opinions. In economic policy, Khrushchev made moderate efforts to decentralize economic planning, but the consumer sector improved only marginally. The ever-growing defense budget and the space program made major demands on the nation's productive resources.

Khrushchev redirected Stalin's agricultural policy. The Soviet Union could not feed its own people. Khrushchev removed the most restrictive regulations on private cultivation, but the agricultural problem continued to grow.

By 1964, Communist Party leaders had concluded that Khrushchev had tried to do too much too soon and had done it poorly. His foreign policy, culminating in the backdown over the Cuban missile crisis, appeared a failure. On October 16, 1964, Khrushchev was forced to resign. Leonid Brezhnev (1906–1982) emerged as his successor.

BREZHNEV

The Soviet government became more repressive after 1964. Intellectuals enjoyed less freedom, and Jewish citizens were harassed. The internal repression gave rise to a dissident movement. A few Soviet citizens dared to criticize the regime for violating the human rights provisions of the 1975 Helsinki Accords. The dissidents included the Nobel Prize–winning physicist Andrei Sakharov (1921–1989). The Soviet government responded with more repression.

In foreign policy, the Brezhnev years witnessed attempts both to reach accommodation with the United States and to continue to expand Soviet influence and maintain Soviet leadership of the Communist movement. Growing spending on defense sqeezed the consumer side of the economy.

In December 1979, the Soviet Union invaded Afghanistan for reasons that still remain unclear. The Afghanistan invasion exacerbated tensions with the United States and tied the hands of the Soviet government in Eastern Europe. Soviet hesitation to react to events in Poland during the 1980s stemmed in part from the military committment in Afghanistan and from the condemnation the invasion provoked from Western European Communists and from many governments. The Soviet government also lost support at home as its army became bogged down and suffered steady losses.

COMMUNISM AND SOLIDARITY IN POLAND

In July 1980, the Polish government raised meat prices. The result was strikes across the country. In August, a strike at the Lenin shipyard at Gdansk spread to other shipyards, transport facilities, and factories. The strikers, led by Lech Walesa (b. 1944), refused to negotiate through the government-controlled unions. The Gdansk strike ended on August 31 after the government promised the workers the right to organize an independent union, Solidarity. Less than a week later the Polish Communist head of state was replaced.

In the summer of 1981, for the first time in any European Communist state, secret elections for the Polish party congress permitted real choices among the

Mujahidin. Muslim guerrilla warriors are pictured here with a captured Soviet armored vehicle in January 1980 near Afghanistan's border with Pakistan. The Soviet invasion of Afghanistan in 1979 met with fierce resistance and sparked a sharp response from the United States, which halted sales of wheat to the Soviet Union and boycotted the Olympic Games held in Moscow in 1980.

C. Spengler/Sygma.

candidates. Poland remained a Communist state, but real debate was temporarily permitted within the party congress. This experiment ended in December 1981. General Wojciech Jaruzelski (b.1923) became head of the party, and martial law was declared.

GORBACHEV ATTEMPTS TO REDIRECT THE SOVIET UNION

By the time of Brezhnev's death in 1982, the Soviet system seemed incapable of meeting the needs of its people or pursuing a successful foreign policy. But no observers expected rapid change in the Soviet Union or its satellites.

However, in 1985, Mikhail S. Gorbachev (b. 1931) came to power and immediately set about making the most remarkable changes that the Soviet Union had witnessed since the 1920s. His reforms unleashed forces that within seven years would force him to retire and end both Communist rule and the Soviet Union itself.

Initially, Gorbachev and his supporters challenged the way the party and bureaucracy managed the Soviet government and economy. Under the policy of **perestroika**, or restructuring, they proposed major economic and political reforms. The centralized economic ministries were streamlined. By early 1990, Gorbachev had even begun to advocate private ownership of property. He and his advisers considered policies to move the economy rapidly toward a free market. However, the Soviet economy, instead of growing, stagnated and even declined. Shortages of food, consumer goods, and housing became chronic. Old-fashioned Communists blamed these results on the abandonment of centralized planning, while democratic critics blamed them on overly slow reform.

Gorbachev also allowed public criticism of Soviet history and Soviet Communist Party policy. This development was termed **glasnost**, or openness. In factories, workers were permitted to criticize party officials and the economic plans of the party and the government. Censorship was relaxed and free expression encouraged. Dissidents were released from prison. In 1988, a new constitution permitted contested elections. After real political campaigning, the Congress of People's Deputies was elected in 1989 and then formally elected Gorbachev as president.

The Soviet Union was a vast empire of diverse nationalities. Some had been conquered under the tsars; others had been seized by Stalin. Glasnost quickly brought to the fore the discontents of all such peoples. Gorbachev proved inept in addressing these ethnic complaints.

1989: YEAR OF REVOLUTIONS IN EASTERN EUROPE

In 1989, Soviet domination and Communist rule in Eastern Europe ended. None of these revolutions could have taken place without the refusal of the Soviet Union to intervene militarily as it had done in 1956 and 1968. For the first time since the end of World War II, the peoples of Eastern Europe could shape their own political destiny. Once they realized the Soviets would stand back, thousands of citizens denounced Communist Party domination and asserted their desire for democracy.

The generally peaceful character of most of these revolutions was not inevitable. It may have resulted from the shock with which the world responded to the violent repression of prodemocracy protesters in Beijing's Tienanmen Square in May 1989. The Communist Party officials of Eastern Europe and the

---

perestroika Meaning "restructuring." Attempt in the 1980s to reform the Soviet government and economy.

glasnost Meaning "openness." Policy initiated by Mikhail Gorbachev in the 1980s of permitting open criticism of the policies of the Soviet Communist Party.

WHY DID communist regimes collapse so easily in Eastern Europe in 1989?

Soviet Union clearly decided that they could not offend world opinion with a similar attack.

SOLIDARITY REEMERGES IN POLAND

During the mid-1980s, Poland's government relaxed martial law. By 1984, leaders of Solidarity began again to work for free trade unions and democratic government. New dissenting organizations emerged. Poland's economy continued to deteriorate. In 1988, new strikes occurred. This time the communist government failed to reimpose control. Solidarity was legalized.

Jaruzelski, with the tacit consent of the Soviet Union, promised free elections to parliament. When elections were held in 1989, the Communists lost overwhelmingly to Solidarity candidates. On August 24, 1989, after negotiating with Lech Walesa, Jaruzelski named Tadeusz Mazowiecki (b. 1927) the first non-Communist prime minister of Poland since 1945. The appointment was made with the express approval of Gorbachev.

HUNGARY MOVES TOWARD INDEPENDENCE

Hungary had for some time shown the greatest national economic independence of the Soviet Union in Eastern Europe. The Hungarian government had emphasized the production of food and consumer goods. In early 1989, as events unfolded in Poland, the Hungarian Communist government permitted independent political parties and free travel between Hungary and Austria, opening the first breach in the Iron Curtain. Thousands of East Germans then moved through Hungary and Austria to West Germany.

In May 1989, Premier Janos Kadar (1912–1989) was voted from office by the parliament. In October, Hungary promised free elections. By 1990, a coalition of democratic parties governed the country.

THE BREACH OF THE BERLIN WALL AND GERMAN REUNIFICATION

In the autumn of 1989, demonstrations erupted in East German cities. The streets filled with people demanding an end to Communist Party rule.

Gorbachev told the leaders of the East German Communist Party that the Soviet Union would no longer support them. They resigned, making way for a younger generation of Communist Party leaders who promised reforms. They convinced few East Germans, however. In November 1989, the government of East Germany ordered the opening of the Berlin Wall, and thousands of East Berliners crossed into West Berlin. By early 1990, the Communist government of East Germany had been swept away.

The citizens of the two Germanies were determined to reunify. By February 1990, reunification had become a foregone conclusion, accepted by France, Great Britain, the Soviet Union, and the United States.

THE VELVET REVOLUTION IN CZECHOSLOVAKIA

Late in 1989, in "the velvet revolution," Communist rule in Czechoslovakia unraveled. In November, under popular pressure from street demonstrations and well-organized political opposition, the Communist Party began to retreat from office. The patterns were similar to those occurring elsewhere: Old leadership

The Fall of the Berlin Wall. The most dramatic moment in the weeks of the collapse of Communist regimes in Eastern Europe occurred in November 1989 when crowds destroyed the Berlin Wall, the most prominent symbol of the Cold War divisions in Europe.

A.Avarkian/Time Life Pictures/Getty Images, Inc.

29.1
A United Germany in a United Europe (June 5, 1990): Helmut Kohl

resigned, and younger Communists replaced them. The changes they offered were inadequate.

The popular new Czech leader was Václav Havel (b. 1936), a playwright of international standing whom the government had imprisoned. Havel and his group, which called itself Civic Forum, negotiated changes with the government that included an end to the political dominance of the Communist Party and the inclusion of non-Communists in the government. In late December 1989, Havel was elected president.

VIOLENT REVOLUTION IN ROMANIA

The most violent upheaval of 1989 occurred in Romania, where President Nicolae Ceausescu (1918–1989) had governed without opposition for almost a quarter century. Romania was a corrupt, one-party state with total centralized economic planning. Ceausescu, who had long been at odds with the Soviet government, maintained his Stalinist regime in the face of Gorbachev's reforms. He was supported by a loyal security force.

On December 15, troubles erupted in the city of Timisoara in western Romania. The security forces fired on demonstrators, and casualties ran into the hundreds. By December 22, Bucharest was in full revolt. Fighting broke out between the army, which supported the revolution, and the security forces. Ceausescu and his wife attempted to flee the country but were captured and executed on December 25. His death ended the fighting. The provisional government in Bucharest announced the first free elections since the end of World War II.

THE COLLAPSE OF THE SOVIET UNION

WHY DID the Soviet Union collapse?

Gorbachev believed that the Soviet Union could no longer afford to support Communist governments in Eastern Europe. He was beginning to realize that the Communist Party within the Soviet Union was also losing power.

RENUNCIATION OF COMMUNIST POLITICAL MONOPOLY

In early 1990, Gorbachev formally proposed that the Soviet Communist Party abandon its monopoly of power. After intense debate, the Central Committee abandoned the Leninist position that only a single elite party could act as the vanguard of the revolution and forge a new Soviet society.

Gorbachev confronted challenges from three major political forces by 1990. One group—considered conservative in the Soviet context—wanted to maintain the influence of the Communist Party and the Soviet army. They were disturbed by the country's economic stagnation and disorder. They appeared to have significant support. During late 1990 and early 1991, Gorbachev, who himself seems to have been disturbed by the nation's turmoil, began to appoint members of this group to government posts. In other words, Gorbachev seemed to be making a strategic retreat. He apparently believed that these more conservative forces could give him the support he needed against opposition from a second group, led by Boris Yeltsin (b. 1931), who wanted to move quickly to a market economy and a more democratic government. In 1990, Yeltsin was elected president of the Russian Republic, the most important of the Soviet Union's constituent republics. That position gave him a firm political base from which to challenge Gorbachev's authority and increase his own.

The third force was regional unrest, especially from the three Baltic republics of Estonia, Latvia, and Lithuania. During 1989 and 1990, the parliaments of the Baltic republics tried to increase their independence, and Lithuania actually declared itself independent. Discontent also arose in the Soviet Islamic republics in Central Asia. Gorbachev sought to negotiate new constitutional arrangements between the republics and the central government but failed. This may have been the most important reason for the rapid collapse of the Soviet Union.

THE AUGUST 1991 COUP

The turning point came in August 1991 when the conservative forces that Gorbachev had brought into the government attempted a coup. Armed forces occupied Moscow, and Gorbachev himself was placed under house arrest in the Crimea. Yeltsin denounced the coup and asked the world for help.

Within two days the coup collapsed. Gorbachev returned to Moscow, but in humiliation, having been victimized by the groups he had turned to for support. From that point on, Yeltsin steadily became the dominant political figure in the nation. The Communist Party, compromised by its participation in the coup, collapsed. On December 25, 1991, the Soviet Union ceased to exist, Gorbachev left office, and the Commonwealth of Independent States came into being (see Map 32–2).

MAP 32–2

The Commonwealth of Independent States. In December 1991, the Soviet Union broke up into its 15 constituent republics. Eleven of these were loosely joined in the Commonwealth of Independent States. Also shown is the autonomous region of Chechnya, which has waged two bloody wars with Russia in the last decade.

WHAT DOES the breakup of the Soviet Union say about the importance of nationalism in the modern world?

THE YELTSIN YEARS

As president of Russia, Yeltsin was head of the largest and most powerful of the new states, but by 1993 he faced serious problems. Opposition to Yeltsin personally and to his economic and political reforms grew in the Russian Parliament. Its members were mostly former Communists who wanted to slow or halt the movement toward reform. In September 1993, Yeltsin suspended Parliament, which responded by deposing him. The military, however, backed Yeltsin and surrounded the Parliament building. On October 4, 1993, after pro-Parliament rioters rampaged through Moscow, Yeltsin ordered tanks to attack the Parliament building, crushing the revolt.

These actions consolidated Yeltsin's position and authority. The major Western powers supported him. The crushing of Parliament left Yeltsin far more dependent on the military. And the country's continuing economic problems bred unrest. In the December 1993 parlimentary elections, radical nationalists made an uncomfortably strong showing. In 1994 and again after 1999, the central government has found itself at war in the province of Chechnya. In December 1999, Yeltsin, who suffered from poor health, resigned and was succeeded as president by Vladimir Putin. Putin was elected to a full term in April 2000, promising strong leadership.

Putin renewed the war against the rebels in Chechnya, which has resulted in heavy casualties and enormous destruction there, but has also strengthened Putin's political support in Russia itself. After the terrorist attacks on the United States, Putin extended cooperation with the American assault on Afghanistan largely because the Russian government was afraid that Islamic extremism would spread beyond Chechnya to other regions in Russia and to the largely Muslim nations that bordered Russia in Central Asia and the Caucasus.

The Chechen war spawned a major terrorist act. In September 2004, a group of Chechens captured an elementary school in Beslan (in the north Caucasus) and held 1,200 students, teachers, and parents hostage for several days. When government troops stormed the school, approximately 330 hostages were killed. In the wake of this event, Putin has pursued policies of strong governmental centralization that cast doubt on the future of democratic processes in Russia.

THE COLLAPSE OF YUGOSLAVIA AND CIVIL WAR

HOW DID the West respond to the collapse of Yugoslavia?

Yugoslavia was created after World War I. Its borders included six major national groups—Serbs, Croats, Slovenes, Montenegrins, Macedonians, and Bosnians (Muslims)—among whom there have been ethnic disputes for centuries. The Croats and Slovenes are Roman Catholic and use the Latin alphabet. The Serbs, Montenegrins, and Macedonians are Eastern Orthodox and use the Cyrillic alphabet. The Bosnians are Islamic. Most members of each group reside in a region with which they are associated historically—Serbia, Croatia, Slovenia, Montenegro, Macedonia, and Bosnia-Herzegovina—and these regions constituted individual republics within Yugoslavia. Many Serbs, however, lived outside Serbia proper.

Yugoslavia's first Communist leader, Marshal Tito (1892–1980), had acted independently of Stalin in the late 1940s and pursued his own foreign policy. He muted ethnic differences by encouraging a cult of personality around himself and by complex power sharing. After his death, economic difficulties undermined the central government, and Yugoslavia dissolved into civil war.

In the late 1980s, the old ethnic differences came to the fore again in Yugoslav politics. Nationalist leaders—most notably Slobodan Milošević (b. 1941) in Serbia and Franjo Tudjman (1922–1999) in Croatia—gained authority. The Serbs contended that Serbia did not exercise sufficient influence in Yugoslavia and that Serbs living in Yugoslavia but outside Serbia encountered discrimination, especially from Croats. Ethnic tension and violence soon resulted. During the summer of 1991, in the wake of the changes in the former Soviet bloc nations, Slovenia and Croatia declared independence from the central Yugoslav government and were recognized by the European community.

From this point on, violence escalated. By June 1991, full-fledged war had erupted between Serbia and Croatia. At its core, however, the conflict was ethnic; as such, it highlights the potential for violent ethnic conflict within the former Soviet Union.

The conflict took a new turn in 1992 as Croatian and Serbian forces determined to divide Bosnia-Herzegovina. The Muslims in Bosnia—who had lived alongside Serbs and Croats for generations—soon became crushed between the opposing forces. The Serbs in particular, pursuing a policy called "ethnic cleansing," a euphemism redolent of some of the worst horrors of World War II, killed or forcibly moved many Bosnian Muslims.

The United Nations attempted unsuccessfully to mediate the conflict and imposed sanctions, which had little influence. But in 1995, NATO forces carried out strategic air strikes. Later that year, under the leadership of the United States, the leaders of the warring forces completed a peace agreement in Dayton, Ohio, which recognized an independent Bosnia. The terms of the agreement were enforced by the presence of NATO troops.

MAP EXPLORATION

Interactive map: To explore this map further, go to
http://www.prenhall.com/craig/map32.3

MAP 32–3
Ethnic Composition in the Former Yugoslavia. The rapid changes in Eastern Europe during the close of the 1980s intensified long-standing ethnic tensions in the former Yugoslavia. This map shows where Yugoslavia's ethnic population lived in 1991, before internal conflicts escalated.

HOW DOES the Balkans conflict illustrate the importance of ethnic identity in the modern world?

The situation in the former Yugoslavia remained dangerous and deadly. During 1997 and 1998, Serbia moved against ethnic Albanians living in its province of Kosovo. In 1999, NATO again undertook air strikes against Serbian forces, and forced Serbia to withdraw from Kosovo. In 2000, a popular revolution swept the nondemocratic government of Yugoslavia. In 2003, the two remaining Yugoslav republics, Serbia and Montenegro, each become autonomous.

CHALLENGES TO THE ATLANTIC ALLIANCE

After the collapse of the Soviet Union, NATO not only decided to continue, but it expanded its membership to include the Czech Republic, Hungary, and Poland. Its purpose, however, is now ill-defined. Having reluctantly undertaken to settle the civil war in the former Yugoslavia, NATO

WHAT PROBLEMS has Europe faced since the fall of Communism?

Terrorist Bombing, Madrid. Police search for clues from the debris of one of the trains destroyed in the terrorist attack of March 11, 2004.

AP/Wide World photos.

tried to become Europe's internal peacekeeper, but not all its members or the European public supported its assumption of this role.

NATO's uncertain mission and continental Europe's inward looking-tendency shaped reactions to the September 11, 2001, attack by al-Qaeda on the United States. Initially, Europeans deeply sympathized with Americans, but a significant split soon developed over President George W. Bush's response to the terrorist assault.

The September 11 attacks transformed American foreign policy, turning it into what Bush termed "a war on terrorism." In late 2001, the United States attacked and rapidly overthrew the Taliban government of Afghanistan. This destroyed some of al-Qaeda's bases, but not its leadership.

Following the Afghan campaign, the Bush administration asserted a policy of preemptive strikes to deal with potential enemies of the United States. The administration argued that the possibility that weapons of mass destruction (allegedly being developed in Iraq and elsewhere) might fall into the hands of terrorist organizations posed so severe a danger to the United States that it could not wait to respond to an attack but had to take strike first. This was a major departure from previous U.S. foreign policy, and it aroused considerable debate when the Bush administration acted on it by invading Iraq in 2003 (see Chapter 34). Some European governments (notably Bulgaria, Italy, Poland, Spain, and the United Kingdom) supported the move, but other traditional European allies of the United States (particularly, France and Germany) were opposed—as was most of the European public.

Terrorists have struck in Europe and have shown how al-Qaeda-sponsored attacks can influence European politics. On March 11, 2004, at least 190 people were killed in commuter train bombings in Madrid, Spain, and on July 7, 2005, more than fifty were killed by a similar attack in London. The Spanish attack occurred just before a general election. The Spanish government, which had supported the American invasion of Iraq, was voted from office and replaced by one that announced that it would withdraw troops from the conflict.

Profound divisions now exist between the United States and many of its historic postwar allies. Their future relationship will no doubt be determined by more than the issue of the Iraq war. The wider conflict between the West and radical political Islam may will be the factor that shapes the future of the Atlantic alliance, as was the division between a democractic West and a Communist Eastern block in the past.

SUMMARY

The Cold War U.S.–Soviet cooperation did not survive World War II. After 1945, Europe was divided into a Soviet-dominated zone in the East (the Warsaw Pact) and a U.S.-led zone in the West (NATO). U.S.–Soviet rivalry played itself out around the world from the 1950s to the 1980s, although gradually a spirit of détente arose between the two powers, especially under President Ronald Reagan and Soviet leader Mikhail Gorbachev. The Cold War ended with the collapse of Communist rule in Eastern Europe in 1989 and the disappearance of the Soviet Union in 1991.

Postwar European Society Since World War II, European society has been marked by a rise in prosperity and consumerism, more rights and opportunities for women, and moves toward political and economic unification symbolized by the adoption of a common currency, the euro, in 2002 and the publication of a draft constitution for a united Europe in 2003.

The United States The major themes in postwar American history were opposition to communism at home and abroad, the expansion of civil rights to African Americans, and economic prosperity. Politically, the relatively liberal years from the late 1950s through the 1970s were succeeded by a growing conservatism, especially under the presidencies of Ronald Reagan, George Bush, and George W. Bush. Even the Democratic President Bill Clinton was more a centrist than a liberal. After the terrorist attacks of September 11, 2001, the United States embarked on a war on terrorism that led to wars in Afghanistan and Iraq.

Eastern Europe The failure of the Communist regimes in Eastern Europe and the Soviet Union to produce economic prosperity or political liberalization led to their growing unpopularity. Soviet economic difficulties led Mikhail Gorbachev to institute liberal reforms that led to the collapse of the Communist rule first in Eastern Europe, then in the Soviet Union itself. The disappearance of the Soviet Union opened the way for independence in much of the former Soviet Empire. Russia itself has experienced social, economic, and political turmoil under presidents Boris Yeltsin and Vladimir Putin.

In the former Yugoslavia, the end of Communist rule led to dismemberment and civil war. In the 1990s, the NATO powers, led by the United States, intervened to halt the fighting and end a pattern of ethnic atrocities.

IMAGE KEY
for pages 794–795

a. A jazz record by Coleman Hawkins with an explicit civil rights message.

b. A Cuban missile site.

c. A huge euro symbol in a park in Frankfurt's banking district in Germany.

d. A teenager holds a Czech flag and a poster of president Vaclav Havel.

e. A piece of the Berlin Wall.

f. A construction worker building the Berlin Wall in 1961.

g. The European Union Headquarters in Brussels, Belgium.

h. Dr. Martin Luther King, Jr.

i. A toppled statue of Vladimir Lenin in the former Soviet Union.

j. A demonstration in Prague, Czechoslovakia.

REVIEW QUESTIONS

1. What were the causes of the Cold War? What was its effect on the foreign policies of the United States and the Soviet Union?

2. How did the outcome of World War II affect Europe's position in the world? What were the factors behind the movement toward European unification?

3. What were the most important developments in the domestic history of the United states in the last half of the 20th century?

4. What were the causes for the collapse of the Soviet Union? What problems has the collapse of Communist rule led to in Eastern Europe and elsewhere?

5. Why did the old Yugoslavia break apart and slide into civil war? How did the West respond to this crisis?

6. How did the American response to the attacks of September 11, 2001, affect relations with European allies? Why is the behavior of America's allies different now than it was during the Cold War?

KEY TERMS

Cold War (p. 796)
euro (p. 801)
**European Economic
   Community** (p. 801)

European Union (p. 801)
glasnost (p. 810)

Marshall Plan (p. 797)
perestroika (p. 810)

 For additional study resources for this chapter, go to:
www.prenhall.com/craig/chapter32

33

East Asia
The Recent Decades

CHAPTER HIGHLIGHTS

Japan The U.S.-led occupation after World War II established a democratic government and set Japan on the way to its remarkable postwar prosperity. By the twenty-first century, Japan had the second largest economy in the world. Politically, the conservative Liberal Democratic Party has remained dominant, despite occasional electoral losses. Socially Japan has remained stable with the world's highest longevity rate.

China Communist rule was established in 1949. Until his death in 1976, Mao Zedong remained in control of China. Mao broke with the Soviet Union in the 1950s and launched the disastrous Cultural Revolution in 1965. After his death, China opened its economy to free-market reforms. The result has been surging economic growth and rising prosperity. Politically, however, the Communist Party has blocked democratic reform, even using force in 1989 to crush prodemocratic demonstrations.

Taiwan The Nationalist Party set up a separate state in Taiwan under U.S. protection after their defeat in the Chinese civil war in 1949. Since then Taiwan has evolved into a prosperous democratic state. The Chinese government, however, insists that Taiwan is an integral part of China. The status of Taiwan could lead to conflict between the United States and China.

Korea The postwar occupation of Korea by the Soviets and the United States led to its division into the Communist state of North Korea and the pro-Western South Korea. This division survived the Korean War of 1950–1953. The prosperity of democratic South Korea contrasts with the poverty and hunger of North Korea. Although contacts between the two Koreas have increased, the North remains a closed society.

Vietnam From the end of World War II until the 1970s, Vietnam was almost continuously involved in war, first against the reimposition of French colonial rule, then against the United States and its South Vietnamese allies. North Vietnam's victory over the South in 1975 reunified the country, but Vietnam remains relatively poor, only slowly moving toward economic liberalization.

CHAPTER QUESTIONS

HOW DID the postwar occupation change Japan politically?

WHY DID Mao launch the Cultural Revolution?

HOW DO U.S. and Chinese policies toward Taiwan differ?

HOW DID South Korean and North Korean postwar developments differ?

HOW DOES the recent history of Vietnam illustrate the legacies of both Colonialism and the Cold War?

毛主席语录
QUOTATIONS FROM
CHAIRMAN
MAO TSE-TUNG

可口可乐
商標

CHAPTER OUTLINE

- Japan
- China
- Taiwan
- Korea
- Vietnam

The history of East Asia since the end of World War II can be divided into two phases (see Map 33–1). In the first phase, from 1945 to 1980, several East Asian nations became Communist but achieved only a small improvement in the conditions of their peoples. In stark contrast, the nations that used a mixture of state guidance and market-oriented economies made the region as a whole the most dynamic in the postwar world.

The second phase of postwar East Asian history began in the 1980s and continues to the present. During the 1980s, those nations that had prospered continued to grow. But during the 1990s, a recession rippled through East Asia and growth halted or slowed.

The most remarkable positive changes occurred in China, which, even while maintaining a Communist dictatorship, introduced many features of a market economy. The result was explosive growth and social change. Vietnam adopted a weaker version of the same policies. Only North Korea resisted the changes sweeping the rest of the Communist world, and as its entered the 21st century, its people suffered hunger and misery.

JAPAN

HOW DID the postwar occupation change Japan politically?

By early 1945, most Japanese were poor, hungry, and ill-clothed. Cities were burnt out, factories scarred by bombings; ships had been sunk, railways were dilapidated, and trucks and cars were scarce. On August 15, 1945, the emperor broadcast Japan's surrender to the Japanese people. They expected a harsh and vindictive occupation, but when they found it constructive, their receptivity to new democratic ideas and their repudiation of militarism led one Japanese writer to label the era "the second opening of Japan."

THE OCCUPATION

General Douglas MacArthur was the Supreme Commander for the Allied powers in Japan, and the occupation forces were mostly American. The chief concern of the first phase of the occupation was demilitarization and democratization. Civilians and soldiers abroad were returned to Japan and the military was demobilized. Wartime leaders were brought to trial for "crimes against humanity." Shinto was disestablished as the state religion, labor unions were encouraged, and the holding companies of **zaibatsu** combines were dissolved. Land reform expropriated landlord holdings and sold them to landless tenants at a fractional cost.

The new constitution, written by MacArthur's headquarters and passed into law by the Japanese Diet, fundamentally changed Japan's polity in five respects:

1. A British-style parliamentary state was established along with an American-style independent judiciary and a federal system of prefectures with elected governors.

2. Women were given the right to vote.

3. The rights to life, liberty, the pursuit of happiness, a free press, and free assembly were guaranteed.

4. Article 9, the no-war clause, stipulated, "The Japanese people forever renounce war as a sovereign right of the nation."

5. The constitution defined a new role for the emperor as "the symbol of the state deriving his position from the will of the people with whom resides sovereign power."

zaibatsu Groups of Japanese companies, or "trusts," that had a common ownership and dominated the economy of prewar Japan.

The Japanese people accepted the new constitution and embraced democracy with uncritical enthusiasm. To create a climate in which the new democracy

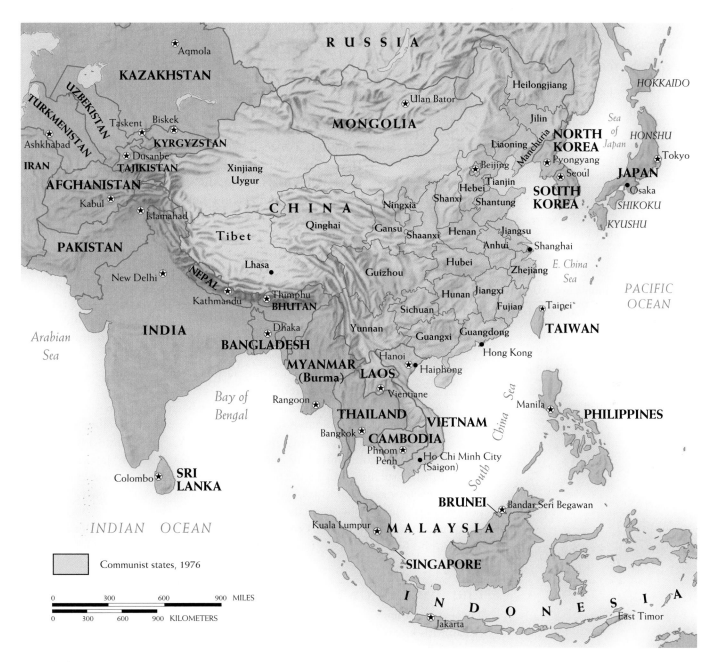

MAP 33–1
Contemporary Asia.

WHICH NATIONS in East Asia are Communist today?

could flourish, the occupation in its second phase turned to Japan's economic recovery. It dropped plans to deconcentrate big business further, encouraged the Japanese government to curb inflation, and cracked down on Communist unions. The United States also gave Japan $2 billion in economic aid.

The outbreak of the Korean War in 1950 diverted American military attention away from Japan, and the Japanese cabinet and Diet began to assume more responsibility for the country. When Japan regained its sovereignty in April 1952, the changeover was hardly noticeable in the daily life of the Japanese people. On the same day as the peace treaty, Japan signed a security treaty with the United

Japan Since 1945

1945	Japan surrenders
1946	Peace and security treaties
1948–1954	Yoshida ministries
1950–1953	Korean War
1955	Liberal and Democratic Parties merge
1955–1973	Double-digit economic growth
1972	Japan recognizes the People's Republic of China
1973–1989	Economic growth continues at slower pace
1991	Bubble bursts and recession begins
1991	Socialists lose Diet seats
1994–1996	Non-LDP coalitions govern; LDP-led coalitions reestablished
2001	Koizumi Junichir becomes prime minister
2003	Japan sends troops to Iraq

LDP Liberal Democratic Party. A conservative party that has dominated postwar Japanese politics.

States, which became the cornerstone of Japan's minimalist defense policy.

PARLIAMENTARY POLITICS

Japan's postwar politics can be divided into three periods. The first, from 1945 to 1955, was the continuation of prewar party politics as modified to fit the new political environment. Two conservative parties, the Liberals and the Democrats, and the Japanese Socialist Party emerged. For most of this first decade, the Liberals held power.

In the long second period from 1955 to 1993, the Liberal Democratic Party (**LDP**), which was formed by a merger of the two conservative parties, held power and the Japanese Socialist Party was the permanent opposition.

The LDP became identified as the party that was rebuilding Japan and maintaining Japan's security through close ties with the United States. Despite the cozy relationships that developed between the LDP and business, periodic scandals, and a widespread distrust of politicians, the Japanese people voted to keep it in power. Rule by a single party for such a long period provided an unusual continuity in government policies.

A third era of politics began with the 1993 election. The notable feature of this era was the decline and fall of the left. The end of the Cold War and the worldwide rejection of Marxism contributed to the demise of socialism in Japan, and the Communist Party also slumped. The collapse of the left inaugurated an era of multiparty conservative politics, but the LDP remains the largest party. Japanese politics were plagued by scandals and factional strife during the 1990s, but the major issue was the economy. Concern for the economy has strengthened opposition to the LDP and raised the posibility that a two-party system might emerge as Japan's future.

ECONOMIC GROWTH

The extraordinary story of the economic rise of East Asia after World War II began with Japan. Several factors explain this growth. An infrastructure of banking, marketing, and manufacturing skills had carried over from prewar Japan. The international situation was also favorable: oil was cheap, access to raw materials and export markets was easy, and American sponsorship gained Japan early entry into international financing organizations. A tradition of frugality created a rate of savings close to 20 percent, which helped reinvestment.

A revolution in education contributed as well. By the early 1980s, almost all middle-school graduates went on to high school, and a rising percentage went on to higher education. By the early 1980s, Japan was graduating more engineers than the United States. (The annual output of law schools in the United States equals the total number of lawyers in Japan.) This upgrading of human capital and channeling of its best minds into productive careers let Japan tap the huge backlog of technology that had developed in the United States during and after the war years. After "improvement engineering," Japan sold its products to the world.

Another factor was an abundance of high-quality, cheap labor provided by a postwar baby boom. Workers quickly moved from agriculture to industry, and labor organizations proved no bar to economic growth. (In 2005, only about one-fifth of the labor force belonged to unions.) The government also aided manufacturers with tariff protection, foreign exchange, and special depreciation allowances. Industries engaged in advanced technologies benefited from cheap loans, subsidies, and research products of government laboratories. Critics who spoke of "Japan Inc." as though Japan were a single gigantic corporation overstated the case, but government was more supportive of business than it was regulative.

By 1973, the Japanese economy had become "mature." Double-digit growth gave way to 4 percent growth. Smokestack industries declined while service industries, pharmaceuticals, specialty chemicals, scientific equipment, computers, and robots grew. Japan's trade began to generate huge surpluses. The surpluses were generated mainly by the appetite of world markets for Japanese products, but they were also a result of protectionist policies that the United States and Europe insisted be abolished.

Even slower growth, or no growth at all, characterized the 1990s. Japanese had bid up the price of corporate shares and land to unrealistic levels, and in 1991, the "bubble" burst. As banks and individuals retrenched, the economy slowed. Unemployment rose from the usual 1.5 to more than 5 or 6 percent, and hidden unemployment was higher. Newspapers accused the government of inaction, but the scale of the problem was enormous. The Japanese were unwilling to shoulder new taxes and preferred instead to increase their savings. No political party dared propose new taxes or a bailout of the banks.

Some saw the recession as a necessary correction of speculative excesses and believed that Japan could export its way out of recession. While domestic consumption sank, exports rose, and Japan's favorable balance of trade grew. The Japanese excelled in quality and efficiency of production, and in 2002 an export-led recovery began. It was linked with the soaring Chinese economy.

At the start of the third millennium, Japan's economy was second only to the United States—slightly larger than the economies of the rest of Asia combined. Japan has achieved a European level of affluence through the peaceful development of human resources in a free society (see Figure 33–1).

SOCIETY AND CULTURE

The triple engines of change in postwar Japan were occupation reforms, economic growth, and a rapid expansion of higher education. Together, they produced deep cultural strains and social dislocations. In 1945, almost half of the population lived in villages rooted in the past; half a century later most Japanese lived in cities, and a tiny portion of the population raised the food that fed the rest. In 1945, arranged marriages and three-generation extended families were common. Now, nuclear families and "love matches" are the rule. Consumerism increased, and the status of women rose. Reforms imposed during the American occupation gave women the right to vote, legal equality, and equal inheritance rights. As women were admitted to prestigious universities and embarked on careers, the average age of marriage rose and more wives worked outside the home. Divorce rates also tripled. Prospering in the new Japan

Nissan Motors Assembly Line. An almost completely automated assembly line at Nissan Motors' Zama factory is shown here. The high cost of labor in Japan makes such robot-intensive production economical.

Reuters/Susumu Takahashi/Archive Photos.

Figure 33-1

A Comparison of Japan with Germany and France in the Year 2005 (IMF Estimates)		
	GDP (in billions)	Population (in millions)	Per Capita GDP
Germany	$2,769	83	$33,575
France	$2,052	64	$33,111
Total	$4,821	147	$32,796 (average)
Japan	$4,759	127	$37,241

depended on education, and a rigorous system of examinations determined admission at every level. The enormous prewar gap between the tiny educated elite and the masses disappeared as 90 percent of Japanese came to see themselves as middle class. This fostered democracy and a new respect for personal autonomy helped diminish some traditional ethnic prejudices. The highly disciplined lifestyle encouraged by the educational system and corporate culture, however, created a phenomenon called *karoshi*, or death from overwork.

The most serious social problem facing Japan today is the aging of its population. By 2010, there will be fewer than two workers for every retired person. A recurring question is how the old will be supported and how they will vote in elections. All developed nations have experienced a comparable shift in demographics, but the imbalance is particularly severe in Germany, Italy, and Japan. Japan is crowded, and some see its current low birthrate as an opportunity to reduce population. Many illegal immigrants, however, come from other parts of Asia to take lowly jobs that the Japanese despise.

The cultural strains produced by Japan's rapid transformation have dislocated some people and created followings for new religions. One aberrant apocalyptic cult released nerve gas in a Tokyo subway in 1995. Yet traditions of lifetime employment, a low crime rate, stable families, and a flourishing artistic culture (which excels at Western as well as traditional Japanese arts) testify to Japan's remarkable success at recovering from the devastation of World War II.

JAPAN AND THE WORLD

Japan has three sets of critical international relationships. The first is with the world. On this front it defends the free trade on which its economy depends, but also excels as a donor of foreign aid. Its second relationship is with its neighbors in East Asia. For reasons of history and proximity, it is particularly sensitive to developments in China, Korea, the Russian Far East, and Taiwan. China's growing military strength is a concern. Japan's third critical relationship is with the United States. The two nations are major trading partners, and the security treaty concluded between them in 1952 is the cornerstone of Japan's defense planning. Japan, however, feels increasingly vulnerable in light of the nuclear arsenals of its neighbors, and should its trust in the U.S. "nuclear umbrella" waver, it would quickly become a nuclear power.

WHY DID Mao launch the Cultural Revolution?

CHINA

The story of China after 1949 is rooted in theories about economics and population. Marx rejected the Malthusian hypothesis that population growth tends to outstrip food production as a myth of capitalist societies, and Mao Zedong agreed and closed down the population studies institutes at China's universities. From 1949 until 1981, China's population increased from 550 million to nearly 1 billion. Growth in the Chinese economy was eaten up by all the new mouths, and in 1981 China adopted a policy of one child per family. Thereafter the increase slowed, but population exceeded 1.3 billion in 2005.

SOVIET PERIOD (1950–1960)

Civil war in China ended in 1949 as the last troops of Chiang Kai-shek (Jiang Jieshi) fled to Taiwan. The People's Republic of China was proclaimed in October. In the decade that followed, the Soviet model was adopted for the government, the army, the economy, and higher education.

Areas inhabited by Tibetans, Uighur Turks, Mongols, and other minorities were occupied by the Chinese army and settled by Chinese immigrants. Political consolidation then followed. The Communist Party held the key levers of power in the government, army, and security forces. Mao was chairman of the party and head of state. He ruled through the Politboro and a system of regional, provincial, and district committees with party cells in every village, factory, school, and government office. Party members were exhorted to enforce the local enactment of government policies. Economic reconstruction was attempted on a massive scale, with the help of the Soviet Union, which sent financial aid as well as engineers and planners.

Rural society underwent two fundamental changes: land redistribution and then collectivization. In the early 1950s, hundreds of thousands of landlords were killed and their holdings redistributed to the landless. Subsequently, all lands were seized by the state and collectivized.

During the early 1950s, intellectuals and universities also became a target for "thought reform," brainwashing. This involved study and indoctrination in Marxism, group pressures to produce an atmosphere of insecurity and fear, followed by confession, repentance, and reacceptance by society. The indoctrination was intended to strengthen party control and mobilize human energies on behalf of the state.

By the late 1950s, Mao was disappointed with the results of collectivization, and in 1958, he resorted to mass mobilization to unleash the productive energies of the people, a policy called the **Great Leap Forward**. Campaigns were organized to accomplish vast projects, and village-based collective farms gave way to communes of 30,000 persons or more. The results were disastrous. Between 1958 and 1962, 20 to 30 million Chinese reportedly starved to death. Policies were modified, but agricultural production continued to fall, plagued by the ills of low incentives and collective responsibility.

Sino-Soviet relations also deteriorated. Disputes arose over borders. China was dissatisfied with Soviet aid. The Soviet Union condemned the Great Leap Forward as "leftist fanaticism" and resented Mao's view of himself, after Stalin's death, as the foremost exponent of world communism. In 1960, the Soviet Union halted economic aid and withdrew its engineers from China. Each country deployed about a million troops along their mutual border. The Sino-Soviet split was arguably the single most important development in postwar international politics.

The years between 1960 and 1965 saw conflicting trends. The failure of the Great Leap Forward led some Chinese leaders to turn away from Mao's reckless radicalism toward more moderate policies. Mao remained head of the party but had to give up his post as head of state. Yet even as the government moved toward realistic goals and stable bureaucratic management, a new mass movement was begun to promote ideological indoctrination.

THE GREAT PROLETARIAN CULTURAL REVOLUTION (1965–1976)

In 1965, Mao again emerged to dominate Chinese politics. He feared that the Chinese revolution—his revolution—would end up as a Soviet-style bureaucratic

China Since 1949	
1949	Communist victory; People's Republic of China
1950	Sino-Soviet alliance; China invaded Tibet
1953	First Five-Year Plan
1958	Great Leap Forward
1960–1963	Sino-Soviet split
1965–1976	Cultural Revolution
1972	Nixon visit to Beijing
1976	Mao Zedong dies
1978	Deng Xiaoping in power
1989	Tienanmen Square incident
1997	Deng Xiaoping dies
1998–2001	China's economy grows while rest of Asia in recession

Great Leap Forward Mao's disastrous attempt to modernize the Chinese economy in 1958.

Cultural Revolution. Participants in this march hold a banner of Mao Zedong.
Archive Photos.

Cultural Revolution Movement launched by Mao between 1965 and 1976 against the Soviet-style bureaucracy that had taken hold in China. It involved widespread disorder and violence.

communism run for the benefit of officials. So he called for a new revolution to create a truly egalitarian culture.

Obtaining army support, Mao urged students and teenagers to form bands of Red Guards to carry out a new **Cultural Revolution**. Mao's sayings, the "Little Red Book," assumed the status of scripture. Universities were shut down as student factions fought. Teachers were beaten, imprisoned, and humiliated. Books were burned and art destroyed. Homes were ransacked for foreign books and Chinese who had studied abroad were persecuted. Red Guards beat to death those viewed as reactionaries. High officials were purged. Chinese today recall these events as a species of mass hysteria that defies understanding.

Eventually Mao tired of the violence and near anarchy. In 1968 and 1969 he called in the army. Millions of students and intellectuals were sent to the countryside to work on farms. Worsening relations with the Soviet Union also made China's leaders desire greater stability at home. When President Richard Nixon proposed a renewal of ties, China responded. Nixon visited Beijing in 1972, opening a new era of diplomatic relations.

The second phase of the Cultural Revolution between 1969 and 1976 was moderate only in comparison with what had gone before. On farms and in factories, ideology was still substituted for economic incentives. Universities reopened, but students were admitted by class background, not examination. In 1971, the so-called Gang of Four, which included Mao's wife and was abetted by the aging Mao, came to power.

CHINA AFTER MAO

Political Developments Mao's death in 1976 brought immediate changes. The Gang of Four and their radical supporters were arrested. In their place, Deng Xiaoping (1904–1997) emerged as the dominant figure in Chinese politics. Deng ousted his enemies, rehabilitated those purged during the Cultural Revolution, and put his supporters in power. After the lunacy of the Cultural Revolution, a "normal" Communist Party dictatorship was a relief. The people could now enjoy a measure of security and material improvement. There continued, however, a tension between the determination of the ruling party to maintain its grip on power and its desire to obtain the benefits of liberalization.

Universities returned to normal in 1977. Entrance examinations were reinstituted, purged teachers returned to their classrooms, and scholars were sent to study in Japan and the West. Students began to demand still greater freedoms with the hope that they would lead to political democracy.

The new spirit came to a head in April and May of 1989, when hundreds of thousands of students, workers, and people from all walks of life demonstrated for democracy in Tienanmen Square in Beijing and in dozens of other cities. The government sent in tanks and troops. Hundreds of students were killed, and leaders who did not escape abroad were jailed. The event defined the political climate in China for the decade that followed: freedom was allowed in most areas of life, but no challenge to Communist Party rule was tolerated.

Economic Growth   In the economic sphere, China's leaders repudiated the policies of Mao. Deng's great achievement in the years after 1978 was to demonstrate in China the superiority of market incentives to central planning.

In China's villages, as the farm household became the basic unit of production, grain production rose. But when farmers living near cities found it more profitable to abandon grains in favor of speciality crops, the government worried about growing dependence on imported grains. In 2003, it established subsidies to promote grain production.

State-operated enterprises, which often ran at a loss and employed twice the labor needed to run them efficiently, were a constant drain on China's state-owned banks. As the free market sector grew faster, their share of production declined. Finally, the government announced that "state ownership" would give way to "public ownership." The costs of such privatization would be high—defaulted loans, bankruptcies, unemployed workers, and a sudden rise in pensioners, but the drain on the state budget would end. The contribution of state-owned enterprises to total industrial production declined from 40 to 31 percent from 1997 to 2003, but much of this was due to rapid growth in the market sector of the economy.

The main driver of the new economy was the free market sector. After 1980, the Chinese economy grew faster than any other Asian economy. Exports skyrocketed. New enterprises surged in special economic zones along the coasts, and the tide of enterprise swept inland. Yet in the hinterlands large regions lagged behind. To achieve growth, the government was willing to tolerate personal and regional inequities.

The factors that fueled this growth were clear: China used tariffs to shield its markets while making use of cheap labor to flood foreign markets with goods and build up its currency reserves–which in 2003 were second only to those of Japan. China joined the World Trade Organization in 2001; since then its protectionism has become less blatant.

Social Change   During the Mao years, farmers had been tied to their collective or village. Cities were closed to those without residence permits. City dwellers were members of "units" that provided their members with jobs, housing, food, child care, medical services, and pensions. Party cadres exercised near total control over the unit's members. Block organizations reported any infractions of "socialist morality" to the authorities.

Under Deng, controls were loosened. The "unit" diminished in importance as food became widely available in free markets and apartments were sold to their inhabitants on easy terms. As workers with higher salaries began to provide for their own needs, life became freer and more enjoyable. The market economy placed a premium on individual decisions and initiatives.

The new prosperity and changing mores became increasingly evident. By the 1990s, Chinese designers were holding fashion shows in Shanghai and

Goddess of Democracy and Freedom.
Student activists construct a "Goddess of Democracy and Freedom," taking the Statue of Liberty as their model. The goddess was in place in Tienanmen Square shortly before tanks drove students from the square in June 1989.

Reuters/Ed Nachtrieb/Archive Photos.

 29.4
Deng Xiaoping, A Market Economy for Socialist Goals

Shanghai Street Scene. Bikers and cars move in separate lanes. New highrise buildings are in the background. Note the three-wheel bike transporting lumber in the foreground.

Jeff Greenberg/PhotoEdit.

Beijing. Young people associated freely. The "household treasures" of the 1960s, radios and bicycles, gave way to stoves and refrigerators, washing machines and color televisions. Motorbikes and privately owned cars competed in crowded streets with the flow of bicycles. Private restaurants opened, and travel for pleasure became commonplace. The awareness of most Chinese that their living standard has improved sharply over the past two decades shapes their attitudes.

But the new wealth was unevenly distributed. The more successful entrepreneurs bought houses, cars, microwaves, computers, and cell phones. They traveled abroad and sent their children to private schools. But many barely scraped by, and in the hinterlands, poverty and hardship remained the rule.

China and the World   From the 1950s to the 1970s, China isolated itself from the rest of the world. The Sino-Soviet split defined its relations to the north, and the Cold War defined its relations with Japan, South Korea, Taiwan and the United States. It aided North Vietnam during America's Vietnam War, but then briefly invaded Vietnam. During the 1980s, trade ties with the non-Communist world led China to look outward and adopt more moderate policies. In the 1990s, foreign relations improved across the board. Relations with Russia became amicable, and China welcomed investment from Taiwan and South Korea. China also worked to improve ties with Southeast Asia.

China's relations with the United States were difficult. U.S. military alliances with Japan, South Korea, Taiwan, and the non-Communist nations of Southeast Asia were the main countervailing force to Chinese hegemony in the region, and China resented the U.S. presence in what it considered its sphere of influence. A new relationship began to be forged when President Nixon visited China in 1972. In 1979, the United States extended diplomatic recognition to China.

From the 1980s, trade with the United States was vital to China's economic growth, and it became more so during the 1990s as the rest of East Asia slipped into recession. Imbalance of trade between the two nations displeases the United States, as does Chinese piracy of U.S. movies, computer software, and CDs. The United States is also critical of Chinese human rights abuses, nuclear testing, and arms sales. Nonetheless, the United States hopes that a deeper Chinese engagement with the United States and the rest of the world will lead to better relations. A generational change in Chinese leadership took place when Hu Jintao became premier in 2003, but apart from a slightly more open style of governance, it is not clear what the change will mean (see "U.S. Foreign Policy: A Chinese Dissident's View").

HOW DO U.S. and Chinese policies toward Taiwan differ?

TAIWAN

Taiwan is a mountainous island less than a hundred miles off the coast of central China. A little larger than Massachusetts, it has a population of 22 million. Originally a remote and backward part of the Qing Empire, Taiwan became a Japanese colony in 1895. The Japanese colonial government suppressed opium and bandits, eradicated epidemic diseases, built roads and railroads, reformed the land system, and improved agriculture. It also introduced mass education and light industries.

HISTORY'S VOICES

U.S. FOREIGN POLICY: A CHINESE DISSIDENT'S VIEW

Wei Jingsheng, a Chinese advocate of democratic rights, was deported to the United States in late 1997. A year later, in The New York Times *op-ed page essay, he criticized U.S. policy as pandering to Chinese tyranny.*

SHOULD U.S. foreign policy be used to promote human rights even in poor countries with cultural traditions different from the West? Or should the United States avoid interference in the domestic politics of other nations and aim primarily at furthering American economic and security goals? What can foreign policy achieve? Where should the balance be struck?

CHINA'S DIVERSIONARY TACTICS

One year ago, after 18 years in a Chinese prison, I was "released" and sent here. A Chinese official said that if I ever set foot in China again, I would immediately be returned to prison. . . .

The State Department, in a report last January, used my forced exile as evidence that China was taking "positive steps in human rights" and that "Chinese society continued to become more open." These "positive steps" led the United States and its allies to oppose condemnation of China at a meeting of the United Nations Commission on Human Rights in April. In the months that followed, President Clinton and other Western leaders traveled to China, trumpeting increased economic ties and muting criticism on human rights.

Thus, without fear of sanction, the Chinese Government intensified its repression in 1998. Once the leaders achieved their diplomatic victories, they turned to their main objective: the preservation of tyrannical power. This year, about 70 people are known to have been arrested. . . .

Li Peng, the speaker of the National People's Party Congress, declared recently, "If an organization's purpose is to promote a multiparty system in China and to negate the leadership prerogatives of the Chinese Communist Party, then it will not be permitted to exist."

This statement clearly shows that the Communist Party's primary objective is to sustain its tyranny, and to do so it must deny the people basic rights and freedoms. We must measure the leaders' progress on human rights not by the "release" of individuals but by the people's ability to speak, worship and assemble without official interference and persecution.

Source: Wei Jingsheng, *The New York Times*, 24 December 1998. Copyright © 1998 by *The New York Times*. Reprinted by permission.

Anticolonial feelings rose slowly, but the Taiwanese were happy to see the Japanese leave in 1945. Kuomintang (Guomindang) officials, however, looted the economy and ruled harshly. By the time Jiang Jieshi and 2 million other military and civilian mainlanders fled to the island in 1949, its economy and society were in disarray. Taiwanese hated their new rulers and even compared them unfavorably to the Japanese.

In the mid-1950s, order was restored, and rapid economic growth followed. By the late 1990s, Taiwan had the healthiest economy in recession-ridden Asia.

Taiwan's politics was authoritarian until Jiang Jieshi died in 1976. Taiwan then moved toward representative government. In 1987, martial law ended and opposition parties were permitted.

In 1996, Li Denghui, a native Taiwanese, was elected president in what was, as he put it, "the first free election in 5,000 years of Chinese history."

Since 1949, the Communist government in Beijing had claimed that Taiwan was a province of China controlled by a "bandit" government. It did not rule out taking Taiwan by force and refused diplomatic relations with any nation maintaining such ties with Taiwan. From the outbreak of the Korean War in 1950 until 1979, Taiwan was a protégé of the United States. In 1979, however, the United States broke off relations with Taipei and recognized Beijing as the sole government of a China that included Taiwan. But the United States continued to trade with Taiwan and to sell it arms, and curiously, it was during the years of diplomatic limbo after the 1979 break that Taiwan's economy grew and its society became democratic.

Both China and the United States are, at the start of the 21st century, apprehensive about Taiwan. China fears that a prosperous, democratic Taiwan would have legitimacy in the eyes of the world and no wish to rejoin the mainland. The United States fears that an increasingly powerful China might try to use military force to retake the island. Many in the U.S. Congress believe that the United States could not stand by and allow that to happen.

KOREA

Korea was annexed by Japan in 1910. The imposition of colonialism on a people with a high indigenous culture and a strong sense of national identity engendered a powerful anticolonial nationalism. After World War II, Korea was divided into a Communist north and a non-Communist south. When a civil war ensued, the United States entered the conflict to stem the spread of communism.

KOREA AS A JAPANESE COLONY

Japan introduced measures designed to make Korea into a model colony. A land survey and land tax reform clarified land ownership. Infectious diseases dropped, and the population grew from 14 million in 1910 to 24 million in 1940. Attendance at schools became widespread. New money was issued and banks established. A huge investment was made in roads, railways, telegraph lines, hydroelectric power, nitrogenous fertilizer plants, and mining. Koreans who studied at Japanese universities brought new knowledge back to Korea. By the 1930s a modern culture was forming in Korea's cities.

Being a Japanese colony was a hard road to modernity, for the colonial government was authoritarian. The government's goal was to make Korea a subordinate part of imperial Japan. Any benefits to the Koreans were incidental. Education was given in Japanese. In government, banking, or industry, Koreans were relegated to the lower echelons. The colonial regime suppressed all nationalist movements and political opposition. The police were brutal. Koreans were pressured to adopt Japanese names, drafted to fight in Japan's wars, and sent to labor in Japan. "Comfort women" were recruited, sometimes forcibly, to service Japanese troops. Only in recent years has this bitter colonial legacy begun to subside.

NORTH AND SOUTH

With Japan's defeat in 1945, U.S. forces occupied Korea south of the 38th parallel and Soviet troops occupied the north. Two separate states developed. In the south, the United States settled for the anti-Communist government of Syngman Rhee (1875–1965), a long-term nationalist leader whose party won the May 1948 election. Many of Rhee's officials and officers had served the Japanese. His government was strongly supported by conservative Koreans and those who had fled the north.

In the north, the Russians established a Communist government under Kim Il-Sung (1912–1994) in 1948 and withdrew its troops from North Korea—now the

---

HOW DID South Korean and North Korean postwar developments differ?

QUICK REVIEW

Two Koreas
- After defeat of Japan in 1945, U.S. troops occupied the south and Soviet troops occupied the north
- U.S. supported government of Syngman Rhee in south
- Soviets supported government of Kim Il-Sung in north

26.6
General Douglas MacArthur, Report to Congress, April 19, 1951: "Old Soldiers Never Die"

Democratic People's Republic of Korea. During 1949 and early 1950, the United States also withdrew most of its troops from the south, part of a general disengagement from continental Asia that followed the Communist victory in China.

CIVIL WAR AND U.S. INVOLVEMENT

On June 25, 1950, North Korea invaded the south. The North Korean leader had received Stalin's permission for the invasion and a promise from Mao to send Chinese troops if the United States entered the war. His plan was for a quick victory, but the United States saw the invasion as an act of aggression by world communism. It rushed troops from Japan to South Korea and obtained U.N. backing.

During the first months of the war, the unprepared American and South Korean forces were driven southward into a small area around Pusan (see Map 33–2). But then, amphibious units landed at Inchon and drove deep into North Korea. American policy shifted from containment of communism to a roll-back. China then sent in "volunteers" to rescue the beleaguered North Koreans and pushed the overextended U.N. forces back to a line close to the 38th parallel. The war ended with an armistice on July 27, 1953. Thereafter, the two Koreas maintained a hostile peace. The 142,000 American casualties made the war the fourth largest in U.S. history.

RECENT DEVELOPMENTS

North Korea remained a closed, authoritarian state with a planned economy. It stressed heavy industry, organized its farmers in collectives, and controlled education and the media. Shortages of food, clothing, and other necessities were chronic. The cult of personality surrounding "the great leader" Kim Il-Sung developed beyond that of even Stalin or Mao. His son, "the beloved leader" Kim Jong-il (b. 1942), succeeded his father in 1994—the only hereditary succession in a Communist state.

In South Korea, Rhee was forced to retire in 1960. There followed 27 years of rule by two generals, Park Chung-hee and Chun Doo-hwan. Their rule was semi-authoritarian: Opposition parties were legal and active but their leaders were often jailed. Park and Chun promoted economic growth. They supported business and expanded higher education, emphasizing science and technology. Labor was disciplined, hardworking, and cheap. The United States gave large amounts of aid and provided an open market for Korean exports. These factors produced double-digit growth. By the 1990s, South Korea had moved into the ranks of developed nations, and by 2005 it had become the world's 11th largest economy.

Industrialization and urbanization produced an affluent and educated middle class that resented authoritarian rule. In 1987, Chun's term ended, and a free election was held. Despite the fact that Chun's hand-picked successor, Roh Tae-woo, became president, most Koreans saw the election as an opening to democracy. This was confirmed four years later when Kim Young-sam, a moderate politician, was elected president, purged the generals who had supported Park and Chun, and launched investigations into his predecessors' finances. In 1995, Chun and Roh were sent to prison, but later released. Kim Dae-jung was elected

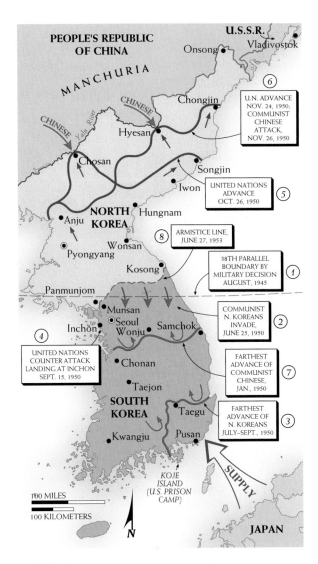

MAP 33–2
Korea, 1950–1953. This map indicates the major developments in the bitter three-year struggle that followed the North Korean invasion of South Korea in 1950.

WHY DID the Korean War end in stalemate?

The Two Kims. South Korean President Kim Dae-jung traveled to Pyongyong in June 2000 to promote his "sunshine policy." As he departs he hugs Kim Jong-il, the North Korean leader. But when the North Korean leader failed to respond with a visit to Seoul or with an easing of tensions, sunshine turned to rain, and Kim Dae-jung's popularity sagged.

Koren Pool/Yonhap/AP/Wide World Photos.

HOW DOES the recent history of Vietnam illustrate the legacies of both Colonialism and the Cold War?

27.7
Views of a Viet Cong Official
27.8
An American Prisoner of War

Viet Minh Communist-dominated popular front organization formed by Ho Chi Minh to establish an independent Vietnamese republic.

president in 1997, the first successful opposition candidate. He took office with high hopes but encountered insurmountable difficulties. As the economy sagged, the public became unsettled. Kim adoped a "sunshine policy" of openness, reconciliation, and material aid toward North Korea, an initiative that won him a Nobel Peace Prize in 1998. When North Korea failed to reciprocate, however, Kim's popularity declined.

In 2002, another opposition politician, Roh Moohyun, became president. In March 2004, the conservative majority party in the National Assembly voted to impeach him, but the public showed its disapproval in the April elections by giving Roh's party a majority of the assembly's seats. Returned to office, Roh was critical of the United States and open to closer relations with China and North Korea.

Since the Korean War, South Korea had been allied with the United States, which guaranteed its defense. North Korea was backed by the Soviet Union and China. But after the collapse of the Soviet Union, Russia lost interest in its ally, and China was drawn closer to South Korea for economic reasons.

North Korea, increasingly isolated, has a poor record. Its economy is in shambles, and its government has engaged in assassinations, conterfeiting, drug smuggling, and kidnapping. A Pakistan connection has enabled it to begin to develop nuclear weapons. China, Japan, South Korea, and the United States have tried to persuade North Korea to renounce nuclear arms, but as of 2004, the futures of negotiations and the North Korean state were unclear.

VIETNAM

THE COLONIAL BACKDROP

The Nguyen dynasty that reunited Vietnam in 1802 proved no match for France. France completed its conquest of Vietnam and Cambodia by 1883 and added Laos in 1893.

In many ways, Indochina was a classic case of colonialism: people of one race and culture, for the sake of economic benefits and national glory, controlling and exploiting a people of another race and culture in a far-off land. To obtain access to the country's natural resources, the French built harbors, roads, and a railway. They established rubber and tea plantations, introduced modern mining technology to extract coal, and built breweries, rice and paper mills, and glass and cement factories. Native workers were paid low wages. In the south, 3 percent of landowners owned 45 percent of the land and received 60 percent of the crop. Rice consumption by peasants declined. More than 80 percent of the population was illiterate.

Under the French, only clandestine opposition parties survived. The most skilled organizer of such parties was Ho Chi Minh (1892–1969), who founded the Indochinese Communist Party in 1930. Shortly before the outbreak of the Pacific War, the Japanese occupied Vietnam. Ho, who in 1941 had formed the **Viet Minh** (League for the Independence of Vietnam) as a popular front organization to resist the Japanese, proclaimed the Democratic Republic of Vietnam in 1945. Since then, the history of Vietnam can be seen in terms of three cycles of war followed by two decades of peace.

THE ANTICOLONIAL WAR

The first war lasted from 1946 to 1954. On one side was the Viet Minh, led by Ho. It was controlled by Communists but also included representatives of nationalist parties. On the other side were the French and their conservative Vietnamese allies. The French lost a major battle at Dien Bien Phu in 1954 and departed in defeat.

A conference at Geneva divided the country into a Communist north and a non-Communist south. In the south, Ngo Dinh Diem, a non-Communist nationalist, established the Republic of Vietnam.

THE VIETNAM WAR

The second cycle of war was from 1959 to 1975 and involved the United States. During the 1940s, the United States, which opposed colonialism, urged the French to reach an accommodation with Ho Chi Minh. But after the rise of Communist China, the United States came to see French actions in Vietnam as an attempt to stem the tide of communism. When the French withdrew, it supported Diem.

Fighting began with guerrilla warfare in the south and eventually became a full-scale war between the north and the south (see Map 33–3). The north received material aid from the Soviet Union and China. The south was supported by the United States, whose forces increased to more than half a million in 1969. Despite such massive assistance, South Vietnam—and the United States—lost the war. In January 1973, a ceasefire was arranged in Paris, and two months later the last U.S. troops left. Fighting then broke out anew between north and south; the South Vietnamese forces collapsed in 1975, and the country was reunited under the Hanoi government in the north. Saigon was renamed Ho Chi Minh City. Thousands of South Vietnamese were sent to labor camps or fled their homeland.

Many explanations have been offered for the loss of the war: South Vietnam was ethnically and religiously diverse and difficult to govern; its governments were often corrupt and enjoyed minimal support from their people; some Vietnamese viewed the United States, like France, as a colonial occupier; South Vietnam's armies did not fight as well as their opponents; and the jungle terrain of Vietnam blunted the technological edge of the American forces.

WAR WITH CAMBODIA

Vietnam's third cycle of war was with its neighbor, Cambodia. Pol Pot (1926–1998) and the Communist **Khmer Rouge** ("Red Cambodia") had come to power in 1975. His government evacuated cities and towns, abolished money and trade, banned Buddhism, and killed an estimated 1 million people, roughly 15 percent of the total population.

Clashes occurred between Khmer Rouge troops and Vietnamese troops along their common border. Historically, Vietnam was Cambodia's traditional enemy, as China was Vietnam's. In 1978, Vietnam occupied much of Cambodia, and the next year, Vietnam set up a puppet government. Most Cambodians

MAP EXPLORATION

Interactive map: To explore this map further, go to
http://www.prenhall.com/craig/map33.3

MAP 33–3

Vietnam and its Southeast Asian Neighbors. The map identifies important locations associated with the war in Vietnam.

WHICH NEIGHBORING countries were most affected by the Vietnam War?

Khmer Rouge Meaning "Red Cambodia." Radical Communist movement that ruled Cambodia from 1975 to 1978.

Genocide. A worker cleans a skull excavated from a mass grave in Cambodia. The Khmer Rouge, under Pol Pot, murdered about one-sixth of the Cambodian population. Doctors, teachers, and other educated people were especially targeted.

AP Wide World Photos.

accepted Vietnamese rule, for they feared Pol Pot more than they hated Vietnam. But Cambodia failed to completely suppress Pol Pot's guerilla forces.

In its international relations, the unified Vietnam of 1975 became an ally of the Soviet Union. Relations with China, never good, worsened. In 1979, China invaded four northern provinces. Vietnamese troops repelled the invaders, but losses were heavy on both sides. Border shellings and attacks continued for years thereafter.

RECENT DEVELOPMENTS

The collapse of the Soviet Union destroyed Vietnam's primary international relationship. Vietnam's leaders also became aware that victories in wars were hollow so long as their people remained destitute.

In 1989, Vietnam withdrew from its costly occupation of Cambodia. A United Nations-sponsored government representing contending Cambodian factions took charge. In 1997, a pro-Vietnamese Communist leader, Hun Sen, staged a coup and took over. His position was strengthened when Pol Pot died in 1998 and the Khmer Rouge collapsed.

By the mid-1990s, Vietnam's relations with China had improved. In 1995, Vietnam joined ASEAN (Association of Southeast Asian Nations), reestablished diplomatic relations with the United States, and moved toward "normal" relations with the rest of the world.

At home, the Communist Party-dominated government monopolized political power, controlled the army, police, and media, and supported a large sector of state-run industries. But it also encouraged the growth of a market economy, and the production of consumer goods grew. Between 1991 and 1996, the economy achieved an average growth of more than 8 percent and received more offers of foreign investment than it could absorb. By 1996, shops in Vietnam were full of food and goods, when only 10 years earlier there had been famine in some areas. Much of the credit for this belongs to the liberal, pluralistic, cosmopolitan south.

But all was not rosy. The economy grew, but so did population. With 82 million people, Vietnam is one of the world's most densely populated nations. A high percentage of labor was agricultural, and in the countryside barter was not uncommon. The gap in the standard of living between urban and rural Vietnamese also increased. Foreign investors were drawn to Vietnam by cheap labor but were put off by the shortages, delays, red tape, and financial bottlenecks they encountered.

SUMMARY

Japan   The U.S.-led occupation after World War II established a democratic government and set Japan on the way to its remarkable postwar prosperity. By the 21st century, Japan had the second largest economy in the world. Socially, Japan has remained stable and healthy with the world's highest longevity rate.

China Communist rule was established in 1949. Until his death in 1976, Mao Zedong remained in control of China. Mao broke with the Soviet Union in the 1950s and launched the disastrous Cultural Revolution in 1965. After his death, China opened its economy to free-market reforms. The result has been surging economic growth and rising prosperity. Politically, however, the Communist Party has blocked democratic reform, even using force in 1989 to crush pro-democratic demonstrations.

Taiwan The Nationalist Chinese set up a separate state in Taiwan under U.S. protection after their defeat in the Chinese civil war in 1949. Since then Taiwan has evolved into a prosperous democratic state. The Chinese government, however, insists that Taiwan is an integral part of China. The future of Taiwan could lead to conflict between the United States and China.

Korea The postwar occupation of Korea by the Soviets and the United States led to its division into the Communist state of North Korea and the pro-Western South Korea. This division survived the Korean War of 1950–1953. The prosperity of democratic South Korea contrasts with the poverty and hunger of North Korea. Although contacts between the two Koreas have increased, the North remains suspicious and largely closed to the world.

Vietnam From the end of World War II until the 1970s, Vietnam was almost continuously involved in war, first against the reimposition of French colonial rule, then against the United States and its South Vietnamese allies. North Vietnam's victory over South Vietnam in 1975 reunified the country, but Vietnam remains poor and the communist government has resisted political or economic liberalization.

IMAGE KEY
for pages 818–819

a. Cover of a Japanese comic book.
b. A highway interchange and bridge over the Huangpu River in Shanghai, China.
c. A North Korean national meeting to commemorate the 91st birthday of late-president Kim Il-Sung.
d. South Korean president Kim Dae-jung, right, and North Korean leader Kim Jong II.
e. Mao Zedong's little red book.
f. A prototype of a bottle for selling Coca-Cola in China.
g. An American-built F-14 Tomcat.
h. Young Chinese children march in the streets while carrying red banners during the Cultural Revolution.

REVIEW QUESTIONS

1. Is postwar Japan better understood in terms of a return to the liberalism of the 1920s, or as a fresh start based on occupation reforms? Why did the occupation of Japan go so smoothly and the recent American occupation of Iraq so poorly?

2. Is China after 1949 better understood as an outgrowth of its earlier history or in the context of a comparison with the Soviet Union and other Communist states?

3. What background factors shaped Korea and Vietnam in the period after World War II? How did the Cold War affect these countries?

KEY TERMS

Cultural Revolution (p. 826)   **Khmer Rouge** (p. 833)   **Viet Minh** (p. 832)
Great Leap Forward (p. 825)   **LDP** (p. 822)   *zaibatsu* (p. 820)

 For additional study resources for this chapter, go to:
www.prenhall.com/craig/chapter33

34 Postcolonialism and Beyond: Latin America, Africa, Asia, and the Middle East

CHAPTER HIGHLIGHTS

The Postcolonial World   Since 1945 the European colonial empires have disappeared from Africa and Asia and have been replaced by a multitude of independent states. These states have had to adjust their political and economic relations first to one or other of the superpowers during the Cold War and then, since the disappearance of the Soviet Union, to the West.

Latin America   Most Latin American countries remain politically and economically dependent on the United States. Except in Cuba, no revolutionary movement has been able to overturn the traditional structure of Latin American society. Despite social and economic problems, Argentina and Brazil have managed to move from military rule to stable, democratic, civilian government.

Africa   Independent Africa has faced severe problems: overpopulation, poverty, the absence of an educated middle class, tribal and class conflict, arbitrary boundaries, disease, economic dependence, and political instability. The challenge for Africa as a whole is to build a truly civil society and achieve economic health and political stability.

The Middle East   Oil and the Muslim reaction to the creation of the state of Israel have dominated the history of the Middle East since the 1940s. While the possession of vast deposits of oil has made some Middle Eastern governments wealthy, it has not led to the creation of prosperous democratic societies. The existence of Israel has inflamed the Middle East for more than five decades. Although peace efforts have made some progress, the cycle of terror and retaliatory violence has persisted, and it is unclear whether a viable Palestinian state can be created.

Political Islamism, although not a monolithic movement, has proved increasingly disruptive to the region and the entire world.

In the wake of the terrorist attacks of September 11, 2001, the United States finds itself increasingly embroiled in a chaotic and unstable region of the world.

CHAPTER QUESTIONS

WHAT ARE the two main developments that have occurred in the postcolonial world since 1945?

WHERE IN Latin America did the major attempts to establish revolutionary governments occur?

WHAT ARE the most serious problems that Africa faces in the twenty-first century?

HOW DID the creation of the state of Israel affect the history of the modern Middle East?

HOW HAS the growth of Hindu nationalism affected Indian politics?

CHAPTER OUTLINE

• Beyond the Postcolonial Era
• Latin America Since 1945
• Postcolonial Africa
• Central, South, and Southeast Asia
• The Postcolonial Middle East

The last half of the 20th century saw Europe eclipsed by the rise of the two superpowers—the United States and the Soviet Union—and then witnessed the collapse of the latter (see Chapter 32). The same era witnessed the end of the age of Western colonialism, challenges to European and superpower imperialism, and the emergence of new nations in Africa and Asia.

Two developments in non-Western regions have major implications for the future. East Asia, Japan, and China have emerged as major political and economic powers. Radical Islamic movements present a political and military challenge across much of the globe. The period of colonialism that began in earnest in the 17th century was a relatively brief episode in world history. The last significant colonial holdings were given their independence in the 1960s, but the legacies of colonialism—positive as well as negative—continue to have major impacts.

BEYOND THE POSTCOLONIAL ERA

WHAT ARE the two main developments that have occurred in the postcolonial world since 1945?

I
t could be argued that with the passing of **apartheid** in South Africa, the postcolonial era has also ended. What we shall witness in the future are waves of economic growth, such as that of the early 1990s in much of East Asia; the forging of dramatic new political alignments, both regional and transregional; internal struggles in country after country to build political systems that allow the development of civil society and limit the destructive domination of oligarchic or dictatorial regimes; and, most dramatically, the determination of radical Islam to confront Western and, in particular, American influences.

Since 1945, two distinct developments have occurred in the postcolonial world. The first—in a process that is generally termed *decolonization*—was the emergence of the various parts of Africa and Asia from the direct administration of foreign powers (see Map 34–1). The second was the organization of those previous colonial dependencies as independent states with greater or lesser degrees of stability.

The latter phase has gone through four stages: the influence of Cold War rivalries on the new states, the economic effects of **globalization**, progress in the spread of the ideals of civil society and participatory government, and finally a resurgence of cultural and religious traditions. This may lead to a **clash of civilizations**, a bloody assertion of ethnic and cultural chauvinism, or the discovery of common values and concerns that leads to the emergence of a more nuanced view of the world as a domain in which diverse peoples learn to get along.

Protest. The globalization of the world economy has sparked hostile political reaction. Numerous groups demonstrate at the World Trade Organization meetings to protest the development of previously untouched parts of the world, which they claim causes environmental damage and expanded wealth for the developed nations and unemployment and poverty elsewhere.
AP Wide World Photos.

LATIN AMERICA SINCE 1945

D
uring the last half century, the nations of Latin America have experienced divergent paths of political and economic change. Their leaders have tried to alleviate their people's dependence on the more developed nations. At best, these efforts have had mixed results; at worst, they have led to repression and tragedy.

Before World War II, the states of Latin America had been economically dependent on the United States and Western Europe. Beginning in the 1950s, Latin America became an arena for confrontations between the United States and the Soviet Union.

During this era attempts were made to expand the industrial base and agricultural production of the various national economies.

MAP EXPLORATION

Interactive map: To explore this map further, go to **http://www.prenhall.com/craig/map34.1**

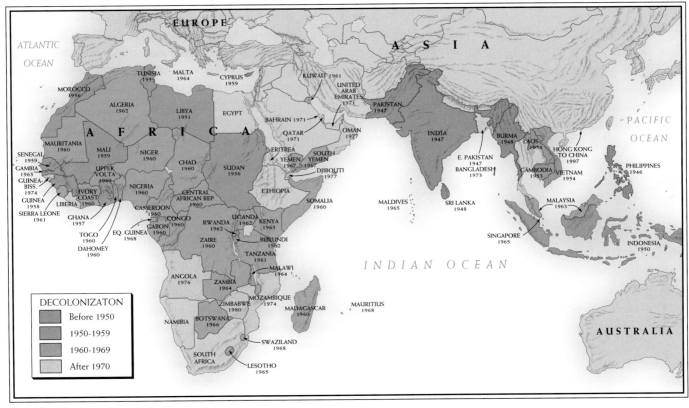

MAP 34–1
Decolonization Since World War II.   The Western powers' rapid retreat from imperialism after World War II is graphically shown on this outline map covering half the globe, from West Africa to the Southwest Pacific.

HOW ARE the effects of colonialism still present in Africa and Asia today?

Financing came from U.S. and Western European banks or from Soviet subsidies. Enormous debts were contracted that made Latin American economies virtual prisoners to the fluctuations of world interest rates and international banks or to Soviet subsidies. These new relationships, however, did not alter the underlying character of most Latin American economies, which remain exporters of agricultural commodities and mineral resources. Since the 1970s, Latin America has also shipped massive amounts of cocaine to the United States and Europe. This has led to political turmoil and civil war in Columbia.

A culture of poverty continues to be the most dominant social characteristic of the area. Migration into the cities from the countryside has caused urban overcrowding and slums inhabited by the desperately poor. The standards of health and nutrition have often fallen. The growth of service industries in the cities has also fostered the emergence of a professional, educated middle class that often wants to imitate the lifestyle of their social counterparts in the United States and Western Europe. This new professional middle class has displayed little taste for radical politics, social reform, or revolution. They and the more traditional elites were willing, especially during the 1960s and 1970s, to support military governments pledged to maintain the status quo.

Political events in Latin America led to the establishment of authoritarian governments of both the left and the right and to a retreat from the model of

WHERE IN Latin America did the major attempts to establish revolutionary governments occur?

apartheid "Apartness." Term referring to racist policies enforced by the White-dominated regime that existed in South Africa from 1948 to 1992.

globalization Term used to describe the increasing economic and cultural interdependence of societies around the world.

clash of civilizations Political theory, most often identified with Harvard political scientist Samuel P. Huntington, which contends that conflict between the world's religio-cultural traditions or "civilizations" increasingly dominates world affairs.

parliamentary democracy. Only Mexico, Colombia, Venezuela, and Costa Rica remained parliamentary states throughout this period. Elsewhere, two paths of political development were followed. In Cuba and Nicaragua, and briefly in Chile, revolutionary Socialist governments with close ties to the Soviet Union were established. Elsewhere, often in response to the fear of revolution or communism, military governments held power, sometimes punctuated with brief interludes of civilian rule. Such were the situations in Argentina, Bolivia, Brazil, Chile, Peru, and Uruguay. Governments of both the left and the right engaged in political repression.

These political changes fostered new roles for the military and the Roman Catholic Church. Latin American armies have played key political roles since the wars of independence. But since World War II, they have frequently assumed the direct government of nations rather than using indirect influence. Many Roman Catholic priests and bishops have protested inequalities and attacked political repression. Certain Roman Catholic theologians have combined traditional Christian concern for the poor with Marxist ideology to formulate what is called a **liberation theology**. This Latin American theological initiative has been attacked by the Vatican.

Since the 1980s, Latin America has changed significantly. Several nations have moved toward democratization and free-market economies. This marks a sharp departure from the 1930s and 1940s, when the state itself was seen as largely responsible for economic development. Yet in most nations, the military keeps a watchful eye on democratic developments and possible disorder. The end of the Cold War brought to a close one source of external political challenge, but the internal social problems of these nations continue to raise difficulties for their governments. In several nations, drug-producing cartels have challenged the authority of governments themselves.

REVOLUTIONARY CHALLENGES

There were four major attempts among the nations of Latin America to establish revolutionary governments pursuing major social and economic change. They occurred in Cuba in 1959, in Chile in 1970, in Nicaragua in 1979, and in Peru in the 1980s. Each involved a Marxist political organization, and each, with the exception of the Shining Path revolutionary movement in Peru, sought a close relationship with the Soviet Union. The establishment of these governments provoked active resistance by the United States and opposition to social and political change from traditional elites across Latin America.

The Cuban Revolution   Cuba had remained a colony until the Spanish-American War of 1898. Thereafter, it achieved independence within a sphere of U.S. influence that took the form of economic domination and military intervention. The governments of the island were ineffective and corrupt. During the 1950s, Fulgencio Batista (1901–1973), a dictator supported by the United States, ruled Cuba.

Historically, Cuba had been politically restive. On July 26, 1953, Fidel Castro Ruz (b. 1926), the son of a wealthy landowner, his close associate, Ernesto Che Guevara, and others attacked a government army barracks. The revolutionary movement that he thereafter came to lead in exile took its name from that date: the Twenty-Sixth of July Movement. In 1956, Castro and a handful of followers landed in Cuba. They took refuge in the Sierra Maestra mountains and attacked Batista's forces. Batista fled Cuba on New Year's Day in 1959. In January, Castro arrived in Havana as the revolutionary victor.

liberation theology Effort by certain Roman Catholic theologians to combine Marxism with traditional Christian concern for the poor.

Castro undertook the most extensive political, economic, and social reconstruction seen in recent Latin American history. He rejected parliamentary democracy and governed Cuba in an authoritarian manner. The revolutionary government carried out major land redistribution. Both small landowners and large state farms were established.

The Cuban Revolution spurned an industrial economic model and concentrated on the agricultural sector. Sugar preserved its leading role, and the Cuban economy remained monocultural. The sugar industry depended on large Soviet subsidies and on the Soviet-bloc nations for its market. In that respect, the Cuban economy did not escape the cycle of external dependence.

In foreign affairs, the Cuban Revolution was characterized by a sharp break with the United States and a close relationship with the Soviet Union. Castro aligned himself with the Cuban Communist Party and with the Soviet bloc. The United States was hostile toward Castro and toward the presence of a Communist state less than a hundred miles from Florida. In 1961, the United States and Cuban exiles launched the unsuccessful Bay of Pigs invasion. The close Cuban relationship to the Soviet Union led to the missile crisis of 1962, the most dangerous incident of the Cold War. In the late 1970s and the 1980s, a dialogue of sorts was undertaken between Cuba and the United States, but mutual distrust continues.

Fidel Castro. The Cuban dictator is shown here waving to cheering crowds acknowledging his triumph over the Batista regime on January 1, 1959.

UPI/Corbis-Bettmann.

With the collapse of the Soviet Union and the end of the Cold War, the future of Castro's Cuba has become uncertain. Cuba remains the only state closely associated with the former Soviet bloc that has not experienced political or economic reform. Subsidies that flowed from the Soviet Union to support the Cuban economy, however, have ended, creating a shortage of consumer goods. The Marxist political and economic ideology stands discredited throughout the world, but the aging Castro's leadership remains intact. Cuba must confront the need for a successor to Castro. It also must confront the need for economic reform and find a new role in a Latin American order in which the issues of the Cold War are no longer relevant. One hint of new direction came in 1998 when the Castro government permitted a highly publicized visit from Pope John Paul II.

Throughout the Cold War, Cuba assumed an importance far greater than its size might suggest. After 1959, it served as a center for the export of Communist revolution and it sent troops to Angola in the late 1970s. The U.S. government sought to prevent the establishment of a second Cuba in Latin America. That goal led to intervention in other revolutionary situations and to support for authoritarian governments in Latin America.

Chile   Until the 1970s, Chile was the most enduring model of parliamentary democracy in Latin America. During the 1960s, however, Chilean politics became polarized. Unemployment rose at an alarmic rate. There was labor unrest and popular resentment of the economic domination of Chile by large U.S. corporations.

The situation came to a head in 1970 when Salvador Allende (1908–1973), the candidate of the left-wing political coalition and a Marxist, was elected president. His coalition did not control the Chilean congress, nor did it have the support of the military. The center and right-wing political groups took a watch-and-wait attitude. Allende nationalized some businesses. Other policies were blocked in the congress, and Allende had to govern by decree. By this device he began to expropriate foreign property, much of which belonged to U.S. corporations. This policy frightened the Chilean owners of small and medium-sized businesses, but did not satisfy workers. Inflation ballooned. Harvests were poor.

In the autumn of 1973, Allende found himself governing a nation in turmoil without significant domestic political support and with many foreign enemies. He proved unwilling to make political compromises or to change his policies. The army became hostile. The government of the United States was disturbed by the prospect of a Marxist nation on the western coast of South America. The Nixon administration supported the discontent within the Chilean army. In mid-September 1973, an army coup overthrew Allende, who was killed in the presidential palace.

Thereafter, for 15 years Chile was governed by a military junta under General Augusto Pinochet (b. 1915). The military government pursued a close relationship with the United States and resisted Marxism in the hemisphere. It established a state-directed free-market economy and reversed the expropriations of the Allende years. There was also harsh political repression.

In a referendum held in late 1988, Chileans rejected Pinochet's bid for another term as president. Democratization was relatively smooth. Civilian rule has included efforts to investigate the political repression of the Pinochet years. Thousands of cases of torture and murder have been revealed. The Chilean government itself moved slowly, not wishing to revisit the most controversial era of the nation's history. In 1999, while Pinochet was visiting Great Britain, Spain indicted him and sought his extradition to stand trial for the disappearance of Spanish citizens under his rule. He was arrested, but ultimately returned to Chile, where he was judged too sick to stand trial.

The Sandinista Revolution in Nicaragua   In the summer of 1979, a Marxist guerrilla force, the **Sandinistas**, overthrew the corrupt dictatorship of the Somoza family in Nicaragua. The Somozas had governed Nicaragua as their personal preserve since the 1930s with support from the United States. The Sandinistas established a collective government that pursued social and economic reform and reconstruction. The movement—with Roman Catholic priests on its leadership council—epitomized the new political and social forces in Latin America. However, the revolutionary government confronted significant domestic political opposition and military challenge from the contra guerrilla movement.

The government of the United States, particularly under the Reagan administration (1981–1989), was hostile toward the Sandinistas. America provided both direct and indirect aid to the opposition guerrillas. The U.S. government feared the spread of Marxist revolutionary activity in Central America, a fear reinforced by the close ties between the revolutionary government and the Soviet Union. For the United States, the Sandinista government represented in Central America a problem analogous to that of Cuba a generation earlier.

Sandinista rule came to a relatively quick end. In early 1990, after a negotiated peace settlement with the contras, they lost the presidential election to an opposition coalition and relinquished power peacefully.

PURSUIT OF STABILITY UNDER THREAT OF REVOLUTION

Argentina   In 1955, the Argentine army revolted against the Perón dictatorship and Juan Perón (1895–1974) went into exile. Two decades of economic stagnation and social unrest followed. In 1973, Perón was recalled from exile in a desperate attempt to restore stability, but died about a year later.

Sandinistas Marxist guerrilla force that overthrew the Somoza dictatorship in Nicaragua in 1979.

By 1976, the army had undertaken direct rule. There was widespread repression; thousands of citizens disappeared, never to be heard of again. In April 1982, General Leopoldo Galtieri (b. 1926) launched a disastrous invasion of the Islas Malvinas (Falkland Islands). Argentina was defeated by Britain, and the military junta discredited.

In 1983 civilian rule was restored, and Argentina set out on the road to democratization. Under President Raul Alfonsín (b. 1927), many of the former military figures responsible for the years of repression received prison sentences. Alfonsín also sought more real political authority for the Argentine congress. Argentina has provided the most extensive example in Latin America of the restoration of democratic practices after military rule. Peaceful elections and transitions of governments have occurred for two decades despite serious economic difficulties. In 2001, however, it became clear that Argentina would be unable to repay its foreign debts, and rising unemployment, a currency devaluation, and drastic cuts in basic government services have subsequently led to political turmoil.

Brazil   In 1964, the military assumed the direct government of Brazil and did not fully relinquish it until the mid-1980s. The military government stressed order and used repression to maintain it. The army itself, however, was divided. Many officers were concerned that the corruption of everyday politics would undermine the army's reputation and esprit de corps. Consequently, within the army itself, certain forces sought to restore a more democratic government. In 1985, civilian government returned under the military's watchful eye.

The military government fostered denationalized industrial development. Non-Brazilian corporations were invited to spearhead the drive toward industrialization. Brazil opted for an industrialism guided and dominated from the outside. One result was a massive foreign debt, the servicing and repayment of which have become perhaps Brazil's most important national problem. Brazil also became the major industrialized nation in Latin America. Its industrialization, however, was guided and dominated from outside and led to the accumulation of a massive foreign debt that now constitutes Brazil's most important national problem. Industrialization has also had a huge impact on the Brazilian rain forest. By 1998, large landowners, encouraged by subsidies and tax incentives, had cleared 12 percent of Brazil's rain forest.

The question now is how the social changes wrought by industrialism, such as growing urbanization, will receive political accommodation. In Brazil, as in Argentina, economic and social pressures have spawned conditions ripe for political agitation. It was just that possibility that led both the traditional and the new professional elites to support authoritarian government in the past.

In 1990, Fernando Collor de Mello was elected president. He advocated privatization and allowing market forces to stimulate growth. In 1992, however, he was impeached on charges of corruption. In 1995, Fernando Henrique Cardoso won the presidency and pursued economic policies devised by technocrats, who hoped to achieve economic growth with stability. By 2003, however, Brazil's economy had slowed sharply, and in that year Luiz Inácio Lula da Silva became the first person from a working-class background to be elected Brazil's president. He has attempted to combine socialist concern for social services with an austere economic policy.

Mexico   Institutionally, Mexico has undergone few political changes since World War II. In theory, the government continued to pursue the goals of the revolution. Power remained in the control of the Partido Revolucionario Institucional (PRI).

Zapatistas. Named after the revolutionary hero Emiliano Zapata (depicted on the banner), the Zapatistas demanded rights for the impoverished Native American population of Mexico, especially in the southern state of Chiapas where this photograph was taken in 1997.

AP/Wide World Photos.

Yet shifts had occurred under this apparently stable surface. The government retreated from some of the aims of the revolution and appeared conservative when compared to Marxist states. In the early 1950s, certain large landowners were exempted from the expropriation and redistribution of land. The Mexican government maintained relations with Cuba and the other revolutionary regimes of Latin America but also resisted Marxist doctrines in Mexico. When necessary, it arrested malcontents.

Mexico experienced an oil boom from 1977 to 1983, but the world oil glut burst that bubble. The aftermath revealed the absence of stable growth. Like so many other states in the region, Mexico amassed large foreign debts and thus surrendered real economic independence.

In 1988, the PRI encountered a challenge at the polls. Opposition candidates received much of the vote in a hotly contested election. The PRI remained in power but with the knowledge that it would not be able to dominate the political scene as it had done. Thereafter, the leadership began to decentralize the party. President Carlos Salinas moved to privatize economic enterprise. He also favored free-trade agreements. The most important of these was the North American Free Trade Agreement (NAFTA), which created a vast free-trade area including Mexico, Canada, and the United States. In 1991, Salinas made new accommodations with the Roman Catholic Church, thus moving away from the traditional anticlericalism of Mexican politics. By 1991, the PRI appeared to have regained its former political ascendancy.

However, in 1994 Mexico underwent political shocks. Troops had to quell armed rebellion in Chiapas. During the election that year, the leading candidate was assassinated and party members were charged with complicity in the deed. Party corruption received increased publicity. Early in 1995, Mexico suffered a major economic downturn, and only loans from the United States saved the economy. Ernesto Zedillo, elected president in 1994, blamed Salinas and his family for the situation, and the corruption of the Salinas government became public. The government faced further unrest in Chiapas, growing power among drug lords, and turmoil within the governing party itself. In 2000, the PRI lost the election for the presidency, though it has remained the most powerful party in the Mexican legislature.

CONTINUITY AND CHANGE IN RECENT LATIN AMERICAN HISTORY

The most striking feature about the history of the past four decades in Latin America is its tragic continuity with the region's previous history. Revolution has brought moderate social change, but at the price of authoritarian government, economic stagnation, and dependence on foreign powers. Real independence has not been achieved. Throughout the region for much of the period, parliamentary democracy has been fragile; it was the first element of national life to be sacrificed to the conflicting goals of socialism, economic growth, or resistance to revolution.

Recent trends toward democratization and market economics may, however, mark a break in that pattern. The region could enjoy healthy economic growth if inflation can be contained and investment fostered. The challenge will be to see that the fruits of any new prosperity are shared in a way that prevents resentment and turmoil. Furthermore, as in the past, economic turmoil far from Latin America may harm it. Each time such turmoil has occurred, the governments of Latin America, like the current government of Mexico, have found themselves economically dependent on either the United States or Europe.

POSTCOLONIAL AFRICA

Nowhere is the dramatic continuity between often arbitrary colonial territories and emergent independent states clearer than in Africa. Most of its modern nations are direct inheritors of their colonial predecessors' boundaries, and the former colonial capitals have become the new national capitals, even though the colonial frontiers had little to do with the boundaries of traditional tribal territories or indigenous states. If nationalism was a European export to the rest of the world, Africa provides striking examples of how attractive it can be as a motive for supratribal and transregional state formation.

African nationalism can be dated generally to the period between the two world wars, when regional opposition to colonial occupation began to be replaced by large-scale movements. World War II proved a catalyst for African nationalism, both among Africans themselves and for Europe, which was largely disposed to give up its colonial empires after the war.

THE TRANSITION TO INDEPENDENCE

In 1950, apart from Egypt, only Liberia, Ethiopia, and White-controlled South Africa were sovereign states. By 1980, no African state (with the exception of two tiny Spanish holdings on the Moroccan coast) was ruled by a European state, although South Africa and Namibia continued to be dominated by Whites. Native sons, such as Patrice Lumumba (1925-1961) in the Congo became symbols of African self-determination and freedom from foreign domination (see "The Pan-African Congress Demands Independence").

The actual transition from colonial administrative territories to independent national states was less fraught with conflict and bloodshed than one might have expected. The most protracted and bloody wars of independence from European overlords were the guerrilla struggles fought in French Algeria from 1955 to 1962; in Portuguese Angola and Mozambique from 1961 to 1975; and in Zaire (formerly the Belgian Congo), Zambia (formerly Northern Rhodesia), and Zimbabwe (formerly Southern Rhodesia) from 1960 to 1980. Usually, however, the transfer of power was relatively peaceable.

The same cannot be said of the internal conflicts that often arose after colonial withdrawal. Much of the instability in emergent African states has been a legacy of both the colonial powers' minimal efforts to prepare their subjects for self-government and the haphazard 19th-century

WHAT ARE the most serious problems that Africa faces in the 21st century?

27.4
Kwame Nkrumah, I Speak of Freedom: A Statement of African Ideology

Ethnic Conflict. Rwandan refugees carry their belongings as they stream out of the Mugunga refugee camp in Zaire (Congo) toward Rwanda in one of the many ethnic conflicts that tore apart central Africa in the 1990s.

David Guttenfelder/AP Wide World Photos.

HISTORY'S VOICES

THE PAN-AFRICAN CONGRESS DEMANDS INDEPENDENCE

For more than two centuries before World War II, European powers had dominated or directly ruled large parts of Africa. Before World War II, nationalist political movements came to the fore in a number of these colonial empires. After the war, nationalist movements burgeoned throughout most of the colonial world.

The costs of fighting World War II meant the European powers had less wealth with which to govern their colonies. In addition, the principles of the victorious Allies in Europe were inconsistent with colonialism, as was the foreign policy of the United States, now the dominant Western power.

In the following passage, representatives to the 1945 Fifth Pan-African Congress meeting in Manchester, England, set forth their demand for freedom.

WHAT ARE the social and political goals these African leaders demanded? How did World War II help to allow such goals to be voiced? Why did these leaders believe they deserved to resort to force?

DECLARATION TO THE COLONIAL POWERS

The delegates believe in peace. How could it be otherwise, when for centuries the African peoples have been the victims of violence and slavery? Yet if the Western world is still determined to rule mankind by force, then Africans, as a last resort, may have to appeal to force in the effort to achieve freedom, even if force destroys them and the world.

We are determined to be free. We want education. We want the right to earn a decent living; the right to express our thoughts and emotions, to adopt and create forms of beauty. We demand for Black Africa autonomy and independence so far and no further than it is possible in this One World for groups and peoples to rule themselves subject to inevitable world unity and federation.

We are not ashamed to have been an age-long patient people. We continue willingly to sacrifice and strive. But we are unwilling to starve any longer while doing the world's drudgery, in order to support by our poverty and ignorance a false aristocracy and a discarded imperialism.

We condemn the monopoly of capital and the rule of private wealth and industry for private profit alone. We welcome economic democracy as the only real democracy.

Therefore, we shall complain, appeal and arraign. We will make the world listen to the fact of our condition. We will fight in every way we can for freedom, democracy, and social betterment.

Source: Molefi Kete Asante and Abus S. Abarry, *African Intellectual Heritage: A Book of Sources* (Philadelphia: Temple University Press, 1996), pp. 520–521.

QUICK REVIEW

African Independence

- By 1980, no African state was ruled by a European state
- Transition to independent states was less bloody than expected
- Internal conflicts since independence have led to instability and violence

division of the continent into often arbitrary colonial units. The establishment of new African governments often succeeded only after substantial civil strife.

Few African states had the numbers of educated and experienced native citizens that were needed to staff the apparatuses of a sovereign country, and this alone made for difficult times after independence. Corruption and military coups were rife; the attempt to implement planned economies on a socialist model often brought economic catastrophe; and tribal and regional revolts at times led to civil war.

Most dangerous and costly were the separatist struggles, civil wars, and border clashes between new states that grew out of the independence struggles. The Nigerian civil war of 1967–1970, in which more than 1 million people died, was a bloody example. However, these conflicts tended to ratify the postcolonial state divisions that had almost always kept to the old colonial boundaries (instead of regional or tribal/linguistic divisions within these units).

Every African state has had a different history in the half century since World War II; here we shall look at two cases: Nigeria and South Africa.

Nigeria   Nigeria is the most populous state in Africa, with about 100 million inhabitants. It was formed when the British joined their protectorates of Northern and Southern Nigeria in 1914. Nigeria achieved independence in 1960 and ratified a republican constitution in 1964 that federated the three major provincial regions—the Eastern, Western, and Northern—under a national government based in Lagos, the former British administrative capital. Nigeria's largest ethnic and linguistic groups are the major ones of the same three regions or provinces: Igbo (Ibo) in the Eastern, Yoruba in the Western, and Hausa and Fulani in the Northern. Nigeria's official language is English.

Nowhere was the aftermath of independence bloodier than in Nigeria, which was, at its inception, the most potentially successful state in independent Africa. The three-province federation soon proved to be unworkable, and a 1966 coup brought a military government into power. Its leader, an Ibo, was assassinated within seven months, and Lt. Colonel Yakubo Gawon (b. 1934) took over amid ethnic unrest that ended in massacres in the fall of 1966. Gawon's government subdivided the three provinces into states, but in May 1967, the Eastern Province's assembly empowered its leader, Lt. Colonel Odumegwu Ojukwu (b. 1933), to form the independent state of Biafra out of the three states of the Eastern Province. Ojukwu was an Ibo nationalist but aspired to control lands beyond those of the Ibos—especially the off-shore oil reserves of the Eastern Province. The new Biafran state gained recognition from several African states; and arms and support from France, South Africa, and Portugal. Worldwide propaganda depicted Biafra as a small, brave, mostly Christian country fighting for its survival.

The ensuing two and one-half years saw a bloody civil war. The larger federal forces slowly chipped away at first the non-Ibo regions, then the Ibo heartland of the Biafran state. Famine was a major cause of casualties, and the estimated death toll soared above a million by the time the Biafrans surrendered in January 1970. Out of this brutal conflict, however, came a sense of Nigerian unity, along with a major role for the military in Nigerian politics. The struggle also contributed to the development of African diplomacy and of international aid efforts in Africa.

Gawon was overthrown by another commander in 1975. In the ensuing 25 years, Nigeria has been plagued by political instability, with its leadership passing usually from one military ruler to another. The regime of General Sani Abacha (1993–1998) was especially brutal.

Abacha died in June 1998. Civilian rule was restored in 1999, and a civilian government and elected president ratified and implemented a new constitution. Elections again took place in 2003. There is considerable hope that democratic rule will continue, despite enduring religious communal animosities and ethnic divisions.

South Africa   One of the most tragic chapters in the history of modern Africa has finally been closed: that of White-minority rule in South Africa, with its radical separation of White from non-White peoples in all areas of life as official government policy for nearly 50 years. In the rest of East and southern Africa, minority White-settler governments tried in vain in the postwar period to put down African independence movements. Only in South Africa did they manage, until the 1990s, to sustain a White supremacist state.

From the time the Afrikaner-led National Party (NP) came to power in 1948, the Union of South Africa was governed according to the racist policy of

QUICK REVIEW

Nigeria
- Achieved independence in 1960
- Collapse of three-province federation led to dictatorship and civil war
- Brutality, instability, and corruption have marked Nigerian government since 1975

Nelson Mandela. On May 10, 1994, Nelson Mandela was sworn in as president of South Africa, bringing an end to the apartheid, White minority government that had imprisoned him for 27 years.

David Brauchli/AP/Wide World Photos.

28.2
"The Struggle Is My Life" (1961): Nelson Mandela

apartheid ("apartness"). Until the dismantling of this policy after 1991, the country's White minority (in 1991, 5.4 million persons) ran the country. Its 31 million Blacks, 3.7 million "colored" (of mixed blood), and 1 million Indians were kept strictly segregated—treated, at best, as second-class citizens or, in the case of Blacks, as noncitizens or even nonhumans. This system was maintained by repression, to quell dissent and enforce apartheid laws.

The history of apartheid and its passing is a bloody but triumphant one. In part, as a result of worldwide opposition, South Africa saw itself become isolated from the 1960s onward. Meanwhile, the rest of Africa—including other White-run states like Rhodesia (now Zimbabwe)—progressed to majority, African rule. In 1961, South Africa withdrew from the British Commonwealth of Nations. In the 1960s and 1970s, the government created three tiny "independent homelands" for Blacks inside the country, allowing the White minority to treat Blacks as immigrant "foreigners" in the parts of South Africa where most had to work. The international community refused to recognize the homelands, or "Bantustans." South Africa's isolation was further dramatized when two antiapartheid Black leaders, the Zulu chief Albert Luthuli in 1960 and the Anglican archbishop Desmond Tutu in 1984, were awarded the Nobel Prize for their work against apartheid.

By 1978, when Pieter Botha (b. 1916) came to power, apartheid was failing: The homelands were economic and political catastrophes; the country was in a recession; skilled Whites were emigrating; and South Africa was becoming an international pariah. In the 1980s, internal opposition to apartheid grew.

Beginning in 1986, many nations imposed economic sanctions against the government. Antiapartheid movements in the United States and elsewhere had convinced companies and individuals to divest themselves of investments in South Africa. Strikes by Black workers in 1987 led the government to give virtually unlimited power to its security forces, but the violence created support in the West for a trade embargo of South Africa.

In June 1988, more than 2 million Black workers went on strike to protest new repressive labor laws and a ban on political activity by trade unions and antiapartheid groups. President Botha resigned in August 1989. His replacement, F. W. de Klerk (b. 1936) (also of the NP, but younger and more ready for accommodation), began to dismantle White-only rule and the official structures of apartheid. In February 1990, de Klerk announced radical changes, and a series of landmark government actions followed: lifting of the ban on the African National Congress (ANC), the main antiapartheid organization; release of ANC leader Nelson Mandela after 27 years of imprisonment; and repeal of the Separate Amenities Act, the legal basis for segregation in public places. In 1991, the race registration law was repealed. In March 1992, a Whites-only referendum voted to grant constitutional equality to all races. The NP government under de Klerk's leadership also negotiated with the ANC leader Mandela, and despite terrorist attempts from both Black and White extremists to derail the talks, the two leaders brought their own and 18 other parties of both sides to endorse an interim constitution, which was to be implemented once national elections could be held in which all citizens of South Africa would be enfranchised. (Mandela and de Klerk shared the Nobel Peace Prize for 1993.)

Elections were held in April 1994. The ANC won 63 percent of the vote, and the NP 20 percent, thus relegating apartheid to the slag heap of history. The nonracial constitution of December 1996 offers a new basis for the future, but the new state faces huge problems: one of the world's most extreme income inequalities; insufficient education and economic infrastructure; rampant Black poverty; high unemployment; militant extremist groups; inadequate public services in much of the country; potentially severe water supply and water quality problems; and difficulties in attracting foreign investment. The obstacles will, however, no longer include a state system that holds the majority of the population in bondage.

While the new independent states of Africa have been anything but models, nevertheless Africa did not revert to tiny tribal and regional political units. However, some struggles—such as those in the Sudan, Somalia, Rwanda, Sierra Leone, Congo, and Liberia—are still ongoing, their human consequences catastrophic, and their ultimate outcomes not clear.

THE AFRICAN FUTURE

Most African states have not achieved peace and prosperity. On the other hand, the last 50 years have seen radical change and development. The prospects for government stability are not entirely bleak. Economic problems loom large, but even here progress is being made. In any case, every African state is different; each faces unique problems and must draw on its unique resources. Probably the most serious problems are those with which almost all of Africa's new nations have to contend: overpopulation, poverty, disease, famine, lack of professional and technical expertise, and general economic underdevelopment. In particular, the explosive growth of new urban centers at the expense of rural areas has brought disruptive changes in the continent's traditionally agrarian-based societies, age-old family and tribal allegiances, religious values, and sociopolitical systems. The challenge for African nations in the 21st century is to build a truly civil society and achieve economic health and political stability in the face of internal divisions, exploding population growth, and world-market competition.

CENTRAL, SOUTH, AND SOUTHEAST ASIA— THE ISLAMIC HEARTLAND

HOW DID the creation of the state of Israel affect the history of the modern Middle East?

*T*he lands today dominated or significantly marked by Islamic culture and containing either Muslim majority populations or major Muslim minority numbers stretch from North and West Africa to the Philippines. The various nations of this huge region of Central, South, and Southeast Asia illustrate the many different ways in which Islamic faith and practice may manifest themselves and affect political life.

TURKEY

In Turkey, a non-Arab country, civil society and a democratically elected government has become the norm, despite struggles over the place of religion in society and lapses into military rule. Economically, Turkey has had difficulties, but it and Israel are the most economically advanced countries in the Middle East. With the creation of new Turkic-language-speaking states in Central Asia after the breakup of the Soviet Union, Turkey is making a bid to strengthen its ties with this underdeveloped part of the world.

Geographically and culturally Turkey is part of both Europe and Asia. Istanbul, its main commerical and cultural center, is located in continental Europe. In recent years, Turkey, already a member of NATO, has sought admission to the European Union. Turkey participates in European cultural events, such as soccer competitions and other contests, but the issue of its membership in the EU is controversial. Many Europeans are skeptical about admitting an overwhelmingly Muslim nation ino the union. Turkey's human rights record (particularly with respect to its Kurdish minority), imprisonment of journalists, suppression of freedom of speech, and serious indebtedness to the International Money Fund are also problems. The emergence of various Islamist parties further complicate the political landscape. It remains to be seen with which region Turkey ultimately will align itself.

IRAN AND ITS ISLAMIC REVOLUTION

Iran was ruled from 1925 to 1941 as a monarchy by a former army commander, Reza Khan, who had come to power by military takeover and governed under the old Persian title Shah Reza Pahlavi. Like his contemporary in Turkey, Atatürk (1881–1938), he attempted to introduce modernist economic, educational, and governmental reforms (but, unlike Turkey, favoring monarchy). By the time Russian and British forces deposed Reza in 1941 and installed his son, Muhammad Reza, as shah, the power of the Shi'ite religious leaders, or *ulama*, had been muted and a strong, centralized state established. The son continued his father's secularist state building from the end of World War II until 1978, with one interruption. In 1951, a nationalist revolution established Muhammad Mosaddeq (1881–1967) in control. But in 1953, a counterrevolution, covertly supported by America and Britain, restored the shah. Memory of this continues to make Iranians suspicious of American motives.

In the 1960s, Muhammad Reza Shah was forced to institute land reform and various socialist or populist programs. However, his violent repression of the leftist and especially the religious opposition alienated the Iranian masses, as did his failure to narrow the gap between the wealthy elites and the poor. In 1978, religious leaders and secularist revolutionaries joined forces to overthrow the shah in an uprising fueled by Shi'ite Islamic feeling and symbolism. In 1979, the constitution of a new Islamic republic was adapted under the guidance of the Shi'ite religious leader, or *ayatollah*, Ruhollah Khomeini (1902–1989). A protracted war with Iraq (1980–1988) followed, and the new regime instituted repressive measures against its enemies not unlike those of the shah. Still, the new state—with religious leaders exercising a degree of political power not seen since the 16th century—has survived. Khomeini and his successors, Hashemi Rafsanjani (b. 1934) and Ali Khameini (b. 1939), struggled to combine Muslim values with 20th-century *realpolitik*, a challenge that remains for their successors.

In 1997, a resounding majority in the first real national election since the 1979 revolution brought Mohammad Khatami to the presidency. Khatami, a moderate cleric and former minister of culture, has tried to steer a moderate, more liberal course for Iran. Many think his administration marks progress toward a more stable, more internationally engaged government in Iran, but the wide-ranging reforms that people expected have failed to materialize. There have been sporadic, unsuccessful student protests against the

ayatollah Major Shi'ite religious leader.

Khomeini. The bearded ayatollah waves to a cheering throng in Tehran, Iran in February 1979.

Reuters/Corbs-Bettmann.

clerical government, and in 2003, Shirin Ebadi, an Iranian lawyer, won the Nobel Peace Prize for her efforts to improve the status of women in Iran.

AFGHANISTAN AND THE FORMER SOVIET REPUBLICS

North of Iran, 40 million Central Asian Muslims predominate in the broad region that stretches across the south-central reaches of the former USSR between the Crimea and China, and 30 million or more Muslims live in Chinese Central Asia. These people have sustained their religious and intellectual traditions in the face of Russian and Chinese imperialism, and when the Soviet Union collapsed in 1990, they established many separate, independent nations. They are loosely connected through the Commonwealth of Independent States (CIS), which contains Kazakhstan, Kyrgyzstan, Tajikistan, Turkmenistan, Uzbekistan, Azerbaijan, Georgia, and Moldova. These Central Asian Islamic republics had little time or infrastructure to manage their transition to independence. It remains to be seen whether they can avoid economic collapse and ethnic or regional conflict to become politically viable.

Afghan Women. Shortly after the Taliban was driven out of Kabul in November 2001, several Afghan women, one unveiled, venture out in the street.

Reuters/Corbis-Bettmann.

The Soviet invasion of Afghanistan in 1979 (see Chapter 32) drew thousands of fundamentalist Muslims to Afghanistan to fight for the eviction of the Russians, whom they regarded as Western imperialists. Conservative Arab states, which wanted to divert the energies of their religious extremists, and the United States, which saw this in the context of the Cold War, supported them, and they succeeded by the late 1980s. The Soviets' withdrawal created a power vacuum that had been filled by 1998 by the *Taliban*. They imposed a version of Islamic law, which mandated strict regimentation of women and public executions and mutilations for criminal offenses. They also allowed Muslim terrorists known as *al-Qaeda* ("Base") to establish training camps in their country. These camps produced the terrorists who attacked the United States on September 11, 2001. A U.S. response to those attacks was a military campaign that overthrew the Taliban's regime.

INDIA

India, a largely Hindu state, and Pakistan, a largely Muslim state, gained independence in 1947 after the British agreed to divide the subcontinent. Hindu-Muslim communal violence and disputes over Kashmir and other areas have plagued the two states ever since. The displacement of Muslims from the new India as well as Hindus and Sikhs from the new Pakistan—about 8 million people in each case—was a tragedy with lingering consequences. Five underground nuclear tests carried out by India in mid-May 1998, were followed by Pakistani tests two weeks later. The crises that continue to flare between the two nations now involve the threat of a nuclear exchange.

Mohandas Gandhi's (1869–1948) Congress Party has dominated Indian politics since his assassination in 1948. Jawaharlal Nehru (1889–1964) kept India neutral during the era of the Cold War and saw India through the critical period of reorganization as an independent state. He reduced the communal hatreds, religious zealotry, and regional tensions that followed partition, and he promoted the

QUICK REVIEW

Nehru Dynasty
- Jawaharlal Nehru (1889–1964): First prime minister of India
- Indira Gandhi (1917–1984): Daughter of Nehru, prime minister of India (1966–1977)
- Rajiv Gandhi (1944–1991): Son of Indira Gandhi, prime minister of India (1984–1989)

economic development of his overpopulated new nation. Hindi and English were set as the national languages, and Nehru's resolute opposition to caste privilege helped increase equality of citizenship.

Nehru's successor, Lal Bahadur Shastri (1904–1966), saw India through a war and standoff with Pakistan in 1965. His successor, Nehru's daughter, Indira Gandhi (1917–1984; no relation to Mohandas Gandhi), continued her father's policies. In 1971, she guided India to a victory over Pakistan that led to the creation of Bangladesh in place of East Pakistan. This war, and the subsequent development of an atomic bomb with Russian help, made India the major power in South Asia, but Gandhi's failure to improve India's general economic health undermined her popularity. In 1977, she and the Congress Party were ousted by the voters. Three years later, she was reelected and served as prime minister until efforts to quell Sikh separatism led to her assassination in 1984 by two Sikhs from her own guard.

Rajiv Gandhi (1944–1991), Indira's son, succeeded her. He managed the thorny Sikh issue and worked to resolve problems with Pakistan, but charges of corruption led to the fall of his government. V.P. Singh (b. 1931) succeeded him as prime minister, and when Singh resigned, Gandhi again ran for office. During the campaign, he was assassinated by a Sri Lankan Tamil suicide bomber. The leader of the Congress Party, P. V. Narasimha Rao, was then asked to form a government. He made substantial economic progress and dealt successfully with a wide variety of communal and separatist problems. In 1997, Vice President K. R. Narayanan assumed the presidency, and he and his party were displaced in 2004 by an unexpected Congress Party victory.

India, the world's largest functioning democracy, faces major problems: mass poverty and disease, separatist movements, and runaway population growth—to mention only a few. The growing strength of militant Hindu nationalists and fundamentalists and new outbreaks of communal violence between Hindus and India's large Muslim minority pose serious threats to the country's political stability.

PAKISTAN AND BANGLADESH

The architect and first president of Pakistan, Muhammad Ali Jinnah (1876–1948), oversaw the creation of a Muslim state that then consisted of widely separated East and West Pakistan, the two predominantly Muslim areas of northwest India and East Bengal. In 1971, East Pakistan seceded to form a new Islamic nation, Bangladesh. Indian and Bangladeshi relations are troubled, but the main political division in the subcontinent remains that between India and Pakistan.

Pakistan's efforts to balance religious and secular ideologies and solve massive economic problems have been hampered by bloodshed, military coups, and periodic lapses into dictatorship. The most recent brought Zia ul-Haqq (1924–1988) to power in 1977. The elections of November 1988, following his death in a suspicious air crash, restored parliamentary government. This government was headed by the first female leader of a modern Islamic state, Benazir Bhutto (b. 1953), the daughter of the man whom Zia ul-Haqq overthrew and executed. The president dismissed her government in August 1990. Benazir returned to the prime ministership, only to be deposed by the president on charges of corruption in 1996 and convicted in 1999. In 1999, General Parviz Musharraf, Chief of Army Staff, took over as chief executive, and he and his country are confronting direct challenges from radical Islam.

INDONESIA AND MALAYSIA

The new East Indies state of Indonesia came into being in 1949 as a nominal republic. It succeeded the long Dutch and brief Japanese domination of the East Indies. The much smaller territory of Malaya, a federation under a rotating monarch, received its independence from British colonial rule in 1957. It was later joined by the states of Sarawak and Sabah in northern Borneo, forming the federation of Malaysia.

Indonesia is the largest Muslim country in the world and must reach a consensus among its disparate and scattered parts on how its religious faith is to be reconciled with secularist government. The overriding problem for Malaysia is the cleft between the largely Chinese and partly Indian non-Muslim minority on the one hand and the largely Muslim majority of Malay and other indigenous peoples on the other.

THE POSTCOLONIAL MIDDLE EAST

 o other part of the postcolonial world so dominates international concern and conflict as the Middle East. The issues have arisen as a result of the new nations established in the region since World War I.

NEW NATIONS IN THE MIDDLE EAST

The modern Middle East arose from the fall of the Ottoman Empire and the intervention in the region by Western powers, which carved out new nations and protectorates. Egypt, Iraq, and Saudi Arabia became sovereign states after World War I; Lebanon and Syria were given independence by France during World War II. In 1948, Great Britain abandoned its protectorate over Palestine, and the United Nations recognized the state of Israel. Subsequently, other Arab states gained independence: Jordan, 1946; Libya, 1951; Morocco and Tunisia, 1956; Algeria, 1962; and, by 1971, Yemen, Oman, and the small Arabian Gulf states (see Map 34–2).

These states all share the classical Arabic written language (*fusha*), but the spoken colloquial language ('*amiyya*) varies from place to place. Attempts to create pan-Arab alliances or federations have failed primarily because of regional differences and political interests, but appeals to Arab nationalism remain powerful.

In the wake of World War II, many proponents of Arab nationalism, such as Gamal Abdul Nasser of Egypt (1918–1970), were sympathetic to socialism or the Soviet Union. But because socialism and communism were Western ideologies, the orientation of left-leaning Arab nationalists was no less Western than that of Arabs friendly to the United States. The overt atheism of Soviet communism was equally offensive to devout Arab Muslims.

Not all the new states were on the same footing. Oil, for instance, made Saudi Arabia wealthy and powerful and the Gulf states, such as Kuwait, rich, but not powerful. States that lacked oil, such as Egypt, Jordan, and Syria, were burdened by large impoverished populations. All the Arab governments, however, worked out arrangements with local Muslim authorities. The Saudi royal family modernized Arabia's infrastructure, but turned its educational system over to a rigorist, puritanical form of Islam called *Wahhabism.* The Egyptian government played different Islamic groups against one another. These governments retained the support of prosperous, devout middle-class Muslims while doing little about the plight of the poor.

HOW HAS the growth of Hindu nationalism affected Indian politics?

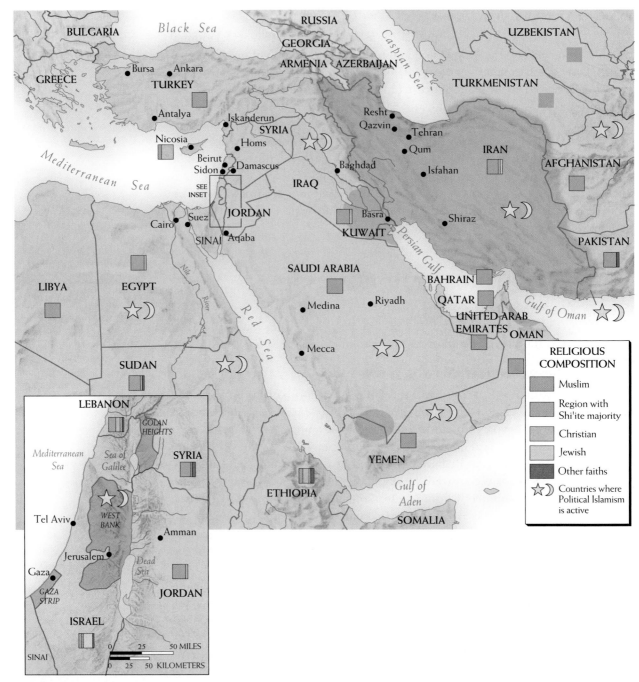

MAP 34–2

The Modern Middle East and the Distribution of Major Religious Communities.   The inset map shows Israel and the occupied territories.

HOW HAS religion shaped the Arab-Israeli conflict?

THE ARAB-ISRAELI CONFLICT

Nowhere have the effects of the West's interventions in the Middle East been more sharply felt than in the creation of the state of Israel in the former British mandate territory of Palestine (1948). The British Balfour Declaration of 1917 supported establishment of a national homeland for the Jews in Palestine, but by 1920 there were only about 60,000 Jews (one-tenth the number of Arabs) in Palestine.

The interwar years saw increasing Jewish settlement and growing communal conflict. Immigration of Jews, largely from Eastern Europe, increased in the

27.5
Israel's Proclamation of Independence

1920s and 1930s. Britain's efforts to restrict it in 1936 tragically prevented many Jews from escaping the Nazi Holocaust. After the war, the Zionist movement received a tremendous boost from Jews worldwide and the Allied nations, which felt the need to atone for the Holocaust by securing a refuge for Jews. The dream of return to the Holy Land had a long history in Judaism.

Under the Ottomans, the Holy Land had been the home of Arabic-speaking Palestinians, primarily Muslims, but also Christians and Jews. None of these had a hand in determing the fate of their land. The Palestinians understandably do not to see why they should be displaced, either because of another people's historic religious attachment to the land or as reparation for Europe's sins against the Jews. Jews, however, felt a desperate need for a homeland where they might be safe from future persecutions and persistent anti-Semitism.

By 1945, Britain was beset in Palestine by Jews seeking to settle there and by Jewish underground and terrorist organizations aiming to oust the British. In 1947, the British turned the problem over to the United Nations. The U.N. called for partition of the mandate territory into a Jewish and an Arab state. The Arab states refused to accept the U.N. resolution, but in May 1948, Jews in Palestine proclaimed the independent state of Israel. Egypt, Iraq, Jordan, Lebanon, Saudi Arabia, and Syria promptly attacked Israel but lost to the better-armed, better trained, and more resolute Israelis. The Israeli-Arab war of 1948–1949 won the Jews not only the U.N.-proposed territory, but also a substantial portion of that proposed for a Palestinian state. The creation of Israel subjected some Palestinians to Israeli rule or occupation and produced a massive Palestinian refugee problem. Another war in 1967 and the aftermaths of two subsequent *intifadahs* further swelled refugee ranks.

The Arab nations and the Palestinian people have generally not accepted Israel's right to exist as a state, and Israel (supported by the United States) has aggressively sought to ensure its survival, often by means that defy world opinion and international laws applying to **occupied territories**. The most serious military confrontations have been: the Suez Crisis of 1956, when Israel (and briefly France and England) invaded the Sinai; the 1967 June war (the "Six Day War"), when Israel occupied the Sinai, the Golan Heights, and the West Bank (of the Jordan River); the October (Yom Kippur) war of 1973, when the Egyptians and Syrians staged a surprise attack on Israel; and the Israeli invasions of Lebanon in 1978 and 1982 to extricate anti-Israeli terrorist refuges. Since the fall of 2000, the region has spiraled into an abyss of violence with repeated Israeli military assaults on towns and refugee camps in the West Bank and Gaza and regular Palestinian extemist suicide attacks on mainly civilian targets. The highly provocative construction by Israel of a massive "separation wall" through the West Bank is currently (2004) impinging on more Palestinian territory as an effort to protect Israelis from suicide bombings.

Israel has responded to extremist terrorist attacks and civilian resistance such as the *intifadah* ("uprising," or literally, "shaking"), in the occupied territories with air and commando raids on Arab states thought to support Palestinian terrorism; with repressive, measures against the Palestinian populations in the occupied territories, and a hard-line stance against negotiation over the status of

intifadah Literally, "shaking." Uprisings by the Palestinians against Israeli occupation.

occupied territories Land occupied by Israel as a result of wars with its Arab neighbors in 1948–1949, 1967, and 1973.

Confrontation. An Israeli settler in prayer shawl carries his American M16 assault rifle past a group of Palestinians in Hebron, who sit in front of a shuttered shop where a large Star of David has been painted.

Kevin Lamarque/Getty Images, Inc./Hulton Archive Photos.

Intifadah. A Palestinian boy hurls a slingshot in the Gaza strip. Though Israel withdrew its forces from Gaza in the summer of 2005, the future for Palestinians is rife with fear and uncertainty.

the territories seized in 1967. The United States has pulled back from serious efforts to mediate.

Arab and some non-Arab states have have supported guerrilla groups attacking Israel and have refused until recently to deal directly with Israel. However, in the late 1970s, Gamal Abdel Nasser's successor, Egyptian President Anwar Sadat (1918–1981), broke ranks and, through the mediation of U.S. President Jimmy Carter (b. 1924), dealt directly with Israel's prime minister Menachem Begin (1913–1994). The Camp David Accords (1978 and 1979) formally concluded peace between the two countries, but in 1981, Sadat was assassinated by Egyptian Muslim extremists. His successor, Husni Mubarak (b. 1928), continued to honor the treaty.

Recent Israeli military actions in the occupied territories were provoked by, but in turn have brought on, more Palestinian terrorist bombings in Israel and abroad. Arabs and many Muslims outside the Arab world have come to view Jews, without distinction, as oppressors and enemies, and many Jews around the world have similarly vilified all Arabs and Muslims.

Some events of recent years gave at least brief hope for resolution of the conflict. In 1991, in the wake of the Gulf War that followed Iraq's invasion of Kuwait, the parties to the Arab-Israeli conflict began peace negotiations. The result was the 1993 Middle East Peace Agreement, or the Oslo Agreement, which promised a negotiated settlement and the creation of an independent Palestinian state alongside Israel. But there has been little substantive progress made in the 11 years since the 1993 agreement. Jordan and Egypt agreed in 1994 to a peace treaty with Israel, but some other Arab states remain unwilling to negotiate. Israel, for its part, has continued actions that preclude formation of a viable state on contiguous territory, and extremists on both sides pose obstacles to the success of the peace initiative. In November 1995, a Jewish Israeli extremist assassinated Prime Minister Yitzhak Rabin for trying to make peace. Then, in the run-up to the Israeli elections of May 29, 1996, Palestinian extremists carried out a series of savage bombings on buses and in crowded shopping areas. This helped a Likud conservative hard-liner, Benjamin Netanyahu (b. 1949), win over Rabin's Labor successor, Shimon Peres, by a margin of less than 1 percent and cast more uncertainty on peace prospects. The Netanyahu regime repeatedly took rigid stands and provocative actions involving settlements and territorial claims. The Palestinian Authority, which was created by the 1993 peace agreement, did not behave any better. Under Yasser Arafat (1929–2004), it grew steadily more corrupt, ineffective, and out of touch with its constituencies. Despite the efforts of both Palestinian and Israeli security forces, Palestinian guerrillas of the extremist wing of the resistance organization Hamas have slaughtered Israeli civilians in a sustained effort to torpedo the **peace process**. These terrorist attacks have exacerbated the already dire plight of thousands of Palestinian families, keeping them in the poverty that recruits new volunteers for the extremist resistance groups.

In March 2000, Ariel Sharon, a former army general, became prime minister. His administration has been marked by an escalation of violence on both sides, but he has proposed that Israel withdraw from Gaza and close Israeli settlements in that region. His government has also begun to erect a fence separating Israeli and Palestinian territory. Arafat's death in late 2004 may present a new opportunity for negotiations with the new Palestinian president, Mahmoud Abbas.

MIDDLE EASTERN OIL

Oil, or black gold, has been a blessing and a curse for the Middle East. Since its discovery in Iran in 1908 and the beginning of its production in Saudi Arabia in 1939, the world demand for oil has surged. The Arab and other oil-rich Third

peace process Efforts, chiefly led by the United States, to broker a peace between the state of Israel and the PLO.

World states—such as Indonesia, Iran, Nigeria, and Venezuela—have used oil to their advantage in international diplomacy since the mid-1970s. Oil has given peripheral and virtually unknown countries of the Sahara or the Arabian deserts major influence over the world of international banking and finance. Middle Eastern oil supplies are so important that the United States and European nations were willing, in partnership with some Arab countries, to go to war to reverse Iraq's invasion of Kuwait in 1990.

The economic benefits of oil are obvious, but they have not inevitably conferred political benefits on the people in the Middle East. The Middle East has been subject to considerable foreign involvement in its affairs from Europe, the United States, and the former Soviet Union, which has sometimes been detrimental to its political development.

THE RISE OF POLITICAL ISLAMISM

The increase in the global importance of the oil-producing states of the Middle East has coincided with a surging movement there and elsewhere for the revival of pristine Muslim values and reformation of Muslim societies. Many Muslims have sought to return to the "fundamentals" of Islam, which they see as a means for rejuvenating societies corrupted by Western secularist and materialist values. A major new element in Muslim revivalism is a consciousness of being a viable response to the destructive influence of Western-style "modernity."

Much of the appeal of Islamist groups everywhere is their willingness and ability to address the needs of the underclasses in Middle Eastern, North African, and Asian cities and countries. Where governments of Muslim-majority countries have failed to provide social services such as housing, medical care, education, and jobs, the Islamist groups have succeeded. While the world press reports only on the relatively small fringe groups of Islamist extremists, Muslims at the grass-roots level have watched while the major Islamist groups in the dictatorships or military regimes under which most of them live provide services for which the state has long abdicated responsibility.

Such Muslim fundamentalism—or more correctly, "Islamist reformism"— motivated the overthrow of the the shah of Iran in 1978, the Muslim Brethren movement in Egypt and elsewhere, the Welfare Party in Turkey, and many other groups, from Morocco to the Persian Gulf and beyond the Middle East. All such Islamist groups see themselves as traditionalist, as true to basic Muslim values and norms. Whether these movements will bring lasting change to Islamic societies is an open issue, but there is no question about their current attraction and influence.

European expansion over much of the globe brought far more social and political change than religious or even cultural change to the Islamic world. Globally it promoted European-style nationalism and the idea of the nation-state, post-Enlightenment ideals of individual liberties and rights and representative government, and the concept of religious faith as a private matter separate from citizenship. Such ideas proved revolutionary in the Islamic world, especially in this century.

Parts of the Islamic world in the 20th century have a checkered history of autocratic governments that were as far removed from their citizenries as any medieval or premodern dynasty. Experiments with European-style parliamentary government have only rarely taken hold; nor have either liberal democratic or Marxist-socialist ideals proven viable for the long term. Until recently, however, little of the political discourse in Islamic lands has given serious thought to *Islamic* alternatives.

The postcolonial independence of many national states divorced politics from Islamic religious traditions and norms. Where leaders had previously claimed Muslim faith and allegiance, some espoused secular ideologies and ignored religion except to use it as a political weapon. In the late 20th and early 21st centuries, Islamic religious allegiance has commonly been invoked to bolster a ruler's claim to legitimacy and to cloak mundane objectives and programs in pious garb. In short, the recent past has seen no realization of an "ideal" Islamic state in which religious and political authority are conjoined. Even in the postrevolutionary Islamic Republic of Iran a clear division exists between political realities and religious standards. However, sincerely the latter are claimed as the basis of state policy, no one can miss the frequent stretching of norms to justify pragmatic political decisions. When we look at the Islamist movements of recent decades, we find that the calls for a congruence of religion and politics in the Islamic world trace less to some kind of ideal model of a religious state or so-called **theocracy** than to a sorely felt need for simple social and political justice. The cries for a "jihad" of Muslims are aimed less often outward than inward, less at foreign "devils" and more at domestic tyrants, corruption, and social and economic injustice. The most international and widely influential of all contemporary Islamic revivalist or reform movements, the Tabligh-i Jama'at, is explicitly apolitical. It aims to convert the individual to true submission *(islam)* not lip service on the principle that reform of the world begins with oneself.

As for those reform movements that are avowedly political, be they activist but nonviolent (the majority) or extremist and violent (the minority), they feed on the deep sense of socioeconomic and political injustice that citizens of most Islamic countries rightfully feel. When such feelings go over the edge, the result is extremism and terrorism. Osama bin Laden, the disposessed Saudi millionare who founded and has led al-Qaeda, from the 1990s to the present, stunned the world by using U.S. civilian airliners to destroy the World Trade Center towers and part of the Pentagon building on September 11, 2001. His motive was revenge for the American military presence in Saudi Arabia, the American-led blockade of Iraq, and the American support of Israel against the Palestinians.

These carefully executed and massively destructive attacks have involved the U.S. military ever more deeply in the Middle East and Central Asia. In October 2001, the United States attacked the Taliban government of Afghanistan, rapidly overthrew it, and dispersed, but did not destroy, al-Qaeda's organization. Whether this military response to the threat of terrorism will be successful remains to be seen. Further U.S. intervention followed in 2003 with the invasion of Iraq.

IRAQ AND U.S. INTERVENTION

The modern nation of Iraq was established after World War I. Iraq as such had never been a distinct political unit and until 1921 was primarily a geographic term, referring to today's southern Iraq. Postwar imperial concern and the potential of oil under Iraqi soil motivated the British government to oversee the creation of an Iraq that they felt would best protect their interests in the region. Given the disparate ethnic and religious groups in the country, the British could not find a suitable native leader. Therefore, they imported a politician from Arabia, Faysal ibn Husayn, crowned him first king of the Hashemite monarchy. The dynasty ruled until 1958, with the help of British advisers, soldiers, and a

theocracy State ruled by religious leaders who claim to govern by divine authority.

British-dominated consortium of oil companies.

Iraqis developed a sense of national identity that led them to resent the foreign presence in their country, and in 1958, a bloody coup, led by Abd al-Karim Qasem, terminated the monarchy. By 1979, the Ba'ath party had become the dominant force in Iraq politics, bringing Saddam Hussein to the start of his tyrannical reign. Following a long, bloody, and unsuccessful war with Iraq (1980–1988), Saddam Hussein invaded and occupied Kuwait (1990). After an international military coalition under the leadership of the United States (in Operation Desert Storm) expelled the Iraqi army from Kuwait, Iraq became an international pariah. It was subject to economic sanctions monitored by the United Nations until 1998, when the Iraqi government expelled the U.N. inspectors.

Terrorist Attack. On September 11, 2001 a terrorist attack targeted the World Trade Center Towers in New York City. In this photograph the first of the twin towers is in flames as the second plane heads directly toward the second tower. In a very brief time both towers collapsed with the loss of nearly 3,000 lives.

Masatomo Kuriya, Corbis/Sygma.

The U.S. government adopted a policy of regime change in Iraq during the last years of the Clinton administration, though it did little to carry out that policy. In the wake of the September 11, 2001, terrorist attacks, however, the Bush administration decided that Saddam Hussein had to be overthrown to remove the threat of Iraqi weapons of mass destruction. During late 2002 and early 2003, the U.S. and British governments sought to obtain passage of the U.N. Security Council resolutions that would require Iraq to disarm on its own or to face disarmament by military force. When opposition from France and Russia blocked the resolution, Australia, Great Britain, and the United States, with more then 40 other nations (the "Coalition of the Willing") invaded Iraq. After three weeks of fighting that began in mid-March 2003, the Coalition removed Saddam Hussein from power.

The invasion of Iraq occasioned considerable international opposition, most notably from France, Germany and Russia, and pro-voked large antiwar demonstrations in the United States and other parts of the world. The war has created strains within the European Union and NATO and begun a new era in international relations.

Traffic Cop. A U.S. Marine directs Iraqi civilians in the northern city of Kirkuk in April 2003.

Sebastian Bolesch/Das Fotoarchiv/ Peter Arnold, Inc.

Currently, it is immensely difficult to ensure peace and stability in Iraq. Many Iraqis have resisted occupation by foreign forces and historical factors militate against formation of a new unified government. The unpreparedness of the Americans and their allies to deal with the chaos of postwar Iraq has exacerbated matters, and the failure to find weapons of mass destruction in Iraq led to wide questioning of the rationale for the war. Throughout Iraq an insurgency has been launched

against the Coalition forces and against Iraqis who cooperate with the coalition and the recently installed Iraqi government. However, President George W. Bush, who was reelected in 2004, has vowed to continue to pursue his existing policies in the Middle East. In late January 2005, an election was held in Iraq under conditions of insurgent attacks to elect the assembly that wrote a new constitution, in October 2005 the constitution was ratified. The challenge of securing general internal support for the construction of democratic processes now confronts the Iraqi government and American policy makers.

IMAGE KEY
for pages 836–837

a. A fifty-gallon oil drum.

b. A statue of deposed Iraqi leader Saddam Hussein is toppled by American forces in April, 2003.

c. Bangladeshi women with a cellular phone.

d. Former South African president Nelson Mandela.

e. Zapatistas demonstrate in Mexico.

f. Ernesto "Che" Guevera.

g. Late Palestinian leader Yasser Arafat.

h. Rwandan refugees.

i. As Tower One burns, another hijacked airliner aims for Tower Two of the World Trade Center, September 11, 2001.

SUMMARY

The Postcolonial World Since 1945, the European colonial empires have disappeared from Africa and Asia and have been replaced by a multitude of independent states. These states had to adjust their political and economic relations to one or the other of the superpowers during the Cold War and then, since the disappearance of the Soviet Union, to the West.

Latin America Most Latin American countries remain politically and economically dependent on the United States. Except in Cuba, no revolutionary movement has been able to overturn the traditional structure of Latin American society. Despite social and economic problems, Argentina and Brazil have managed to move from military rule to stable democratic, civilian government. In Mexico, the long dominance of the PRI ended in 2000.

Africa Independent Africa has faced severe problems: overpopulation, poverty, the absence of an educated middle class, tribal and class conflict, arbitrary boundaries, disease, economic dependence, and political instability. The challenge for Africa as a whole is to build a truly civil society and achieve economic health and political stability.

The Middle East Oil and Muslim reaction to the creation of the state of Israel have dominated the history of the Middle East since the 1940s. While the possession of vast deposits of oil has made some Middle Eastern governments wealthy, it has not led to the creation of prosperous democratic societies. Although efforts by the United States to sponsor an Arab-Israeli peace have made some progress, the cycle of terror and retaliatory violence has persisted.

Political Islamism, although not a monolithic movement, has proved increasingly disruptive to the region and the entire Islamic world.

In the wake of the terrorist attacks of September 11, 2001, the United States finds itself increasingly embroiled in a chaotic and unstable region of the world.

REVIEW QUESTIONS

1. How did the superpower rivalry of the Cold War affect Latin America? How successful has the worldwide trend toward democratization been in Latin America?

2. What factors contributed to the spread of decolonization in sub-Saharan Africa? Why were the newly independent states so fragile? What was the apartheid regime in South Africa? How was it dismantled, and what problems does the new South Africa face?

3. What roles does Islam play in Iran, Pakastan, Malaysia, and Turkey? What does the influence of Islam in these regions suggest about the power of religious tradition in modern politics and society?

4. How have interventions by European powers and the United States affected the modern Middle East? How did the Arab-Israeli conflict begin? How has it developed?

5. What is political Islamism? Why has it taken so radical a course? Why has the United States become its primary target? How did the United States respond to the attacks of September 11, 2001?

KEY TERMS

apartheid (p. 839)

ayatollah (p. 850)

clash of civilizations (p. 839)

globalization (p. 839)

intifadah (p. 855)

liberation theology (p. 840)

occupied territories (p. 855)

peace process (p. 856)

Sandinistas (p. 842)

theocracy (p. 857)

 For additional study resources for this chapter, go to:
www.prenhall.com/craig/chapter34

Visualizing The Past

Imperialism and Race in Modern Art

HOW HAVE the experiences of imperialism and race influenced modern and contemporary art in both style and technique?

The second half of the 19th century witnessed the "second wave" of European imperialism. The United States and Japan also participated in the frenzy of the industrialized powers to obtain the labor and natural resources of other regions. Colonizers focused their attention on regions such as China, the African interior, and the Pacific Islands, which were not yet firmly ensconced in older colonial empires.

The colonial experience has been an important legacy in Western and non-Western art alike, in terms of providing artistic themes, but also in the influence of Western techniques in painting and sculpture on indigenous artists. The result has been an original and imaginative blending of styles and techniques that in turn have greatly influenced Western artists.

Paul Gauguin, "Where do we come from? What are we? Where are we going?" (1897), Oil on canvas.
Gauguin was one of the last French impressionist painters of the late 19th century. Like colonists, he imagined the people of French Tahiti as a kind of "noble savage" among whom he would find the primitive, spiritually pure lifestyle he sought. Race thus is central to his depiction of the Tahitians, but always in an idealized vision of peace and simplicity.

Museum of Fine Arts, Boston, Mass./A.K.G., Berlin/Super Stock.

▼

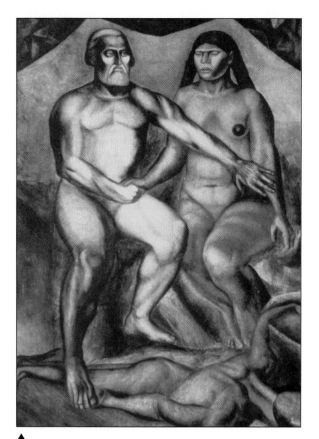

▲

José Clemente Orozco, "Cortés y Malinzin," (1926), fresco.
Orozco, in his fresco of the great Spanish conquistador Hernan
Cortés and Cortés' Indian translator and concubine, Malinzin
(Malinche), deals with themes of race, conquest, and gender in a
much less idealized way than Gauguin. Both the style and theme of
this work reflect the often uneasy but creative mixing of Western
and Indian genes and culture that characterizes Mexico's *mestizo*
society.

Photography: Angel Hurtado, Art Museum of the Americas, OAS. © Orozco
Valladares Family. Reproduction authorized by the Instituto Nacional de Bellas Artes.

**Penny Siopis, "Cape of Good Hope—
A History Painting," 1989–1990.**
As in the image of Cortés, the naked female form, signifying the
violated body of the colonized people, is at the heart of Penny
Siopis's conception of
the experience of
South African Blacks
under White rule.
Siopis's figure literally
embodies the suffer-
ing of all Black South
Africans, but also their
dignity and patience,
in stark contrast to the
decadent, voyeuristic
whites presumably
viewing the painting.
Courtesy of the University
of the Witwatersand,
Jahannesburg, South
Africa.

▼

**Taguchi Beisaku, "Strange-looking Manchurian Horsemen on an Expedition to Observe the Japanese Camp in the
Distance near Sauhoku (Sokako)" 1894.**
Japan also entered the race for colonial possessions in the last decade of the 19th century. Two wars, one with China (1894–1895)
and the other with Russia (1904–1905), resulted in the 1905 Treaty of Portsmouth that earned Japan control of Manchuria,
hegemony over Korea, and outright annexation of Sakhalin Island. In this Japanese painting from the period, we see two
Manchurian horsemen portrayed as barbaric and ghoulish.

▼

Taguchi Beisaku, Japanese, 1864–1903.
Strange-looking Manchurian horsemen
on an expedition to observe the
Japanese camp in the distance near
Sauhoku (Sokako) Japanese, Meiji
era probably published late 1894.
Woodblock print; ink and color
on paper. Vertical oban triptych:
37 × 71.2 cm (14 9/16 × 28 1/16 in.)
Courtesy, Museum of Fine Arts, Boston.
Jaen S. and Frederic A. Sharf Collection
2000.255. Reproduction with permission.
© 2003 Museum of Fine Arts, Boston.
All Rights Reserved.

A Chronological Survey of World History

Enlightenment, Revolution, and Modernity

1750 – 1850

1850 – 1914

EUROPE

1756–1763   Seven Years' War
1783   Peace of Paris, ending American Revolution
1789   French Revolution begins
1804–1814   Napoleon's empire
1814–1815   Congress of Vienna
1832   First British Reform Act
1837–1901   Queen Victoria of England
1848   Revolutions across Europe

1854–1856   The Crimean War
1861   Italy unified
1861   Emancipation of Russian serfs
1866   Austro-Prussian War; creation of Dual Monarchy of Austria-Hungary in 1867
1870–1871   Franco-Prussian War; German Empire proclaimed in 1871
1882   Triple Alliance
1905   Revolution in Russia
1914   World War I begins in Europe

NEAR EAST/ASIA

1757   British victory at Plassey, in Bengal
1772–1833   Ram Mohan Roy, Hindu reformer in India
1794–1925   Qajar shahs in Iran
1805–1849   Muhammad Ali in Egypt
ca. 1839–1880   Tanzimat reforms, Ottoman Empire
1839–1897   Muslim intellectual Jamal al-Din Al-Afghani

1857–1858   Sepoy Rebellion, India
1869   Suez Canal completed
1869–1948   Mohandas (Mahatma) Gandhi
1876–1949   Muhammad Ali Jinnah, "founder of Pakistan"
1882   English occupation of Egypt
1886   India National Congress formed
1889–1964   Jawaharlal Nehru
1899   Ottoman sultan grants concession to Germany to extend railway to Baghdad
1908   "Young Turk" Revolt, Turkey

EAST ASIA

1787–1793   Matsudaira Sadanobu's reforms in Japan
1789   White Lotus Rebellion in China
1835–1908   Empress Dowager Tz'u-hsi
1839–1842   Opium War

1850–1873   Taiping and other rebellions, China
1853–1854   Commodore Perry "opens" Japan to the West
1860s   Establishment of treaty ports in China
1870s–1890s   Self-Strengthening movement in China
1889   Meiji Constitution in Japan
1894–1895   Sino-Japanese War
1898–1900   Boxer Rebellion in China
1904–1905   Russo-Japanese War
1910   Japan annexes Korea
1911   Republican Revolution begins in China

AFRICA

1754–1817   Usman Dan Fodio, founder of Sultanate in northern and central Nigeria
1762   End of Funj sultanate in eastern Sudanic region
1806   British take Cape Colony from the Dutch
1817–1828   Zulu chief Shaka reigns
1830–1847   French invasion of Algeria
1830s   Dutch settlers, the Boers, expand northward from Cape Colony
1848–1885   Sudanese Madhi, Muhammad Ahmad

1856–1884   King Mutasa of Buganda reigns
1880s   Mahdist revival and uprising in Sudan
1880   French protectorate in Tunisia and the Ivory Coast
1885   British control Nigeria and British East Africa
1894   French annex Dahomey
1899   German East Africa; British in Sudan
1899–1902   Boer War
1900   Nigeria a British Crown colony
1907   Union of South Africa formed
1911   Liberia becomes a virtual U.S. protectorate
1914   Ethiopia the only independent state in Africa

THE AMERICAS

1776   American Declaration of Independence
1791   First ten amendments to U.S. Constitution (Bill of Rights) ratified
1791   Negro slave revolt in French Santo Domingo
1804   Haitian independence
1808–1824   Wars of independence in Latin America
1822   Brazilian independence
1847   Mexican War

1854   Kansas-Nebraska Act
1856   Dred Scott Decision
1859   Raid on Harper's Ferry
1860   Abraham Lincoln elected U.S. president
1861–1865   U.S. Civil War
1862–1867   French invasion of Mexico
1863   Emancipation Proclamation in United States
1865–1877   Reconstruction
1880s   Slavery eliminated in Cuba and Brazil
1898   Spanish-American War
1901   Theodore Roosevelt elected U.S. president
1910–1917   Mexican Revolution
1912   Woodrow Wilson elected U.S. president

Empires and Cultures of the Ancient World

3000 B.C.E	1500 B.C.E	500 B.C.E	300 B.C.E	1 C.E.

EUROPE

3000 B.C.E	1500 B.C.E	500 B.C.E	300 B.C.E	1 C.E.
ca. 2500–1100 Minoan civilization	ca. 1100–800 Greek "dark ages"	480–479 Persian invasion of Greece	264 Rome rules all of Italy	96–180 The good emperors rule Rome
ca. 1600–1100 Mycenaean civilization on Greek mainland	800 Etruscan civilization begins in Italy	478 Foundation of Delian League/Athenian Empire	146 Rome destroys Carthage; rules all of western Mediterranean	180–284 Breakdown of the Pax Romana
	ca. 750–550 Rise of the polis	431–404 Peloponnesian Wars	44–31 Civil wars destroy Roman Republic	306–337 Constantine reigns
	594 Solon's legislation at Athens	338 Battle of Chaeronia; Macedonian conquest of Greece	31 Rome rules Mediterranean	313 Edict of Milan
	509 Foundation of the Roman Republic	336–323 Career of Alexander the Great	31 b.c.e.–14 c.e. Principate of Augustus	325 Council of Nicaea
	508 Democracy established in Athens			391 Theodosius makes Christianity the official imperial religion
				ca. 400–500 The Germanic invasions
				426 The City of God, by Augustine
				476 The last Western emperor is deposed

NEAR EAST/ASIA

3000 B.C.E	1500 B.C.E	500 B.C.E	300 B.C.E	1 C.E.
ca. 3500–3000 Emergence of Sumerian city–states	ca. 1500 Aryan peoples migrate into northwestern India	ca. 540–468 Vardhamana Mahavira, founder of Jain tradition	ca. 300 Founding of Seleucid dynasty in Anatolia, Syria, and Mesopotamia; Ptolemaic dynasty in Egypt	30 Crucifixion of Jesus
ca. 3000 Emergence of civilization along the Nile River	960–933 Rule of Hebrew king Solomon	334 Alexander begins conquest of the Near East; invades India in 327	269–232 Mauryan emperor Ashoka patronizes Buddhism	70 Romans destroy the Temple at Jerusalem
ca. 2300 Emergence of Harappan civilization in Indus valley	ca. 628–551 Life of Zarathushtra	321–181 Mauryan Empire in India	247 b.c.e.–224 c.e. Parthian dynasty controls Persia	216–277 Mani
2276–2221 Sargon of Akkad creates the first Mesopotamian Empire	ca. 537–486 Siddhartha Gautama		180 b.c.e.–320 c.e. India politically divided	ca. 224 Fall of Parthians, rise of Sasanids, in Persia
2000 Epic of Gilgamesh	559–529 Cyrus the Great creates the Persian Empire			ca. 320–500 Gupta dynasty, India
50 Hammurabi's code				ca. 400 Chandra Gupta conquers western India
				ca. 450 The Huns invade India

EAST ASIA

3000 B.C.E	1500 B.C.E	500 B.C.E	300 B.C.E	1 C.E.
4000 Neolithic cultures in China	1027–771 Western Chou dynasty, China	ca. 500–200 Rise of Mohist, Taoist, and Legalist schools of thought in China	256–206 Ch'in dynasty in China	25–220 The Later Han dynasty, China
3000–300 Jōmon culture in Japan	771–256 Eastern Chou dynasty in China	401–256 Period of the Warring States in China	221 Ch'in emperor unites all of China	ca. 220–590 Spread of Buddhism in China
766–1050 Hang dynasty in China with city–states and writing	ca. 771 Iron Age territoria states in China	ca. 300 Old Stone Age Jōmon culture in Japan replaced by Yayoi culture	206 b.c.e.–8 c.e. Former Han dynasty in China	220–589 Six Dynasties period in China
1	551–479 Confucius in China		179–104 Han philosopher Tung Chung-shu	ca. 300–500 Barbarian invasions of China
19			145–90 Han historian Ssu-ma Chien	ca. 300–680 Archaic Yamato state in Japan
			141–187 Emperor Wu Ti of China reigns	

AFRICA

3000 B.C.E	1500 B.C.E	500 B.C.E	300 B.C.E	1 C.E.
00 Practice of agriculture spreads from Nile river valley to the Sudan	750 Kushite king Kashta conquers Upper Egypt		25 Romans sack Kushite capital of Napata	ca. 200 Camel first used for trans-Saharan transport
2000 Ivory and gold trade between Kush (Nubia) and Egypt	ca. 720 Kushite king Piankhy completes conquest of Egypt		00 b.c.e.–1 c.e. Probable first Indonesian migrations to east African coast	ca. 200–900 Expansion of Bantu people
ca. 1500 Practice of agriculture spreads from the Sudan to Abyssinia and the savanna region	ca. 600 Meroitic period of Kushan civilization begins			ca. 250 Aksum (Ethiopia) controls the Red Sea trade
				ca. 300–400 Rise of kingdom of Ghana
				a. 350 Kush ceases to exist

THE AMERICAS

3000 B.C.E	1500 B.C.E	500 B.C.E	300 B.C.E	1 C.E.
ca. 4000 Maize already domesticated in Mexico	ca. 1500–800 Olmec civilization in Mesoamerica	ca. 500–20 Founding of Monte Alban		ca. 200–600 Early Intermediate period in Andean South America; Moche and Nazca cultures
	a. 800–200 Chavín (Early) Horizon in Andean South America			ca. 150–900 Classic period. Dominance of Teotihuacán in central Mexico, Tikal in southern Yucatán

Consolidation and Interaction of World Civilizations

500 C.E – 800	800 – 1100	1100 –1300	1300 –1500

EUROPE

500 C.E – 800	800 – 1100	1100 –1300	1300 –1500
511 Death of Clovis, Frankish ruler of Gaul **529** Benedict of Nursia founds Benedictine Order **590–604** Pontificate of Gregory I, "The Great" **768–814** Charlemagne	**ca. 800–1000** Invasions of England and the Carolingian Empire (Vikings, Magyars, and Muslims) **843** Treaty of Verdun **910** Cluny Monastery founded **1019–1054** Yaroslav the Wise reigns; peak of Kievan Russia **1054** Schism between Latin and Greek churches **1066** Norman Conquest of England **1073–1085** Investiture controversy **1096–1270** The Crusades	**1154–115** Frederick Barbarosa invades Italy **1182–1226** St. Francis of Assisi **1198–1216** Pontificate of Innocent III **ca. 1100–1300** Growth of trade and towns **1215** Magna Carta granted **ca. 1225–1274** St. Thomas Aquinas **265–1321** Dante Alighieri	**1337** Hundred Years' War begins **ca. 1340–1400** Geoffrey Chaucer **1347–1349** The Black Death **1375–1527** The Italian Renaissance **1485** Battle of Bosworth Field; accession of Henry Tudor to the throne of England **1492** Columbus's first voyage to the New World

NEAR EAST/ASIA

500 C.E – 800	800 – 1100	1100 –1300	1300 –1500
527–565 Justinian's reign **531–579** Reign of Chosroes Anosharvian in Iran **ca. 570–632** Muhammad **622** The Hijra **616–657** Reign of Harsha **651** Death of last Sasanid ruler **661–750** Umayyad dynasty **680** Death of Al-Husayn at Karbala **ca. 710** First Muslim invasion of India **750–1258** Abbasid dynasty **786–809** Caliph Harun Al-Rashid reigns	**800–120** Period of feudal overlordship in India **900–1100** Golden age of Muslim learning **909–1171** Fatimids in North Africa and Egypt **945–1055** Buyid rule in Baghdad **994–1186** Ghaznavid rule in northwestern India, Afghanistan, and Iran **1055–1194** Seljuk rule in Baghdad **1071** Seljuk Turks capture Jerusalem **1081–1118** Byzantine emperor Alexius Comnenus reigns **ca. 1000–1300** Turko-Afghan raids into India	**1174–1193** Saladin reigns **1192** Muslim conquerors end Buddhism in India **1206–1526** Delhi Sultanate in India **ca. 1220** Mongol invasions of Iran, Iraq, Syria, India **1258** Hulagu Khan, Mongol leader, conquers Baghdad **1260–1335** Il-Khans rule Iran	**1250–1517** Mamluk rule in Egypt **1366–1405** Timur (Tamerlane) reigns **1405–1494** Timurids rule in Transoxiana and Iran **1453** Byzantine Empire falls to the Ottoman Turks

EAST ASIA

500 C.E – 800	800 – 1100	1100 –1300	1300 –1500
589–618 Sui dynasty reunifies China **607** Japan begins embassies to China **618–907** Tang dynasty in China **701–762** Li Po, Tang poet **710–784** Nara court, Japan's first permanent capital **712** Records of Ancient Matters, in Japan **713–756** Emperor Hsuan Tsung reigns in China **755** An Lu-shan rebellion in China **794–1185** Heian (Kyoto) court in Japan	**856–1086** Fujiwara dominate Heian court **960–1279** Sung dynasty in China **ca. 1000** *Pillow Book* by Shohōnagon and *Tale of Genji* by Murasaki Shikibu **1037–1101** Su Tung-p'o, Sung poet	**1130–1200** Chu Hsi, Song philosopher **1167–1227** Genghis Khan, founder of Mongol Empire **1185–1333** Kamakura shogunate in Japan **1274–1281** Mongol invasions of Japan **1279–1368** Mongol (Yuan) dynasty in China	**1336–1467** Ashikaga shogunate in Kyoto **1368–1644** Ming dynasty in China **1405–1433** Voyages of Cheng Ho **1467–1568** Warring States era in Japan **1472–1529** Wang Yang-ming, Ming philosopher

AFRICA

500 C.E – 800	800 – 1100	1100 –1300	1300 –1500
ca. 500 States of Takrur and Ghana founded **ca. 500–700** Political and commercial ascendancy of Aksum (Ethiopia) **ca. 600–1500** Extensive slave trade from sub-Saharan Africa to Mediterranean **ca. 700–800** Ghanians begin to supply gold to Mediterranean **ca. 700–900** States of Gao and Kanem **ca. 800** Appearance of the Kanur people around Lake Chad	**ca. 800–900** Decline of Aksum **ca. 900–1100** Kingdom of Ghana; capital city, Kumbi Saleh **ca. 1000–1100** Islam penetrates sub-Saharan Africa **1000–1500** "Great Zimbabwe" center of Bantu Kingdom in southeastern Africa	**ca. 1100–1897** Kingdom of Benin in tropical rain forest region **1194–1221** Kanem Empire achieves greatest expansion **1203** Kingdom of Ghana falls to Sosso people **1230–1255** King Sundiata, first ruler of Mali Empire **ca. 1230–1450** Kingdom of Mali Empire	**1307–1332** Mansa Musa, greatest king of Mali **1490s** Europeans establish trading posts on western African coast **mid-1400s** Decline of Mali Empire; creation of Songhai Empire **1468** Sonni Ali captures Timbuktu **1476–1507** Reign of King Mai Ali of Bornu in central Sudan **1493–1528** Songhai ruler Askia Muhammed reigns; consolidates Songhai Empire

THE AMERICAS

500 C.E – 800	800 – 1100	1100 –1300	1300 –1500
ca. 150–900 Classic period. Dominance of Teotihuacán in central Mexico, Tikal in southern Yucatán	**ca. 600–1000** Middle (Huari/Tiwanaku) Horizon in Andean South America	**ca. 800–1400** Chimu Empire on north coast of Peru	**1325** Founding of Aztec capital **1428–1519** Period of Aztec expansion **1492** European encounter with America **1519** Cortes conquers Aztec Empire **ca. 1350–1533** Inca Empire in Peru **1533** Pizarro executes Inca ruler Atahualpa

The World in Transition

1500 – 1600   1600 – 1700   1700 – 1800

EUROPE

1500 – 1600	1600 – 1700	1700 – 1800

1517–1555 Protestant Reformation
1533–1584 Ivan the Terrible of Russia reigns
1540 Jesuit Order founded by Ignatius Loyola
1543–1727 Scientific Revolution
1556–1598 Philip II of Spain reigns
1558–1603 Elizabeth I of England reigns
1562–1598 French Wars of Religion
1581 The Netherlands declares its independence from Spain
1588 Defeat of the Spanish Armada
1589–1610 Henry IV, founds Bourbon dynasty, France

618–1648 Thirty Years' War
1640–1688 Frederick William, the Great Elector, reigns in Brandenburg-Prussia
1642–1646 Puritan Revolution in England
1643–1715 Louis XIV of France reigns
1682–1725 Peter the Great of Russia reigns
1688 Glorious Revolution in England
1690 *Second Treatise of Civil Government* by John Locke

1701 Act of Settlement provides for Protestant succession to English throne
1702–1713 War of Spanish Succession
1740–1748 War of Austrian Succession
1756–1763 Seven Years' War
ca. 1750 Industrial Revolution begins in England
1772 First partition of Poland
1789 First French Revolution
1793 and 1795 Last two partitions of Poland

NEAR EAST/ASIA

500–1722 Safavid Shi'ite rule in Iran
1512–1520 Ottoman ruler Selim I
1520–1566 Ottoman ruler Suleiman the Magnificent
1525–1527 Babur founds Mughal dynasty in India
1540 Hungary under Ottoman rule
1556–1605 Akbar the Great of India reigns
1571 Battle of Lepanto; Ottomans defeated
ca. 1571–1640 Safavid philosopher-writer Mullah Sadra
1588–1629 Shah Abbas I of Iran reigns

1628–1657 Shah Jahan reigns; builds Taj Mahal as mausoleum for his beloved wife
1646 Founding of Maratha Empire
1648 Delhi becomes the capital of Mughal Empire
1658–1707 Shah Aurangzeb, the "World Conqueror," reigns in India
1669–1683 Last military expansion by Ottomans: 1669, seize Crete; 1670s, the Ukraine; 1683, Vienna

1700 Sikhs and Marathas bring down Mughal Imperial Power
1708 British East India Company and New East India Company merge
1722 Last Safavid ruler forced to abdicate
1724 Rise in the Deccan of the Islamic state of Hyderabad
1725 Nadir Shah of Afganhistan becomes ruler of Persia
1739 Persian invasion of northern India, by Nadir Shah
1748–1761 Ahmad Shah Durrani of Afghanistan invades India
1757 British victory at Plassey, in Bengal

EAST ASIA

1500–1800 Commercial revolution in Ming-Ch'ing China; trade with Europe; flourishing of the novel
1543 Portuguese arrive in Japan
1568–1600 Era of unification follows end of Warring States Era, Japan
1587 Spanish arrive in Japan
1588 Hideyoshi's sword hunt in Japan
1592–1598 Ming troops battle Hideyoshi's army in Korea

1600 Tokugawa Ieyasu wins battle of Sekigahara, completes unification of Japan
1600–1868 Tokugawa shogunate in Edo
1630s Seclusion adopted as national policy in Japan
1644–1694 Bashō Japanese poet
1644–1911 Ch'ing (Manchu) dynasty in China
1661-1722 K'ang Hsi reign in China
1673–1681 Revolt of southern generals in China
1699 British East India Company arrives in China

1701 Forty-seven ro-nin incident in Japan
1716–1733 Reforms of Tokugawa Yoshimune in Japan
1737–1795 Reign of Ch'ien Lung in China
1742 Christianity banned in China
1784 American traders arrive in China
1787–1793 Matsudaira Sadanobu's reforms in Japan
1798 White Lotus Rebellion in China

AFRICA

1506 East coast of Africa under Portuguese domination
1507 Mozambique founded by Portuguese
1517 Spanish crown authorizes slave trade to its South American colonies; rapid increase in importation of slaves to the New World
1554–1659 Sa'did Sultanate in Morocco
1575 Union of Bornu and Kanem by Idris Alawma
1591 Songhai Empire collapses

1600s English, Dutch, and French enter the slave trade
1619 First African slaves in North America land in Virginia
1652 First Cape Colony settlement of Dutch East India Company
1660–1856 Omani domination of East Africa

1702 Asiento Guinea Trade Company founded for slave trade between Africa and the Americas
1700s Transatlantic slave trade at its height
1741–1856 United Sultanate of Oman and Zanzibar
1754–1817 Usman Dan Fodio, founder of sultanate in northern and central Nigeria
1762 End of Funj Sultanate in eastern Sudanic region

THE AMERICAS

1519 Conquest of the Aztecs by Cortes
1533 Pizarro begins his conquest of the Incas
1536 Spanish under Mendoza arrive in Argentina
1544 Lima becomes capital of the viceroyalty of Peru
1584 Sir Walter Raleigh sends expedition to Roanoke Island (North Carolina)

1607 The London Company establishes Jamestown Colony
1608 Champlain founds Quebec
1619 Slave labor introduced at Jamestown (Virginia)

1733 Georgia founded as last English colony in North America
1739–1763 Era of trade wars in Americas between Great Britain and the French and Spanish
1763 Peace of Paris establishes British government in Canada
1776–1781 American Revolution
1783–1830 Simón Bolívar, Latin American soldier, statesman
1789 U.S. Constitution
1791 Negro slave revolt in French Santo Domingo
1791 Canada Constitution Act divides the country into Upper and Lower Canada

The Birth of Civilization

	8000 B.C.E	3500 B.C.E	1500 B.C.E	1000 B.C.E	500 B.C.
EUROPE	End of Paleolithic introduction of farming	Copper Age	Bronze Age	**624–545** Thales of Miletus **ca. 611–546** Anaximander **ca. 546** Anaximenes	**469–399** Socrates **429–347** Plato **384–322** Aristotle **435–404** Great Peloponnesian War **ca. 460–400** Thucydides **ca. 400** Hippocrates of Cos **384–322** Demosthenes
NEAR EAST/ASIA	**ca. 8000** Neolithic Revolution, Mesopotamia	**ca. 3500** Development of Sumerian Cities **ca. 3000** Development of Writing in Mesopotamia **ca. 2800–2370** Early Dynastic period of Sumerian city–states **ca. 2370** Sargon establishes Akkadian dynasty and empire **ca. 2250–1750** Indus (Harappan) civilization; writing first appears in India **ca. 2125–2027** Third dynasty of Ur **ca. 2000–1800** Establishment of Amorites in Mesopotamia **ca. 1800–1500** Aryan peoples invade northwestern India **ca. 1792–1750** Reign of Hammurabi **ca. 1550** Establishment of Kassite dynasty at Babylon	**ca. 1500–1000** Rig-Vedic period, India **ca. 1400–1200** Hittite Empire **ca. 1100** Rise of Assyrian Power	**ca. 1000–961** Reign of King David **ca. 961–922** Reign of King Solomon **ca. 1000–500** Late Vedic period, India **ca. 1000–800/600** Composition of Brahmanas **ca. 800–500** Composition of major Upanishads **ca. 700–500** Probable reintroduction of writing **732–722** Assyrian conquest of Syria-Palestine **722** Assyrian conquest of Israel (Northern Kingdom) **612** Destruction of Assyrian capital at Nineveh **612–539** Neo-Babylonian (Chaldean) Empire **586** Destruction of Jerusalem fall of Judah (southern king dom); Babylonian captivity **539** Restoration of Temple; return of exiles **540–ca. 468** Mahavira **ca. 566–ca. 486** Siddhartha Gautama, the Buddha	**ca. 400 b.c.e.–200 c.e.** Composition of great epics, the *Mahabharata* and *Ramayana*
EAST ASIA	**4000 b.c.e.** Neolithic Revolution	**2205–1766** Xia dynasty **1766** Bronze Age city–states **1766–1050** Shang dynasty	**1050–256** Zhou dynasty	**771** Iron Age territorial states **551–479** Confucius	**500** Age of philosophers **370–290** Mencius **Fourth century** Laozi **221** China is unified under the Qin
AFRICA		**3100–2700** Early Dynastic period, Egypt **ca. 3000** Writing first appears in Egypt **2700–2200** Old Kingdom (III–VI) **2200–2025** First Intermediate period **2025–1630** Middle Kingdom **1630–1550** Second Intermediate period **1550–1075** New Kindom		**671** Assyrian conquest of Egypt	
THE AMERICAS	**ca. 4000** Neolithic revolution in Mexico	**ca. 2750** Monumental architecture at Aspero	**1500–400** The Olmec	**800 b.c.e.–200 c.e.** Chavin (Early) Horizon	**200 b.c.e.–750 c.e.** The Classic period in central Mexico **150 b.c.e.–900 c.e.** The Classic period of Mayan civilization in the Yucatán and Guatemala

Global Conflict and Change

1914 – 1970   1970 – 2005

EUROPE

1914 – 1970		1970 – 2005	
1917	Bolsheviks seize power, Russia	1972	British Impose direct rule on N. Ireland
1919	Versailles Settlement	1972	Israeli Olympic athletes killed by Arab terrorists
1922	Mussolini seizes power, Italy	1974	Portuguese dictatorship deposed
1933	Hitler comes to power	1977	Brezhnev president of USSR
1936	Spanish Civil War begins	1979	Margaret Thatcher becomes British prime minister
1939	World War II begins	1980	Solidarity Movement in Poland
1945	World War II ends	1984	Mikhail Gorbachev introduces *glasnost* in USSR
1948	Berlin blockade and airlift	1989	Berlin Wall demolished
1949	NATO treaty; Russia detonates atomic bomb	1990	Germany unified
1955	Warsaw Pact	1991	Failed coup in Soviet Union; Yeltsin emerges as leader of Russia
1956	Soviets crush Hungarian revolt	1993	Czechoslovakia divides into two republics
1957	EEC founded	1995	Dayton Peace Accords end war in Bosnia
1958	Charles de Gaulle comes to power in France	2000	Putin elected president of Russia
1961	Berlin Wall erected	2005	Angela Merkl becomes chancellor of Germany
1968	Soviets invade Czechoslovakia		

NEAR EAST/ASIA

1914 – 1970		1970 – 2005	
1922	British leave Egypt	1973	Arab-Israeli October War
\1922–1938	Mustafa Kemal first president of Turkey	1973	OPEC oil embargo
1928	The Muslim Brotherhood founded	1978	Iranian revolution
1947	Indian Independence; creation of Pakistan	1979	Egyptian-Israeli Peace Treaty
1949	State of Israel founded	1979	Iran takes U.S. hostages
1953	Mosaddeq overthrown in Iran	1979	Soviets invade Afghanistan
1954–1970	Abdel Nasser leads Egypt	1980–1988	Iran-Iraq War
1956	Suez Crisis	1981	Egypt's Sadat assassinated
1966	Indira Gandhi becomes prime minister of India	1982	Israel invades Lebanon
1967	Israeli-Arab June War	1989	Soviets leave Afghanistan
		1990–1991	Gulf War

EAST ASIA

1914 – 1970		1970 – 2005	
1919	May 4th Movement in China	1959–1975	Vietnam War
1925	Universal male suffrage in Japan	1965–1976	Cultural Revolution devastates China
1928–1937	Nationalist government in China	1972	President Nixon visits China
1931	Japan occupies Manchuria	1976	Death of Mao Zedong
1937–1945	Japan at war with China	1978–1989	New Economic policies of Deng Xiaoping in China
1941	Japan attacks Pearl Harbor	1988	Japan's GNP second in world
1945	Japan surrenders	1989	China crushes pro-democracy demonstrations in Beijing
1949	People's Republic of China founded	1991–1992	Political scandals and plummeting stock market in Japan
1950	N. Korea invades S. Korea	2004	Tsunami strikes Indian Ocean
1952	U.S. ends occupation of Japan		
1959–1960	Sino-Soviet split		

AFRICA

1914 – 1970		1970 – 2005	
1919	Pan-African Congress in Paris	1967–1970	Nigerian Civil War
1935	Mussolini invades Ethiopia	1974	Drought and famine in Africa
1942–1945	World War II engulfs North Africa	1974	Emperor Haile Selassie of Ethiopia is deposed
1955–1962	Wars of independence in French Algeria	1974–1975	Portugal grants independence to Guinea, Angola, Mozambique, Cape Ver
1956	Sudan gains independenc	1980	Southern Rhodesia (Zimbabwe) gains independence from Britain
1956	Morocco and Tunisia gain independence	1984	Bishop Desmond Tutu awarded Nobel Peace Prize
1957	Ghana an independent state	1985	U.S. economic sanctions against South Africa
1960	Belgian Congo granted independence	1992	Nelson Mandela freed from prison in South Africa
1963	Kenya becomes an independent republic	1994	Nelson Mandela elected president of South Africa
1965	Revolution in Kenya	2004	Ellen Johnson–Sirleaf becomes woman president of Liberia

THE AMERICAS

1914 – 1970		1970 – 2005	
1917	U.S. enters World War I	1970	Allende elected in Chile
1930–1945	Vargas dictatorship in Brazil	1972	Nixon visits China and USSR
1932	FDR U.S. president	1973	Watergate scandal breaks
1938	Mexico nationalizes oil industry	1973	Perón reelected, Argentina
1941	U.S. enters World War II	1973	Chile's Allende overthrown
1945	Death of FDR	1979	Revolution in Nicaragua and El Salvador
1946	Perón elected president in Argentina	1980	Reagan elected president
1954	U.S. Supreme Court outlaws segregation	1983	Argentine military government overthrown
1955	Perón overthrown	1983	End of Mexican oil boom
1956	Montgomery bus boycott	1988	Major arms agreement between U.S. and USSR
1959	Fidel Castro comes to power in Cuba	1991	Gulf War
1962	Cuban Missile Crisis	1992	Clinton elected president
1964	Passage of Civil Rights Act	1994	Revolt in Chiapas, Mexico
1965	U.S. expands Vietnam commitment	1998	Pope visits Cuba
1968	Martin Luther King and Robert Kennedy assassinated	2001	Terrorists attack the U. S.
		2005	New Orleans devastated by Hurricane Katrina

absolutism Term applied to strong centralized continental monarchies that attempted to make royal power dominant over aristocracies and other regional authorities.

Acropolis Religious and civic center of Athens. It is the site of the Parthenon.

Afrikaans New language, derived from Dutch, that evolved in the 17th- and 18th-century Cape Colony.

agape Meaning "love feast." A common meal that was part of the central ritual of early Christian worship.

agora Greek marketplace and civic center. It was the heart of the social life of the polis.

agricultural revolution Innovations in farm production that began in the eighteenth century and led to a scientific and mechanized agriculture.

amir/emir Islamic military commander.

Amitabha Buddha Buddhist Lord of the Western Paradise, or Pure Land.

Annam Chinese term for Vietnam.

Anschluss Meaning "union." Annexation of Austria by Germany in March 1938.

anti-Semitism Prejudice, hostility, or legal discrimination against Jews.

apartheid "Apartness," the term referring to racist policies enforced by the White-dominated regime that existed in South Africa from 1948 to 1992.

apostolic primacy Doctrine that the popes are the direct successors to the Apostle Peter and as such heads of the church.

appeasement Anglo-French policy of making concessions to Germany in the 1930s to avoid a crisis that would lead to war. It assumed that Germany had real grievances and Hitler's aims were limited and ultimately acceptable.

Areopagus Governing council of Athens, originally open only to the nobility. Named after the hill on which it met.

Arianism Belief formulated by Arius of Alexandria (ca. 280–336 C.E.) that Jesus was a created being, neither fully man nor fully God, but something in between.

aristocratic resurgence Eighteenth-century aristocratic efforts to resist the expanding power of European monarchies.

Aryans Indo-European people who invaded India and Iran in the second and first millenia B.C.E.

assignats Government bonds based on the value of confiscated church lands issued during the early French Revolution.

Atman-Brahman The unchanging, infinite principle of reality in Indian religion.

Atomists School of ancient Greek philosophy founded in the fifth century B.C.E. by Leucippus of Miletus and Democritus of Abdera. It held that the world consists of innumerable, tiny, solid, indivisible, and unchangeable particles called atoms.

Augustus Title given to Octavian in 27 B.C.E. and borne thereafter by all Roman emperors.

ausgleich Meaning "compromise." Agreement between the Habsburg emperor and the Hungarians to give Hungary considerable administrative autonomy in 1867. It created the Dual Monarchy, or Austria-Hungary.

Axis Alliance between Nazi Germany and Fascist Italy. Also called the Pact of Steel.

ayatollah Major Shi'ite religious leader.

bakufu "Tent government." Military regime that governed Japan under the shoguns.

bazaari Iranian commercial middle class.

bhakti Hindu devotional movements.

Black Death Bubonic plague that killed millions of Europeans in the 14th century.

Black Legend Argument that Spanish treatment of Native Americans was uniquely inhumane.

Blitzkrieg Meaning "war by lightening strokes." German tactic early in World War II of employing fast-moving, massed armored columns supported by air power to overwhelm the enemy.

bodhisattva A "Buddha to be" who postpones his own nirvana until he has helped all other beings become enlightened.

Bolsheviks Meaning the "majority." Term Lenin applied to his faction of the Russian Social Democratic Party. It became the Communist Party of the Soviet Union after the Russian Revolution.

Boxers Nationalistic Chinese religious society that attacked foreigners and their encroachments on China in the late 19th century.

boyars Russian nobility.

Brahmanas Texts dealing with the ritual application of the Vedas.

Bronze Age The name given to the earliest civilized era, ca. 4000 to 1000 B.C.E. The term reflects the importance of the metal bronze for the people of this age in making weapons and tools.

caliphate Spiritual and temporal rule of the Muslim community.

calpulli Wards into which the Aztec capital, Tenochtitlan, was divided.

cantonments Segregation of areas in which Europeans lived in British-ruled India from those areas inhabited by native Indians.

Catholic emancipation Grant of full political rights to Roman Catholics in Britain in 1829.

Catholic Meaning "universal." The body of belief held by most Christians enshrined within the church.

caudillo Latin American strongman, or dictator, usually with close ties to the military.

Censorate Branch of the imperial Chinese government that acted as a watchdog, reporting instances of misgovernment directly to the emperor and remonstrating when it considered the emperor's behavior improper.

censor Official of the Roman republic charged with conducting the census and compiling the lists of citizens and members of the Senate.

Chartism First large-scale European working-class political movement. It sought political reforms that would favor the interests of skilled British workers in the 1830s and 1840s.

chiaroscuro Use of shading to enhance naturalness in painting and drawing.

chicha Maize beer brewed by the mamakuna for the Inca elite.

chun-tzu The Confucian term for a person who behaves ethically, in harmony with the cosmic order.

civilization A form of human culture marked by urbanism, metallurgy, and writing.

clash of civilizations Political theory, most often identified with Harvard political scientist Samuel P. Huntington, which contends that conflict between the world's religio-cultural traditions or "civilizations" increasingly dominates world affairs.

Cold War Ideological and geographical struggle between the United States and its allies and the USSR and its allies that began after World War II and lasted until the dissolution of the USSR in 1989.

collectivization Bedrock of Stalinist agriculture, which forced Russian peasants to give up their private farms and work as members of collectives, large agricultural units controlled by the state.

conquistadores Meaning "conquerors." Spanish conquerors of the New World.

Consulate French government dominated by Napoleon from 1799 to 1804.

Convention French radical legislative body from 1792 to 1794.

Council of Nicaea Council of Christian bishops at Nicaea in 325 C.E. that formulated the Nicene Creed, a statement of Christian belief that rejected Arianism in favor of the doctrine that Christ is both fully human and fully divine.

Counter-Reformation Sixteenth-century reform movement in the Roman Catholic Church in reaction to the Protestant Reformation.

Creole A person of European descent born in Latin America or the Caribbean.

Crusades Religious wars directed by the church against infidels and heretics.

Cultural Revolution Movement launched by Mao between 1965 and 1976 against the Soviet-style bureaucracy that had taken hold in China. It involved widespread disorder and violence.

culture The ways of living built up by a group and passed on from one generation to another.

cuneiform A writing system invented by the Sumerians that used a wedge-shaped stylus, or pointed tool, to write on wet clay tablets that were then baked or dried (*cuneus* means "wedge" in Latin). The writing was also cut into stone.

Curia Papal government.

daimyo Japanese territorial lord.

Daoism A Chinese philosophy that teaches that wisdom lies in becoming one with the *Dao*, the "way," which is the creative principle of the universe.

debt peonage Requirement that laborers remain and continue to work on a hacienda until they had paid their debts to the owner for goods bought from him on credit.

deism Belief in a rational God who had created the universe, but then allowed it to function without his interference according to the mechanisms of nature and a belief in rewards and punishments after death for human action.

Delian League Alliance of Greek states under the leadership of Athens that was formed in 478–477 B.C.E. to resist the Persians.

demesne Part of a manor that was cultivated directly for the lord of the manor.

devshirme System under the Ottoman Empire that required each province to furnish a levy of Christian boys who were raised as Muslims and became soldiers in the Ottoman army.

dharma Moral law or duty.

diaspora Dispersion of an originally homogeneous people or culture. Among the many diasporas in world history, some of the most famous are the Jewish, the Chinese, the African, the Irish, and the Armenian.

Diet of Worms Meeting of the representatives (diet) of the Holy Roman Empire, presided over by the Emperor Charles V at the German city of Worms in 1521, at which Martin Luther was ordered to recant his ninety-five theses. Luther refused and was declared an outlaw although he was protected by the Elector of Saxony and other German princes.

Diet Bicameral Japanese parliament.

divine right of kings Theory that monarchs are appointed by and answerable only to God.

domestic or putting-out system of textile production Method of producing textiles in which agents furnished raw materials to households whose members spun them into thread and then wove cloth, which the agents sold as finished products.

Duce Meaning "leader." Mussolini's title as head of the Fascist Party.

Duma Russian parliament, after the revolution of 1905.

dynastic cycle Term used to describe the rise, decline, and fall of China's imperial dynasties.

ego According to Freudian theory, the part of the mind that mediates between the impulses of the id and the asceticism of the superego and allows the personality to cope with the inner and outer demands of its existence.

empiricism Use of experiment and observation derived from sensory evidence to construct scientific theory or philosophy of knowledge.

enclosures Consolidation or fencing in of common lands by British landlords to increase production and achieve greater commercial profits. It also involved the reclamation of waste land and the consolidation of strips into block fields.

encomienda Grant by the Spanish crown to a colonist of the labor of a specific number of Indians for a set period of time.

Enlightenment Eighteenth-century movement led by the philosophes that held that change and reform were both desirable through the application of reason and science.

Epicureans School of philosophy founded by Epicurus of Athens (342–271 B.C.E.). It sought to liberate people from fear of death and the supernatural by teaching that the gods took no interest in human affairs and that true happiness consisted in pleasure, which was defined as the absence of pain.

equestrians Literally "cavalrymen" or "knights." In the earliest years of the Roman republic, those who could afford to serve as mounted warriors.

Estado Novo "New state" based on political stability and economic and social progress supposedly established by the dictator Getulio Vargas after 1937.

Etruscans A people of central Italy who exerted the most powerful external influence on the early Romans.

Eucharist Meaning "thanksgiving." Celebration of the Lord's Supper. Considered the central ritual of worship by most Christians. Also called Holy Communion.

euro Common currency created by the EEC in the late 1990s.

European Economic Community Economic association formed by France, Germany, Italy, Belgium, the Netherlands, and Luxembourg in 1957. Also known as the Common Market.

European Union New name given to the EEC in 1993. It included most of the states of Western Europe.

Fabians British Socialists in the late 19th and early 20th centuries who sought to achieve socialism through gradual, peaceful, and democratic means.

family economy Basic structure of production and consumption in preindustrial Europe.

fascism Political movements that tend to be antidemocratic, anti-Marxist, antiparliamentary, and often anti-Semitic. Fascists were invariably nationalists and exhalted the nation over the individual. They supported the interests of the middle class and rejected the ideas of the French Revolution and 19th-century liberalism. The first fascist regime was founded by Benito Mussolini (1883–1945) in Italy in the 1920s.

fealty Oath of loyalty by a vassal to a lord, promising to perform specified services.

feudal society Social, political, military, and economic system that prevailed in the Middle Ages and beyond in some parts of Europe.

fief Land granted to a vassal in exchange for services, usually military.

Fourteen Points President Woodrow Wilson's (1856–1924) idealistic war aims.

Führer Meaning "leader." Title taken by Hitler when he became dictator of Germany.

gentry In China, a largely urban, landowning class that represented local interests and functioned as quasi-bureaucrats under the magistrates.

ghazis Warriors who carried Islam by force of arms to pagan groups.

ghettos Separate communities in which Jews were required by law to live.

glasnost Meaning "openness." Policy initiated by Mikhail Gorbachev in the 1980s of permitting open criticism of the policies of the Soviet Communist Party.

globalization Term used to describe the increasing economic and cultural interdependence of societies around the world.

Glorious Revolution Largely peaceful replacement of James II by William and Mary as English monarchs in 1688. It marked the beginning of constitutional monarchy in Britain.

Golden Horde Name given to the Mongol rulers of Russia from 1240 to 1480.

Grand Mufti Chief religious authority of the Ottoman Empire. Also called "the Shaykh of Islam."

Great Depression Prolonged worldwide economic downturn that began in 1929 with the collapse of the New York Stock Exchange.

Great Leap Forward Mao's disastrous attempt to modernize the Chinese economy in 1958.

Great Purges Imprisonment and execution of millions of Soviet citizens by Stalin between 1934 and 1939.

Great Reform Bill (1832) Limited reform of the British House of Commons and expansion of the electorate to include a wider variety of the propertied classes. It laid the groundwork for further orderly reforms within the British constitutional system.

Great Schism Appearance of two and at times three rival popes between 1378 and 1415.

Great Trek Migration between 1835 and 1847 of Boer pioneers (called *voortrekkers*) north from British-ruled Cape Colony to establish their own independent republics.

guild Association of merchants or craftsmen that offered protection to its members and set rules for their work and products.

Guomindang (GMT) China's Nationalist Party, founded by Sun Zhongshan.

hacienda Large landed estates in Spanish America.

hadith Saying or action ascribed to Muhammad.

Hajj Pilgrimage to Mecca that all Muslims are enjoined to perform at least once in their lifetime.

Harappan Term used to describe the first civilization of the Indus Valley.

Hegira Flight of Muhammad and his followers from Mecca to Medina in 622 C.E. It marks the beginning of the Islamic calendar.

heliocentric theory The theory, now universally accepted, that the Earth and the other planets revolve around the sun. First proposed by Aristarchos of Samos (310–230 B.C.E.).

Helots Hereditary Spartan serfs.

heretics Persons whose religious beliefs differ from the official doctrines of their faith.

hieroglyphics The complicated writing script of ancient Egypt. It combined picture writing with pictographs and sound signs. Hieroglyph means "sacred carvings" in Greek.

Hindu Term applied to the diverse social, racial, linguistic, and religious groups of India.

Holocaust Nazi extermination of millions of European Jews between 1940 and 1945. Also called the "final solution to the Jewish problem."

Holy Roman Empire Revival of the old Roman Empire, based mainly in Germany and northern Italy, that endured from 870 to 1806.

home rule Advocacy of a large measure of administrative autonomy for Ireland within the British Empire between the 1880s and 1914.

hoplite phalanx Basic unit of Greek warfare in which infantrymen fought in close order, shield to shield, usually eight ranks deep.

Huguenots French Calvinists.

humanism Study of the Latin and Greek classics and of the Church Fathers both for their own sake and to promote a rebirth of ancient norms and values.

humanitas Roman name for a liberal arts education.

id According to Freudian psychoanalysis, the part of the mind that consists of amoral, irrational, driving instincts for sexual gratification, aggression, and physical and sensual pleasure.

imam Islamic prayer leader.

impact of modernity Effect of western political, economic, and social ideas and institutions on traditional societies.

imperator Under the Roman republic, the title given to a victorious general. Under Augustus and his successors, it became the title of the ruler of Rome, meaning "emperor."

imperium In ancient Rome, the right to issue commands and to enforce them by fines, arrests, and even corporal and capital punishment.

import substitution Replacement of imported goods with those manufactured domestically.

Indo-European A widely distributed language group that includes most of the languages spoken in Europe, Persian, Sanskrit, and their derivatives.

Indo-Greeks Bactrian rulers who broke away from the Seleucid Empire to found a state that combined elements of Greek and Indian civilizations.

indulgences Remission of the temporal penalty of punishment in purgatory that remained after sins had been forgiven.

Industrial Revolution Mechanization of the European economy that began in Britain in the second half of the 18th century.

intifadah Literally, "shaking." Uprisings by the Palestinians against Israeli occupation.

Islam "Submission." Religion founded by the prophet Muhammad.

Italia Irredenta Meaning "unredeemed Italy." Italian-speaking areas that had been left under Austrian rule at the time of the unification of Italy.

Jacobins Radical republican party during the French Revolution that displaced the Girondists.

Jains Indian religious community that teaches compassion for all beings.

Janissaries Elite Ottoman troops who were recruited through the *devshirme*.

jatis The many subgroups that make up the Hindu caste system.

jihad "Struggle in the path of God." Although not necessarily implying violence, it is often interpreted to mean holy war in the name of Islam.

July Monarchy French regime set up after the overthrow of the Bourbons in July 1830.

Junkers Noble landlords of Prussia.

Ka'ba A black meteorite in the city of Mecca that became Islam's holiest shrine.

Kabuki Realistic form of Japanese theater similar to English Elizabethan drama.

Kalahari A large desert in southwestern Africa that partially isolates southern Africa from the rest of the continent.

kamikaze "Divine winds" that sank a portion of the invading Mongol fleet in Japan in 1281.

karma Indian belief that every action has an inevitable effect. Good deeds bring good results; evil deeds have evil consequences.

Khmer Rouge Meaning "Red Cambodia." Radical Communist movement that ruled Cambodia from 1975 to 1978.

kleindeutsch Meaning "small German." Argument that the German-speaking portions of the Habsburg Empire should be excluded from a united Germany.

Kristallnacht Meaning "crystal night" because of the broken glass that littered German streets after the looting and destruction of Jewish homes, businesses, and synagogues across Germany on the orders of the Nazi Party in November 1938.

La Reforma The 19th-century Mexican liberal reform movement that opposed Santa Ana's dictatorship and sought to foster economic progress, civilian rule, and political stability. It was strongly anticlerical.

laissez-faire French phrase meaning "allow to do." In economics, the doctrine of minimal government interference in the working of the economy.

latifundia Large plantations for growing cash crops owned by wealthy Romans.

LDP Liberal Democratic Party. A conservative party that has dominated postwar Japanese politics.

League of Nations Association of sovereign states set up after World War I to pursue common policies and avert international aggression.

Lebensraum "Living space," Nazi plan to colonize and exploit eastern Europe.

Legalism Chinese philosophical school that argued that a strong state was necessary to have a good society.

levée en masse French revolutionary conscription (1792) of all males into the army and the harnessing of the economy for war production.

liberalism In the 19th century, support for representative government dominated by the propertied classes and minimal government interference in the economy.

liberation theology Effort by certain Roman Catholic theologians to combine Marxism with traditional Christian concern for the poor.

logos Divine reason, or fire, which according to the Stoics, was the guiding principle in nature.

Long Count Mayan calendar that dated from a fixed point in the past.

Long March Flight of the Chinese communists from their nationalist foes to northwest China in 1934.

Luftwaffe German air force in World War II.

madrasa Islamic college of higher learning.

Magna Carta The "Great Charter" limiting royal power, which the English nobility forced King John to sign in 1215.

Magna Graecia Meaning "Great Greece" in Latin. The name given by the Romans to southern Italy and Sicily because there were so many Greek colonies in the region.

Magyars Majority ethnic group in Hungary.

Mahabharata and Ramayana Two classical Indian epics.

Mahayana The "Great Vehicle" for salvation in Buddhism. It emphasized the Buddha's infinite compassion for all beings.

mamakuna Inca women who lived privileged but celibate lives and had important economic and cultural roles.

Mandate of Heaven The Chinese belief that heaven entrusts or withdraws a ruler's or a dynasty's right to govern.

Manichaeism A dualistic and moralistic view of reality in which good and evil, spirit and matter warred with each other.

mannerism A style of art in the mid to late 16th century that permitted artists to express their own "manner" or feelings in contrast to the symmetry and simplicity of the art of the High Renaissance.

manors Village farms owned by a lord.

Marshall Plan U.S. program, named after Secretary of State George C. Marshall, that provided economic aid to Europe after World War II.

Marxism Theory of Karl Marx (1818–1883) and Friedrich Engels (1820–1895) that history is the result of class conflict, which will end in the inevitable triumph of the industrial proletariat over the bourgeoisie and the abolition of private property and social class.

Meiji restoration Overthrow of the Tokugawa *bakufu* in Japan in 1868 and the transfer, or "restoration," of power to the imperial government under the Emperor Meiji.

Mein Kampf Meaning "My Struggle." Hitler's statement of his political program, published in 1924.

Mensheviks Meaning the "minority." Term Lenin applied to the majority moderate faction of the Russian Social Democratic Party opposed to him and the Bolsheviks.

mercantilism Term used to describe close government control of the economy that sought to maximize exports and accumulate as much precious metals as possible to enable the state to defend its economic and political interests.

Mesoamerica Region of North America that extends from the central part of modern Mexico to Central America.

Mesopotamia Modern Iraq. The land between the Tigris and Euphrates Rivers.

Messiah The redeemer whose coming, Jews believed, would establish the kingdom of God on earth. Christians considered Jesus to be the Messiah (Christ means Messiah in Greek).

mestizos Persons of mixed Native American and European descent.

Mexica Aztecs' name for themselves.

mfecane Period of widespread warfare and chaos among Bantu peoples in east-central Africa during the early 19th century.

millets Small self-governing communities within the Ottoman Empire.

Minoan Bronze Age civilization that arose in Crete in the third and second millennia B.C.E.

mita Inca system of forced labor in return for gifts and ritual entertainments.

Mitimaqs Communities whom the Incas forced to settle in designated regions for strategic purposes.

monotheism The worship of one universal God.

Moors Spanish and Portuguese term for Muslims.

Mughals Descendants of the Mongols who established an Islamic empire in India in the 16th century with its capital at Delhi.

mujtahid Shi'ite religious-legal scholar.

mulattos Persons of mixed African and European descent.

Mycenaean Bronze Age civilization of mainland Greece that was centered at Mycenae.

"mystery" religions Cults of Isis, Mithra, and Osiris, which promised salvation to those initiated into the secret or "mystery" of their rites.

nacionalismo Right-wing Argentine nationalist movement that arose in the 1930s and resembled European fascism.

National Studies Japanese intellectual tradition that emphasized native Japanese culture and institutions and rejected the influence of Chinese Confucianism.

nationalism Belief that one is part of a nation, defined as a community with its own language, traditions, customs, and history that distinguish it from other nations and make it the primary focus of a person's loyalty and sense of identity.

natural selection According to Darwin, the process in nature by which only the organisms best adapted to their environment tend to survive and transmit their genes, while those less adapted tend to be eliminated.

neocolonial economy Economic relationship between a former colonial state and countries with more developed economies in which the former colony exports raw materials to and imports manufactured goods from the more developed nations.

Neo-Daoism A revival of Daoist "mysterious learning" that flourished as a reaction against Confucianism during the Han dynasty.

Neolithic Revolution The shift beginning 10,000 years ago from hunter-gatherer societies to settled communities.

New Economic Policy (NEP) Limited revival of capitalism, especially in light industry and agriculture, introduced by Lenin in 1921 to repair the damage inflicted on the Russian economy by the civil war and War Communism.

New Imperialism Extension in the late 19th and early 20th centuries of Western political and economic dominance to Asia, the Middle East, and Africa.

Nicene Creed A declaration of faith that the Council of Nicaea hoped would be endorsed by all Christians.

Nilotic Africa The lands along the Nile River.

ninety-five theses Document posted on the door of Castle Church in Wittenberg, Germany on October 31, 1517 by Martin Luther protesting, among other things, the selling of indulgences.

nirvana In Buddhism the attainment of release from the wheel of karma.

Nō play Highly stylized form of Japanese drama in which the chorus provides the narrative line as in classical Greek plays.

oba Title of the king of Benin.

obsidian Hard volcanic glass that was widely used in Mesoamerica.

occupied territories Land occupied by Israel as a result of wars with its Arab neighbors in 1948–1949, 1967, and 1973.

Old Regime Term applied to the pattern of social, political, and economic relationships and institutions that existed in Europe before the French Revolution.

orthodox Meaning "holding the right opinions." Applied to the doctrines of the Catholic Church.

orthopraxy Correct practice of a religion.

Paleolithic Age The earliest period when stone tools were used, from about 1,000,000 to 10,000 B.C.E. From the Greek meaning "old stone."

Panhellenic Meaning "all-Greek." The sense of cultural identity that all Greeks felt in common with each other.

pan-Islamism Movement that advocates that the entire Muslim world should form a unified political and cultural entity.

Pan-Slavic movement Effort to create a nation or federation that would embrace all the Slavic peoples of Eastern Europe.

Papal States Territory in central Italy ruled by the pope until 1870.

parlement French regional court dominated by hereditary nobility. The most important was the Parlement of Paris, which claimed the right to register royal decrees before they could become law.

Parliamentary monarchy Form of limited monarchy developed in England.

patricians Hereditary upper class of early republican Rome.

peace process Efforts, chiefly led by the United States, to broker a peace between the state of Israel and the PLO.

Peloponnesian Wars Protracted struggle between Athens and Sparta to dominate Greece between 465 and Athens' final defeat in 404 B.C.E.

peninsulares Native-born Spaniards who immigrated from Spain to settle in the Spanish colonies.

perestroika Meaning "restructuring." Attempt in the 1980s to reform the Soviet government and economy.

Perónism Authoritarian, nationalist movement founded in Argentina in the 1940s by the dictator Juan Perón.

pharaoh The god-kings of ancient Egypt. The term originally meant "great house" or palace.

Pharisees Group that was most strict in its adherence to Jewish law.

philosophes Eighteenth-century writers and critics who forged the new attitudes favorable to change. They sought to apply reason and common sense to the institutions and societies of their day.

pipiltin Aztec bureaucrats and priests.

pirs Shi'ite holy men.

plantation economy Economic system stretching between Chesapeake Bay and Brazil that produced crops, especially sugar, cotton, and tobacco, using slave labor on large estates.

plebeians Hereditary lower class of early republican Rome.

plenitude of power Teaching that the popes have power over all other bishops of the church.

pochteca Aztec merchants.

pogroms Organized riots against Jews in the Russian Empire.

polis The basic Greek political unit. Usually, but incompletely, translated as "city-state," the Greeks thought of the polis as a community of citizens theoretically descended from a common ancestor.

polytheism The worship of many gods.

Popular Front Government of all left-wing parties that took power in France in 1936 to enact social and economic reforms.

populares Roman politicians who sought to pursue a political career based on the support of the people rather than just the aristocracy.

positivism Philosophy of Auguste Comte that science is the final, or positive, stage of human intellectual development because it involves exact descriptions of phenomena, without recourse to unobservable operative principles, such as gods or spirits.

Pragmatic Sanction Legal basis negotiated by Emperor Charles VI (r. 1711–1740) for the Habsburg succession through his daughter Maria Theresa (r. 1740–1780).

PRI The Institutional Revolutionary Party, which emerged from the Mexican revolution of 1911 and governed Mexico until the end of the 20th century.

proletarianization Process whereby independent artisans and factory workers lose control of the means of production and of the conduct of their own trades to the owners of capital.

Ptolemaic system Pre-Copernican explanation of the universe, which placed the Earth at the center of the universe.

Punic Wars Three wars between Rome and Carthage for dominance of the western Mediterranean that were fought from 264 B.C.E. to 146 B.C.E.

Pure Land Buddhism Variety of Japanese Buddhism that maintained that only faith was necessary for salvation.

Puritans English Protestants who sought to "purify" the Church of England of any vestiges of Catholicism.

Quechua Inca language.

quipu Knotted string used by Andean peoples for recordkeeping.

Qur'an "A reciting." Islamic bible, which Muslims believe God revealed to the prophet Muhammad.

racism Pseudoscientific theory that biological features of race determine human character and worth.

raja An Indian king.

raj The years from 1858 to 1947 during which India was governed directly by the British Crown.

Ramadan Month when Muslims must fast during daylight hours.

Reconquista Christian reconquest of Spain from the Muslims from 1000 to 1492.

Reformation Sixteenth-century religious movement that sought to reform the Roman Catholic Church and led to the establishment of Protestantism.

regular clergy Monks and nuns who belong to religious orders.

Reichstag German parliament, which existed in various forms, until 1945.

Reign of Terror Period between the summer of 1793 and the end of July 1794 when the French revolutionary state used extensive executions and violence to defend the Revolution and suppress its alleged internal enemies.

relativity Theory of physics, first expounded by Albert Einstein in 1905, in which time and space exist not separately, but rather as a combined continuum.

Renaissance Revival of ancient learning and the supplanting of traditional religious beliefs by new secular and scientific values that began in Italy in the 14th and 15th centuries.

repartimiento Labor tax in Spanish America that required adult male Native Americans to devote a set number of days a year to Spanish economic enterprises.

revisionism Advocacy among 19th-century German Socialists of achieving a humane socialist society through the evolution of democratic institutions, not revolution.

Sahara The world's largest desert. It extends across Africa from the Atlantic to the eastern Sudan. Historically, the Sahara has hindered contact between the Mediterranean and sub-Saharan Africa.

Sahel An area of steppe and semi-desert that borders the Sahara.

samsara The endless cycle of existence, of birth, and rebirth.

samurai Professional Japanese warriors.

Sandinistas Marxist guerrilla force that overthrew the Somoza dictatorship in Nicaragua in 1979.

sans-culottes Meaning "without breeches." The lower-middle classes and artisans of Paris during the French Revolution.

satraps Governors of provinces in the Persian Empire.

savannah An area of open woodlands and grassy plains.

Schlieffen Plan Germany's plan for achieving a quick victory in the West at the outbreak of World War I by invading France through Belgium and Luxembourg.

Scholasticism Method of study based on logic and dialectic that dominated the medieval schools. It assumed that truth already existed; students had only to organize, elucidate, and defend knowledge learned from authoritative texts, especially those of Aristotle and the Church Fathers.

Scientific Revolution Sweeping change in the scientific view of the universe that occurred in the West in the 16th and 17th centuries.

scramble for Africa Late 19th century takeover of most of Africa by European powers.

secular clergy Parish clergy who did not belong to a religious order.

serfs Peasants tied to the land they tilled.

Shaanxi banks Private commercial banks in China under the Manchus.

Shahanshah "King of kings," the title of the Persian ruler.

Shari'a Islamic religious law.

Shi'a Muslims who trace their beliefs to the caliph Ali, who was assassinated in 661 C.E.

Shintō "The way of the gods." The animistic worship of the forces of nature that is the indigenous religion of Japan.

shōgun Military official who was the actual ruler of Japan in the emperor's name from the late 1100s until the mid-19th century.

Silk Road Trade route from China to the West that stretched across Central Asia.

Sophists Professional teachers who emerged in Greece in the mid-fifth century B.C.E. who were paid to teach techniques of rhetoric, dialectic, and argumentation.

soviets Workers' and soldiers' councils formed in Russia during the revolution.

spinning jenny Machine invented in England by James Hargreaves around 1765 to mass-produce thread.

Stele (also Stela) An upright stone or slab within inscribed surface, used as a monument or as a commemorative tablet.

steppe peoples Nomadic tribespeople who dwelled on the Eurasian plains from eastern Europe to the borders of China and Iran. They frequently traded with or invaded more settled cultures.

Stoics Philosophical school founded by Zeno of Citium (335–263 B.C.E.) that taught that humans could only be happy with natural law.

streltsy Professional troops who made up the Moscow garrison. They were suppressed by Peter the Great.

studia humanitatis During the Renaissance, a liberal arts program of study that embraced grammar, rhetoric, poetry, history, philosophy, and politics.

stupa A Buddhist shrine.

suffragettes British women who lobbied and agitated for the right to vote in the early 20th century.

Sufi Movement within Islam that emphasizes the spiritual and mystical.

sultan Muslim royal title that means "authority."

Sunna "Tradition." Dominant Islamic group.

superego According to Freud, the part of the mind that embodies the external moral imperatives and expectations imposed on the personality by society and culture.

Swahili Language and culture that developed from the interaction of native Africans and Arabs along the East African coast.

symposion Carefully organized drinking party that was the center of Greek aristocratic social life. It featured games, songs, poetry, and even philosophical disputation.

syncretism In religion, the equating or combining of deities.

Table of Ranks Official hierarchy established by Peter the Great in imperial Russia that equated a person's social position and privileges with his rank in the state bureaucracy or army.

taille Direct tax on the French peasantry.

Taiping rebellion A 19th-century revolt against China's Manchu dynasty that was inspired by quasi-Christian ideas and that led to enormous suffering and destruction before its collapse in 1868.

tennō "Heavenly emperor." The official title of the emperor of Japan.

tetcutin Subordinate Aztec lords.

tetrarchy Diocletian's (r. 306–337 C.E.) system for ruling the Roman Empire by four men with power divided territorially.

The *Iliad* and the *Odyssey* Epic poems by Homer about the "Dark Age" heroes of Greece who fought at Troy. The poems were written down in the eighth century B.C.E. after centuries of being sung by bards.

theocracy State ruled by religious leaders who claim to govern by divine authority.

Theravada The "Way of the Elders." A school of Buddhism that emphasized the monastic ideal.

Thermidorean Reaction Reaction against the radicalism of the French Revolution that began in July 1794. Associated with the end of terror and establishment of the Directory.

Third Estate Branch of the French Estates General representing all of the kingdom outside the nobility and the clergy.

three-field system Medieval innovation that increased the amount of land under cultivation by leaving only one-third fallow in a given year.

tlatoani An Aztec ruler.

transubstantiation Doctrine that the entire substances of the bread and wine are changed in the Eucharist into the body and blood of Christ.

treaty ports Chinese ports ruled by foreign consuls where foreigners enjoyed commercial privileges and immunity from Chinese laws.

Trekboers White livestock farmers in Cape Colony.

tribunes Roman officials who had to be plebeians and were elected by the plebeian assembly to protect plebeians from the arbitrary power of the magistrates.

Tripartite Pact Alliance between Japan and Nazi Germany and Fascist Italy that was signed in 1940.

ulama "Persons with correct knowledge." Islamic scholarly elite who served a social function similar to the Christian clergy.

Umma Islamic community.

"unequal treaties" Agreements imposed on China in the 19th century by European powers, the United States, and Japan that granted their citizens special legal and economic privileges on Chinese soil.

Upanishads Vedic texts most concerned with speculation about the universe.

Urdu-Hindi Language that combines Persian-Arabic and native Indian elements. Urdu is the Muslim version of the language; Hindi is the Hindu version.

uzama Order of hereditary chiefs in Benin.

varnas The four main classes that form the basis for Hindu caste relations.

vassal Person granted an estate or cash payments in return for accepting the obligation to render services to a lord.

Vedas Sacred texts of the ancient Aryan invaders of India. The Rig Veda is the oldest material in the Vedas.

vernacular Everyday language spoken by the people as opposed to Latin.

Viet Minh Communist-dominated popular front organization formed by Ho Chi Minh to establish an independent Vietnamese republic.

War Communism Economic policy adopted by the Bolsheviks during the Russian civil war to seize the banks, heavy industry, railroads, and grain.

war guilt clause Clause of the Versailles Treaty, which assigned responsibility for World War I solely to Germany.

water frame Water-powered device invented by Richard Arkwright to produce a more durable cotton fabric. It led to the shift in the production of cotton textiles from households to factories.

Weimar Republic German democratic regime that existed between the end of World War I and Hitler's coming to power in 1933.

White Russians Russians who opposed the Bolsheviks (the "Reds") in the Russian Civil War of 1918–1921.

Works Progress Administration New Deal program created by the Roosevelt administration in 1935 that provided relief for the unemployed in the industrial sector during the Great Depression in the United States.

yangban Elite Korean families of the Choson period.

zaibatsu Groups of Japanese companies, or "trusts," that had a common ownership and dominated the economy of prewar Japan.

Zen A form of Buddhism, which taught that Buddha was only a man and exhorted each person to attain enlightenment by his or her own efforts.

Zionism Movement to create a Jewish state in Palestine (the Biblical Zion).

Zoroastrianism A quasi-monotheistic Iranian religion founded by Zoroaster (ca. 628–551 B.C.E.) who preached a message of moral reform and exhorted his followers to worship only Ahura Mazda, the Wise Lord.

CHAPTER 1

General Prehistory

P. BOGUCKI, *The Origins of Human Society* (1999). An excellent summary of recent scholarship on the earliest origins of human societies.

F. BRAY, *The Rice Economies: Technology and Development in Asian Societies* (1986). Still the best authority on the origins of rice cultivation and its effect on the develepment of ancient Asia.

M. EHRENBERG, *Women in Prehistory* (1989). An account of the role of women in early times.

C. FREEMAN, *Egypt, Greece and Rome: Civilizations of the Ancient Mediterranean* (2004). Good comparative study of Egypt with Greece and Rome.

D. C. JOHNSON and M. R. EDEY, *Lucy: The Beginning of Mankind* (1981). An account of the African origins of humans.

S. M. NELSON, ed., *Ancient Queens: Archaeological Explorations* (2003). Reassesses women rulers and female power in the ancient world.

S. M. NELSON and M. ROSEN-AYALON, *In Pursuit of Gender: Worldwide Archaeological Approaches* (2002). Essays on gender and the archaeology of the ancient world.

D. L. NICHOLS and T. H. CHARLTON, eds., *The Archaeology of CityStates: Cross-cultural Approaches* (1997). One of a growing body of books and essay collections employing cross-cultural and comparative approaches to world history and archaeology.

M. OLIPHANT, *The Atlas of the Ancient World: Charting the Great Civilizations of the Past* (1992). An excellent comprehensive atlas of the ancient world.

P. L. SHINNIE, *Ancient Nubia* (1996). A study of the African state most influenced by Egyptian culture.

Near East

M. E. AUBER, *The Phoenicians and the West* (1996). A new study of an important sea-going people who served as a conduit between East and West.

BEN-TOR, ed., *The Archaeology of Ancient Israel* (1992). A useful and up-to-date survey.

J. BOTTÉRO, *Everyday Life in Ancient Mesopotamia* (2001). Interesting vignettes of ancient Mesopotamian life.

H. CRAWFORD, *Sumer and the Sumerians* (1991). A discussion of the oldest Mesopotamian civilization.

I. FINKELSTEIN and N. A. SILBERMAN, *The Bible Unearthed: Archaeology's New Vision of Ancient Israel and the Origin of its Sacred Texts* (2001). An interesting discussion of the insights of recent archaeological finds on the history of the Bible and ancient Israel.

G. LEICK, *Mesopotamia: The Invention of the City* (2002). Good discussion of the urban history of ancient Mesopotamia.

J. N. POSTGATE, *Early Mesopotamia* (1992). An excellent study of Mesopotamian economy and society from the earliest times to about 1500 B.C.E., helpfully illustrated with drawings, photos, and translated documents.

D. B. REDFORD, *Akhenaten* (1987). A study of the controversial religious reformer.

W. F. SAGGS, *The Might That Was Assyria* (1984). A history of the northern Mesopotamian Empire and a worthy companion to the author's account of the Babylonian Empire in the south.

M. VAN DE MIEROOP, *A History of the Ancient Near East, ca. 3000–323 B.C.* (2004). An up-to-date comprehensive survey of ancient Near Eastern history.

India

D. P. AGRAWAL, *The Archaeology of India* (1982). A fine survey of the problems and data. Detailed, but with excellent summaries and brief discussions of major issues.

C. CHAKRABORTY, *Common Life in the Rigveda and Atharvaveda—An Account of the Folklore in the Vedic Period* (1977). An interesting attempt to reconstruct everyday life in the Vedic period from the principal Vedic texts.

J. R. McINTOSH, *A Peaceful Realm: The Rise and Fall of the Indus Civilization* (2002). Discusses what archaeologists have managed to unearth so far regarding Harrapan civilization.

W. D. O'FLAHERTY, *The Rig Veda: An Anthology* (1981). An excellent selection of Vedic texts in prosaic but very careful translation, with helpful notes on the texts.

J. E. SCHWARTZBERG, ed., *A Historical Atlas of South Asia* (1978). The definitive reference work for historical geography. Includes chronological tables and substantive essays.

R. THAPAR, *Early India: From the Origins to A.D. 1300* (2003). A comprehensive introduction to the early history of India.

China

M. LOEWE and E. SHAUGHNESSY eds., *The Cambridge History of Ancient China: From the Origins of Civilization to 221 B.C.* (1999). A comprehensive and authoritative history of ancient China.

K. C. CHANG, *The Archeology of Ancient China*, 4th ed. (1986). The standard work on the subject.

K. C. CHANG, *Art, Myth, and Ritual, The Path to Political Authority in Ancient China* (1984). A study of the relation between shamans, gods, agricultural production, and political authority during the Shang and Zhou dynasties.

N. DI COSMO, *Ancient China and its Enemies: The Rise of Nomadic Power in East Asian History* (2002). An excellent study of the relationship between China and nomadic peoples that was a powerful force in shaping Chinese and Central Asian history.

C. Y. Hsu, *Western Chou Civilization* (1988).

D. N. Keightley, *The Origins of Chinese Civilization* (1983).

M. E. Lewis, *Sanctioned Violence in Early China* (1990).

X. Q. Li, *Eastern Zhou and Qin Civilizations* (1986). This work includes fresh interpretations based on archaeological finds.

Americas

R. L. Burger, *Chavín and the Origins of Andean Civilization* (1992). A lucid and detailed account of the rise of civilization in the Andes.

M. D. Coe and R. Koontz, *Mexico: From the Olmecs to the Aztecs* (2002). Good survey of ancient Mexico.

D. Drew, *The Lost Chronicles of the Maya Kings* (1999). Fine introduction to the history of Maya civilization.

V. W. Fitzhugh and A. Crowell, *Crossroads of Continents: Cultures of Siberia and Alaska* (1988). Covers the area where the immigration from Eurasia to the Americas began.

R. Ford, ed., *Prehistoric Food Production in North America* (1985). Examines the origins of agriculture in the Americas.

P. D. Hunt, *Indian Agriculture in America: Prehistory to the Present* (1987). Includes a discussion of preconquest agriculture.

A. Knight, *Mexico: From the Beginning to the Spanish Conquest* (2002). First of a three-volume comprehensive history of Mexico.

C. Morris and A. Von Hagen, *The Inka Empire and Its Andean Origins* (1993). An overview of Andean civilization with excellent illustrations.

M. Moseley, *The Incas and Their Ancestors: The Archaeology of Ancient Peru* (1992). An overview of Peruvian archaeology.

J. A. Sabloff, *The New Archaeology and the Ancient Maya* (1990). A lively account of recent research in Maya archaeology.

I. Silverblatt, *Moon, Sun, and Witches: Gender Ideologies and Class in Inca and Colonial Peru* (1987). A controversial but thought-provoking discussion of Incan ideas about gender.

CHAPTER 2

China

R. Berstein, *Ultimate Journey: Retracing the Path of an Ancient Buddhist Monk who Crossed Asia in Search of Enlightenment* (2001). Discusses the diffusion of Buddhism from India to China.

H. G. Creel, *What Is Taoism? And Other Studies in Chinese Cultural History* (1970).

W. T. de Bary et al., *Sources of Chinese Tradition* (1960). A reader in China's philosophical and historical literature. It should be consulted for the later periods as well as for the Zhou.

H. Fingarete, *Confucius—The Secular as Sacred* (1998).

Y. L. Fung, *A Short History of Chinese Philosophy*, ed. by D. Bodde (1948). A survey of Chinese philosophy from its origins down to recent times.

A. Graham, *Disputers of the Tao* (1989).

D. Hawkes, *Ch'u Tz'u: The Songs of the South* (1985).

D. C. Lau, trans., *Lao-tzu, Tao Te Ching* (1963).

D. C. Lau, trans., *Confucius, The Analects* (1979).

C. Li, ed., *The Sage and the Second Sex: Confucianism, Ethics, and Gender* (2000). A good introduction to gender and ethics in Confucian thought.

B. I. Schwartz, *The World of Thought in Ancient China* (1985).

A. Waley, *Three Ways of Thought in Ancient China* (1956). An easy yet sound introduction to Confucianism, Daoism, and Legalism.

A. Waley, *The Book of Songs* (1960).

B. Watson, trans., *Basic Writings of Mo Tzu, Hsun Tzu, and Han Fei Tzu* (1963).

B. Watson, trans., *The Complete Works of Chuang Tzu* (1968).

H. Welch, *Taoism, The Parting of the Way* (1967).

India

A. L. Basham, *The Wonder That Was India*, rev. ed. (1963). Still unsurpassed by more recent works. Chapter VII, "Religion," is a superb introduction to the Vedic Aryan, Brahmanic, Hindu, Jain, and Buddhist traditions of thought.

W. N. Brown, *Man in the Universe: Some Continuities in Indian Thought* (1970). A penetrating yet brief reflective summary of major patterns in Indian thinking.

W. T. de Bary et al., *Sources of Indian Tradition* (1958). 2 vols. Vol. I, *From the Beginning to 1800*, ed. and rev. by Ainslie T. Embree (1988). Excellent selections from a variety of Indian texts, with good introductions to chapters and individual selections.

P. Harvey, *An Introduction to Buddhism* (1990). Chapters 1–3 provide an excellent historical introduction.

T. J. Hopkins, *The Hindu Religious Tradition* (1971). A first-rate, thoughtful introduction to Hindu religious ideas and practice.

K. Klostermaier, *Hinduism: A Short History* (2000). A relatively compact survey of the history of Hinduism.

J. M. Koller, *The Indian Way* (1982). A useful, wide-ranging handbook of Indian thought and religion.

R. H. Robinson and W. L. Johnson, *The Buddhist Religion*, 3rd ed. (1982). An excellent first text on the Buddhist tradition, its thought and development.

R. C. Zaehner, *Hinduism* (1966). One of the best general introductions to central Indian religious and philosophical ideas.

Israel

A. Bach, ed., *Women in the Hebrew Bible: A Reader* (1999). Excellent introduction to the ways in which biblical scholars are exploring the role of women in the Bible.

Bright, *A History of Israel* (1968), 2nd ed. (1972). One of the standard scholarly introductions to biblical history and literature.

W. D. Davies and L. Finkelstein, eds., *The Cambridge History of Judaism*. Vol. I, *Introduction: The Persian Period* (1984). Excellent essays on diverse aspects of the exilic period and later.

J. Neusner, *The Way of Torah: An Introduction to Judaism* (1979). A sensitive introduction to the Judaic tradition and faith.

The Oxford History of the Biblical World, M. D. Coogan, ed. (1998).

Greece

The Cambridge Companion to Greek and Roman Philosophy, D. Sedley ed., (2003).

G. B. Kerferd, *The Sophistic Movement* (1981). An excellent description and analysis.

J. Lear, *Aristotle: The Desire to Understand* (1988). A brilliant yet comprehensible introduction to the work of the philosopher.

T. E. Rihil, *Greek Science* (1999). Good survey of Greek science incorporating recent reseach on the topic.

J. M. Robinson, *An Introduction to Early Greek Philosophy* (1968). A valuable collection of the main fragments and ancient testimony to the works of the early philosophers, with excellent commentary.

G. Vlastos, *The Philosophy of Socrates* (1971). A splendid collection of essays illuminating the problems presented by this remarkable man.

G. Vlastos, *Platonic Studies*, 2nd ed. (1981). A similar collection on the philosophy of Plato.

G. Vlastos, *Socrates, Ironist and Moral Philosopher* (1991). The results of a lifetime of study by the leading interpreter of Socrates in our time.

Comparative Studies

(Increasingly world historians are looking at ancient civilizations in relationship to each other rather than as isolated entities to try to understand commonalities and differences in social and cultural development.)

W. Doniger, *Splitting the Difference: Gender and Myth in Ancient Greece and India* (1999).

G. E. R. Lloyd, *The Ambitions of Curiosity: Understanding the World in Ancient Greece and China* (2002).

G. E. R. Lloyd, *The Way and the Word: Science and Medicine in Early China and Greece* (2002).

T. McEvilley, *The Shape of Ancient Thought: Comparative Studies of Greek and Indian Philosopies* (2002).

CHAPTER 3

The Rise of Greek Civilization

P. Cartledge, *The Spartans* (2003). A readable account of this enigmatic people.

J. Chadwick, *The Mycenaean World* (1976). A readable account by a man who helped decipher Mycenaean writing.

R. Drews, *The Coming of the Greeks* (1988). A fine discussion of the Greeks' arrival as part of the movements of the Indo-European peoples.

J. V. Fine, *The Ancient Greeks* (1983). An excellent survey that discusses historical problems and the evidence that gives rise to them.

M. I. Finley, *World of Odysseus*, rev. ed. (1965). A fascinating attempt to reconstruct Homeric society.

P. Green, *Xerxes at Salamis* (1970). A lively and stimulating history of the Persian War.

D. Hamel, *Trying Neaira* (2003). A lively account of the events surrounding a famous jury trial that sheds interesting light on Athenian society in the fourth century B.C.E.

V. D. Hanson, *The Western Way of War* (1989). A brilliant and lively discussion of the rise and character of the hoplite phalanx and its influence on Greek society.

V. D. Hanson, *The Other Greeks* (1995). A revolutionary account of the Greek invention of the family farm and its centrality for the shaping of the *polis*.

D. Kagan, *The Great Dialogue: A History of Greek Political Thought from Homer to Polybius* (1965). A discussion of the relationship between the Greek historical experience and political theory.

W. K. Lacey, *The Family in Ancient Greece* (1984).

J. F. Lazenby, *The Defense of Greece, 490–479 B.C.* (1993). A new and valuable study of the Persian Wars.

J. F. McGlew, *Tyranny and Political Culture in Ancient Greece* (1993). A recent account of political developments in the Archaic period.

O. Murray, *Early Greece* (1980). A lively and imaginative account of the early history of Greece to the end of the Persian War.

A. M. Snodgrass, *The Dark Age of Greece* (1972). A good examination of the archaeological evidence.

B. S. Strauss, *The Battle of Salamis: The Naval Encounter That Saved Greece and Western Civilization* (2004). A lively account of the major naval battle of the Persian Wars and its setting.

A. G. Woodhead, *Greeks in the West* (1962). An account of the Greek settlements in Italy and Sicily.

W. J. Woodhouse, *Solon the Liberator* (1965). A discussion of the great Athenian reformer.

S. G. Miller, *Ancient Greek Athletics* (2004). The most complete and most useful account of the subject.

Classical and Hellenistic Greece

W. Burkert, *Greek Religion* (1987). An excellent study by an outstanding student of the subject.

J. R. Lane Fox, *Alexander the Great* (1973). An imaginative account that does more than the usual justice to the Persian side of the problem.

Y. Garlan, *Slavery in Ancient Greece* (1988). An up-to-date survey.

P. Green, *Alexander to Actium: The Historical Evolution of the Hellenistic Age* (1990). A remarkable synthesis of political and cultural history.

C. D. Hamilton, *Agesilaus and the Failure of Spartan Hegemony* (1991). An excellent biography of the king who was the central figure in Sparta during its domination in the fourth century B.C.E.

N. G. L. Hammond, *Philip of Macedon* (1994). A new biography of the founder of the Macedonian Empire.

N. G. L. Hammond and G. T. Griffith, *A History of Macedonia*, Vol. 2, *550–336 B.C.* (1979). A thorough account of Macedonian history that focuses on the careers of Philip and Alexander.

R. Just, *Women in Athenian Law and Life* (1988). An account of women's place in Athenian society.

D. Kagan, *The Peloponnesian War* (2003). A narrative history of the war.

B. M. W. Knox, *The Heroic Temper: Studies in Sophoclean Tragedy* (1964). A brilliant analysis of tragic heroism.

D. M. Lewis, *Sparta and Persia* (1977). A valuable discussion of relations between Sparta and Persia in the fifth and fourth centuries B.C.E.

A. A. Long, *Hellenistic Philosophy: Stoics, Epicureans, Sceptics* (1974). An account of Greek science in the Hellenistic and Roman periods.

R. Meiggs, *The Athenian Empire* (1972). A fine study of the rise and fall of the empire, making excellent use of inscriptions.

J. J. Pollitt, *Art and Experience in Classical Greece* (1972). A scholarly and entertaining study of the relationship between art and history in classical Greece, with excellent illustrations.

J. J. Pollitt, *Art in the Hellenistic Age* (1986). An extraordinary analysis that places the art in its historical and intellectual context.

E. W. Robinson, *Ancient Greek Democracy* (2004). A stimulating collection of ancient sources and modern interpretations.

D. M. Schaps, *Economic Rights of Women in Ancient Greece* (1981).

B. S. Strauss, *Athens After the Peloponnesian War* (1987). An excellent discussion of Athens' recovery and of the nature of Athenian society and politics in the fourth century B.C.E.

B. S. Strauss, *Fathers and Sons in Athens* (1993). An unusual synthesis of social, political, and intellectual history.

V. Tcherikover, *Hellenistic Civilization and the Jews* (1970). A fine study of the impact of Hellenism on the Jews.

G. Vlastos, *Socrates, Ironist and Moral Philosopher* (1991). The results of a lifetime of study by the leading interpreter of Socrates in our time.

CHAPTER 4

Iran

M. Boyce, *Zoroastrians: Their Religious Beliefs and Practices* (1979). The most recent survey, organized historically and based on extensive research.

M. Boyce, ed. and trans., *Textual Sources for the Study of Zoroastrianism* (1984). Well-translated selections from a broad range of ancient Iranian materials.

J. M. Cook, *The Persian Empire* (1983). Survey of the Achaemenid period.

J. Curtis, *Ancient Persia* (1989). Excellent portfolio of photographs of artifacts and sites, with a clear historical survey of the arts and culture of ancient Iran.

W. D. Davies and L. Finklestein, ed., *The Cambridge History of Judaism*, Vol. 1, Introduction; "The Persian Period". Good articles on Iran and Iranian religion as well as Judaism.

J. Duchesne-Guillemin, trans., *The Hymns of Zarathushtra*, trans. by M. Henning (1952, 1963). The best short introduction to the original texts of the Zoroastrian hymns.

R. N. FRYE, *The Heritage of Persia* (1963, 1966). A first-rate survey of Iranian history to Islamic times: readable but scholarly.

R. GHIRSHMAN, *Iran* (1954). Good material on culture, society, and economy as well as politics and history.

W. W. MALANDRA, trans. and ed., *An Introduction to Ancient Iranian Religion: Readings from the Avesta and Achaemenid Inscriptions* (1983). Helpful especially for texts of inscriptions relevant to religion.

India

A. L. BASHAM, *The Wonder That Was India*, rev. ed. (1963). Excellent material on Mauryan religion, society, culture, and history.

A. L. BASHAM, ed., *A Cultural History of India* (1975). A fine collection of historical-survey essays by a variety of scholars. See Part I, "The Ancient Heritage" (Chapters 2–16).

N. N. BHATTACHARYYA, *Ancient Indian History and Civilization: Trends and Perspectives* (1988). Covers Mauryan and Gupta times as well as earlier periods, with chapters on political systems, cities and villages, ideology and religion, and art.

W. T. DE BARY et al., COMP., *Sources of Indian Tradition*, 2nd ed. (1958). Vol. I: *From the Beginning to 1800*, ed. and rev. by Ainslie T. Embree (1988). Excellent selections from a wide variety of Indian texts, with good introductions to chapters and selections.

B. ROWLAND, *The Art and Architecture of India: Buddhist/Hindu/Jain*, 3rd rev. ed. (1970). The standard work, lucid and easy to read. Note Part Three, "Romano-Indian Art in North-West India and Central Asia."

V. A. SMITH, ed., *The Oxford History of India*, 4th rev. ed. by Percival Spear et al. (1981), pp. 71–163. A dry, occasionally dated historical survey. Includes useful reference chronologies.

R. THAPAR, *Ashoka and the Decline of the Mauryans* (1973). The standard treatment of Ashoka's reign.

R. THAPAR, *A History of India, Part I* (1966), pp. 50–108. Three chapters that provide a basic survey of the period.

S. WOLPERT, *A New History of India*, 2nd ed. (1982). A basic survey history. Chapters 5 and 6 cover the Mauryans, Guptas, and Kushans.

Greek and Asian Dynasties

A. K. NARAIN, *The Indo-Greeks* (1957. Reprinted with corrections, 1962). The most comprehensive account of the complex history of the various kings and kingdoms.

F. E. PETERS, *The Harvest of Hellenism* (1970), pp. 222–308. Helpful chapters on Greek rulers of the Eastern world from Seleucus to the last Indo-Greeks.

J. W. SEDLAR, *India and the Greek World: A Study in the Transmission of Culture* (1980). A basic work that provides a good overview.

D. SINOR, ed., *The Cambridge History of Early Inner Asia* (1990). See especially Chapters 6 and 7.

CHAPTER 5

P. BOHANNAN AND P. CURTIN, *Africa and Africans*, rev. ed. (1971). An enjoyable and enlightening discussion of African history and prehistory and of major African institutions (e.g., arts, family life, religion).

R. BULLIET, *The Camel and the Wheel* (1990). Explains why the camel was chosen over the wheel as a means of transport in the Sahara.

P. CURTIN, S. FEIERMANN, L. THOMPSON, AND J. VANSINA, *African History* (1978). Probably the best survey history. The relevant portions are chapters 1, 2, 4, 8, and 9.

T. R. H. DAVENPORT, *South Africa: A Modern History*, 3rd rev. ed. (1987). Chapter 1 gives excellent summary coverage of prehistoric southern Africa, the Khoisan peoples, and the Bantu migrations.

B. DAVIDSON, *The African Past* (1967). A combination of primary-source selections and brief secondary discussions trace sympathetically the history of the diverse parts of Africa.

P. GARLAKE, *The Kingdoms of Africa* (1978). A lavishly illustrated set of photographic essays that provide a helpful introduction to the various historically important areas of precolonial Africa.

E. GILBERT AND J. REYNOLDS, *Africa in World History* (2004). The best new survey of African history, placing it in a global context.

R. W. JULY, *Precolonial Africa: An Economic and Social History* (1975). A very readable, topically arranged study. See especially "The Savannah Farmer," "The Bantu," "Cattlemen," and "The Traders" chapters.

H. LOTH, *Woman in Ancient Africa*, trans. by S. Marnie (1987). An interesting survey of legal, familial, cultural, and other aspects of women's roles.

R. OLIVER, *The African Experience* (1991). A masterly, balanced, and engaging sweep through African history. The chapters on prehistory and early history are outstanding summaries of the results and implications of recent research.

I. VAN SERTIMA, *Black Women in Antiquity* (1984, 1988). Studies of queens, goddesses, matriarchy, and other aspects of the role and status of women in Egyptian, Ethiopian, and other African societies of the past.

CHAPTER 6

From Republic to Empire

R. BAUMANN, *Women and Politics in Ancient Rome* (1995). A Study of the role of women in roman public life.

A. H. BERNSTEIN, *Tiberius Sempronius Gracchus: Tradition and Apostasy* (1978). A new interpretation of Tiberius's place in Roman politics.

T. J. CORNELL, *The Beginnings of Rome: Italy and Rome from the Bronze Age to the Punic Wars, c. 1000–264 B.C.* (1995). A consideration of the royal and early republican periods of Roman history.

T. CORNELL AND J. MATTHEWS, *Atlas of the Roman World* (1982). Much more than the title indicates, this book presents a comprehensive view of the Roman world in its physical and cultural setting.

J-M. DAVID, *The Roman Conquest of Italy* (1997). A good analysis of how Rome united Italy.

A. GOLDSWORTHY, *Roman Warfare* (2002). A good military history of Rome.

A. GOLDSWORTHY, *In the Name of Rome: The Men Who Won the Roman Empire* (2004). The story of Rome's greatest generals in the republican and imperial periods.

E. S. GRUEN, *Diaspora: Jews Amidst Greeks and Romans* (2002). A fine study of Jews in the Hellenistic and Roman world.

E. S. GRUEN, *The Hellenistic World and the Coming of Rome* (1984). A new interpretation of Rome's conquest of the eastern Mediterranean.

W. V. HARRIS, *War and Imperialism in Republican Rome, 327–70 B.C.* (1975). An analysis of Roman attitudes and intentions concerning imperial expansion and war.

A. KEAVENEY, *Rome and the Unification of Italy* (1988). The story of how Rome organized her defeated opponents.

S. LANCEL, *Carthage, A History* (1995). Includes a good account of Rome's dealings with Carthage.

J. F. LAZENBY, *Hannibal's War: A Military History of the Second Punic War* (1978). A careful and thorough account.

F.G.B. MILLAR, *The Crowd in Rome in the Late Republic* (1999). A challenge to the view that only aristocrats counted in the late republic.

M. PALLOTTINO, *The Etruscans*, 6th ed. (1974). Makes especially good use of archaeological evidence.

H. H. SCULLARD, *A History of the Roman World 753–146 B.C.*, 4th ed. (1980). An unusually fine narrative history with useful critical notes.

G. WILLIAMS, *The Nature of Roman Poetry* (1970). An unusually graceful and perceptive literary study.

Imperial Rome

W. BALL, *Rome in the East: The Transformation of an Empire* (2001). A thorough account of the influence of the East on Roman history.

T. BARNES, *The New Empire of Diocletian and Constantine* (1982).

K. R. BRADLEY, *Slavery and Society at Rome* (1994). A study of the role of slaves in Roman life.

P. BROWN, *The Rise of Western Christendom: Triumph and Diversity, 200–1000* (1996). A vivid picture of the spread of Christianity by a master of the field.

A. FERRILL, *The Fall of the Roman Empire, The Military Explanation* (1986). An interpretation that emphasizes the decline in the quality of the Roman army.

K. GALINSKY, *Augustan Culture* (1996). A work that integrates art, literature, and politics.

A. H. M. JONES, *The Later Roman Empire*, 3 vols. (1964). A comprehensive study of the period.

D. KAGAN, ed., *The End of the Roman Empire: Decline or Transformation?* 3rd ed. (1992). A collection of essays discussing the problem of the decline and fall of the Roman Empire.

J. E. LENDON, *Empire of Honor, The Art of Government in the Roman World* (1997). An original and path-breaking interpretation.

E. N. LUTTWAK, *The Grand Strategy of the Roman Empire* (1976). An original and fascinating analysis by a keen student of modern strategy.

R. MACMULLEN, *Roman Social Relations, 50 B.C. to A.D. 284* (1981).

R. MACMULLEN, *Corruption and the Decline of Rome* (1988). A study that examines the importance of changes in ethical ideas and behavior.

R. W. MATHISON, *Roman Aristocrats in Barbarian Gaul: Strategies for Survival* (1993). An unusual slant on the late empire.

J.F. MATTHEWS, *Laying Down the Law: A Study of the Theodosian Code* (2000). A study of the importance of Roman law as a source for the understanding of Roman history and civilization.

W. A. MEEKS, *The Origins of Christian Morality: The First Two Centuries.* An account of the shaping of Christianity in the Roman Empire.

F. MILLAR, *The Emperor in the Roman World, 31 B.C.–A.D. 337* (1977). A study of Roman imperial government.

F. MILLAR, *The Roman Empire and Its Neighbors*, 2nd ed. (1981).

H. M. D. PARKER, *A History of the Roman World from A.D. 138 to 337* (1969). A good survey.

M. I. ROSTOVTZEFF, *Social and Economic History of the Roman Empire*, 2nd ed. (1957). A masterpiece whose main thesis has been much disputed.

V. RUDICH, *Political Dissidence Under Nero, The Price of Dissimulation* (1993). A brilliant exposition of the lives and thoughts of political dissidents in the early empire.

E. T. SALMON, *A History of the Roman World, 30 B.C. to A.D. 138* (1968). A good survey.

R. SYME, *The Roman Revolution* (1960). A brilliant study of Augustus, his supporters, and their rise to power.

R. SYME, *The Augustan Aristocracy* (1985). An examination of the new ruling class shaped by Augustus.

L. A. THOMPSON, *Romans and Blacks* (1989).

CHAPTER 7

D. BODDE, *China's First Unifier* (1938). A study of the Qin unification of China, viewed through the Legalist philosopher and statesman LiSi.

T. T. CH'U, *Law and Society in Traditional China* (1961). Treats the sweep of Chinese history from 202 B.C.E. to 1911 C.E.

T. T. CH'U, *Han Social Structure* (1972).

A. COTTERELL, *The First Emperor of China* (1981). A study of the first Qin emperor.

R. COULBORN, *Feudalism in History* (1965). One chapter interestingly compares the quasi feudalism of the Zhou with that of the Six Dynasties period.

J. K. FAIRBANK, E. O. REISCHAUER, AND A. M. CRAIG, *East Asia: Tradition and Transformation* (1989). A fairly detailed single-volume history covering China, Japan, and other countries in East Asia from antiquity to recent times.

J. GERNET, *A History of Chinese Civilization* (1982). A survey of Chinese history.

D.A. GRAFF AND R. HIGHAM, *A Military History of China* (2002).

C. Y. HSU, *Ancient China in Transition* (1965). On social mobility during the Eastern Zhou era.

C. Y. HSU, *Han Agriculture* (1980). A study of the agrarian economy of China during the Han dynasty.

J. LEVI, *The Chinese Emperor* (1987). A novel about the first Qin emperor based on scholarly sources.

M. LOEWE, *Everyday Life in Early Imperial China* (1968). A social history of the Han dynasty.

J. NEEDHAM, *The Shorter Science and Civilization in China* (1978). An abridgment of the multivolume work on the same subject with the same title—minus Shorter—by the same author.

S. OWEN, ed. and Trans., *An Anthology of Chinese Literature: Beginnings to 1911* (1996).

I. ROBINET, *Taoism: Growth of a Religion* (1987).

M. SULLIVAN, *The Arts of China* (1967). An excellent survey history of Chinese art.

D. TWITCHETT AND M. LOEWE, eds., *The Ch'in and Han Empires, 221 B.C.E.–C.E. 220* (1986). Vol. 1 of *The Cambridge History of China*.

Z. S. WANG, *Han Civilization* (1982).

B. WATSON, *Ssu-ma Ch'ien, Grand Historian of China* (1958). A study of China's premier historian.

B. WATSON, *Records of the Grand Historian of China*, Vols. 1 and 2 (1961). Selections from the *Shiji* by Sima Qian.

B. WATSON, *The Columbia Book of Chinese Poetry* (1986).

F. WOOD, *The Silk Road: Two Thousand Years in the Heart of Asia* (2003). A lively narrative combined with photographs and paintings.

A. WRIGHT, *Buddhism in Chinese History* (1959).

Y. S. YU, *Trade and Expansion in Han China* (1967). A study of economic relations between the Chinese and their neighbors.

CHAPTER 8

General

P. BOL, *This Culture of Ours* (1992). An insightful intellectual history of the Tang through the Song dynasties.

J. CAHILL, *Chinese Painting* (1960). An excellent survey.

J. K. FAIRBANK AND M. GOLDMAN, *China: A New History* (1998). The summation of a lifetime engagement with Chinese history.

F. A. KIERMAN JR., AND J. K. FAIRBANK, eds., *Chinese Ways in Warfare* (1974). Chapters by different authors on the Chinese military experience from the Zhou to the Ming.

Sui and Tang

P. B. EBREY, *The Aristocratic Families of Early Imperial China* (1978).

D. MCMULLEN, *State and Scholars in T'ang China* (1988).

S. OWEN, *The Great Age of Chinese Poetry: The High T'ang* (1980).

S. OWEN, trans. and ed., *An Anthology of Chinese Literature: Beginnings to 1911* (1996).

E. G. PULLEYBLANK, *The Background of the Rebellion of An Lu-shan* (1955). A study of the 755 rebellion that weakened the central authority of the Tang dynasty.

E. O. REISCHAUER, *Ennin's Travels in T'ang China* (1955). China as seen through the eyes of a ninth-century Japanese Marco Polo.

E. H. SCHAFER, *The Golden Peaches of Samarkand* (1963). A study of Tang imagery.

SO. TEISER, *The Ghost Festival in Medieval China* (1988). On Tang popular religion.

D. TWITCHETT, ed., *The Cambridge History of China*, Vol. III: *Sui and T'ang China, 589–906 Part 1*, (1979).

G. W. WANG, *The Structure of Power in North China During the Five Dynasties* (1963). A study of the interim period between the Tang and the Song dynasties.

A. F. WRIGHT, *The Sui Dynasty* (1978).

Song

B. BIRGE, *Women, Property, and Confucian Reaction in Song and Yuan China (960–1366)* (2002). The rights of women to property—whether in the form of dowries or inheritances—were considerable during the Song but declined thereafter.

C. S. CHANG AND J. SMYTHE, *South China in the Twelfth Century* (1981). China as seen through the eyes of a twelfth-century Chinese poet, historian, and statesman.

E. L. DAVIS, *Society and the Supernatural in Song China* (2001).

J. W. HAEGER, ed., *Crisis and Prosperity in Song China* (1975).

R. HYMES, *Statesmen and Gentlemen* (1987). On the transformation of officials into a local gentry elite during the twelfth and thirteenth centuries.

R. HYMES, *Way and Byway: Taoism, Local Religion, and Models of Divinity in Sung and Modern China* (2002).

M. ROSSABI, *China Among Equals* (1983). A study of the Liao, Qin, and Song Empires and their relations.

W. M. TU, *Confucian Thought, Selfhood as Creative Transformation* (1985).

K. YOSHIKAWA, *An Introduction to Song Poetry*, trans. by B. Watson (1967).

Yuan

T. T. ALLSEN, *Mongol Imperialism* (1987).

J. W. DARDESS, *Conquerors and Confucians: Aspects of Political Change in Late Yuan China* (1973).

DE RACHEWILTZ, trans., *The Secret History of the Mongols: A Mongolian Epic Chronicle of the Thirteenth Century* (2003). A new translation of a key historical work on the life of Genghis.

H. FRANKE AND D. TWITCHETT, eds., *The Cambridge History of China*, Vol. VI: *Alien Regimes and Border States, 710–1368* (1994).

J. D. LANGLOIS, *China Under Mongol Rule* (1981).

R. LATHAM, trans., *Travels of Marco Polo* (1958).

H. D. MARTIN, *The Rise of Chingis Khan and His Conquest of North China* (1981).

D. MORGAN, *The Mongol Empire and its Legacy* (1999). Genghis, the several khanates, and the aftermath of empire.

P. RATCHNEVSKY, *Genghis Khan, His Life and Legacy* (1992). The rise to power of the Mongol leader, with a critical consideration of historical sources.

CHAPTER 9

M. ADOLPHSON, *The Gates of Power: Monks, Courtiers, and Warriors in Premodern Japan* (2000). A new interpretation stressing the importance of temples in the political life of Heian and Kamakura Japan.

B.L. BATTEN, *To the Ends of Japan: Premodern Frontiers, Boundaries, and Interactions.* (2003). An interesting treatment of Heian Japan, topic by topic.

C. BLACKER, *The Catalpa Bow* (1975). An insightful study of folk Shinto.

R. BORGEN, *Sugawara no Michizane and the Early Heian Court* (1986). A study of a famous courtier and poet.

D. M. BROWN, ed., *The Cambridge History of Japan: Ancient Japan* (1993). This series of six volumes sums up several decades of research on Japan.

D. BROWN AND E. ISHIDA, eds., *The Future and the Past* (1979). A translation of a history of Japan written in 1219.

The Cambridge History of Japan, D.M. BROWN, ed.; Vol. 1, *Ancient Japan*, W. McCullough and D. H. Shively eds; Vol. 2, *Heian Japan*, K. Yamamura, ed. Vol. 3, *Medieval Japan*. Fine multi-author works.

M. COLLCUTT, *Five Mountains* (1980). A study of the monastic organization of medieval Zen.

T.D. CONLON, *State of War: The Violent Order of Fourteenth Century Japan* (2003). Compare Conlon's account with those of Souyri and Friday.

P. DUUS, *Feudalism in Japan* (1969). An easy survey of the subject.

W. W. FARRIS, *Population, Disease, and Land in Early Japan, 645–900* (1985). An innovative reinterpretation of early history.

W. W. FARRIS, *Heavenly Warriors: The Evolution of Japan's Military, 500–1300* (1992).

W. W. FARRIS, *Sacred Texts and Buried Treasures* (1998). Studies of Japan's prehistory and early history, based on recent Japanese research.

K. F. FRIDAY, *Samurai, Warfare and the State in Early Medieval Japan* (2004). Weapons and warfare in Japan from the tenth to fourteenth centuries.

A. E. GOBLE, *GōDaigo's Revolution* (1996). A provoking account of the 1331 revolt by an emperor who thought emperors should rule.

J. W. HALL, *Government and Local Power in Japan, 500–1700: A Study Based on Bizen Province* (1966). A splendid and insightful book.

J. W. HALL AND T. TOYODA, *Japan in the Muromachi Age* (1977). Another collection of essays.

D. KEENE, ed., *Anthology of Japanese Literature from the Earliest Era to the Mid-Nineteenth Century* (1955).

D. KEENE, ed., *Twenty Plays of the Nō Theatre* (1970).

T. LAMARRE, *Uncovering Heian Japan: An Archeology of Sensation and Inscription* (2000). The "archeology" in the title refers to digging into literature.

I. H. LEVY, *The Ten Thousand Leaves* (1981). A fine translation of Japan's earliest collection of poetry.

J. P. MASS AND W. HAUSER, eds., *The Bakufu in Japanese History* (1985). Topics in *bakufu* history from the twelfth to the nineteenth centuries.

I. MORRIS, trans., *The Pillow Book of Sei Shōnagon* (1967). Observations about the Heian court life by the Jane Austen of ancient Japan.

S. MURASAKI, *The Tale of Genji*, trans. by A. Waley (1952). A comparison of this translation with that of Seidensticker is instructive.

S. MURASAKI, *The Tale of Genji*, trans. by E. G. Seidensticker (1976). The world's first novel and the greatest work of Japanese fiction.

R. J. PEARSON et al., eds., *Windows on the Japanese Past: Studies in Archaeology and Prehistory* (1986).

D. L. PHILIPPI, trans., *Kojiki* (1968). Japan's ancient myths.

J. PIGGOT, *The Emergence of Japanese Kingship* (1997).

E. O. REISCHAUER, *Ennin's Diary, the Record of a Pilgrimage to China in Search of the Law and Ennin's Travels in T'ang China* (1955).

E. O. REISCHAUER AND A. M. CRAIG, *Japan: Tradition and Transformation* (1989). A more detailed work covering the sweep of Japanese history from the early beginnings through the 1980s.

H. SATO, *Legends of the Samurai* (1995). Excerpts from various tales and writings.

D. H. SHIVELY and W. H. MCCULLOUGH, eds., *The Cambridge History of Japan: Heian Japan* (1999).

D. T. SUZUKI, *Zen and Japanese Culture* (1959).

H. TONOMURA, *Community and Commerce in Late Medieval Japan* (1992).

R. TSUNODA, W. T. DE BARY, AND D. KEENE, comps., *Sources of the Japanese Tradition* (1958). A collection of original religious, political, and philosophical writings from each period of Japanese history. The best reader. A new edition should be out soon.

H. P. VARLEY, *Imperial Restoration in Medieval Japan* (1971). A study of the 1331 attempt by an emperor to restore imperial power.

A. WALEY, trans., *The Nō Plays of Japan* (1957). Medieval dramas.

K. YAMAMURA, ed., *Cambridge History of Japan: Medieval Japan* (1990).

CHAPTER 10

Iran

M. BOYCE, *Zoroastrians: Their Religious Beliefs and Practices* (1979). A detailed survey by the current authority on Zoroastrian religious history. See Chapters 7–9.

M. BOYCE, ed. and trans., *Textual Sources for the Study of Zoroastrianism* (1984). A valuable anthology with an important introduction that includes Boyce's arguments for a revision of the dates of Zoroaster's life (to between 1400 and 1200 B.C.E.).

R. N. FRYE, *The Heritage of Persia* (1963). Still one of the best surveys, Chapter 6 deals with the Sasanid era.

R. GHIRSHMAN, *Iran* (1954 [orig. ed. 1951]). An introductory survey of similar extent to Frye, but with differing material also.

R. GHIRSHMAN, *Persian Art: The Parthian and Sasanid Dynasties* (1962). Superb photographs, and a very helpful glossary of places and names. The text is minimal.

GEO WIDENGRAN, *Mani and Manichaeism* (1965). Still the standard introduction to Mani's life and the later spread and development of Manichaeism.

India

A. L. BASHAM, *The Wonder That Was India* (1963). The best survey of classical Indian religion, society, literature, art, and politics.

W. T. DE BARY et al., comp., *Sources of Indian Tradition*, 2nd ed. (1958), Vol. I, *From the Beginning to 1800*, ed. and rev. by Ainslie T. Embree (1988). Excellent selections from a wide variety of Indian texts, with good introductions to the text selections.

S. DUTT, *Buddhist Monks and Monasteries of India* (1962). The standard work. See especially Chapters 3 ("Bhakti") and 4 ("Monasteries Under the Gupta Kings").

D. G. MANDELBAUM, *Society in India* (1972). 2 vols. The first two chapters in Volume I of this study of caste, family, and village relations are a good introduction to the caste system.

B. ROWLAND, *The Art and Architecture of India: Buddhist/Hindu/Jain*, 3rd rev. ed. (1970). See the excellent chapters on Sungan, Andhran, and other early Buddhist art (6–8, 14), the Gupta period (15), and the Hindu Renaissance (17–19).

V. A. SMITH, *The Oxford History of India*, 4th rev. ed. (1981). See especially pages 164–229 (the Gupta period and following era to the Muslim invasions).

R. THAPAR, *A History of India, Part I* (1966), pp. 109–193. Three chapters covering the rise of mercantilism, the Gupta "classical pattern," and the southern dynasties to ca. 900 C.E..

P. YOUNGER, *Introduction to Indian Religious Thought* (1972). A sensitive attempt to delineate classical concerns of Indian religious thought and culture.

CHAPTER 11

O. GRABAR, *The Formation of Islamic Art* (1973). A critical and creative interpretation of major themes in the development of distinctively Islamic forms of art and architecture.

A. HOURANI, *A History of the Arab Peoples* (1991). A masterly survey of the Arabs down through the centuries and a clear picture of many aspects of Islamic history and culture that extend beyond the Arab world.

H. KENNEDY, *The Prophet and the Age of the Caliphates: The Islamic Near East from the Sixth to the Eleventh Century* (1986). The best survey of early Islamic history.

I. LAPIDUS, *A History of Islamic Societies* (1988). A comprehensive overview of the rise and development of Islam all over the world.

F. E. PETERS, *Muhammad and the Origins of Islam* (1994). A balanced analysis of the life of Muhammad.

F. RAHMAN, *Major Themes of the Qur'an* (1980). The best introduction to the basic ideas of the Qur'an and Islam, seen through the eyes of a perceptive Muslim modernist scholar.

F. SCHUON, *Understanding Islam* (1994). Compares the Islamic worldview with Catholic Christianity. A dense, but intellectually stimulating, discussion.

M. SELLS, *Approaching the Qur'an. The Early Revelations* (1999). A fine introduction and new translations of some of the more common earlier Qur'anic revelations.

B. STOWASSER, *Women in the Qur'an, Traditions and Interpretation* (1994). An outstanding systematic study of statements regarding women in the Qur'an.

CHAPTER 12

K. ARMSTRONG, *Muhammad: A Biography of the Prophet* (1992). Strong on religion.

R. BARTLETT, *The Making of Europe, 950–1350* (1992). A study of the way immigration and colonial conquest shaped the Europe we know.

M. BLOCH, *Feudal Society*, Vols. 1 and 2, trans. by L. A. Manyon (1971). A classic on the topic and as an example of historical study.

P. BROWN, *Augustine of Hippo: A Biography* (1967). Late antiquity seen through the biography of its greatest Christian thinker.

J. H. BURNS, *The Cambridge History of Medieval Political Thought c. 350–c. 1450* (1991). The best scan.

R. H. C. DAVIS, *A History of Medieval Europe: From Constantine to St. Louis* (1972). Unsurpassed in clarity.

R. FLETCHER, *The Barbarian Conversion: From Paganism to Christianity* (1998). Up-to-date survey.

J. B. GLUBB, *The Great Arab Conquests* (1995). Jihadists.

G. GUGLIELMO, ed., *The Byzantines* (1997). Updates key issues.

D. GUTAS, *Greek Thought, Arabic Culture* (1998). A comparative intellectual history.

G. HOLMES, Ed., *The Oxford History of Medieval Europe* (1992). Overviews of Roman and northern Europe during the "Dark Ages."

B. LEWIS, *The Middle East: A Brief History of the Last 2,000 Years* (1995)

C. MANGO, *Byzantium: The Empire of New Rome* (1980).

J. MARTIN, *Medieval Russia 980–1584* (1995). A concise narrative history.

R. MCKITTERICK, ed., *Carolingian Culture: Emulation and Innovation* (1994). Fresh essays.

J.J. NORWICH, *Byzantium: The Decline and Fall* (1995).

J.J. NORWICH, *Byzantium: The Apogee* (1997). The whole story in two volulmes.

R.I. PAGE, *Chronicles of the Vikings: Records, Memorials, and Myths* (1995). Sources galore.

F. ROBINSON, ed., *The Cambridge Illustrated History of the Islamic World* (1996). Spectacular.

S. RUNCIMAN, *Byzantine Civilization* (1970). Succinct, comprehensive account by a master.

P. SAWYER, *The Age of the Vikings* (1962). Old but solid account.

C. STEPHENSON, *Medieval Feudalism* (1969). Excellent short summary and introduction.

L. WHITE JR., *Medieval Technology and Social Change* (1962). Often fascinating account of how primitive technology changed life.

H. WOLFRAM, *The Roman Empire and Its Germanic Peoples* (1997). Challenging, but most rewarding.

CHAPTER 13

The Islamic Heartlands

L. AHMED, *Women and Gender in Islam. Historical Roots of a Modern Debate* (1992). A good historical survey of the status of women in Middle Eastern societies.

J. BERKEY, *The Formation of Islam. Religion and Society in the Near East 600–1800* (2002). An interesting new synthesis foducing on political and religious trends.

C. E. BOSWORTH, *The Islamic Dynasties: A Chronological and Genealogical Handbook* (1967). A handy reference work for dynasties and families important to Islamic history in all periods and places.

M. A. COOK, *Commanding Right and Forbidding Wrong in Islamic Thought* (2001). A masterful anaylsis of the development of Islamic law.

P. K. HITTI, *History of the Arabs*, 8th ed. (1964). Still a useful English resource, largely for factual detail. See especially Part IV, "The Arabs in Europe: Spain and Sicily."

A. HOURANI, *A History of the Arab Peoples* (1991). The newest survey history and the best, at least for the Arab Islamic world.

S. K. JAYYUSI, ed., *The Legacy of Muslim Spain*, 2 vols. (1994). A comprehensive survey of the arts, politics, literature, and society by experts in various fields.

B. LEWIS, ed., *Islam and the Arab World* (1976). A large-format, heavily illustrated volume with many excellent articles on diverse aspects of Islamic (not simply Arab, as the misleading title indicates) civilization through the premodern period.

D. MORGAN, *The Mongols* (1986). A recent and readable survey history.

J. J. SAUNDERS, *A History of Medieval Islam* (1965). A brief and simple, if sketchy, introductory survey of Islamic history to the Mongol invasions.

India

W. T. DE BARY et al., comp., *Sources of Indian Tradition*, 2nd ed. (1958), Vol. I, *From the Beginning to 1800*, ed. and rev. by Ainslie T. Embree (1988). Excellent selections from a wide variety of Indian texts, with good introductions to chapters and individual selections.

S. M. IKRAM, *Muslim Civilization in India* (1964). The best short survey history, covering the period 711 to 1857.

R. C. MAJUMDAR, gen. ed., *The History and Culture of the Indian People*, Vol. VI, *The Delhi Sultanate*, 3rd ed. (1980). A comprehensive political and cultural account of the period in India.

F. ROBINSON, ed., *The Cambridge History of India, Pakistan, Bangladesh, Sri Lanka, Nepal, Bhutan, and the Maldives* (1989). A very helpful quick reference source with brief but well-done survey essays on a wide range of topics relevant to South Asian history down to the present.

A. WINK, *Al-Hind: The Making of the Indo-Islamic World*, Vol. 1 (1991). The first of five promising volumes to be devoted to the Indo-Islamic world's history. This volume treats the seventh to eleventh centuries.

Southeast Asia

L. ANDAYA, *The World of Maluku: Eastern Indonesia in the Early Modern Period* (1993). A comprehensive view of the formation of what is now Indonesia.

B. W. ANDAYA AND L. ANDAYA, *A History of Malaysia* (1982). A good overiew of Indonesia's smaller but critical northern neighbor.

J. SIEGEL, *Shadow and Sound: The Historical Thought of a Sumatran People* (1979). An excellent analysis tracing the relation between foreign influences and local practice.

CHAPTER 14

B. S. BAUER, *The Development of the Inca State* (1992). An important new work that emphasizes archaeological evidence over the Spanish chronicles in accounting for the emergence of the Inca Empire.

F. F. BERDAN, *The Aztecs of Central Mexico: An Imperial Society* (1982). An excellent introduction to the Aztecs.

R. E. BLANTON, S. A. KOWALEWSKI, G. FEINMAN, AND J. APPEL, *Ancient Mesoamerica: A Comparison of Change in Three Regions* (1981). Concentrates on ancient Mexico.

K. O. BRUHNS, *Ancient South America* (1994). A clear discussion of the archaeology and civilization of the region with emphasis on the Andes.

R. L. BURGER, *Chavín and the Origins of Andean Civilization* (1992). A detailed study of early Andean prehistory by one of the leading authorities on Chavín.

R. M. CARMACK, J. GASCO, AND G. H. GOSSEN, *The Legacy of Mesoamerica: History and Culture of a Native American Civilization* (1996). A survey of Mesoamerica from its origins to the present.

I. CLENDINNEN, *Aztecs: An Interpretation* (1995). A fascinating attempt to reconstruct the Aztec world.

M. D. COE, *Breaking the Maya Code* (1992). The story of the remarkable achievement of deciphering the ancient Maya language.

M. D. Coe, *The Maya* (1993). The best introduction.

M. D. Coe, *Mexico from the Olmecs to the Aztecs* (1994). A wide-ranging introductory discussion.

G. Conrad and A. A. Demarest, *Religion and Empire: The Dynamics of Aztec and Inca Expansionism* (1984). An interesting comparative study.

S. D. Gillespie, *The Aztec Kings* (1989).

R. Hassig, *Aztec Warfare.*

J. Hyslop, *Inka Settlement Planning* (1990). A detailed study.

M. León-Portilla, *Fifteen Poets of the Aztec World* (1992). An anthology of translations of Aztec poetry.

M. E. Miller, *The Art of Mesoamerica from Olmec to Aztec* (1986). A well-illustrated introduction.

C. Morris and A. Von Hagen, *The Inka Empire and Its Andean Origins* (1993). A clear overview of Andean prehistory by a leading authority. Beautifully illustrated.

M. E. Mosely, *The Incas and Their Ancestors: The Archaeology of Peru* (1992). Readable and thorough.

J. A. Sabloff, *The Cities of Ancient Mexico* (1989). Capsule summaries of ancient Mesoamerican cultures.

J. A. Sabloff, *Archaeology and the Maya* (1990). A look at changing views of the ancient Maya.

L. Schele and M. E. Miller, *The Blood of Kings* (1986). A rich and beautifully illustrated study of ancient Maya art and society.

R. S. Sharer, *The Ancient Maya*, 5th ed. (1994). A classic. Readable, authoritative, and thorough.

M. P. Weaver, *The Aztecs, Maya, and Their Predecessors* (1993). A classic textbook.

CHAPTER 15

L. B. Alberti, *The Family in Renaissance Florence*, trans. by R. N. Watkins (1962). A contemporary humanist, who never married, explains how a family should behave.

E. Amt, ed., *Women's Lives in Medieval Europe: A Source-book* (1992). Outstanding collection of sources.

H. Baron, *The Crisis of the Early Italian Renaissance*, Vols. 1 and 2 (1996). New edition of an old, major work, setting forth the civic dimension of Italian humanism.

G. Barraclough, *The Origins of Modern Germany* (1963). Penetrating political narrative.

S. Bramly, *Discovering the Life of Leonard da Vinci* (1991). The man and the genius.

G. Brucker, *Renaissance Florence* (1983). Still one of the best introductions.

G. Bull, *Michelangelo: A Biography* (1995). Recent life in full.

J. Burckhardt, *The Civilization of the Renaissance in Italy* (1867). The famous classic that still has as many defenders as detractors.

S. Flanagan, *Hildegard of Bingen, 1098–1179: A Visionary Life* (1995). A most interesting German woman.

E. Hallam, ed., *Chronicles of the Crusades* (1989). All nine!

D. Herlihy, *Medieval Households* (1985). Survey of Middle Ages that defends the medieval family against modern caricatures.

D. Herlihy and C. Klapisch-Zuber, *Tuscans and Their Families* (1985). Important work based on unique demographic data that gives the reader an appreciation of quantitative history.

G. Holmes, *Renaissance* (1996). An expert's take on the subject.

J. C. Holt, *Magna Carta*, 2nd ed. (1992). The famous document and its interpretation by succeeding generations.

J. Huizinga, *The Waning of the Middle Ages: A Study of the Forms of Life, Thought, and Art in France and the Netherlands in the Dawn of the Renaissance* (1924). A classic study of "mentality" at the end of the Middle Ages.

L. Jardine, *Worldly Goods: A New History of the Renaissance* (1996). The material side of the Renaissance.

M. King, *Women of the Renaissance* (1991). Women's presence and creativity.

W. H. McNeill, *Plagues and Peoples* (1976). The Black Death in a broader context.

R. I. Moore, *The Formation of a Persecuting Society: Power and Deviance in Western Europe, 950–1250* (1987). A sympathetic look at heresy and dissent.

T. Noonan, *Contraception: A History of Its Treatment by the Catholic Theologians and Canonists* (1967). A fascinating account of medieval theological attitudes toward sexuality and sex-related problems.

J. Riley-Smith, ed., *Oxford Illustrated History of the Crusades* (1995) Lucid, gorgeous, and up-to-date.

J. Weisheipl, *Friar Thomas* (1980). Biography of Saint Thomas Aquinas, both the man and the theologian.

CHAPTER 16

M. Brecht, *Martin Luther: His Road to Reformation, 1483–1521* (1985). Best on young Luther.

C. Brown, et al., *Rembrandt: The Master and His Workshop* (1991) A great master's art and influence.

R. Briggs, *Witches and Neighbors: A History of European Witchcraft* (1996). A readable introduction.

E. DUFFY, *The Stripping of the Altars* (1992). Strongest argument yet that there was no deep reformation in England.

H. O. EVENNETT, *The Spirit of the Counter Reformation* (1968). The continuity and independence of Catholic reform.

HANS-JÜRGEN GOERTZ, *The Anabaptists* (1996). Best treatment of minority Protestants.

O. P. GRELL AND A. CUNNINGHAM, *Health Care and Poor Relief in Protestant Europe* (1997) The civic side of the Reformation.

M. HOLT, *The French Wars of Religion, 1562–1629* (1995). Scholarly appreciation of religious side of the story.

J. C. HUTCHISON, *Albrecht Durer* (1990). The life behind the art.

H. JEDIN, *A History of the Council of Trent*, Vols. 1, 2 (1957–1961). Comprehensive, detailed, and authoritative.

M. KITCHEN, *The Cambridge Illustrated History of Germany* (1996). Comprehensive and accessible.

A. KORS AND E. PETERS, eds., *European Witchcraft, 1100–1700* (1972). Classics of witch belief.

W. MACCAFFREY, *Elizabeth I* (1993). Magisterial study.

G. MATTINGLY, *The Armada* (1959). A masterpiece, novel-like in style.

D. MCCOLLOCH, *The Reformation* (2004). No stone unturned, with English emphasis.

H. A. OBERMAN, *Luther: Man Between God and Devil* (1989). Authoritative biography

J. W. O'MALLEY, *The First Jesuits* (1993). Extremely detailed account of the creation of the Society of Jesus and its original purposes.

S. OZMENT, *The Age of Reform 1250–1550: An Intellectual and Religious History of Late Medieval and Reformation Europe* (1980). Broad, lucid survey.

S. OZMENT, *When Fathers Ruled: Family Life in Reformation Europe* (1983). Effort to portray the constructive side of Protestant thinking about family relationships.

S. OZMENT, *The Bürgermeister's Daughter: Scandal in a Sixteenth Century German Town* (1996). What a woman could do at law in the sixteenth century.

G. PARKER, *The Thirty Years' War* (1984). Large, lucid survey.

J. H. PARRY, *The Age of Reconnaissance* (1964). A comprehensive account of explorations from 1450 to 1650.

W. PRINZ, *Durer* (1998). Latest biography of Germany's greatest painter.

J. J. SCARISBRICK, *Henry VIII* (1968). The best account of Henry's reign.

G. STRAUSS, ed. and trans., *Manifestations of Discontent in Germany on the Eve of the Reformation* (1971). A rich collection of sources for both rural and urban scenes.

H. WUNDER, *He Is the Sun, She Is the Moon: Women in Early Modern Germany* (1998). Best study of early modern women.

CHAPTER 17

J. ABUN-NASR, *A History of the Maghrib in the Islamic Period* (1987). The most recent North African survey. Pages 59–247 are relevant to this chapter.

D. BIRMINHAM, *Central Africa to 1870* (1981). Chapters from the *Cambridge History of Africa* that give a brief, lucid overview of developments in this region.

P. BOHANNAN AND P. CURTIN, *Africa and Africans*, rev. ed. (1971). Accessible, topical approach to African history, culture, society, politics, and economics.

P. D. CURTIN, S. FEIERMANN, L. THOMPSON, AND J. VANSINA, *African History* (1978). An older, but masterly survey. The relevant portions are Chapters 6–9.

R. ELPHICK, *Kraal and Castle: Khoikhoi and the Founding of White South Africa* (1977). An incisive, informative interpretation of the history of the Khoikhoi and their fateful interaction with European colonization.

R. ELPHICK AND H. GILIOMEE, *The Shaping of South African Society, 1652–1820* (1979). A superb, synthetic history of this crucial period.

J. D. FAGE, *A History of Africa* (1978). Still a readable survey history.

M. HISKETT, *The Development of Islam in West Africa* (1984). The standard survey study of the subject. Of the relevant sections (Chapters 1–10, 12, 15), that on Hausaland, which is treated only in passing in this text, is noteworthy.

R. W. JULY, *Precolonial Africa: An Economic and Social History* (1975). Chapter 10 gives an interesting overall picture of slaving in African history.

R. W. JULY, *A History of the African People*, 3rd ed. (1980). Chapters 3–6 treat Africa before about 1800 area by area; Chapter 7 deals with "The Coming of Europe."

I. M. LEWIS, Ed., *Islam in Tropical Africa* (1966), pp. 4–96. Lewis's introduction is one of the best brief summaries of the role of Islam in West Africa and the Sudan.

D. T. NIANI, ed., *Africa from the Twelfth to the Sixteenth Century, UNESCO General History of Africa*, Vol. IV (1984). Many survey articles cover the various regions and major states of Africa in the centuries noted in the title.

R. OLIVER, *The African Experience* (1991). A masterly, balanced, and engaging survey, with outstanding syntheses and summaries of recent research.

J. A. Rawley, *The Transatlantic Slave Trade: A History* (1981). Impressively documented, detailed, and well-presented survey history of the Atlantic trade; little focus on African dimensions.

A. F. C. Ryder, *Benin and the Europeans: 1485–1897* (1969). A basic study.

John K. Thornton, *The Kingdom of Kongo: Civil War and Transition, 1641–1718* (1983). A detailed and perceptive analysis for those who wish to delve into Kongo state and society in the seventeenth century.

M. Wilson and L. Thompson, eds., *The Oxford History of South Africa*, Vol. I., *South Africa to 1870* (1969). Relatively detailed, if occasionally dated, treatment.

CHAPTER 18

I. Berlin, *Many Thousands Gone: The First Two Centuries of Slavery in North America* (1998); *Generations of Captivity: A History of African American Slaves* (2003). Two volumes representing the most extensive and important recent treatment of slavery in North America.

R. Blackburn, *The Making of New World Slavery from the Baroque to the Modern 1492–1800* (1997). An extraordinary work.

B. Cobo, *History of the Inca Empire* (1979). A major discussion.

N. D. Cook, *Born to Die: Disease and New World Conquest, 1492–1650* (1998) A survey of the devastating impact of previously unknown diseases on the native populations of the Americas.

P. D. Curtin, *The Atlantic Slave Trade: A Census* (1969). Remains a basic work.

D. B. Davis, *The Problem of Slavery in Western Culture* (1966). A brilliant and far-ranging discussion.

H. L. Gates Jr. and W. L. Andrews, eds., *Pioneers of the Black Atlantic: Five Slave Narratives from the Enlightenment 1772–1815* (1998). An anthology of autobiographical accounts.

S. Gruzinski, *The Conquest of Mexico: The Incorporation of Indian Societies into the Western World, 16th–18th Centuries* (1993). Interprets the experience of Native Americans, from their own point of view, during the time of the Spanish conquest.

L. Hanke, *Bartolomé de Las Casas: An Interpretation of His Life and Writings* (1951). A classic work.

R. Harms, *The Diligent: A Voyage through the Worlds of the Slave Trade* (2002). A powerful narrative of the voyage of a French slave trader.

J. Hemming, *The Conquest of the Incas,* (1970). A lucid account of the conquest of the Inca Empire and its aftermath.

J. Hemming, *Red Gold: The Conquest of the Brazilian Native Americans, 1500–1760* (1978). A careful account with excellent bibliography.

H. Klein, *The Middle Passage: Comparative Studies in the African Slave Trade* (1978). A far-ranging overview of the movement of slaves from Africa to the Americas.

M. Leon-Portilla, ed., *The Broken Spears: The Aztec Account of the Conquest of Mexico* (1961). A collection of documents recounting the experience of the Aztecs from their own point of view.

P. Manning, *Slavery and African Life: Occidental, Oriental, and African Slave Trades* (1990). An admirably concise economic-historical synthesis of the evidence, with multiple tables and statistics to supplement the magisterial analysis.

A. Pagden, *Lords of All the World: Ideologies of Empire in Spain, Britain, and France* c. 1500–c. 1800 (1995). An effort to explain the imperial thinking of the major European powers.

S. B. Schwartz, *Sugar Plantations in the Formation of Brazilian Society: Bahia, 1550–1835* (1985). A broad-ranging study of the emergence of the plantation economy.

I. K. Steele, *The English Atlantic, 1675–1740s: An Exploration of Communication and Community* (1986). An exploration of culture and commerce in the transatlantic world.

S. J. Stein, *Peru's Indian Peoples and the Challenge of Spanish Conquest: Huamanga to 1640* (1983). A work that examines the impact of the conquest of the Inca empire over the scope of a century.

H. Thomas, *Conquest: Montezuma, Cortés, and the Fall of Old Mexico* (1993). A splendid modern narrative of the event with careful attention to the character of the participants.

H. Thomas, *The Slave Trade: The Story of the Atlantic Slave Trade: 1440–1870* (1999). A sweeping narrative overview.

J. Thornton, *Africa and Africans in the Making of the Atlantic World, 1400–1680* (1992). A discussion of the role of Africans in the emergence of the transatlantic economy.

N. Wachtel, *The Vision of the Vanquished: The Spanish Conquest of Peru Through Indian Eyes, 1530–1570* (1977). A presentation of Incan experience of conquest.

CHAPTER 19

China

D. Bodde and C. Morris, *Law in Imperial China* (1967). Focuses on the Qing dynasty (1644–1911).

T. Brook, *The Confusions of Pleasure: Commerce and Culture in Ming China* (1988).

C. S. Chang and S. L. H. Chang, *Crisis and Transformation in Seventeenth Century China: Society, Culture, and Modernity* (1992).

P. CROSSLEY, *Translucent Mirror: History and Identity in Qing Imperial Ideology* (1999).

W. T. DE BARY, *Learning for One's Self: Essays on the Individual in Neo-Confucian Thought* (1991). A useful corrective to the view that Confucianism is simply a social ideology.

M. C. ELLIOTT, *The Manchu Way: The Eight Banners and Ethnic Identity in Late Imperial China* (2001). The latest word; compare to Crossley above.

M. ELVIN, *The Pattern of the Chinese Past: A Social and Economic Interpretation* (1973). A controversial but stimulating interpretation of Chinese economic history in terms of technology. It brings in earlier periods as well as the Ming, Qing, and modern China.

J. K. FAIRBANK, ed., *The Chinese World Order: Traditional China's Foreign Relations* (1968). An examination of the Chinese tribute system and its varying applications.

H. L. KAHN, *Monarchy in the Emperor's Eyes: Image and Reality in the Ch'ien-lung Reign* (1971). A study of the Chinese court during the mid-Qing period.

P. KUHN, *Soulstealers: The Chinese Sorcery Scare of 1768* (1990).

LI YU, *The Carnal Prayer Mat*, trans. by P. Hanan (1990).

F. MOTE AND D. TWITCHETT, eds., *The Cambridge History of China: The Ming Dynasty 1368–1644*, Vols. VI (1988) and VII (1998).

S. NAQUIN, *Peking Temples and City Life, 1400–1900* (2000).

S. NAQUIN AND E. S. RAWSKI, *Chinese Society in the Eighteenth Century* (1987).

J. B. PARSONS, *The Peasant Rebellions of the Late Ming Dynasty* (1970).

P. C. PERDUE, *Exhausting the Earth, State and Peasant in Hunan, 1500–1850* (1987).

D. H. PERKINS, *Agricultural Development in China, 1368–1968* (1969).

E. RAWSKI, *The Last Emperors: A Social History of Qing Imperial Institutions* (1998).

M. RICCI, *China in the Sixteenth Century: The Journals of Matthew Ricci, 1583–1610* (1953).

W. ROWE, *Hankow* (1984). A study of a city in late imperial China.

G. W. SKINNER, *The City in Late Imperial China* (1977).

J. D. SPENCE, *Ts'ao Yin and the K'ang-hsi Emperor: Bondservant and Master* (1966). An excellent study of the early Qing court.

J. D. SPENCE, *Emperor of China: A Self-Portrait of K'ang-hsi* (1974). The title of this readable book does not adequately convey the extent of the author's contribution to the study of the early Qing emperor.

J. D. SPENCE, *Treason by the Book* (2001). An account of the legal workings of the authoritarian Qing state that reads like a detective story.

L. A. STRUVE, trans. and ed., *Voices from the Ming-Qing Cataclysm* (1993). A reader with translations of Chinese sources.

F. WAKEMAN, *The Great Enterprise* (1985). On the founding of the Manchu dynasty.

Japan

M. E. BERRY, *Hideyoshi* (1982). A study of the sixteenth-century unifier of Japan.

M. E. BERRY, *The Culture of Civil War in Kyoto* (1994). On the Warring States era.

H. BOLITHO, *Treasures Among Men: The Fudai Daimyo in Tokugawa Japan* (1974). A study in depth.

H. BOLITHO, *Bereavement and Consolation: Testimonies from Tokugawa Japan* (2003). Instances of how Tokugawa Japanese handled the death of a child.

C. R. BOXER, *The Christian Century in Japan, 1549–1650* (1951).

The Cambridge History of Japan, Vol. 4 J.W. Hall (ed.), *Early Modern Japan* (1991). A multi-author work.

M. CHIKAMATSU, *Major Plays of Chikamatsu*, trans. by D. Keene (1961).

R. P. DORE, *Education in Tokugawa Japan* (1965).

G. S. ELISON, *Deus Destroyed: The Image of Christianity in Early Modern Japan* (1973). A brilliant study of the persecutions of Christianity during the early Tokugawa period.

J. W. HALL AND M. JANSEN, eds., *Studies in the Institutional History of Early Modern Japan* (1968). A collection of articles on Tokugawa institutions.

J. W. HALL, K. NAGAHARA, AND K. YAMAMURA, eds., *Japan Before Tokugawa* (1981).

S. HANLEY, *Everyday Things in Premodern Japan: The Hidden Legacy of Material Culture* (1997).

H. S. HIBBETT, *The Floating World in Japanese Fiction* (1959). An eminently readable study of early Tokugawa literature.

M. JANSEN, ed., *The Nineteenth Century*, Vol. 5 in *The Cambridge History of Japan* (1989).

K. KATSU, *Musui's Story* (1988). The life and adventures of a boisterous, no-good samurai of the early nineteenth century. Eminently readable.

D. KEENE, trans., *Chushingura, the Treasury of Loyal Retainers* (1971). The puppet play about the forty-seven rōnin who took revenge on the enemy of their former lord.

O.G. LIDIN, *Tanegashima: The Arrival of Europe in Japan* (2002). The impact of the musket and Europeans on sixteenth-century Japan.

M. MARUYAMA, *Studies in the Intellectual History of Tokugawa Japan*, trans. by M. Hane (1974). A seminal work in this field by one of modern Japan's greatest scholars.

J.L. MCCLAIN, et. al., *Edo and Paris: Urban Life and the State in the Early Modern Era* (1994). Comparison of city life and government role in capitals of Tokugawa Japan and France.

K. W. NAKAI, *Shogunal Politics* (1988). A brilliant study of Arai Hakuseki's conceptualization of Tokugawa government.

P. NOSCO, ed., *Confucianism and Tokugawa Culture* (1984). A lively collection of essays.

H. OOMS, *Tokugawa Village Practice: Class, Status, Power, Law* (1996).

A. RAVINA, *Land and Lordship in Early Modern Japan* (1999). A sociopolitical study of three Tokugawa domains.

I. SAIKAKU, *The Japanese Family Storehouse*, trans. by G. W. Sargent (1959). A lively novel about merchant life in seventeenth-century Japan.

G. B. SANSOM, *The Western World and Japan* (1950).

J. A. SAWADA, *Confucian Values and Popular Zen* (1993). A study of *Shingaku*, a popular Tokugawa religious sect.

C. D. SHELDON, *The Rise of the Merchant Class in Tokugawa Japan* (1958).

T. C. SMITH, *The Agrarian Origins of Modern Japan* (1959). On the evolution of farming and rural social organization in Tokugawa Japan.

P. F. SOUYRI, *The World Turned Upside Down: Medieval Japanese Society* (2001). After a running start from the late Heian period, an analysis of the overthrow of lords by their vassals.

R. P. TOBY, *State and Diplomacy in Early Modern Japan: Asia in the Development of the Tokugawa Bakufu* (1984).

C. TOTMAN, *Tokugawa Ieyasu: Shōgun* (1983).

C. TOTMAN, *Green Archipelago, Forestry in Preindustrial Japan* (1989).

H. P. VARLEY, *The Ō'nin War: History of Its Origins and Background with a Selective Translation of the Chronicle of Ō'nin* (1967).

K. YAMAMURA AND S. B. HANLEY, *Economic and Demographic Change in Preindustrial Japan, 1600–1868* (1977).

Korea

T. HATADA, *A History of Korea* (1969).

W. E. HENTHORN, *A History of Korea* (1971).

KI-BAIK LEE, *A New History of Korea* (1984).

P. LEE, *Sourcebook of Korean Civilization*, Vol. I (1993).

Vietnam

J. BUTTINGER, *A Dragon Defiant, a Short History of Vietnam* (1972).

NGUYEN DU, *The Tale of Kieu* (1983).

N. TARLING, ed., *The Cambridge History of Southeast Asia* (1992).

K. TAYLOR, *The Birth of Vietnam* (1983).

A. B. WOODSIDE, *Vietnam and the Chinese Model* (1988).

CHAPTER 20

F. ANDERSON, *The Crucible of War: The Seven Years' War and the Fate of Empire in British North America, 1754–1766* (2000) A splendid narrative and analysis.

J. BLUM, *Lord and Peasant in Russia from the Ninth to the Nineteenth Century* (1961). Remains a thorough and wide-ranging discussion.

P. BURKE, *The Fabrication of Louis XIV* (1992). Examines the manner in which the public image of Louis XIV was forged in art.

P. BUSHKOVITCH, *Peter the Great: The Struggle for Power, 1671–1725* (2001). Replaces previous studies.

L. COLLEY, *Britons: Forging the Nation, 1707–1837* (1992) A major study of the making of British nationhood.

P. DEANE, *The First Industrial Revolution,* (1999). A well-balanced and systematic treatment.

J. DE VRIES, *European Urbanization 1500–1800* (1984). The most important and far-ranging of recent treatments of the subject.

W. DOYLE, *The Old European Order, 1660–1800* (1992). The most thoughtful treatment of the subject.

R. J. W. EVANS, *The Making of the Habsburg Monarchy, 1550–1700: An Interpretation* (1979). Places much emphasis on intellectual factors and the role of religion.

D. FRASER, *Frederick the Great: King of Prussia* (2001) Excellent on both Frederick and eighteenth-century Prussia.

E. HOBSBAWM, *Industry and Empire: The Birth of the Industrial Revolution* (1999). A survey by a major historian of the subject.

K. HONEYMAN, *Women, Gender and Industrialization in England, 1700–1850* (2000). Emphasizes how certain work or economic roles became associated with either men or women.

O. H. HUFTON, *The Poor of Eighteenth-Century France, 1750–1789* (1975). A brilliant study of poverty and the family economy.

L. HUGHES, *Russia in the Age of Peter the Great* (1998). An excellent account.

D. I. KERTZER AND M. BARBAGLI, *The History of the European Family: Family Life in Early Modern Times, 1500–1709* (2001). A series of broad-ranging essays covering the entire Continent.

S. KING AND G. TIMMONS, *Making Sense of the Industrial Revolution: English Economy and Society, 1700–1850* (2001). Examines the Industrial Revolution through the social institutions that brought it about and were changed by it.

M. KISHLANSKY, *A Monarchy Transformed: Britain 1603–1714* (1996) An excellent synthesis.

P. LANGFORD, *A Polite and Commercial People: England 1717–1783* (1989). An excellent survey of mid-eighteenth-century Britain covering social history as well as politics, the overseas wars, and the American Revolution.

A. LOSSKY, *Louis XIV and the French Monarchy* (1994). The most recent major analysis.

F. E. MANUEL, *The Broken Staff: Judaism Through Christian Eyes* (1992). An important discussion of Christian interpretations of Judaism.

M. A. MEYER, *The Origins of the Modern Jew: Jewish Identity and European Culture in Germany, 1749–1824* (1967). A general introduction organized around individual case studies.

D. UNDERDOWN, *Fire from Heaven: Life in an English Town in the Seventeenth Century* (1992). A lively account of how a single English town experienced the religious and political turmoil of the century.

D. VALENZE, *The First Industrial Woman* (1995). An elegant work exploring the manner in which industrialization transformed the work of women.

J. WEST, *Gunpower, Government, and War in the Mid–Eighteenth Century* (1991). A study of how warfare touched much government of the day.

CHAPTER 21

S. S. BLAIR AND J. BLOOM, *The Art and Architecture of Islam, 1250–1800* (1994). A fine survey of the period for all parts of the Islamic world.

R. CANFIELD, ed., *Turko-Persia in Historical Perspctive* (1991). A good general collection of essays.

K. CHELEBI, *The Balance of Truth* (1957). A marvelous volume of essays and reflections by probably the major intellectual of Ottoman times.

W. T. DE BARY et al., comp., *Sources of Indian Tradition*, 2nd ed. (1958),Vol. I, *From the Beginning to 1800*, ed. and rev. by Ainslie T. Embree (1988). Excellent selections from a wide variety of Indian texts, with good introductions to chapters and individual selections.

S. FAROQI, *Towns and Townsmen of Ottoman Anatolia* (1984). Examines the changing balances of economic power between the urban and rural areas.

C. H. FLEISCHER, *Bureaucrat and Intellectual in the Ottoman Empire: The Historian Mustafa Ali (1541–1600)* (1986). A major study of Ottoman intellectual history.

G. HAMBLY, *Central Asia* (1966). Excellent survey chapters (9–13) on the Chaghatay and Uzbek (Shaybanid) Turks.

R. S. HATTOX, *Coffee and Coffee-Houses: The Origins of a Social Beverage in the Medieval Near East* (1985). A fascinating piece of social history.

M. G. S. HODGSON, *The Gunpowder Empires and Modern Times*, Vol. 3 of *The Venture of Islam*, 3 vols. (1974). Less ample than Vols. 1 and 2 of Hodgson's monumental history, but a thoughtful survey of the great post-1500 empires.

S. M. IKRAM, *Muslim Civilization in India* (1964). Still the best short survey history, covering the period from 711 to 1857.

H. INALCIK, *The Ottoman Empire: The Classical Age 1300–1600* (1973). An excellent, if dated, survey with solid treatment of Ottoman social, religious, and political institutions.

H. INALCIK, *An Economic and Social History of the Ottoman Empire, 1300–1914* (1994). A masterly survey by the dean of Ottoman studies today.

C. KAFADAR, *Between Two Worlds: The Construction of the Ottoman State* (1995). A readable analysis of theories of Ottoman origins and early development.

N. R. KEDDIE, ed., *Scholars, Saints, and Sufis: Muslim Religious Institutions in the Middle East Since 1500* (1972). A collection of interesting articles well worth reading.

M. MUJEEB, *The Indian Muslims* (1967). The best cultural study of Islamic civilization in India as a whole, from its origins onward.

G. NECIPOGLU, *Architecture, Ceremonial, and Power: The Topkapi Palace in the Fifteenth and Sixteenth Centuries* (1991). A superb analysis of the symbolism of Ottoman power and authority.

L. PIERCE, *The Imperial Harem: Women and Sex in the Ottoman Empire* (1993). Ground-breaking study on the role of women in the Ottoman Empire.

D. QUATARERT, *An Economic and Social history of the Ottoman Empire 1300–1914* (1994). The authoritative account of Ottoman economy and society.

J. RICHARDS, *The Mughal Empire*, Vol. 5 of *The New Cambridge History of India* (1993). A impressive synthesis of the varying interpretations of the Mughal India.

S. A. A. RIZVI, *The Wonder That Was India*, Vol. II (1987). A sequel to Basham's original *The Wonder That Was India*; treats Mughal life, culture, and history from 1200 to 1700.

F. ROBINSON, *Atlas of the Islamic World Since 1500* (1982). Brief, excellent historical essays, color illustrations with detailed accompanying text, and chronological tables, as well as precise maps, make this a refreshing general reference work.

R. SAVORY, *Iran Under the Safavids* (1980). A solid and readable survey.

S. J. SHAW, *Empire of the Gazis: The Rise and Decline of the Ottoman Empire, 1280–1808*, Vol. I of *History of the Ottoman Empire and Modern Turkey* (1976). A solid historical survey with excellent bibliographic essays for each chapter and a good index.

CHAPTER 22

D. BEALES, *Joseph II: In the Shadow of Maria Theresa, 1741–1780* (1987). The best treatment in English of the early political life of Joseph II.

M. BIAGIOLI, *Galileo Courtier: The Practice of Science in the Culture of Absolutism* (1993). A major revisionist work that emphasizes the role of the political setting on Galileo's career and thought.

D. D. BIEN, *The Calas Affair: Persecution, Toleration, and Heresy in Eighteenth-Century Toulouse* (1960). Classic treatment of the famous case.

T. C. W. BLANNING, *The Culture of Power and the Power of Culture: Old Regime Europe 1660–1789* (2002). The strongest treatment of the relationship of eighteenth-century cultural changes and politics.

R. DARNTON, *The Literary Underground of the Old Regime* (1982). Classic essays on the world of printers, publishers, and booksellers.

P. DEAR, *Revolutionizing the Sciences: European Knowledge and Its Ambitions, 1500–1700* (2001). A broad-ranging study of both the ideas and institutions of the new science.

I. DE MADARIAGA, *Catherine the Great: A Short History* (1990). A good brief biography.

S. GAUKROGER, *Francis Bacon and the Transformation of Early-Modern Philosophy* (2001). An excellent, accessible introduction.

J. GLEIXK, *Isaac Newton* (2003) The best brief biography.

D. GOODMAN, *The Republic of Letters: A Cultural History of the French Enlightenment* (1994). Concentrates on the role of salons.

I. HARRIS, *The Mind of John Locke: A Study of Political Theory in Its Intellectual Setting* (1994). The most comprehensive recent treatment.

J. L. HEILBRON, *The Sun in the Church: Cathedrals as Solar Observatories* (2000). A remarkable study of the manner in which Roman Catholic cathedrals were used to make astsronomical observations and calculations.

K. J. HOWELL, *God's TwoBooks: Copernican Cosmology and Biblical Interpretqation in Early Modern Science* (2003) Best introduction to early modern issues of science and religion.

J. MELTON, *The Rise of the Public in Enlightenmen Europe* (2001). A superb overview of the emergence of new institutions which made the expression of a broad public opinion possible in Europe.

T. MUNCK, *The Enlightenment: A Comparative Social History 1721–1794* (2000). A clear introduction to the social background making possible the spread of Enlightenment thought.

S. MUTHU, *Enlightenment against Empire* (2003) A study of philosophes who criticized the European empires of their day.

D. OUTRAM, *The Enlightenment* (1995). An excellent brief introduction.

R. PORTER, *The Creation of the Modern World: The Untold Story of the British Enlightenment* (2001) A superb, lively overview.

P. RILEY, *The Cambridge Companion to Rousseau* (2001). Excellent accessible essays by major scholars.

E. ROTHCHILD, *Economic Sentiments: Adam Smith, Condorcet, and the Enlightenment* (2001). A sensitive account of Smith's thought and its relationship to the social questions of the day.

S. SHAPIN, *The Scientific Revolution* (1996). An important revisionist survey emphasizing social factors.

L. STEINBRÜGGE, *The Moral Sex: Woman's Nature in the French Enlightenment* (1995). Emphasizes the conservative nature of Enlightenment thought on women.

P. ZAGORIN, *How the Idea of Religious Toleration Came to the West* (2003) An excellent exploration of the rise of toleration.

CHAPTER 23

R. ANSTEY, *The Atlantic Slave Trade and British Abolition, 1760–1810* (1975). A standard overview that emphasizes the role of religious factors.

B. BAILYN, *The Ideological Origins of the American Revolution* (1967). An important work illustrating the role of English radical thought in the perceptions of the American colonists.

K. M. BAKER, *Inventing the French Revolution: Essays on French Political Culture in the Eighteenth Century* (1990). Important essays on political thought before and during the revolution.

K. M. BAKER AND C. LUCAS, eds., *The French Revolution and the Creation of Modern Political Culture*, 3 vols. (1987). A splendid collection of important original articles on all aspects of politics during the revolution.

R. J. BARMAN, *Brazil: The Forging of a Nation, 1798–1852* (1988). The best coverage of this period.

C. BECKER, *The Declaration of Independence: A Study in the History of Political Ideas* (1922). Remains an important examination of the political and imperial theory of the Declaration.

J. F. BERNARD, *Talleyrand: A Biography* (1973). A useful account.

L. BETHELL, *The Cambridge History of Latin America*, Vol. 3 (1985). Contains an extensive treatment of independence.

R. BLACKBURN, *The Overthrow of Colonial Slavery, 1776–1848* (1988). A major discussion quite skeptical of the humanitarian interpretation.

T. C. W. BLANNING, ed., *The Rise and Fall of the French Revolution* (1996). A wide-ranging collection of essays illustrating the debates over the French Revolution.

J. BROOKE, *King George III* (1972). The best biography.

R. COBB, *The People's Armies* (1987). The major treatment in English of the revolutionary army.

O. CONNELLY, *Napoleon's Satellite Kingdoms* (1965). The rule of Napoleon and his family in Europe.

E. V. DA COSTA, *The Brazilian Empire* (1985). Excellent coverage of the entire nineteenth-century experience of Brazil.

D. B. DAVIS, *The Problem of Slavery in the Age of Revolution, 1770–1823* (1975). A transatlantic perspective on the issue.

F. FEHÉR, *The French Revolution and the Birth of Modernity* (1990). A wide-ranging collection of essays on political and cultural facets of the revolution.

A. FORREST, *The French Revolution and the Poor* (1981). A study that expands consideration of the revolution beyond the standard social boundaries.

M. GLOVER, *The Peninsular War, 1807–1814: A Concise Military History* (1974). An interesting account of the military campaign that so drained Napoleon's resources in western Europe.

J. GODECHOT, *The Counter-Revolution: Doctrine and Action, 1789–1804* (1971). An examination of opposition to the revolution.

A. GOODWIN, *The Friends of Liberty: The English Democratic Movement in the Age of the French Revolution* (1979). A major work that explores the impact of the French Revolution on English radicalism.

L. HUNT, *Politics, Culture, and Class in the French Revolution* (1986). A series of essays that focus on the modes of expression of the revolutionary values and political ideas.

W. W. KAUFMANN, *British Policy and the Independence of Latin America, 1802–1828* (1951). A standard discussion of an important relationship.

E. KENNEDY, *A Cultural History of the French Revolution* (1989). An important examination of the role of the arts, schools, clubs, and intellectual institutions.

M. KENNEDY, *The Jacobin Clubs in the French Revolution: The First Years* (1982). A careful scrutiny of the organizations chiefly responsible for the radicalizing of the revolution.

M. KENNEDY, *The Jacobin Clubs in the French Revolution: The Middle Years* (1988). A continuation of the previously listed study.

H. KISSINGER, *A World Restored: Metternich, Castlereagh and the Problems of Peace, 1812–1822* (1957). A provocative study by an author who became an American secretary of state.

G. LEFEBVRE, *The Coming of the French Revolution* (trans. 1947). A classic examination of the crisis of the French monarchy and the events of 1789.

G. LEFEBVRE, *Napoleon*, 2 vols., trans. by H. Stockhold (1969). The fullest and finest biography.

J. LYNCH, *The Spanish American Revolutions, 1808–1826* (1986). An excellent one-volume treatment.

P. MAIER, *American Scripture: Making the Declaration of Independence* (1997). Stands as a major revision of our understanding of the Declaration.

G. MASUR, *Simón Bolívar* (1969). The standard biography in English.

S. E. MELZER AND L. W. RABINE, eds., *Rebel Daughters: Women and the French Revolution* (1992). A collection of essays exploring various aspects of the role and image of women in the French Revolution.

M. MORRIS, *The British Monarchy and the French Revolution* (1998). Explores the manner in which the British monarchy saved itself from possible revolution.

R. MUIR, *Tactics and the Experience of Battle in the Age of Napoleon* (1998). Examines the wars from the standpoint of the soldiers in combat.

H. NICOLSON, *The Congress of Vienna* (1946). A good, readable account.

T. O. OTT, *The Haitian Revolution, 1789–1804* (1973). An account that clearly relates the events in Haiti to those in France.

R. R. PALMER, *Twelve Who Ruled: The Committee of Public Safety During the Terror* (1941). A clear narrative and analysis of the policies and problems of the committee.

R. R. PALMER, *The Age of the Democratic Revolution: A Political History of Europe and America, 1760–1800*, 2 vols. (1959, 1964). An impressive survey of the political turmoil in the transatlantic world.

C. Proctor, *Women, Equality, and the French Revolution* (1990). An examination of how the ideas of the Enlightenment and the attitudes of revolutionaries affected the legal status of women.

A. J. Russell-Wood, ed., *From Colony to Nation: Essays on the Independence of Brazil* (1975). A series of important essays.

P. Schroeder, *The Transformation of European Politics, 1763–1848* (1994). A fundamental treatment of the diplomacy of the era.

T. E. Skidmore and P. H. Smith, *Modern Latin America*, 4th ed. (1997). A very useful survey.

A. Soboul, *The Parisian Sans-Culottes and the French Revolution, 1793–94* (1964). The best work on the subject.

A. Soboul, *The French Revolution* (trans. 1975). An important work by a Marxist scholar.

D. G. Sutherland, *France, 1789–1825: Revolution and Counterrevolution* (1986). A major synthesis based on recent scholarship in social history.

T. Tackett, *Religion, Revolution, and Regional Culture in Eighteenth-Century France: The Ecclesiastical Oath of 1791* (1986). The most important study of this topic.

T. Tackett, *Becoming a Revolutionary: The Deputies of the French National Assembly and the Emergence of a Revolutionary Culture (1789–1790)* (1996). The best study of the early months of the revolution.

J. M. Thompson, *Robespierre*, 2 vols. (1935). The best biography.

D. K. Van Key, *The Religious Origins of the French Revolution: From Calvin to the Civil Constitution, 1560–1791* (1996). Examines the manner in which debates within French Catholicism influenced the coming of the revolution.

M. Walzer, ed., *Regicide and Revolution: Speeches at the Trial of Louis XVI* (1974). An important and exceedingly interesting collection of documents with a useful introduction.

I. Woloch, *The New Regime: Transformations of the French Civic Order, 1789–1820s* (1994). An important overview of just what had and had not changed in France after the quarter century of revolution and war.

G. Wood, *The Radicalism of the American Revolution* (1991). A major interpretation.

CHAPTER 24

I. Berlin, *Generations of Captivity: A History of African-American Slaves* (2003) A major work.

D. Blackbourn, *The Long Nineteenth Century: A History of Germany, 1780–1918* (1998). An outstanding survey.

D. G. Creighton, *John A. MacDonald* (1952, 1955). A major biography of the first Canadian prime minister.

D. Donald, *Lincoln* (1995). Now the standard biography.

R. B. Edgerton, *Death or Glory: The Legacy of the Crimean War* (2000). Multifaceted study of a badly mismanaged war that transformed many aspects of European domestic politics.

M. Holt, *The Rise and Fall of the American Whig Party: Jacksonian Politics and the Onset of the Civil War* (2003) An extensive survey of the Jacksonian era.

R. Kee, *The Green Flag: A History of Irish Nationalism* (2001). A vast survey.

W. Lacquer, *A History of Zionism* (1989). The most extensive one-volume treatment.

M. B. Levinger, *Enlightened Nationalism: The Transformation of Prussian Political Culture, 1806–1848* (2002). A major work based on the most recent scholarship.

J. M. McPherson, *The Battle Cry of Freedom: The Civil War Era* (1988). An excellent one-volume treatment.

D. Morton, *A Short History of Canada* (2001). Useful popular history.

J. P. Parry, *The Rise and Fall of Liberal Government in Victorian Britain* (1994). An outstanding study.

A. Plessis, *The Rise and Fall of the Second Empire, 1852–1871* (1985). A useful survey of France under Napoleon III.

D. M. Potter, *The Impending Crisis, 1848–1861* (1976) A penetrating study of the coming of the American Civil War.

A. Sked, *Decline and Fall of the Habsburg Empire 1815–1918* (2001). A major, accessible survey of a difficult subject.

D. M. Smith, *Cavour* (1984). An excellent biography.

C. P. Stacey, *Canada and the Age of Conflict* (1977, 1981). A study of Canadian foreign relations.

D. Wetzel, *A Duel of Giants: Bismarck, Napoleon III, and the Origins of the Franco-Prussian War* (2001). Broad study based on most recent scholarship.

CHAPTER 25

M. Adas, *Machines as the Measure of Men: Science, Technology, and Ideologies of Western Dominance* (1989). The best single volume on racial thinking and technological advances as forming ideologies of European colonial dominance.

A. Ascher and P. A. Stolypin, *The Search for Stability in Late Imperial Russia* (2000). A broad-ranging biography based on extensive research.

I. Berlin, *Karl Marx: His Life and Environment*, 4th ed. (1996). A classics volume that remains an excellent introduction.

Janet Browne, *Charles Darwin*, 2 vols. (2002) An eloquent, accessible biography.

J. Burrow, *The Crisis of Reason: European Thought, 1848–1914* (2000). The best overview available.

A. D. CHANDLER JR., *The Visible Hand: Managerial Revolution in American Business* (1977). Remains the best discussion of the innovative role of American business.

A. CLARKE, *The Struggle for the Breeches: Gender and the Making of the British Working Class* (1995). An examination of the manner in which industrialization made problematical the relationships between men and women.

W. CRONIN, *Nature's Metropolis: Chicago and the Great West, 1848–1893* (1991) The best examination of any major American nineteenth-century city.

P. GAY, *Freud: A Life for Our Time* (1988). The new standard biography.

R. F. HAMILTON, *Marxism, Revisionism, and Leninism: Explication, Assessment, and Commentary* (2000). A contribution from the perspective of a historically minded sociologist.

S. HAHN, *A Nation under Our Feet: Black Political Struggles in the Rural South from Slavey to the Great Migration* (2003). A major synthesis.

A. HOURANI, *Arab Thought in the Liberal Age 1789–1939* (1967). A classic account, clearly written and accessible to the nonspecialist.

D. I. KERTZER AND M. BARBAGLI, eds., *Family Life in the Long Nineteenth Century, 1789–1913: The History of the European Family* (2002). Wide-ranging collection of essays.

J. T. KLOPPENBERG, *Uncertain Victory: Social Democracy and Progressivism in European and American Thought* (1986). An extremely important comparative study.

J. KÖHLER, *Zarathustra's Secret: The Interior Life of Friedrich Nietzsche* (2002). A controversial new biography.

L. KOLAKOWSKI, *Main Currents of Marxism: Its Rise, Growth, and Dissolution*, 3 vols. (1978). Especially good on the last years of the nineteenth century and the early years of the twentieth.

P. KRAUSE, *The Battle for Homestead, 1880–1892* (1992). Examines labor relations in the steel industry.

D. LANDES, *The Wealth and Poverty of Nations: Why Some Are So Rich and Some So Poor* (1998). A major international discussion of the subject.

M. McGERR, *A Fierce Discontent: The Rise and Fall of the Progressive Moevement in America 1870–1920* (2003). The best recent synthesis.

E. MORRIS, *Theodore Rex* (2002). Major survey of Theodore Roosevelt's presidency and personality.

A. PAIS, *Subtle Is the Lord: The Science and Life of Albert Einstein* (1983). Remains the most accessible scientific biography.

J. RENDALL, *The Origins of Modern Feminism: Women in Britain, France and the United States, 1780–1860* (1985). A well-informed introduction.

R. SERVICE, *Lenin: A Biography* (2002). Based on new sources and will no doubt become the standard biography.

R. M. UTLEY, *The Indian Frontier and the American West, 1846–1890* (1984). A broad survey of the pressures of white civilization against Native Americans.

D. VITAL, *A People Apart: The Jews In Modern Europe, l789–1939* (1999). A deeply informed survey.

CHAPTER 26

S. ARROM, *The Women of Mexico City, 1790–1857* (1985). A pioneering study.

E. BERMAN, ed., *Women, Culture, and Politics in Latin America* (1990). Useful essays.

L. BETHELL, ed., *The Cambridge History of Latin America*, 8 vols. (1992). The single most authoritative coverage, with extensive bibliographical essays.

V. BULMER-THOMAS, *The Economic History of Latin America Since Independence* (1994). A major study in every respect.

E. B. BURNS, *The Poverty of Progress: Latin America in the Nineteenth Century* (1980). Argues that the elites suppressed alternative modes of cultural and economic development.

E. B. BURNS, *A History of Brazil* (1993). The most useful one-volume treatment.

D. BUSHNELL AND N. MACAULAY, *The Emergence of Latin America in the Nineteenth Century* (1994). A survey that examines the internal development of Latin America during the period.

R. CONRAD, *The Destruction of Brazilian Slavery, 1850–1889* (1971). A good survey of the most important problem in Brazil in the second half of the nineteenth century.

R. CONRAD, *World of Sorrow: The African Slave Trade to Brazil* (1986). An excellent survey of the subject.

E. V. DA COSTA, *The Brazilian Empire: Myths and Histories* (1985). Essays that provide a thorough introduction to Brazil during the period of empire.

H. S. FERNS, *Britain and Argentina in the Nineteenth Century* (1968). Explains clearly the intermeshing of the two economies.

M. FONT, *Coffee, Contention, and Change in the Making of Modern Brazil* (1990). Extensive discussion of the problems of a single-commodity economy.

R. GRAHAM, *Britain and the Onset of Modernization in Brazil* (1968). Another study of British economic dominance.

S. H. HABER, *Industry and Underdevelopment: The Industrialization of Mexico, 1890–1940* (1989). Examines the problem of industrialization before and after the revolution.

G. HAHNER, *Emancipating the Female Sex: The Struggle for Women's Rights in Brazil, 1850–1940* (1990). An extensive examination of a relatively understudied issue in Latin America.

C. H. HARING, *Empire in Brazil: A New World Experiment with Monarchy* (1958). Remains a useful overview.

J. HEMMING, *Amazon Frontier: The Defeat of the Brazilian Indians* (1987). A brilliant survey of the experience of Native Americans in modern Brazil.

R. A. HUMPHREYS, *Latin America and the Second World War*, 2 vols. (1981–1982). The standard work on the topic.

F. KATZ, ed., *Riot, Rebellion, and Revolution in Mexico: Social Base of Agrarian Violence, 1750–1940* (1988). Essays that put the violence of the revolution in a longer context.

A. KNIGHT, *The Mexican Revolution*, 2 vols. (1986). The best treatment of the subject.

S. MAINWARING, *The Catholic Church and Politics in Brazil, 1916–1985* (1986). An examination of a key institution in Brazilian life.

M. C. MEYER AND W. L. SHERMAN, *The Course of Mexican History* (1995). An excellent survey.

M. MORNER, *Adventurers and Proletarians: The Story of Migrants in Latin America* (1985). Examines immigration to Latin America and migration within it.

J. PAGE, *Perón: A Biography* (1983). The standard English treatment.

D. ROCK, *Politics in Argentina, 1890–1930: The Rise and Fall of Radicalism* (1975). The major discussion of the Argentine Radical Party.

D. ROCK, *Argentina, 1516–1987: From Spanish Colonization to Alfonsin* (1987). Now the standard survey.

D. ROCK, ed., *Latin America in the 1940s: War and Postwar Transitions* (1994). Essays examining a very difficult decade for the continent.

R. M. SCHNEIDER, *"Order and Progress": A Political History of Brazil* (1991). A straightforward narrative with helpful notes for further reading.

T. E. SKIDMORE, *Black into White: Race and Nationality in Brazilian Thought* (1993). Examines the role of racial theory in Brazil.

P. H. SMITH, *Argentina and the Failure of Democracy: Conflict Among Political Elites. 1904–1955* (1974). An examination of one of the major political puzzles of Latin American history.

S. J. STEIN AND B. H. STEIN, *The Colonial Heritage of Latin America: Essays on Economic Dependence in Perspective* (1970). A major statement of the dependence interpretation.

D. TAMARIN, *The Argentine Labor Movement, 1930–1945: A Study in the Origins of Perónism* (1985). A useful introduction to a complex subject.

H. J. WIARDA, *Politics and Social Change in Latin America: The Distinct Tradition* (1974). Excellent essays that stress the ongoing role of Iberian traditions.

J. D. WIRTH, ed., *Latin American Oil Companies and the Politics of Energy* (1985). A series of case studies.

J. WOLFE, *Working Women, Working Men: São Paulo and the Rise of Brazil's Industrial Working Class, 1900–1955* (1993). Pays particular attention to the role of women.

J. WOMACK, *Zapata and the Mexican Revolution* (1968). A classic study.

CHAPTER 27

General Works

S. COOK, *Colonial Encounters in the Age of High Imperialism* (1996). A good introduction to the imperial enterprise in Africa and Asia.

D. K. FIELDHOUSE, *The West and the Third World. Trade, Colonialism, Depedence and Development* (1999). Addresses whether colonialism was detrimental or beneficial to colonized peoples.

P. HOPKIRK, *The Great Game: The Struggle for Empire in Central Asia* (1992). Focuses on the political and economic rivalries of the imperial powers.

India

A. AHMAD, *Islamic Modernism in India and Pakistan, 1857–1964* (1967). The standard survey of Muslim thinkers and movements in India during the period.

C. A. BAYLY, *Indian Society and the Making of the British Empire, The New Cambridge History of India*, II. 1 (1988). One of several major contributions of this author to the ongoing revision of our picture of modern Indian history since the eighteenth century.

A. GHOSH, *In an Antique Land. History in the Guise of a Traveler's Tale* (1992). An anthropologist traces the footsteps of a premodern slave traveling with his master from North Africa to India. A gripping tale of premodern life in the India Ocean basin and also of contemporary Egypt.

R. GUHA, ed., *Subaltern Studies: Writings on South Asian History and Society* (1982). Essays on the colonial period that focus on the social, political, and economic history of "subaltern" groups and classes (hill tribes, peasants, etc.) rather than only the elites of India.

S. N. HAY, ed., "Modern India and Pakistan," Part VI of Wm. Theodore de Bary et al., eds., *Sources of Indian Tradition*, 2nd ed. (1988). A superb selection of primary-source documents with brief introductions and helpful notes.

F. ROBINSON, ed., *The Cambridge Encyclopedia of India, Pakistan, Bangladesh, Sri Lanka, Nepal, Bhutan, and the*

Maldives (1989). A fine collection of survey articles by various scholars, organized into topical chapters ranging from "Economies" to "Cultures."

Central Islamic Lands

J. J. DONAHUE AND J. L. ESPOSITO, eds., *Islam in Transition: Muslim Perspectives* (1982). An interesting selection of primary-source materials on Islamic thinking in this century.

W. CLEVELAND, *A History of the Modern Middle East*, 3rd ed. (2004). A balanced and well-organized overview of modern Middle Eastern history.

A. DAWISHA, *Arab Nationalism in the Twentieth Century. From Triumph to Despair* (2003). A good overview of the development of Arab nationalism.

S. DERINGIL, *The Well-Protected Domains: Ideology and the Legitimation of Power in the Ottoman Empire, 1876–1909* (1998). An impressive study on nationalism and reform in the Ottoman Empire.

D. F. EICKELMAN, *Knowledge and Power in Morocco: The Education of a Twentieth-Century Notable* (1985). A fascinating study of traditional Islamic education and society in the twentieth century through a social biography of a Moroccan religious scholar and judge.

A. HOURANI, *Arabic Thought in the Liberal Age, 1798–1939* (1967). The standard work, by which all subsequent scholarship on the topic is to be judged.

N. R. KEDDIE, *An Islamic Response to Imperialism* (1968). A brief study of al-Afghani, the great Muslim reformer, with translations of a number of his writings.

B. LEWIS, *The Emergence of Modern Turkey*, 2nd ed. (1968). A concise but thorough history of the creation of the Turkish state, including nineteenth-century background.

J. O. VOLL, *Islam: Continuity and Change in the Modern World* (1982). Chapters 1–6. An interpretive survey of the Islamic world since the eighteenth century. Its emphasis on eighteenth-century reform movements is especially noteworthy.

Africa

A. A. BOAHEN, *Africa Under Colonial Domination, 1880–1935* (1985). Vol. VII of the *UNESCO General History of Africa*. Excellent chapters on various regions of Africa in the period. Chapters 3–10 detail African resistance to European colonial intrusion in diverse regions.

W. CARTEY AND M. KILSON, eds., *The Africa Reader: Colonial Africa* (1970). Original source materials give a vivid picture of African resistance to colonial powers, adaptation to foreign rule, and the emergence of the African masses as a political force.

P. CURTIN, S. FEIERMANN, L. THOMPSON, AND J. VANSINA, *African History* (1978). The relevant portions are Chapters 10–20.

B. DAVIDSON, *Modern Africa: A Social and Political History* (1989). A very useful survey of African history.

J. D. FAGE, *A History of Africa* (1978). The relevant chapters, which give a particularly clear overview of the colonial period, are 12–16.

B. FREUND, *The Making of Contemporary Africa: The Development of African Society Since 1800* (1984). A refreshingly direct synthetic discussion and survey that take an avowedly, but not reductive, materialist approach to interpretation.

T. PAKENHAM, *The Scramble for Africa* (1991). An excellent analysis of the imperialist age in Africa.

A. D. ROBERTS, ed., *The Colonial Moment in Africa: Essays on the Movement of Minds and Materials, 1900–1940* (1986). Chapters from *The Cambridge History of Africa* treating various aspects of the colonial period in Africa, including economics, politics, and religion.

CHAPTER 28

China

P. M. COBLE, *The Shanghai Capitalists and the Nationalist Government, 1927–1937* (1980).

L. E. EASTMAN, *The Abortive Revolution: China Under Nationalist Rule, 1927–1937* (1974).

L. E. EASTMAN, *Seeds of Destruction: Nationalist China in War and Revolution, 1937–1949* (1984).

M. ELVIN AND G. W. SKINNER, *The Chinese City Between Two Worlds* (1974). A study of the late Qing and Republican eras.

J. W. ESHERICK, *The Origins of the Boxer Rebellion* (1987).

S. ETŌ, *China's Republican Revolution* (1994).

J. K. FAIRBANK AND M. GOLDMAN, *China, a New History* (1998). A survey of the entire sweep of Chinese history; especially strong on the modern period.

J. K. FAIRBANK AND D. TWITCHETT, eds., *The Cambridge History of China*. Like the premodern volumes in the same series, the volumes on modern China represent a survey of what is known. Volumes 10–15, which cover the history from the late Qing to the People's Republic, have been published, and the others will be available soon. The series is substantial. Each volume contains a comprehensive bibliography.

J. FITZGERALD, *Awakening China: Politics, Culture, and Class in the Nationalist Revolution* (1996).

C. HAO, *Chinese Intellectuals in Crisis: Search for Order and Meaning, 1890–1911* (1987).

W. C. KIRBY, ed., *State and Economy in Republican China* (2001).

P. A. KUHN, *Rebellion and Its Enemies in Late Imperial China: Militarization and Social Structure, 1796–1864* (1980). A study of how the Confucian gentry saved the Manchu dynasty after the Taiping Rebellion.

P. KUHN, Origins of the Modern Chinese State (2002).

J. LEVENSON, *Liang Ch'i-ch'ao and the Mind of Modern China* (1953). A classic study of a major Chinese reformer and thinker.

LU XUN, *Selected Works* (1960). Novels, stories, and other writings by modern China's greatest writer.

S. NAQUIN, *Peking: Temples and City Life, 1400–1900* (2000).

E. O. REISCHAUER, J. K. FAIRBANK, AND A. M. CRAIG, *East Asia: Tradition and Transformation* (1989). A detailed text on East Asian history. Contains ample chapters on Japan and China and shorter chapters on Korea and Vietnam.

H. Z. SCHIFFRIN, *Sun Yat-sen, Reluctant Revolutionary* (1980). A biography.

B. I. SCHWARTZ, *Chinese Communism and the Rise of Mao* (1951). A classic study of Mao, his thought, and the Chinese Communist Party before 1949.

B. I. SCHWARTZ, *In Search of Wealth and Power: Yen Fu and the West* (1964). A fine study of a late-nineteenth-century thinker who introduced Western ideas into China.

J. D. SPENCE, *The Gate of Heavenly Peace: The Chinese and Their Revolution, 1895–1980* (1981). Historical reflections on twentieth-century China.

J. D. SPENCE, *The Search for Modern China* (1990). A thick text but well written.

M. SZONYI, *Practicing Kinship: Lineage and Descent in Late Imperial China* (2002).

S. Y. TENG AND J. K. FAIRBANK, *China's Response to the West* (1954). A superb collection of translations from Chinese thinkers and political figures, with commentaries.

T. H. WHITE AND A. JACOBY, *Thunder Out of China* (1946). A view of China during World War II by two who were there.

Japan

G. AKITA, *Foundations of Constitutional Government in Modern Japan* (1967). A study of Itō Hirobumi in the political process leading to the Meiji constitution.

G. C. ALLEN, *A Short Economic History of Modern Japan* (1958).

A. E. BARSHAY, *The Social Sciences in Modern Japan: the Marxian and Modernist Traditions* (2004). Different interpretations of history.

J. R. BARTHOLOMEW, *The Formation of Science in Japan* (1989). The pioneering English-language work on the subject.

W. G. BEASLEY, *Japanese Imperialism, 1894–1945* (1987). Excellent short book on subject.

G. M. BERGER, *Parties Out of Power in Japan, 1931–1941* (1977). An analysis of the condition of political parties during the militarist era.

G.L. BERNSTEIN, *Recreating Japanese Women, 1600–1945* (1991).

The Cambridge History of Japan, The Nineteenth Century, M.B. Jansen, ed. (1989); *The Twentieth Century*, P. Duus, ed. (1988). Multi-author works.

A. M. CRAIG, *Chōshū in the Meiji Restoration* (2000). A study of the Chōshū domain, a Prussia of Japan, during the period 1840–1868.

A. M. CRAIG AND D. H. SHIVELY, eds., *Personality in Japanese History* (1970). An attempt to gauge the role of individuals and their personalities as factors explaining history.

P. DUUS, *Party Rivalry and Political Change in Taisho Japan* (1968). A study of political change in Japan during the 1910s and 1920s.

P. DUUS, *The Abacus and the Sword, the Japanese Penetration of Korea, 1895–1910* (1995). A thoughtful analysis.

S. ERICSON, *The Sound of the Whistle: Railroads and the State in Meiji Japan* (1996). An economic and social history of railroads, an engine of growth and popular symbol.

Y. FUKUZAWA, *Autobiography* (1966). Japan's leading nineteenth-century thinker tells of his life and of the birth of modern Japan.

A. GARON, *The State and Labor in Modern Japan* (1987). A fine study of the subject.

C. N. GLUCK, *Japan's Modern Myths: Ideology in the Late Meiji Period* (1988). A brilliant study of the complex weave of late Meiji thought.

A. GORDON, *The Evolution of Labor Relations in Japan: Heavy Industry, 1853–1955* (1985). A seminal work.

B. R. HACKETT, *Yamagata Aritomo in the Rise of Modern Japan, 1932–1922* (1973). History as seen through the biography of a central figure.

I. HALL, *Mori Arinori* (1973). A biography of Japan's first minister of education.

T. R. H. HAVENS, *The Valley of Darkness: The Japanese People and World War II* (1978). Wartime society.

C. IRIYE, *After Imperialism: The Search for a New Order in the Far East, 1921–1931* (1965). (Also see other studies by this author.)

D. M. B. JANSEN AND G. ROZMAN, eds., *Japan in Transition from Tokugawa to Meiji* (1986). Contains fine essays.

W. JOHNSTON, *The Modern Epidemic: A History of Tuberculosis in Japan* (1995). A social history of a disease.

E. KEENE, Ed., *Modern Japanese Literature, An Anthology* (1960). A collection of modern Japanese short stories and excerpts from novels.

F. Y.T. MATSUSAKA, *The Making of Japanese Manchuria, 1904–1932* (2001). On railroad strategies in empire building.

J. W. MORLEY, ed., *The China Quagmire* (1983). A study of Japan's expansion on the continent between 1933 and 1941. (For diplomatic history, see also the many other works by this author.)

R. H. MYERS AND M. R. PEATTIE, eds., *The Japanese Colonial Empire, 1895–1945* (1984).

T. NAJITA, *Hara Kei in the Politics of Compromise, 1905–1915* (1967). A study of one of Japan's greatest party leaders.

K. OHKAWA AND H. ROSOVSKY, *Japanese Economic Growth: Trend Acceleration in the Twentieth Century* (1973).

M. RAVINA, *The Last Samurai: The Life and Battles of Saigo Takamori* (2004). Unlike the movie, this account of the Satsuma uprising is historical.

G. SHIBA, *Remembering Aizu* (1999). A stirring auto-biographical account of a samurai youth whose domain lost in the Meiji Restoration.

K. SMITH, *A Time of Crisis: The Great Depression and Rural Revitalization* (2001). An intellectual history of village movements during the 1930s.

J. J. STEPHAN, *Hawaii Under the Rising Sun* (1984). Japan's plans for rule in Hawaii.

R. H. SPECTOR, *Eagle Against the Sun: The American War with Japan* (1985). A narrative of World War II in the Pacific.

E. P. TSURUMI, *Factory Girls: Women in the Thread Mills of Meiji Japan* (1990). A sympathetic analysis of the key component of the Meiji labor force.

W. WRAY, *Mitsubishi and the N. Y. K., 1870–1914* (1984). The growth of a shipping *zaibatsu*, with analysis of business strategies, the role of government and imperialist involvements.

CHAPTER 29

L. ALBERTINI, *The Origins of the War of 1914*, 3 vols. (1952, 1957). Discursive but invaluable.

V. R. BERGHAHN, *Germany and the Approach of War in 1914* (1973). A work similar in spirit to both of Fischer's (see below) but stressing the importance of Germany's naval program.

R. BOSWORTH, *Italy and the Approach of the First World War* (1983). A fine analysis of Italian policy.

S. B. FAY, *The Origins of the World War*, 2 vols. (1928). The most influential of the revisionist accounts.

F. FISCHER, *Germany's Aims in the First World War* (1967). An influential interpretation that stirred a great controversy in Germany and around the world by emphasizing Germany's role in bringing on the war.

F. FISCHER, *War of Illusions* (1975). A long and diffuse book that tries to connect German responsibility for the war with internal social, economic, and political developments.

D. FROMKIN, *Europe's Last Summer: Who Started the Great War in 1914?* (2004). A lively account that fixes on the final crisis in July 1914.

J. N. HORNE, *Labour at War: France and Britain, 1914–1918* (1991). An examination of a major issue on the home fronts.

J. JOLL, *The Origins of the First World War* (1984). A brief but thoughtful analysis.

P. KENNEDY, *The Rise of the Anglo-German Antagonism 1860–1914* (1980). An unusual and thorough analysis of the political, economic, and cultural roots of important diplomatic developments.

W. L. LANGER, *European Alliances and Alignments*, 2nd ed. (1966). A splendid diplomatic history of the years 1871–1890.

W. L. LANGER, *The Diplomacy of Imperialism* (1935). A continuation of the previous study for the years 1890–1902.

D. C. B. LIEVEN, *Russia and the Origins of the First World War* (1983). A good account of the forces that shaped Russian policy.

A. MOMBAUER, *The Origins of the First World War. Controversies and Consensus* (2002). A fascinating survey of the debate over the decades and the current state of the question.

R. PIPES, *A Concise History of the Russian Revolution* (1996). A one-volume version of a scholarly masterpiece.

Z. STEINER, *Britain and the Origins of the First World War* (1977). A perceptive and informed account of the way British foreign policy was made in the years before the war.

H. STRACHAN, *The First World War* (2004). A fine one-volume account of the war.

A. J. P. TAYLOR, *The Struggle for Mastery in Europe, 1848–1918* (1954). Clever but controversial.

S. R. WILLIAMSON, JR., *Austria-Hungary and the Origins of the First World War* (1991). A valuable study of a complex subject.

CHAPTER 30

W. S. ALLEN, *The Nazi Seizure of Power: The Experience of a Single German Town, 1930–1935*, rev. ed. (1984). A classic treatment of Nazism in a microcosmic setting.

J. BARNARD, *Walter Reuther and the Rise of the Auto Workers* (1983). A major introduction to the new American unions of the 1930s.

K. D. BRACHER, *The German Dictatorship* (1970). A comprehensive treatment of both the origins and the functioning of the Nazi movement and government.

A. BULLOCK, *Hitler: A Study in Tyranny*, rev. ed. (1964). The best biography.

M. BURLEIGH AND W. WIPPERMAN, *The Racial State: Germany 1933–1945* (1991). Emphasizes the manner in which racial theory influenced numerous areas of policy.

R. CONQUEST, *The Great Terror: Stalin's Purges of the Thirties* (1968). The best treatment of the subject to this date.

G. CRAIG, *Germany, 1866–1945* (1978). A major survey.

I. DEUTSCHER, *The Prophet Armed* (1954), *The Prophet Unarmed* (1959), and *The Prophet Outcast* (1963). Remains the major biography of Trotsky.

I. DEUTSCHER, *Stalin: A Political Biography*, 2nd ed. (1967). The best biography in English.

B. EICHENGREEN, *Golden Fetters: The Gold Standard and the Great Depression, 1919–1939* (1992). A remarkable study of the role of the gold standard in the economic policies of the interwar years.

E. EYCK, *A History of the Weimar Republic*, 2 vols. (trans. 1963). The story as narrated by a liberal.

M. S. FAUSOLD, *The Presidency of Herbert Hoover* (1985). An important treatment.

G. FELDMAN, *The Great Disorder: Politics, Economics, and Society in the German Inflation, 1914–1924* (1993). The best work on the subject.

S. FITZPATRICK, *Stalin's Peasants: Resistance and Survival in the Russian Village After Collectivization* (1994). A pioneering study.

P. FUSSELL, *The Great War and Modern Memory* (1975). A brilliant account of the literature arising from World War I during the 1920s.

J. K. GALBRAITH, *The Great Crash* (1979). A well-known account by a leading economist.

R. GELLATELY, *The Gestapo and German Society: Enforcing Racial Policy, 1933–1945* (1990). A discussion of how the police state supported Nazi racial policies.

H. J. GORDON, *Hitler and the Beer Hall Putsch* (1972). An excellent account of the event and the political situation in the early Weimar Republic.

R. HAMILTON, *Who Voted for Hitler?* (1982). An examination of voting patterns and sources of Nazi support.

J. HELD, ed., *The Columbia History of Eastern Europe in the Twentieth Century* (1992). Individual essays on each country.

P. KENEZ, *The Birth of the Propaganda State: Soviet Methods of Mass Mobilization, 1917–1929* (1985). An examination of the manner in which the Communist government inculcated popular support.

B. KENT, *The Spoils of War: The Politics, Economics, and Diplomacy of Reparations, 1918–1932* (1993). A comprehensive account of the intricacies of the reparations problem of the 1920s.

D. LANDES, *The Unbound Prometheus: Technological Change and Industrial Development in Western Europe from 1750 to the Present* (1969). Includes an excellent analysis of both the Great Depression and the few areas of economic growth.

B. LINCOLN, *Red Victory: A History of the Russian Civil War* (1989). An excellent narrative account.

M. MCAULEY, *Bread and Justice: State and Society in Petrograd, 1917–1922* (1991). A study that examines the impact of the Russian Revolution and Leninist policies on a major Russian city.

D. J. K. PEUKERT, *Inside Nazi Germany: Conformity, Opposition, and Racism in Everyday Life* (1987). An excellent discussion of life under Nazi rule.

R. PIPES, *The Unknown Lenin: From the Secret Archives* (1996). A collection of previously unpublished documents that indicated the repressive character of Lenin's government.

P. PULZER, *Jews and the German State: The Political History of a Minority, 1848–1933* (1992). A detailed history by a major historian of European minorities.

L. J. RUPP, *Mobilizing Women for War: German and America Propaganda, 1939–1945* (1978). Although concentrating on a later period, it includes an excellent discussion of general Nazi attitudes toward women.

A. M. SCHLESINGER, JR., *The Age of Roosevelt*, 3 vols. (1957–1960). The most important overview.

D. M. SMITH, *Mussolini's Roman Empire* (1976). A general description of the Fascist regime in Italy.

D. M. SMITH, *Italy and Its Monarchy* (1989). A major treatment of an important neglected subject.

A. SOLZHENITSYN, *The Gulag Archipelago*, 3 vols. (1974–1979). A major examination of the labor camps under Stalin by one of the most important contemporary Russian writers.

R. J. SONTAG, *A Broken World, 1919–1939* (1971). An exceptionally thoughtful and well-organized survey.

A. J. P. TAYLOR, *English History, 1914–1945* (1965). Lively and opinionated.

H. A. TURNER JR., *German Big Business and the Rise of Hitler* (1985). An important major study of the subject.

H. A. TURNER JR., *Hitler's Thirty Days to Power* (1996). A narrative of the events leading directly to the Nazi seizure of power.

L. YAHIL, *The Holocaust: The Fate of European Jewry, 1932–1945* (1990). A major study of this fundamental subject in twentieth-century history.

CHAPTER 31

A. ADAMTHWAITE, *France and the Coming of the Second World War,* 1936–1939 (1977). A careful account making good use of the French archives.

E. R. BECK, *Under the Bombs: The German Home Front,* 1942–1945 (1986). An interesting examination of a generally unstudied subject.

R. S. BOTWINICK, *A History of the Holocaust,* 2nd ed., 2002. A brief but broad and useful account of the causes, character and results of the Holocaust.

A. BULLOCK, *Hitler: A Study in Tyranny,* rev. ed. (1964). A brilliant biography.

W. S. CHURCHILL, *The Second World War,* 6 vols. (1948–1954). The memoirs of the great British leader.

A. CROZIER, *The Causes of the Second World War,* 1997. An examination of what brought on the war.

R. B. FRANK, *Downfall: The End of the Imperial Japanese Empire,* 1998. A thorough, well-documented account of the last months of the Japanese empire and the reasons for its surrender.

J. L. GADDIS, *We Now Know: Rethinking Cold War History* (1998). A fine account of the early years of the Cold War making use of new evidence emerging since the collapse of the Soviet Union.

J. L. GADDIS, P. H. GORDON, E. MAY, eds., *Cold War Statesmen Confront the Bomb: Nuclear diplomacy Since 1945* (1999). A collection of essays discussing the effect of atomic and nuclear weapons on diplomacy since WW II.

M. GILBERT, *The Holocaust: A History of the Jews of Europe During the Second World War* (1985). The best and most comprehensive treatment.

A. IRIYE, *Pearl Harbor and the Coming of the Pacific War* (1999). Essays on how the Pacific war came about, including a selection of documents.

J. KEEGAN, *The Second World War* (1990). A lively and penetrating account by a master military historian.

I. KERSHAW, *Hitler: 1889–1936: Hubris* (1999) and *Hitler: 1936–1945: Nemesis* (2001). An outstanding two-volume biography.

W. F. KIMBALL, *Forged in War: Roosevelt, Churchill, and the Second World War,* (1998). A study of the collaboration between the two great leaders of the West based on a thorough knowledge of their correspondence.

W. MURRAY AND A. R. MILLETT, *A War to be Won: Fighting the Second World War,* (2000). A splendid account of the military operations in the war.

R. OVERY, *Why the Allies Won* (1997). An anlysis of the reasons for the victory of the Allies with special emphasis on technology.

N. RICH, *Hitler War Aims,* 2 vols. (1973–1974). The best study of the subject in English.

H. THOMAS, *The Spanish Civil War,* 3rd ed. (1986). The best account in English.

P. WANDYCZ, *The Twilight of French Eastern Alliances,* 1926–1936 (1988). A well-documented account of the diplomacy of central and eastern Europe in a crucial period.

G. L. WEINBERG, *A World at Arms: A Global History of World War II* (1994). A thorough and excellent narrative account.

CHAPTER 32

B. S. ANDERSON AND J. P. PINSSER, *A History of Their Own: Women in Europe from Prehistory to the Present,* Vol. 2 (1988). A broad-ranging survey.

R. BERNSTEIN, *Out of the Blue: The Story of September 11, 2001 from Jihad to Ground Zero* (2002). An excellent account by a gifted journalist.

A. BROWN, *The Gorbachev Factor* (1996). An important commentary by an English observer.

D. CALLEO, *Rethinking Europe's Future* (2003) A daring book by an experienced commentator.

J. L. GADDIS, *What We Know Now* (1997). Examines the Cold War in light of newly released documents.

D. J. GARROW, *Bearing the Cross: Martin Luther King, Jr. and the Southern Leadership Conference 1955–1968* (1986). The best work on the subject.

W. HITCHCOCK, *Struggle for Europe: The Turbulent History of a Divided Continent,* 1945–2002 (2003). The best overall narrative now available

D. KEARNS, *Lyndon Johnson and the American Dream* (1976). A useful biography.

J. KEEP, *The Last of the Empires: A History of the Soviet Union,* 1956–1991 (1995). A clear narrative.

M. MANDELBAUM, *The Ideas That Conquered the World: Peace, Democracy, and Free Markets* (2002). An important analysis by a major commentator on international affairs.

J. MANN, *The Rise of the Vulcans: The History of Bush's War Cabinet* (2004). An account of the major foreign policy advisors behind the invasion of Iraq.

R. MANN, *A Grand Delusion: America's Descent into Vietnam* (2001). The best recent narrative.

J. McCORMICK, *Understanding the European Union: A Concise Introduction* (2002) Outlines the major features.

N. NAIMARK, *Fires of Hatred: Ethnic Cleansing in Twentieth-Century Europe* (2002). A remarkably sensitive treatment of a tragic subject.

R. SAWKA AND ANNE STEVENS, eds., *Contemporary Europe* (2000). A collection of essays on major topics.

G. STOKES, ed., *From Stalinism to Pluralism: A Documentary History of Eastern Europe Since 1945* (1996). An important collection of documents that are not easily accessible elsewhere.

M. WALKER, *The Cold War and the Making of the Modern World* (1994). A major survey.

CHAPTER 33

China

R. BAUM, *Burying Mao: Chinese Politics in the Age of Deng Xiaoping* (1996).

A. CHAN, R. MADSEN, J. UNGER, *Chen Village under Mao and Deng* (1992).

J. CHANG, *Wild Swans: Three Daughters of China* (1991). An intimate look at recent Chinese society through three generations of women. Immensely readable.

J. FENG, *Ten Years of Madness: Oral Histories of China's Cultural Revolution* (1996).

J. FEWSMITH, *China Since Tiananmen: The Politics of Transition* (2001). Focus is on the rise to power of Jiang Zemin and Chinese politics during the nineties.

B. M. FROLIC, *Mao's People: Sixteen Portraits of Life in Revolutionary China* (1987).

T. GOLD, *State and Society in the Taiwan Miracle* (1986). The story of economic growth in postwar Taiwan.

M. GOLDMAN, *Sowing the Seeds of Democracy in China: Political Reform in the Deng Xiaoping Era* (1994).

A. IRIYE, *China and Japan in the Global Setting* (1992).

D. M. LAMPTON, *Same Bed, Different Dreams: Managing U.S.–China Relations, 1989–2000* (2001).

H. LIANG, *Son of the Revolution* (1983). An autobiographical account of a young man growing up in Mao's China.

K. LIEBERTHAL, *Governing China, from Revolution Through Reform* (2004).

B. LIU, *People or Monsters? and Other Stories and Reportage from China After Mao* (1983). Literary reflections on China.

R. MACFARQUHAR AND J. K. FAIRBANK, eds., *The Cambridge History of China*, Vol. 14, *Emergence of Revolutionary China* (1987), and Vol. 15, *Revolutions Within the Chinese Revolution, 1966–1982* (1991).

L. PAN, *Sons of the Yellow Emperor: A History of the Chinese Diaspora* (1990). A pioneer study that treats not only Southeast Asia but the rest of the world as well.

M. R. RISTAINO, *Port of Last Resort: The Diaspora Communities of Shanghai* (2001).

T. SAICH, *Governance and Politics of China* (2004).

H. WANG, *China's New Order* (2003). Translation of a work by a Qinghua University professor, a liberal within the boundaries of what is permissable in China.

G. WHITE, ed., *In Search of Civil Society: Market Reform and Social Change in Contemporary China* (1996).

M. WOLF, *Revolution Postponed: Women in Contemporary China* (1985).

ZHANG X. AND SANG Y., *Chinese Lives: An Oral History of Contemporary China* (1987).

Japan

G. L. BERNSTEIN, *Haruko's World: A Japanese Farm Woman and Her Community* (1983). A study of the changing life of a village woman in postwar Japan.

T. BESTOR, *Neighborhood Tokyo* (1989). A portrait of contemporary urban life in Japan.

G. L. CURTIS, *The Logic of Japanese Politics: Leaders, Institutions, and the Limits of Change* (1999).

G. L. CURTIS, *Policymaking in Japan: Defining the Role of Politicians* (2002).

M. H. CUSUMANO, *The Japanese Automobile Industry* (1985). A neat study of the postwar business strategies of Toyota and Nissan.

R. P. DORE, *City Life in Japan* (1999). A classic, reissued.

R. P. DORE, *Land Reform in Japan* (1959). Another classic.

S. GARON, *Molding Japanese Minds: The State in Everyday Life* (1997).

S. M. GARON, *The Evolution of Civil Society from Meiji to Heisei* (2002). That is to say, from the mid–nineteenth century to the present day.

A. GORDON, ed., *Postwar Japan as History* (1993).

H. HIBBETT, ed., *Contemporary Japanese Literature: An Anthology of Fiction, Film, and Other Writing Since 1945* (1977). Translations of postwar short stories.

Y. KAWABATA, *The Sound of the Mountain* (1970). Sensitive, moving novel by Nobel author.

J. NATHAN, *Sony, the Private Life* (1999). A lively account of the human side of growth in the Sony Corporation.

D. OKIMOTO, *Between MITI and the Market* (1989). A discussion of the respective roles of government and private enterprise in Japan's postwar growth.

S. PHARR, *Losing Face: Status Politics in Japan* (1996).

E. F. VOGEL, *Japan as Number One: Lessons for America* (1979). While dated and somewhat sanguine, this remains an insightful classic.

Korea and Vietnam

B. CUMINGS, *Korea, The Unknown War* (1988).

B. CUMINGS, *The Origins of the Korean War* (Vol. 1, 1981; Vol. 2, 1991).

B. CUMINGS, *The Two Koreas: On the Road to Reunification?* (1990).

C. J. ECKERT, *Korea Old and New, A History* (1990). The best short history of Korea, with extensive coverage of the postwar era.

C. J. ECKERT, *Offspring of Empire: The Koch'ang Kims and the Colonial Origins of Korean Capitalism, 1876–1945* (1991).

G. M. T. KAHIN, *Intervention: How America Became Involved in Vietnam* (1986).

S. KARNOW, *Vietnam: A History*. rev. ed. (1996).

L. KENDALL, *Shamans, Housewives, and Other Restless Spirits: Women in Korean Ritual and Life* (1985).

K. B. LEE, *A New History of Korea* (1984). A translation by E. Wagner and others of an outstanding Korean work covering the full sweep of Korean history.

T. LI, *Nguyen Cochinchina: South Vietnam in the Seventeenth and Eighteenth Centuries* (1998).

D. MARR, *Vietnam 1945: The Quest for Power* (1995).

C. W. SORENSEN, *Over the Mountains Are Mountains* (1988). How peasant households in Korea adapted to rapid industrialization.

A. WOODSIDE, *Vietnam and the Chinese Model* (1988). Provides the background for Vietnam's relationship to China.

CHAPTER 34
Latin America

P. BAKEWELL, *A History of Latin America: c. 1450 to the Present* (2003). An up-to-date survey.

A. CHOMSKY et al., *The Cuba Reader: History, Culture, Politics* (2004). Very useful, broad-ranging anthology.

J. DOMINGUEZ AND M. SHIFTER, *Contructing Democratic Governance in Latin America* (2003). Contains individual country studies.

G. JOSEPH et al. , *The Mexico Reader: History, Culture, Politics*(2003). Excellent introduction to major issues.

P. LOWDEN, *Moral Opposition to Authoritarian Rule in Chile* (1996). A discussion of Chilean politics from the standpoint of human rights.

J. PRESTON AND S. DILLON, *Opening Mexico: The Making of a Democracy* (2004). Excellent analysis of recent developments in Mexico.

H. WIRARDA, *Democracy and Its Discontents: Development, Interdependence, and U.S. Policy in Latin America* (1995). A useful overview.

Africa

B. DAVIDSON, *Let Freedom Come* (1978). Remains a thought commentary of African independence.

R. W. JULY, *A History of the African People,* 5th ed. (1995). Provides a careful and clear survey of post–World War I history and consideration of nationalism.

J. HERBST, *States and Power in Africa* (2000). Relates current issues of African state-building to those before to the colonial era.

J. H. LATHAM, *Africa, Asia, and South America Since 1800: A Bibliographic Guide* (1995). A valuable tool for finding materials on the topics in this chapter.

N. MANDELA, *Long Walk to Freedom: The Autobiography of Nelson Mandela* (1995). Autobiography of the African leader who transformed South Africa.

L. THOMPSON, *A History of South Africa* (2001). The best survey.

N. VAN DE WALLE, *African Economies and the Politics of Perm anent Crisis, 1979–1999* (2001). Exploration of difficulties of African economic development.

India and Pakistan

O. B. JONES, *Pakistan: Eye of the Storm* (2003). Best recent introduction.

R. RASHID, *Taliban: Militant Islam, Oil and Fundamentalism in Central Asia* (2001). Analysis of radical Isalmist regime in Afghanistan.

R. W. STERN, *Changing India: Bourgeois Revolution on the Subcontinent* (2003). Overview of forces now changing Indian society.

S. WOLPERT, *A New History of India* (2003). The closing chapters of this fine survey history are particularly helpful in orienting the reader in postwar Indian history until the mid-1980s.

Islam and the Middle East

A. AHMED, *Discovering Islam. Making Sense of Muslim Hisotry and Society,* rev. ed. (2003). An excellent and readable overivew of Islamic– Western relations.

J. ESPOSITO, *The Islamic Threat: Myth or Reality,* 2nd ed. (1992). A useful corrective to some of the polemics against Islam and Muslims today.

J. J. ESPOSITO, ed., *The Oxford Encyclopedia of Islam* (1999). A thematic survey of Islamic history, particularly strong in the Modern Era.

D. Fromkin, *A Peace to End All Peace: The Fall of the Ottoman Empire and the Creation of the Modern Middle East* (2001). Very good on the impact of World War I on the region.

G. Fuller, *The Future of Political Islam* (2003). A very good overview of Islamist ideology by a former CIA staff member.

J. Keay, *Sowing the Wind: The Seeds of Conflict in theMiddle East* (2003). A balanced account.

N. R. Keddie, *Modern Iran. Roots and Results of Revolution* (2003). Chapters 6–12 focus on Iran from 1941 through the first years of the 1978 revolution and provide a solid overview of history in this era.

G. Kepel, *Jihad: The Trail of Political Islam* (2002). An extensive treatment by a leading French scholar of the subject.

(44.5 × 54.5 cm), Yale Center for British Art, Paul Mellon Collection/Bridgeman Art Library (B1977.14.118); Getty Images Inc. - Stone Allstock; Japan Airlines Photo; Unidentified Artist. The Emperor Ch'ien Lung (1736–1795) as a Young Man. Colors on silk. H. 63-1/2 in. W. 30-1/2 in. © The Metropolitan Museum of Art, Rogers Fund, 1942. (42.141.8). Photograph © 1980 The Metropolitan Museum of Art; Embassy of Kenya; © Hulton-Deutsch Collection/CORBIS.

Chapter 16 a. Dorling Kindersley/British Museum; c. Rijksmuseum, Amsterdam; d. Huntington Library; e. Art Resource, NY, The Branch Libraries, The New York Public Library, Astor, Lenox and Tilden Foundations; f. © Art Resource, NY; g. Musee Cantonal Des Beaux Arts, Palais de Rumine, Lausanne; h. Bibliotheque Publique et Universitaire, Geneva; i. National Portrait Gallery, London.

Chapter 17 a. Dorling Kindersley Media Library; c. Mapungubwe Museum; d. © Frank Willet; e. UN/DPI PHOTO/Jeffrey Fox; f. Cliche Bibliotheque nationale de France—Paris; g. Photograph by Eliot Elisofon, National Museum of African Art, Eliot Elisofon Archives, Smithsonian Institution, Washington DC; h. Courtesy Entwistle Gallery, London; j. Robert Aberman and Barbara Heller/Art Resource, NY; k. Werner Forman Archive/Art Resource, NY.

Chapter 18 a. "The Fortunate Slave" An illustration of African Slavery in the early 18th century by Douglas Grant (1968). From "Some Memoirs of the Life of Job," by Thomas Bluett, 1734. Photo by Robert D. Rubic/Precision Chromes, Inc. The New York Times Library, Research Libraries; b. Courtesy, American Antiquarian Society; d. Guy Ryecart/Dorling Kindersley Media Library; e. Courtesy of The University of Texas Archives. The UT Institute of Texan Cultures at San Antonio; f. Chas Howson/Dorling Kindersley Media Library; g. Dorling Kindersley Media Library; h. Samuel Scott, "Old Custom House Quay" Collection. V&A IMAGES, THE VICTORIA AND ALBERT MUSEUM, LONDON; i. The Granger Collection; j. Hulton/Corbis/Bettmann; k. Fur traders and Indians: engraving, 1777. c. The Granger Collection, New York; l. Glenbow Museum.

Chapter 19 a. Dorling Kindersley Media Library; c. Box: Carved lacquer box with cover decorated with scene of sages in a garden. Chinese, Yongle (1403–1429). Carved red lacquer over wood. 7.9 × 26.6 cm. China. freer Gallery of Art. Smithsonian Institution, Washington, D.C.: Purchase, F1953.64a; d. Karaori kimono. Middle Edo period, c. 1700. Brocaded silk. Tokyo National Museum; e. Tai Chin, "Fisherman on an Autumn River", (1390–1460). Painting. Ink and color on paper. 18-1/8 × 291-1/4 in. (46 × 740 cm). Courtesy of the Freer Gallery of Art, Smithsonian Institution, Washington, D.C.; f. Albert Craig; g. Melon-shaped Ewer, Stoneware. Koryo Dynasty, ca. 12th century H. 9" × Diam. 19-1/2" Korea. The Avery Brundage Collection, Asian Art Museum of San Francisco; h. Roger Phillips/ Dorling Kindersley Media Library; i. © Metropolitan Museum of Art, Rogers Fund, 1942, (42.141.8); j. Giraudon/Art Resource, NY; k. © 1996. All rights reserved. Courtesy of Museum of Fine Arts, Boston.

Chapter 20 a. Francois Boucher (1703 – 1770), "Breakfast" Louvre, Paris, France. Copyright Scala/Art Resource; b. Mary Evans Picture Library Ltd.; c. Kunsthistorisches Museum, Vienna; d. Art Resource, NY; e. Dorling Kindersley/The Museum of English Rural Life; f. Art Resource/Musee du Louvre; g. General James Wolfe's expedition against Quebec in 1759; English engraving. 1760. The Granger Collection, NY; h. By permission of the Master and Fellows of Sidney Sussex College, Cambridge; i. The Granger Collection; j. The Granger Collection.

Part 5 Timeline, top to bottom, left to right: Anonymous, France, 18th century, "Seige of the Bastille, 14 July, 1789." Obligatory mention of the following: Musee de la Ville de Paris, Musee Carnavalet, Paris, France. Bridgeman-Giraudon/Art Resource, NY; Bildarchiv Preubischer Kulturbesitz; Corbis/Bettmann; Bettmann/ Corbis; The Granger Collection, New York.

Part 5 Timeline, top to bottom, left to right: "Col. James Todd on elephant Indian painting" ca. 1880. E.T. Archive, Victoria and Albert Museum; © Hulton-Deutsch Collection/CORBIS; © Christie's Images/Corbis.

Chapter 21 a. Bichitr, "Jahangir Preferring a Sufi Shaikh to Kings", ca. 1660-70. Album page. Opaque watercolor, gold, and ink on paper. 25.3 cmH × 18.1 cm W (10" × 7 1/8"). Courtesy of the Freer Gallery of Art, Smithsonian Institution, Washington, DC.; b. Opaque watercolor, ink, and gold on paper, 34.2 × 21.5 cm, Arthur M. Sackler Gallery, Smithsonian Institution, Washington DC. Lent by the Art and History Trust, LTS 1995. 2,80; c. Mart Nieuwland/Omni Photo Communications, Inc.; d. Getty Images, Inc. – All Stock; e. Tony Sterling © Dorling Kindersley; f. Arifi, "suleymanname," Topkapi Palace Museum, 11 1517, fol. 31b, photograph courtesy of Talat Halman; g. Michel Gotin/Ouzebekistan; h. Super Stock; i. Corbis/Bettmann.

Chapter 22 a. Dorling Kindersley/The Wallace Collection; b. Bildarchiv Preussischer Kulturbesitz; c. Corbis Bettman; d. The Granger Collection; e. © Bettmann/CORBIS; f. Sir Godfrey Kneller, *Sir Isaac Newton*, 1702. Oil on canvas. The Granger Collection; g. The Granger Collection; h. The Granger Collection; e. SuperStock, Inc.; j. The Granger Collection, New York.

Part 6 Timeline, top to bottom, left to right: Bildarchiv Preubischer Kulturbesitz; Bildarchiv Preubischer Kulturbesitz; Corbis/Bettmann; © Hulton-Deutsch Collection/CORBIS; Bridgeman Art Library, London/SuperStock, Inc.; SuperStock, Inc.

Part 6 Timeline, top to bottom, left to right: Bildarchiv Preubischer Kulturbesitz; Shosai Ginko (Japanese, act. 1874–1897), View of the Issuance of the State Constitution in the State Chamber of the New Imperial Palace, March 2, 1889 (Meiji 22), Ink and color on paper, 14 1/8 × 28 3/8 in. The Metropolitan Museum of Art, Gift of Lincoln Kirstein, 1959 (JP3233-3235) Photograph © The Metropolitan Museum of Art; Dorling Kindersley Media Library; The Granger Collection.

Chapter 23 a. Execution of Louis XVI. Aquatint. French, 18th century. Musee de la Ville de Paris, Musee Carnavalet, Paris, France. Giraudon/Art Resource, N.Y.; b. Corbis Bettmann; c. Corbis Bettmann; d. Francisco de Goya, "Los fusilamientos del 3 de mayo, 1808" 1814. Oil on canvas, 8'6" × 11'4" © Museo Nacional del Prado, Madrid; e. The Granger Collection; f. Austrian Archive/Corbis; g. Biblioteque Nationale Paris. France/ Giraudon/Art Resource, NY; h. Mary Evans Picture Library, Ltd.; i. Hulton-Deutsch Collection/Corbis; j. The Granger Collection; k. Muse de la Ville de Paris, Musee Carnavalet/Giraudon/Art Resource, NY.

Chapter 24 a. The Art Archive/Picture Desk, Inc./Kobal Collection; b. Library of Congress; c. Library of Congress; d. Corbis/Bettmann; e. Art Resource/Bildarchiv P_reussischer Kulturbesitz; f. The Granger Collection, NY; g. Roger Violett; Getty Images Inc. – Liaison; h. Bildarchiv Preussicher Kulturbesitz/Original: Friedrichsruher Fassung, Bismark Musuem; i. Roger Viollett; Getty Images, Inc.—Liaison; j. The Granger Collection, New York.

Chapter 25 a. Corbis Bettmann; b. Photo RMN/Senice Photographique des Muses Nationaux, Paris; c. Georges Seurat, (French 1859 – 1891), "A Sunday on La Grande Jatte 1884" 1884-86, Oil on canvas, 207.6 × 308 cm. Helen Birch Bartlett Memorial Collection, 1926.224 © The Art Institute of Chicago. All Rights Reserved; d. Corbis Bettmann; e. Oil on canvas, 283 cm × 550 cm. Civica Galleria d'Arte Moderna-Milano. Photo by Marcello Saporetti; f. The Granger Collection, NY; g. Getty Images Inc.; h. Art Resource/Bildarchiv Preussischer Kulturbesitz; i. Leeds Museums and Art Galleries (City Museum) UK/Bridgeman Art Library; j. Mary Evans Picture Library.

Chapter 26 a. Geoff Brightling, Dorling Kindersley Media Library; b. Corbis/ Bettmann; c. Dorling Kindersley Media Library; d. Diego Rivera, "Orgy – Night of the Rich" (La Orgia – La noche de los ricos), 1926. Mural, 2.05 × 1.54 m. Court of Fiestas, Level 3, North Wall. Secretaria de Education Publica, Mexico City, Mexico. Schalkwijk/Art Resource, NY © Banco de Mexico Diego Rivera; e. Geoff Brightling; Dorling Kindersley Media Library; f. Corbis Bettmann; g. © Corbis; h. Corbis Bettmann; i. Corbis Bettmann; j. UPI/Corbis Bettmann.

Chapter 27 a. © Stockbyte; b. Giraud Philippe; Corbis/Sygma; c. Caravan with Ivory, French Congo, (now the Republic of the Congo). Robert Visser (1882–1894). c. 1890–1900, postcard, collotype. Publisher unknown, c. 1900. Postcard 1912. Image No. EEPA 1985-140792. Eliot Elisofon Photographic Archives. National Museum; d. By permission of the British Library; e. AP/Wide World Photos; f. The Granger Collection, New York; g. The Granger Collection; f. Brown Brothers; h. Getty Images Inc.—Hulton Archive Photos.

Chapter 28 a. Jean-Loup Charmet; b. Corbis/Bettmann; c. Coll. Ministry of Foreign Affairs, Tokyo, Japan; d. Shoes for bound feet. China, Asia circa 1900–1910. Qing Dynasty. Silk, leather 9.5 cm high, 12.5 cm. Dora O. Mitchell Collection. Museum of Anthropology, University of Missouri-Columbia. Daniel S. Glover, photographer; e. Hulton Picture Library/Bettman; Corbis/Bettmann; f. Courtesy of the Library of Congress. Gift of Mrs. E. Crane Chadbourne; 1930; g. Stock Montage, Inc./Historical Pictures Collection;h. Martin Plomer; Dorling Kindersley Media Library.

Part 7 Timeline, top to bottom, left to right: The Granger Collection; Pablo Picasso , 'Guernica' 1937, Oil on canvas. 11'5 1/2 × 25'5 3/4. Museo Nacional Centro de Arte Reina Sofia/ © 2004 Estate of Pablo Picasso/Artists Rights Society (ARS), New York; Getty Images Inc. - Hulton Archive Photos; Corbis/Bettmann.

Part 7 Timeline, top to bottom, left to right: Corbis/Sygma; Corbis/Bettmann; Corbis/Bettmann; Getty Images Inc. - Hulton Archive Photos; AP/Wide World Photos.

Chapter 29 a. Karl Shone; Dorling Kindersley Media Library; b. Corbis/Bettmann; c. Imperial War Museum, London; d. Andy Crawford; Dorling Kindersley Media Library; e. Alexander Gerasimov "Lenin at the Tribune" 1930. Tretyakov Gallery, Moscow, Russia. Scala/Art Resource, NY; f. Dorling Kindersley Media Library; g. Richard Ward/Dorling Kindersley Media Library; h. The Granger Collection; i. Musee des Blindes; j. Corbis Bettmann.

Chapter 30 a. © Scheufler Collection/CORBIS; b. Bildarchiv Preubischer Kulturbesitz; c. Corbis/Bettmann; d. The Granger Collection; e. Dorling Kindersley/ The Museum of the Revolution; e. Grosz George (1893–1959) ©VAGA, NY. Stuetzen der Gesellschaft (Pillars of Society), 1926. Oil on Canvas, 200,0 × 108,0 cm. Photo: Joerg P. Anders. Nationalgalerie, Staatliche Museen zu Berlin, Berlin, Germany; f. Getty Images Inc.—Hulton Archive Photos; f. Corbis/Bettmann; g. Bildarchiv Preubischer Kulturbesitz; h. © Leonard de Selva/CORBIS; i. Corbis Bettmann.

Chapter 31 a. © Bettmann/CORBIS; b. Corbis Bettmann; c. Dorling Kindersley/The Imperial War Museum; d. Corbis/ Bettmann; e. The Granger Collection; f. Corbis/Bettmann; g. Getty Images Inc.—Hulton Archive Photos; h. Corbis Bettmann.

Chapter 32 a. Dorling Kindersley Media Library; b. Corbis/ Bettmann; d. © Owen Franken/CORBIS; e. Telepress Syndicate Agency; Corbis/Bettmann; f. Corbis/Bettmann; g. Van Parys; Corbis/Sygma; h. SuperStock, Inc.; i. Corbis/Sygma; j. Peter Turnley; Corbis/Bettmann; k. Reuters; Corbis/Bettmann.

Chapter 33 a. Clive Streeter/Dorling Kindersley Media Library; b. China Tourism Press/Xie Guang Hui/ Getty Images; c. CORBIS-NY; d. Koren POOL/ Yonhap; AP/Wide World Photos; e. Dave Bartruff/CORBIS; f. Corbis/Bettmann CORBIS-NY; g. Photographer's Mate 3rd Class Todd Frantom; U.S. Navy News Photo; h. Corbis/Bettmann.

Chapter 34 a. Dorling Kindersley Media Library; b. Markus Matzel/Das Fotoarchiv/Peter Arnold, Inc.; c. AP Wide World Photos; d. David Brauchli/AP/Wide World Photos; e. AP/Wide World Photos; f. Roberto & Osvaldo Salas; Getty Images, Inc.—Liaison; f. M & E Bernheim; Woodfin Camp & Associates; g. UPI; Corbis/Bettmann; h. David Guttenfelder; AP/Wide World Photos; i. Masatomo Kuriya, Corbis/Sygma.

WORLD HISTORY DOCUMENTS CD-ROM

SINGLE PC LICENSE AGREEMENT AND LIMITED WARRANTY

READ THIS LICENSE CAREFULLY BEFORE OPENING THIS PACKAGE. BY OPENING THIS PACKAGE, YOU ARE AGREEING TO THE TERMS AND CONDITIONS OF THIS LICENSE. IF YOU DO NOT AGREE, DO NOT OPEN THE PACKAGE. PROMPTLY RETURN THE UNOPENED PACKAGE AND ALL ACCOMPANYING ITEMS TO THE PLACE YOU OBTAINED THEM.

1. **GRANT OF LICENSE AND OWNERSHIP:** THE ENCLOSED COMPUTER PROGRAMS <<AND DATA>> ("SOFTWARE") ARE LICENSED, NOT SOLD, TO YOU BY PEARSON EDUCATION, INC. PUBLISHING AS PEARSON PRENTICE HALL ("WE" OR THE "COMPANY") AND IN CONSIDERATION OF YOUR PURCHASE OR ADOPTION OF THE ACCOMPANYING COMPANY TEXTBOOKS AND/OR OTHER MATERIALS, AND YOUR AGREEMENT TO THESE TERMS. WE RESERVE ANY RIGHTS NOT GRANTED TO YOU. YOU OWN ONLY THE DISK(S) BUT WE AND/OR OUR LICENSORS OWN THE SOFTWARE ITSELF. THIS LICENSE ALLOWS YOU TO USE AND DISPLAY YOUR COPY OF THE SOFTWARE ON A SINGLE COMPUTER (I.E., WITH A SINGLE CPU) AT A SINGLE LOCATION FOR ACADEMIC USE ONLY, SO LONG AS YOU COMPLY WITH THE TERMS OF THIS AGREEMENT. YOU MAY MAKE ONE COPY FOR BACK UP, OR TRANSFER YOUR COPY TO ANOTHER CPU, PROVIDED THAT THE SOFTWARE IS USABLE ON ONLY ONE COMPUTER.

2. **RESTRICTIONS:** YOU MAY NOT TRANSFER OR DISTRIBUTE THE SOFTWARE OR DOCUMENTATION TO ANYONE ELSE. EXCEPT FOR BACKUP, YOU MAY NOT COPY THE DOCUMENTATION OR THE SOFTWARE. YOU MAY NOT NETWORK THE SOFTWARE OR OTHERWISE USE IT ON MORE THAN ONE COMPUTER OR COMPUTER TERMINAL AT THE SAME TIME. YOU MAY NOT REVERSE ENGINEER, DISASSEMBLE, DECOMPILE, MODIFY, ADAPT, TRANSLATE, OR CREATE DERIVATIVE WORKS BASED ON THE SOFTWARE OR THE DOCUMENTATION. YOU MAY BE HELD LEGALLY RESPONSIBLE FOR ANY COPYING OR COPYRIGHT INFRINGEMENT THAT IS CAUSED BY YOUR FAILURE TO ABIDE BY THE TERMS OF THESE RESTRICTIONS.

3. **TERMINATION:** THIS LICENSE IS EFFECTIVE UNTIL TERMINATED. THIS LICENSE WILL TERMINATE AUTOMATICALLY WITHOUT NOTICE FROM THE COMPANY IF YOU FAIL TO COMPLY WITH ANY PROVISIONS OR LIMITATIONS OF THIS LICENSE. UPON TERMINATION, YOU SHALL DESTROY THE DOCUMENTATION AND ALL COPIES OF THE SOFTWARE. ALL PROVISIONS OF THIS AGREEMENT AS TO LIMITATION AND DISCLAIMER OF WARRANTIES, LIMITATION OF LIABILITY, REMEDIES OR DAMAGES, AND OUR OWNERSHIP RIGHTS SHALL SURVIVE TERMINATION.

4. **LIMITED WARRANTY AND DISCLAIMER OF WARRANTY:** COMPANY WARRANTS THAT FOR A PERIOD OF 60 DAYS FROM THE DATE YOU PURCHASE THIS SOFTWARE (OR PURCHASE OR ADOPT THE ACCOMPANYING TEXTBOOK), THE SOFTWARE, WHEN PROPERLY INSTALLED AND USED IN ACCORDANCE WITH THE DOCUMENTATION, WILL OPERATE IN SUBSTANTIAL CONFORMITY WITH THE DESCRIPTION OF THE SOFTWARE SET FORTH IN THE DOCUMENTATION, AND THAT FOR A PERIOD OF 30 DAYS THE DISK(S) ON WHICH THE SOFTWARE IS DELIVERED SHALL BE FREE FROM DEFECTS IN MATERIALS AND WORKMANSHIP UNDER NORMAL USE. THE COMPANY DOES NOT WARRANT THAT THE SOFTWARE WILL MEET YOUR REQUIREMENTS OR THAT THE OPERATION OF THE SOFTWARE WILL BE UNINTERRUPTED OR ERROR-FREE. YOUR ONLY REMEDY AND THE COMPANY'S ONLY OBLIGATION UNDER THESE LIMITED WARRANTIES IS, AT THE COMPANY'S OPTION, RETURN OF THE DISK FOR A REFUND OF ANY AMOUNTS PAID FOR IT BY YOU OR REPLACEMENT OF THE DISK. THIS LIMITED WARRANTY IS THE ONLY WARRANTY PROVIDED BY THE COMPANY AND ITS LICENSORS, AND THE COMPANY AND ITS LICENSORS DISCLAIM ALL OTHER WARRANTIES, EXPRESS OR IMPLIED, INCLUDING WITHOUT LIMITATION, THE IMPLIED WARRANTIES OF MERCHANTABILITY AND FITNESS FOR A PARTICULAR PURPOSE. THE COMPANY DOES NOT WARRANT, GUARANTEE OR MAKE ANY REPRESENTATION REGARDING THE ACCURACY, RELIABILITY, CURRENTNESS, USE, OR RESULTS OF USE, OF THE SOFTWARE.

5. **LIMITATION OF REMEDIES AND DAMAGES:** IN NO EVENT, SHALL THE COMPANY OR ITS EMPLOYEES, AGENTS, LICENSORS, OR CONTRACTORS BE LIABLE FOR ANY INCIDENTAL, INDIRECT, SPECIAL, OR CONSEQUENTIAL DAMAGES ARISING OUT OF OR IN CONNECTION WITH THIS LICENSE OR THE SOFTWARE, INCLUDING FOR LOSS OF USE, LOSS OF DATA, LOSS OF INCOME OR PROFIT, OR OTHER LOSSES, SUSTAINED AS A RESULT OF INJURY TO ANY PERSON, OR LOSS OF OR DAMAGE TO PROPERTY, OR CLAIMS OF THIRD PARTIES, EVEN IF THE COMPANY OR AN AUTHORIZED REPRESENTATIVE OF THE COMPANY HAS BEEN ADVISED OF THE POSSIBILITY OF SUCH DAMAGES. IN NO EVENT SHALL THE LIABILITY OF THE COMPANY FOR DAMAGES WITH RESPECT TO THE SOFTWARE EXCEED THE AMOUNTS ACTUALLY PAID BY YOU, IF ANY, FOR THE SOFTWARE OR THE ACCOMPANYING TEXTBOOK. BECAUSE SOME JURISDICTIONS DO NOT ALLOW THE LIMITATION OF LIABILITY IN CERTAIN CIRCUMSTANCES, THE ABOVE LIMITATIONS MAY NOT ALWAYS APPLY TO YOU.

6. **GENERAL:** THIS AGREEMENT SHALL BE CONSTRUED IN ACCORDANCE WITH THE LAWS OF THE UNITED STATES OF AMERICA AND THE STATE OF NEW YORK, APPLICABLE TO CONTRACTS MADE IN NEW YORK, EXCLUDING THE STATE'S LAWS AND POLICIES ON CONFLICTS OF LAW, AND SHALL BENEFIT THE COMPANY, ITS AFFILIATES AND ASSIGNEES. THIS AGREEMENT IS THE COMPLETE AND EXCLUSIVE STATEMENT OF THE AGREEMENT BETWEEN YOU AND THE COMPANY AND SUPERSEDES ALL PROPOSALS OR PRIOR AGREEMENTS, ORAL, OR WRITTEN, AND ANY OTHER COMMUNICATIONS BETWEEN YOU AND THE COMPANY OR ANY REPRESENTATIVE OF THE COMPANY RELATING TO THE SUBJECT MATTER OF THIS AGREEMENT. IF YOU ARE A U.S. GOVERNMENT USER, THIS SOFTWARE IS LICENSED WITH "RESTRICTED RIGHTS" AS SET FORTH IN SUBPARAGRAPHS (A)-(D) OF THE COMMERCIAL COMPUTER-RESTRICTED RIGHTS CLAUSE AT FAR 52.227-19 OR IN SUBPARAGRAPHS (C)(1)(II) OF THE RIGHTS IN TECHNICAL DATA AND COMPUTER SOFTWARE CLAUSE AT DFARS 252.227-7013, AND SIMILAR CLAUSES, AS APPLICABLE.

SHOULD YOU HAVE ANY QUESTIONS CONCERNING THIS AGREEMENT OR IF YOU WISH TO CONTACT THE COMPANY FOR ANY REASON, PLEASE CONTACT IN WRITING: LEGAL DEPARTMENT, PRENTICE HALL, 1 LAKE STREET, UPPER SADDLE RIVER, NJ 07450 OR CALL PEARSON EDUCATION PRODUCT SUPPORT AT 1-800-677-6337.